# Le — Surréalisme, ≠ c'est — moi!



KUNSTHALLE wien

VERLAG *für* MODERNE KUNST

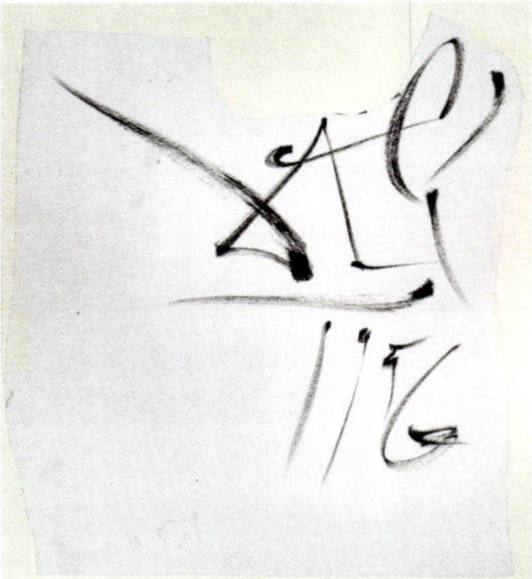

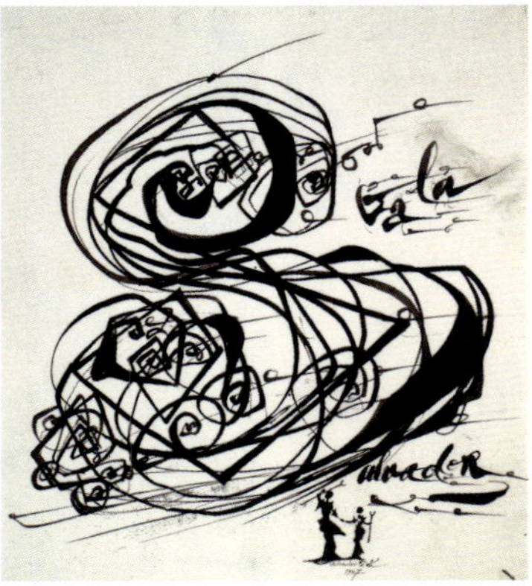

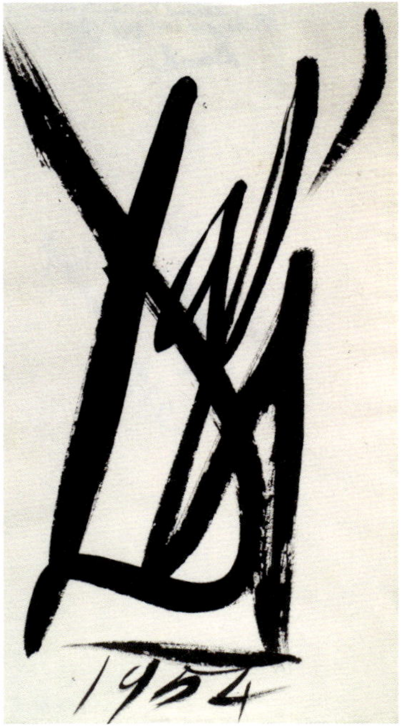


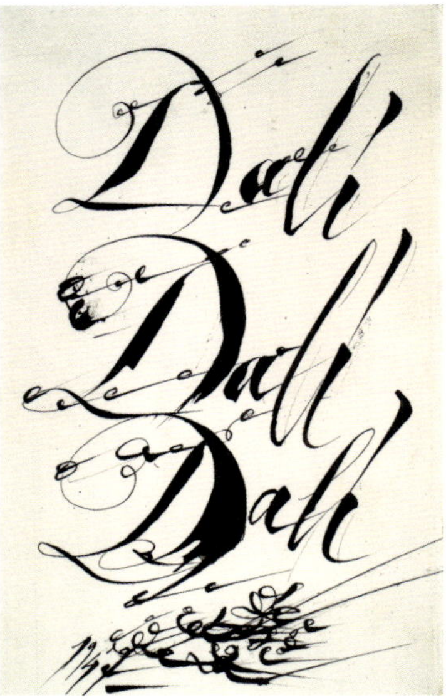




Salvador Dalí,
Entwürfe für Katalog-Titelseiten/sketches for exhibition catalogue covers, 1956 / 1947 / 1947 / 1954

4
Vorwort/Foreword

10
Gerald A. Matt
Le Surréalisme, c'est moi! Ein Ausstellungsparcours/
Le Surréalisme, c'est moi! An exhibition parcours

44
Belinda Grace Gardner
Aquarium der Wunder/Aquarium of Wonders

100
August Ruhs
Le Mal d'Aurore – Das frühe Leid der Kindheit?/
Le Mal d'Aurore – The early Suffering of Childhood?

174
David Lomas
You Take My Place in this Showdown: Salvador Dalí und Glenn Brown/You Take My Place in this Showdown: Salvador Dalí with Glenn Brown

220
Catherine Millet
Dalí und ich/Dalí and me

239
Wolfgang Fetz
Dalí – Warhol

262
Schuldige Augen
Glenn Brown im Gespräch mit Gerald A. Matt und Katarzyna Uszynska/Guilty Eyes
Glenn Brown in Conversation with Gerald A. Matt and Katarzyna Uszynska

277
Stummfilm Aquarium Markus Schinwald im Gespräch mit Lucas Gehrmann/Silent movie: Aquarium
Markus Schinwald in Conversation with Lucas Gehrmann

288
Dalí gegenüber sterbe ich sprichwörtlich vor Neid
Francesco Vezzoli im Gespräch mit Caroline Corbetta/
In front of Dalí I am literally sick with envy Francesco Vezzoli in conversation with Caroline Corbetta

288
Synne Genzmer
Hommage/Homage

292
Angst zersplittert einen
Louise Bourgeois im Gespräch mit Gerald A. Matt/
Fear fragments you
Louise Bourgeois in Conversation with Gerald A. Matt

295
Anhang/Appendix

# Vorwort/Foreword

It's like being with royalty or circus people.
Andy Warhol über Salvador Dalí

Exzentriker, Wahnsinniger, Genie? Wie kaum ein anderer Künstler des 20. Jahrhunderts löste Salvador Dalí (1904–1989) mit seinem Œuvre und seinem provokanten Auftreten die Grenzen zwischen Kunst und Leben, Originalität und Kommerz auf. Seine Visionen vom Surrealismus, der ästhetischen Verschmelzung von Traum und Wirklichkeit, die sich im Wahnbild, Fieber- und Rauschzustand oder Delirium äußert, setzte er in nahezu allen künstlerischen Medien um und darüber hinaus in der Inszenierung seiner selbst. Dalí gehört nicht nur zu den berühmtesten Malern seiner Generation, der im altmeisterlichen Stil die Prinzipien seiner sogenannten „paranoisch-kritischen Methode" anwandte und weltweit an seinen Motiven wiedererkannt wird. Dalí war auch einer der ersten Künstler, der sich mit Design, Kino und Massenmedien auseinandersetzte und Vermarktungsstrategien verfolgte, die heute vorrangig mit dem Namen Andy Warhol assoziiert werden. Dem Verfahren der Surrealisten um André Breton, die mit der *écriture automatique* die Bildwelt des Unbewussten über einen passiven Zustand des Ich zu evozieren versuchten, setzte Dalí einen demonstrativen Individualismus entgegen und reagierte polemisch auf die von der Gruppe vorgebrachten politischen Vorwürfe und den Ausschluss seiner Person: „Ich bin kein Surrealist. Ich bin der Surrealismus. Surrealismus ist keine Partei oder Marke; es ist ein Geisteszustand, für jeden einzigartig, der von keiner Vereinigung, Tabus, oder Moral beeinflusst werden kann. Es ist die totale Freiheit und das absolute Recht zu träumen." Für den Multimedia-Künstler, der sich auf fast jedem Feld der Kulturproduktion betätigte, der Bühnenbilder, Parfümflakons und Schmuck entwarf, mit Luis Buñuel, Alfred Hitchcock und Walt Disney arbeitete, Werbespots drehte, in Fernsehshows auftrat und seine Gemälde als Covermotive für *Vogue*, *Harper's Bazaar* und *Town & Country* zur Verfügung stellte, war Surrealismus eine Lebensweise. Dalí machte sich unzählige Rollen zu Eigen und kultivierte seinen Auftritt, der zur Marke und schließlich zur Karikatur wurde.

Zu Dalís 100. Geburtstag schrieb Peter Bürger: „Dalí, der 1989 starb, hat bisher noch keinen Ort in der Kunst des 20. Jahrhunderts gefunden." Die Ausstellung der Kunsthalle Wien akzentuiert Dalís kontrovers wahrgenommenes Schaffen im Spiegel zeitgenössischer Kunst neu und verweist auf Affinitäten, die vielseitige Berührungspunkte mit der gegenwärtigen Kunstwelt sichtbar machen: Rund 70 ausgewählte Werke von Salvador Dalí stehen den international etablierten Positionen von Louise Bourgeois, Glenn Brown, Markus Schinwald und Francesco Vezzoli gegenüber. Der Ausstellungsparcours führt durch atmosphärisch inszenierte Räume, wo diese vier künstlerischen Positionen exemplarisch in Dialog zu Dalí treten, um aktuelle Tendenzen und Varianten surrealer Ästhetik zu diskutieren. Markus Schinwald schuf eigens für die Ausstellung eine Arbeit, die sich mit der Verfremdung von Perspektive beschäftigt. Seine Installation eines wassergefüllten Schaukastens nimmt Bezug auf Dalís populär-surrealen Erlebnisraum, den er 1939 für die Weltausstellung in New York mit einem von lebenden Nixen animierten Schwimmbecken ausstattete. Als

Objekte in einer Art Wunderkammer präsentiert, visualisieren die Skulpturen und Zeichnungen von Louise Bourgeois den psychoanalytischen Zugang zum Bildnerischen, das in Träumen zum Vorschein kommende Unbewusste. Glenn Brown macht die Kunstgeschichte und ihre Maltradition zum Thema seiner Kunst: Technisch virtuos ausgeführte Gemälde verhandeln die Begriffe von Rezeption und Appropriation, Postmoderne und Manierismus anhand illusionistischer Farboberflächen. Francesco Vezzolis Arbeit ist inspiriert vom Phänomen der Berühmtheit, das sich medial konstruierter Projektionsflächen von Fantasien und Wünschen bedient. Die ausgewählten Künstler teilen mit Dalí das Interesse an der Darstellung von irrationalem Wissen und der Frage nach einer Realität zwischen Traum und Wirklichkeit.

*Le Surréalisme, c'est moi!* setzt die Ausstellungsreihe der Kunsthalle Wien fort, die das Werk großer Künstler aus der ersten Hälfte des 20. Jahrhunderts über philosophische, kunsthistorische und soziologische Diskurse in einen spannungsreichen Dialog zwischen künstlerischer Moderne und Gegenwartskunst stellt, um letztlich die Frage nach der Rolle von Kunst und Künstler in der Gesellschaft immer wieder neu zu stellen. Die von Dalí ausgegangenen noch wirksamen Impulse, die visionären, oftmals verkannten Aspekte seines außergewöhnlich vielseitigen Schaffens haben ebenso aktuelle Tendenzen des Surrealistischen beeinflusst wie auf Strategien des Kunstmarkts vorausgewiesen. Dalí brachte seinen eigenen Mythos hervor, trat als Provokateur und Tabubrecher auf und hinterlässt ein künstlerisches Œuvre, dessen stilistische Multiplizität und eigenwilliger Anachronismus die Gültigkeit der Kategorisierung von Avantgarde und Kitsch vor dem Hintergrund veränderter gesellschaftspolitischer Vorzeichen und einem damit einhergehenden Wandel ästhetischer Werte anhaltend hinterfragt.



Danken möchte ich an dieser Stelle allen, die zur Realisierung dieses ambitionierten Projektes beigetragen haben: An erster Stelle sei den teilnehmenden Künstlern und ihren Teams gedankt, die sich bei der Konzeption und Umsetzung der Raumgestaltung sehr engagiert haben: Glenn Brown mit Edgar Laguinia, Markus Schinwald, Francesco Vezzoli mit Luca Corbetta und Gioele Amaro. Ein besonders herzlicher Dank gilt dem Studio von Louise Bourgeois mit Jerry Gorovoy und Wendy Williams, die seit Beginn der Ausstellungsvorbereitung unser Vorhaben unterstützt und eine fantastische Auswahl von Werken von den vierziger Jahren bis 2008 zur Verfügung gestellt haben. Großer Dank gilt allen privaten Leihgebern, die sich oftmals nur schwer, wenn dies auch nur für kurze Zeit ist, von ihren Dalí-Werken getrennt haben und allen Museen für ihre großzügigen Leihgaben. Danken möchte ich den Autoren, die diese Publikation mit aufschlussreichen und für die Dalí-Rezeption sehr wichtigen Essays und Künstlergesprächen bereichert haben: Wolfgang Fetz, Belinda Grace Gardner, Lucas Gehrmann, David Lomas, August Ruhs. Gedankt sei auch Catherine Millet sehr herzlich für den Textauszug aus ihrem inspirierenden Buch *Dalí und Ich* und Caroline Corbetta, Lucas Gehrmann und Katarzyna Uszynska für ihre Interviewbeiträge. Ich danke Chris Goennawein für das großartige Katalogdesign, mit dem er Dalís Sinn für Altertümlichkeiten in eine zeitgenössische Form gegossen hat. Ebenso sei Silvia Jaklitsch sehr herzlich gedankt für die Aufnahme des Buches in das Verlagsprogramm des Verlags für moderne Kunst Nürnberg und ihre warmherzige Begeisterung für die Inhalte dieser Publikation. Dem Team der Kunsthalle Wien danke ich für die umsichtige und engagierte Umsetzung dieser Ausstellung: Claudia Bauer, Katharina Baumgartner, Johannes Diboky, Isabella Drozda, Lucas Gehrmann, Synne Genzmer, Katharina Murschetz, Barbara Nowy, Iris Spah, Viola Wagner und Michael Würges.

**Gerald A. Matt**
**Kurator der Ausstellung**
**Direktor der Kunsthalle Wien**

It's like being with royalty or circus people.
Andy Warhol on Salvador Dalí

Eccentric, madman, genius? To an extent greater than almost any other artist of the 20th century, Salvador Dalí (1904–1989) dissolved the borders between art and life, originality and commerce. His visions of Surrealism and the aesthetic fusion of dream and reality, which expresses itself as hallucination, fever and frenzy or delirium, were manifested in almost all artistic media and also in his self-dramatisation. Dalí is not only one of the most famous painters of his generation, who implemented the principles of his so-called paranoïac-critical method in the style of the Old Masters and is recognised for his motifs all over the world; Dalí was also one of the first artists to concern himself with design, cinema and mass media, and followed marketing strategies that are now mainly associated with the name Andy Warhol. The techniques of the Surrealists centering around André Breton, which tried to evoke the images of the unconscious through a passive condition of the ego using *écriture automatique*, were confronted by Dalí with a demonstrative individualism, as he reacted polemically to the political accusations and the exclusion of his person from the group by saying: "I am not a Surrealist. I am Surrealism. Surrealism is not a party or a label; it is a state of mind, unique, to each his own, that can be affected by no party line, taboo, or morality. It is the total freedom to be and the right to absolute dreaming." For this multimedia artist, who was active in almost every area of art production, designing stage sets, perfume bottles and jewellery, working with Hitchcock and Walt Disney, filming advertising spots, appearing on TV shows and making his paintings available as cover art for *Vogue*, *Harper's Bazaar* and *Town & Country*, Surrealism was a way of life. Dalí took over a huge range of roles and cultivated his appearance, which became a brand and, ultimately, a caricature.

On Dalí's 100th birthday, Peter Bürger wrote: "Dalí, who died in 1989, has still not found a place in the art of the 20th century." The exhibition at Kunsthalle Wien re-emphasises the controversial perception of Dalí's creativity in the mirror of contemporary art, and points to affinities that make the many kinds of contact points with the present-day art world visible: about 70 selected works by

Salvador Dalí are juxtaposed against the internationally established positions of Louise Bourgeois, Glenn Brown, Markus Schinwald and Francesco Vezzoli. The course of the exhibition leads one through atmospherically staged spaces, where four artistic positions are placed as examples in a dialogue with Dalí to discuss current trends and variants of surreal aesthetics. Markus Schinwald created a work especially for the exhibition, involving the alienation of perspectives. His installation of a display case filled with water makes reference to Dalí's popular surreal perceptual space, which he fitted out with a swimming pool animated by living water nymphs in 1939 for the World Fair in New York. As objects displayed in a kind of cabinet of curiosities, the sculptures and drawings of Louise Bourgeois visualise the psychoanalytical approach to imagery, the unconscious manifested in dreams. Glenn Brown takes art history and its painting tradition as the theme of his art: paintings executed with the skill of a virtuoso re-negotiate the concepts of reception and appropriation, and Post-modernism and Mannerism, based on illusionistically covered patches of colour. Francesco Vezzoli's work is inspired by the phenomenon of fame, using projection spaces of fantasy and desire constructed via various media. The artists exhibited share with Dalí an interest in visualising irrational knowledge, and the question of a reality somewhere between dream and reality.

*Le Surréalisme, c'est moi!* continues the series of exhibitions at Kunsthalle Wien, setting the work of great artists from the first half of the 20th century (involving philosophical, art-historical and sociological questions) into an exciting dialogue between artistic modernism and contemporary art, so as to ultimately pose – both repeatedly and freshly – the question of the role of art and artists in society and popular culture. The impact of Dalí's work is still effective: the visionary, often misunderstood aspects of his extraordinarily versatile creativity influenced contemporary trends of Surrealism no less than they affected and anticipated strategies of the art market. Dalí gave birth to his own myth, acted as a provocateur and breaker of taboos, and left an artistic oeuvre whose stylistic multiplicity and eccentric anachronism cast doubt on the validity of categorising the avant-garde and kitsch against the background of altered socio-political omens and an associated change in aesthetic taste.

At this point, I would like to thank all those who contributed to the implementation of this ambitious project: our first thanks goes out to the participating artists and their teams, who demonstrated utmost commitment in the conception, realisation and shaping of spaces: Glenn Brown with Edgar Laguinia; Markus Schinwald; Francesco Vezzoli with Luca Corbetta and Gioele Amaro. We are especially grateful to the studio of Louise Bourgeois with Jerry Gorovoy and Wendy Williams, who, from the beginning, supported our project and made a fantastic selection of works from the 1940s to the year 2008 available. We are very grateful to all private lenders, who some-times found it very hard to part with their Dalís, even for this short period of time, and to all museums for their generous loans. I also wish to thank all the authors who enriched this publication with insightful essays and artist interviews that are extremely important for the reception of Dalí: Wolfgang Fetz,

Belinda Grace Gardner, Lucas Gehrmann, David Lomas, and August Ruhs. Big thanks also go out to Catherine Millet for the excerpt from her inspirational book, *Dalí and Me*, and to Carolina Corbetta, Lucas Gehrmann and Katarzyna Uszynska for the interviews they contributed. I thank Chris Goennawein for the superb design of the catalogue, where he has molded Dalí's sense of antiquities into a contemporary form. Big thanks to Silvia Jaklitsch as wellfor integrating the book into the publication programme of the Verlag für moderne Kunst in Nuremberg and her warm-hearted enthusiasm for the contents of this publication. I thank the team at Kunsthalle Wien for their careful and committed realisation of this exhibition: Claudia Bauer, Katharina Baumgartner, Johannes Diboky, Isabella Drozda, Lucas Gehrmann, Synne Genzmer, Katharina Murschetz, Barbara Nowy, Iris Spah, Viola Wagner and Michael Würges.

Gerald A. Matt
Curator of the exhibition
Director of Kunsthalle Wien



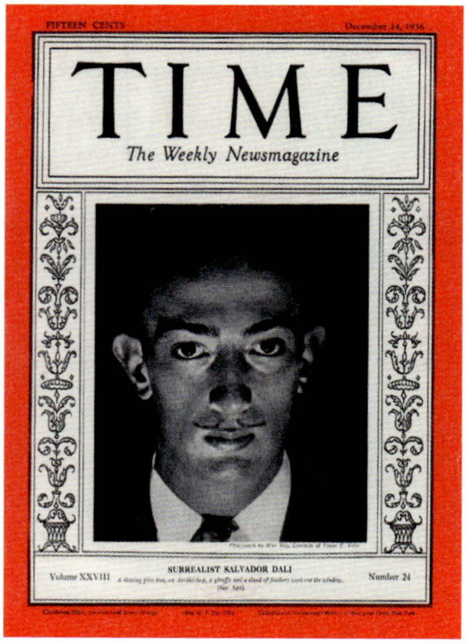


Salvador Dalí, Fotografie von/photograph by Man Ray auf dem Cover/ on the cover of *Time*, 14/12/1936

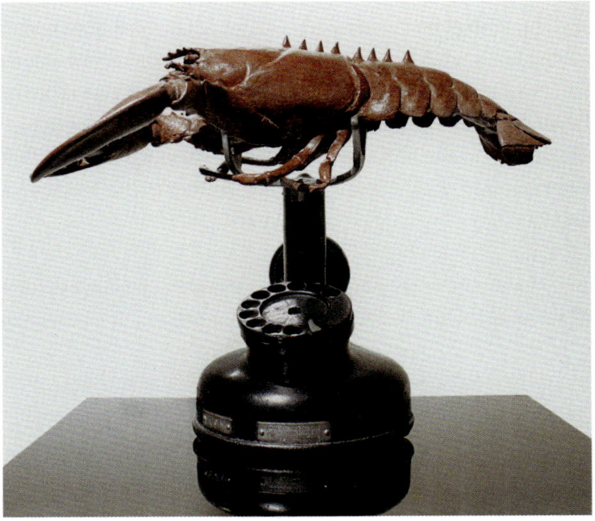

Salvador Dalí,
*Téléphone-homard ou Téléphone aphrodisiaque*, 1936



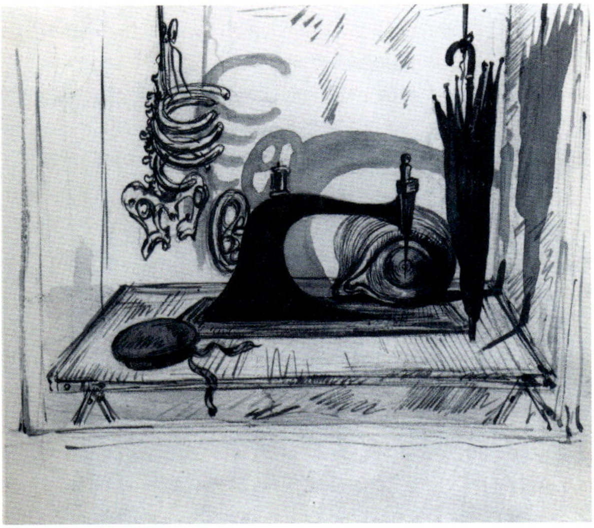

Salvador Dalí,
*Homenaje a Lautréamont*, c. 1945

# Gerald A. Matt
# Le Surréalisme, c'est moi!
# Ein Ausstellungsparcours

„Das Bild ist eine reine Schöpfung des Geistes. Es kann nicht aus dem Vergleich, vielmehr nur aus der Annäherung von zwei mehr oder weniger voneinander entfernten Wirklichkeiten geboren werden. Je entfernter die Beziehungen dieser Wirklichkeiten zueinander sind, desto stärker wird das Bild sein."

> Pierre Reverdy, in: André Breton, „Manifeste du Surréalisme", in: *La Révolution surréaliste*, Nr. 1/1924.

Die Kritik an der „sogenannten kartesianischen Welt, die uns umgibt", an einer „unhaltbaren Welt [...] wogegen jede Form des Aufstands gerechtfertigt" sei,

> André Breton, *Entretiens – Gespräche*, hg. v. U. Hörner & W. Kiepe. Amsterdam, Dresden 1996, S. 121.

propagierte André Breton. Dabei ging es ihm vor allem auch um den „Aufstand" gegen den überkommen-traditionellen Schönheitsbegriff. Die in seinem *Manifeste du Surréalisme* (1924) zitierte Aussage seines Freundes Pierre Reverdy entspricht dabei ganz dem von Breton selbst so genannten „hasard objectif", der Annäherung zweier in ihrer „Binnenlogik" konträrer Ideen oder Dinge, die aus ihrer Begegnung heraus wie zwei verschiedene aufeinanderprallende Kräfte eine ungeahnte neue Kraft entfalten – eine Synthese, welche die Grenze zwischen „Subjekt" und „Objekt", zwischen Traum beziehungsweise Unterbewusstsein und Wirklichkeit aufhebt. So ist Reverdys Aussage nichts anderes als ein Pamphlet gegen die kartesianische Vernunft. Das Ziel ist die Auflösung der Grenze zwischen Kunst und Leben bis hin zu ihrer gegenseitigen fruchtbaren Verflüssigung.

# Gerald A. Matt
# Le Surréalisme, c'est moi!
# An exhibition parcours

"The image is a pure creation of the mind. It cannot be born from a comparison but from an encounter of two more or less distant realities. The more the relationship between the two juxtaposed realities is distant and true – the greater is the emotional power and poetic reality..."

> Pierre Reverdy, in André Breton, „Manifeste du Surréalisme," in *La Révolution surréaliste*, no. 1/1924.

André Breton propagated a critique of the "putative Cartesian world that surrounds us" of an "unsustainable world – against which every form of revolution [is] justified."

> André Breton, *Entretiens – Gespräche*, ed. by U. Hörner & W. Kiepe, Amsterdam, Dresden, 1996, 121.

His most central concern, in this instance, is the revolt against the established, traditional notion of beauty. The statement quoted above, by his friend Pierre Reverdy, published in Breton's 1924 *Manifeste du Surréalisme* (Surrealist Manifesto) corresponds fully to Breton's own socalled "hasard objectif" (loosely translated: objective chance encounters). Thus the coming together of two elements, which for the very inner logic of contrary ideas or things is an encounter in which extremely different powers collide against each other, unfurls a new unforeseen, undreamt of power – a synthesis which eradicates the borders between 'subject' and 'object,' between dream (i.e. the unconscious) and reality. As a consequence, Reverdy's statement here is nothing less than a pamphlet against Cartesian reason. Its purpose is to dissolve the borders between art and life so they seep into mutual,

Dieser Perspektivenwechsel – der „Durchbruch von der ‚Denkform' zur ‚Lebensform'", wie es Ernst Cassirer einmal nannte – geht auf das letzte Drittel des 19. Jahrhunderts zurück. Literarisch wird diese Haltung in den 1870 in Paris erschienenen *Les Chants de Maldoror* des Isidore Ducasse, genannt Comte de Lautréamont, formuliert, welche von Breton 1919 im *Journal Literature* nachgedruckt und seither als Poetik der Übertretung (Gilbert Lascaolt) berühmt und vielfältigst rezipiert wurden. „Mit diesem Text vollzog sich eine Volte hinsichtlich dessen – was künftig als Schönheit zu gelten habe […], es ist die generelle Weigerung, Künstlerisches nach konventionellen ästhetischen Kriterien zu beurteilen", wie Steffen Dietzsch anmerkt. Lautréamonts diesbezügliche poetische Neubestimmungen waren vorderhand degoutant, provokativ und nihilistisch – „schön" etwa „wie das Zittern der Hand bei Alkoholsucht".

Comte de Lautréamont, *Les Chants de Maldoror*, 5. Ch., 2. Kap. Paris 1870 [ed. Re Soupault, Heidelberg 1954, S. 211].

Die meistzitierte Passage aus Lautréamonts Gesängen ist allerdings die vergleichsweise liebevolle Beschreibung der Schönheit eines Knaben: „Er ist sechzehn Jahre und vier Monate alt. Er ist so schön wie die Einziehbarkeit der Raubvogelkrallen; oder auch wie die Unschlüssigkeit der Muskelbewegungen in den Wunden der Weichteile der hinteren Genicksgegend; oder vielmehr wie jene perpetuelle Rattenfalle, die von dem gefangenen Tier selbst immer von Neuem gespannt, allein und unaufhörlich Nagetiere fangen kann und die sogar unter Stroh versteckt arbeitet; und vor allem wie die unvermutete Begegnung einer Nähmaschine und eines Regenschirms auf einem Seziertisch!"

cross-fertilising and fruitful liquefaction. This change of perspective – the "breakthrough of 'thought form' to 'life form'" (Ernst Cassirer) – refers back to the last third of the $19^{th}$ century. In literary terms this attitude appeared in Paris in 1870 with *Les Chants de Maldoror* by Isadore Ducasse, known as the Comte de Lautréamont, which Breton reprinted in his 1919 *Journal Literature* and that has since been renowned as the poetics of transgression (Gilbert Lascaolt) garnering the most diverse acclaim. "What takes place in this text is a volte face regarding – what is to be considered beauty in the future […], it is the general refusal to judge the artistic by conventional aesthetic criteria," remarked Steffen Dietzsch. In this regard Lautréamont's poetical reclassification was at first sight, disgusting, provocative and nihilistic – "beautiful," for instance, "like the trembling hand of alcohol addiction."

Comte de Lautréamont, *Les Chants de Maldoror*, 5. Ch., Paris 1870 [ed. Re Soupault, Heidelberg, 1954, 211].

The most frequently quoted passage from Lautréamont's chants is the comparatively loving description of the beauty of a male youth: "He is sixteen years and four months old! He is as handsome as the retractability of the claws of birds of prey; or again, as the uncertainty of the muscular movements of wounds in the soft parts of the posterior cervical region; or rather as the perpetual rat trap, re-set each time by the trapped animal, that can catch rodents indefinitely and works even when hidden beneath straw; and especially as the fortuitous encounter upon a dissecting table of a sewing-machine and an umbrella!"

Ebd., 6. Ch., 2. Kap., I [ed. Re Soupault, Heidelberg 1954: S. 250] („[...] beau comme la rencontre fortuite sur une table de dissection d'une machine à coudre et d'une parapluie!")

Unter den surrealistischen Malern gibt es kaum einen, der Lautréamonts Gesänge nicht illustriert hat. 1934 lieferte auch Salvador Dalí seinen Beitrag – einen Radierzyklus, der in seiner Gesamtheit in der Ausstellung *Le Surréalisme, c'est moi!* zu sehen ist und der für Dalís wohl wichtigstes grafisches Werk gehalten werden kann. Eine 1945 entstandene Hommage an Lautréamont Dalís (*Homenaje a Lautréamont*, Abb. S. 9), welche jene berühmte Begegnung „von zwei mehr oder weniger voneinander entfernten Wirklichkeiten" auf einem Seziertisch zum Gegenstand hat, bildet den gleichsam programmatischen Einstieg in diese Ausstellung. *Le Surréalisme, c'est moi!* – ein Zitat Dalís – verweist als Ausstellungstitel nicht allein auf den Protagonisten Dalí und seinen ausgeprägten Sinn zur Selbstdarstellung, sondern es soll auch der darin ironisch gebrochene und dennoch ausgesprochene hegemoniale Anspruch des Surrealismus (als „Staat/Etat" also, ungeachtet einmal seines Sonnenkönigs) angedeutet werden: Elementare Gedanken, Ideen und Praktiken des Surrealismus haben bis heute nicht nur Aktualität in weiten außerkünstlerischen Feldern (etwa als Gegenmodelle zu einer noch immer primär kartesianisch geprägten Welt), sondern beeinflussen auch viele wichtige Positionen der bildenden Kunst, ohne dass diese als „surreal(istisch)" im Sinne eines Ismus zu bezeichnen wären.
Anhand von vier ausgewählten Positionen zeitgenössischer bildender Kunst sollen in jeweiliger Gegenüberstellung mit Werken



Ibid., 6. Ch., 250 ("[...] beau comme la rencontre fortuite sur une table de dissection d'une machine à coudre et d'une parapluie!")

Hardly a Surrealist painter was not to illustrate Lautréamont's chants. In 1934 Salvador Dalí made his contribution – a cycle of etchings, in its entirety on view at the exhibition *Le Surréalisme, c'est moi!,* one which can be regarded as the most important of his graphic works. Also Dalí's homage to Lautréamont (*Homenaje a Lautréamont*, 1945, ill. 9), actually creates an image of that famous encounter "of two more or less distant realities" on a dissecting table and at the same time renders a programmatic introduction to this exhibition. *Le Surréalisme, c'est moi!* – a Dalí quote – as exhibition title refers not only to the protagonist Dalí and his acute sense of self-promotion but also implies the ironic, broken and nonetheless hegemonic claim of Surrealism (i.e. L'Etat/the State is me, irrespective of its once sun king): to this day elementary thoughts, ideas and practices of Surrealism, have not just influenced the current day situation in broad areas outside of or extra to artistic fields (for instance as antitheses to a world still primarily formed by Cartesian thought) but also mould many important positions of the visual arts, without them being described as "Surreal(istic) in the sense of an 'ism'."
Works from four selected positions of contemporary visual art have been set in particular confrontation to works by Dalí (in this instance therefore they are not chance encounters but ones founded on extensive research and discussions with the artists, who in the final selection turned out not just to be significant artist personalities, but all shared an admiration

Dalís (diesmal sind diese Begegnungen nicht zufällig, sondern basieren auf ausgedehnten Recherchen und Gesprächen mit Künstlerinnen und Künstlern, die in einer finalen Auswahl signifikanter und an Dalí interessierter Künstlerpersönlichkeiten endeten) einige wesentliche Parameter surrealistischen Denkens und Handelns und insbesondere im Hinblick auf die Arbeit, das Denken und die Praxis des wohl bekanntesten Surrealisten Dalí auf ihre „Nachhaltigkeit", ja auch auf eine Art Comeback hin untersucht werden. Dabei geht es vorrangig um die Bedeutung des Unterbewussten, die Auflösung der Grenzen zwischen Hoch- und Populärkultur, die Rezeption kunstgeschichtlicher Themen und Techniken sowie um die Erfindung des Künstlers als (Medien-)Star. Wenn Dalí hierbei tatsächlich für den Surrealismus steht, liegt dies vor allem daran, dass er das Prinzip des „hasard objectif" nicht nur vertritt, sondern gleichsam alle denkbaren, voneinander entfernten Wirklichkeiten in sich vereint – und Surrealismus dadurch lebte und verkörperte wie kein anderer. So ließ er seine Legende auch nicht erst um sich herum entstehen, sondern brachte sie gleich selbst hervor. „Ein Leben lang spielt er der Welt den Exzentriker vor, der an der Grenze des Wahnsinns lebt, den großen Provokateur und Tabubrecher. Er liefert den Medien die lebende Karikatur des genialen Künstlers, zwirbelt seinen Schnurrbart hoch und reißt die Augen auf. Wie steht dazu die Arbeit dieses Malers und Zeichners, der die akademischen Techniken perfekt beherrscht?"

Peter Bürger, „Zum Malen verdammt. War Salvador Dalí wirklich wahnsinnig?", in: *Die Zeit*, Feuilleton, 6. 5. 2004.

of Dalí). As a result a few essential parameters with Surrealist thought and activity, with particular regard to the work, thought and practice of Dalí, the most renowned of the Surrealists, investigate its "sustainability," indeed with a view to a kind of come back. What is of most concern here is the meaning of the subconscious, the dissolving of the boundaries between high and popular culture, the reception of art historical subjects and techniques as well as the discovery of the artist as (media) star.
If Dalí actually does stand for Surrealism here then it is above all due to the fact that he does not just simply represent the "hasard objectif" but merges, as it were, all thinkable realities more or less distant from one another – and in so doing he lives and embodies Surrealism as no other. Thus he does not simply let the legend build up around him but creates it himself directly. "Life-long he acted-out the world of the eccentric, someone who lived on the borders of madness, the grand provocateur and taboo-breaker. He gave to the media the living caricature of an ingenious artist, curled his moustache upward and opened his eyes wide. How does one view the work of this painter and draughtsman who mastered academic techniques to perfection?"

Peter Bürger, "Zum Malen verdammt. War Salvador Dalí wirklich wahnsinnig?," in *Die Zeit*, Feuilleton, 6. 5. 2004.

"A blazing pine tree, an Archbishop, a giraffe and a cloud of feathers went out the window," read the caption of New York's *Time* magazine dated 14th December 1936 (ill. p. 8), featuring on its cover a reproduction of Man Ray's photographic portrait of the "Surrealist Salvador

„A blasing pine tree, an Archbishop, a giraffe and a cloud of feathers went out the window", untertitelte das New Yorker Magazin *Time* vom 14. Dezember 1936 ein auf dem Cover wiedergegebenes Porträtfoto des „Surrealist[en] Salvador Dalí" von Man Ray (Abb. S. 8). Diese Ausgabe der *Time* bildet den Prolog zur Ausstellung, gemeinsam mit einigen Zeichnungen, dem Buch Lautréamonts, der schon genannten Hommage Dalís an dessen Autor sowie dem *Hummer-Telefon* von 1936 (Abb. S. 9), das die auf einer Antimonie basierenden Motive von Regenschirm und Nähmaschine ins Skulpturale transferiert. Nicht zuletzt wird damit auf jenen vielgesichtigen Künstler hingewiesen, über den André Parinaud 1973 schrieb: „Dalí sagt nie *je,* sondern *jeux* [frz. je – ich; jeux – Spiele]. Denn Dalí ist das Ja und das Nein, der Widerspruch selbst, die Herausforderung. Wenn Dalí ‚ich' sagt, so spricht nicht Dalí, sondern nur *ein* möglicher Dalí, den ich kenne und aus den tausend anderen, die er verkörpert, heraushöre."

**André Parinaud, *Comment on devient Dalí, les aveux inavouables de Salvador Dalí*, 1973; deutsch: *So wird man Dalí*, 1974, 1986.**

Salvador Dalís Beitrag für die New Yorker Weltausstellung von 1939, der Pavillon *Dream of Venus* (Abb. S. 24–39), ist nicht nur von Zitaten aus der Kunstgeschichte und dem eigenen Werk des Künstlers geradezu überladen, sondern in seinem Inneren vor allem ein Spektakel zwischen Wasserballett, Varieté- und Puppentheater. Überliefert ist dieses surreale Gesamtereignis durch Fotografien von Eric Schaal, welche vereinzelt publiziert und in dieser Form auch von Markus Schinwald gesichtet wurden. Dieser greift für seinen Beitrag



Dalí." Together with various drawings, Lautréamont's book, the already mentioned homage to the author by Dalí and the *Lobster Telephone* (1936, ill. p. 9), this edition of *Time* magazine forms a prologue to the exhibition – to refer to the multi-facetted artist about whom André Parinaud wrote in 1973: "Dalí never says je, but always jeux [French: je – I; jeux – play/game]. For Dalí is the yes and the now, the contradiction itself, the challenge. When Dalí says 'I' it is not Dalí who speaks, but one possible Dalí, whom I know that I hear, out of the thousand others that he embodies."

**André Parinaud, *Comment on devient Dalí, les aveux inavouables de Salvador Dalí*, 1973.**

Salvador Dalí's contribution to the New York World Fair in 1939 – a pavilion titled *Dream of Venus* (ill. pp. 24–37), not only featured quotes from art history and the artists' own works emblazoned around it, but its interior offered a spectacle somewhere between water ballet, variety and puppet theatre. This traditional surreal total incident is documented through the occasionally published photographs of Eric Schaal. For his contribution to the exhibition, Markus Schinwald, first and foremost, takes on the glass water container to present scenarios for the animation of the inanimate. Dali achieves his spectacle with real "ballerinas" diving through water and costumed display mannequins and other "accessories," whereas Schinwald transfers this concept using a pair of catfish sporting with a "black beard" in front of a (at least conceived of) stage set: an aquarium recessed into a wall. Hence Schinwald confronts Dalí's spectacle with a quite contemplative situation – in this respect literally as Eric Schaal's photographic documentation

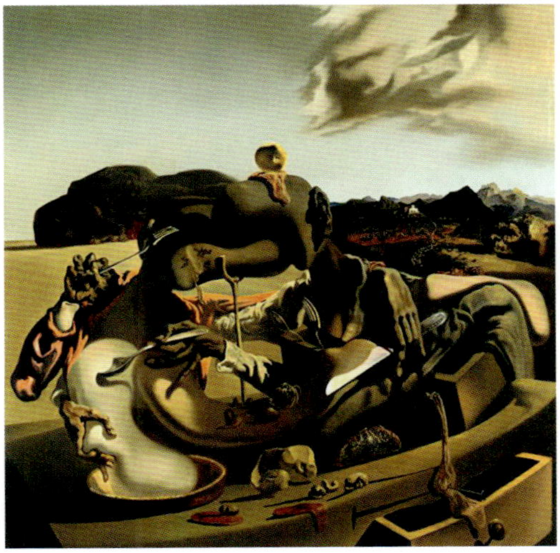

Abb./ill. 1, Salvador Dalí,
*Herbstlicher Kannibalismus/Autumnal Cannibalism*, 1936
Öl auf Leinwand/oil on canvas
65,1 × 65,1 cm

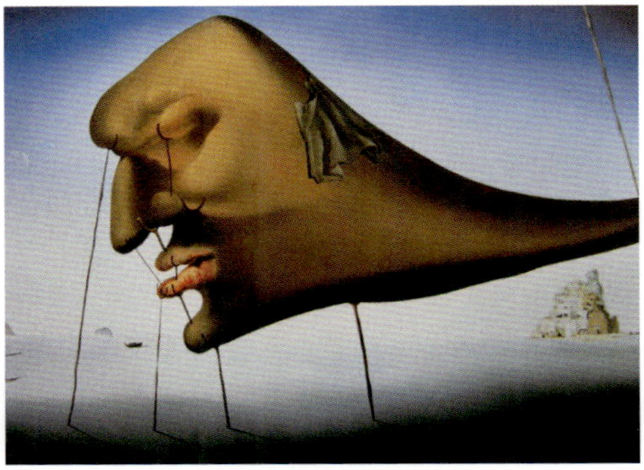

Abb./ill. 3, Salvador Dalí,
*Der Schlaf/Sleep*, 1937
Öl auf Leinwand/oil on canvas
51 × 78 cm

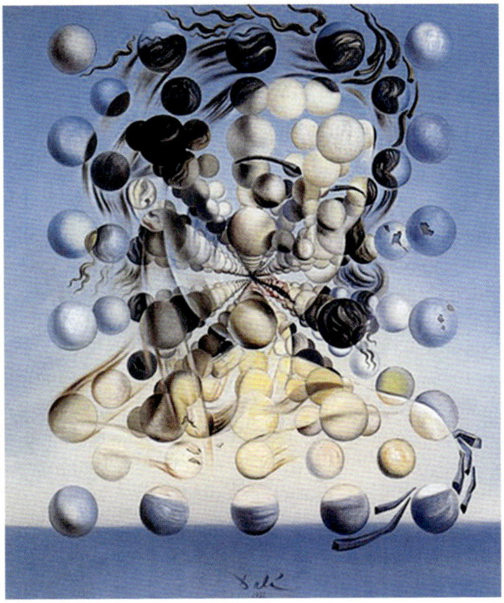

Abb./ill. 2, Salvador Dalí,
*Galatea of the Spheres*, 1952
Öl auf Leinwand/oil on canvas
65 × 54 cm

zur Ausstellung vor allem die gläsernen Wasserbehälter als Szenarien zur Belebung des Unbelebten auf. Was bei Dalí durchs Wasser tauchende reale „Ballerinen" sowie kostümierte Schaufensterpuppen und andere „Accessoires" leisteten, übernimmt bei Schinwald ein Marmorantennenwelsfischpärchen mit „schwarzem Bart" vor einem (zumindest konzipierten) Bühnenbild: ein in die Wand eingelassenes Aquarium. Dem Spektakel Dalís stellt Schinwald eine gänzlich kontemplative Situation gegenüber – und dies insofern wörtlich, als Eric Schaals Fotodokumentationen des Dalí'schen *Venus*-Pavillons im selben Ausstellungsraum als Projektionen vis-à-vis über die Wand takten. Schinwald referenziert hierbei nicht allein auf das theatralisch-filmische Moment bei Dalí, indem er es entschleunigt und ihm auch jede (narrative) Handlung entzieht, er reagiert auch auf den populärkulturellen Anteil in Dalís Szenario, indem er sich eines Objektes bedient, das sich so gut wie in „jedem Haushalt" befindet, zugleich aber fast nie Gegenstand der Kunst ist: das Aquarium. In erster Linie geht es Schinwald dabei aber einmal mehr um den Film und seine Phänomenologie: „Meine Filme haben keinen Anfang und kein Ende. Sie bestehen eigentlich nur aus Mitte. Es ist eine Art Pseudo-Narration, in der bestimmte Handlungen zwar angedeutet, aber nicht zu Ende gebracht werden; eine Art künstliche Ruine, so als würde man in einem Drehbuch die Szenen, die die Handlung vorantreiben, einfach wegnehmen und nur den Rest übrig lassen."

Markus Schinwald, zitiert aus: *Edward Hopper, Western Motel*, hg. von Gerald A. Matt, Ausst.-Kat. Kunsthalle Wien 2008, S. 112.



of the Dalí *Venus* Pavilion is synchronised in the same exhibition space, vis-a-vis on the wall. Here Schinwald reflects not just on the theatrical filmic moment of Dalí, in that he completely decelerates it and deprives it of every (narrative) action, likewise he reacts to the popular cultural aspect in Dalí's scenario by using an object that one could find in virtually "every household" but which simultaneously is virtually never an object used in art – the aquarium. Of prime concern to Schinwald here is actually film and its phenomenology: "My films have no beginnings and no end. They consist, basically, just of the middle bit. It is a kind of pseudo narrative, where certain actions are hinted at, but not brought to any conclusion."

Markus Schinwald, quoted from *Edward Hopper, Western Motel*, ed. by Gerald A. Matt, Exh. cat. Kunsthalle Wien 2008, 112.

The nightmarish etchings for *Les Chants de Maldoror* that Dalí completed for the publisher Albert Skira, in which Dalí rendered the evil other, the deviant and perverse, rage and destruction, the deformation and decay of his reference surround a "room within a room" closed to the outside and accessible through two entrances. The graphic narration of Maldoror – who as Dalí once wrote "negated everything, father, mother, destiny, love, ideals in order only to think of himself" and ultimately "overshadowed" Dalí's own life – circles, in the exhibition, a "retrospective curiosity cabinet" featuring works by Louise Bourgeois, who continually worked on her own similarly problematic stories of childhood and youth. These have been combined into a

Die albtraumhaften Radierungen zu den Gesängen des Maldoror, die Dalí für den Verleger Albert Skira gefertigt hat und in denen Dalí dem bösen Anderen in sich, dem Abartigen und Abwegigen, dem Furor und der Zerstörung, der Deformation und dem Verfall seine Reverenz erweist, umgeben einen nach außen abgeschlossenen, nur durch zwei Zugänge betretbaren „Raum im Raum". Die grafische Erzählung zu Maldoror, der, wie Dalí einmal schrieb, „alles verleugnet hat, Vater, Mutter, Vorsehung, Liebe, Ideal, um nur noch an sich selbst zu denken" und der schließlich auch Dalís Leben „überschattet" hat, umkreist in der Ausstellung eine „retrospektive Wunderkammer" mit Werken von Louise Bourgeois, die ihre eigene, gleichermaßen problematische Kindheits- und Jugendgeschichte immer wieder künstlerisch aufarbeitet und zu einer Art visuellem Tagebuch vereinigt. Die Ausstellung präsentiert über Zeichnungen und Objekte von 1945 bis zu ihrem Tode – einer umfassenden Werkschau gleich – die unterschiedlichsten Aspekte ihres Œuvres. „Mein Vater redete pausenlos. Ich hatte nie Gelegenheit, etwas zu sagen. Da habe ich angefangen, aus Brot kleine Sachen zu formen. Wenn jemand immer redet und es sehr weh tut, was die Person sagt, dann kann man sich so ablenken. Man konzentriert sich darauf, etwas mit seinen Fingern zu machen. Diese Figuren waren meine ersten Skulpturen, und sie repräsentieren eine Flucht vor etwas, was ich nicht hören wollte. [...] Es war eine Flucht vor meinem Vater. Ich habe zahlreiche Arbeiten zu dem Thema ‚The Destruction of the Father' gemacht. Ich vergebe nicht und ich vergesse nicht. Das ist das Motto, das meine Arbeit nährt", sagte Louise Bourgeois im Alter von 95 Jahren. In den Vitrinen der Kammer sind

kind of visual journal which through drawings and objects presents the most various aspects of her artistic work – an all-embracing body of work – dating from 1945 to her death. "My father talked non-stop. I never had the opportunity to say a thing. Then I began to shape little things out of bread. If someone talks all the time and it really hurts what that person says, then I can distract myself this way. One concentrates on making something with one's fingers. These figures were my first sculptures and they represent a flight from something I didn't want to hear. [...] It was a flight from my father. I have made numerous works on the subject 'The Destruction of the Father.' I don't forgive and I don't forget. That is the motto which nourishes my work,"

„Dieses zwingende Bedürfnis zu arbeiten. Louise Bourgeois, ein Potrait", in *Kulturzeit extra*, 8. 7. 2006.

said Louise Bourgeois at the age of 95. Over 50 works by Louise Bourgeois have been put together in the cabinet's vitrines, small-scale sculptures which now and then register Dalíesque motifs and forms such as *Soft Landscape I* (1967, ill. p. 83), *Untitled (Clocks)* (1944, ill. p. 74) and *Topiary* (2005, ill. p. 93) – a woman's body with an acorn leaf for a head recalling Dalí's Gala portrait of flowers (*Flores surrealistas*, 1938, ill. p. 125). Selected objects represent the entire breadth of Louis Bourgeois' thematic and material vocabulary, sublimated variants of amputated, oppressed, fragmented bodies mistreated by nails or knives, which speak of wounds and pain. In neighbourhood some works of Dalí, amongst them the drawing of a Sphinx and an object metamorphosed somewhere between tower and human elucidate

„Dieses zwingende Bedürfnis zu arbeiten. Louise Bourgeois, ein Potrait", in: *Kulturzeit extra*, 8. 7. 2006.

über 50 Werke von Louise Bourgeois versammelt, kleinformatige Skulpturen, deren Motive und Formen immer wieder eine Nähe zu Dalí erkennen lassen wie *Soft Landscape I* (1967, Abb. S. 83), *Untitled (Clocks)* (1944, Abb. S. 74) oder *Topiary* (2005, Abb. S. 93) – ein Frauenkörper mit einem Ahornblatt als Kopf, der an Dalís Gala-Porträt aus Blumen erinnert (*Flores surrealistas*, 1938, Abb. S. 125). In der ganzen Bandbreite des Themen- und Materialvokabulars von Louise Bourgeois repräsentieren die ausgewählten Objekte sublimierte Varianten des amputierten, geschundenen, fragmentierten, von Nägeln oder Messern malträtierten Körpers, der von Verwundung und Schmerz spricht. Dazwischen gesellen sich einige Werke Dalís, unter anderem die Zeichnung einer Sphinx (*Esfinge*, c. 1947, Abb. S 71) und eines metamorphotischen Objektes zwischen Turm und Mensch (*Estudio*, 1942, Abb. S. 73), welche die Bezüge, aber auch die Gegensätze zwischen den Traumobsessionen von Salvador Dalí und Louise Bourgeois verdeutlichen. Die unterschiedlichen psychologischen Hintergründe ebenso wie das ästhetische Spannungsverhältnis verdichten sich in der Gegenüberstellung von zwei signifikanten Skulpturen in der Mitte des Raumes. Bourgeois' *Lady in Waiting* (2003, Abb. S. 76), eine Spinne auf einem Fauteuille, eingeschlossen in eine kabinenartige Box, ist ebenso mit Femininität wie Gewalttätigkeit besetzt, denn die stählernen Beine wachsen aus dem weichen Textilkörper heraus, indem sie diesen durchbohren. Seine Assemblage *Objet scatologique à fonctionnement symbolique*, auch bekannt als *Galas Schuh* (1930, Rekonstruktion

the relationship as well as the contradictions between the dream obsessions of both Salvador Dalí and Louise Bourgeois. The differing psychological backgrounds become particularly vivid in the confrontation of two significant sculptures in the middle of the room. Bourgeois' *Lady in Waiting* (2003, ill. p. 76), a spider on an easy chair, enclosed in a cabin-like box, is as charged with femininity as it is with violence, as the steely legs grow out of the soft textile body which also bore through it. The assemblage *Objet scatologique à fonctionnement symbolique* also known as *Gala's Shoe* (1930, reconstruction 1973, ill. p. 87) was understood by Dalí to be an erotically charged object translating Freud's notion of fetishism into an artistic form: a woman's red shoe, modelling clay, a glass of milk, a brush without bristles, sugar cubes, a spoon, and pubic hair.
The conflict-burdened debate with sexuality, power and fear find their continuation through the exhibition: from Dalí's painting *The Tower* (1936, ill. p. 121) via his *Colossus of Rhodes* (1954, ill. p. 120), in which human or, better said, male images of omnipotence find their gigantic or rather phallic orientation, to Dalí's dream sequences for Hitchcock's film *Spellbound* (1945, ill. p. 225). *Spellbound*, a film in which through his love for his analyst played by Ingrid Bergman and their work on his repressed trauma (the alleged murder of a colleague), the protagonist Gregory Peck not only regains his memory and identity but through a thrilling linking up of psychoanalytical and criminological methods, also solves a murder case. At the centre point of the Daliesque dream sequence in *Spellbound* is an enormous stage- scenery-like curtain covered with innumerable eyes. This work, in which

1973, Abb. S. 87), verstand Dalí als erotisch besetztes Objekt und Übersetzung von Freuds Begriff des Fetischismus in eine künstlerische Form: ein roter Damenschuh, Knetmasse, ein Milchglas, eine Bürste ohne Borsten, Zuckerwürfel, ein Löffel, Schamhaare. Die konfliktreiche Auseinandersetzung mit Sexualität, Macht und Angst findet ihre Fortsetzung im weiteren Ausstellungsparcours: von Dalís Gemälde *Der Turm* (1936, Abb. S. 121) über seinen *Koloss von Rhodos* (1954, Abb. S. 120), in denen menschliche oder wohl besser noch männliche Allmachtsvorstellungen ihre gigantomanische beziehungsweise phallische Orientierung finden, zu Dalís Traumvisionen für Hitchcocks Film *Spellbound* (1945, Abb. S. 225). *Spellbound*, ein Film, in dem der Protagonist Gregory Peck über seine Liebe zur Analytikerin Ingrid Bergmann und der gemeinsamen Aufarbeitung seines verdrängten Traumas, dem vermeintlichen Mord an einem Kollegen, nicht nur seine Erinnerung und seine Identität wiedergewinnt, sondern auch in einer spannenden Vernetzung psychoanalytischer und kriminalistischer Methoden den Mordfall aufklärt. Im Mittelpunkt der Dalí' schen Traumsequenzen für *Spellbound* steht ein riesiger, mit unzähligen Augen bedeckter, bühnenbildhaft gestalteter Vorhang. Dieses Werk Dalís, das die Bildvision fixierender Augen eines imaginären Betrachters ins Riesenhafte der Kinoleinwand erweitert, fasziniert Glenn Brown ebenso wie die Verwandlung des Auges in eine Art Raumschiff in Dalís *The Eye* (1945, Abb. S. 135), das einer entseelten, dunklen, unfreundlichen und vom Leben befreiten Welt zu entschweben scheint und seinen Widerhall in Browns Science-Fiction-Motiven und außerirdischen Landschaften findet. Wie Dalí liebt Brown

Dalí furthers his visionary image of the imaginary viewer with fixating eyes on a mammoth cinema screen, fascinated Glenn Brown. Likewise the transformation of the eye in a kind of space ship in Dalí's *The Eye* (1945, ill. 135), which appears floating loose from life and freed from a soulless, dark, unfriendly world finds its echoes in Brown's science fiction motifs and alien landscapes. Like Dalí, Brown loves art historical references; they coincide in their interest in painters such as El Greco, Velázquez and William Blake. Glenn Brown's work is influenced by a scepticism toward reality and its representability and continually falls back on high painterly intensity and quality, on strategies of illusion ranging from deceptive trompe l'œil effects through confusing shifts in dimension, to startling effects of paint. Brown's still-lives, landscapes and portraits settle between dream and nightmare, illusion and reality, and seem to be distant from space and time and, like Dalí's landscapes, become mirages of an unreal world. When observing Brown's works one is reminded inevitably of the list made up by Alfred H. Barr, who curated the 1936 exhibition at the New York Museum of Modern Art, *Fantastic Art, Dada, Surrealism,* and which implied the "fundaments, techniques and medium of these movements."

Alfred H. Barr jr, *Fantastic Art, Dada, Surrealism,* New York, 1947, 65–66.

Fundaments which Gustav Rene Hocke in his book *Die Welt als Labyrinth* (The World as Labyrinth) takes up again as "Mannerist."

kunsthistorische Bezüge: im Interesse für Maler wie El Greco, Velázquez oder William Blake treffen sich beide. Glenn Browns Arbeit ist beseelt von der Skepsis an der Wirklichkeit und ihrer Darstellbarkeit und greift immer wieder mit hoher malerischer Intensität und Qualität auf Strategien der Illusion zurück, von täuschenden Trompe l'œil-Effekten über verwirrende Dimensionsverschiebungen bis hin zu überraschenden Farbeffekten. Auch Browns Stillleben, Landschaften und Porträts siedeln zwischen Traum und Albtraum, Illusion und Realität und scheinen wie Dalís Landschaften fern von Raum und Zeit zu sein, Trugbilder einer unwirklich gewordenen Welt. Beim Betrachten der Arbeiten Browns wird man unweigerlich an jene von Alfred H. Barr jr. erstellte Auflistung für die von ihm 1936 im New Yorker Museum of Modern Art kuratierte Ausstellung *Fantastic Art, Dada, Surrealism* erinnert, welche die „Grundsätze, Techniken und Mittel"

Vgl. Alfred H. Barr jr, *Fantastic Art, Dada, Surrealism*, New York 1947, S. 65–66.

dieser Bewegungen beinhaltet; Grundsätze, die von Gustav René Hocke als „manieristisch" in seinem Buch *Die Welt als Labyrinth* wieder aufgegriffen werden.

Gustav René Hocke, *Die Welt als Labyrinth. Manier und Manie in der europäischen Kunst*. Reinbek bei Hamburg 1987.

Einige dieser Kategorien sind beispielsweise die fantastische Perspektive, die Bewegung des Unbeseelten und die Metamorphose, die Isolierung anatomischer Fragmente, die Vereinigung



Gustav René Hocke, *Die Welt als Labyrinth. Manier und Manie in der europäischen Kunst*, Reinbek bei Hamburg, 1987.

Some of these categories are the fantastic perspectives, the movement of the inanimate and the metamorphosis, the isolation of anatomical fragments, the unification of the incoherent, wonder and anomalies, organic abstractions, fantastic construction and dream images. Brown is not interested in the originals, but in the already altered copies, which he, however, does not copy but like in his painting *Oscillate Wildly* (1999, ill. p. 136–137) with direct reference to Dalí's work *Autumnal Cannibalism* (1936, ill. 1) he alienates, distorts, enlarges or, as in his latest photographic works, allows to go out of focus. The play on pictorial illusion continues in the abstract metamorphoses of paintings such as *International Velvet* (2004, ill. p. 127) and *Come All Ye Rolling Minstrels* (2009, ill. p. 128), whose iridescent paint surfaces present the abject body as a vegetal organ in a placeless space. Dalí describes the dissolving of the human silhouette in *Flores surrealistas* with motif-like means – a bouquet of flowers – also referred to by Brown in his painting *Architecture and Morality* (2004, ill. p. 122) –, or in the painting *Gala of the Spheres* (1952, ill. 2) as geometric exploded surfaces of three-dimensional spheres which contradict the unity of the face by an atomised form.
In consequence, the encounter of Francesco Vezzoli's Dalí portrait is based on a photograph by Horst P. Horst (*Le Surréalisme, c'est moi! (Portrait of Salvador Dalí with Jewels and Tears, After Horst)*, 2009, ill. p. 210), which positions the star artist between saintly worship and an ironic kitsch rendering and Andy Warhol's

des Inkohärenten, Wunder und Anomalien, organische Abstraktionen, fantastische Konstruktionen und Traumbilder.
Doch Brown interessieren nicht die Originale, sondern deren bereits veränderte Kopien, die er jedoch nicht kopiert, sondern wie sein direkt auf Dalís Werk *Herbstlicher Kannibalismus* (1936, Abb. 1) Bezug nehmendes Gemälde *Oscillate Wildly* (1999, Abb. S. 136–137) verfremdet, verzerrt, vergrößert oder wie in seinen neuesten fotografischen Werken bis zur Unschärfe verfließen lässt. Das Spiel mit der piktoralen Illusion setzt sich in den abstrakten Metamorphosen seiner Gemälde wie *International Velvet* (2004, Abb. S. 127) oder *Come All Ye Rolling Minstrels* (2009, Abb. S. 128) fort, die mit schillernden Farboberflächen den Widerwillen erregenden Körper als vegetabiles Organ im ortlosen Raum darstellen. Die Auflösung der menschlichen Silhouette beschreibt Dalí in seinen *Flores surrealistas* mit motivischen Mitteln – einem Blumenstrauß – auf die auch Glenn Brown in seinem Gemälde *Architecture and Morality* (2004, Abb. S. 122) zurückgreift oder im Gemälde *Gala of the Spheres* (1952, Abb. 2) als geometrisch zersprengte Oberfläche aus dreidimensional dargestellten Kugeln, die der Einheit des Gesichtes eine atomisierte Form entgegenhalten.
In Folge begegnen sich Francesco Vezzolis Dalí-Porträt, das basierend auf einer Fotografie von Horst P. Horst (*Le Surréalisme, c'est moi! (Portrait of Salvador Dalí with Jewels and Tears, After Horst)*, 2009, Abb. S. 210), den Starkünstler zwischen heiligenbildhafter Verehrung und verkitschter Ironisierung positioniert, und Andy Warhols *Screen Test* (1966, S. 205) von Dalí, in dem Warhol – vermutlich auf den Wunsch Dalís hin – den Spanier auf den Kopf stellt und

*Screen Test* of Dalí (1966, ill. p. 205), in which Warhol – probably upon Dalí's wish – turns the Spaniard on his head and in doing so bears out the Mannerist-Surrealist principle of "inversion." Programmatic writings of Dalí and a selection from the many magazines which featured Dalí on the front page, showing him in the most various of poses, extend the thematisation and reflection of Dalíesque self-presentation and self-centredness forming the beginning of the artistic and media star cult with which Francesco Vezzoli's works are occupied. Here Dalí utilised his fame extremely early on for the marketing of products such as his self-designed jewellery, his adverts for cars, chocolate, air travel and even the stomach and headache powder Alka-Seltzer, thus Vezzoli renounced on his film *Greed* (2009, ill. p. 216–217) directed by Roman Polański already on to a commercialisable, real product and invented the application of an imaginary perfume as a new artwork. Vezzoli's fascination and obsession with the social and media phenomenon of the star disembogues into an artistic "Hall of Fame" with lush violet drapes that bring to mind a surreal laying-out hall of fame deceased. Hence Vezzoli integrates into Dalí's painting *Sleep* (1936, ill. 3) Elizabeth Taylor's face (*Le sommeil in Hollywood*, 2008, ill. p. 215), from whose dead eyes flow jewellery pieces of congealed tears. In Vezzoli's grove of heroes and heroines – because in the end it is his preference and predominant interest in Hollywood's divas – the ambivalent interests of an entire generation of artists, from Jeff Koons to Julian Schnabel is manifest in yearning and critique. Dalí's eccentricities and genius for presentation find congenial counterpart in the absurd portraits by Philippe Halsman (ill. p. 206–207), damit dem manieristisch-surrealistischen Prinzip der „Inversion“ huldigt. Programmatische Schriften Dalís und eine Auswahl einzelner Covers von den Legionen von Zeitschriften, die Dalí auf die „Frontpage“ setzten und ihn in unterschiedlichsten Posen präsentierten, ergänzen die Thematisierung und Reflexion der Dalí'schen Selbstdarstellung und Selbstbezogenheit, und bilden den Auftakt zu den sich mit dem künstlerischen und medialen Starkult beschäftigenden Arbeiten Francesco Vezzolis. Hatte Dalí seinen Starruhm schon sehr früh für die Vermarktung von Produkten von dem von ihm selbst entworfenen Schmuck bis hin zu Werbungen für Autos, Schokoladen, Flugreisen und gar für das Magen und Kopfwehpulver Alka-Seltzer kommerziell verwertet, so verzichtet der von Vezzoli konzipierte und von Roman Polański gedrehte Film *Greed* (2009, Abb. S. 216–217) bereits auf ein kommerzialisierbares, reales Produkt und erfindet die Bewerbung eines imaginären Parfüms als Kunstwerk neu. Vezzolis Faszination und Obsession für das soziale und mediale Phänomen des Stars mündet in eine mit violetten Vorhängen üppig ausgestaltete künstlerische „Hall of Fame“, die an eine surreale Aufbahrungshalle verblichenen Ruhmes erinnert. So versieht Vezzoli Dalís Gemälde *Der Schlaf* (1936, Abb. 3) mit Elizabeth Taylors Antlitz, aus dessen toten Augen zu Schmuckstücken geronnene Tränen fließen. In Vezzolis Helden- und Heldinnenhain – denn letztlich gelten seine Vorlieben und Interessen vorwiegend den Diven Hollywoods, so nennt er sein Werk auch *Le Sommeil in Hollywood* [Schlaf in Hollywood] (2008, Abb S. 215) – manifestieren sich die ambivalenten Interessen einer ganzen Künstlergeneration von Jeff Koons bis Julian Schnabel

which precede the final filmic sequence of the exhibition. In Jean-Michel Othoniel's video titled *Es bello como el encuentro fortuito entre un paraguas y una máquina de coser* [as handsome as the fortuitous encounter upon a dissecting table of a sewing-machine and an umbrella] (1993, ill. p. 287) the two Maldororish objects of the Surrealist state melt before our eyes. If "the world has become unsustainable" then the concept of an other, dreamed reality is at once obsolete, what remains is an empty unlaid table.

am Scheinwerferlicht des Ruhmes zwischen Sehnsucht und Kritik.
Dalís Exzentrizität und Darstellungsgenie finden ihre kongeniale Entsprechung in den absurden Porträts von Philippe Halsman (Abb. S. 206–207), die der filmischen Schlusssequenz der Ausstellung vorangehen. In Jean-Michel Othoniels Video mit dem Titel *Es bello como el encuentro fortuito entre un paraguas y una máquina de coser* [So schön wie die unvermutete Begegnung einer Nähmaschine und eines Regenschirms auf einem Seziertisch] (1993, Abb. S. 287) schmelzen vor unseren Augen die beiden maldororschen Objekte surrealer Befindlichkeit weg. Wenn „die Welt unhaltbar geworden ist", wird auch die Vorstellung einer anderen geträumten Wirklichkeit alsbald obsolet, was bleibt, ist ein leerer, ungedeckter Tisch.

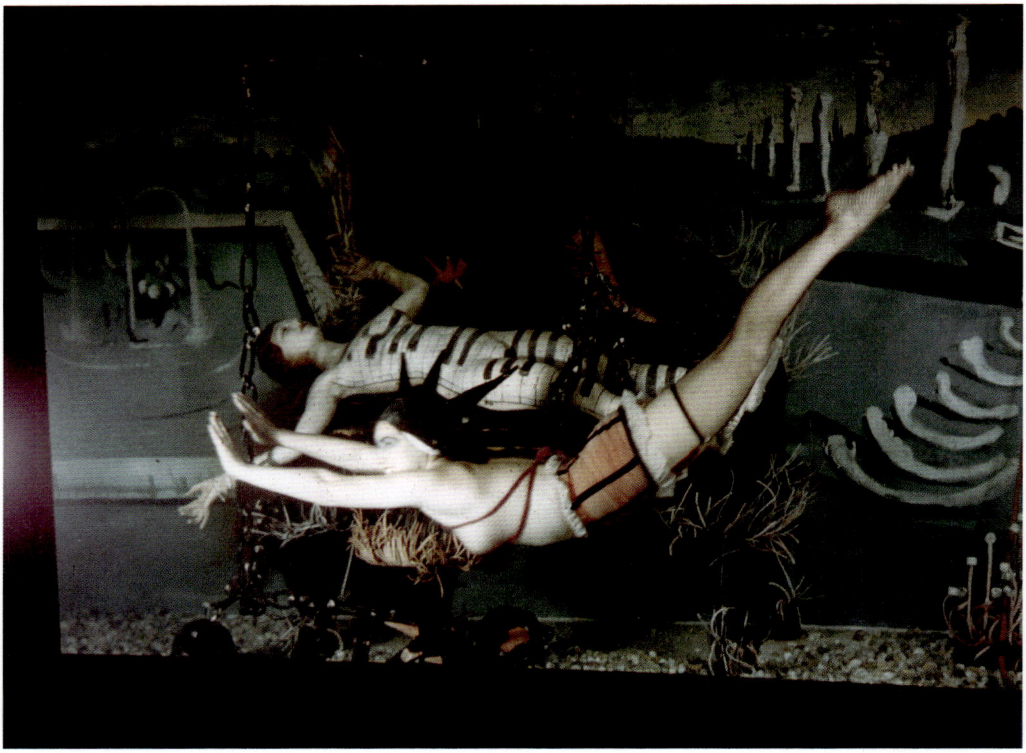

Salvador Dalí,
*Dream of Venus-Pavillon*, 1939,
Fotografien von/photographs by Eric Schaal

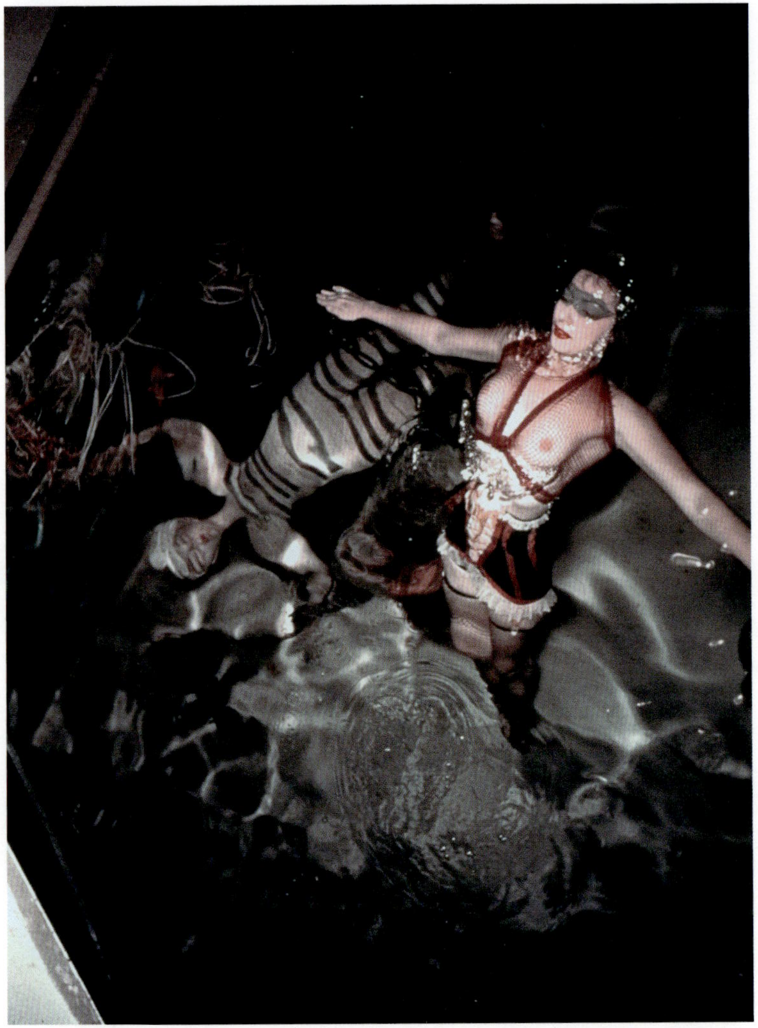

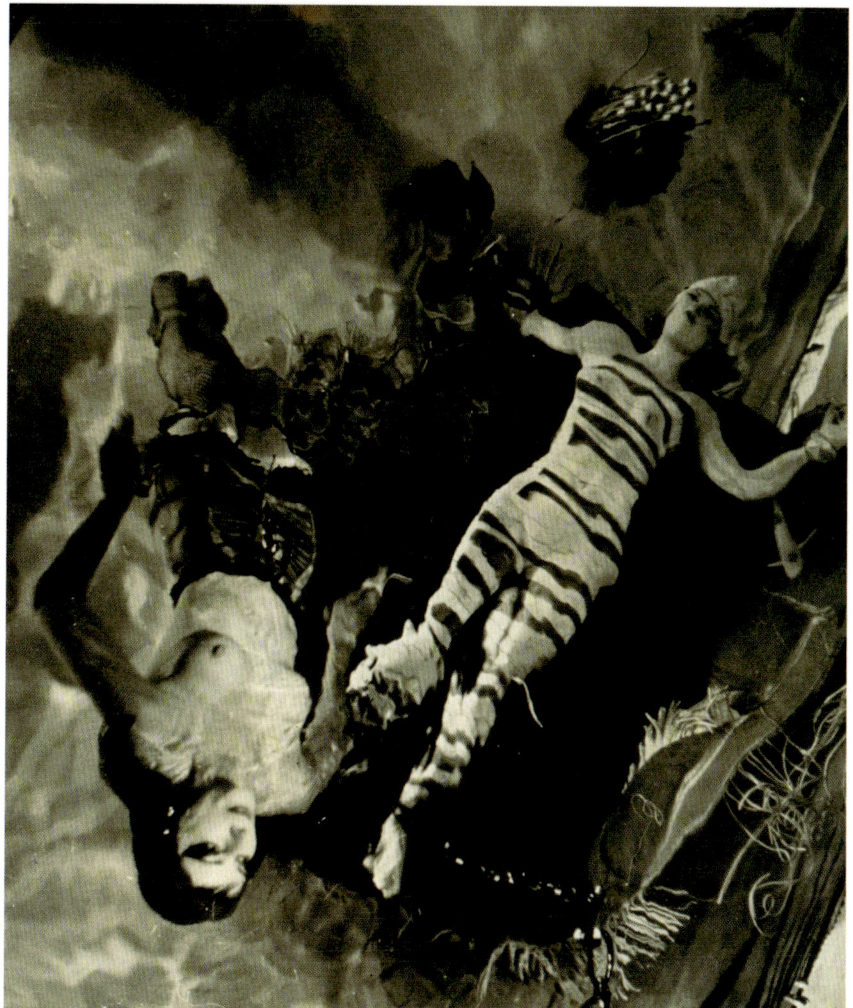

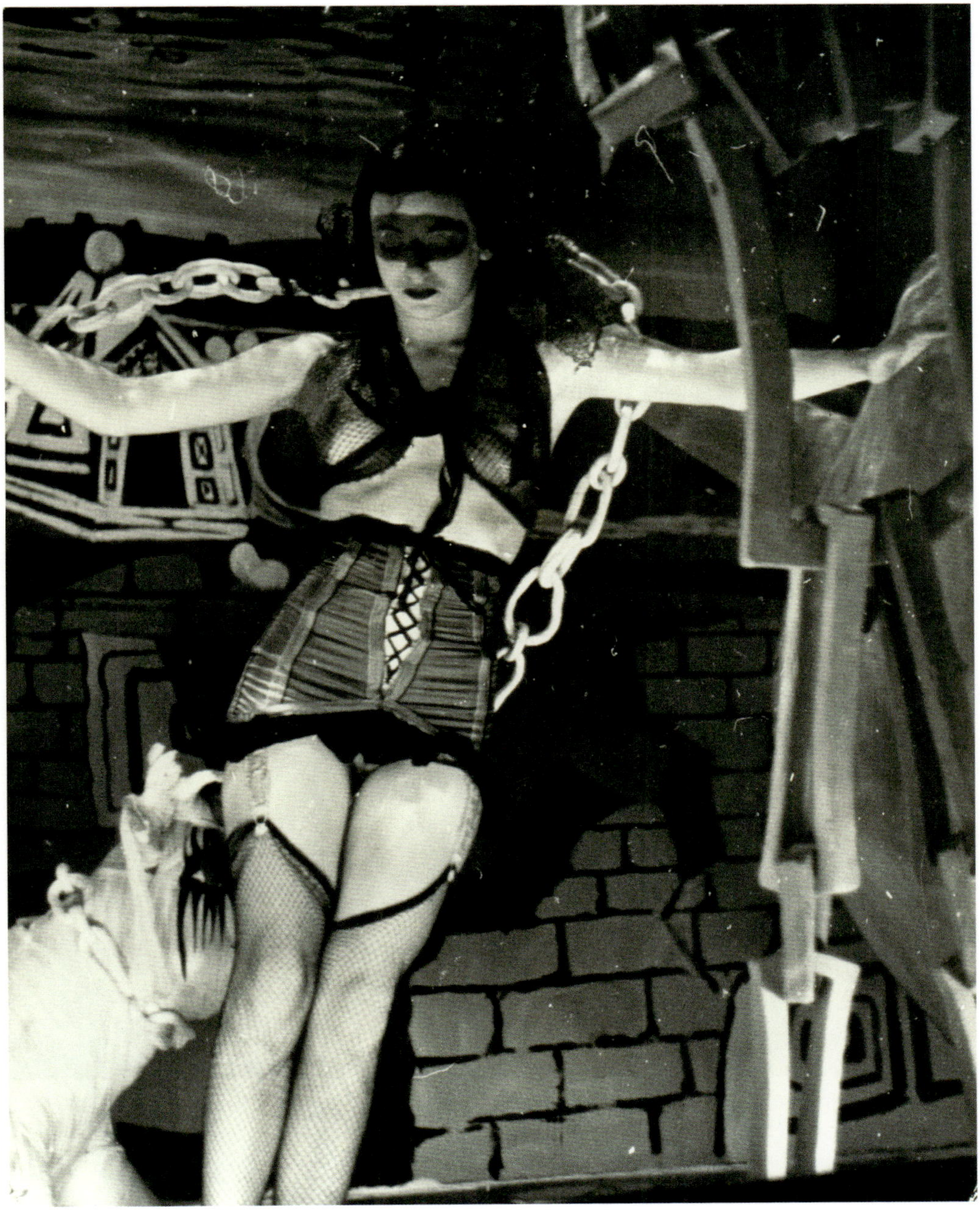

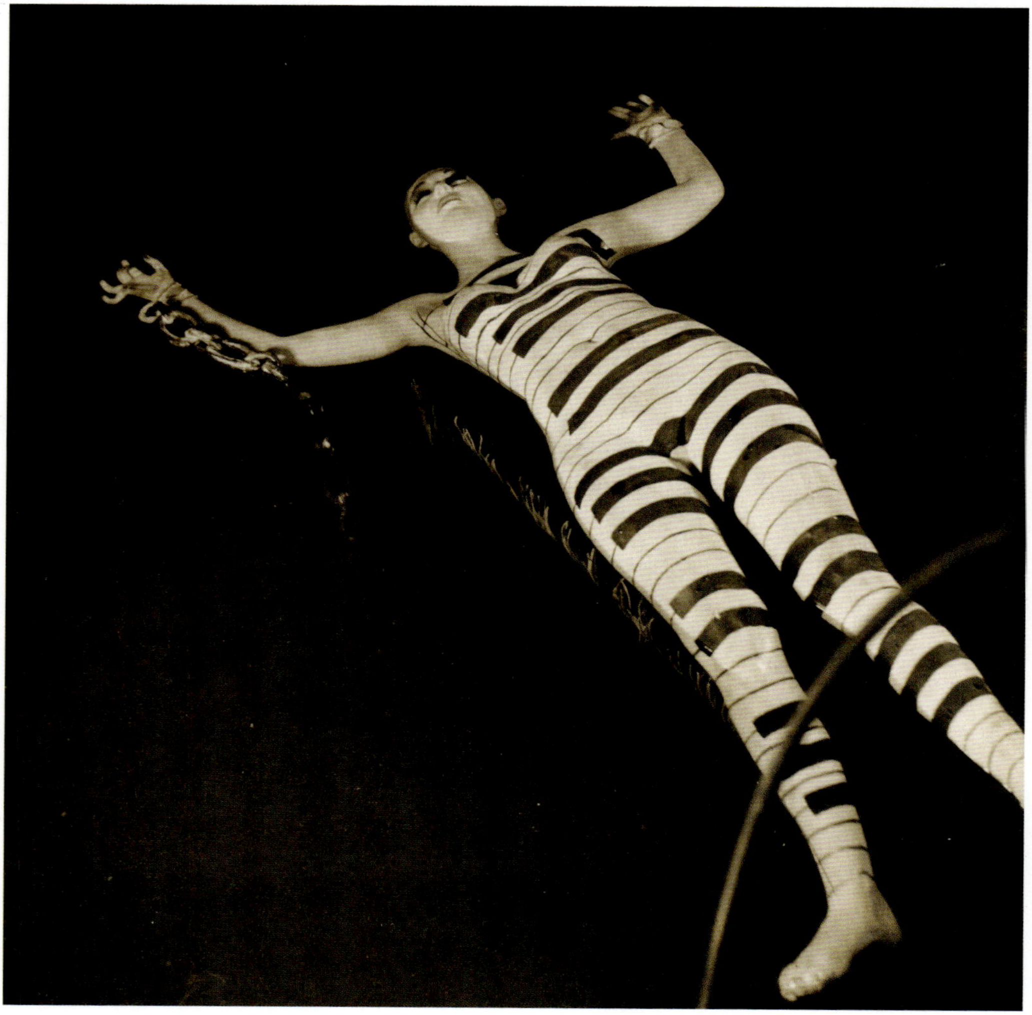

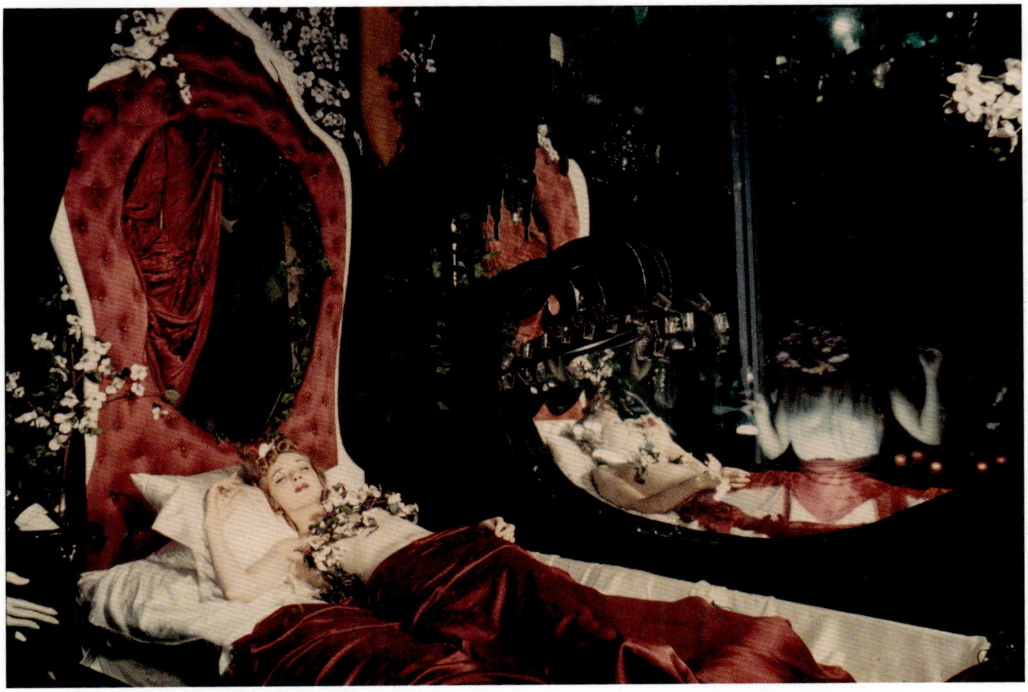

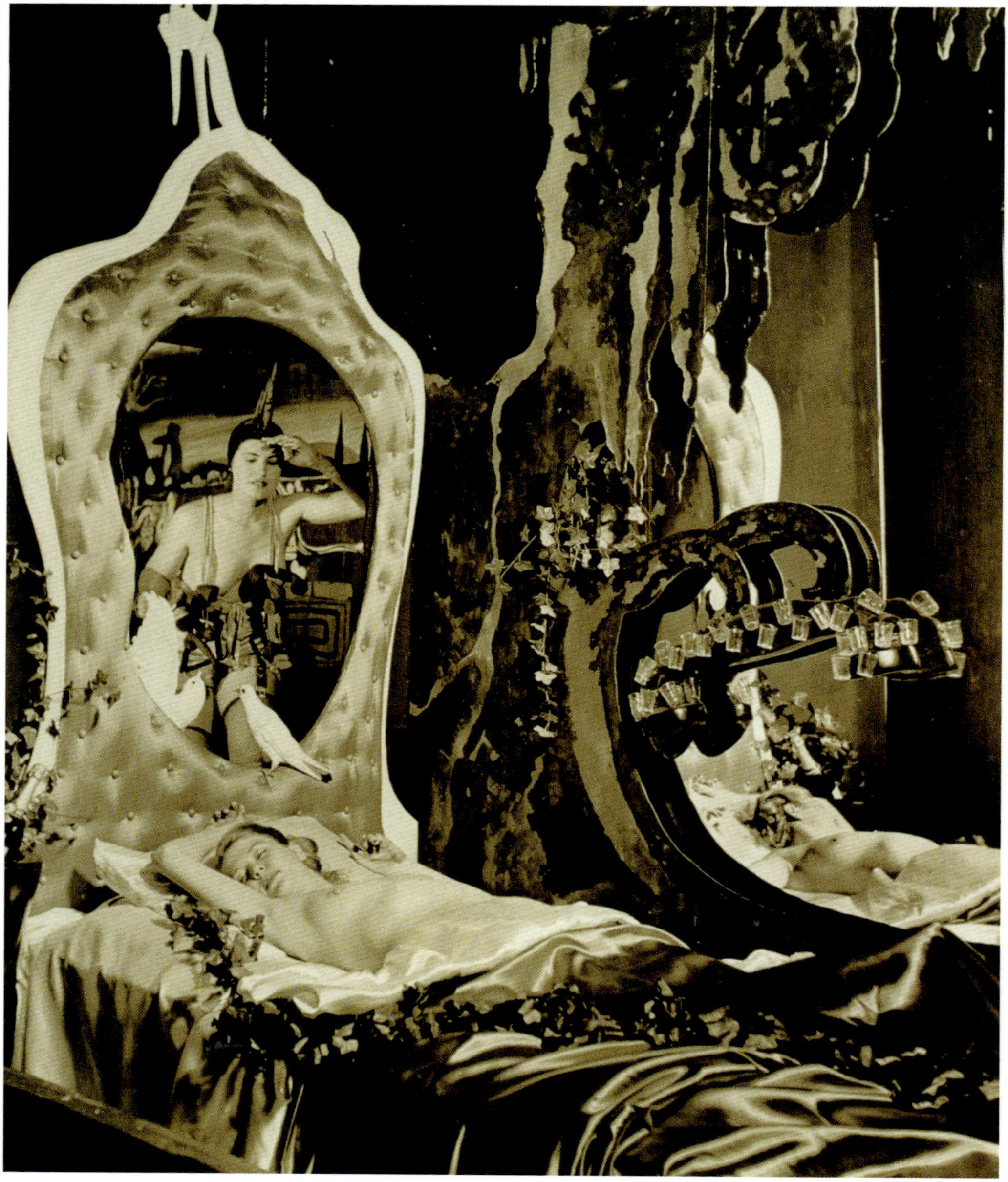

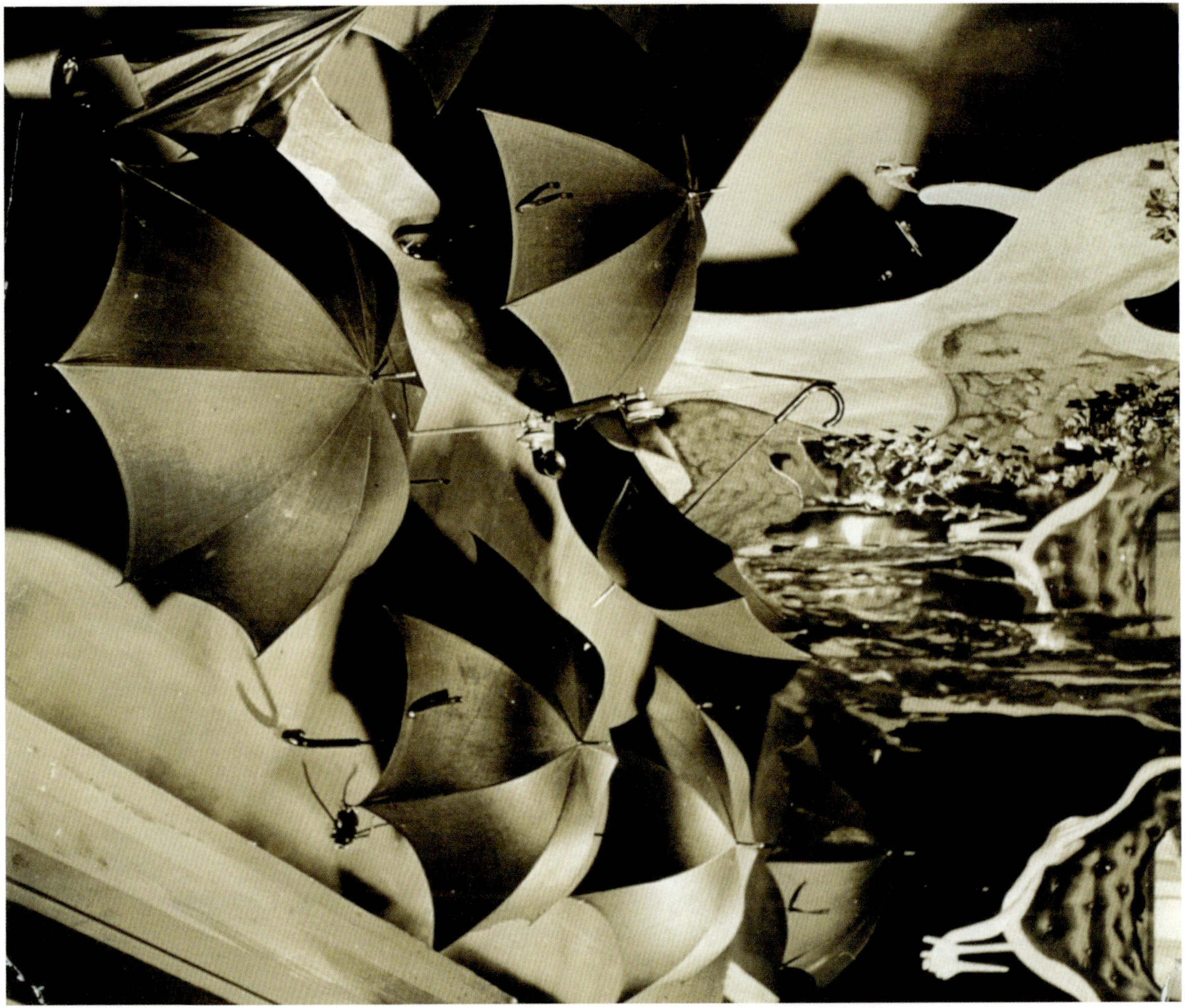

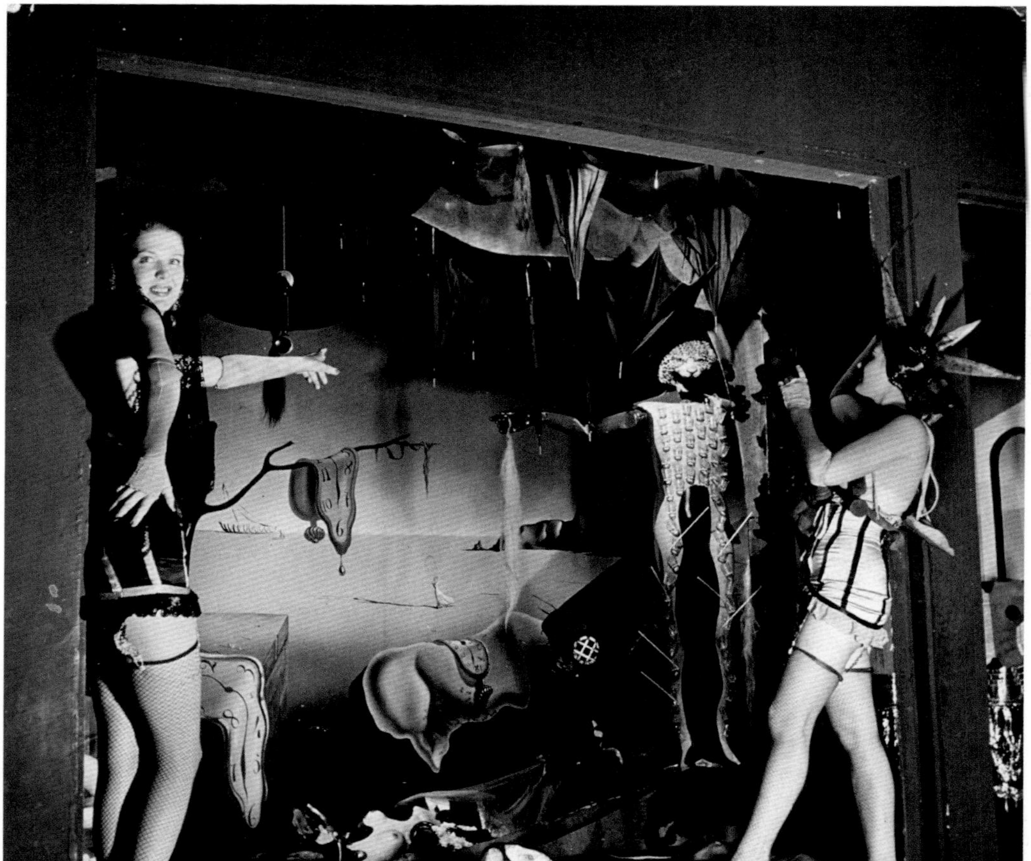

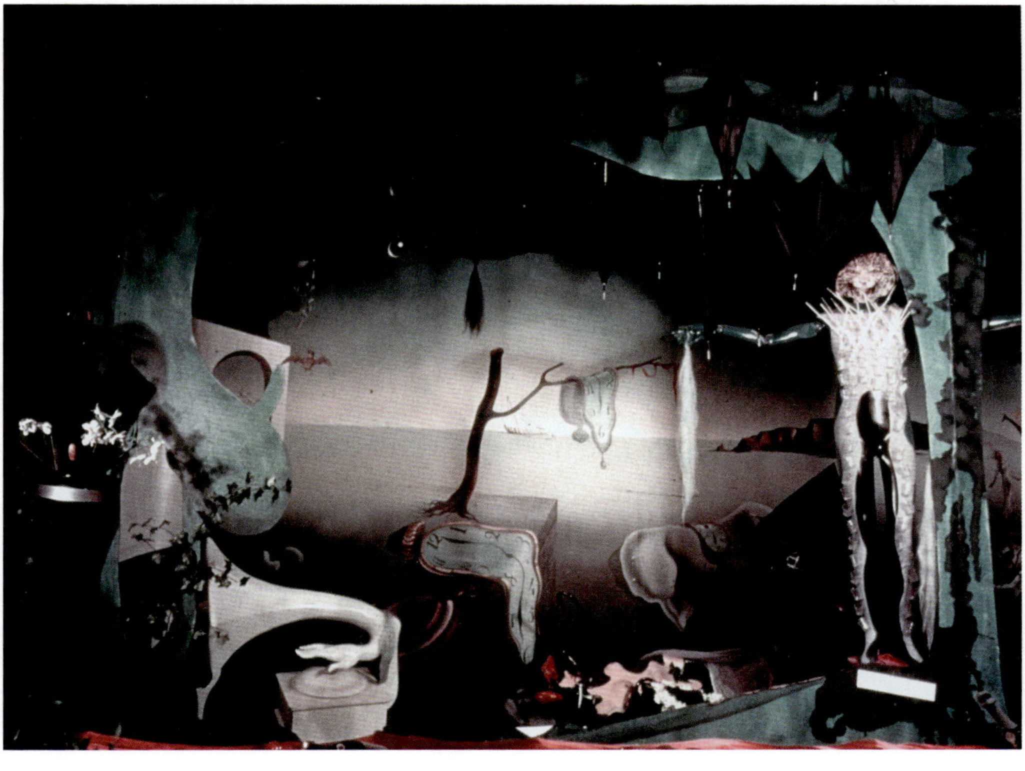

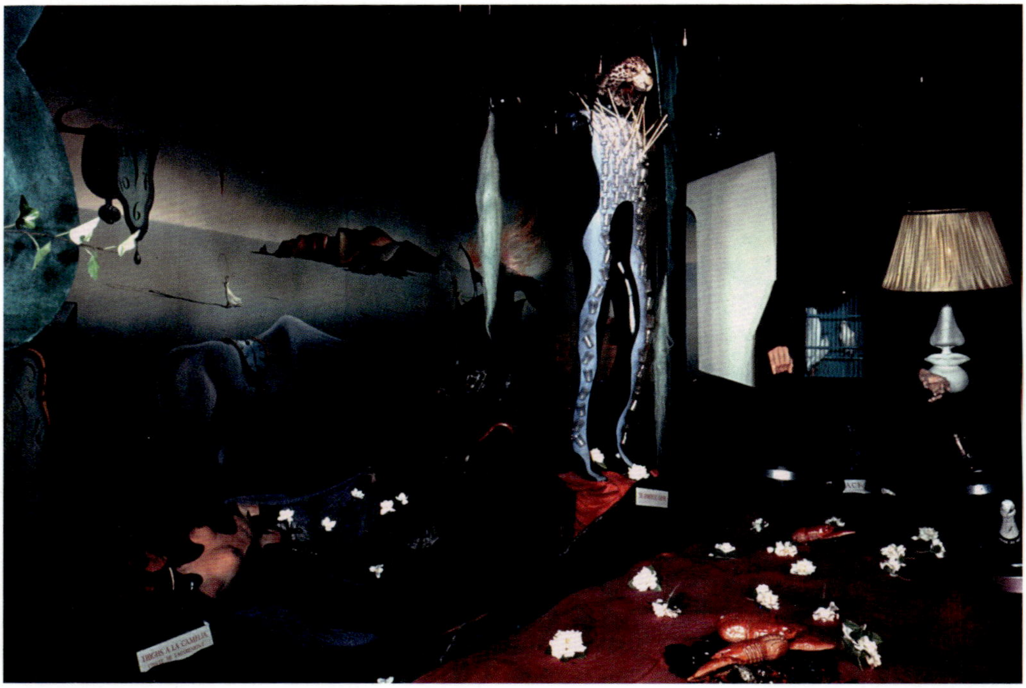

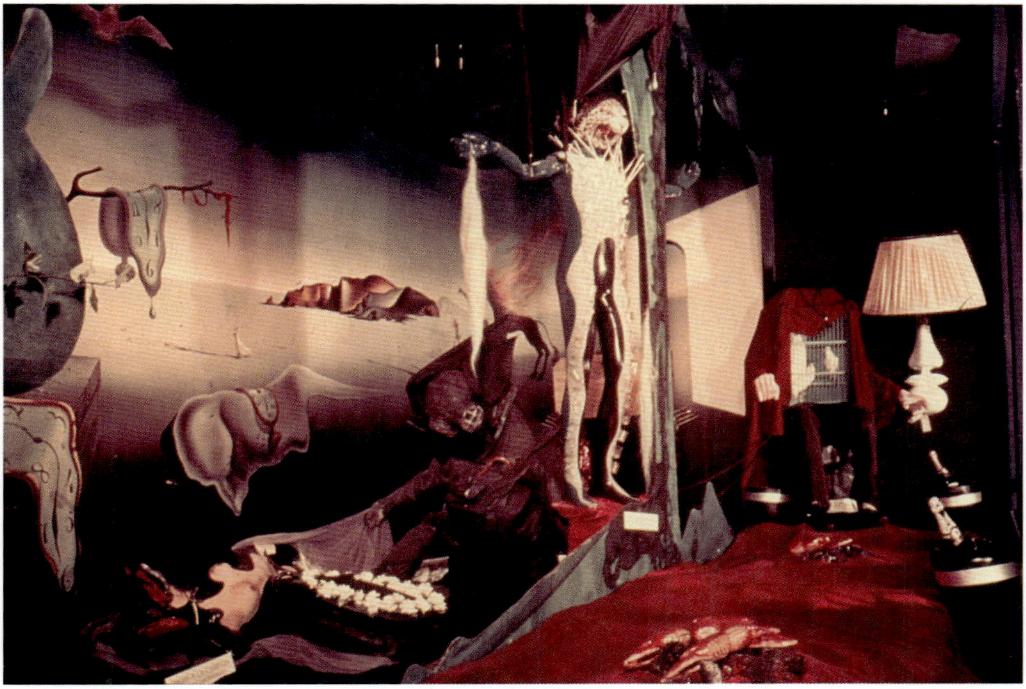

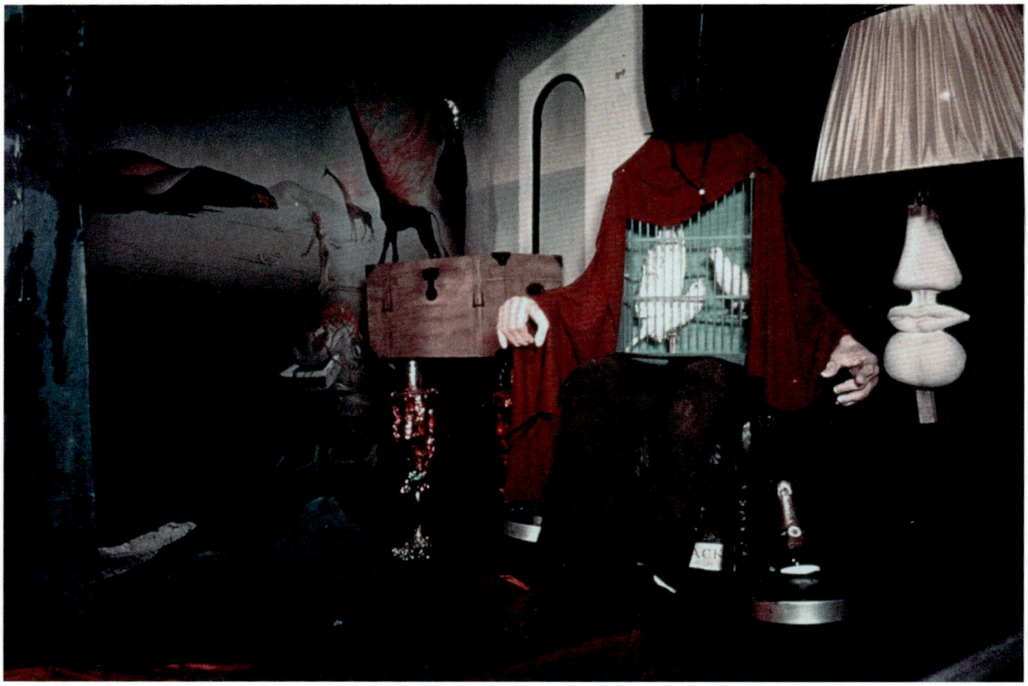

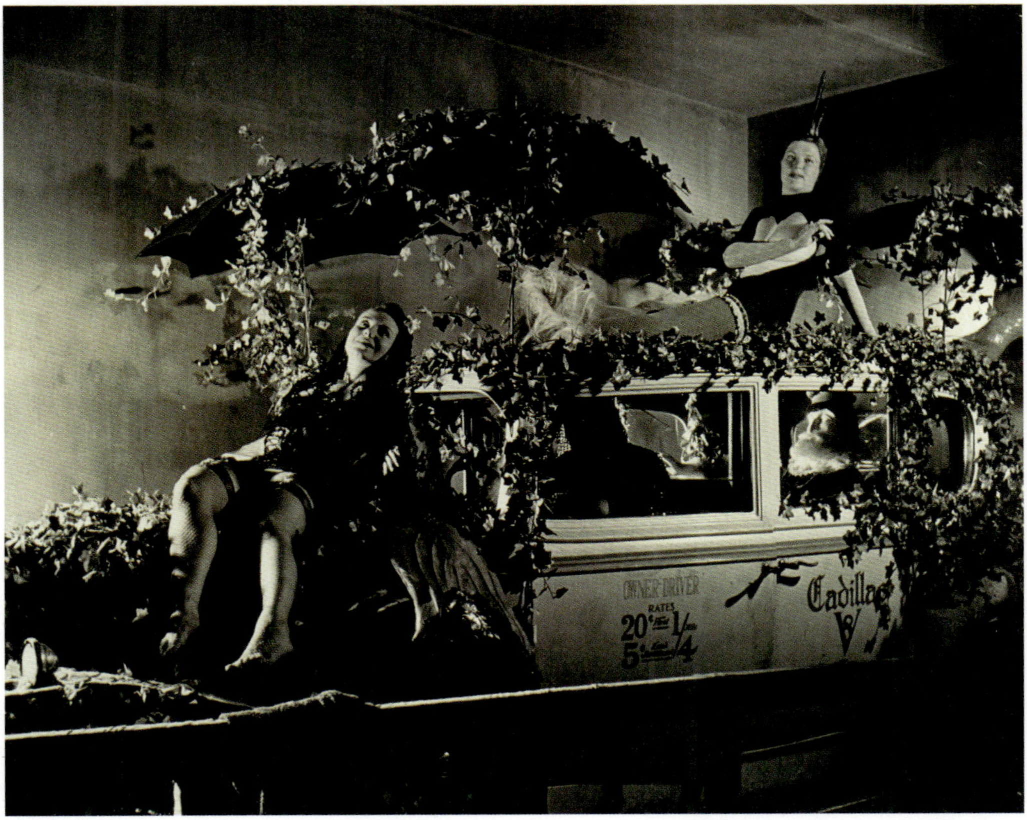
OWNER-DRIVER
RATES

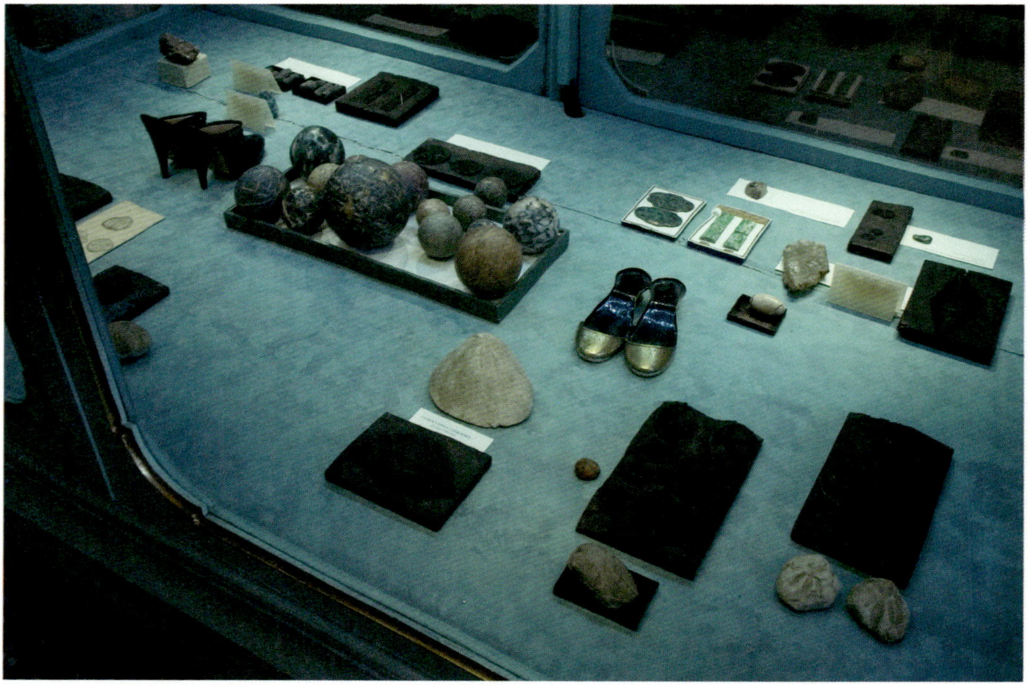

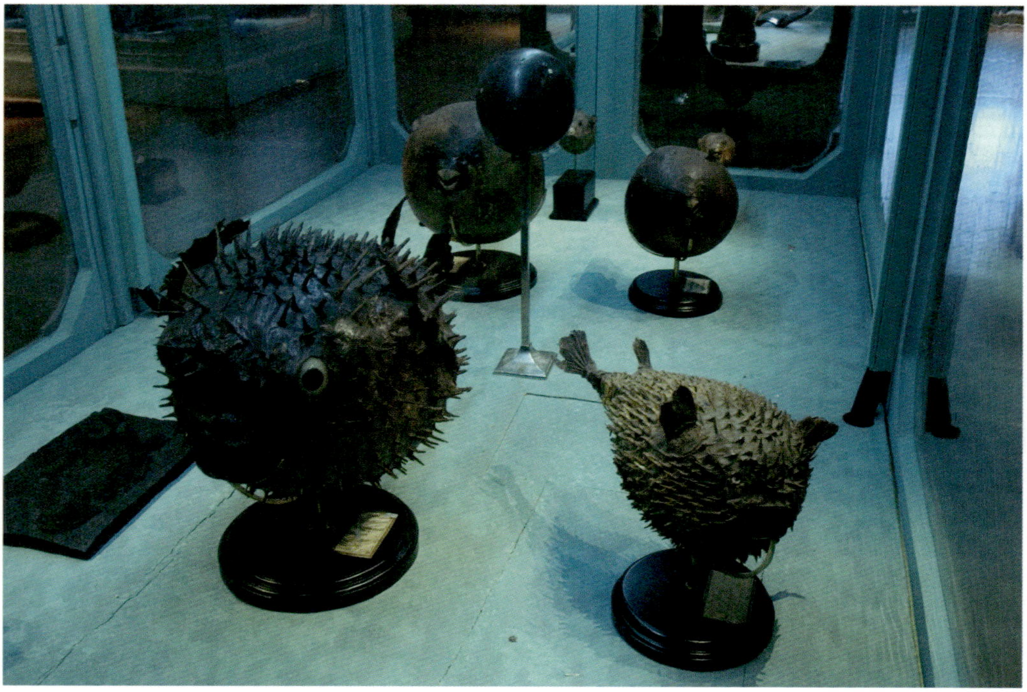



Markus Schinwald,
Installationsansichten/installation views
MAMbo – Museo Palazzo Poggi, Bologna, 2006

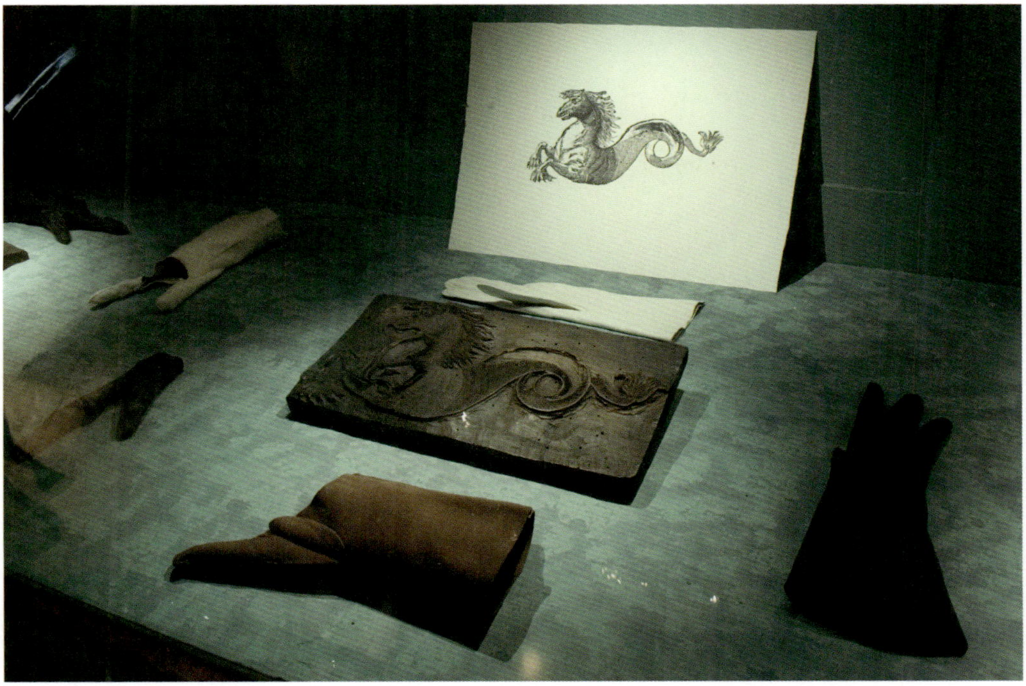

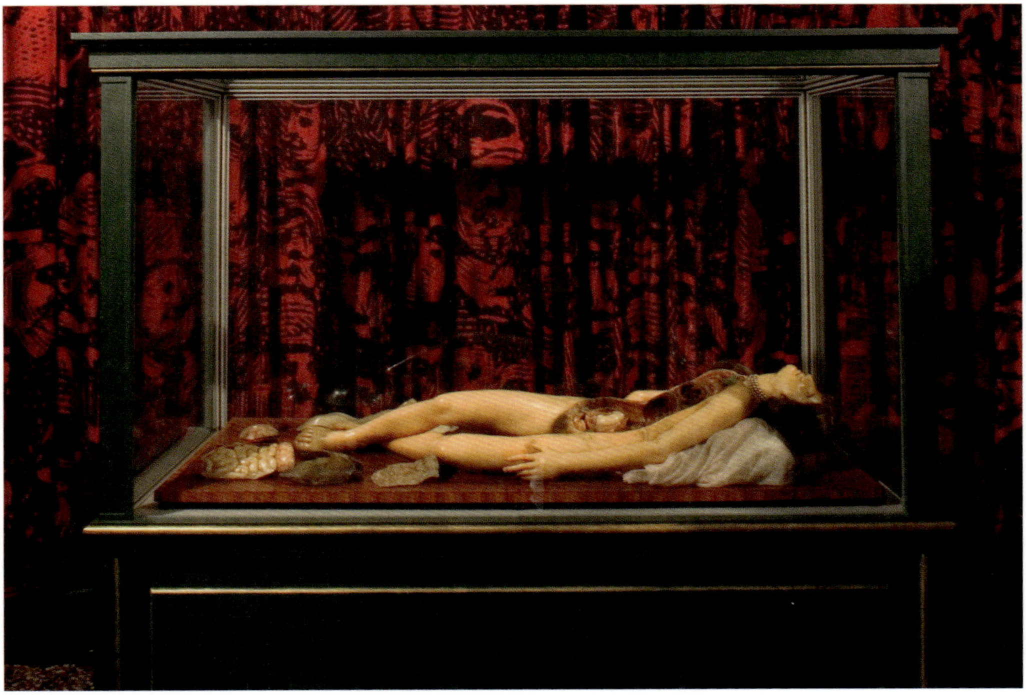

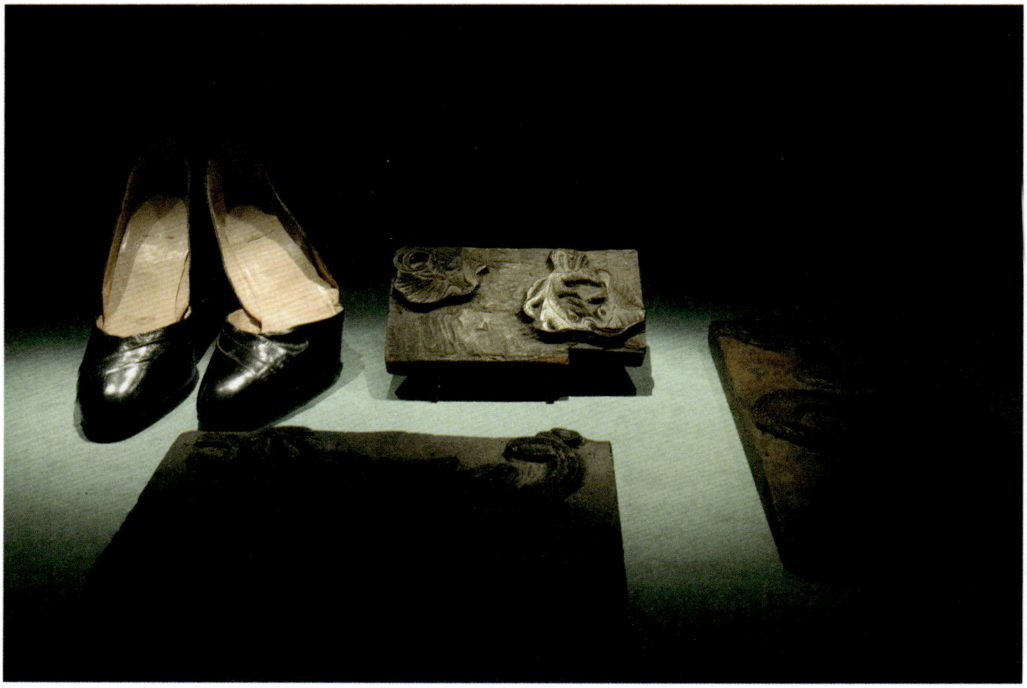



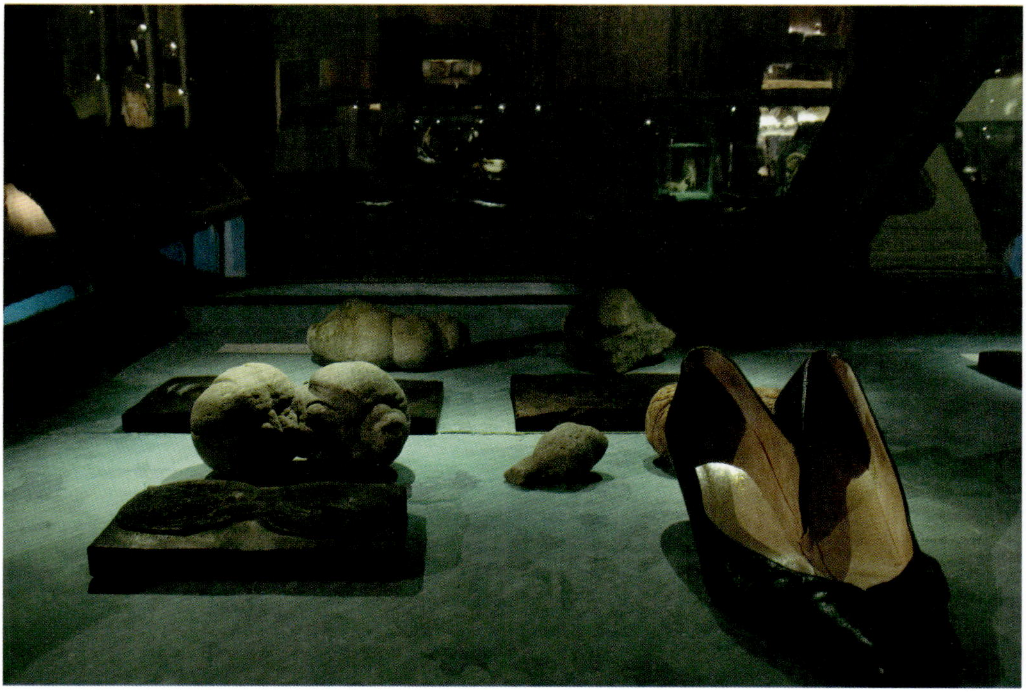

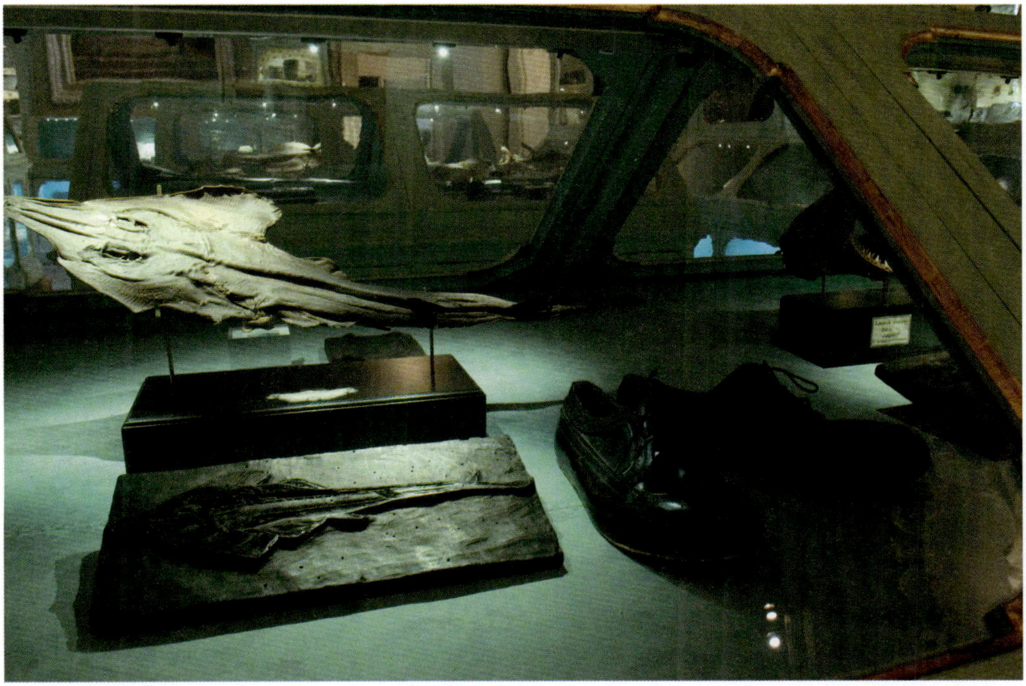

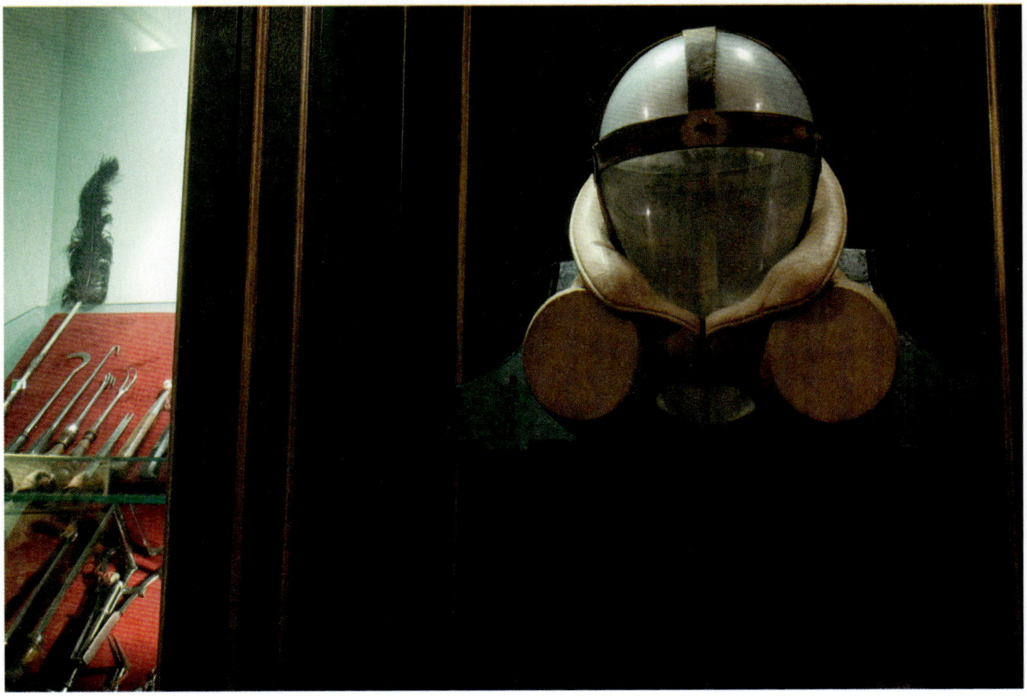

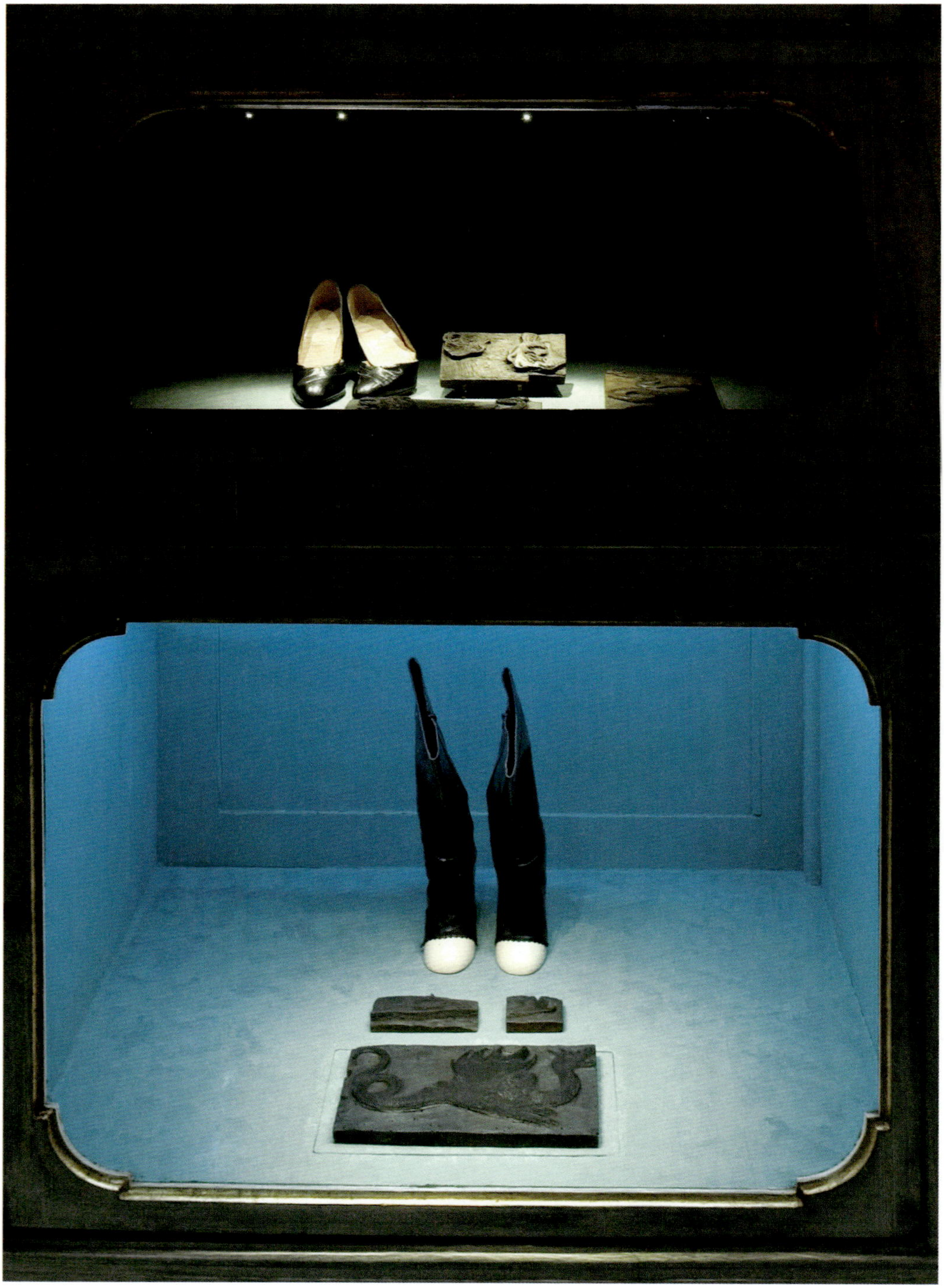

Markus Schinwald,
*Curvings*, *Toes*, 2007

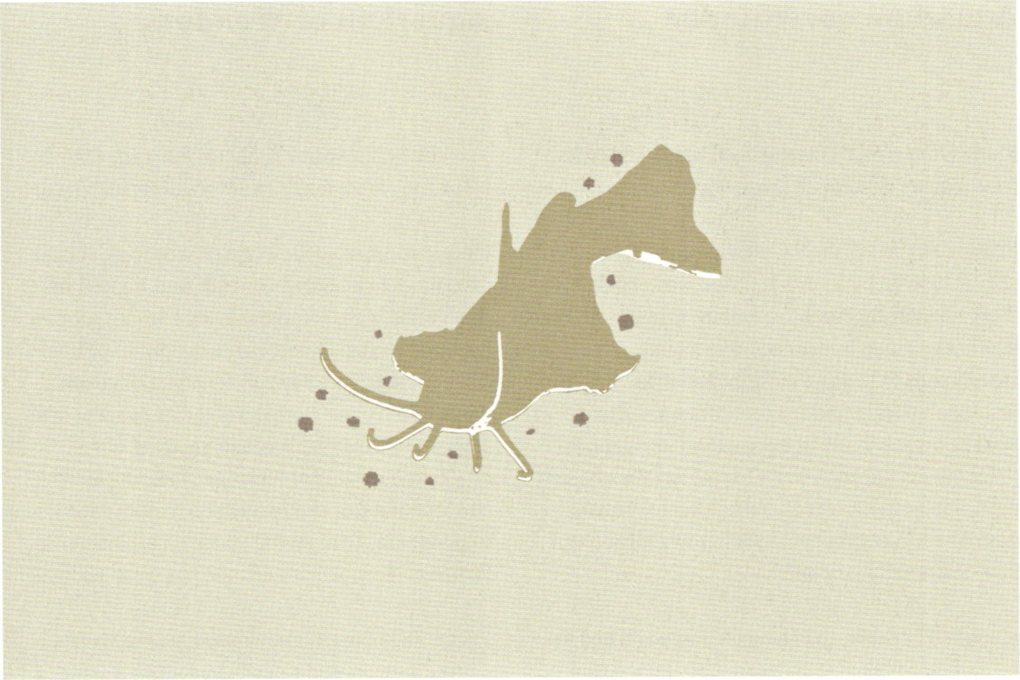

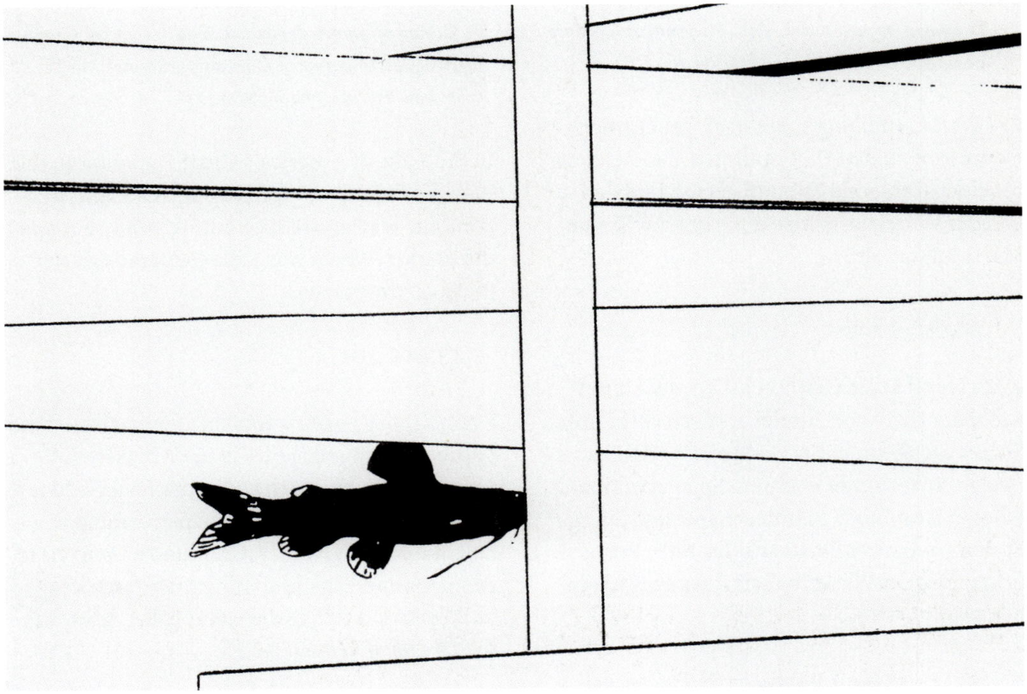



Markus Schinwald,
*Untitled (Aquarium#1)*, 2011

# Belinda Grace Gardner
## Aquarium der Wunder

Markus Schinwalds Replik auf Salvador Dalís New Yorker *Dream of Venus*-Pavillon von 1939

Fraglos bot das bizarre Gebilde nach Entwürfen von Salvador Dalí, das bei der New Yorker Weltausstellung 1939 im Bezirk Queens zu erleben war, einen kuriosen Anblick (Abb. S. 24–37). Der *Dream of Venus*-Pavillon des notorischen Selbstdarstellers und Inszenators surrealistischer Spektakel stach als überbordend-amorphes Bauwerk im Rahmen einer Messe hervor, die sich dem Fortschritt verschrieben hatte, getreu dem Motto: „Aufbau der Welt von morgen mit dem Werkzeug von heute."

Vgl. Fèlix Fanés, „Mannequins, mermaids and the bottoms of the sea. Salvador Dalí and the New York World's Fair of 1939", in: *Salvador Dalí. Dream of Venus*, Ausst.-Kat., Museum of Contemporary Art. North Miami, Florida 2002, S. 47.

Die Weltausstellung sollte nach der Großen Depression in den USA optimistische Zeichen für eine strahlende Zukunft setzen und den von der Wirtschaftskrise noch geschwächten Markt ankurbeln.

Vgl. ebd., S. 44ff.

Auch wenn Dalís Pavillon im „Amusement"-Areal der Expo von allerlei erotisch verbrämten Shows wie Norman Bel Geddes' *Crystal Lassies* (Nackttänzerinnen in einem Spiegelkabinett), Niles T. Granlunds Männerphantasien anregenden *Congress of Beauty* oder Billy Roses erfolgreichem Wasserballett *Aquacade* umgeben war:

Vgl. Lewis Kachur, *Displaying the Marvelous. Marcel Duchamp, Salvador Dalí, and*



# Belinda Grace Gardner
## Aquarium of Wonders

Markus Schinwald's reply to Salvador Dalí's New York *Dream of Venus* pavilion from 1939

Unquestionably, the bizarre structure based on concepts by Salvador Dalí and hosted by the World's Fair in New York City's Queens borough in 1939 was a curious sight to behold (ill. p. 24–37). The *Dream of Venus* pavilion designed by the notorious self-promoter and stager of Surrealist spectacles stood out as an extravagant, amorphous building in the context of a fair that was keenly dedicated to progress, true to the motto: "Building the World of Tomorrow with the Tools of Today."

Cf. Fèlix Fanés, "Mannequins, mermaids and the bottoms of the sea. Salvador Dalí and the New York World's Fair of 1939," in *Salvador Dalí. Dream of Venus*, exhib. cat., Engl transl. by Teresa Brugués, Museum of Contemporary Art, North Miami, Florida, Miami, 2002, 47.

In the wake of America's Great Depression, the World's Fair was to spread optimism and to point the way to a radiant future, while boosting the market, which was still recuperating after the economic crisis.

Cf. ibid., 44ff.

Even if Dalí's pavilion was surrounded by several erotically charged shows in the Amusement Area of the Expo – such as Norman Bel Geddes's *Crystal Lassies* (nude dancers performing in a hall of mirrors), Niles T. Granlund's *Congress of Beauty* (aimed at stimulating male fantasies), or Billy Rose's successful water ballet *Aquacade* – the *Dream of Venus*

*Surrealist Exhibition Installations*. Cambridge, Massachusetts, London 2001, S. 152ff.

Mit seiner Fülle von kunsthistorischen und populärkulturellen Zitaten und Versatzstücken blieb der *Dream of Venus*-Pavillon ein wundersamer Fremdkörper.

Vgl. ebd., S. 129.

Die vielgestaltige, von diversen Öffnungen und Hohlräumen durchbrochene plastische Vorderseite des Pavillons vereinte weibliche Torsi und andere feminine Körperfragmente, Nixenfiguren und korallenartige, aus der Fassade herausragende Greifarme und Hände, die teils wie die häufig bei Dalí auftauchenden Krücken oder Prothesen wirkten.

Vgl. ebd., S. 130 und Fanés. "Mannequins, mermaids and the bottom of the sea", 2002, S. 95.

In Nischen waren Reproduktionen von Leonardo da Vincis *Johannes der Täufer* (mit dem Gesicht der *Mona Lisa* kombiniert) und Sandro Botticellis *Venus* platziert. Letztere ersetzte die ursprünglich von Dalí gewünschte Venusgestalt mit Fischkopf und Frauenbeinen, die den Projektleitern zu befremdlich erschien. Überhaupt geriet der Plan, einen surrealistischen Pavillon für die Weltausstellung zu errichten – ursprünglich eine gemeinsame Idee des jungen Architekten Ian Woodner und des einflussreichen Galeristen und Surrealismus-Verfechters Julien Levy (beide aus New York; Levy zeigte im Frühling 1939 fast zeitgleich zur Eröffnung der Expo auch eine Dalí-Ausstellung) –, schnell aus dem Lot. Es fing schon mit der Forderung des Gummiherstellers und

Cf. Lewis Kachur, *Displaying the Marvelous. Marcel Duchamp, Salvador Dalí, and Surrealist Exhibition Installations*, Cambridge, Massachusetts, London, 2001, 152ff.

pavilion remained a wondrous alien element at the event, with its abundance of quotes and set pieces from art history and popular culture.

Cf. ibid., 129.

On the polymorphic front side of the pavilion, perforated by various apertures and cavities, female torsi and other fragments of the female body were conjoined, together with mermaids, coral-like tentacles and hands jutting out of the facade, partially recalling the crutches and prostheses often found in Dalí's work.

Cf. ibid., p. 130 and Fanés, "Mannequins, mermaids and the bottoms of the sea," 2002, 95.

Reproductions of Leonardo da Vinci's *St. John the Baptist* (combined with the face of *Mona Lisa*) and Sandro Botticelli's *Venus* were situated in niches, the latter replacing Dalí's original Venus figure sporting a fish head and female legs, which, however was considered far too outlandish by the project managers. Indeed, the plan to construct a Surrealist pavilion for the World's Fair, originally a joint idea of the young architect Jan Woodner and the influential gallery owner and supporter of Surrealism Julien Levy (both residents of New York; in spring of 1939, Levy mounted a Dalí exhibition almost simultaneous to the opening of the Expo), quickly went awry. The trouble had already started with the rubber manufacturer and main sponsor of the pavilion, W. M. Gardner, insisting upon an integrated aquarium with mermaids as its chief attraction.

Hauptsponsors des Pavillons W. M. Gardner an, der auf ein integriertes Aquarium mit Nixen als Publikumsmagnet bestanden hatte.

Zur verwickelten Geschichte des Entstehens des Pavillons vgl. Fanés. "Mannequins, mermaids and the bottom of the sea", 2002, S. 61ff. und 67ff.

Selbst Dalís Botticelli-Ersatz-Venus wanderte wenige Wochen nach Eröffnung der Weltausstellung von der Front an die Seite des Pavillons. Aus dem *Traum der Venus* wurde, so Dalí etwas später, „ein schrecklicher Alptraum".

Vgl. Salvador Dalí, *Das geheime Leben des Salvador Dalí*, übers. von Ralf Schiebler. München 1984, S. 465f.

Dennoch traf das damals gerade hoch populäre Wasser-Motiv (samt Aqua-Balletten und herumschwimmenden Grazien) den Geist des Surrealismus im Allgemeinen und den von Salvador Dalí im Besonderen, der das Vordringen in die Tiefen des Meeres mit dem Eintauchen in die Abgründe des Unbewussten gleichsetzte.

Vgl. Kachur. *Displaying the Marvelous*, 2001, S. 137.

Im Pariser Coliseum in Montmartre waren bereits Unterwasser-Nackt-Tänzerinnen aufgetreten – darunter markanterweise auch Jacqueline Lamba, die 1934 den Surrealisten-Wortführer André Breton kennenlernte und heiratete.

Vgl. ebd. S. 137f.

Dalís Variante des Wasserballetts im New Yorker *Venus*-Pavillon geriet trotz der oktroyierten



On the complex history of the pavilion: cf. Fanés, "Mannequins, mermaids and the bottoms of the sea," 2002, 61ff. and 67ff.

Even Dalí's Botticelli-substitute-Venus was moved from the front wall to the side wall of the pavilion a few weeks after the opening of the Fair. As Dalí recalled a short while later, the *Dream of Venus* had turned into "a frightful nightmare."

Cf. Salvador Dalí, *The Secret Life of Salvador Dalí*, transl. by Haakon M. Chevalier, New York, 1942, 376.

Still, the water motif that was highly popular at the time (including aqua-ballets and fair maidens swimming around in pools) corresponded with the spirit of Surrealism and Salvador Dalí's in particular, who compared plunging into the depths of the sea with a descent into the abysses of the unconscious.

Cf. Kachur, *Displaying the Marvelous*, 2001, 137.

In the Paris Coliseum in Montmartre there had already been nude underwater dancers – strikingly including Jacqueline Lamba, whom the spokesman of Surrealism, André Breton, met and married in 1934.

Cf. ibid., 137f.

Despite the changes that were imposed upon it, Dalí's variation of the water ballet in the New York *Dream of Venus* pavilion proved to be a surreal event par excellence, replete with references to the artist's works and performances. A voluminous fish guarded the entrance. The audience

Abänderungen zu einem surrealen Ereignis par excellence, das vor Verweisen auf Werke und Aktionen des Künstlers strotzte. Der Eingang wurde von einem voluminösen Fisch bewacht. Das Interieur betrat das Publikum durch ein Tor aus gespreizten Frauenbeinen und flanierte dann an zwei in die Wand eingelassenen Glasbehältern von je 11 Metern Länge vorbei: Als erstes gelangte man zu einem mit Wasser gefüllten Riesenaquarium, in dem "echte Nixen" vor dem gemalten Setting eines pompejanischen Ruinen-Szenarios mit diversen grotesken Gummifiguren interagierten. Darauf folgte ein Trockenbassin, in dem sich die Liebesgöttin befand, versunken in ihre Träume und flankiert von Spiegeln und einer Hüterin ihres Schlafes, die den Zeigefinger warnend an die Lippen hielt.

Vgl. ebd. S. 143.

Den Hintergrund bildete ein Remake des von zerfließenden Uhren bestimmten Dalí-Werks *Die Beständigkeit der Erinnerung* (1931), erweitert um Giraffen und ein hybrides Schubladen-Wesen im Stil des ebenfalls von Dalí geschaffenen Gemäldes *Die Brennende Giraffe* (1936–1937).

Die Glaskästen, die wie „Schaufenster in einem rechteckigen Grundriss arrangiert waren"

Vgl. Fèlix Fanés, „Dream of Venus", in: *It's all Dalí. Film, Fashion, Photography, Design, Advertising, Painting*, Ausst.-Kat., Museum Boijmans van Beuningen. Rotterdam 2005, S. 186.

und damit auch an Dalís „Tag"- und „Nacht"-Inszenierung für die Auslagen des New Yorker Kaufhauses Bonwit-Teller kurz vor der Weltausstellung anknüpften, ergänzten sich dialek-

entered the interior through a portal consisting of parted female legs, wandering past two glass basins, both spanning a length of eleven meters respectively. First, the viewers arrived at a gigantic aquarium filled with water, in which real-life mermaids were interacting with various grotesque rubber figures before a painted setting featuring a scenario with Pompeian ruins. Next came a dry basin, in which the goddess of love could be seen live, absorbed in her dreams and flanked by mirrors, while the guardian of her sleep raised her finger to her lips in warning.

Cf. ibid., 143.

The background consisted of a remake of Dalí's melting watches from *The Persistence of Memory* (1931), including additional giraffes and a hybrid creature with inserted drawers in the style of *The Burning Giraffe* (1936–37), also created by Dalí.

The glass cases, which "similar to window displays were arranged on a rectangular-type floor plan,"

Cf. Fèlix Fanés, "Dream of Venus," in *It's all Dalí. Film, Fashion, Photography, Design, Advertising, Painting*, exhib. cat., Museum Boijmans van Beuningen, Rotterdam, 2005, 186.

were also reminiscent of Dalí's *Night* and *Day* window scenarios conceived for the New York department store Bonwit Teller, and presented shortly before the World's Fair, dialectically complementing one another by setting movement against stillness and the state of wakefulness against that of dreams. In the shop window installation, Dalí had combined, together tisch, insofern sie Bewegung und Ruhe, Wach- und Traumzustände gegeneinander setzten. In der Schaufensterinstallation hatte Dalí neben allerhand anderen eine mit Persianerfell ausgekleidete Badewanne, Spiegel, Hände und gefundene Schaufensterpuppen aus der Ära um 1900 kombiniert. Gerade die „doppelte Tendenz (technischer Anachronismus und psychischer Atavismus)" sieht Dalí-Spezialist Fèlix Fanés als ursächlich für die „beunruhigende" Qualität im Werk des Künstlers.

Vgl. Fanés, "Mannequins, mermaids and the bottom of the sea", 2002, S. 37.

Dalí selbst deutet sein Faible für atmosphärisch aufgeladene Altertümlichkeiten wie folgt: „Weit davon entfernt, ein sogenanntes nutzloses, mumifiziertes Ding' zu sein, das die pseudointellektuelle Wahrnehmung für harmlos hält und ironisch in die Rumpelkammer der Geschichte ausmustert, ist der Anachronismus im Gegen-teil eine wahrhaft lebendige Sache aus Fleisch und Knochen."

Salvador Dalí, zit. nach Fanés, ebd.

In der „Feuchtzone" des *Dream of Venus*-Pavillons lag eine gefesselte Gummipuppe, deren Körper mit schwarzweißem Tastenmuster bedeckt war, auf einem Klavier, deren Körper mit schwarz-weißem Tastenmuster bedeckt war, daneben lugte eine weitere Gestalt aus Kettenelementen hervor. Eine in Bandagen eingewickelte Kuh, ein Kamin, Schreibmaschinen und ein Geflecht von Telefonhörern, die wie Seetang im Wasser waberten, gehörten zu den eigentümlichen Attributen, mit denen die Nixen-Schwimmerinnen ihre Unterwasser-



with other items, an astrakhan-clad bathtub, mirrors, hands, and found mannequins dating from around 1900. According to the Dalí specialist Fèlix Fanés, it was particularly the "double tendency (technical anachronism and psychic atavism)" that made his work so disturbing.

Cf. Fanés, "Mannequins, mermaids and the bottoms of the sea," 2002, 37.

Dalí himself perceived his passion for atmospherically charged anachronisms as "far from being this so-called useless 'mummified thing' that pseudointellectual experience believes harmless, rejecting it ironically into the 'boxroom' of the times, [but] on the contrary, a true living thing, a thing that has flesh and bones."

Salvador Dalí, quoted after Fanés, ibid.

In the "wet' zone" of the *Dream of Venus* pavilion, a shackled rubber doll whose body was covered with the black-and-white pattern of a keyboard was lying supine on a piano; next to it another figure consisting of chain elements jutted forth. A cow wrapped in bandages, a fire place, typewriters, and intertwining telephone receivers, which were drifting in the water like seaweed, were among the peculiar attributes with which the mermaid swimmers performed their underwater roles. In the "dry zone," in turn, apart from Venus slumbering upon a bed of glowing coals covered by abundant foliage, a number of reprises of works could be found, which Dalí and his colleagues had presented in the Paris *Exposition Internationale du Surréalisme* at the Galerie Beaux-Arts in 1938 or in

Rollenspiele bestritten. In der „Trockenzone" wiederum fanden sich neben der auf einem von üppigem Blattwerk umrankten Bett aus „glühenden Kohlen" schlummernden Venus etliche Reprisen von Arbeiten, die Dalí und Kollegen bei der Pariser *Exposition Internationale du Surréalisme* in der Galerie Beaux-Arts 1938 oder bei anderer Gelegenheit präsentiert hatten. Auch eine Variante von Dalís magisch-makabrer Installation *Taxi pluvieux* (Regentaxi) aus der *Exposition* von 1938 war zu sehen: ein von Efeu überwuchertes Auto, in dem statt einer von Schnecken bekrochenen weiblichen Puppe eine männliche Figur mit katalanischem Hut saß, die Christoph Columbus repräsentieren sollte.

Vgl. Fanés, ebd., S. 186 und Kachur, *Displaying the Marvelous*, S. 137; S. 142ff.

Der von allen Protagonisten des Surrealismus praktizierte rege Einsatz von (Schaufenster-) Puppen – darunter als prominentes Beispiel Hans Bellmers derangierte *Poupées* – verknüpft im Fall des *Dream of Venus*-Pavillons die Felder des Konsums, der surrealistischen Inszenierung und der Projektion des Unheimlichen im Sinne von Sigmund Freud, dem Dalí 1938 in London begegnet war. Freuds Aufsatz über „Das Unheimliche" (1919) veranschaulichte bekanntlich die potenziell entsetzliche Belebung des Unbelebten am Beispiel der Puppe Olimpia aus E. T. A. Hoffmanns schauerromantischer Erzählung *Der Sandmann*,

Vgl. Sigmund Freund, „Das Unheimliche" (1919), in: Ders.: *Studienausgabe Bd. IV, Psychologische Schriften*, hg. von Alexander Mitscherlich, Angela Richards, James Strachey, Mithrsg. des

other contexts. A version of Dalí's magical, macabre installation *Taxi pluvieux* (Rainy Taxi) from the *Exposition* of 1938 was also on display: an ivy-covered car in which a male figure with a Catalan hat, supposedly representing Christopher Columbus, replaced the original female doll crawling with snails.

Cf. Fanés, "Dream of Venus," 2005, p. 186 and Kachur, *Displaying the Marvelous*, 2001, 137; 142ff.

In the case of the *Dream of Venus* pavilion, the avid use of (shop window) dolls pursued by all protagonists of Surrealism – including, as a prominent example, Hans Bellmer's distorted *Poupées* – brings together the fields of consumption, the Surrealist spectacle, and the projection of the "uncanny" coined by Sigmund Freud, whom Dalí had met in London in 1938. Freud's essay on "The Uncanny" (1919) visualized the potentially terrifying animation of the inanimate, drawing upon the doll Olimpia from E.T.A. Hoffmann's dark Romantic tale "The Sandman,"

Cf. Sigmund Freund, "Das Unheimliche" (1919), in Freud, *Studienausgabe* Bd. IV, *Psychologische Schriften*, Alexander Mitscherlich, Angela Richards, James Strachey (eds.), co-edited by Ilse Grubrich-Simitis, Frankfurt a. M., 1982, 250ff.

where the horror effect is brought about by "the superimposition of the non-living over the living, that is to say, of death over life."

Cf. Fanés, "Mannequins, mermaids and the bottoms of the sea," 2002, 31.

Ergänzungsbandes Ilse Grubrich-Simitis. Frankfurt a. M. 1982, S. 250ff.

in welcher der Gruseleffekt mittels „Überlagerung des Lebendigen durch das Nicht-Lebendige, also des Lebens durch den Tod"

Fanés, „Mannequins, mermaids and the bottom of the sea", 2002, S. 31.

herbeigeführt wird. Der Animation lebloser Gegenstände – das Gebäude des Pavillons, die Puppen, die diversen Accessoires im Wassertank – steht die Wandlung des Belebten in etwas Lebloses gegenüber, ein Prozess, der sich etwa in den „verdinglichten" Tiergestalten und Menschenfiguren, die zu Mobiliar werden, manifestiert.

Dalís Hinter-Glas-Welten des *Dream of Venus*-Pavillons, in der seinerzeitigen Formulierung des Magazins *Art Digest* die „Rekonstruktion eines hochgradig freudianischen Unbewussten über das, was der Broadway als ‚Girl Show' bezeichnet",

Zit. nach Fanés, „Dream of Venus", 2005, S. 185.

entfalteten sich leicht entrückt vom Expo-Geschehen in einer heterotopischen Parallel-Dimension im Sinne von Michel Foucaults Definition „anderer Räume": „So bringt das Theater auf dem Rechteck der Bühne nacheinander eine ganze Reihe von Orten zur Darstellung, die sich gänzlich fremd sind."

Michel Foucault, „Von anderen Räumen", in: *Raumtheorie. Grundlagentexte aus Philosophie und Kulturwissenschaften*, hg. von Jörg Dünne und Stephan Günzel. Frankfurt a. M. 2006, S. 324.

The animation of lifeless objects – the pavilion building, the dolls, the various accessories in the water tank – is countered by the transformation of the animate into the inanimate, a process that becomes manifest, for example, in "objectified" animal and human figures that become pieces of furniture.

Dalí's worlds behind glass in the *Dream of Venus* pavilion, which, according to a phrase printed at the time in the magazine *Art Digest*, represented "a reconstruction of a highly Freudian subconscious through what Broadway called a girl show,"

Quoted after Fanés, "Dream of Venus," 2005, 185.

took effect in a heterotopian parallel dimension slightly removed from the Expo events, in the sense of Michel Foucault's definition of "other spaces": "Thus it is that the theater brings onto the rectangle of the stage, one after the other, a whole series of places that are foreign to one another."

Cf. Michel Foucault, "Of Other Spaces (Des espaces autres, 1967)," first publ. in the French journal *Architecture/Mouvement/Continuité*, Oct. 1984, transl. from the French by Jay Miskowiec, under: http://foucault.info/documents/heteroTopia/foucault.heteroTopia.en.html (accessed: June 7, 2011).

The creation or evocation of the "counter-sites" or "real places [...] outside of all places"

Cf. ibid.

Die Herstellung oder Evokation von jenen Foucaultschen „Gegenräumen" oder „realen Orten jenseits aller Orte"

Michel Foucault, zit. nach Heike Munder, „Heterotopien", in: *Markus Schinwald,* hg. von Agnes Husslein-Arco et al. Belvedere, migros museum für gegenwartskunst. Wien, Zürich 2007, S. 24.

ist auch ein wesentliches ästhetisches Verfahren des österreichischen Künstlers Markus Schinwald. In seinen poetisch-enigmatischen Filmarbeiten, Performances, Skulpturen, Malereien, Architekturen und Installationen greifen Realität und Illusion, Außen- und Innensphären, Belebtes und Unbelebtes, Vertrautes und Traumlogisches ineinander. Doch tritt die abgründige Dialektik, die von den Surrealisten kultiviert wurde und die allen voran Salvador Dalí in seinen zwischen Verführung und Schock-Effekt oszillierenden Inszenierungen auf die Spitze trieb, bei Schinwald leiser, beiläufiger, weniger theatralisch in Erscheinung. Schinwald sucht in seinen Arbeiten nicht das Spektakel, das Dalís Herangehen beherrscht. Seine subtilen Verschiebungen und Dislozierungen dagegen „entführen uns in den eigenen Kosmos einer unheimlichen, nichtsprachlichen Welt und verwandeln scheinbar Alltägliches in etwas Mystisches und Enigmatisches."

Agnes Husslein-Arco, Heike Munder, „Prolog", ebd., S. 9.

Wiederkehrende Motive in Schinwalds Kosmos sind bühnenhafte Architekturen, die mögliche Geschichten andeuten, ohne sie explizit aus-

is also an essential aesthetic procedure of the Austrian artist Markus Schinwald. In his poetic, enigmatic film works, performances, sculptures, paintings, architectural constructions, and installations reality and illusion, outer and inner spheres, the animate and the inanimate, the realms of the commonplace and of dreams converge. However, the allusive dialectic cultivated by the Surrealists and carried to particular extremes by Salvador Dalí with his spectacles oscillating between seduction and shock-effect finds expression, in Schinwald's case, in a much more quiet and offhand manner, and in a less theatrical style. In his works, Schinwald is not seeking the spectacle that is so central to Dalí's approach. His subtle shifts and displacements "take us into the singular cosmos of an eerie, non-verbal world and transform ostensibly everyday things into something mystical and enigmatic."

Cf. Agnes Husslein-Arco and Heike Munder, "Prologue," in Markus Schinwald, exhib. cat., Engl. transl. by Wolfgang Astelbauer, Virginia Dellenbaugh, ed. by Agnes Husslein-Arco, et al., Belvedere, migros museum für gegenwartskunst, Vienna, Zurich, 2007, 13.

Consistent themes in Schinwald's cosmos are stage-like architectural constructs, which suggest possible stories without giving explicit information. Frequently, closed curtains, doors, and walls obstruct the constructions' accessibility. In display cases resembling shop windows, one encounters strange objects that oscillate between deformed pieces of clothing (here, particularly, transformed shoes are employed, recalling the surreal shoe objects of the Swiss artist Meret Oppenheim), zuführen. Des Öfteren ist die Zugänglichkeit der Konstruktionen durch geschlossene Vorhänge, Türen oder Wände verstellt. In schaufensterartigen Vitrinen trifft man auf merkwürdige Gegenstände, die zwischen deformierten Kleidungsstücken (insbesondere kommen hier umgewandelte Schuhe zum Einsatz, welche die surrealen Schuh-Objekte der Schweizer Künstlerin Meret Oppenheim in Erinnerung rufen), Fetischen, Reliquien, Lebewesen und Prothesen changieren. Letztere tauchen gezielt als zarte malerische Eingriffe auf Porträtgemälden des 19. Jahrhunderts auf, die der Künstler auf Floh- und Trödelmärkten findet und mit absonderlichen Bandagen, Mund-Vorrichtungen und Gesichtsgestellen verfremdet und erweitert. Seine aus nostalgisch geschwungenen (Chippendale-)Möbelbeinen geschaffenen Skulpturen verbinden dann das Unbelebte des Einrichtungs- oder prothetischen Gegenstands mit dem Animierten eines menschlichen oder animalischen Geschöpfs. In den genannten Bildern und Objekten kommt zudem das anachronistische Moment, das laut Fanés ursächlich ist für die beunruhigende Wirkung von Dalís Kompositionen, zum Tragen. Das gilt auch für Schinwalds skurrile Puppenfiguren, die in Gestalt von Marionetten und fragmentierten Gliedmaßen oder (Teil-)Masken auftreten und die grotesken Mannechinos der Surrealisten auf eigene Weise weiterführen – und damit auch Freuds puppenhafte Wieder- und Doppelgänger-Wesen der Olimpia heraufbeschwören.

Im enzyklopädisch organisierten Katalog der Schinwald-Ausstellung 2007/2008 in Wien und Zürich hat Thomas Trummer die von dem Künstler auf verschiedenen Ebenen praktizierte



as well as fetishes, relics, living beings, and prostheses. The latter appear in the shape of delicate painted interventions in portrait paintings from the 19th century, which the artist finds at flea and junk markets and disrupts and extends through peculiar bandages, mouth contraptions, and facial racks. The sculptures created by the artist from curved (Chippendale) furniture legs, in turn, conflate the inanimate characteristics of furniture or prosthetic objects with the animate quality of human beings or animals. Furthermore, in the paintings and objects mentioned above, the anachronistic element comes into effect, which, according to Fanés, elicits the disturbing effect of Dalí's compositions. This also applies to Schinwald's mysterious doll figures that appear in the form of marionettes and fragmented extremities or (partial) masks, carrying on the notion of the grotesque mannequins of the Surrealists in a unique manner, while simultaneously evoking Freud's zombie doll and doppelganger Olimpia.

In the catalogue accompanying the Schinwald exhibition in 2007/2008 in Vienna and Zurich, organized encyclopedically, Thomas Trummer has interrelated the method of deconstruction practiced by the artist on a number of levels with a specific form of text interpretation, in the sense of notions conceived by the French philosopher, Jacques Derrida. Accordingly, "it is about a reading that works proactively with displacements, distortions and the presence of time" and "aims at establishing an unending chain of meaning in the text as evidence for the indeterminacy of symbol and knowledge."

Cf. Thomas Trummer, "Deconstruction," ibid., 32.

Methode der Dekonstruktion mit einer spezifischen Form der Textauslegung im Sinne des französischen Philosophen Jacques Derrida in Beziehung gesetzt. Demnach handelt es sich dabei „um eine Lektüre, die Verschiebungen, Verzerrungen und Zeitlichkeit mitdenkt" und „eine unendliche Sinnverkettung im Text als Beleg für die Unbestimmtheit von Zeichen und Wissen ermitteln will".

Thomas Trummer, „Dekonstruktion", ebd., S. 32.

Dieses Verfahren, das keine endgültige Lesart zulässt, findet sich in den Filmarbeiten ebenso wie in raumgreifenden Installationen Schinwalds. So verwandelt sich die scheinbare Liebeserklärung *Diarios (to you)* von 2003 mit ihren traumartigen Bildern und ihrem meditativen, gesprochenen Soundtrack zu einer Art inneren Monolog, der den Bildern zuwiderläuft und auch wieder eine Parallelwelt generiert, während die Figuren in *1st Part Conditional* (2004) an einem altertümlich-gediegen ausgestatteten heterotopischen „Ort jenseits aller Orte" wie in Trance ausharren oder sich sprunghaft und im freien Fall durch diesen hindurch bewegen, derweil einzelne Möbelstücke wie von unsichtbaren Kräften erfasst, in sich zusammenkrachen. In architektonischen Konstruktionen wie dem Setting zur Performance *A Stage Matrix II* (2006) ist das „Verrutschen" der Dinge direkt in dessen inkongruente Öffnungen und Verschließungen eingebaut oder äußert sich im Zerrspiegel eines Sportstudios der anderen Art, wie im Rahmen der Ausstellung *Vanishing Lessons* im Kunsthaus Bregenz 2009 zu erleben. Der Installationsentwurf für den österreichischen Pavillon bei der 54. Venedig-Biennale 2011 seinerseits basiert auf einem

This aesthetic, which at the same time does not permit conclusive interpretations, is to be found in both Schinwald's film works and in his extensive spatial installations. Thus, the supposed declaration of love *Diarios (to you)* from 2003, with its dream-like images and its meditative spoken soundtrack, turns into a kind of inner monologue running counter to the images, again generating a parallel world. Meanwhile, in *1st Part Conditional* (2004), the figures poise as if caught up in trance in a heterotopic place "outside of all places" that is furnished in a sedate, antiquated style, or move around in the space by leaps and bounds or in a free fall, while individual pieces of furniture collapse as if seized by invisible forces. In architectural constructions such as the setting for the performance *A Stage Matrix II* (2006), the "shifts" governing the general dynamic of Schinwald's works are directly built into the objects' incongruent apertures and barriers. Or become apparent, for instance, in the distorting mirror of a very different kind of fitness center, which viewers were able to experience in the context of the exhibition *Vanishing Lessons* at the Kunsthaus Bregenz in 2009. The installation Schinwald conceived for the Austrian Pavilion at the 54th Venice Biennale, 2011, is based upon a labyrinth extending from the ceiling to approximately hip height of the viewers, inducing a broadening of perception through a literal narrowing of the audience's perspective and through spatial disorientation.

Schinwald also plays with the shifts and forms of displacement, around which the aesthetic program of the Surrealists revolves, in numerous ways and on multiple levels. His evasive artistic production reveals a penchant for dolls

Labyrinth, das sich von der Decke bis in Hüfthöhe des Publikums erstreckt und eine Wahrnehmungserweiterung durch buchstäbliche Blickverengung und räumliche Desorientierung erzielt.

Das Spiel mit Verrückungen auf multiplen Ebenen, um die das ästhetische Programm der Surrealisten kreist, betreibt auch Schinwald in mehrfacher Hinsicht. Seine schwer festlegbare künstlerische Produktion zeigt einen Hang zu Puppen und Prothesen, den er ebenso mit Dalí teilt wie dessen Vorliebe für die vitale Subversivität des Anachronistischen und die parallelen Realitäten des Traums. Doch fehlen bei Schinwald die ostentative Thematisierung erotischer Begehrlichkeiten und die „Verdinglichung“ des Weiblichen, die Dalí in Inszenierungen wie dem *Dream of Venus*-Pavillon oder in den zu Möbelstücken mit Schubladen mutierten Venus- und anderen Figuren zum Ausdruck bringt.

Vgl. Fanés, „Dream of Venus“, 2002, S. 87.

Es geht ihm auch nicht um „eine Ergründung des Ödlands unbefriedigter Begierden des Menschen und seiner Träume und Tagträume“, wie sie Dalí als grundlegende Dynamik seines Pavillons genannt hat.

Salvador Dalí, zit. nach ebd., S. 85.

Schinwalds Perspektive ist trotz medialer Brechungen und der Ausweitung in die zweite Wirklichkeit von Film und Fernsehen eher nach innen gerichtet; seine Figuren (von Marionetten bis zu „echten“ Menschen) agieren in Terrains, in denen sie introspektiv in sich selbst kreisen

and prostheses, which he shares with Dalí as he does the latter's proclivity for the vital subversions of anachronisms and the parallel realities of dreams. However, in Schinwald's case, the ostentatious focus upon erotic desires and the "objectification" of the feminine that Dalí gives expression to in spectacles such as the *Dream of Venus* pavilion or in his Venus figures and other personae, which have mutated into furniture pieces with sets of drawers, is missing.

Cf. Fanés, "Mannequins, mermaids and the bottoms of the sea," 2002, 87.

Schinwald is equally disinterested in "an exploration into the wasteland of man's unsatisfied desires and into his dreams and daydreams,"

Quoted after ibid., 85.

which Dalí himself outlined as the fundamental dynamic of his pavilion. In spite of medial refractions and an extension into the second reality of film and TV, Schinwald's perspective is rather introversive. His figures (ranging from marionettes up to "real" people) revolve within themselves in a self-engrossed manner as if inhabiting their own self-contained world. When viewing the works, the recipients are equally thrown back upon themselves: "Attention becomes self-attention, aesthetic experience becomes self-experience, references becomes self-reference."

Cf. Hans Dieter Huber, "Uncanny Lessons. Aesthetic Conditions in the Work of Markus Schinwald," in *Vanishing Lessons*, exhib. cat., Engl. transl. by Nicholas Grindell, Kunsthaus Bregenz. Bregenz, 2009, 103.

wie in einer eigenen, abgeschlossenen Welt. Bei der Betrachtung der Arbeiten werden auch die Rezipienten auf sich selbst zurückgeworfen: „Aus Aufmerksamkeit wird Selbstaufmerksamkeit, aus ästhetischer Erfahrung wird Selbsterfahrung, aus Referenz wird Selbstreferenz."

> Hans Dieter Huber, „Unheimliche Lektionen. Ästhetische Bedingungen im Werk von Markus Schinwald", in: *Vanishing Lessons*, Ausst.-Kat. Kunsthaus Bregenz. Bregenz 2009, S. 95.

Die Bild stiftende Energie, die Dalí und Co. aus den Untiefen des Unbewussten zu schöpfen suchten, kehrt sich bei Schinwald um: „Die Psyche", so Jörg Heiser im Katalog zur Schinwald-Ausstellung 2009 im Kunsthaus Bregenz, „ist nicht ein vorgängiges, archetypisches Innen, von dem im Sinne C. G. Jungs nach außen ‚projiziert' wird, sondern, anders herum, der Ort der Introjektion der sozialen und kulturellen Erfahrungen."

> Jörg Heiser, „Die Marx Brothers im Kunsthaus", ebd., S. 48.

Dass sich Markus Schinwald in seinem Beitrag zu *Le Surréalisme, c'est moi!* in der Kunsthalle Wien vorrangig mit Dalís *Dream of Venus*-Pavillon auseinandersetzt, ist vor dem Hintergrund seines durchgehend architektonisch-räumlich orientierten Werks nur konsequent. In seiner Installation, die eine Lichtbild-Projektion mit kleinformatigen historischen Ansichten von Dalís Pavillon einbezieht, begegnet er dessen Opulenz und Spektakel-Charakter mit extremem Minimalismus. Anknüpfend an seine Schaukästen in früheren Installationen wie *Curvings, Toes* (2007) und zugleich auf Dalís

The creative, image-generating energy, which Dalí and co. sought to draw from the abysses of the unconscious, becomes inverted in Schinwald's work. As Jörg Heiser remarks in the catalogue accompanying the Schinwald exhibition in 2009 at the Kunsthaus Bregenz, "This psyche is not a processual, archetypal inside 'projecting' outwards in the sense of C. G. Jung, but, conversely, the place where social and cultural experience is interjected."

> Cf. Jörg Heiser, "The Marx Brothers at the Kunsthaus," ibid, 55.

Against the backdrop of his consistently architecturally and spatially oriented work, it makes perfect sense that Markus Schinwald should primarily allude to Dalí's *Dream of Venus* pavilion in his contribution to *Le Surréalisme, c'est moi! Homage to Salvador Dalí* at the Kunsthalle Wien. In his installation, which incorporates a slide projection show of small-format historical images of Dalí's pavilion, he replies to the latter's opulence and spectacularity with extreme minimalism. Adopting the display cases of earlier installation works such as *Curvings, Toes* (2007) and simultaneously referring to Dalí's shop window and underwater presentations, Schinwald has inserted an aquarium (dimensions: 140 × 70 × 70 cm) into a dark wall in the exhibition space. Instead of live mermaids and surreal rubber figures, his basin harbors ornamental fish along with an oxygen pump and plants, as well as miniature versions of his own works, which again takes up Dalí's integration of earlier works in the *Dream of Venus* pavilion. In the style of Dalí's painted background panoramas, which expanded the "wet" and "dry" zones of the pavilion,

Schaufenster- und Unterwasser-Präsentationen Bezug nehmend, hat Schinwald ein Aquarium (Maße: 140 × 70 × 70 cm) in eine dunkel gehaltene Wand eingelassen. Statt lebender Nixen und surrealer Gummifiguren beherbergt sein Bassin Zierfische samt Sauerstoffpumpe und Pflanzen sowie Miniatur-Versionen eigener Arbeiten, was wiederum Dalís Integration früherer Werke im *Dream of Venus*-Pavillon aufgreift. In Anlehnung an Dalís gemalte Hintergrund-Panoramen, die die „Feucht-" und „Trocken"-Zonen des Pavillons in die Weite öffneten und narrativ umrahmten, hat Schinwald für seinen gläsernen Unterwasser-Show-Room eine Rückwand-Gestaltung gewählt, die eher als abstrahierte Reflexionsfläche fungiert und das Publikum zum Erfinden eigener Geschichten animiert.



Die Fische, die das Erstaunliche als reales Phänomen sichtbar machen, bilden einen natürlichen Kontrapunkt zur künstlich beziehungsweise künstlerisch geschaffenen Exotik der surrealistischen Inszenierung. Schinwald denkt sich seine „minimalistische Variante" des Dalí-Pavillons „wie ein Bild, das auf der Wand hängt", in dem nichts besonderes passiert und „das eine beruhigende Wirkung" haben soll – wie die Testbilder, die früher nach Sendeschluss im TV liefen.

Markus Schinwald in einem Telefongespräch mit der Autorin am 3. Mai 2011.

Damit nimmt er eine diametral entgegengesetzte Position zu Dalís auf Provokation und Schock angelegten Ansatz ein. Schinwald geht laut eigener Auskunft mit einer „gewissen Distanz" vor und vermeidet das „Pathos" und

giving them scope and a narrative frame, Schinwald has chosen to design the back wall of his underwater showroom as a more abstract surface for reflection, inviting the viewers to invent their own stories.

The fish make the wondrous visible as a phenomenon of real life, and form a natural counterpoint to the artificially or, rather, artistically created exoticism of the Surrealist spectacle. Schinwald perceives his "minimalist version" of the Dalí pavilion "as a picture hanging on the wall," in which nothing special happens and which is aimed at having "a soothing effect" – in the manner of test patterns on TV that used to be broadcast when stations went off air for the night.

Markus Schinwald in a telephone conversation with the author on May 3, 2011.

With this, he takes a diametrically opposed position to Dalí's approach that is aimed at provocation and shock. According to his own remarks, Schinwald proceeds with a "certain distance" and avoids the "pathos" and "plumbing of the depths" characteristic of Surrealism.

Ibid.

Nonetheless, apart from Dalí's pavilion, Philippe Halsman's surreal slapstick photo portrait *Dalí Atomicus* from 1948 (ill. p. 207) had also caught his eye, when conceiving his current work for the Kunsthalle Wien.

In the Halsman's portrait, Dalí is floating about next to his easel, together with an airborne die „Tiefenauslotungen", die dem Surrealismus eigen sind.

Ebd.

Gleichwohl ist ihm vor Konzeption seiner aktuellen Arbeit für die Kunsthalle neben Dalís Pavillon auch Philippe Halsmans slapstickhaft-surreales Foto-Porträt *Dalí Atomicus* von 1948 ins Auge gesprungen (Abb. S.207).

In letzterem hebt Dalí an der Staffelei nebst schwebendem Stuhl ab, während Katzen auf einem Wasserschwall durch den Raum fliegen. Die hier momenthaft eingefangenen Ausfallschritte und Schwebezustände lassen sich in anderen Spielarten auch in einigen Filmarbeiten oder den sich in alle möglichen Verbiegungen hinein begebenden *Contortionists* Schinwalds (aus dessen gleichnamiger, ab 2002 entstehender Fotoserie) entdecken. In seiner labyrinthischen Venedig-Installation lenkt der Künstler die Blickrichtung der Betrachter immer wieder um und gibt somit „Anlass, einen Schritt weiter oder zur Seite"

Ebd.

zu gehen: Ein Vorgehen, das grundsätzlich seine Produktion bestimmt. Angesichts seiner Replik zu Dalís *Venus*-Pavillon ist man ebenfalls aufgefordert, jenen Schritt weiter und zur Seite zu gehen. Es sind die kleinen Verschiebungen, auf die es bei Markus Schinwald ankommt: Die sanften Dislozierungen und überraschenden Brüche, die das Wundersame im Gewöhnlichen, das Surreale im Realen, eine andere Wahrnehmung der Dinge freizusetzen vermögen.

chair, while cats are flying through the space upon a jet of water. The sidesteps and states of suspension captured here can also be discovered in other variations in some of Schinwald's film works or in the range of convolutions carried out by the *Contortionists* (in the photo series of the same title, which the artist started working on in 2002). In his labyrinthian Venice installation, the artist keeps redirecting the viewer's line of vision, thus creating "the occasion to go a step further or to the side":

Ibid.

a course of action that essentially determines his production. In the face of his reply to Dalí's *Dream of Venus* pavilion, one is also called upon as a viewer to go that additional step further or to the side. Markus Schinwald's work depends upon those many small shifts: the gentle dislocations and surprising refractions, which have the power to release the wondrous in the ordinary, the surreal in the real, and another form of perception of the reality we inhabit.

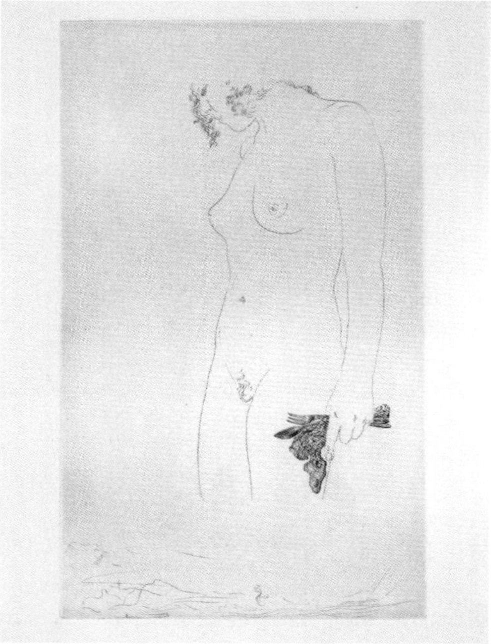

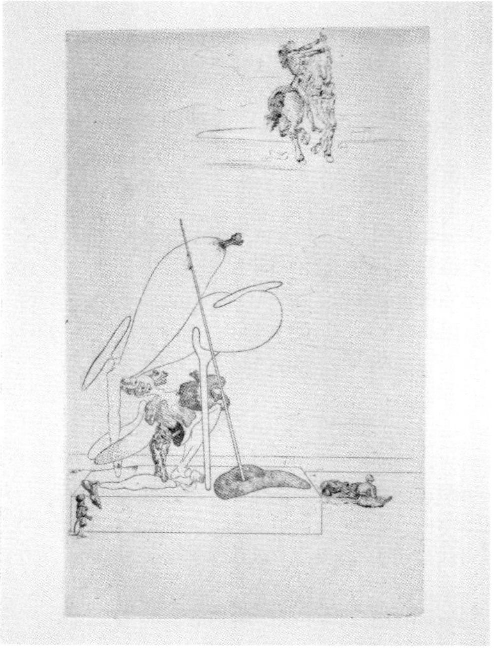

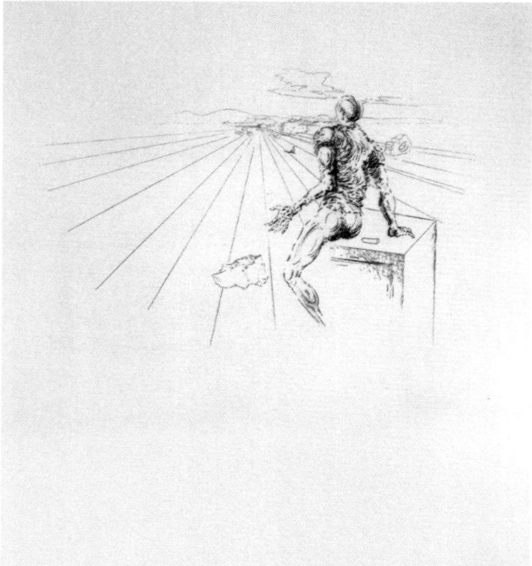

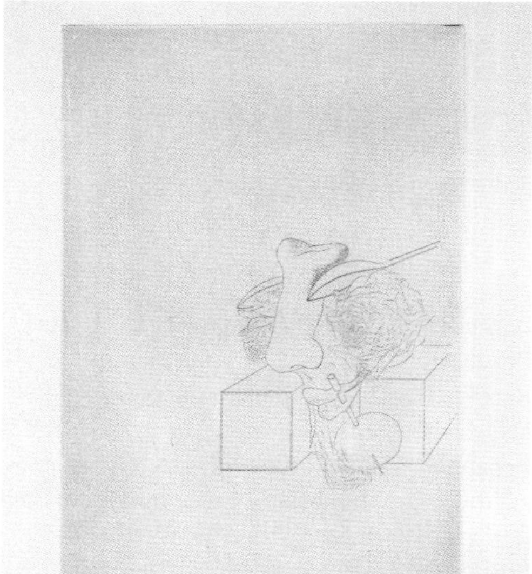

Salvador Dalí,
*Les Chants de Maldoror*, 1933–1934

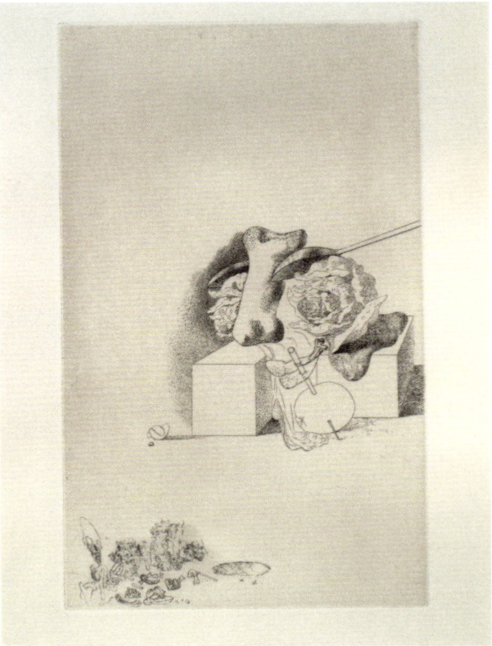

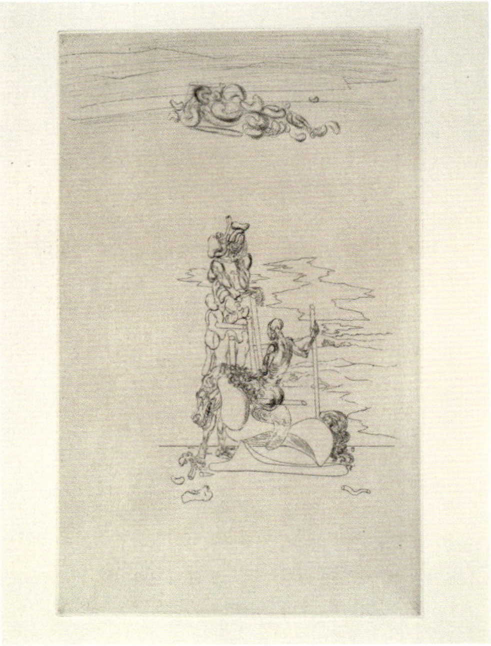

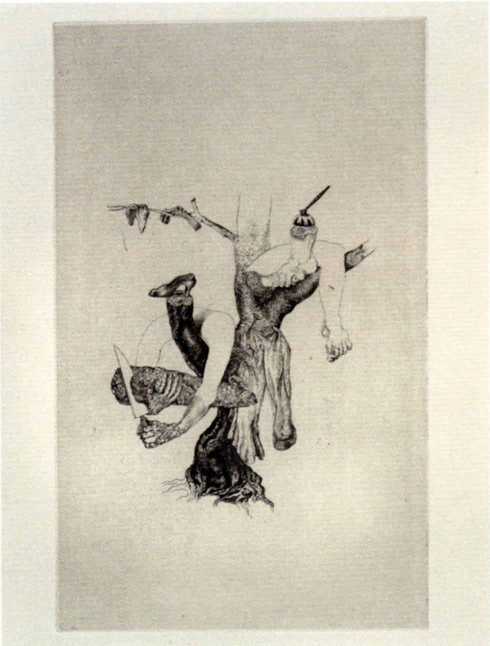

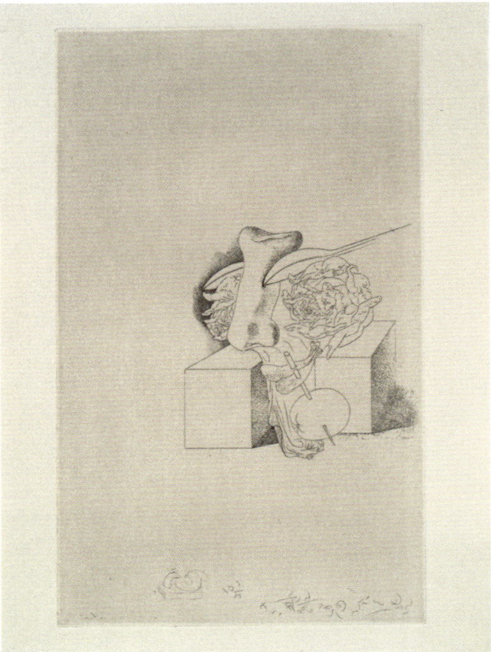

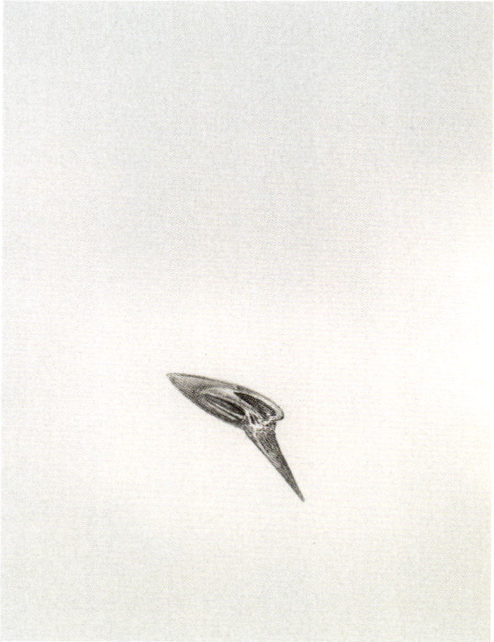

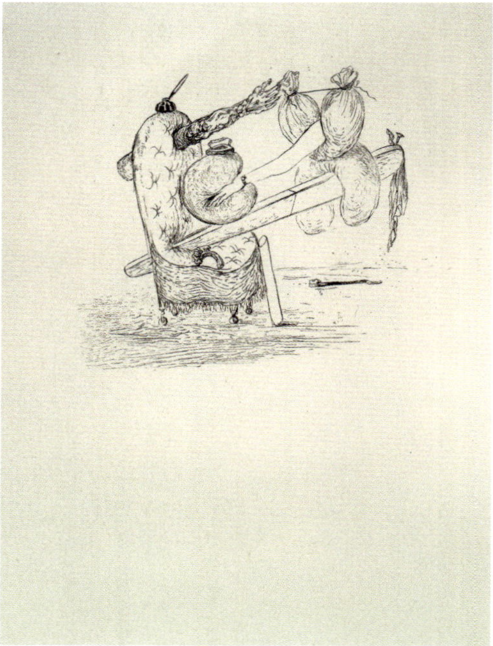



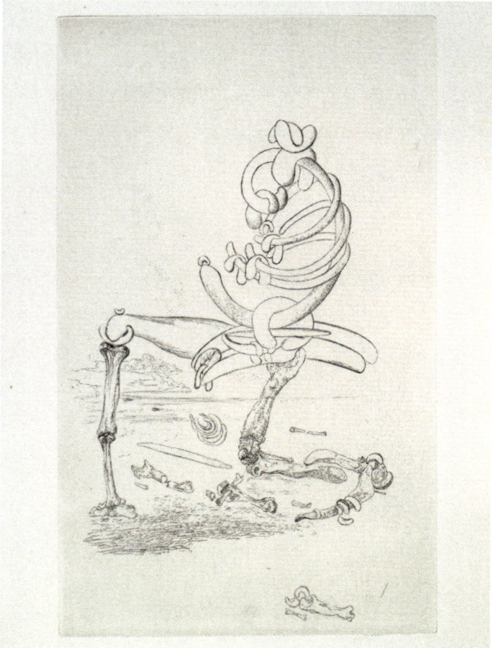

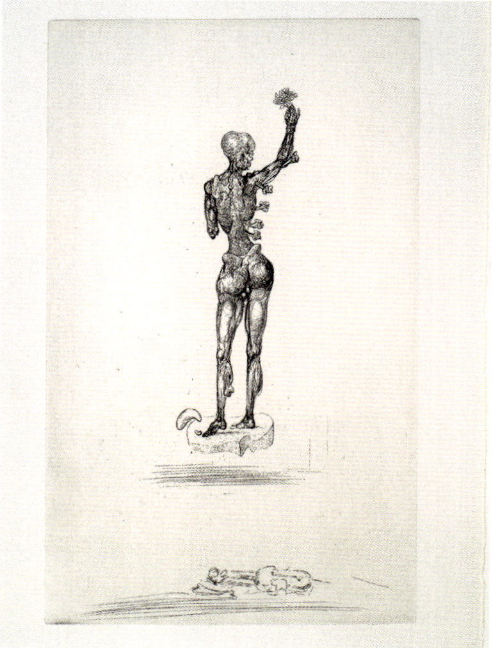

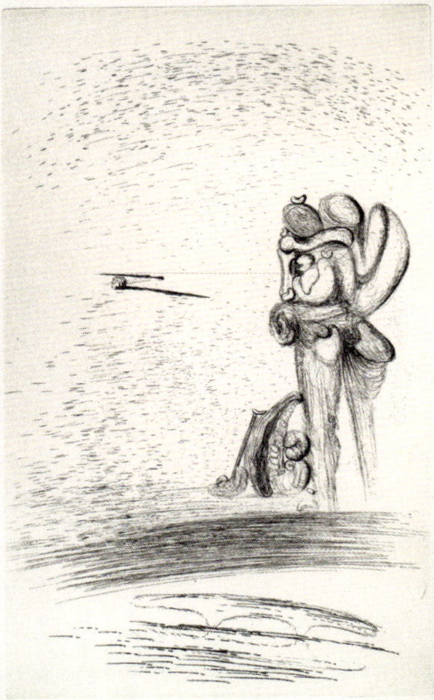
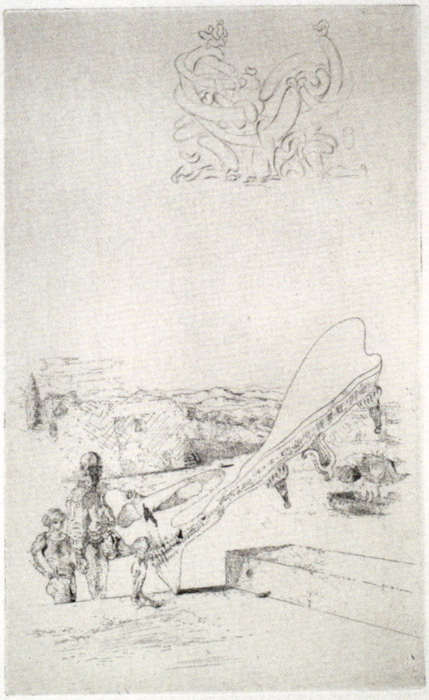
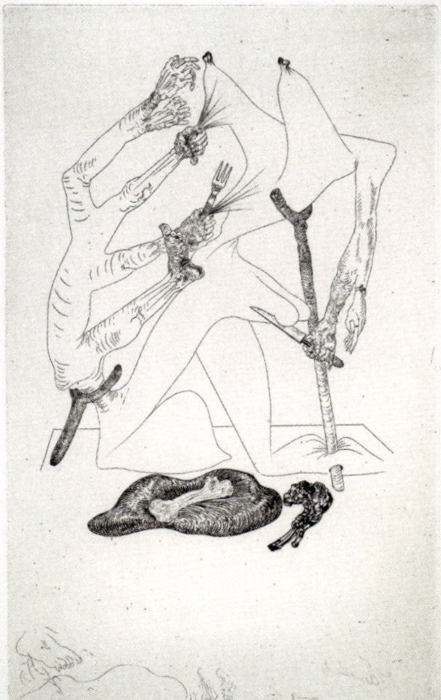
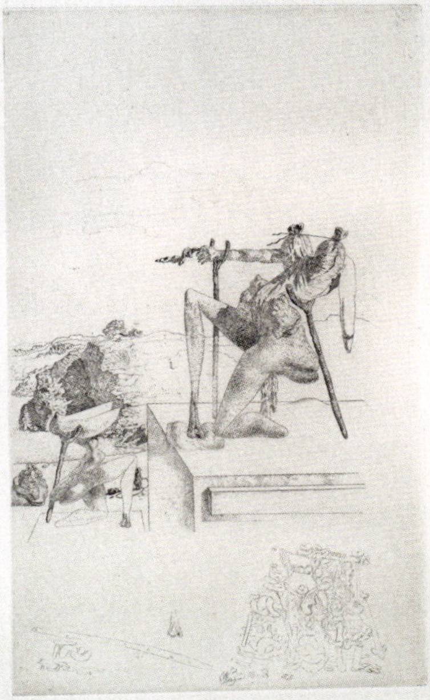

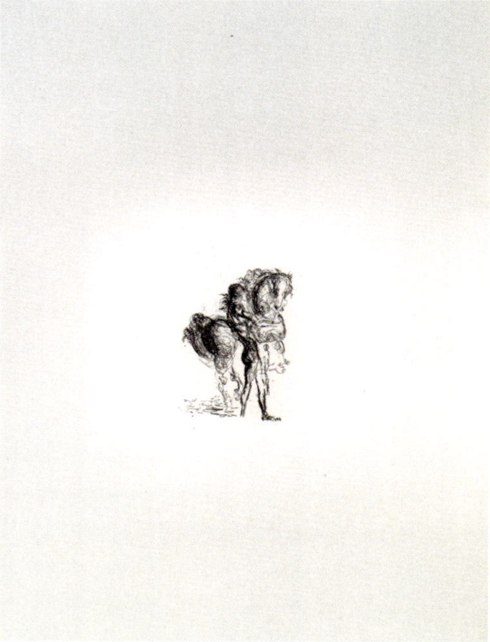

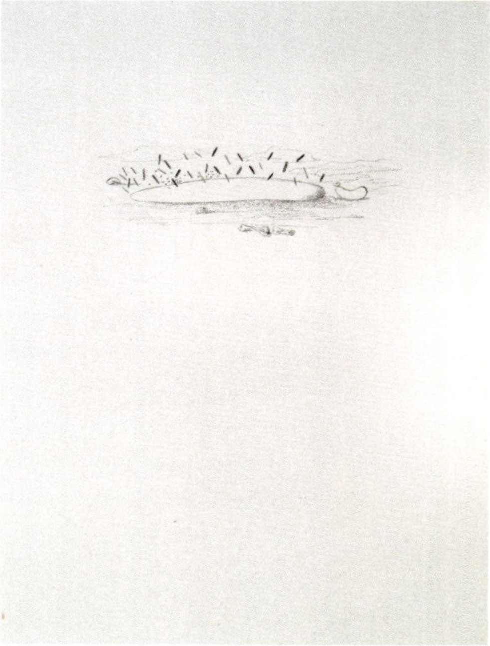

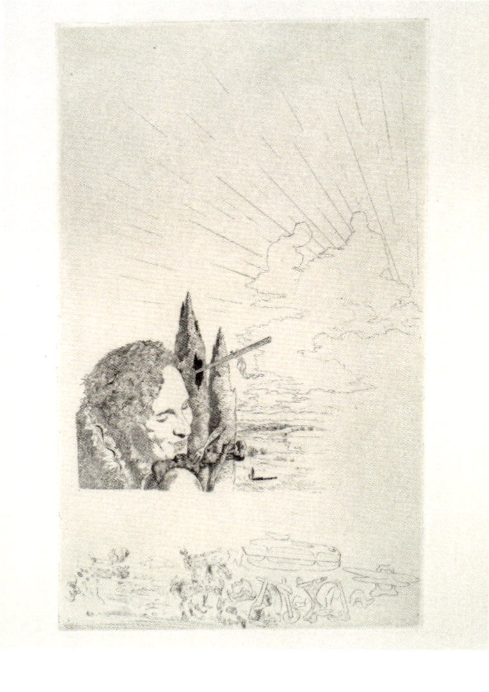

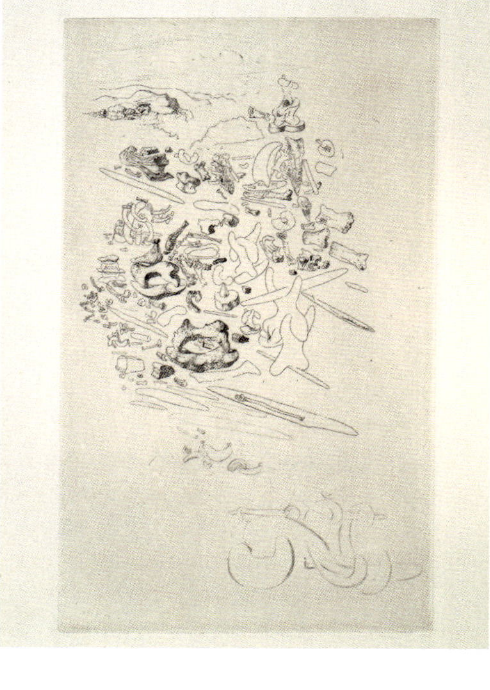

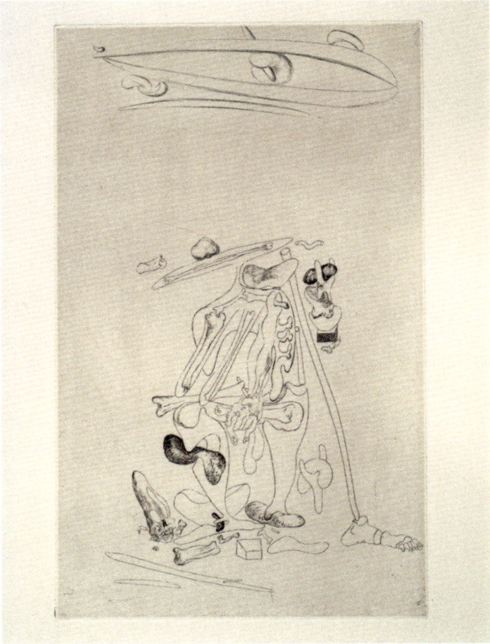

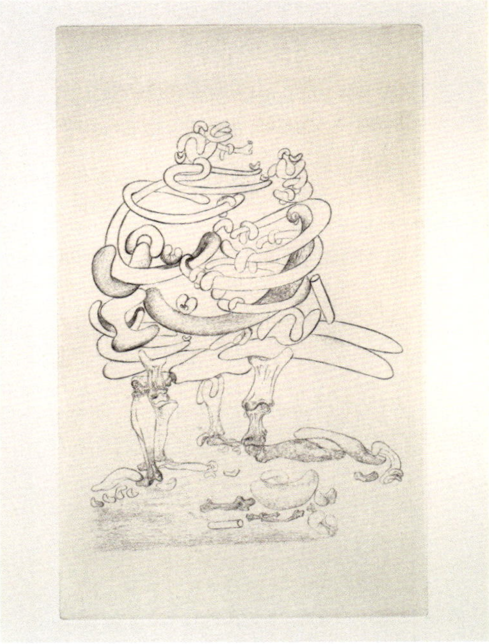

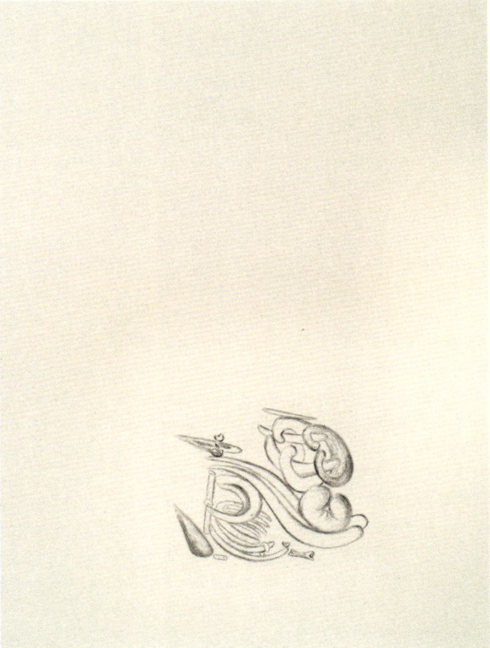

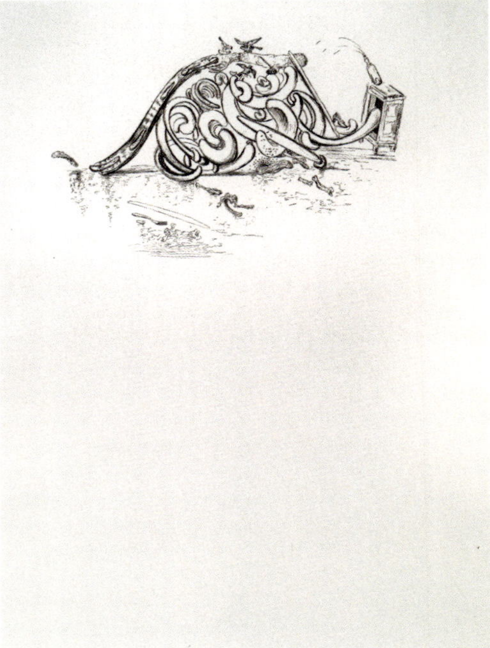

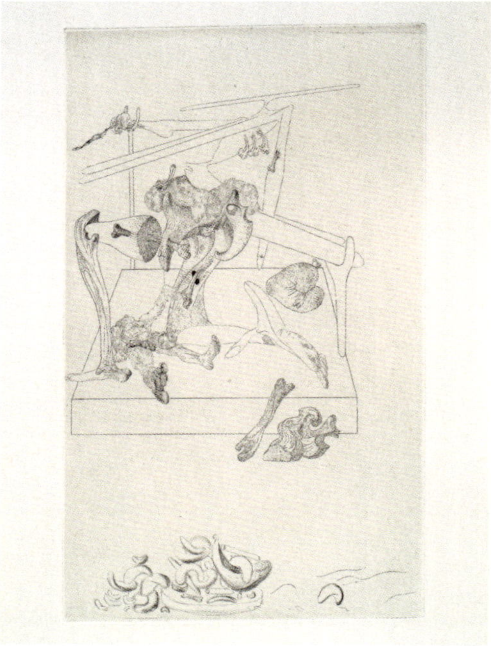

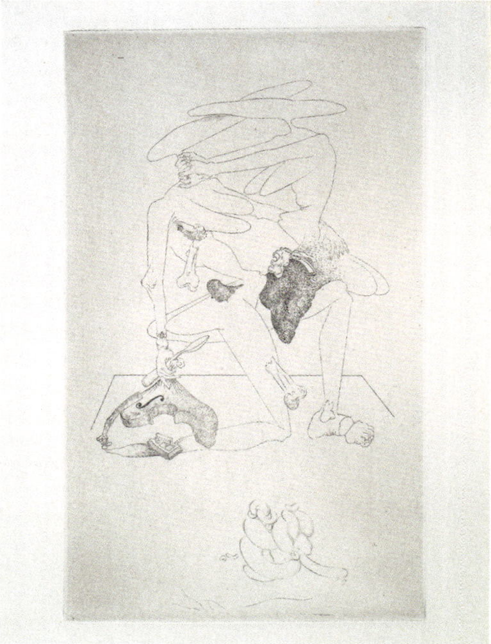

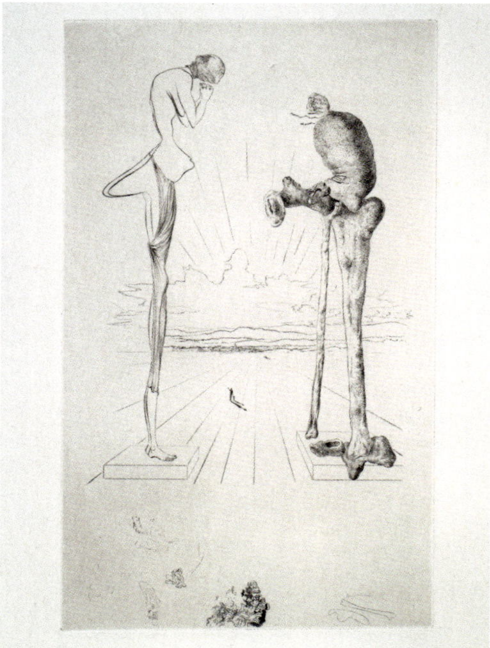

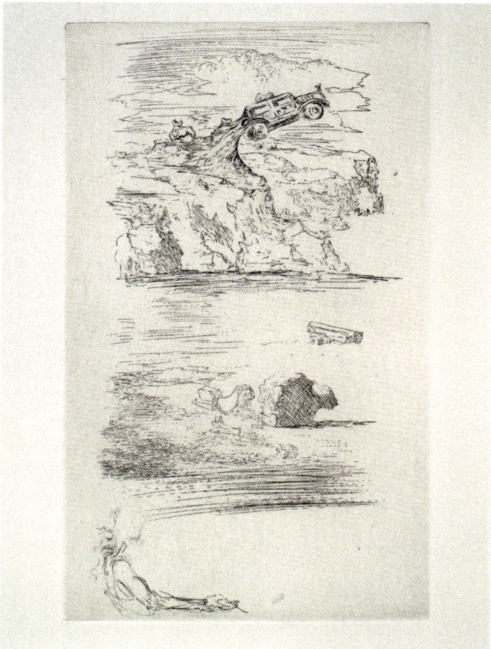

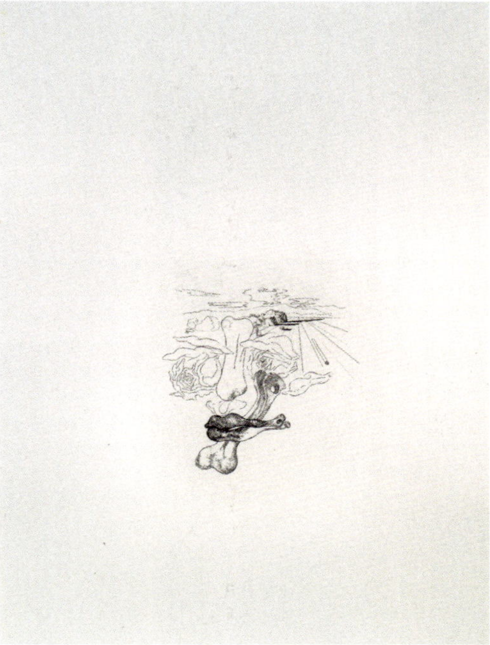
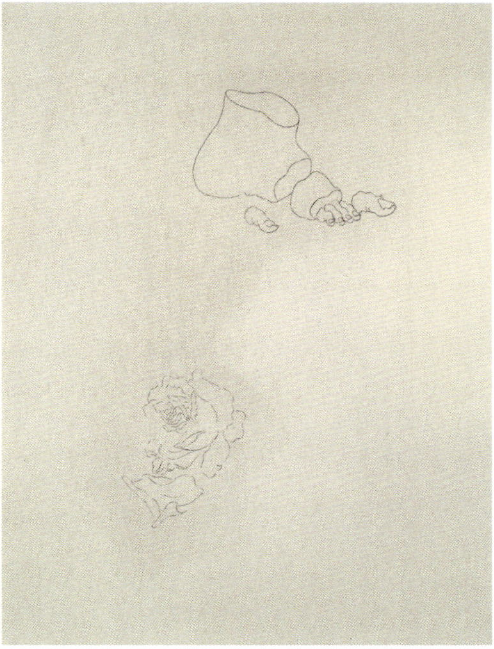
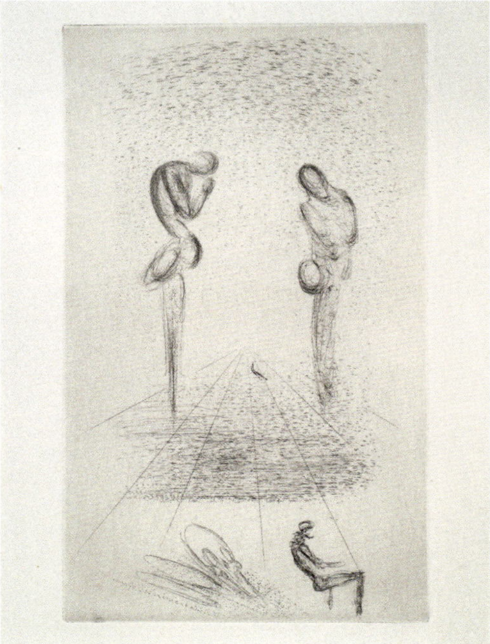
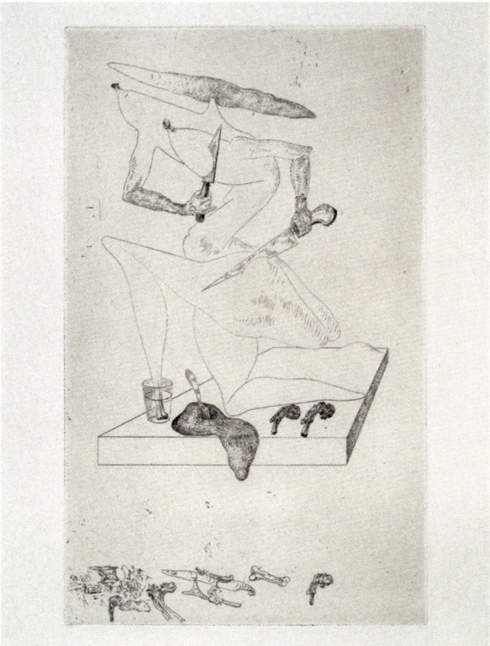

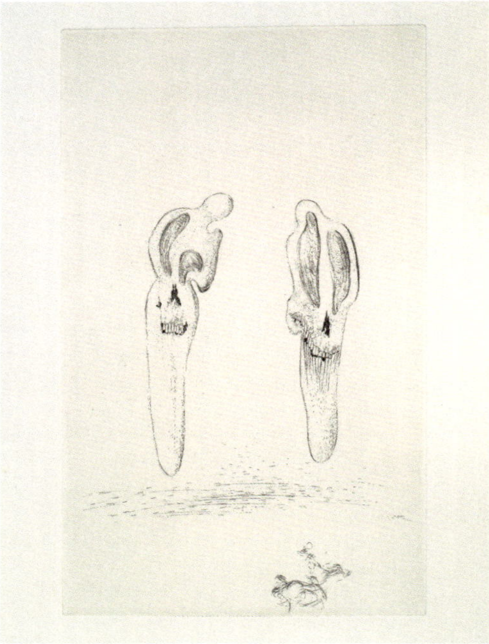

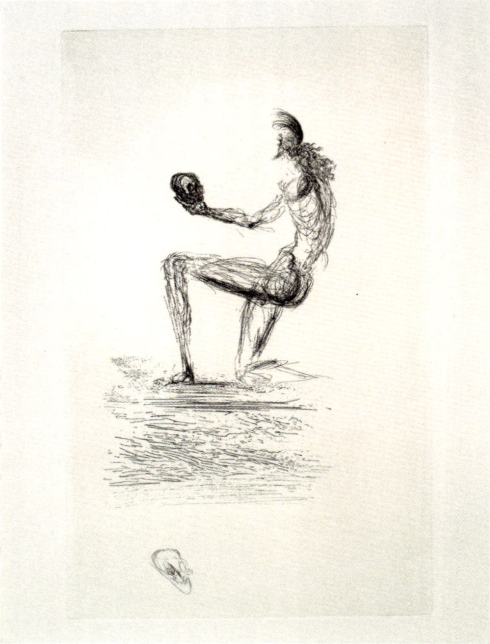



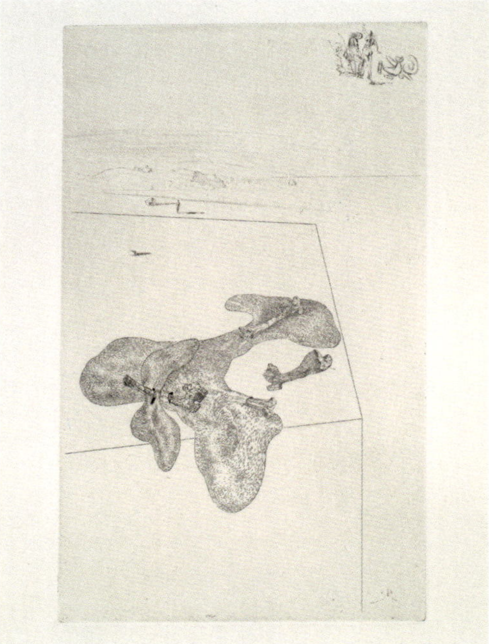

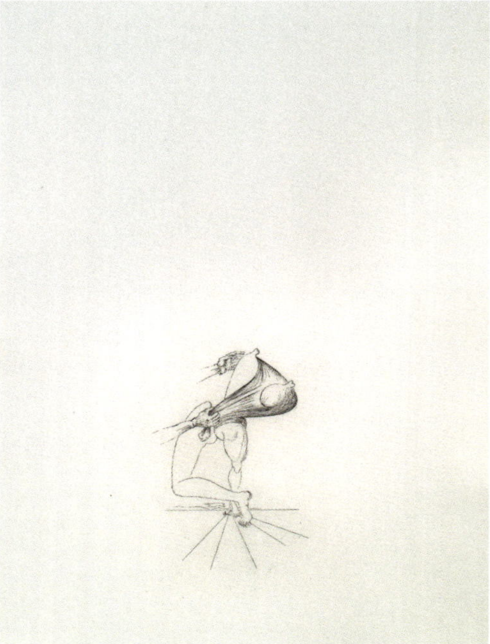

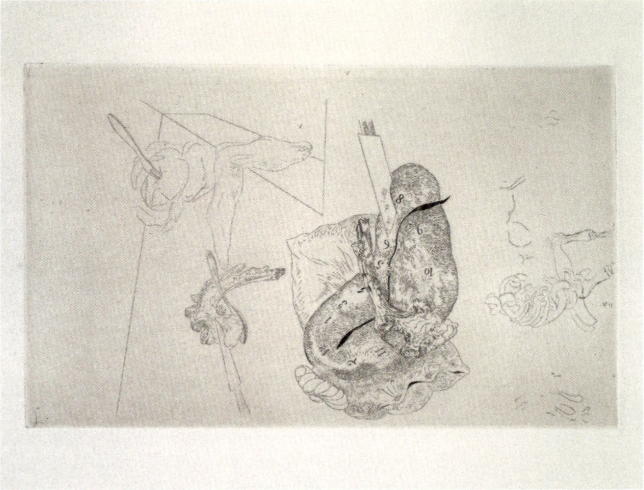

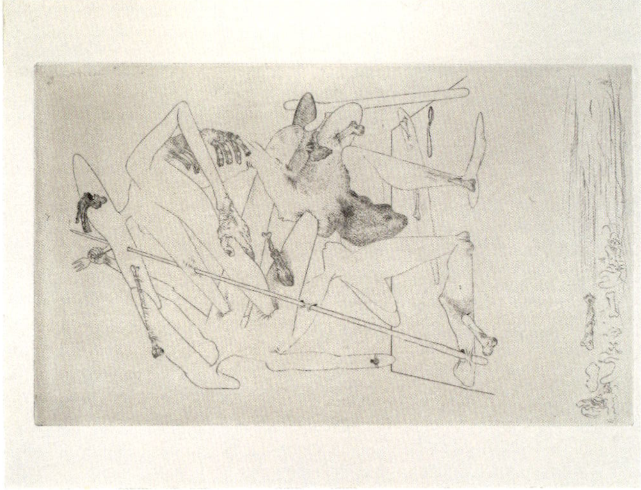

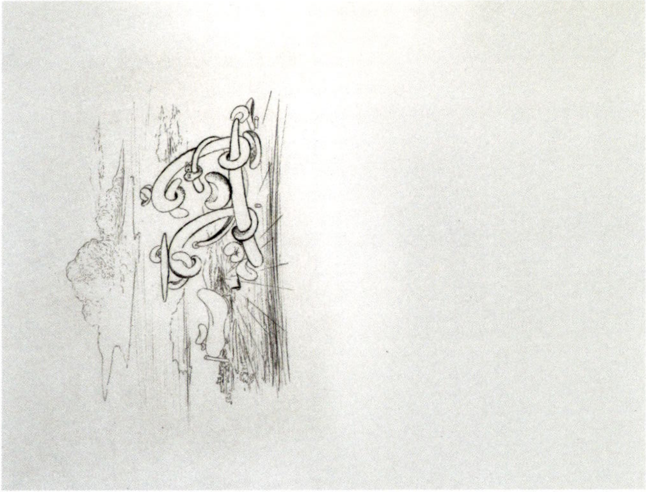

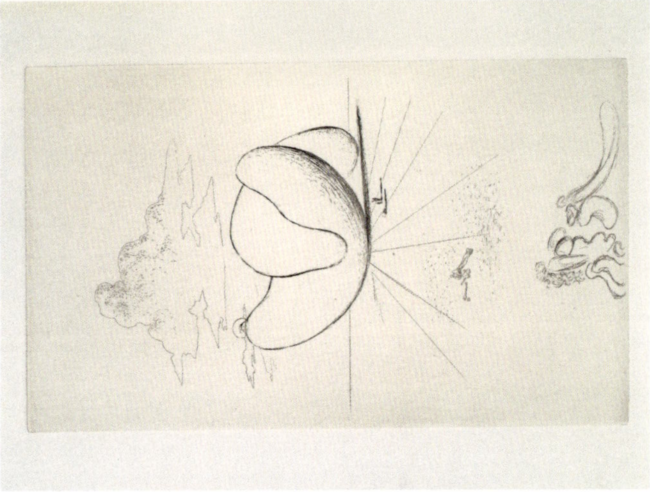

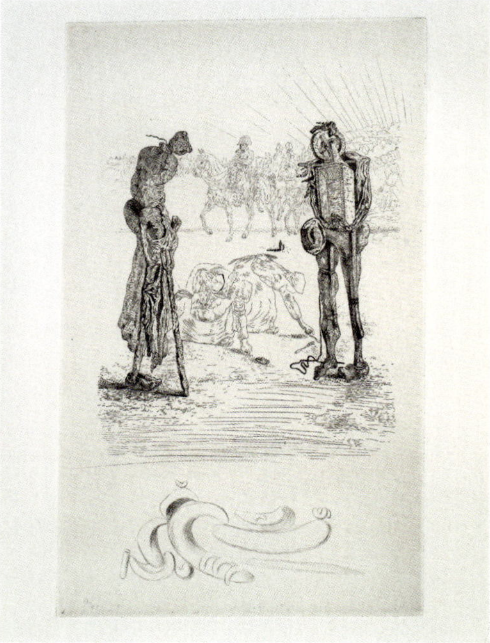

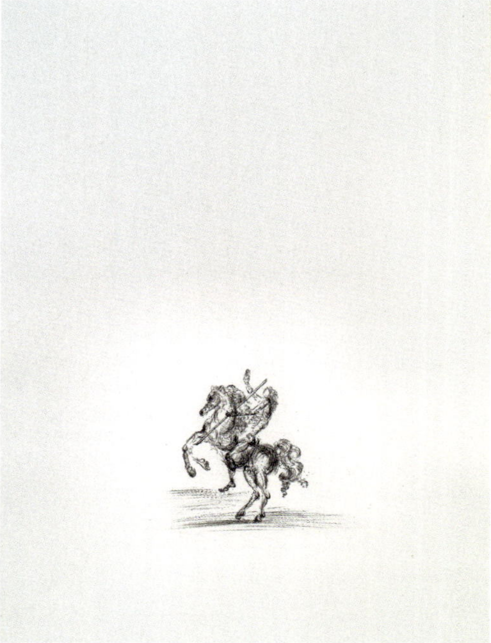



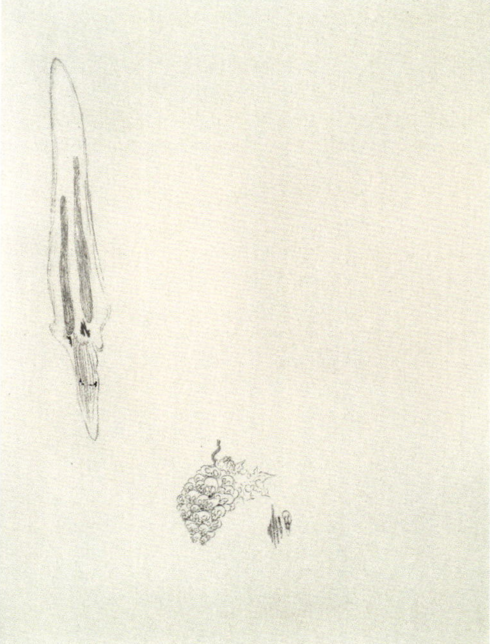

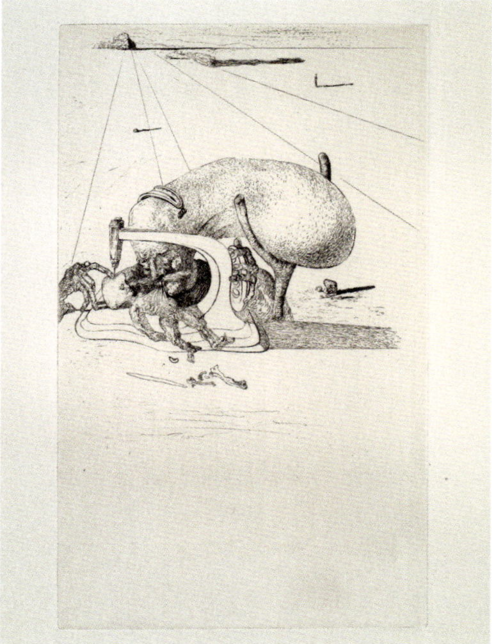

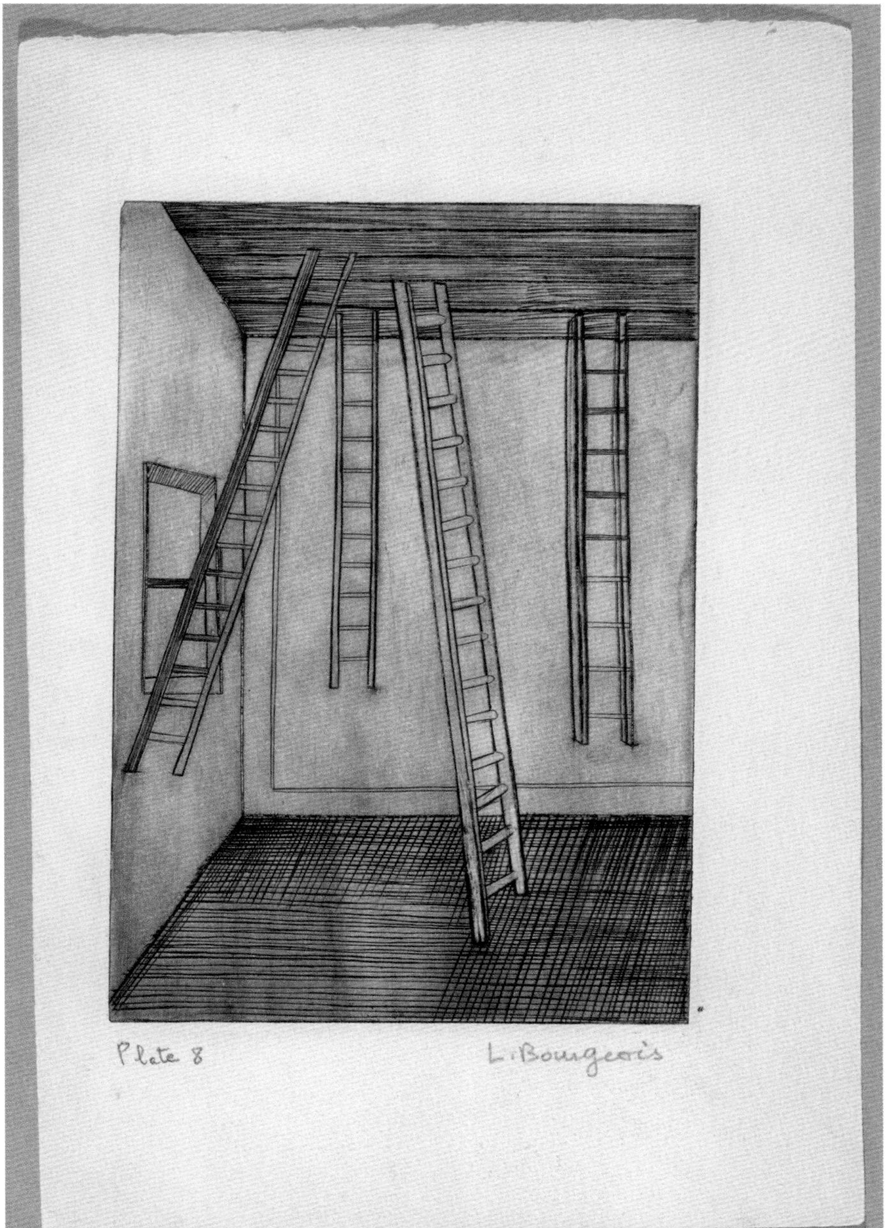


Louise Bourgeois,
*He disappeared into complete silence* (Plate 8), 1947

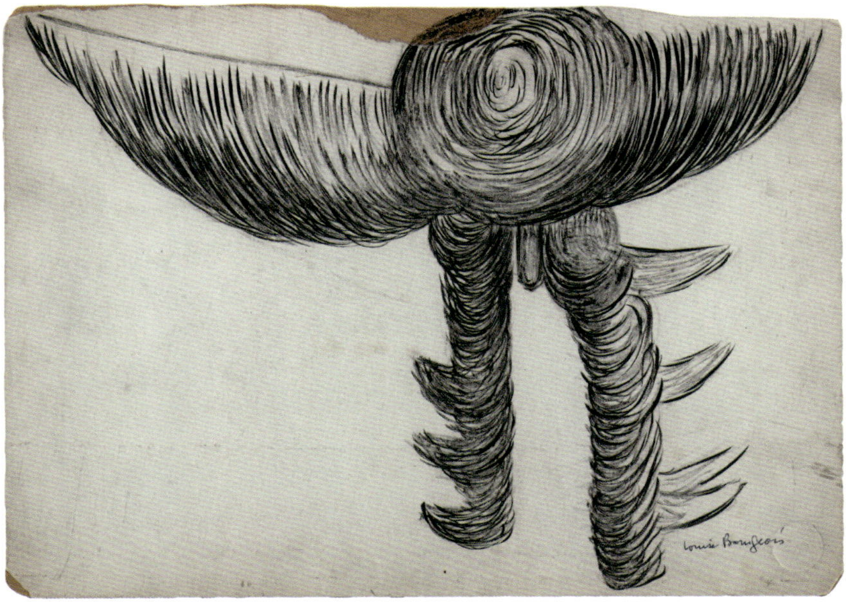


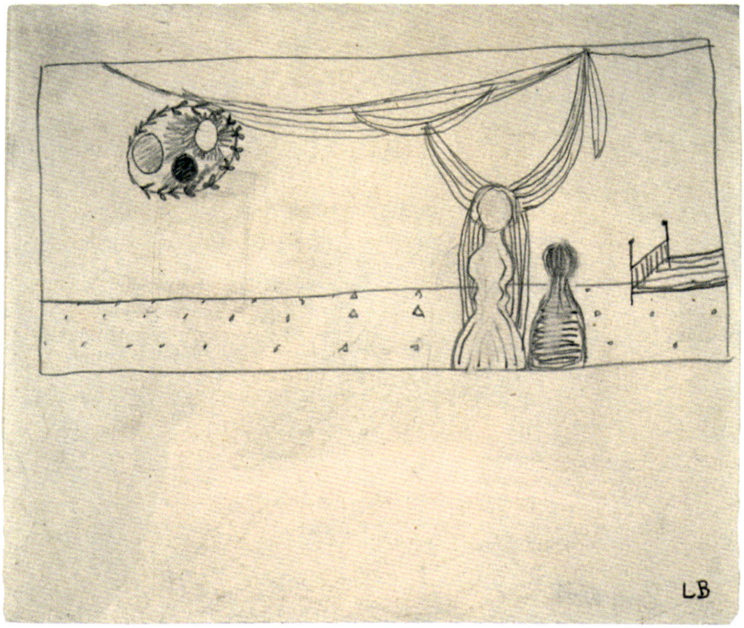


Louise Bourgeois,
*Untitled*, 1947

Louise Bourgeois,
*Untitled*, 1943

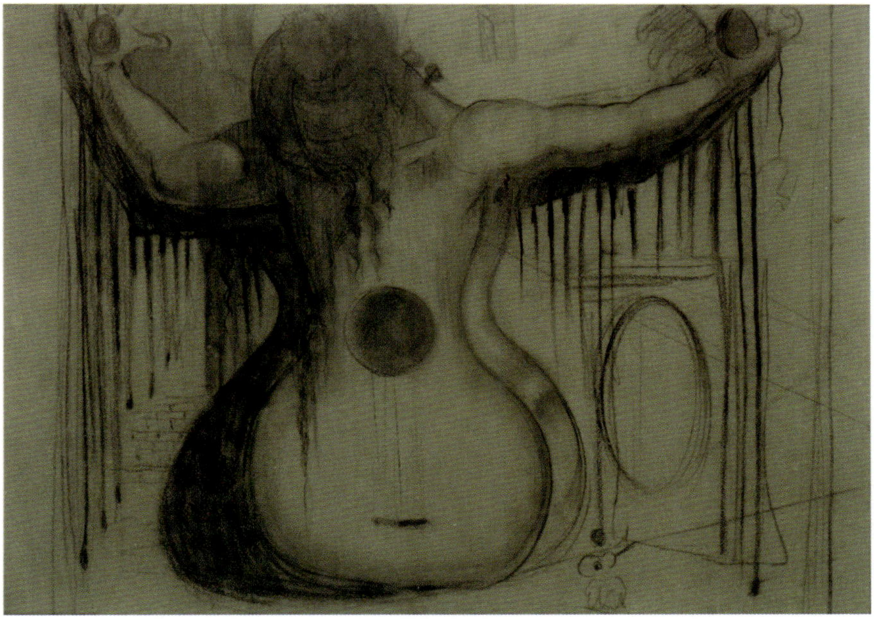

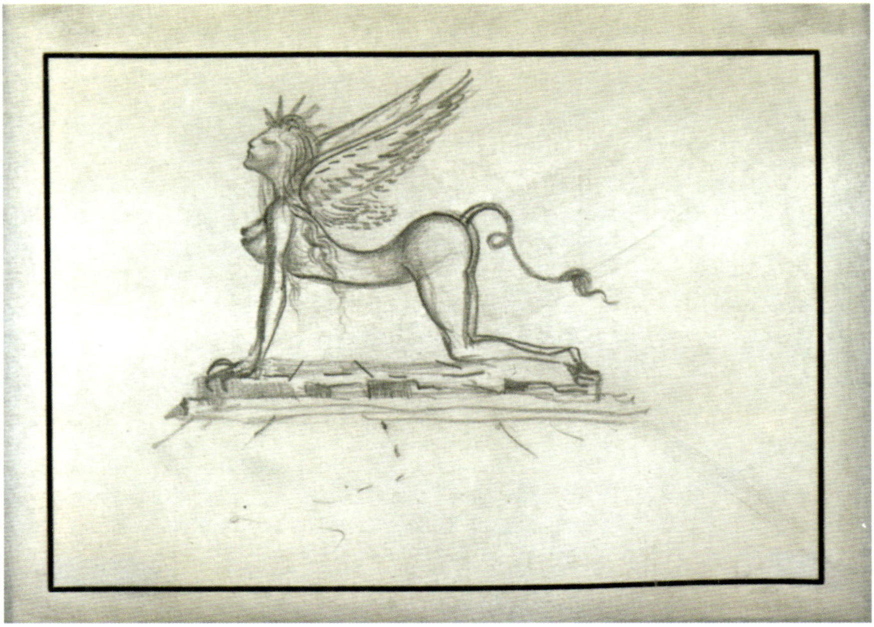



Salvador Dalí,
*Café de Chinitas*, 1943

Salvador Dalí,
*Esfinge*, c. 1947

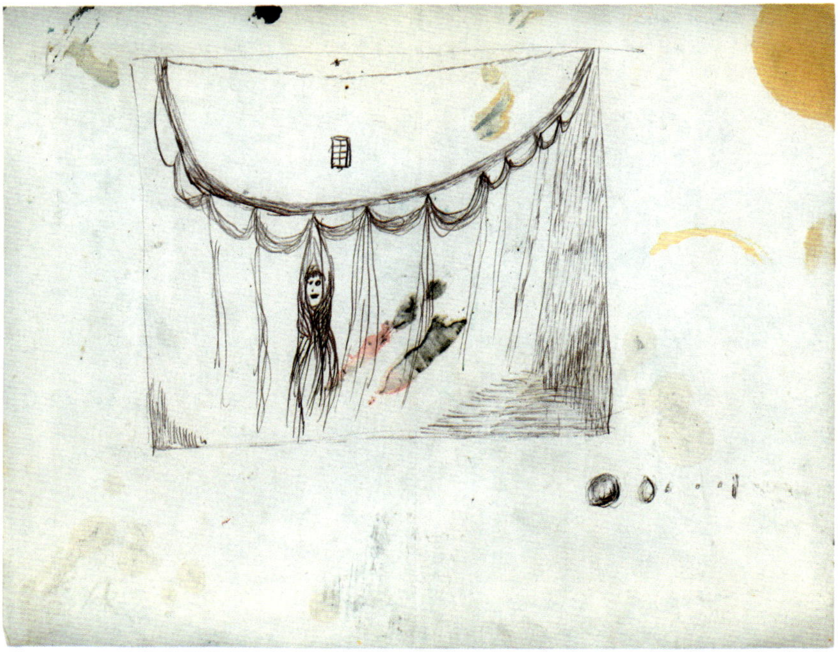

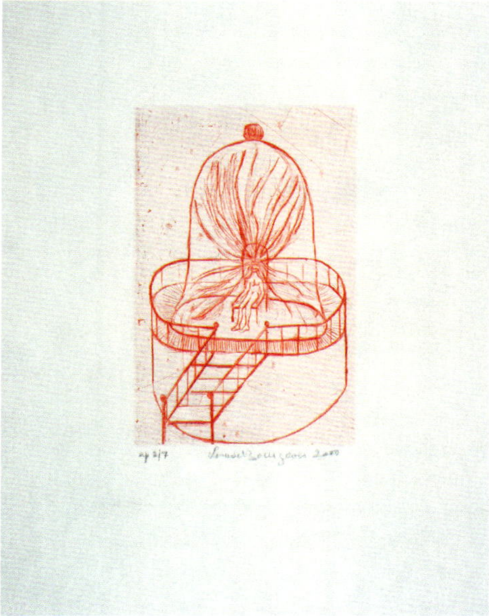

Louise Bourgeois,
*Untitled*, 1946

Louise Bourgeois,
*Hair*, 2000

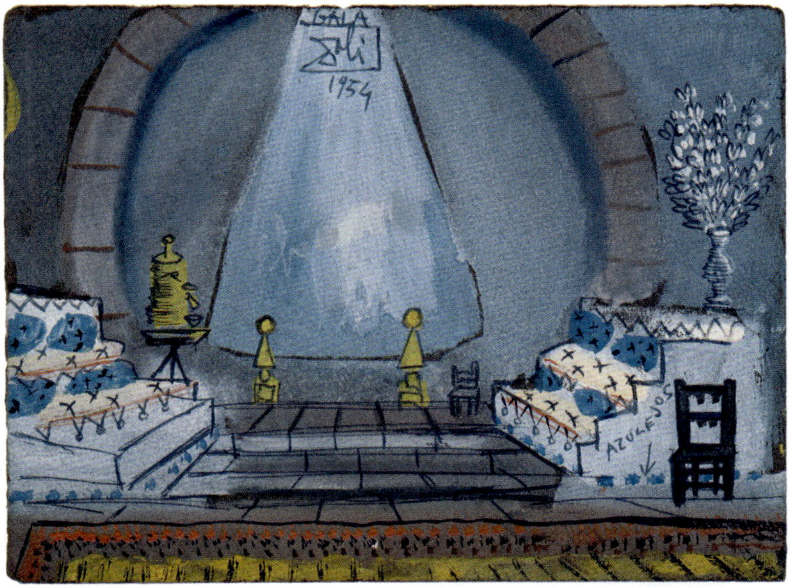


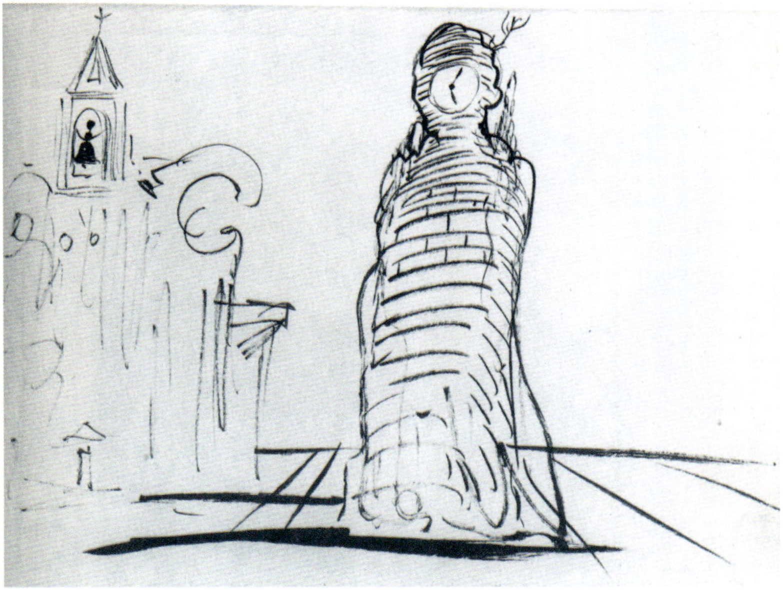

Salvador Dalí, Entwurf für die Neueinrichtung des Schlafzimmers in Dalís Haus in Port Llegat/sketch for the re-accomodation of the bedroom in Dalí's house in Port Llegat, 1954

Salvador Dalí, *Estudio – Croquis para "Romeo y Julieta"*, 1942

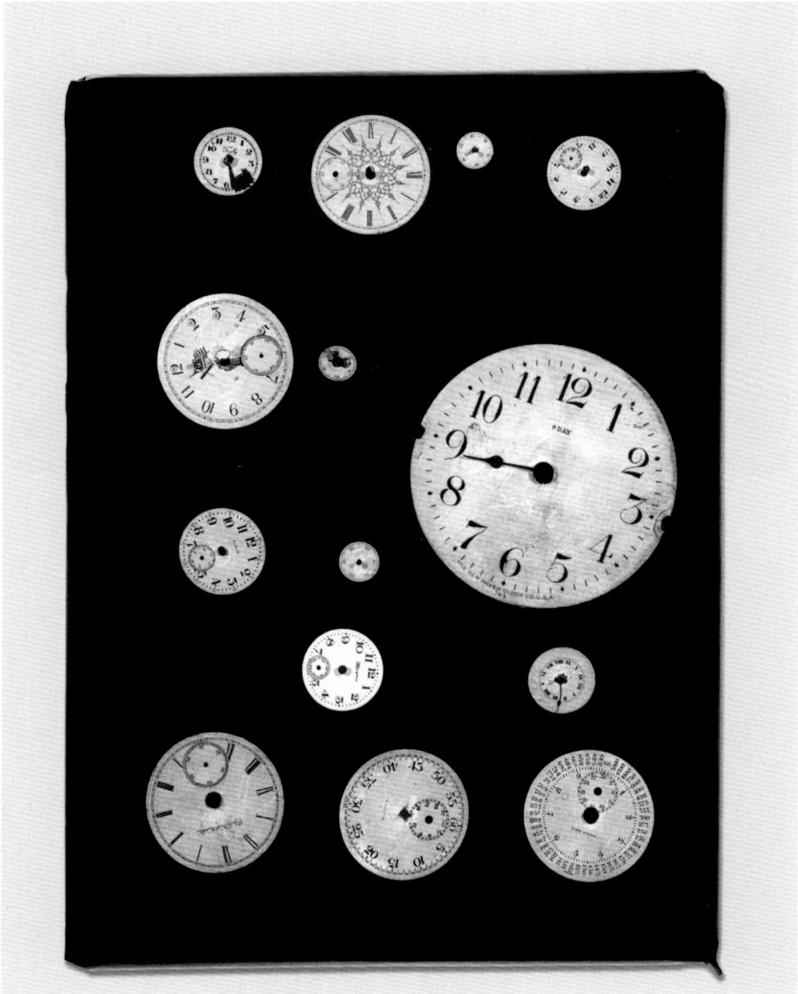

Louise Bourgeois,
*Untitled (Clocks)*, 1944

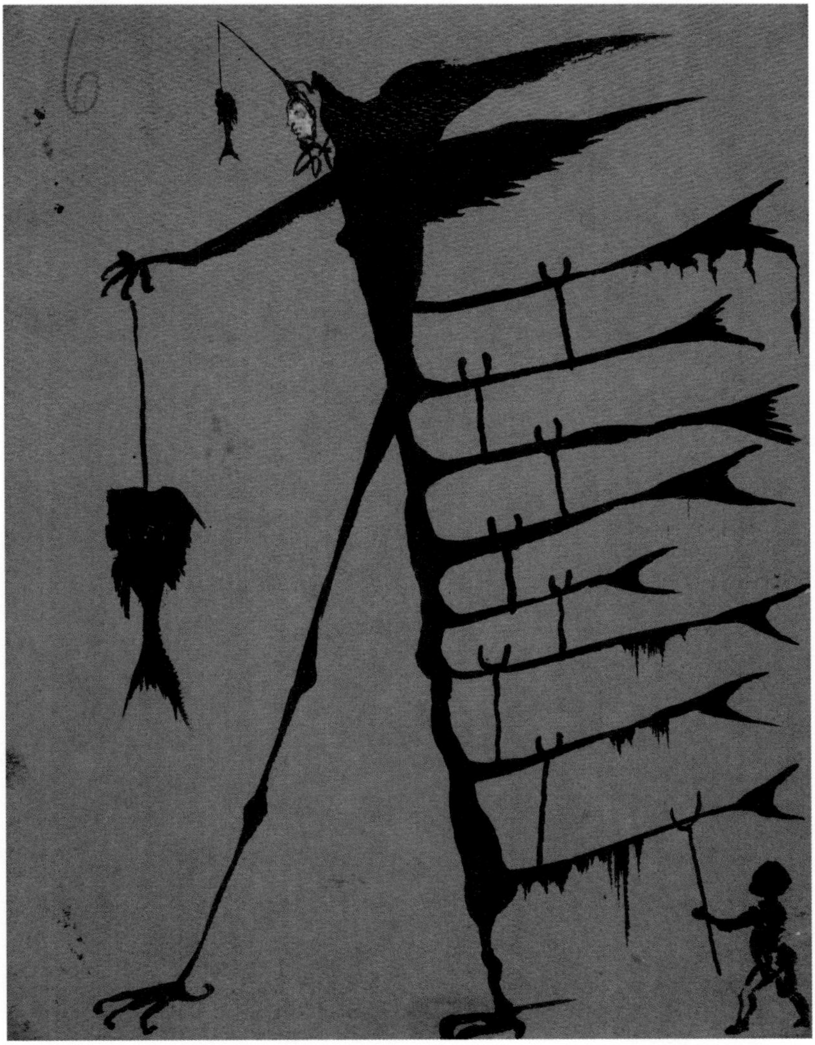

Salvador Dalí,
*Personaje surrealista/Boceto para la escenografía de "Don Juan Tenorio"*, 1950

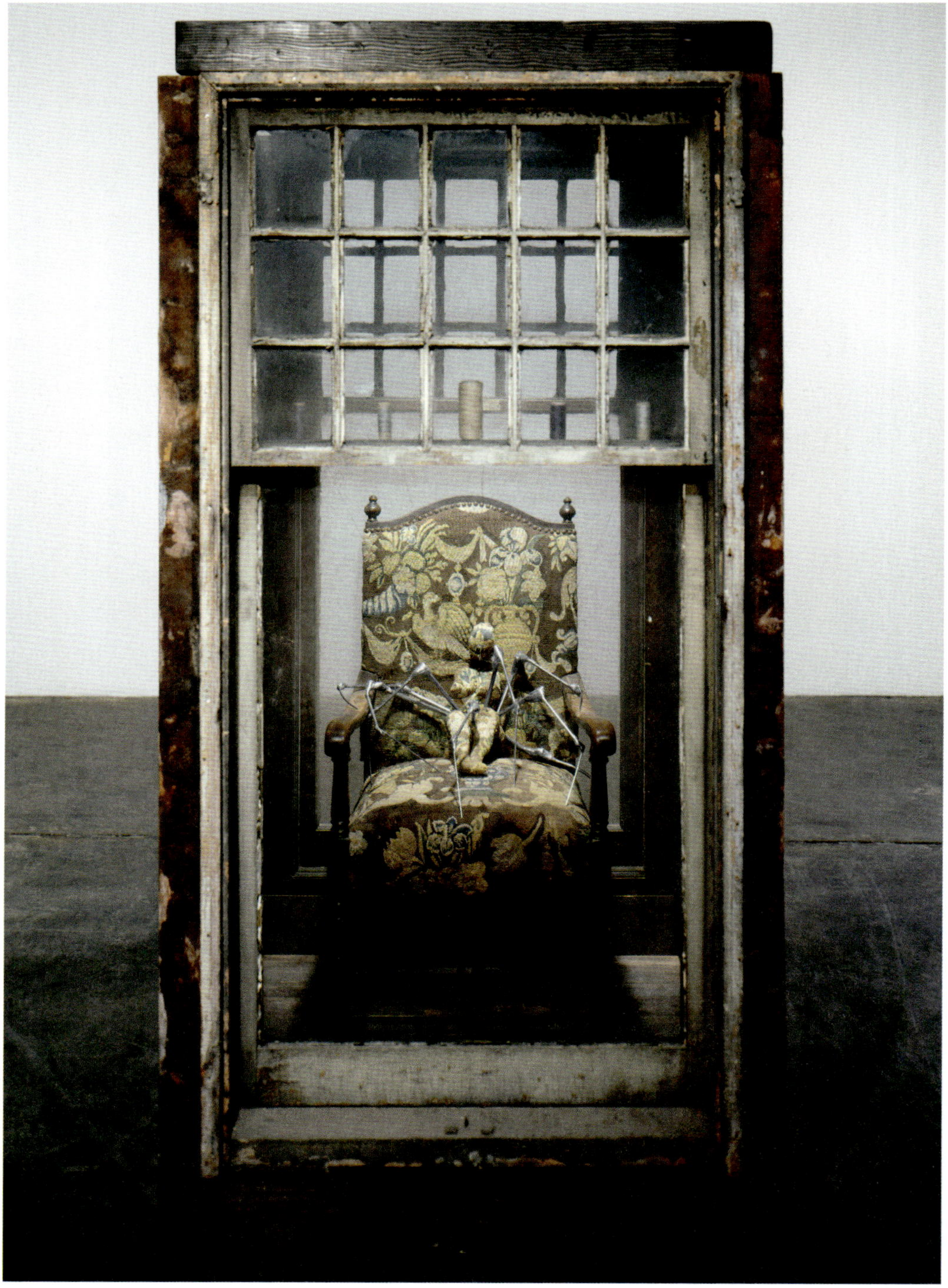

Louise Bourgeois,
*Lady in Waiting*, 2003

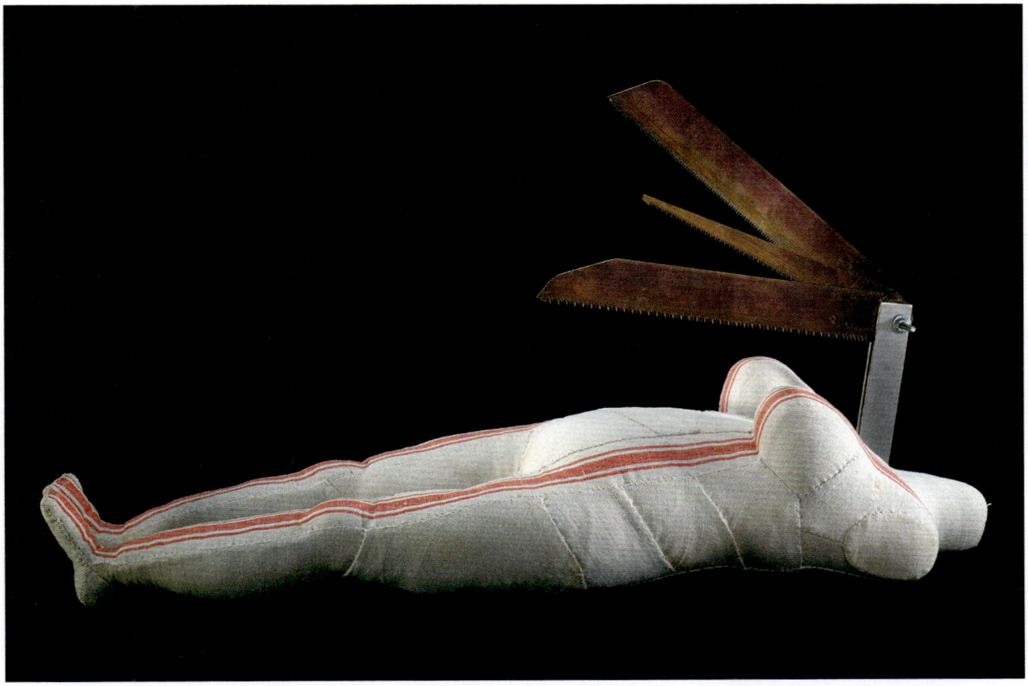

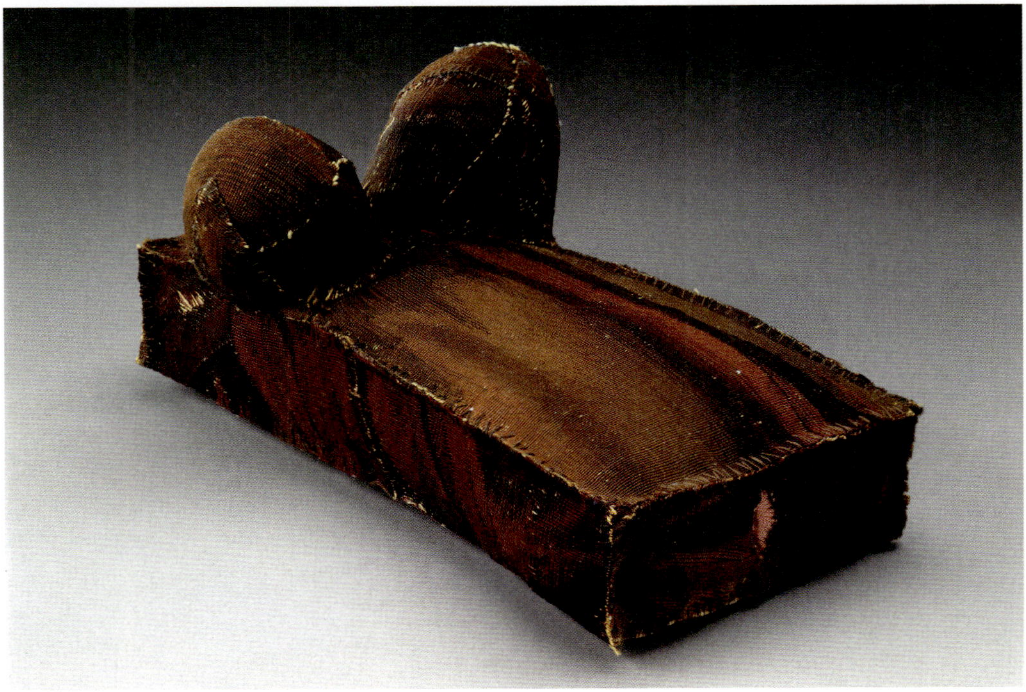

Louise Bourgeois,
*Femme Couteau*, 2002

Louise Bourgeois,
*Femme*, 2005

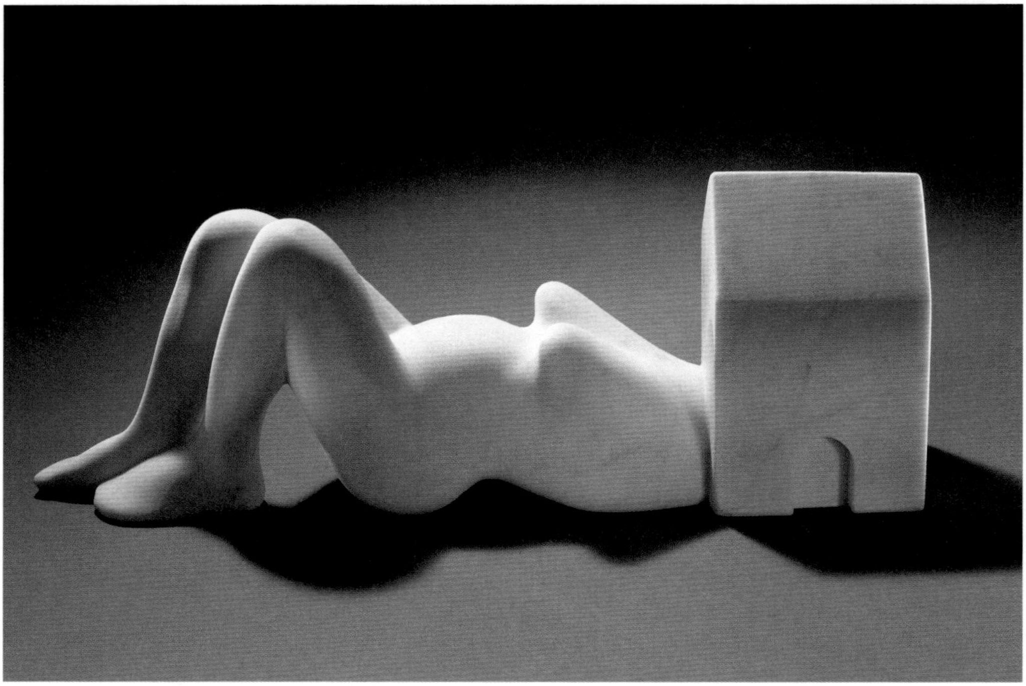

Louise Bourgeois,
*Femme Maison*, 1994

Louise Bourgeois,
*Fallen Woman*, 1981–1996

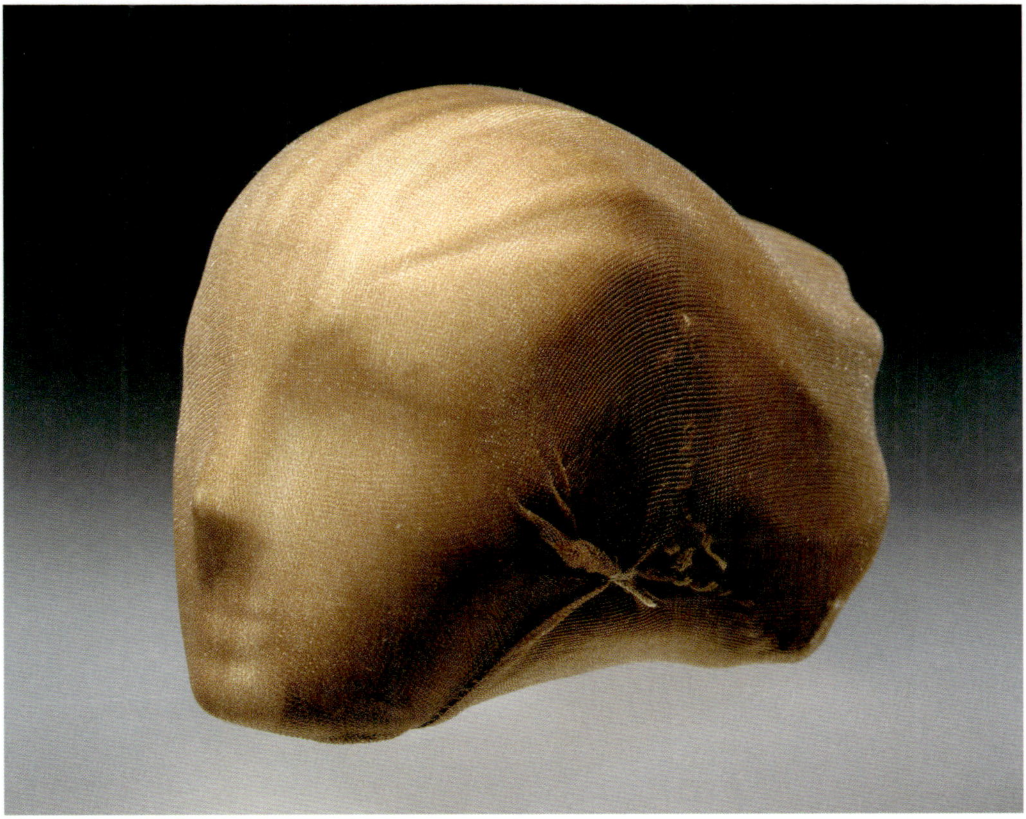

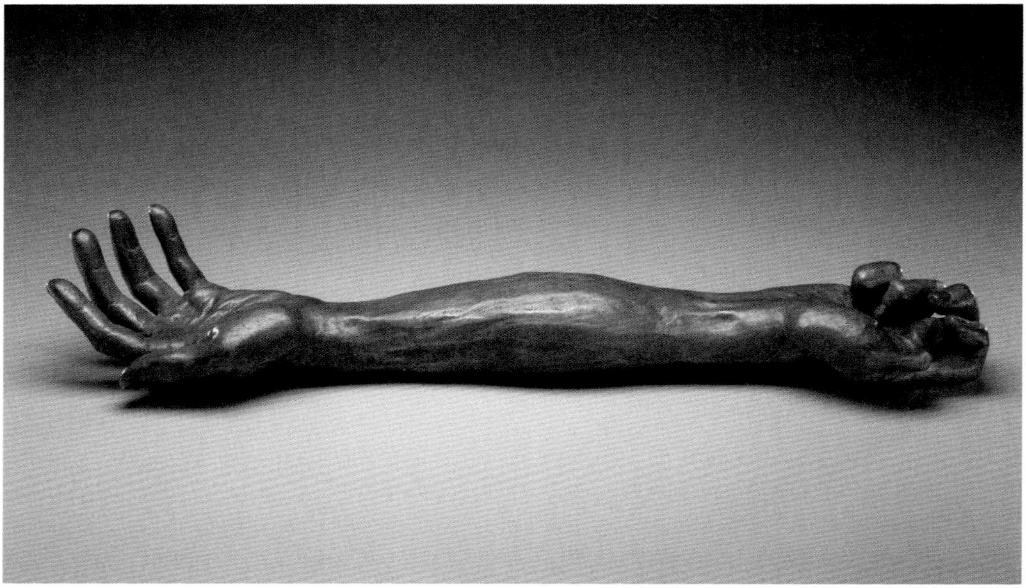



Louise Bourgeois,
*Give or take*, 2002

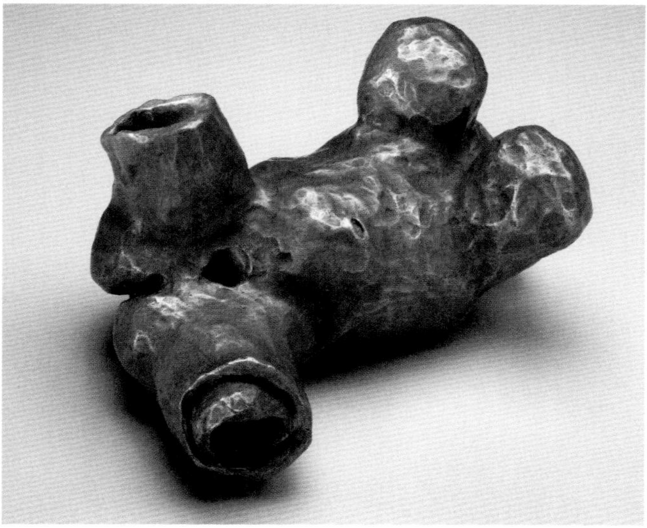

Louise Bourgeois,
*Femme*, 2005

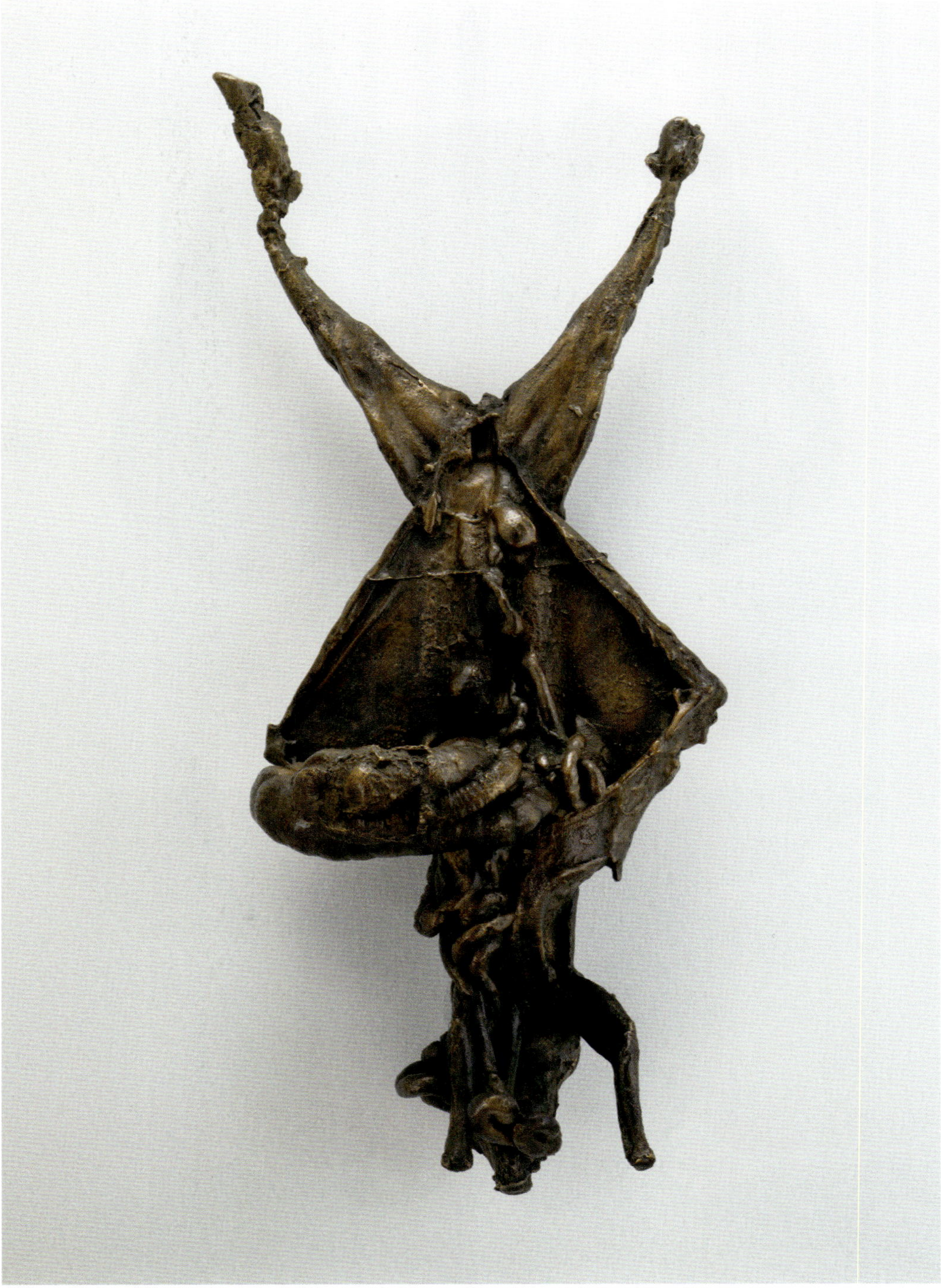



Louise Bourgeois,
*Rabbit*, 1970

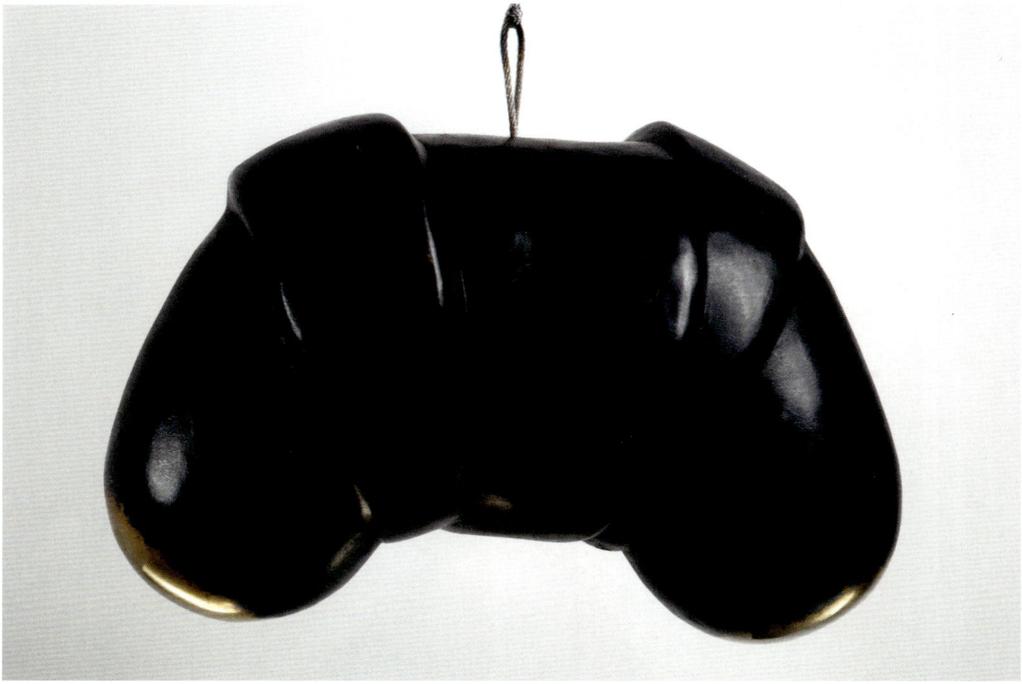



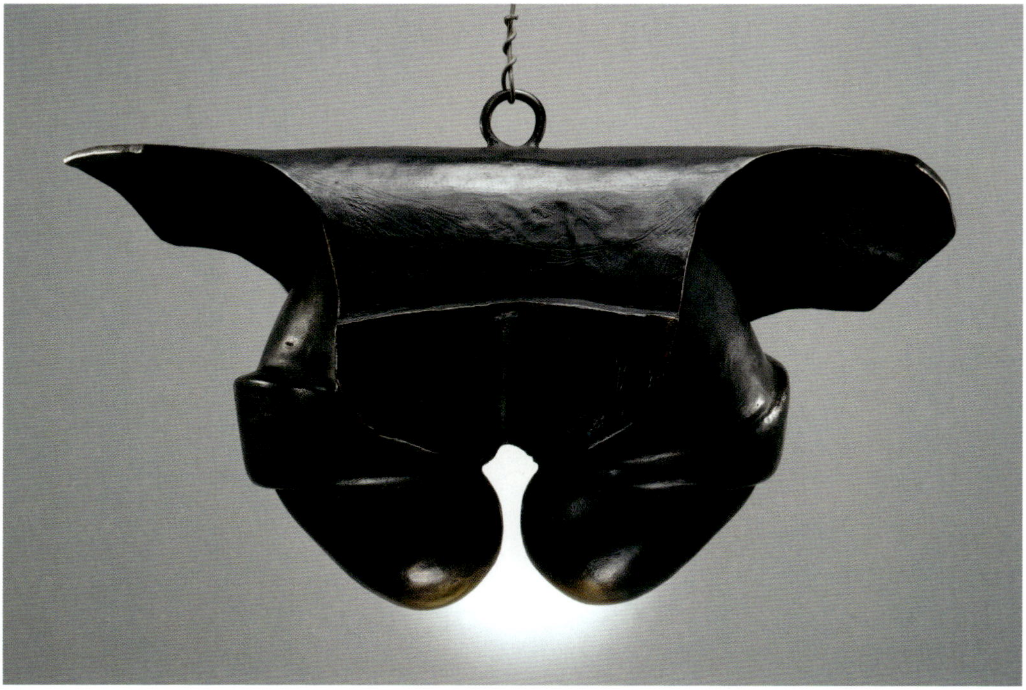

Louise Bourgeois,
*Hanging Janus*, 1968

Louise Bourgeois,
*Hanging Janus with Jacket*, 1968

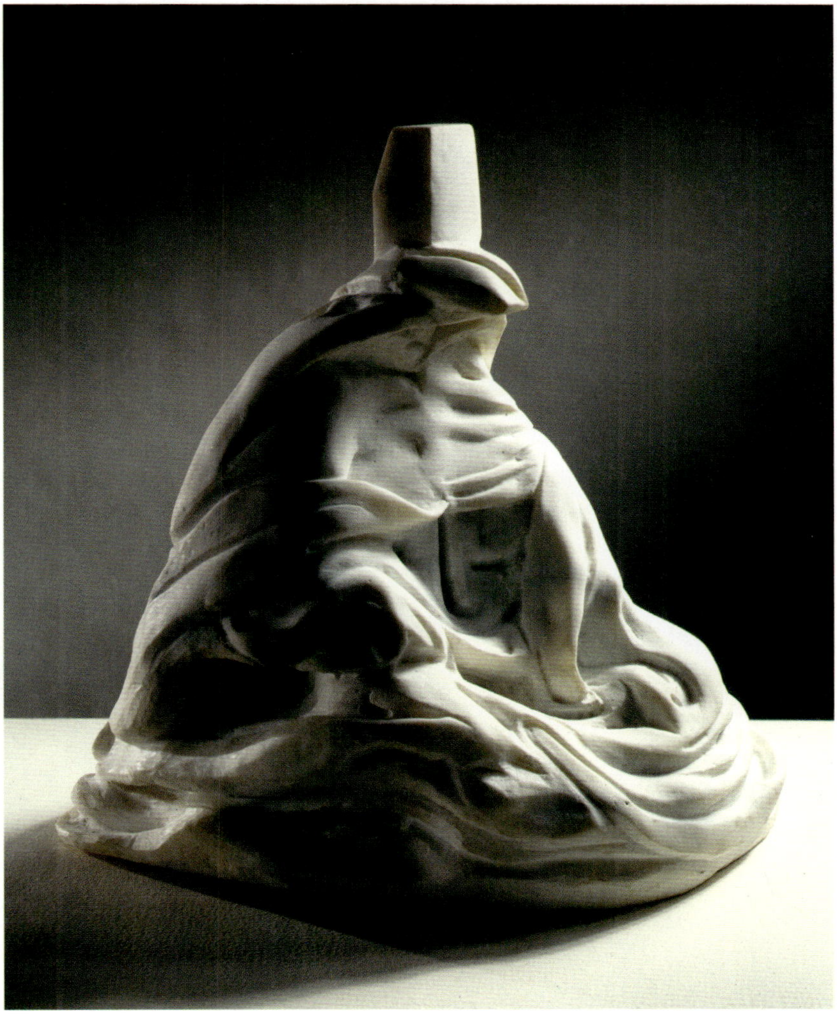

Louise Bourgeois,
*Femme Maison*, 1982

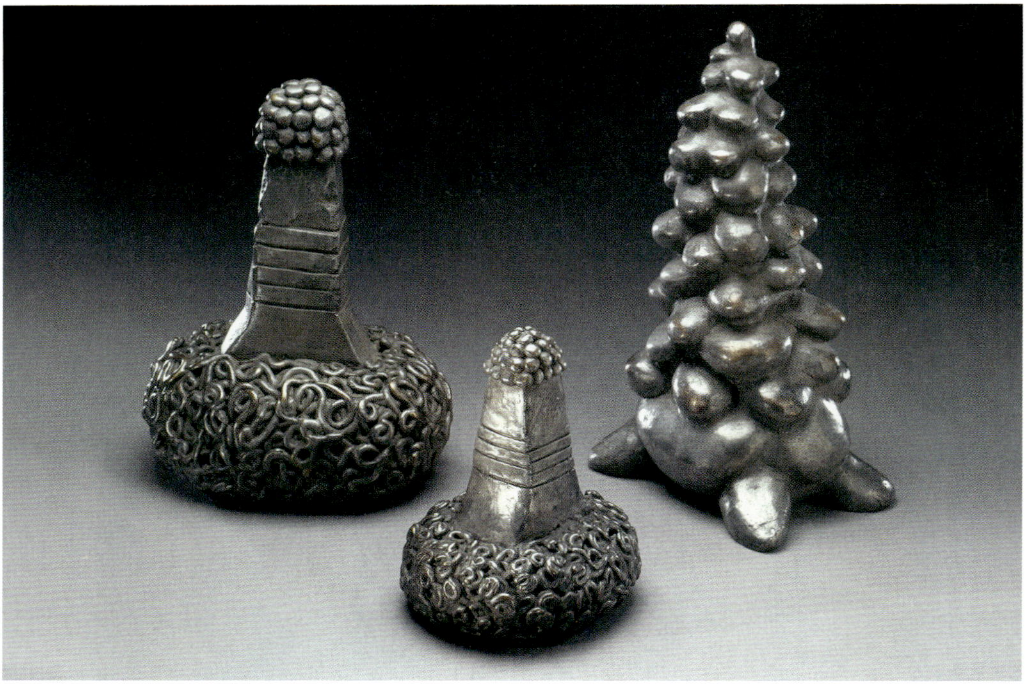



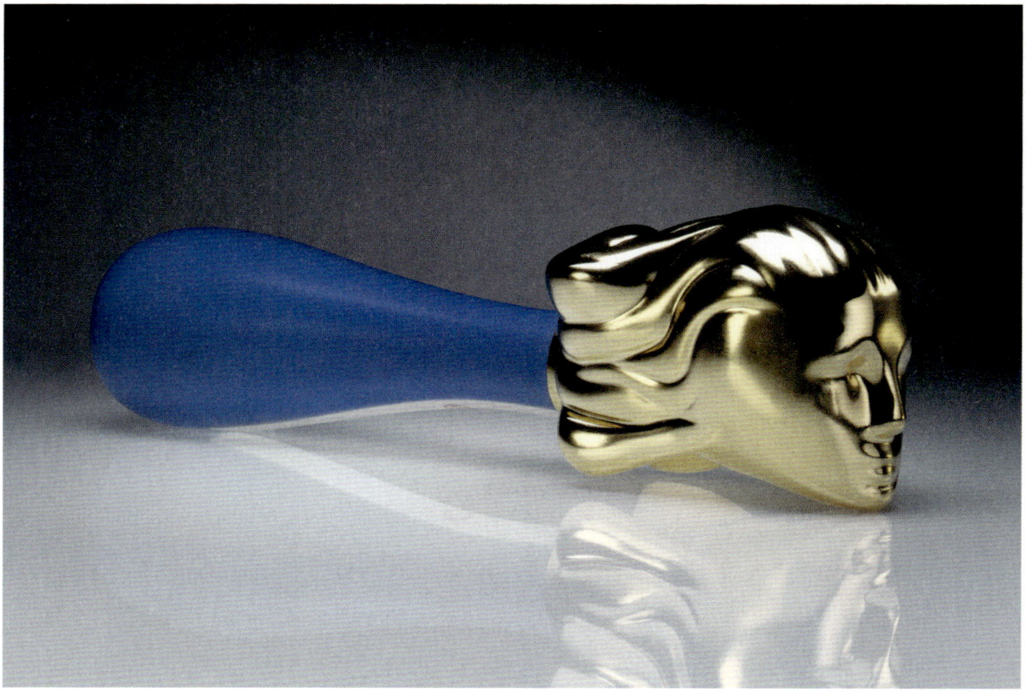

Louise Bourgeois,
*Untitled*, 2001

Louise Bourgeois,
*Fallen Woman*, 1996

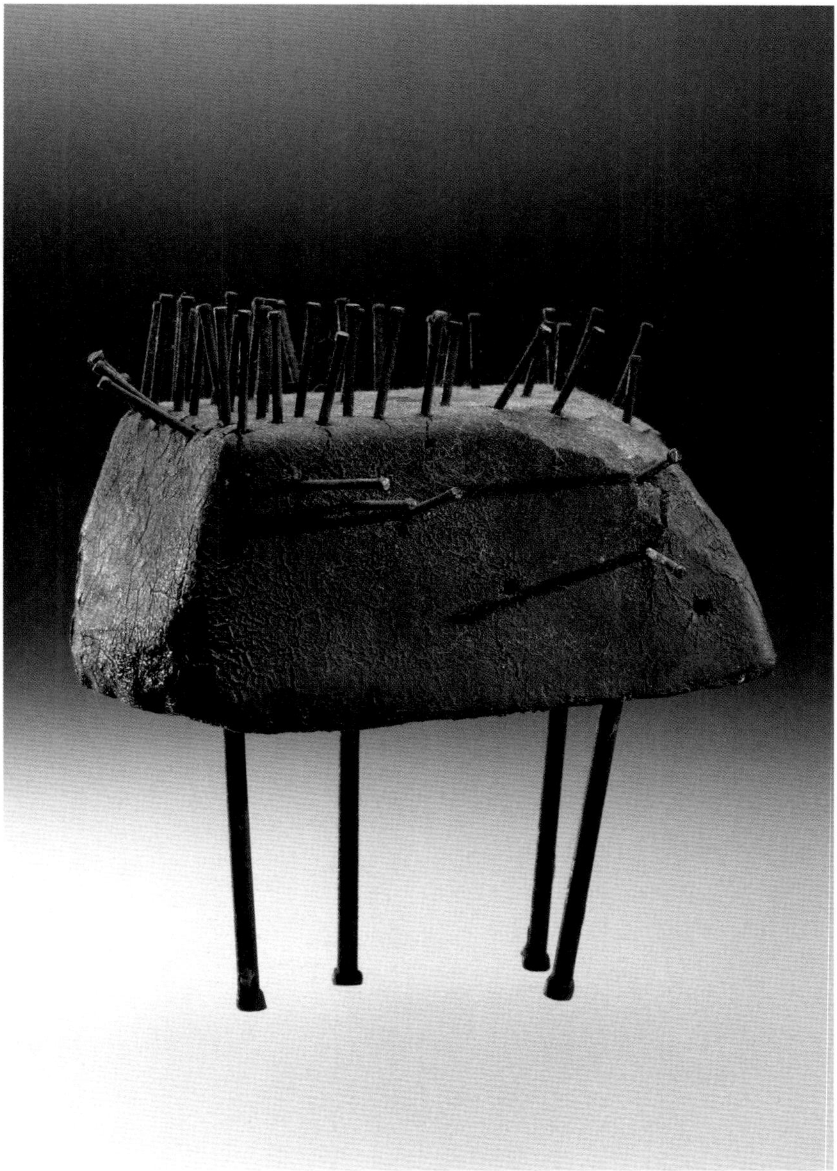

Louise Bourgeois,
*Untitled*, c. 1960

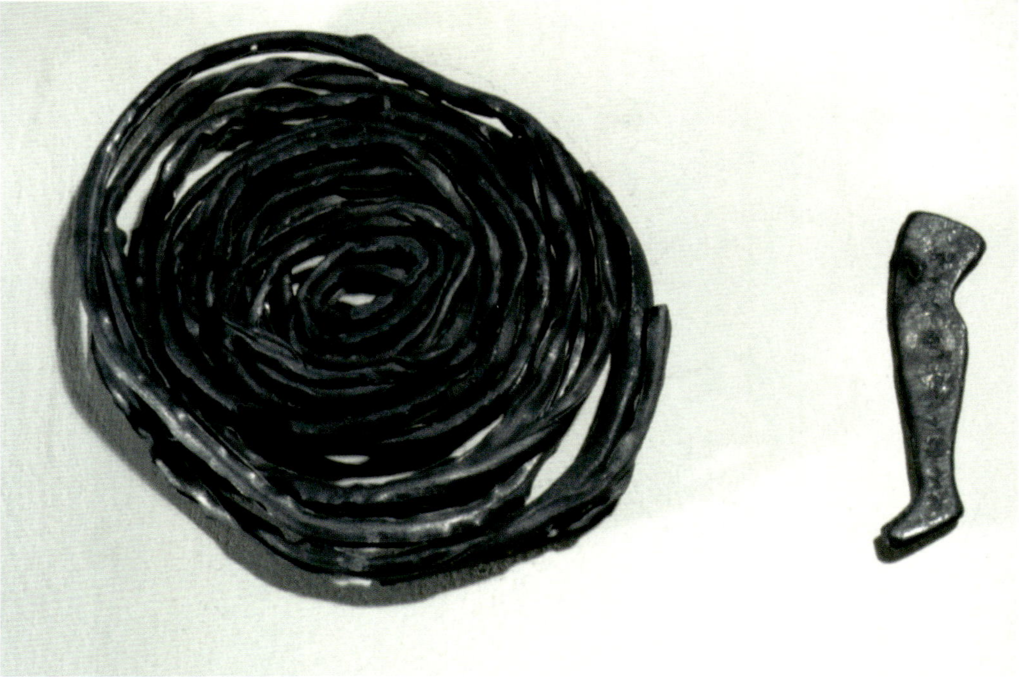



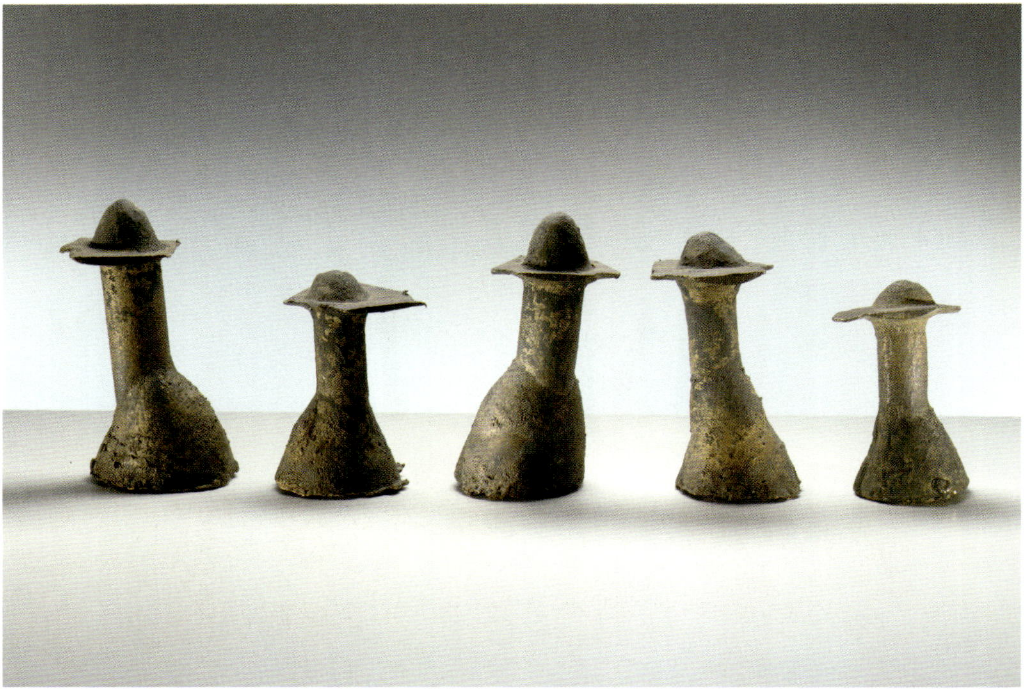

Louise Bourgeois,
*Untitled*, 1965

Louise Bourgeois,
*Untitled*, 1970–1972

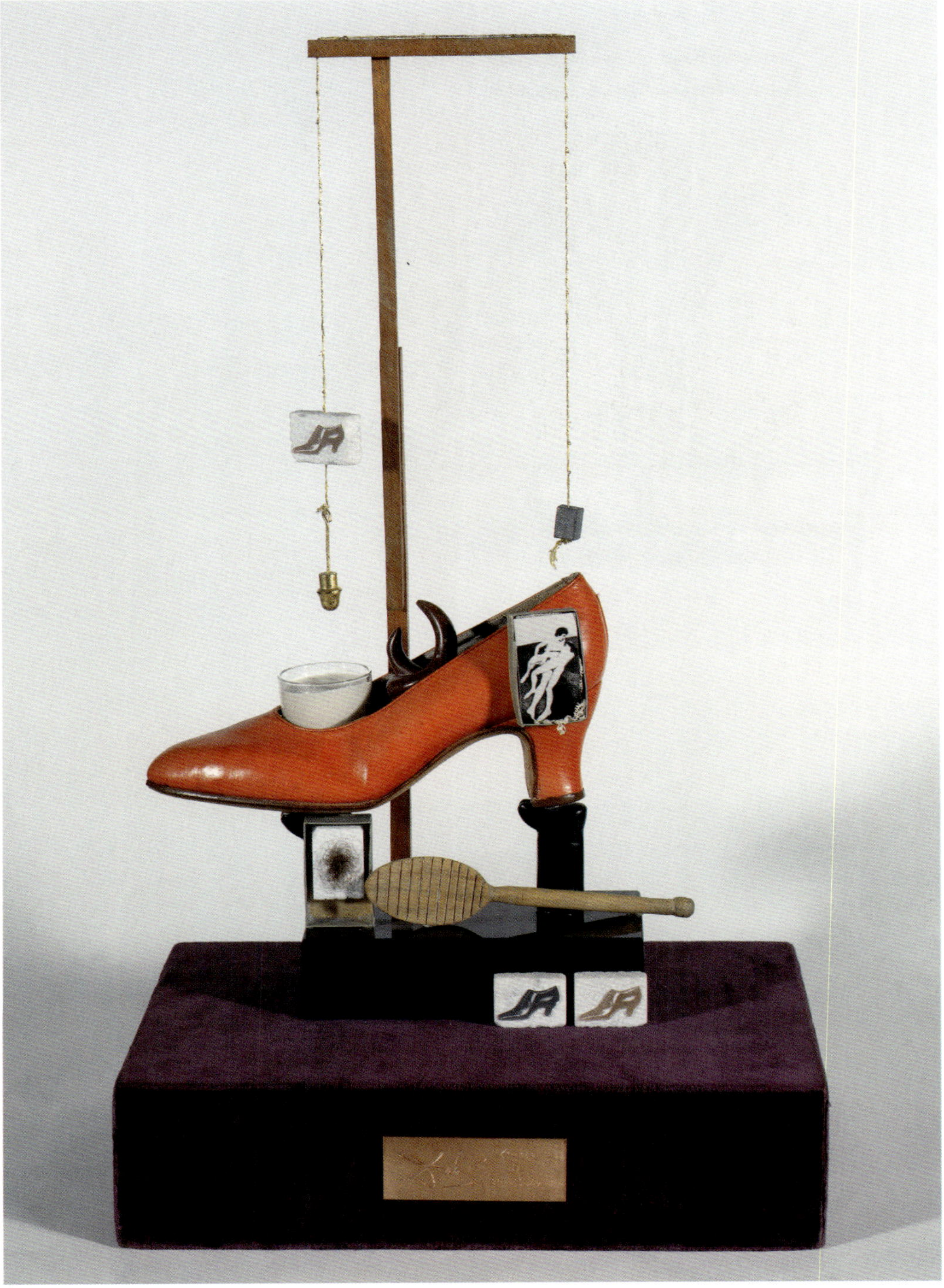

Salvador Dalí,
*Objet scatologique à fonctionnement symbolique (Scatological Object Functioning Symbolically)*, Assemblage 1930 (Rekonstruktion/reconstruction 1973)

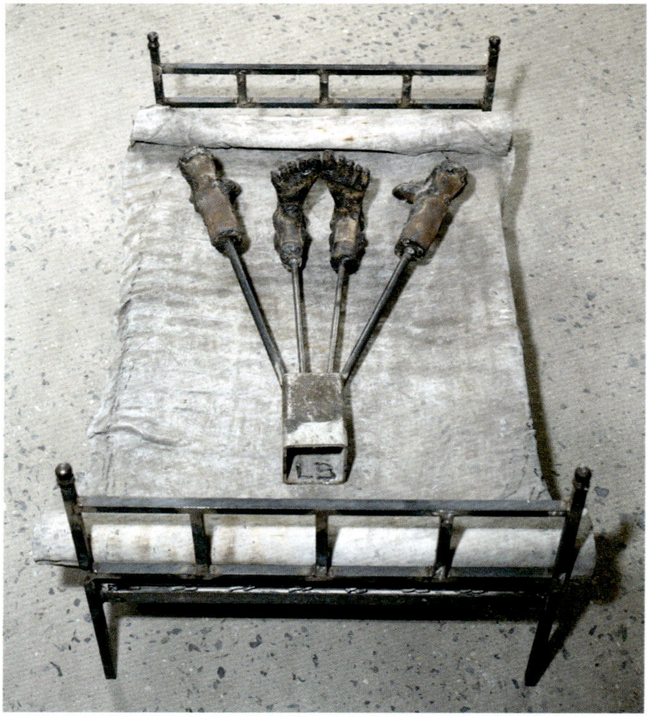

Louise Bourgeois,
*In and out*, 1997

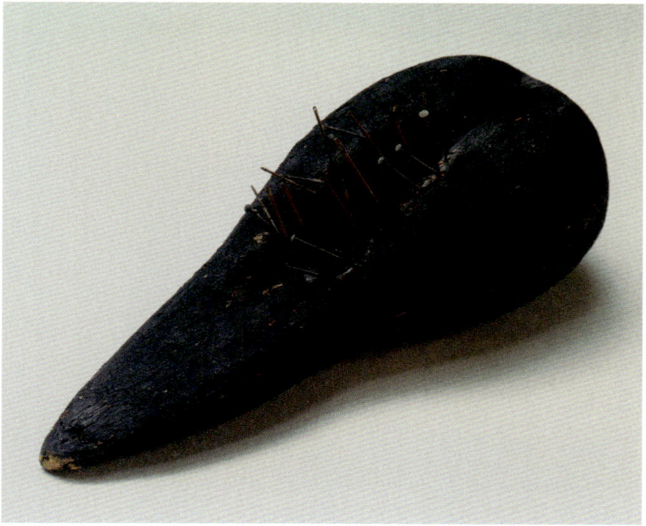

Louise Bourgeois,
*Femme Pieu*, c. 1970

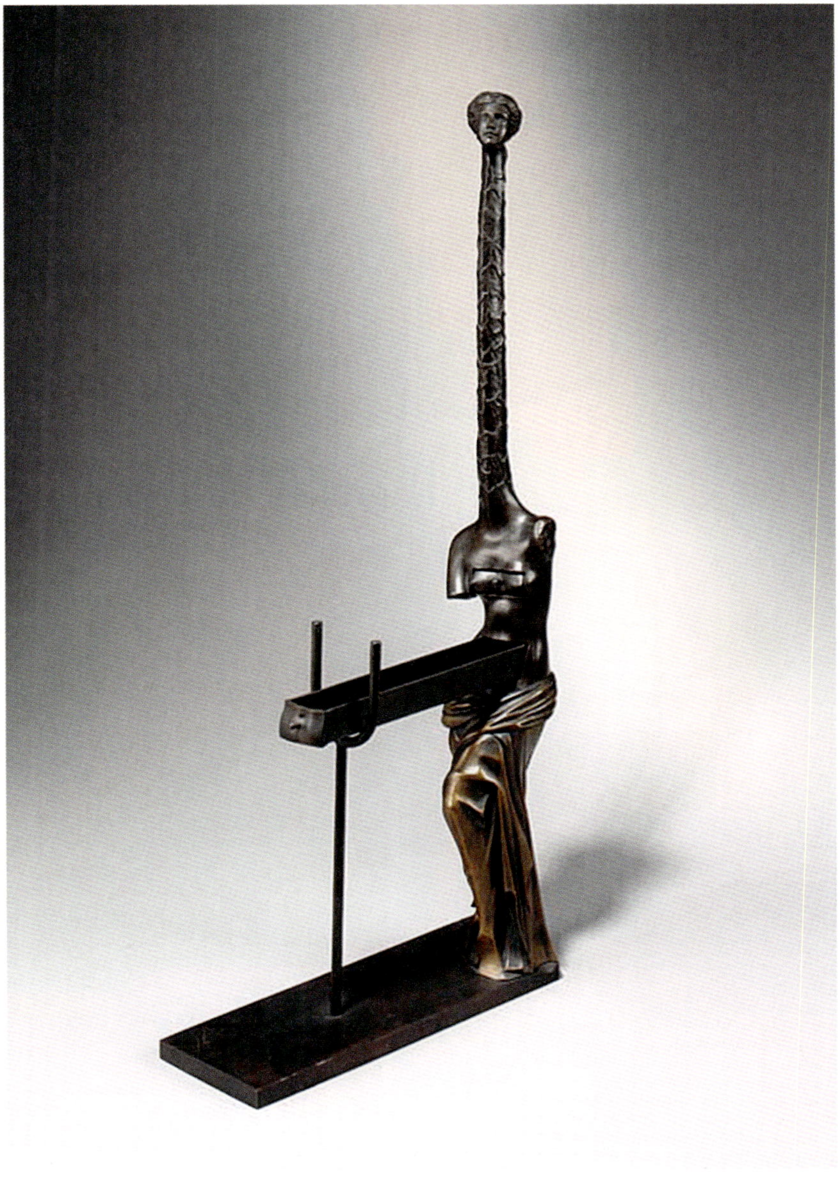

Salvador Dalí,
*Venus à la Giraffe*, 1973

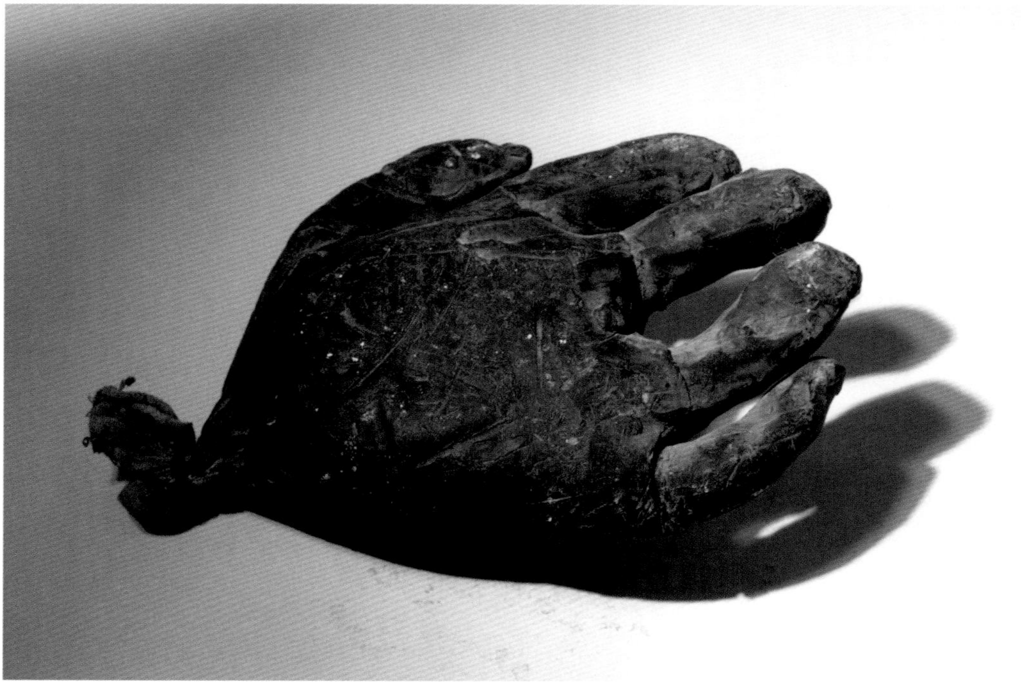

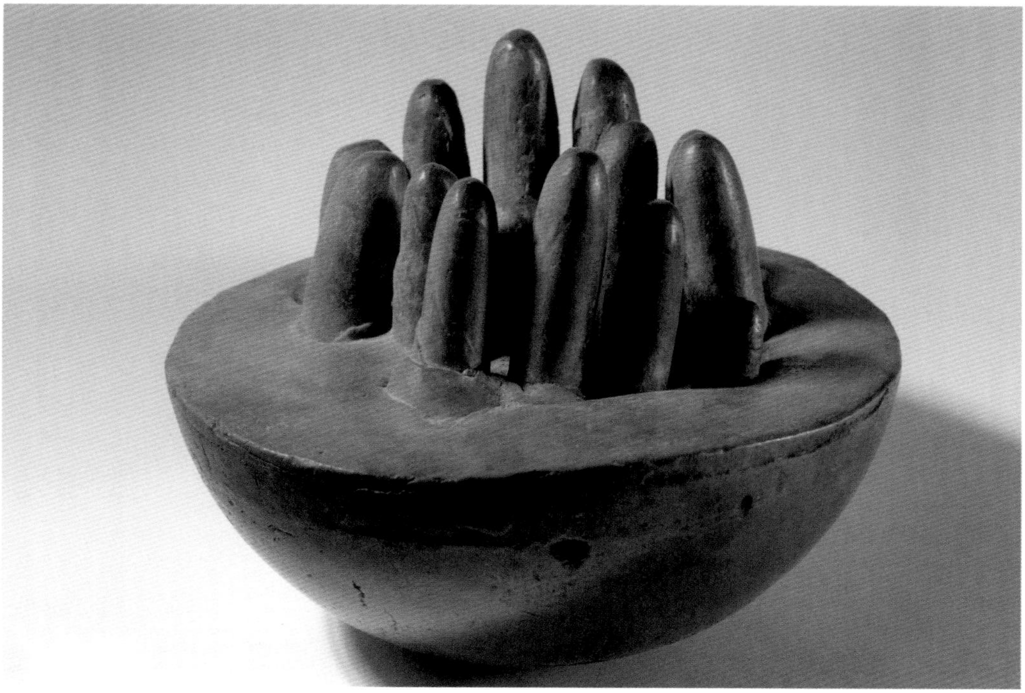



Louise Bourgeois,
*Untitled (Hand)*, 1970

Louise Bourgeois,
*Untitled Germinal*, 1967–1995

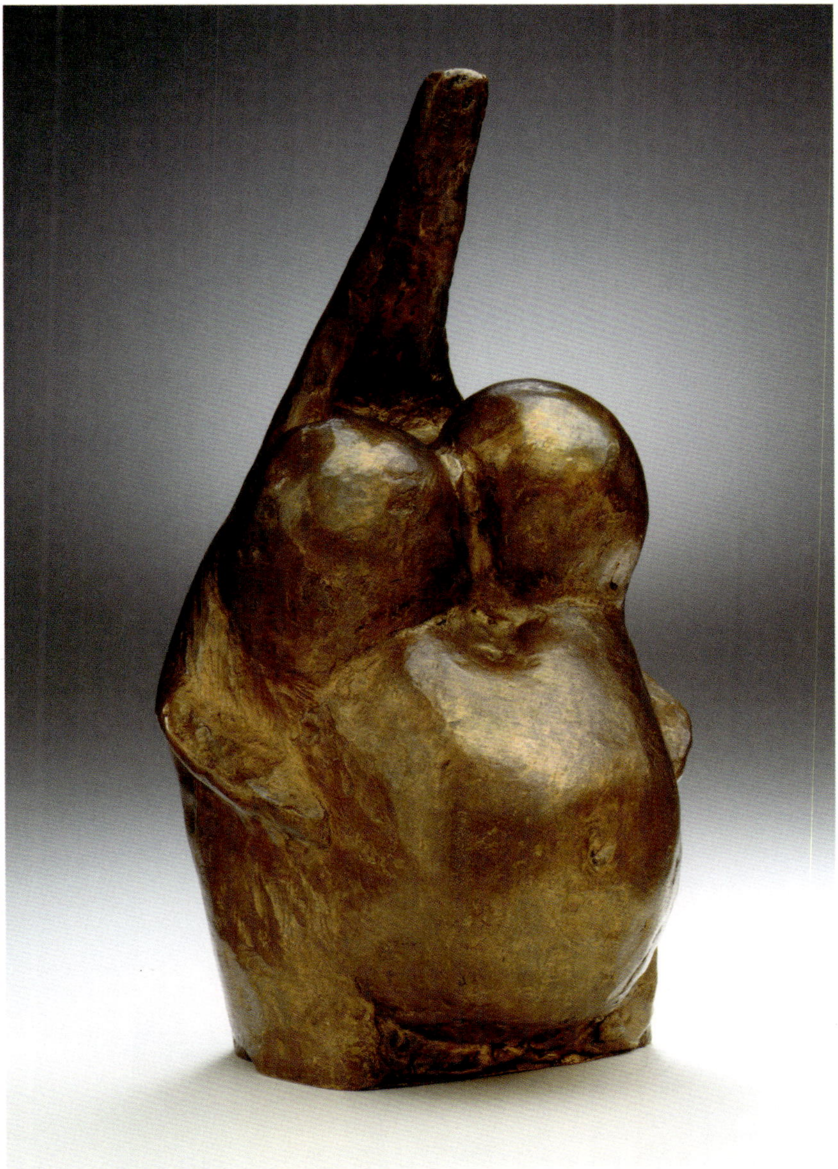

Louise Bourgeois,
*Fragile Goddess*, 1970

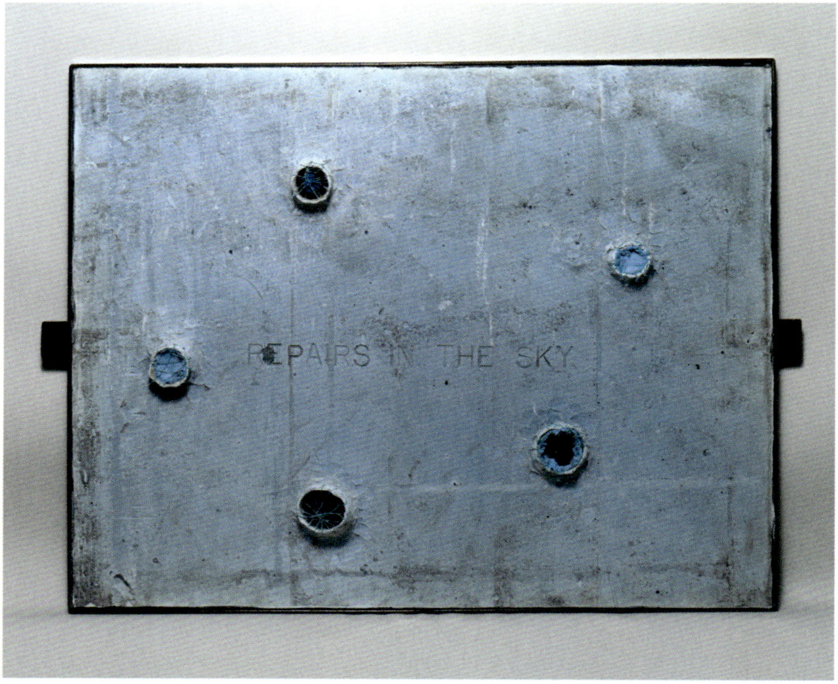


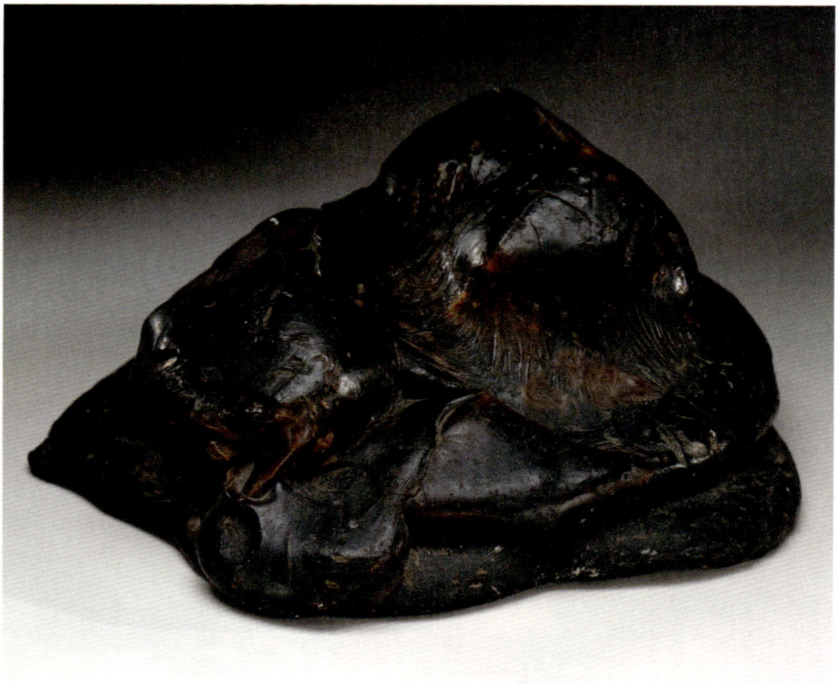

Louise Bourgeois,
*Repairs in the Sky*, 1999

Louise Bourgeois,
*Soft Landscape I*, 1967

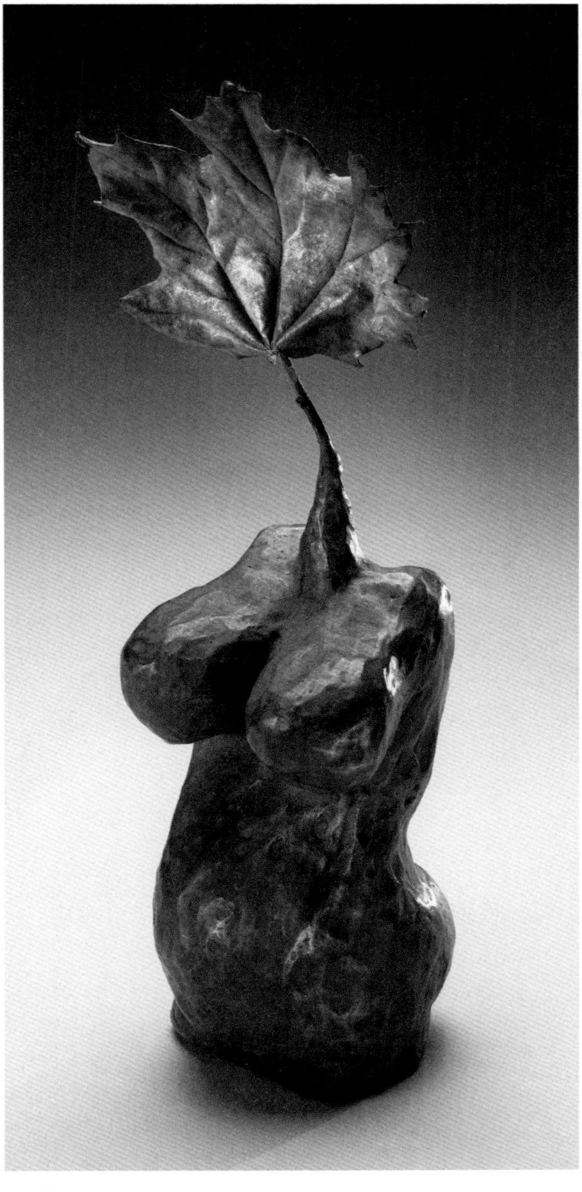

Louise Bourgeois,
*Topiary*, 2005

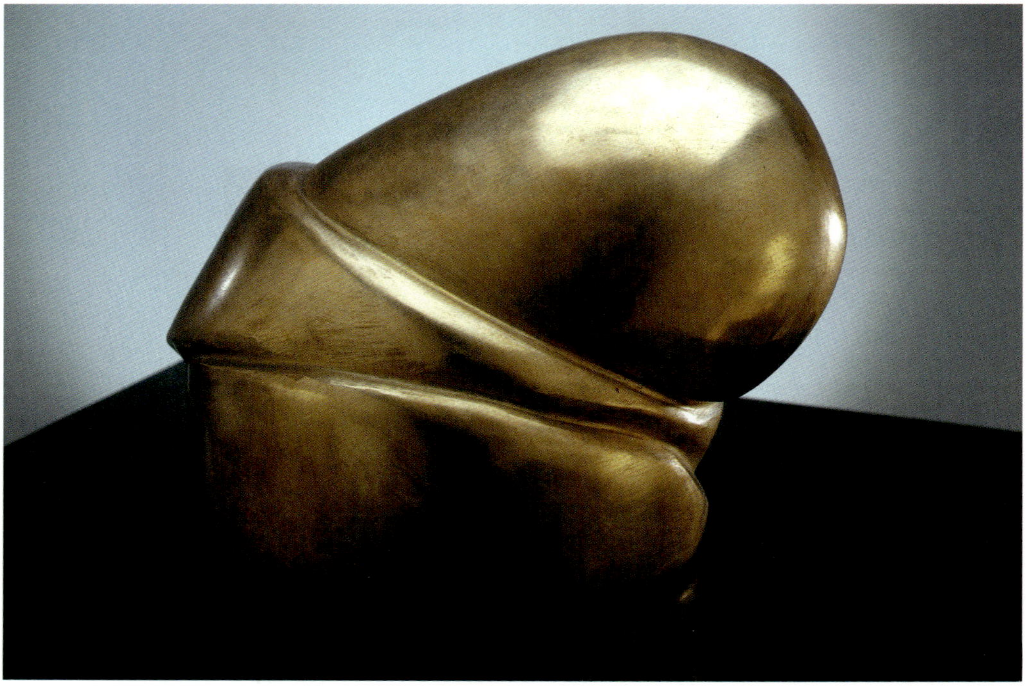

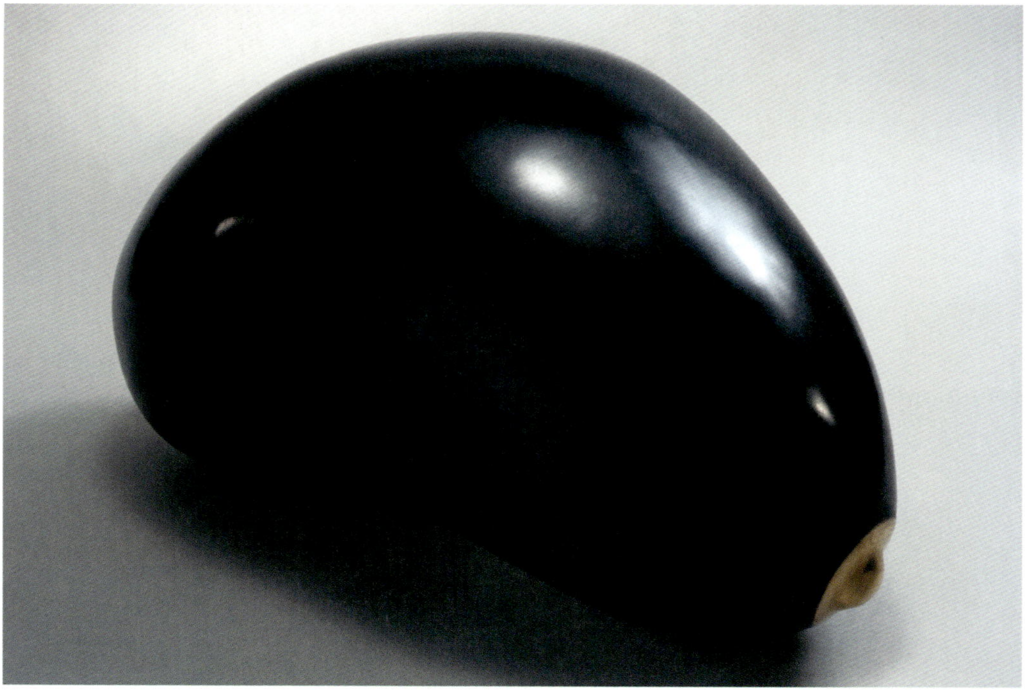

Louise Bourgeois,
*Untitled (Sleep II)*, 1968

Louise Bourgeois,
*The Worm*, 1989

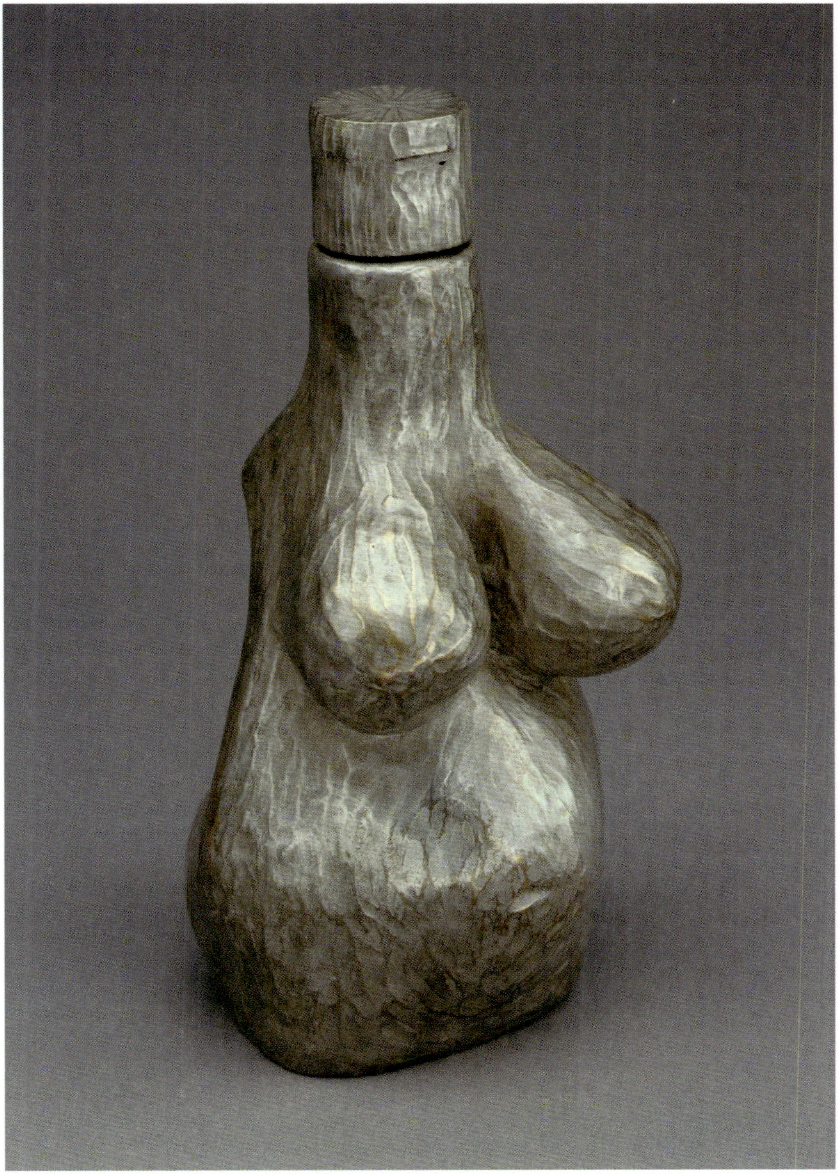

Louise Bourgeois,
*Femme*, 2006

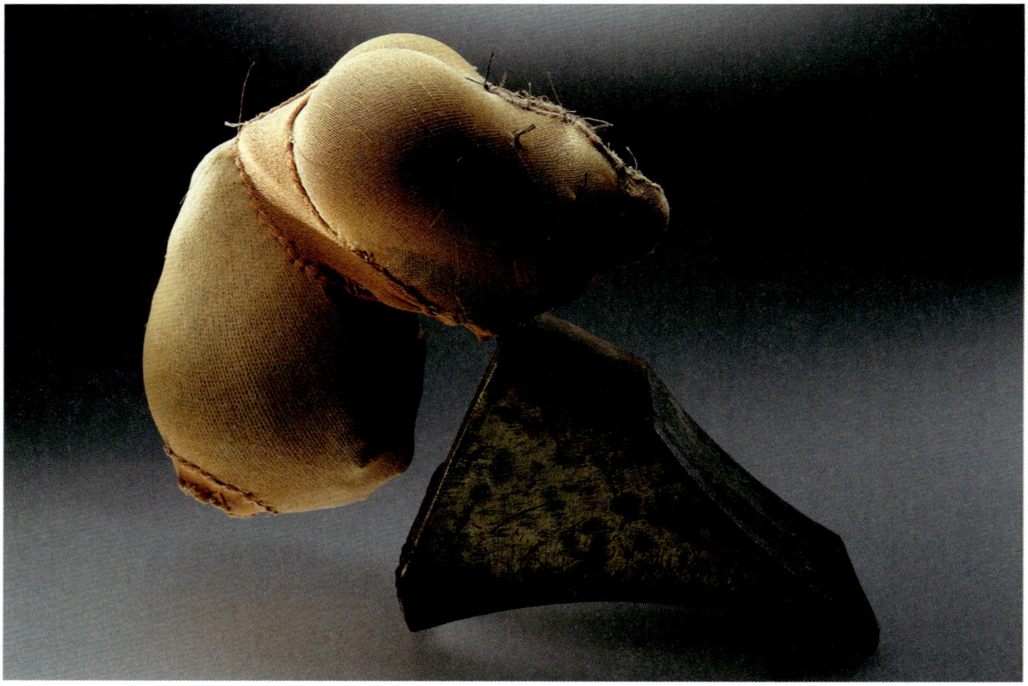

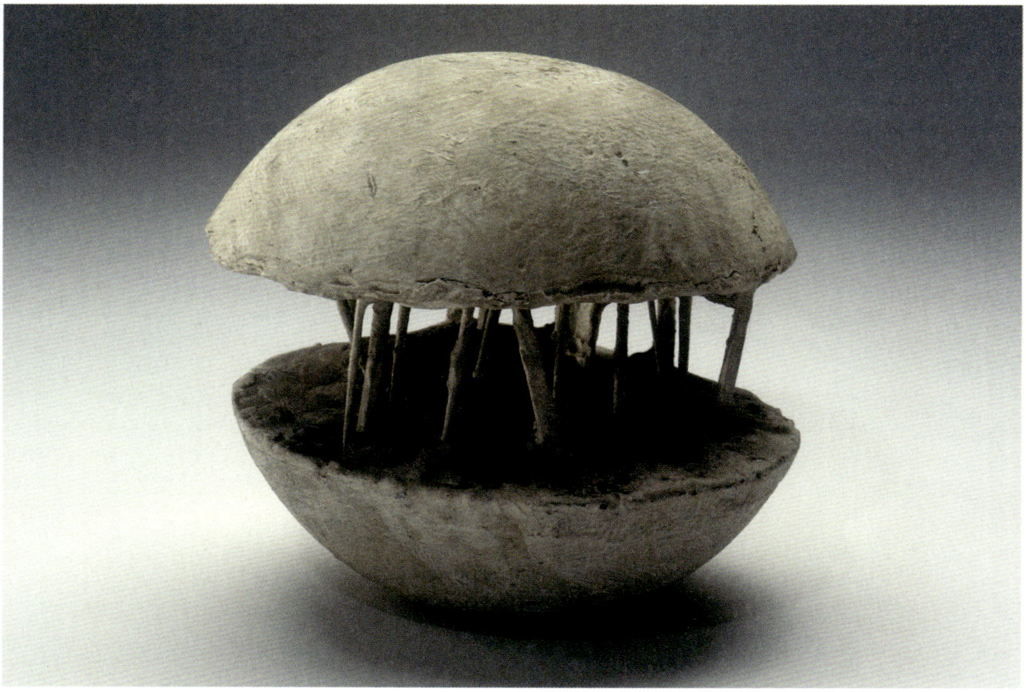

Louise Bourgeois,
*Untitled*, 1997

Louise Bourgeois,
*Untitled*, 1964

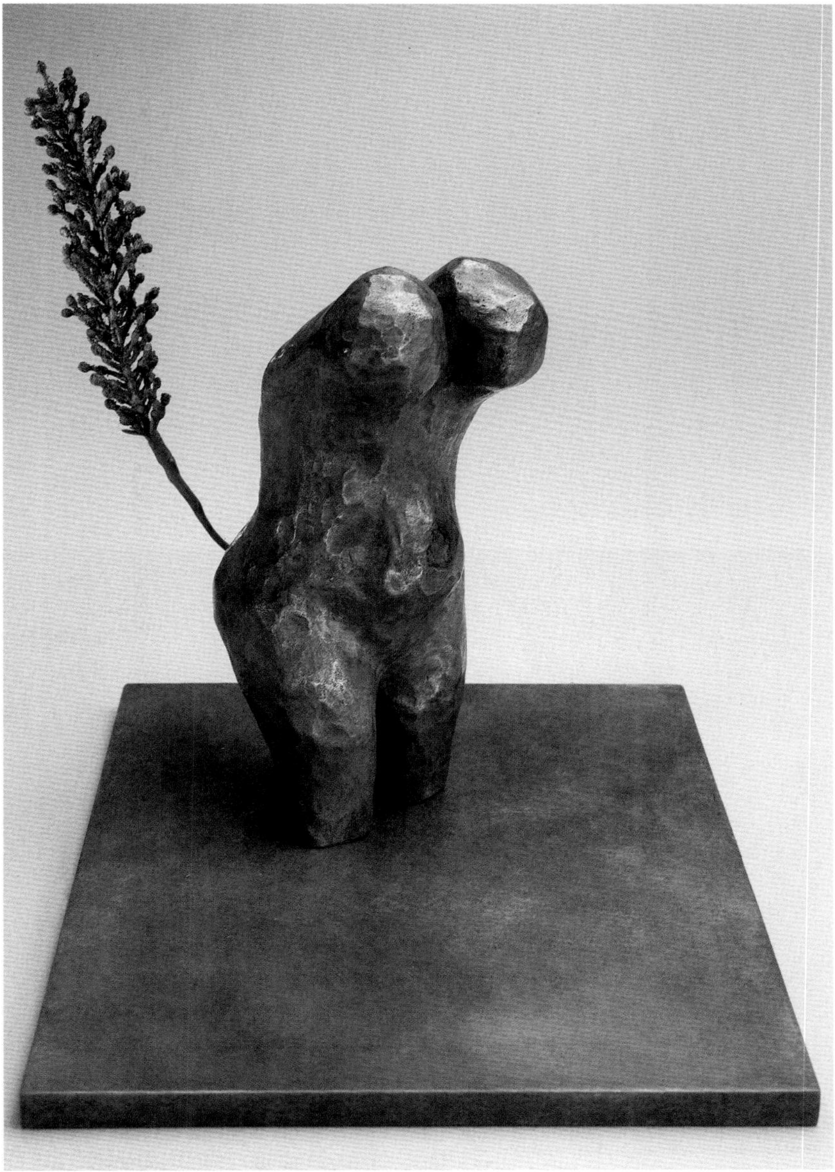

Louise Bourgeois,
*Topiary*, 2005

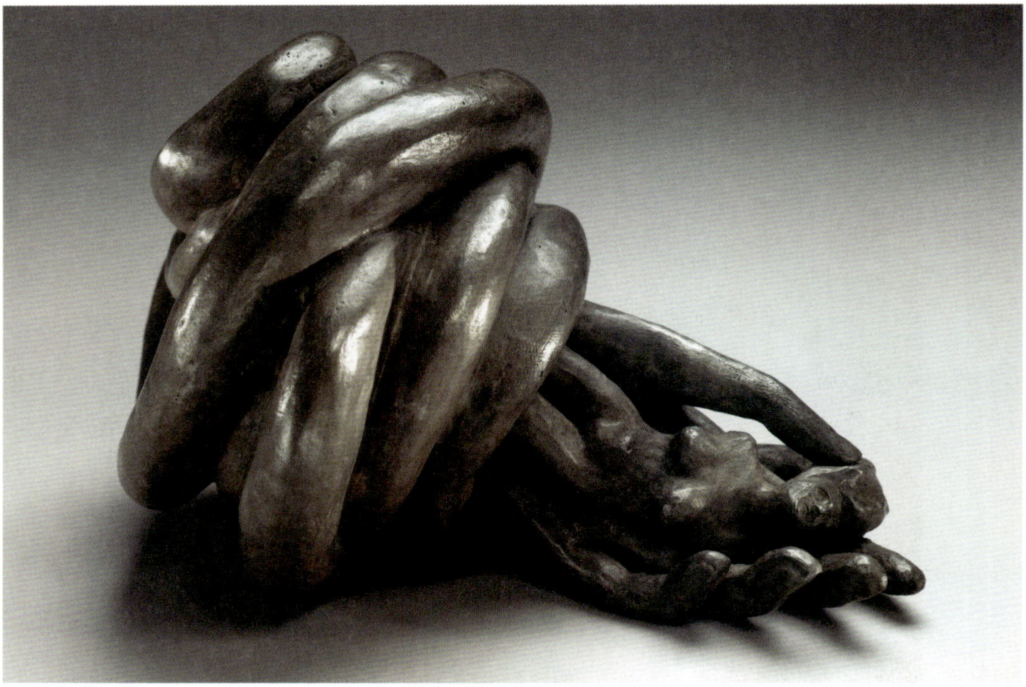

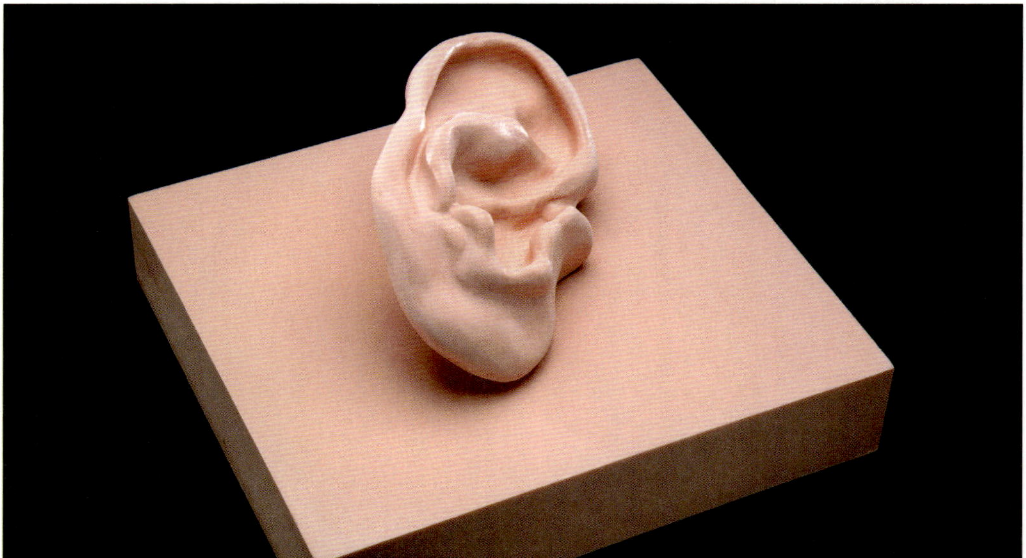

Louise Bourgeois,
*Nature Study*, 1986

Louise Bourgeois,
*Ear*, 2002

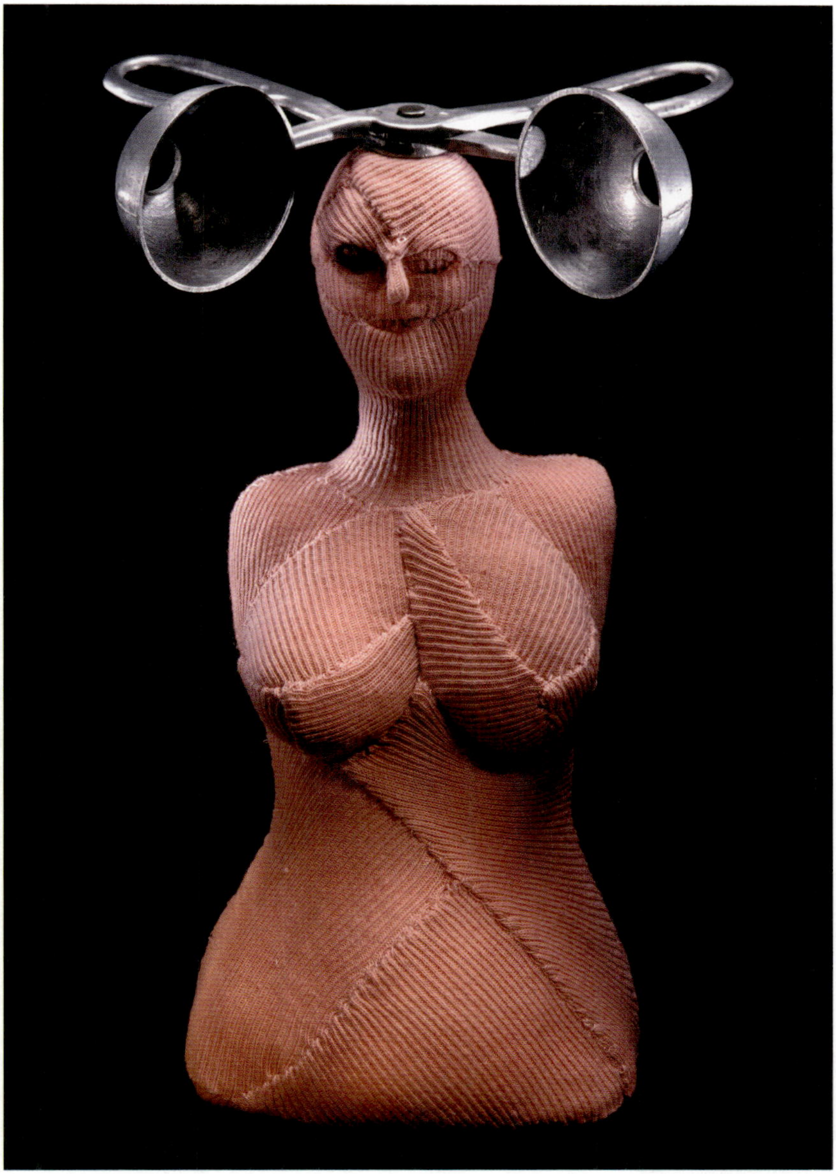



Louise Bourgeois,
*Untitled*, 2002

# August Ruhs
# Le Mal d'Aurore – Das frühe Leid der Kindheit?

Die Annahme, dass das künstlerische und insbesondere das skulpturale Werk von Louise Bourgeois nicht unabhängig von ihrem sublimen Umgang mit dem Begehren des väterlichen Anderen gedacht werden kann, ist autobiografisch gut gestützt. Als donjuaneske Figur par excellence sammelte ihr Vater sowohl Frauen als auch Statuen, was offenbar zu einer unbewussten Identifizierung mit den Objekten seines Begehrens aufseiten der Tochter Anlass gab.

Dieser eher für Frauen typischen Beziehungskonstellation ist eine mehr männliche Relation gegenüberzustellen, welche das Begehren des Anderen energisch zurückweist, um die Illusion einer Unabhängigkeit, einer kompromisslosen Individualität und das Phantasma einer Selbsterzeugung mit bisweilen demiurgischen bis göttlichen Anwandlungen aufrechtzuerhalten. Es wird zu zeigen sein, dass in dieser Hinsicht Salvador Dalí insofern eine paradigmatische Figur darstellt, als seine Identität und Ichhaftigkeit in einer beinahe einzigartigen Verschränkung von Symptom, Werk und Leben besteht.

Annulliert sich im ersten Fall das Subjekt, um ganz im Objekt für einen Anderen aufzugehen, wird im zweiten Fall der Andere ausgelöscht, um sich zum Zweck der eigenen Vervollkommnung des begehrten Objekts zu bemächtigen und es zu vereinnahmen, sodass von ihm nur noch ein Fetisch, ein Abfall, ein skatologisches Objekt ohne reale Funktion übrig bleibt. Als solches dient es nur als Stütze für die Verleugnung des Mangels, der Differenz (insbesondere der Geschlechter), der Begrenzung, des Todes (Abb. S. 87: Salvador Dalí, *Objet scatologique à fonctionnement symbolique*, 1930/1973).



# August Ruhs
# Le Mal d'Aurore – The early Suffering of Childhood?

There are good autobiographical reasons supporting the assumption that Louise Bourgeois's artistic and, in particular, sculptural oeuvre cannot be seen in isolation from her sublime approach to the desire for the fatherly other. Her father was a Don Juan like figure, who collected both women and statues, something that evidently spawned, on the part of his daughter, an unconscious identification with the objects of his desire.

This form of relationship is more typical of women, and in Bourgeois's case needs to be contrasted to a more male relation, one that strongly rebuffs the other's desire in order to maintain the illusion of independence, of an uncompromising individuality and the phantasm of self-generation, at times to the point of a demiurgic if not divine allure. I shall demonstrate below that, in this regard, Salvador Dalí was a paradigmatic figure to the extent that his identity and ego-centricity consisted of an almost unique interlocking of symptom, œuvre and life.

While in the first instance the subject elides itself in order to morph completely into the object of the other, in the latter the other is elided in order to seize control of and appropriate the desired object for the purpose of self-perfection, to such an extent that only a fetish, waste, a scatological object remains, bereft of any real function. As such, it serves only as a support for denying any deficiency, all difference (in particular between the genders), all limitation and death (ill. p. 87: Salvador Dalí, *Objet scatologique à fonctionnement symbolique*, 1930/1973). With her *Arch of Hysteria* installation made in 1992–3 (ill. 1), one of the countless variants on her concern with the theme of hysteria, Louise Bourgeois not only offers an

Mit der 1992/93 geschaffenen Installation *Arch of Hysteria* (Abb. 1), einer der zahlreichen Varianten ihrer Beschäftigung mit dem Thema Hysterie, präsentiert Louise Bourgeois nicht nur ein bemerkenswertes Dokument einer intimen persönlichen Erfahrung, sondern sie inszeniert auch mit beeindruckender Prägnanz einen entscheidenden Moment im Entstehungsprozess der Psychoanalyse, einer Disziplin, welche, abgesehen von ihren klinischen und gesellschaftskritischen Implikationen, auch für die Kunst des 20. Jahrhunderts und da insbesondere für den Surrealismus eine mehr als bedeutsame Rolle spielen sollte.

Je t'aime: Unter der ekstatischen Wölbung des hysterischen Körpers als kopfloses entsubjektiviertes Objekt wissenschaftlicher Zerlegungskunst schreibt sich in der Fachsprache der Leidenschaften und in eindringlicher Wiederholung diese Botschaft ein, die als deformierter Schrei nach Liebe und Anerkennung bislang unerhört geblieben war. Freuds Freilegung dieses verborgenen Begehrens als Grundlage und Wahrheit des seltsamen Gebarens hysterischer Personen war bekanntlich von einer Suche ausgegangen, die den jungen Wiener Neurowissenschaftler, der 1880 als seine erste Arbeit auf psychologischem Terrain John Stuart Mills Essay *Über Frauenemanzipation* übersetzt hatte, nach Paris führte, um sich beim großen Neurologen Charcot in der Hysteriebehandlung unterweisen zu lassen.
Unter dem Hysteriebegriff wurden durch Charcot am Ende des 19. Jahrhunderts verschiedene Phänomene, die bis dahin hauptsächlich vom Mystisch-Religiösen sowie von Theologie und Philosophie verwaltet und darin einerseits als Wunder oder als Besessenheit oder ander-

impressive document of an intimate personal experience, but also stages a decisive moment in the emergence of psychoanalysis with stunning poignancy – a discipline that (apart from its clinical and sociocritical implications) was to have a more-than-important role in 20th century art and, in particular, in Surrealism.

Je t'aime: under the ecstatic curvature of the hysterical body, portrayed as a headless desubjectivized object of scientific dissection, this message is inscribed in the specialist language of the passions and in incisive repetition, a message that until then had gone unheeded by way of a deformed cry for love and recognition. It is well known that Freud uncovered this lost desire as the foundation and truth underlying the strange habits of hysterical individuals, having started with research that took the young Viennese neuroscientist (whose first work in the terrain of psychology had been a translation into German of John Stuart Mill's essay *The Subjection of Women*) to Paris in order to learn from the great neurologist Charcot how to treat hysteria.
At the end of the 19th century, Charcot was using the term 'hysteria' to cover and reclaim for medicine various phenomena that had, until then, mainly been considered mystic/religious, and therefore had come under the dominion of theologists and philosophers, to whom the phenomena were considered either as miracle or obsession, on the one hand, or, on the other, as borderline cases of empirical enquiry. Thus, these phenomena became objects of a clinic that, thanks to the mutual cross-ferti-lization of therapeutic methods and aesthetics, was in the process of merging science and art within its practice.

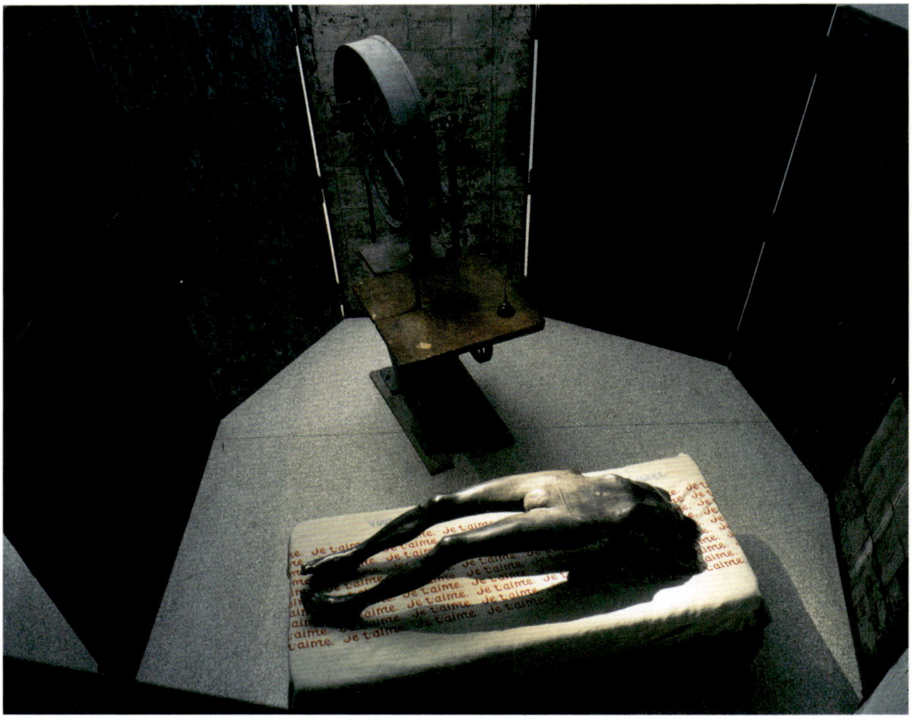


Abb./ill.1: Louise Bourgeois,
*Cell (Arch of Hysteria)*, 1992–1993

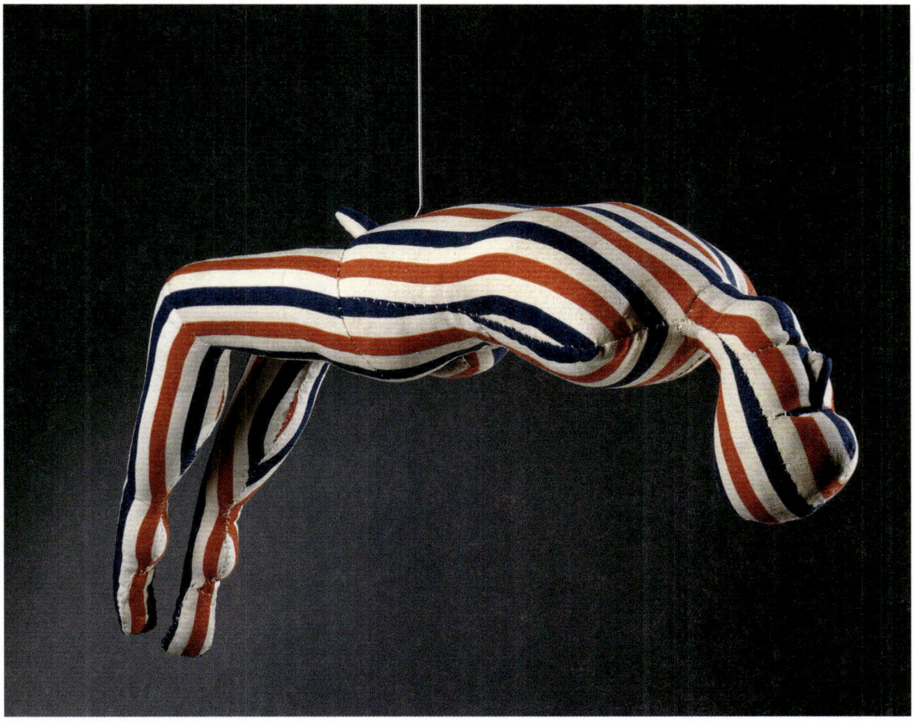

Louise Bourgeois,
*Arch of Hysteria*, 2004

erseits als Grenzfragen der Empirie verstanden wurden, medizinisch wieder vereinnahmt. Dadurch wurden diese Erscheinungen zu Gegenständen einer Klinik, welche gerade im Begriffe war, durch die gegenseitige Durchdringung von Therapeutik und Ästhetik ihren Beitrag zur programmierten Zusammenführung von Wissenschaft und Kunst in sich zu vereinigen. In Charcots klinischem Dispositiv mit seinem zweifachen Gebrauch der Hypnose (Provokation und Zähmung des Anfalls) lernte Freud die Verbindung der Inszenierung des Experiments mit der Kunst der strengen und genauen Beobachtung, welche freilich ganz auf den Blick konzentriert war, kennen. Während die experimentell angewandte Hypnose vorwiegend auf die Reproduktion des hysterischen Anfalls zielte und damit die hysterischen Phänomene entmystifizierte, konzentrierte sich die Beobachtung ganz auf die Herausarbeitung der idealtypischen Symptomatik der Krankheit und forderte deren möglichst exakte Reproduktion im gezeichneten oder fotografierten Bild. Das teilweise Gelingen dieses Vorhabens war natürlich im besonderen Entgegenkommen der für Suggestion stets empfänglichen hysterischen Subjekte begründet. Indem das hysterische Subjekt in seinem vornehmlich imitatorischen Verhalten Reproduktionen lieferte, wobei es nicht nur andere Krankheiten, sondern auch Bilder und Szenen in Form erotischer und/oder religiöser Tableaus nachahmte, gelangte Charcot zur Auffassung, dass Hysteriker immer schon Modell gestanden hätten für Künstler, welchen die Darstellung und Reproduktion menschlicher Leidenschaften ein besonderes Anliegen gewesen sei. In einem solchen Bild einer Solidargemeinschaft von Maler und Modell, zu dem die Allianz



It was from Charcot's clinical method, with its dual use of hypnosis (for both provocation and taming of the attacks), that Freud learned how to combine a staging of the experiment with the art of strict and exact observation, whereby the latter was focused entirely on the gaze. While hypnosis, as applied to experimentation, predominantly sought to reproduce the hysterical attack and thus strip the hysterical phenomenon of the myth surrounding it, observation exclusively sought to elaborate the ideal typical symptoms of the illness and required that they be reproduced as exactly as possible in drawings or photographic images. The partial success of this project stemmed, of course, from the responsiveness of the hysterical individuals, who were always susceptible to suggestion.
Charcot found that the hysterical individual, with his/her primarily imitational behavior, tended to create reproductions not of other illnesses, but of images and scenes in the form of copied erotic and/or religious tableaus. As a result, Charcot suggested that hysterics had always been the model for artists whose special interest lay in representing and reproducing the human passions. Charcot's original wish to become an artist would seem to have found fulfillment in this image of the closed ranks of painter and model (and the alliance of medical master and his 'hysterics' was an analogous counterpart). At any rate, in terms of art history, the creative output of the "atelier" in Paris's Salpêtrière hospital was a key factor in stimulating the invasion of pathological elements into art.

Later, the focus was to lay not only on the recognition and greater estimation of the des medizinischen Meisters mit seinen Hysterikern ein analoges Gegenstück lieferte, scheint sich schließlich auch Charcots ursprünglicher Wunsch, Künstler zu werden, erfüllt zu haben. Als kunsthistorisch bedeutungsvoll darf jedenfalls gelten, dass vom kreativen Schaffen in den „Ateliers" der Pariser Salpêtrière ein wesentlicher Impuls zur Invasion des Pathologischen in der Kunst ausgegangen ist.

Dabei wird es aber später nicht nur um die unter dem Kennzeichen der Art Brut vollzogene Anerkennung und Aufwertung des bildnerischen Schaffens von Geisteskranken gehen, sondern auch um alle die leidenden, deformierten, zerstückelten, abnormen und geschundenen Körper, welche die Bilderwelt des 20. Jahrhunderts dicht besiedeln werden. Dem wird sich schließlich auch noch jenes „psychopathologische" Moment hinzugesellen, das durch Freuds Eintritt in das Kulturleben der neuen Zeit bedingt ist. Dieser Einfluss hat in der Tat die Kunst nicht nur um die durch die Psychoanalyse erschlossene *Psychopathologie des Alltagslebens* bereichert und sie dazu angeregt, auch den Witz und scheinbare Un-Bedeutungen (so etwa im Dadaismus) stärker in den Vordergrund zu rücken, sondern er hat auch über das Phänomen des Traums imaginäre Welten eröffnet, die dem Surrealismus eine konzeptuelle, ideologische und inhaltliche Grundlage geboten haben. Dabei hat sich jenseits der irrealen Bilderwelt auch eine Rationalität mit einer Orientierung am Logos, am Gesetz und an der symbolisch-sprachlichen Verfassung des Unbewussten herausgebildet.
Denn mit Freuds Auftritt auf der therapeutisch-ästhetischen Bühne des auslaufenden 19. Jahrhunderts war ein Paradigmenwechsel

creative output of the mentally disturbed under the label of Art Brut, but also on all the suffering, deformed, hacked, abnormal and beaten bodies that would so densely populate the world of 20th century images. This combination would then be joined by that "psychopathological" element triggered by Freud's entrance into modern cultural life, which has not only definitely enriched art through the *psychopathology of everyday life*, as uncovered by psychoanalysis (encouraging art to more strongly foreground jokes and seemingly insignificant elements, e.g. Dadaism), but, via the phenomenon of the dream, Freud opened up imaginary worlds that provided a conceptual, ideological and substantive basis for Surrealism. Here, beyond the worlds of unreal images, a rationality has emerged that is geared towards the logos, the law and the symbolic/linguistic constitution of the unconscious.
For, when Freud took to the therapeutic-aesthetic stage at the end of the 19th century, it spelled a paradigm change. It signified a rejection of the amphitheatrical showroom in which Charcot's notion of hysteria was situated, and a turn instead toward the medium of announcement. This amounted to a change in aesthetic direction and a shift in perceptual space that, with the transition from the visual to the auditory (the above mentioned and until then unheard of speech through hysterical gesture) explored and deciphered not just the unconscious motivational contexts underlying all neurotic phenomena, but went much further, uncovering and decoding all unconscious formations in the so-called healthy emotional life of us all.
Among the latter, and we can consider them the normal models for emotional disorders, the phenomenon of dreams (as the opposite of

verbunden. Die Abkehr vom amphitheatralischen Schauraum, in welchem die charcotsche Hysterie eingespannt war, und die nunmehrige Hinwendung zum Medium der Verlautbarung bedeutete eine ästhetische Richtungsänderung und einen Wechsel des Wahrnehmungsraumes, welcher durch den Übergang vom Visuellen zum Auditiven das bereits erwähnte und bis dahin unerhörte Sprechen im hysterischen Gebaren und in der Folge nicht nur die unbewussten Motivationszusammenhänge aller neurotischen Phänomene, sondern weit darüber hinausgehend auch alle unbewussten Bildungen im sogenannten gesunden Seelenleben eines jeden Menschen aufspürte und entschlüsselte.

Unter Letzteren, welche man als Normalvorbilder seelischer Störungen betrachten darf, kommt dem Phänomen des Traums (als Gegenstück zur psychotischen Halluzination) eine herausragende Bedeutung zu. Wenn auch Freud seine Arbeit über den Witz aus dem Jahre 1905 (*Der Witz und seine Beziehung zum Unbewußten*) als das eigentliche ästhetische Werk der Psychoanalyse bezeichnet hat, so gebührt der 1900 erschienenen *Traumdeutung* ein solches Attribut ebenso und, sofern man die Frage der Ursprünglichkeit mit einbezieht, darf sie sogar eine Vorrangstellung für sich beanspruchen.

Abgesehen von der Erfassung der beiden Hauptfunktionen des Traums, nämlich einerseits der Wunscherfüllung zu dienen und andererseits Hüter des Schlafes zu sein, ließen sich auf der Grundlage der Unterscheidung zwischen manifesten Trauminhalten und latenten Traumgedanken die allgemeinen Bedeutungsgesetze des Unbewussten, die Determinanten seiner Konstituierung und die Bedingungen



psychotic hallucination) is of outstanding importance. Freud considered his essay on jokes written in 1905 (*Jokes and Their Relation to the Unconscious*) to be the real aesthetic work of psychoanalysis, yet his *Interpretation of Dreams* published in 1900 likewise deserves such credit and, to the extent that one includes the criteria of originality, it can even lay claim to preeminence in this regard.

Quite apart from the definition of the two main functions of dreams; namely, on the one hand to enable wish fulfillment and, on the other, to guard sleep, Freud was able to quite emphatically and vividly elaborate on the general symbolic rules of the unconscious (on the basis of the distinction between manifest dream-content and latent dream-thoughts), the determinants for its constitution, and the conditions and mechanisms for its return to consciousness.

In light of Freud's hypotheses, the two phenomena that cannot be considered separately are the fact that dreams are charged to the point of non-sense with enigmatic meaning and primarily structured as images with a hallucinatory character in a scenic/theatrical guise. Here, questions of sense and meaning initially arise as functions of the unusual representation of the dream, the vividness and sensory nature of which must not solely be derived from the form in which the memories being worked through in dreams are shaped. For dreams are not some non-judging reflex to everyday occurrences, which, taken at face value, already suggests that dreams serve to process latent and concealed content. Unlike other categories of meaning and interpretative traditions, the concealed content in Freud's work is reduced to a wish that the individual is preventing from entering his/her consciousness.

und Mechanismen für seine Wiederkehr ins Bewusstsein besonders prägnant und anschaulich herausarbeiten.

Die bis in den Un-Sinn hineinreichende Aufladung des Traums mit enigmatischem Sinn einerseits, seine mediale Verfasstheit als vorwiegend Bildhaftes mit halluzinatorischem Charakter und szenisch-theatralischer Gestaltung andererseits sind Phänomene, die nicht unabhängig von-einander gedacht werden können. Wobei die Sinn- und Bedeutungsfrage zunächst als Funktion der ungewöhnlichen Traumdarstellung erscheint, deren Anschaulichkeit und Sinnlich-
keit wiederum nicht allein aus der Form abzuleiten ist, in der die Erinnerungen, die der Traum verarbeitet, vorliegen. Denn der Traum ist eben nicht der urteilslose Reflex des Tagesgeschehens, was für sich allein genommen schon die Unterstellung aufkommen lässt, dass er im Dienst der Verarbeitung eines latenten und verborgenen Inhalts stehe. Im Gegensatz zu anderen Sinnkategorien und Deutungstraditionen reduziert sich bei Freud der verborgene Gehalt wie gesagt auf einen vom Bewusstsein ferngehaltenen Wunsch des Subjekts. Während also die visuell dominierte Sinnlichkeit der Erfahrung des (manifesten) Traums zumeist nichts an Klarheit zu wünschen übrig lässt, sind es vor allem die Fiktionalität des Traumgeschehens und die frei von gewohnten Sinnzusammenhängen bestehenden Verknüpfungen seiner imaginären Elemente, die den Träumer nach seinem Erwachen verstören und seinen Wunsch nach Deutung bedingen. Die Vorherrschaft des Imaginären im manifesten Traum lässt das Traumgeschehen auf einer Ebene erscheinen, auf welcher sich auch die

While the visually dominated sensory nature of the experience of the (manifest) dream is usually exceptionally clear, it is above all the fictional status of the dream activity and the linkages of its imaginary elements (freed of the usual semantic context) that disturb the dreamer after awakening and drive his/her wish for interpretation. The prevalence of the imaginary in the manifest dream leads to dream activity appearing on a level at which the visual arts likewise prefer to move. Even where art apparently moves in a desymbolized reality (for example, the many forms of body art), ever beyond the reach of language and meaning, it also challenges interpretation, especially as, given a work's claim to be art in the first place, or rather "artificial," it always references something and is set in a specific context. Located beyond discourses on utility, use and the every-day, art is closely linked to the perception of meaning, and the visual arts also to the desire to "see meaning."
Making meaning visible, visualizing it, is also the function that dream-work has to undergo. In order to do justice to this task, it must make use of many an artifice, with respect to the demand for the consideration of presentability. When searching out aesthetic principles for this work, Freud retrospectively outlined the stages of dream-work in his *Interpretation of Dreams* in order to arrive at the raw material of image generation. He not only captured the signifiers linked more or less coherently in the manifest dream (imaginations) in the search for the signified (sounds and written characters or concepts) in one of many possible discursivities but, also, by tracing the logic of the system and reversing the transformations, twists and distortions, linked them back to the relevant

bildende Kunst mit Vorliebe bewegt. Auch sie, selbst wenn sie sich wie in vielen Formen der Körperkunst scheinbar im entsymbolisierten Realen jenseits von Sprache und Bedeutung aufhält, fordert Interpretation heraus, zumal sie durch ihren Anspruch auf Kunst beziehungsweise Künstlichkeit immer einen Verweisungscharakter in sich trägt und in einen spezifischen Kontext eingebunden ist. Außerhalb von Diskursen der Nützlichkeit, des Gebrauchs, der Alltäglichkeit stehend, ist Kunst eng an die Wahrnehmung von Bedeutung geknüpft und bildende Kunst auch an das Begehren, „Bedeutung zu sehen", gebunden.

Bedeutung zum Sehen und zur Anschaulichkeit zu bringen ist auch die Funktion, der sich die Traumarbeit zu unterziehen hat, wobei sie sich entsprechend der Forderung nach Rücksicht auf Darstellbarkeit so manchen Kunstgriffs bedienen muss, um ihrer Aufgabe gerecht zu werden. Auf der Suche nach den ästhetischen Prinzipien dieser Arbeit hat Freud in seiner *Traumdeutung* die Stationen der Bearbeitung retrograd aufgesucht, um schließlich am Rohmaterial der Bilderzeugung anzukommen.

Die im manifesten Traum mehr oder weniger kohärent verknüpften Signifikate (Vorstellungen) auf der Suche nach Signifikanten (Laut- und Schriftzeichen beziehungsweise Begriffen) hat er damit aber nicht nur in einer von vielen möglichen Diskursivitäten eingefangen, sondern er hat sie, die Logik des Systems aufspürend und die Verwandlungen, Verdrehungen und Entstellungen rückgängig machend, mit den ihnen zugehörigen und ihnen ursprünglichen Signifikanten als latente Traumgedanken wieder verbunden. Der Bedeutungsanspruch des Traums als Appell eines verwirrten Subjekts resultiert aber nicht allein aus der traumatisie-



and thus original signified content, as latent dream-thoughts. The dream's claim to meaning as an appeal made by a confused individual does not just result from the traumatized impact of the autonomous dream activity to which the dreamer is passively exposed, but also arises from the disconcerting impact of an imaginary scenario that correlates to the narcissistic structure, and owing to which the individual feels the threat of losing himself in the images and moreover dissolving in the directness of its hallucinatory character from the 'real'. The reduction of meaning-free space is thus an antidote to that threat and opposes the vortex of unknown meanings which, as some say, creates hell. The accordant interpretation of dreams as a means of giving meaning for disturbing experiences in life is thus one way of shedding or reducing the existential angst and sense of being lost, inextricably bound up with the dream and the dream activity. In addition to the hermeneutic arrest of the vagabonding dream phantasmagoria, there are also clearly efforts in which an artistic foil comes into play in order to effectively combat the exposure to the tyranny of dream activity and gain at least some control over the scenery.

Never were dreams so programmatically and consistently appropriated, the power of their images creatively exploited and their frightening dynamism captured in the stasis of artistic products as they were in Surrealism, which is essentially inconceivable without dreams and above all without dreams in the sense of Freudian insights into them. The Surrealists tried to grant *automatisme psychique* the status of a primary and predominant creative agency, and by resorting to *écriture automatique* sought to attain renden Wirkung eines autonomen Traumgeschehens, dem der Träumende passiv ausgesetzt ist, sondern ergibt sich auch aus der verunsichernden Wirkung eines imaginären, der narzisstischen Struktur korrelierten Szenariums, das das Subjekt bedroht, sich in den Bildern zu verlieren und sich obendrein in der Unvermitteltheit seines halluzinatorischen Realcharakters aufzulösen. Die Reduzierung des bedeutungsfreien Raums ist somit ein Antidot gegen eine derartige Gefahr, eine Gegenkraft gegen den Sog der unbekannten Bedeutungen, der, wie man bisweilen zu sagen pflegt, die Hölle erzeugt. Die derart motivierte Traumdeutung als Sinnstiftung verstörender Seinserfahrung ist somit eine der Möglichkeiten, die mit dem Traum und dem Traumgeschehen untrennbar verbundene existenzielle Angst und Verlorenheit aufzugeben oder zu reduzieren. Neben der hermeneutischen Arretierung der vagabundierenden Traum-Phantasmagorien sind aber auch jene Bemühungen nicht zu übersehen, welche in künstlerischen Dispositiven wirksam sind, um der Auslieferung an die Willkür des Traumgeschehens wirksam zu begegnen und sich wenigstens einer teilweisen Kontrolle der Szenerie zu bemächtigen.

Sich den Traum anzueignen, seine Bildmächtigkeit schöpferisch auszubeuten und seine bedrohliche Dynamik in der Stase künstlerischer Produkte zu bannen wurde nie so programmatisch und konsequent verfolgt wie im Surrealismus, der ohne den Traum und vor allem ohne den Traum im Sinne der freudschen Erkenntnisse letztlich nicht denkbar ist. Wenn auch die Surrealisten versuchten, dem *automatisme psychique* den Status einer erstrangigen und maßgeblichen kreativen Instanz einzu-

a level of poetic objectivity at which, in the process of artistic creation, all understanding and all reason, all taste and every conscious effort of will is avoided. Yet they could not and did not wish to forego the controllability and manipulation of their inner world of signs and images:
"If the Surrealists are widely described as painters of a constantly mutating dream-world, this should not imply that they reproduce their dreams in painting (that would be descriptive and naïve realism) or that each artist uses the elements of dreams to construct a little private world in which to play out some benevolent or malevolent role (this would simply be a 'flight from time'). It means rather that these artists move freely, boldly, and confidently at the borderline between the inner and the outer world, a borderline that is physically and psychologically real ('surreal'), even if it has not yet been adequately defined and determined that they undertake to register precisely what they see and experience there, and that they intervene wherever their evolutionary instincts suggest they should."

Max Ernst, "What is Surrealism?" (1976), in Charles Harrison and Paul Wood (eds.), *Art in Theory*, Oxford, 1993, 493.

It was Salvador Dalí who finally and clearly rejected any dedication to the arbitrary functioning of the imagination – thought as a purpose in itself – or to any cult of introspection, and instead, with his *activité paranoïaque-critique*, extended the hallucination of the dream and the associative automatic thought into the intended and nurtured mania. In so doing, he sought to contribute, in the name of a social revolution, räumen und mit Hilfe der *écriture automatique* zu einer poetischen Objektivität zu gelangen, indem jeder Verstand und jede Vernunft, jeder Geschmack und jede bewusste Willensanstrengung aus dem künstlerischen Schaffensprozess herausgehalten werden sollten, so konnten und wollten sie dennoch nicht auf die Steuer- und Manipulierbarkeit ihrer inneren Zeichen- und Bilderwelt verzichten: „Wenn man also von den Surrealisten sagt, sie seien Maler einer stets wandelbaren Traumwirklichkeit, so darf das nicht etwa heißen, daß sie ihre Träume abmalen (das wäre deskriptiver, naiver Naturalismus), oder daß sich ein jeder aus Traumelementen seine eigene kleine Welt aufbaue, um sich in ihr gütlich oder boshaft zu gebärden (das wäre ‚Flucht aus der Zeit'), sondern daß sie sich auf dem physikalisch und psychisch durchaus realen (‚surrealen'), wenn auch noch wenig bestimmten Grenzgebiet von Innen- und Außenwelt frei, kühn und selbstverständlich bewegen, einregistrieren, was sie dort sehen und erleben und eingreifen, wo ihnen ihre revolutionären Instinkte dazu raten."

Max Ernst, „Was ist Surrealismus?", in: *Als die Surrealisten noch recht hatten. Texte und Dokumente*, hg. von Günter Metken. Stuttgart 1976, S. 324.

Schließlich hat Salvador Dalí jeder Hingabe an das unwillkürliche Funktionieren der Fantasie und des Denkens als einem Selbstzweck und Innerlichkeitskult eine klare Absage erteilt und mit seiner *activité paranoïaque-critique* die Halluzination des Traums und den assoziativen Denkautomatismus in den intendierten und kultivierten Wahn hinein verlängert, womit er

to "systemizing confusion and completely discrediting the real world,"

Peter Gorsen, *Kunst und Krankheit. Metamorphosen der ästhetischen Einbildungskraft*, Frankfurt a. M., 1980, 235.

while at the same time tearing down the divisions between inner and outer worlds, and irrationalizing everyday reality in order to rob dreams of their independence. What scientific research attempts by accessing the dream from the outside (namely, to weaken its autonomy and to conquer its terrain) was something advanced Surrealism evidently had its eye on from the other side, deliberately trying to transform the outer world in line with the model of the dream into precisely the latter.
Beyond all socio-cultural and political implications, Surrealism already contributed to an aesthetics of the dream by exploring the world of iconography in the manifest dream and by attempting to represent it both conceptually and visually, something in which Freud is known to not really have been interested. He concentrated completely on what lay behind, was always searching for the invisible and, in fact, not so much in the midst of the visible, but usually at a different level, always in the process of discerning a narrative beyond the images. Indeed, his efforts primarily focused on an analysis of the transformation as opposed to an analysis of the transformed. It is therefore no big surprise that he judged certain artists who were his contemporaries quite harshly: "Meaning is but little with these men, all they care about is line, shape, agreement of contours. They are given up to the Lustprinzip."

im Namen einer gesellschaftlichen Revolution „die Verwirrung systematisieren und zum vollständigen Verruf der realen Welt“

Peter Gorsen, *Kunst und Krankheit. Metamorphosen der ästhetischen Einbildungskraft*. Frankfurt a. M. 1980, S. 235.

beitragen wollte, gleichzeitig aber auch im Niederreißen der Grenzen von Innenwelt und Außenwelt und in der Irrationalisierung der Alltagsrealität den Traum seiner Eigenständigkeit beraubte. Was wissenschaftliche Forschung durch einen Zugriff von außen versucht, nämlich die Autonomie des Traums zu schwächen und sein Terrain zu erobern, das hat offenbar der fortgeschrittene Surrealismus von der anderen Seite her im Auge gehabt, indem er die Außenwelt bewusst nach dem Vorbild des Traums in einen ebensolchen verwandeln wollte.
Jedoch diesseits soziokultureller und politischer Implikationen hatte der Surrealismus bereits Beiträge zu einer Ästhetik des Traums geliefert, indem er die Ikonografie des manifesten Traums nach ihrer Formenwelt hinterfragte und sie konzeptuell und bildnerisch darzustellen versuchte, wofür Freud bekanntlich kein sonderliches Interesse entwickeln konnte. Ganz auf das stets Dahinterliegende konzentriert, immer auf der Suche nach dem Unsichtbaren und das nicht so sehr inmitten des Sichtbaren, sondern zumeist auf einer anderen Ebene, immer auch die Erzählung jenseits der Bilder aufspürend, galten seine Anstrengungen vornehmlich einer Analyse der Verwandlung gegenüber einer Analyse des Verwandelten. So ist auch sein abschätziges Urteil über bestimmte, ihm zeitgenössische Künstler nicht weiter verwunder-

Letter by Sigmund Freud to Ernest Jones, Feb. 8th, 1914. In *The Complete Correspondence of Sigmund Freud and Ernest Jones 1908–1939*, ed. R. Andrew Paskaukas, Cambridge, 1993, 261.

By contrast, we find manifested in the Surrealists' flood of images (and it corresponded to the flood of ideas in *écriture automatique*) a fascination not only with the wealth of shapes assumed by an untrammeled imagination (such as was offered first and foremost by dreams), but also with those successful metamorphoses that arose through the concurrence or interlocking of imaginary elements, and not by the transformation of thoughts into images. Thus, the Surrealists were by no means interested in contributing to the Freudian interpretation of dreams or in extending Freud's theory of dreams but, instead, in identifying completely with the dream itself, sought to discover in its creative potential, , its aesthetic mechanisms and artifices, its grotesque linkages an artistically enthralling source that could be brought to serve in new artistic creations: "'The accidental encounter between a sewing machine and an umbrella on a dissecting table' (Lautréamont) is now a celebrated, even classic example of the phenomenon discovered by the Surrealists: that the conjunction of two (or more) allegedly quite incompatible elements in an incompatible context sparks off the most powerful poetic insights."

Max Ernst, op. cit., 492.

Behind the joy in these and other cases of surreal craziness, behind the obscene enjoyment of imaginary fusions and "symbolic equations of the anus, eyes, ears, labia, toes, navel, thighs, etc.," lich: „Der Sinn bedeutet diesen Männern nur wenig; sie kümmern sich nur um Linie, Form, Übereinstimmung der Umrisse. Sie frönen dem Lustprinzip."

Brief von Sigmund Freud an Ernest Jones, 08.02.1914, in: Ernest Jones, *Das Leben und Werk von Sigmund Freud*. Bern, Stuttgart, Wien 1982, S. 478.

In der der Ideenflucht der *écriture automatique* entsprechenden Bilderflucht der Surrealisten hingegen manifestierte sich eine Faszination nicht nur am Formenreichtum einer entfesselten Fantasie, wie sie sich vor allem in Träumen darbot, sondern auch an jenen gelungenen Metamorphosen, die sich durch ein Zusammentreffen oder Ineinandergreifen von imaginären Elementen und nicht durch die Verwandlung von Gedanken in Bilder ergaben. So waren also die Surrealisten keineswegs daran interessiert, Beiträge zur freudschen Traumdeutung zu liefern oder Freuds Traumtheorie zu erweitern beziehungsweise zu ergänzen, sondern, ganz identifiziert mit dem Traum selbst, dessen kreatives Potenzial, dessen ästhetische Mechanismen und Kunstgriffe, dessen Groteskkoppelungen als künstlerisches Faszinosum zu entdecken und in den Dienst einer neuen bildnerischen Dichtung zu stellen: „‚Die zufällige Begegnung von Nähmaschine und Regenschirm auf einem Seziertisch' (Lautréamont) ist heute ein allbekanntes, fast klassisch gewordenes Beispiel für das von den Surrealisten entdeckte Phänomen, daß die Annäherung von zwei (oder mehr) scheinbar wesensfremden Elementen auf einem ihnen wesensfremden Plan die stärksten poetischen Zündungen provoziert."



Peter Gorsen, op. cit., 216.

behind the joy in the trompe l'oeil, in the anamorphotic, in the *structuresmolles* and the various pareidolia, indeed even behind the thirst to overthrow the dominant cultural and social relations was, at least for Dalí (who can lay claim to a preeminent position in his genius period that ran through into the 1940s [Wieland Schmied]), the need to adopt isopathic strategies toward the consequences of his precarious biography.
For Dalí's art also ever constituted an attempt at self-healing that consisted largely of playing crazy in order to protect himself against those greater forms of craziness that affected his entire identity and that stemmed from the uncanny question that was posed from the very outset – whether he actually existed in the first place. Dalí (like Vincent van Gogh, Heinrich Schliemann or Hans Henny Jahnn) was among those who bore a heavy fate upon their shoulders by virtue of having entered life to take the place of one who had died: "My brother died at the age of seven from an attack of meningitis, three years before I was born. His death plunged my father and mother into the depths of despair; they found consolation only upon my arrival into the world. My brother and I resembled each other like two drops of water, but we had different reflections."

Salvador Dalí, *The Secret Life of Salvador Dalí*, New York, 1993, 2.

So only in his spirit (which was rooted neither in the reality of the body nor in the symbol of his own name, bordering therefore on mania) could Dalí initially find the basis of an original

Max Ernst, „Was ist Surrealismus?", in: *Als die Surrealisten noch recht hatten. Texte und Dokumente*, hg. von Günter Metken. Stuttgart 1976, S. 324.

Hinter der Freude an solchen und anderen surrealen Verrücktheiten, hinter dem obszönen Genießen imaginärer Verschmelzungen und „Symbolgleichungen von Anus, Augen, Ohren, Schamlippen, Zehen, Nabel, Schenkel usw.",

Peter Gorsen, *Kunst und Krankheit. Metamorphosen der ästhetischen Einbildungskraft*. Frankfurt a. M. 1980, S. 216.

hinter der Lust am Trompe l'œil, am Anamorphotismus, an den *structuresmolles* und an den diversen Pareidolien, schließlich auch hinter der Triebkraft zum Umsturz herrschender kultureller und gesellschaftlicher Verhältnisse lag allerdings für Dalí, der diesbezüglich in seiner bis in die vierziger Jahre reichenden Geniezeit (Wieland Schmied) eine Vorrangstellung beanspruchen durfte, auch die Notwendigkeit isopathischer Strategien gegenüber den Folgen seiner prekären Lebensgeschichte.
Denn Dalís Kunst stellte immer auch einen Selbstheilungsversuch dar, der hauptsächlich darin bestand, Verrücktheiten zu spielen, um sich vor jener größeren Verrücktheit zu schützen, die seine ganze Identität betraf und die auf der von Anfang an bestehenden unheimlichen Frage beruhte, ob er überhaupt existierte.
Denn Dalí gehörte (so wie auch Vincent van Gogh, Heinrich Schliemann oder Hans Henny Jahnn) zu jenen Trägern eines schwerwiegenden Schicksals, welche beim Eintritt ins Leben den Platz eines Toten einzunehmen haben: „Mein Bruder starb mit sieben Jahren an einer Gehirn-

and genuine existence. For his body was the copy of a dead body, and since his first name was also that of his dead brother, and thus was only available qua deceased loan, all that remained to symbolically found his existence was the empty signified, the crazed metaphors onto which he could project his being – his life's project was the attempt to inhabit these. This was also the reason for Dalí's flight into a virtual, spiritual being that dispensed with all material foundations: "I actually have no physical dimensions. My Ego is Dalí."

Salvador Dalí, Andre Parinaud, *Comment on devient Dalí*, Paris, 1973, 302 (translated by August Ruhs).

It was thus initially the name in a generational sequence through which he attempted to forge a more stable identity; it was also the name of a father whom he despised as a person, whom he had to refuse and reject as an impossible role model. It was in this blank space, purged of an unacceptable imago, in this proximity to psychosis, that he had to create himself – and this was a space he set out to defend.
The retention of a significant ego, the almost infinite and inexhaustible activity of his imagination to ward off his fear of dissolution and destruction, not to mention his rebellious rejection of the values, opinions and stances of his epoch being passed down as tradition, truly predestined Dalí for Surrealism, offering his ego yet another home. In order to secure his ideational and phantasmatic existence, it did not suffice him to give Surrealism the status of a reality, but in his declaration "Le Surréalisme, c'est moi!" he uninhibitedly and completely usurped its signified for himself before aban-

hautentzündung, drei Jahre vor meiner Geburt. Sein Tod stürzte meine Eltern in tiefe Verzweiflung; sie fanden Trost nur dadurch, daß ich zur Welt kam. Mein Bruder und ich ähnelten einander wie ein Ei dem anderen, aber wir dachten verschieden."

Salvador Dalí, *Das geheime Leben des Salvador Dalí. Sonderausgabe zum 100. Geburtstag.* München 2004, S. 219.

Nur in seinem Geist also, nur in seinem Denken, das weder im Realen des Körpers noch im Symbol eines eigenen Namens verankert war und daher ans Wahnhafte grenzen musste, konnte Dalí zunächst die Grundlagen eines originellen und genuinen Daseins finden. Denn sein Körper war die Kopie eines toten Körpers, und da ihm auch sein Vorname, der vom toten Bruder auf ihn übergegangen war, nur als abgelebtes Leihgut zur Verfügung stand, blieben zu seiner symbolischen Existenzbegründung nichts als leere Signifikanten, wahnhafte Metaphern, in die er sein Sein projizierte und die zu bewohnen sein Lebensprojekt bestimmen sollte. Daher auch die Flucht Dalís in ein virtuelles, spirituelles Sein, das jede materielle Begründung hinter sich lässt: „Tatsächlich habe ich keine körperlichen Dimensionen. Mein Ich ist Dalí."

Salvador Dalí, *Comment on devient Dalí.* Paris 1973, S. 302 (übers. von August Ruhs).

So war es zunächst der Name in der Generationenfolge, in der er seine Identität stabiler einzurichten versuchte; es war aber auch der Name eines Vaters, den er als Person verachtete und als unmögliches Vorbild zurückweisen



doning that identity for one of egomaniac closure and indivisibility: "On the dial of the clock of history, after the quarter-hour of the 'isms,' the hour of the individual is about to sound! Your hour, Salvador!"

Salvador Dalí, *The Secret Life of Salvador Dalí*, 351.

At a time when madness threatened to breach his defensive bastions and during which, as he confesses in his autobiography, he frittered away his genius in crazy bouts of laughter, meaningless ejaculations and fruitless visions, Gala offered him not only an additional significant support, but also helped him obtain a body and a soul. In Gala's other, loved body, Dalí's crazed being, trammeled as it was to the symbol, found more viable material backbone than it could in the products of his artistic work, which until then were hardly able to provide much more than a transcendental body as ersatz for his lack thereof.
In his complete and perfect identification with Gala, Dalí was then able to find firmer ground under his feet in earthly life: "By signing my pictures as Gala-Dalí, I did nothing other than give an existential truth a name, as I would no longer exist without my twin Gala. Thanks to Gala I had not only achieved a right to my own life, but also the masculine and feminine sides to my genius and the ability to keep my phantasms at a distance. The paranoïac-critical method, that is above all Gala."

Salvador Dalí, *Comment on devient Dalí*, 299 (translated by August Ruhs).

By elaborating on his critical-paranoid activity as a "spontaneous method to gain irrational

und verwerfen musste. In dieser von einer unannehmbaren Imago gereinigten Leerstelle, in dieser Nähe zur Psychose musste er sich also selbst erschaffen und diesen Platz galt es zu verteidigen.
Das Festhalten an einem signifikanten Ich, die gegen seine Angst vor Auflösung und Vernichtung eingesetzte und beinahe grenzenlose und unerschöpfliche Fantasietätigkeit, aber auch seine rebellische Auflehnung gegen die Tradierung von Werten, Anschauungen und Haltungen seiner Epoche prädestinierten Dalí geradezu für den Surrealismus, der seinem Ich eine weitere Behausung bieten sollte. Um sich hier seine ideelle und phantasmatische Existenz zu sichern, genügte es ihm aber nicht, dem Surrealismus Realitätsstatus zu verleihen, sondern er usurpierte auch in seiner Deklaration „Le Surréalisme, c'est moi!" hemmungslos dessen Signifikanten ganz für sich selbst, bevor er auch diese Identität zugunsten einer egomanen Geschlossenheit und Unteilbarkeit verließ: „Nach Ablauf der Viertelstunde der ‚Ismen', sagt das Zifferblatt der Uhr der Geschichte, schlägt jetzt die Stunde des Individuums. Deine Stunde, Salvador!"

> Salvador Dalí, *Das geheime Leben des Salvador Dalí. Sonderausgabe zum 100. Geburtstag.* München 2004, S. 605.

Gala schließlich bot ihm in einer Zeit, in der der Wahnsinn in die Bastionen seiner Abwehr einzubrechen drohte und in der er, wie er autobiografisch einbekennt, sein Genie in verrückten Lachkrämpfen, in sinnlosen Ejakulationen und in fruchtlosen Visionen vergeudete, nicht nur eine weitere signifikante Stütze, sondern sie verhalf ihm auch zu einer Seele und

insight on the basis of the interpretative-critical association of manic phenomena,"

> Salvador Dalí, quoted from Marie-Francoise de Munck, "La méthode paranoia-critique," in *Quarto, Revue de Psychanalyse - Ecole de la Cause freudienne en Belgique*, no. 37–8 (1989), 46 (translated by August Ruhs).

Dalí not only succeeded in bringing his personal psychic chaos under the control of a critical intellect, in giving his artistic oeuvre theoretical underpinnings, but also in providing an original treatise for Surrealism's socio- and cultural-political program in its battle to *conquer the irrational.*
Dalí's spectacular pictorial compositions, his images that can be read in two ways, enigmatic and anamorphic, in which opposites are not dialectically sublated and represented by a third term, but visualized simultaneously, were created and elaborated, on the one hand, with the assistance of his paranoïac-critical method, while, on the other, still able to be explained and justified by the latter. The encounters with psychiatric and psychoanalytical thought unmistakably influenced this creative and intellectual activity. They not least gave clearer contours to how Dalí understood himself and, after he had evidently overcome his fear of introspection, were able to possibly show him with especial emphasis how strongly a person's biography can be expressed in the total sum of his life statements. Analogously to Freud's study on Leonardo da Vinci, these encounters enabled him to track down those childhood memories reflected so unmistakably in his pictures and writings, and in his critical enquiry into his artistic and poetic surroundings.

zu einer Körperlichkeit. In diesem anderen und geliebten Körper Galas konnte Dalís wahnhaftes und an das Zeichen gebundene Sein einen tragfähigeren materiellen Halt finden als in den Produktionen seines künstlerischen Schaffens, die ihm bis dahin kaum mehr als einen transzendenten Körper als Ersatz für seinen Körpermangel bieten konnten.
In seiner umfassenden und vollkommenen Identifizierung mit Gala konnte nun Dalí auch im Irdischen einen festeren Halt finden: „Indem ich meine Bilder mit Gala-Dalí signierte, habe ich nichts anderes getan, als einer existenziellen Wahrheit einen Namen zu geben, da ich ohne meinen Zwilling Gala nicht mehr existieren würde. Durch Gala habe ich nicht nur das Recht zu meinem eigenen Leben errungen, sondern auch den männlichen und weiblichen Anteil meines Genies und die Fähigkeit, gegenüber meinen Phantasmen Abstand zu wahren. Die paranoisch-kritische Methode, das ist vor allem Gala."

Salvador Dalí, *Comment on devient Dalí*. Paris 1973, S. 299 (übers. von August Ruhs).

Mit der Ausarbeitung seiner kritisch-paranoischen Aktivität als „spontaner Methode zu irrationaler Erkenntnis auf der Grundlage der interpretativ-kritischen Assoziation wahnhafter Phänomene"

Salvador Dalí, zit. nach Marie-Francoise de Munck, *La méthode paranoia-critique. Quarto, Revue de Psychanalyse – Ecole de la Cause freudienne en Belgique*, No. 37/38, 1989, S. 46. (Übers. von August Ruhs)



As regards the latter, there is no underestimating the relation that Dalí forged with Isidore Ducasse, an intellectual companion who had come to fame as Comte de Lautréamont and, after a very short life, died a mysterious death in 1870. Considered a trailblazer of modern literature, he was one of the most important stimulating influences for the Surrealists alongside Freud, which is why Dalí even considered him a precursor of psychoanalysis. While his *Songs of Maldoror*, which Lacan considered as madness arguing logically, became a Surrealist cult book, Dalí went even further, viewing the figure of Maldoror as that black brother within himself who, with his polymorphous-perverse constitution, gave voice to the evil, the hatred of everything, the amoral and blasphemous, the joy in cruelty, to nausea celebrated without recourse to an essentially despised traditional aesthetic. By illustrating the *Songs of Maldoror*, Dalí not only found a linguistic/visual overall shape for reports on the basest of human experience, but was able to find a support in his merciless struggle for existence, a god who functioned as a crutch: "For Dalí, Maldoror, 'who denied everything, father, mother, providence, love, ideals, in order only to think of himself,' embodied the total triumph of individuality and artistic self-deification."

Adrian La Salvia, "Der Krake mit dem seidenen Blick: Lautréamont, Breton, Dalí," in Lisa Puyplat et al. (ed.), *Salvador Dalí. Facetten eines Jahrhundertkünstlers*, Würzburg, 2005, 110.

On the feminine side, by contrast (where we are when considering the oeuvre of Louise Bourgeois), the question as to the identity of the artist as individual is different, as are her gelang es Dalí nicht nur, sein persönliches psychisches Chaos nun auch unter die Kontrolle eines kritischen Intellekts zu bringen und gleichzeitig seinem künstlerischen Werk eine theoretische Grundlage zu unterlegen, sondern darüber hinaus dem gesellschafts- und kulturpolitischen Programm des Surrealismus eine originelle Streitschrift für dessen Kampf zur *Eroberung des Irrationalen* zu liefern.

Dalís spektakuläre Bildkompositionen, seine Kippbilder, Vexierbilder und Anamorphosen, in welchen Gegensatzpaare nicht dialektisch aufgehoben und durch ein Drittes repräsentiert wurden, sondern simultan zur Anschauung gelangten, wurden einerseits mit Hilfe seiner paranoisch-kritischen Methode geschaffen und ausgearbeitet, andererseits aber auch durch diese erklärt und gerechtfertigt. Unverkennbar ist dabei der Einfluss, welchen die Begegnungen mit psychiatrischem und psychoanalytischem Denken auf diese schöpferische und intellektuelle Aktivität ausgeübt haben. Sie haben aber nicht zuletzt Dalís Selbstverständnis geschärft und ihm nach offensichtlicher Überwindung seiner Introspektionsangst vielleicht mit besonderem Nachdruck zeigen können, wie stark sich die Lebensgeschichte eines Menschen in allen seinen Lebensäußerungen einprägen kann. So war es ihm auch möglich, analog zu Freuds Arbeit über Leonardo da Vinci, bei sich selbst jene Kindheitserinnerungen aufzuspüren, die sich so unverkennbar in seinen Bildern und Schriften und in seiner Auseinandersetzung mit seiner künstlerischen und dichterischen Umwelt niederschlugen. Was Letzteres betrifft, ist jene Beziehung keineswegs als gering zu erachten, welche Dalí mit Isidore Ducasse verband, einem Gesinnungs-

attempts to solve it. Unlike Dalí, who had to square up to an existential question, one that in terms of its fundamental thrust paraphrases Hamlet's *to be or not to be*, Bourgeois is primarily concerned with the enigma of gender attribution in and through her artistic oeuvre, i.e. the question, "what is a man, what is a woman?." This presupposes a critical enquiry into a differentiated or sexualized body, something that also strongly defines Bourgeois's output. While Dalí transposes his being mainly into abstract signifiers (such as his own name or his artistic agenda) and into images with a discursive structure, Bourgeois seeks artistic expression more strongly in terms of objects and thus is more closely tied to an artistic medium that is manifestly supported by the father's desire for corporeality. In this way, she also comes up against the relativity of gender and of fundamental traits of human identity that precede all things phallic and all spider and cat metaphors. In this regard, desire has no gender. Which is why Louise Bourgeois also introduced the male body into her cell of hysteria, as is expressed in a later version of her *Arch of Hysteria*.

genossen, der als Comte de Lautréamont bekannt geworden war und der nach einem äußerst kurzen Leben 1870 einen mysteriösen Tod erleiden musste. Als bahnbrechend für die moderne Literatur angesehen, bedeutete er für die Surrealisten einen der wichtigsten Impulsgeber neben Freud, wobei Dalí ihm sogar den Status eines Vorläufers der Psychoanalyse einräumte. Waren seine *Gesänge des Maldoror*, welche Lacan als logisch argumentierenden Wahnsinn betrachtete, zu einem surrealistischen Kultbuch geworden, so konnte darüber hinausgehend Dalí in der Figur des Maldoror jenem schwarzen Bruder in ihm selbst begegnen, der in seiner polymorph-perversen Verfasstheit das Boshaft-Böse, den Hass auf alles, das Amoralische und Blasphemische, die Lust an der Grausamkeit und den zelebrierten Ekel ohne Anspruch auf eine letztlich verabscheute traditionelle Ästhetik zur Sprache brachte. Indem er Die *Gesänge des Maldoror* illustrierte, hat Dalí nicht nur Erfahrungsberichte aus den tiefsten Niederungen menschlichen Erlebens in eine sprachlich-bildhafte Gesamtform gebracht, sondern hat sich auch in seinem gnadenlosen Existenzkampf einer Stütze bedienen können, die als eine Art Krückengott fungierte: „Maldoror, ‚der alles verleugnet hat, Vater, Mutter, Vorsehung, Liebe, Ideal, um nur noch an sich selbst zu denken', verkörpert für Dalí den totalen Triumph der Individualität und der künstlerischen Selbstvergottung."

Adrian La Salvia, „Der Krake mit dem seidenen Blick: Lautréamont, Breton, Dalí", in: *Salvador Dalí. Facetten eines Jahrhundertkünstlers*, hg. von Lisa Puyplat et al., Würzburg 2005, S. 110.

Auf der weiblichen Seite hingegen, auf welcher wir dem Werk von Louise Bourgeois gegenüberstehen, ist die Identitätsfrage des Künstlersubjekts mit ihren Lösungsversuchen andersgeartet. Im Gegensatz zu Dalí, der sich einer existenziellen Frage zu stellen hat, einer Frage, die in ihrer Grundsätzlichkeit Hamlets *Sein* oder *Nicht-Sein* paraphrasiert, ist Bourgeois in und mit ihrem Kunstschaffen vornehmlich mit dem Rätsel der Geschlechtlichkeit, d. h. mit der Frage „Was ist ein Mann, was ist eine Frau?" befasst. Dies setzt die Auseinandersetzung mit einem differenzierten bzw. sexuierten Körper voraus, was auch Bourgeois' Schaffen weitgehend bestimmt. Während Dalí sein Sein hauptsächlich in die abstrakten Signifikanten (wie etwa in seinen Eigennamen oder in sein künstlerisches Programm) und in diskursiv gefasste Bilder verlegt, ist Bourgeois Streben nach Ausdruck daher stärker dem Objekthaften und damit einem künstlerischen Medium verpflichtet, welchem das Begehren des Vaters nach Körperlichkeit offensichtlich entgegenkommt. Damit stößt sie aber auch auf den Relativitätscharakter des Geschlechtlichen und auf Grundzüge der menschlichen Identität, welche allem Phallischen und jeder Spinnen- und Katzenmetaphorik vorausgehen. In diesem Sinn hat das Begehren kein Geschlecht. Deshalb hat Louise Bourgeois auch den männlichen Körper in ihre Zelle der Hysterie eingeführt, wie es in einer späteren Version des *Arch of Hysteria* nachdrücklich zum Ausdruck kommt.

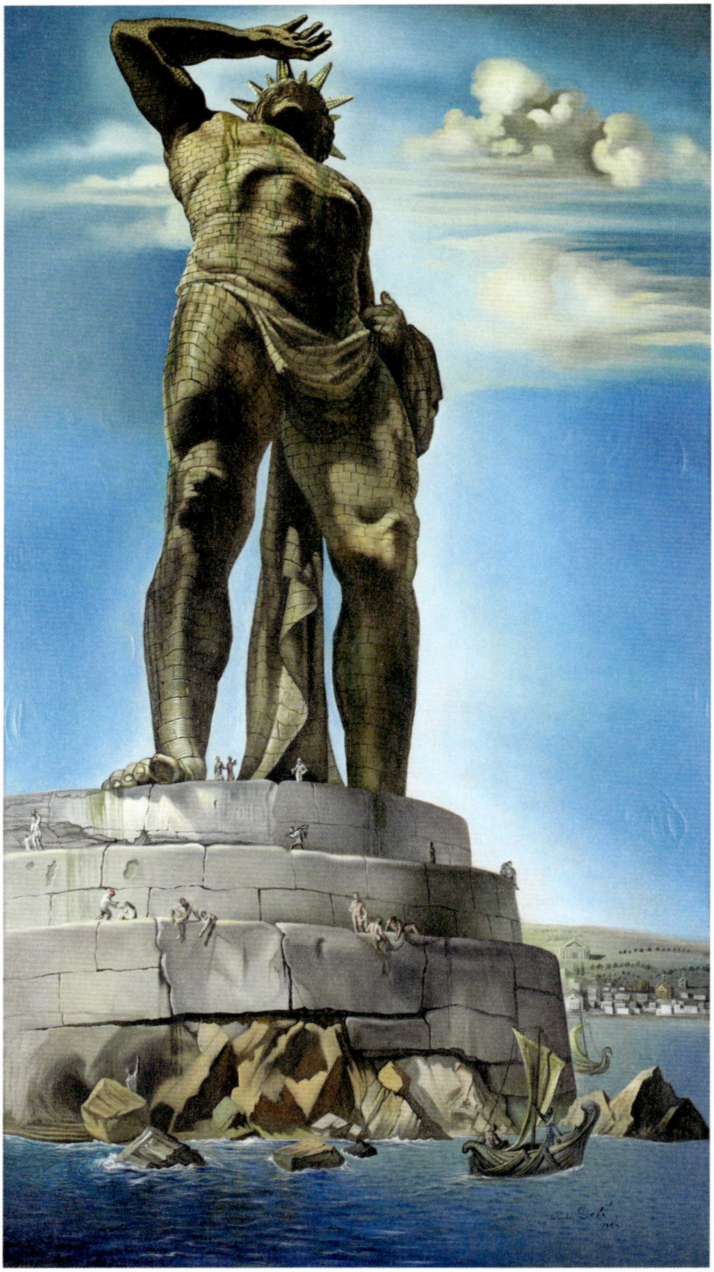

Salvador Dalí,
*Der Koloss von Rhodos*, 1954

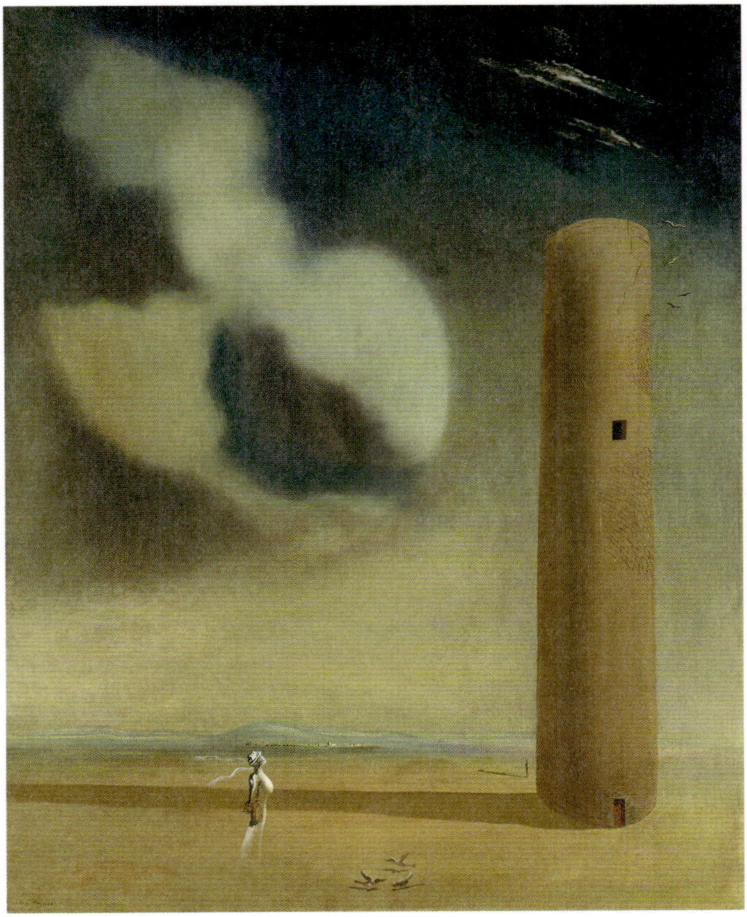

Salvador Dalí,
*La Tour*, 1936

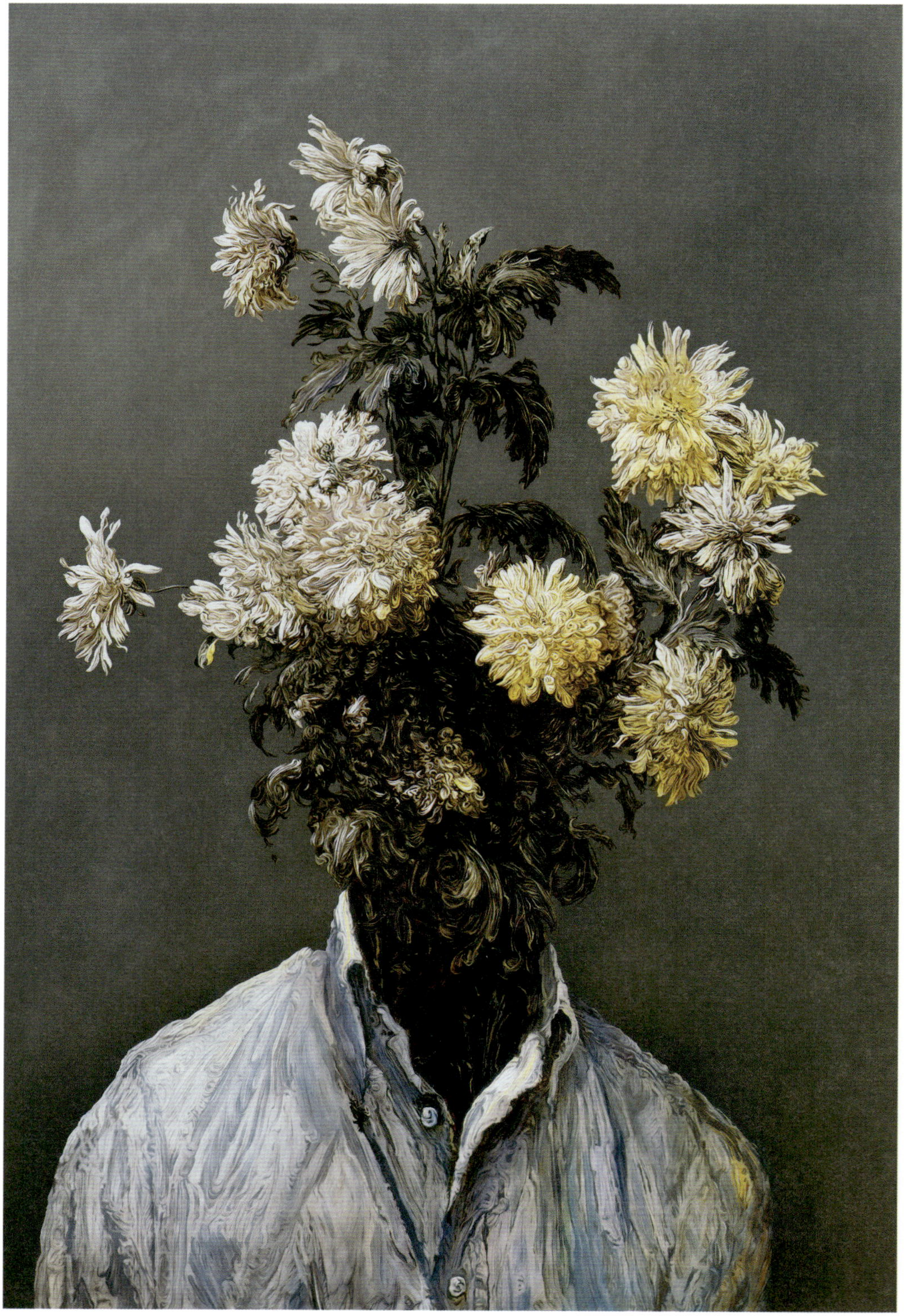

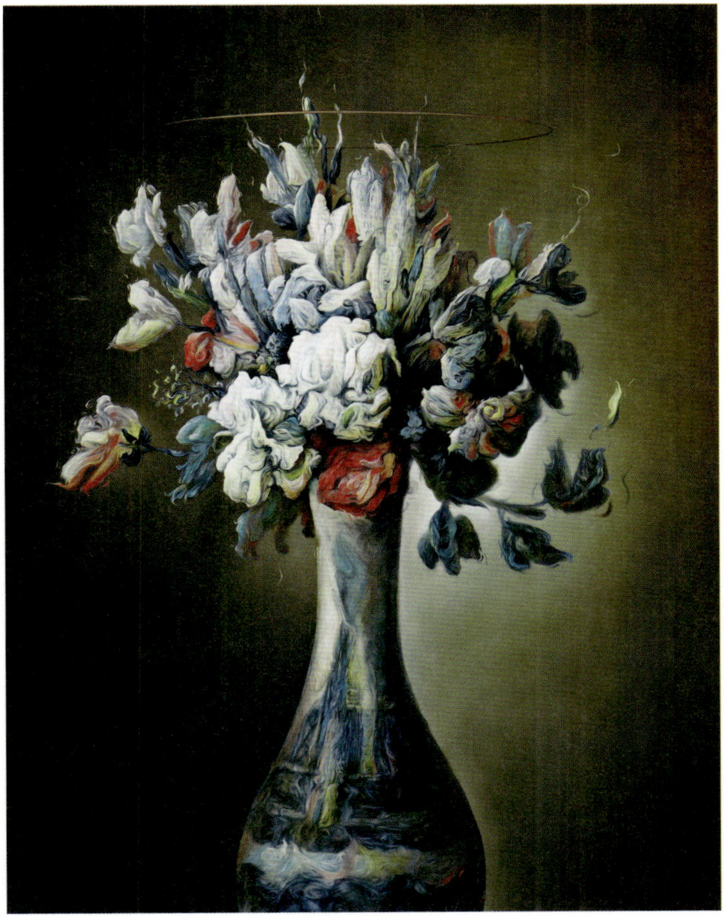



Glenn Brown,
*Architecture and Morality*, 2004

Glenn Brown,
*Natural Selection*, 2010

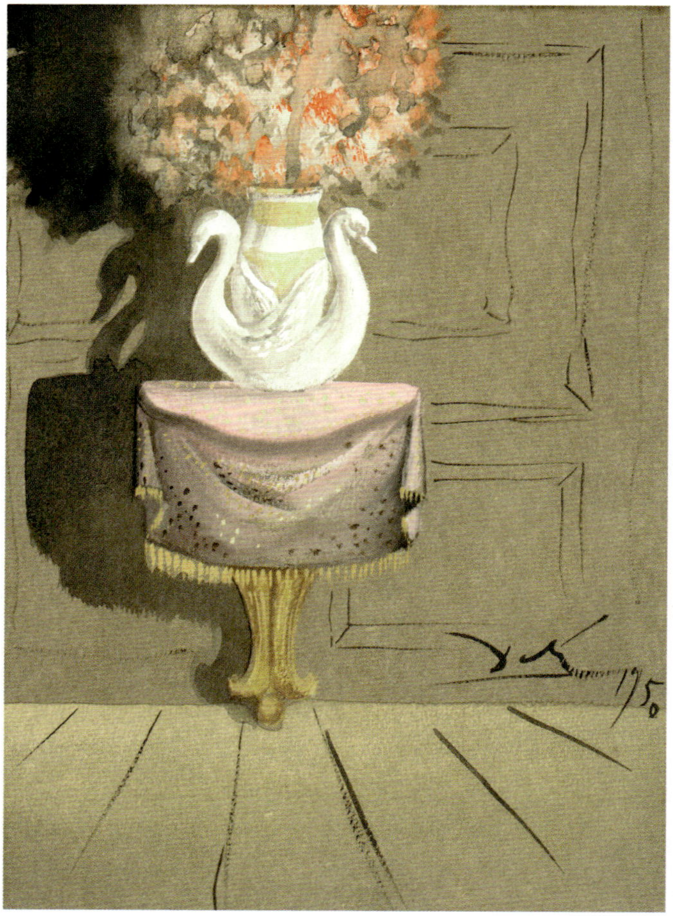

Salvador Dalí,
*Consola con florero de cisnes*, 1950

Salvador Dalí,
*Flores surrealistas (Gala-Narciso)*, 1938

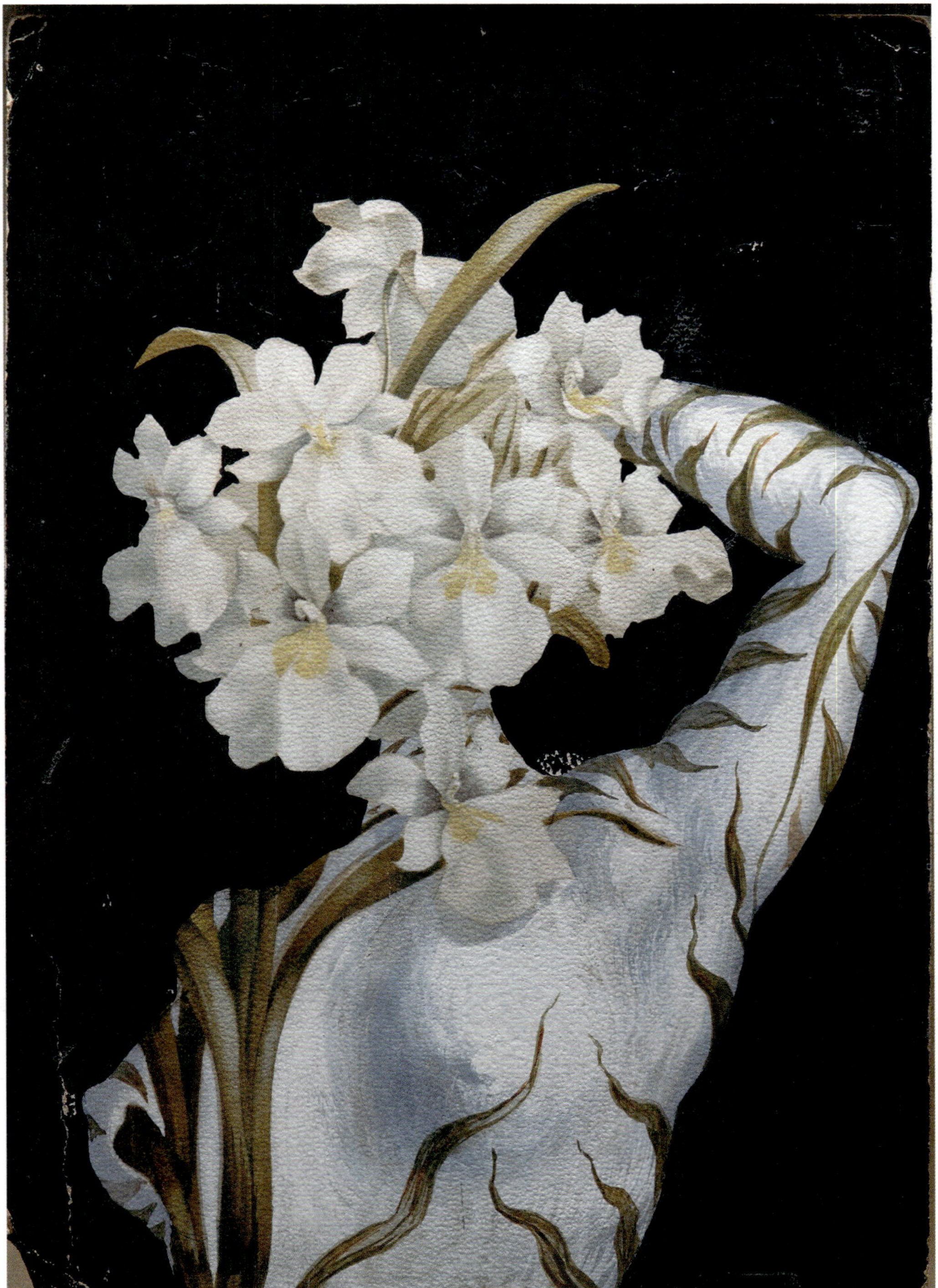

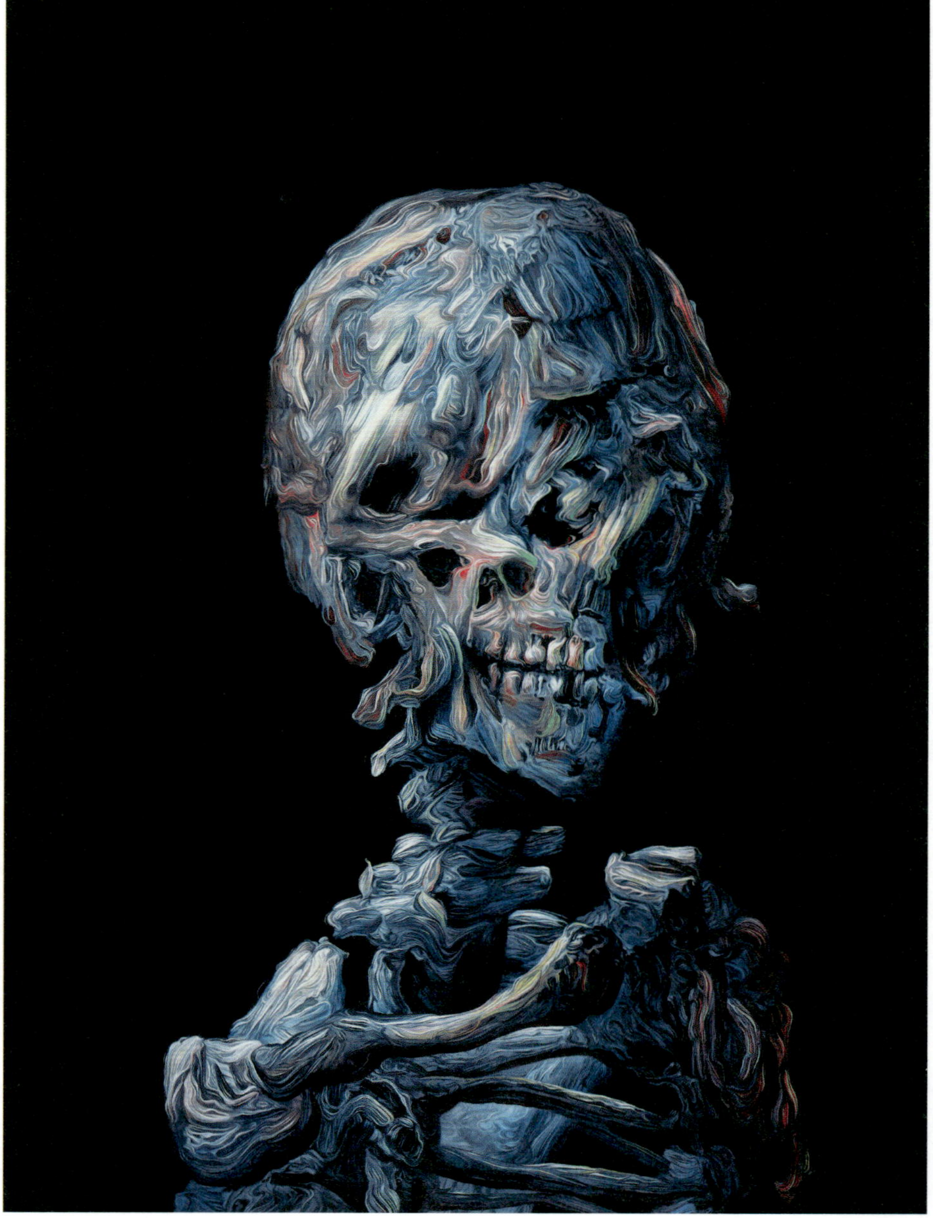

Glenn Brown,
*Theatre*, 2006

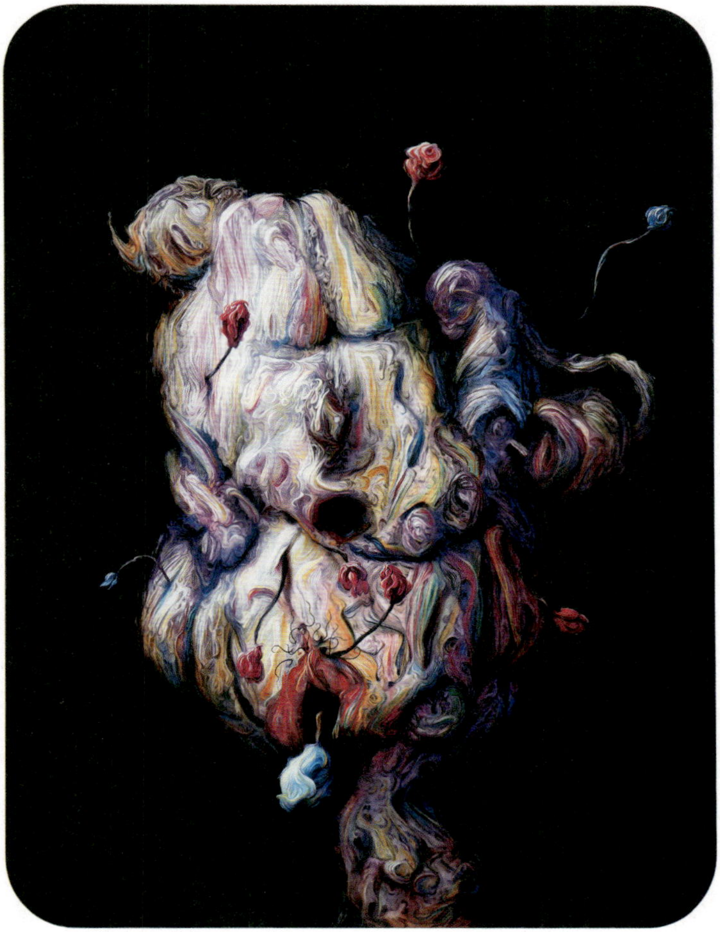

Glenn Brown,
*International Velvet*, 2004

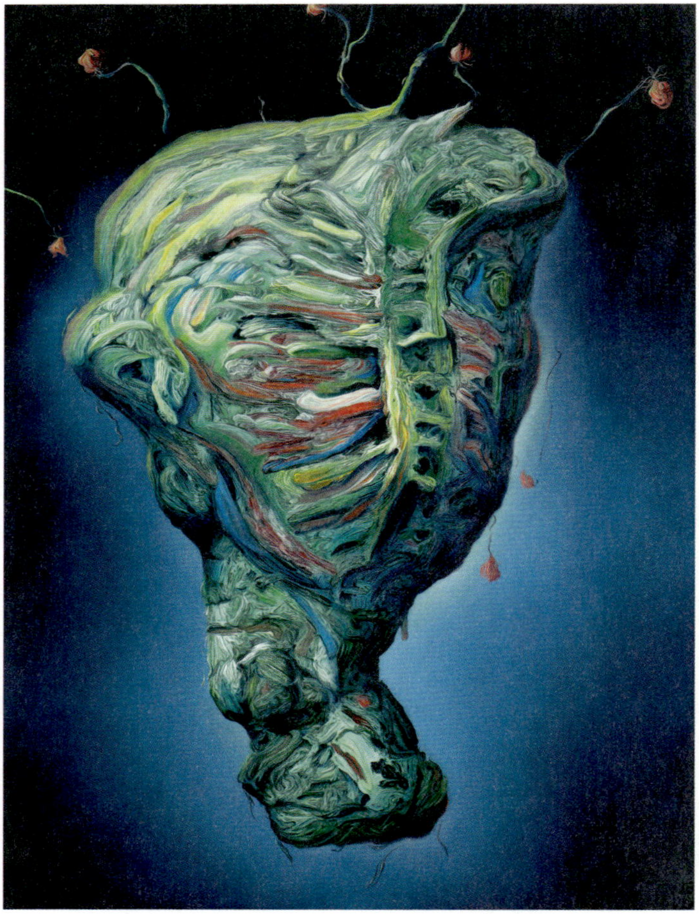

Glenn Brown,
*Come All Ye Rolling Minstrels*, 2009

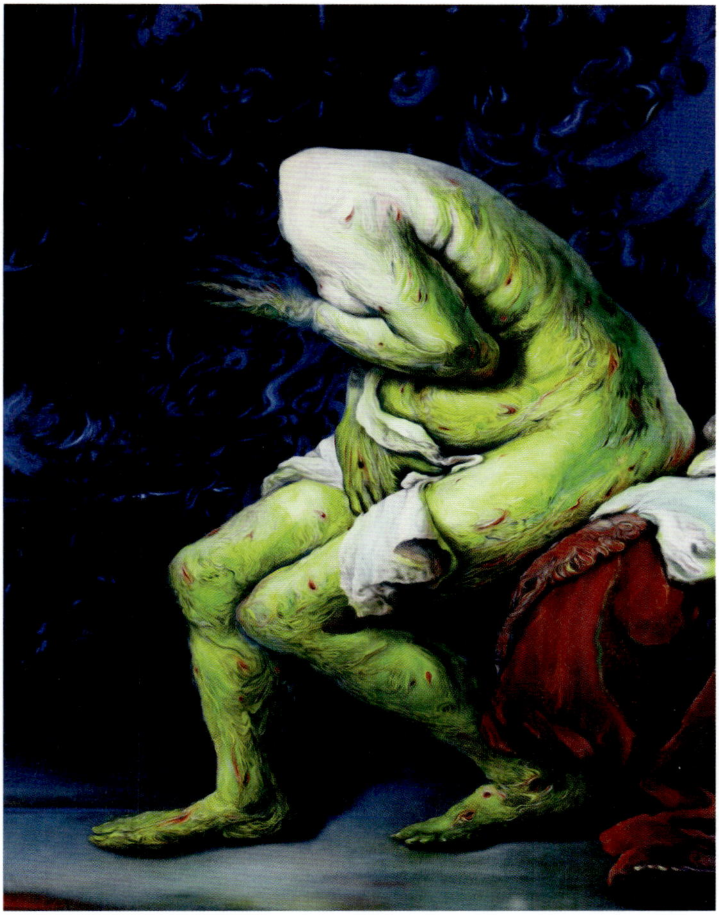

Glenn Brown,
*Nigger of the World*, 2011

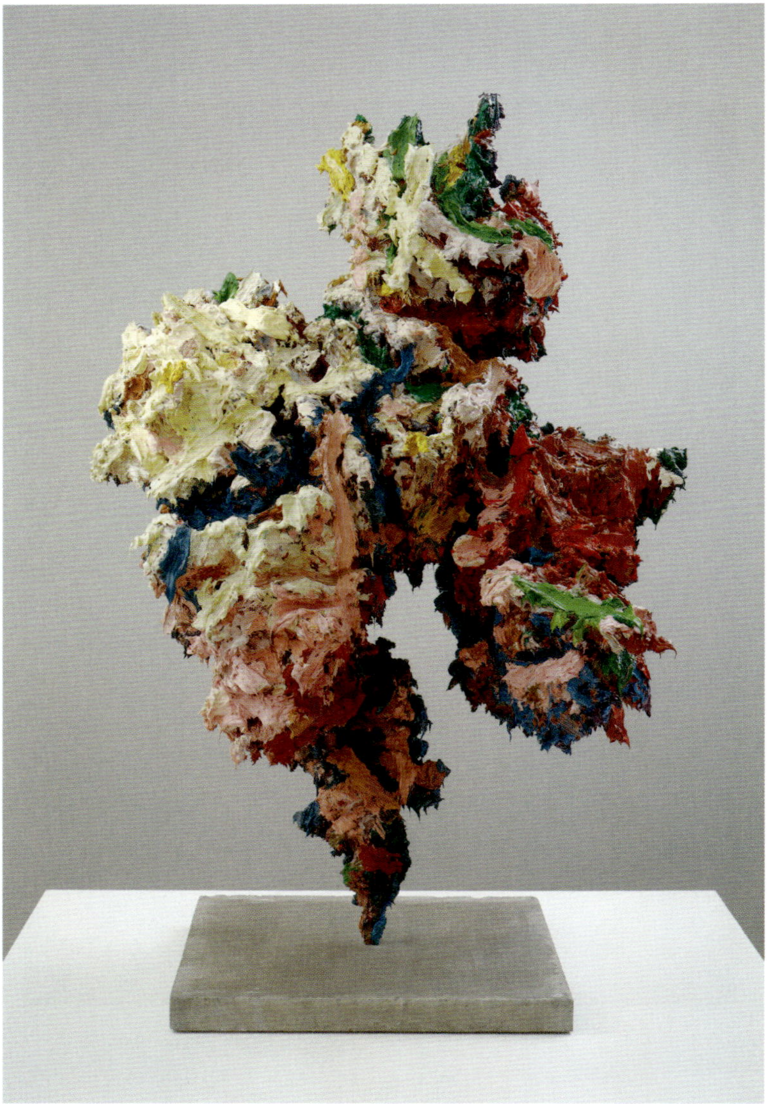

Glenn Brown,
*Woman I*, 2011

Glenn Brown,
*Song to the Siren*, 2009

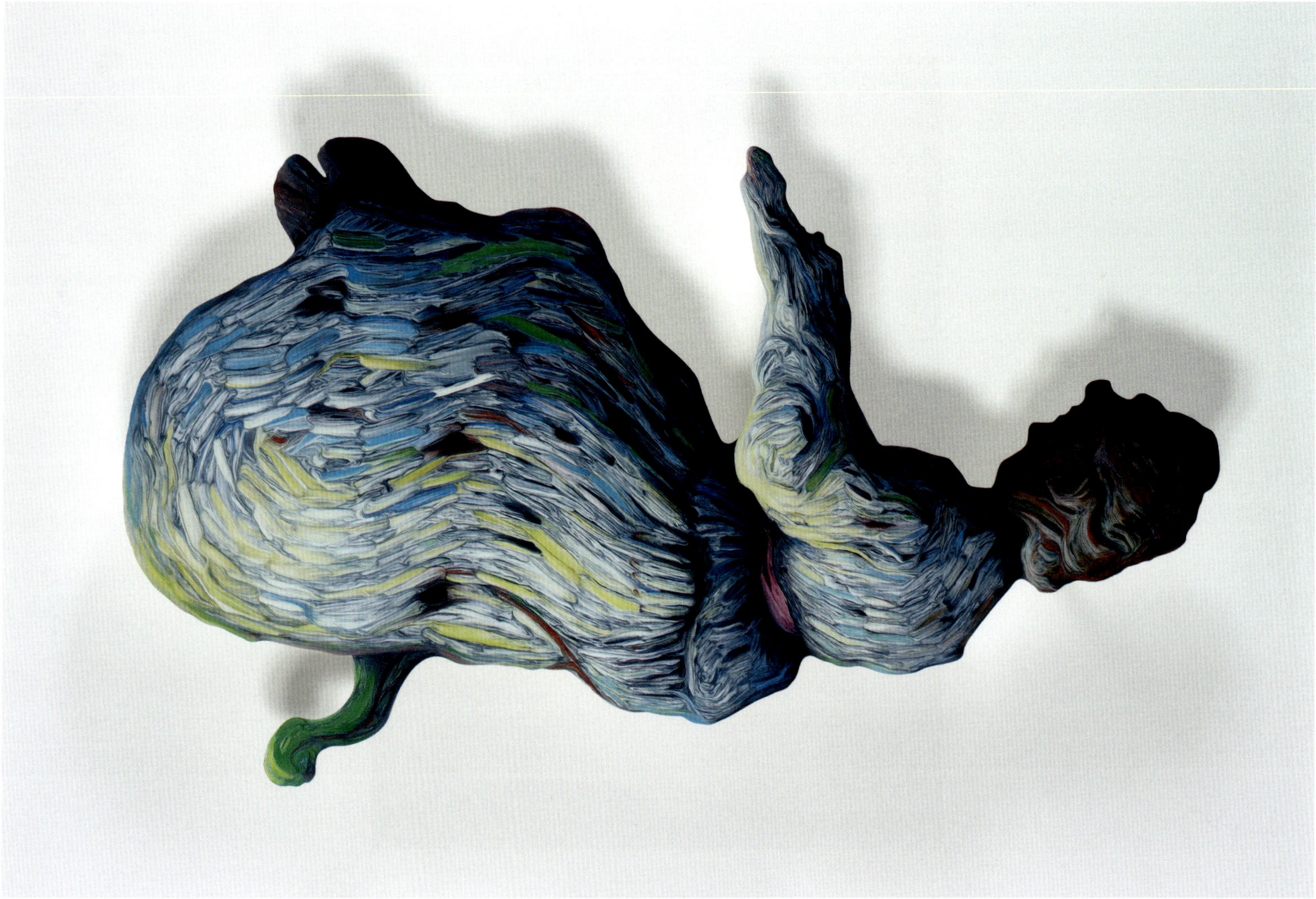

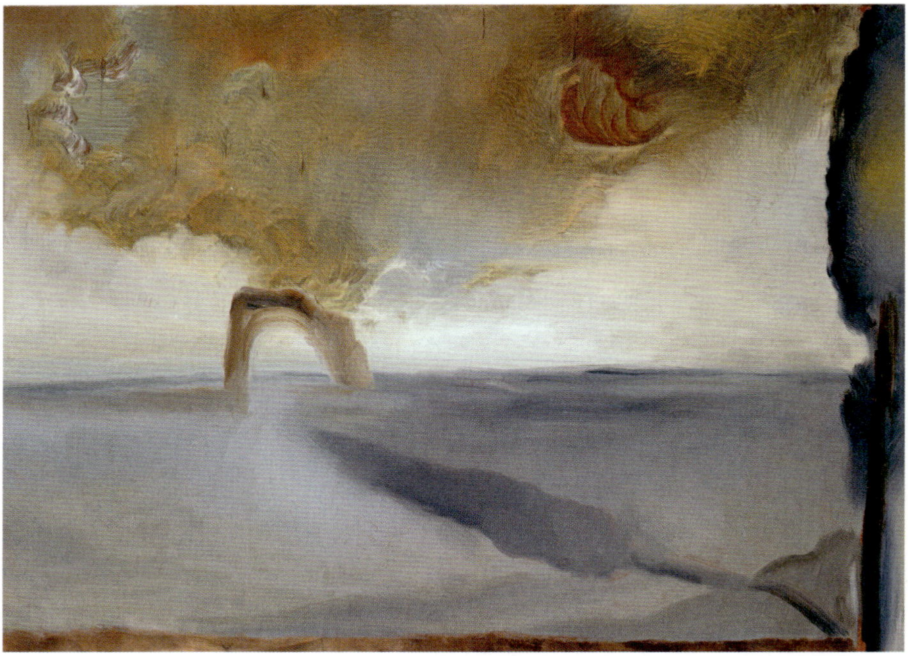

Salvador Dalí,
*Paisaje con ciprés*, 1981

Salvador Dalí,
*Couple aux têtes pleines de nuages*, 1936

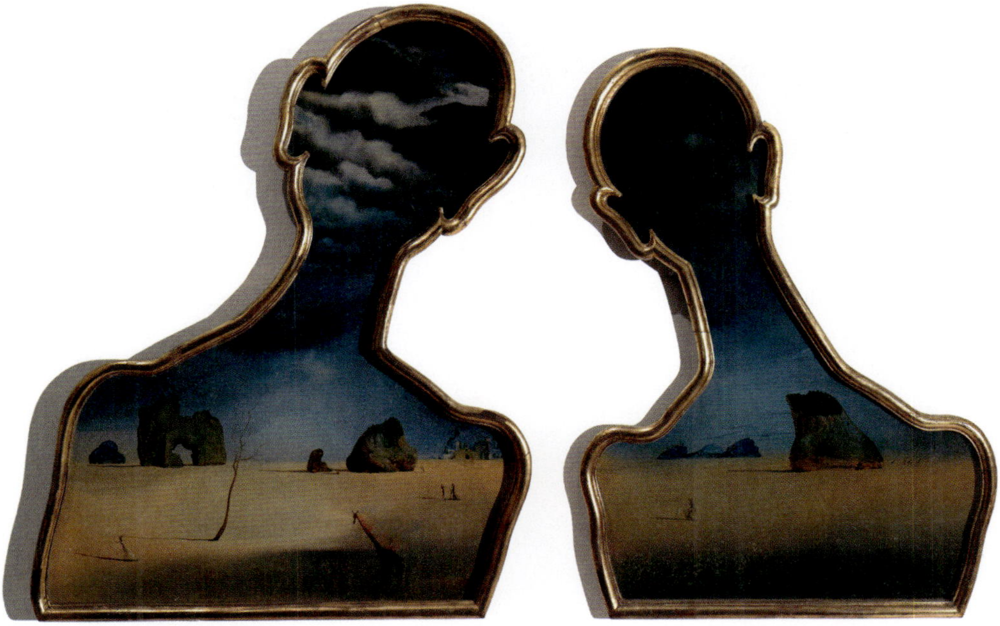

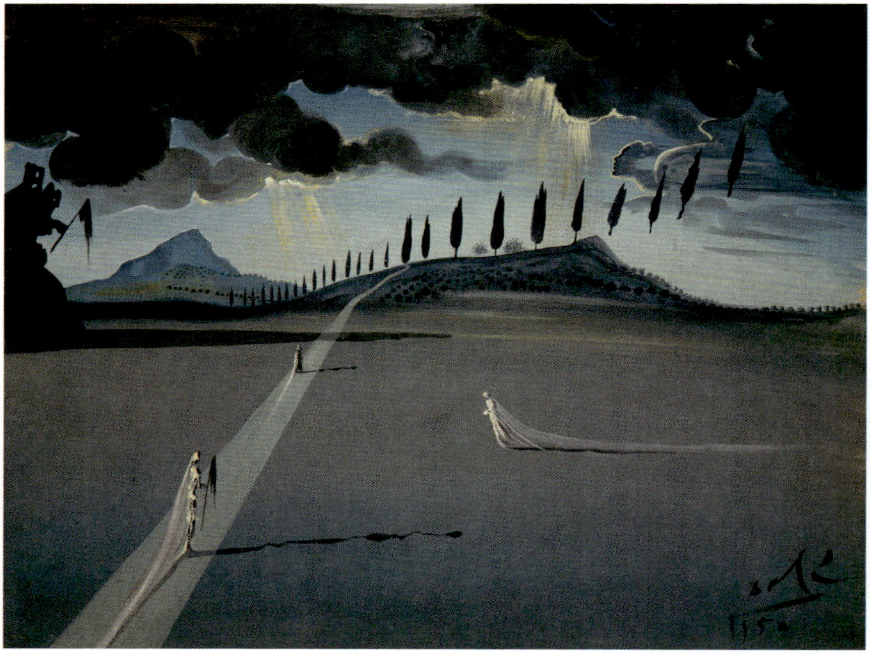

Salvador Dalí,
*Paisaje/Boceto para la escenografía de "Don Juan Tenorio"*, 1950

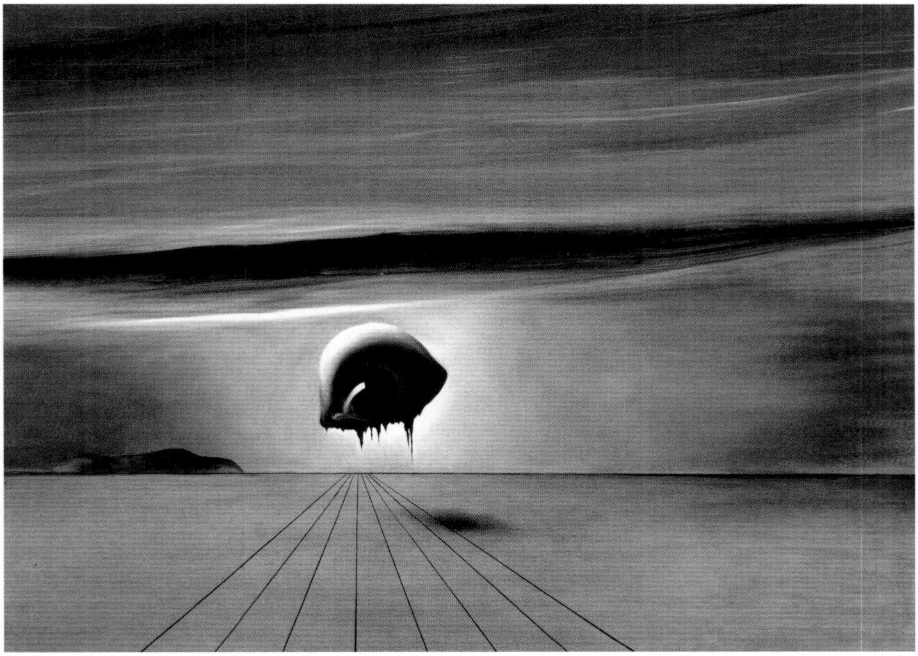

Salvador Dalí,
*The Eye*, 1944

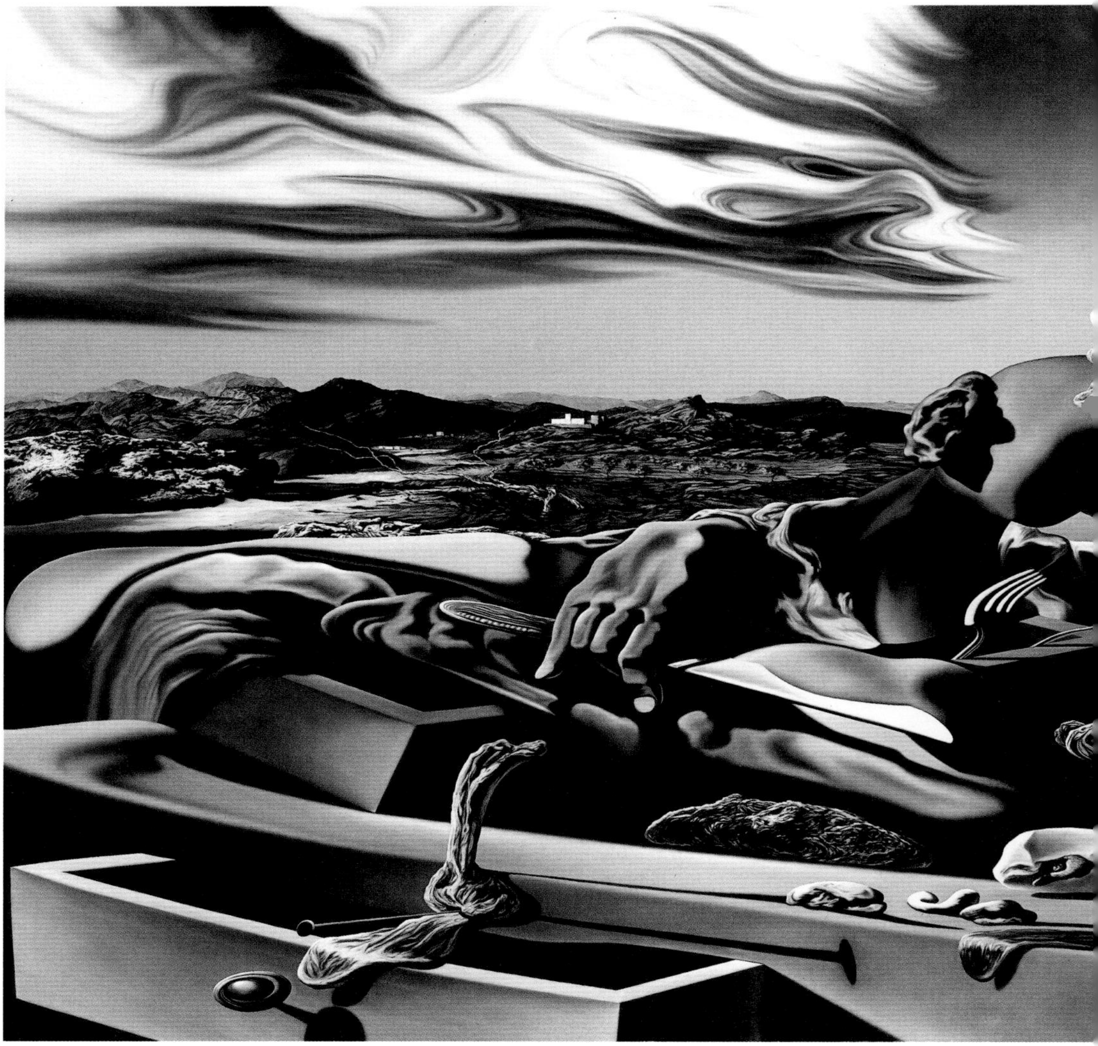

Glenn Brown,
*Oscillate Wildly (after "Autumn Cannibalism", 1936 by Salvador Dalí)*, 1999

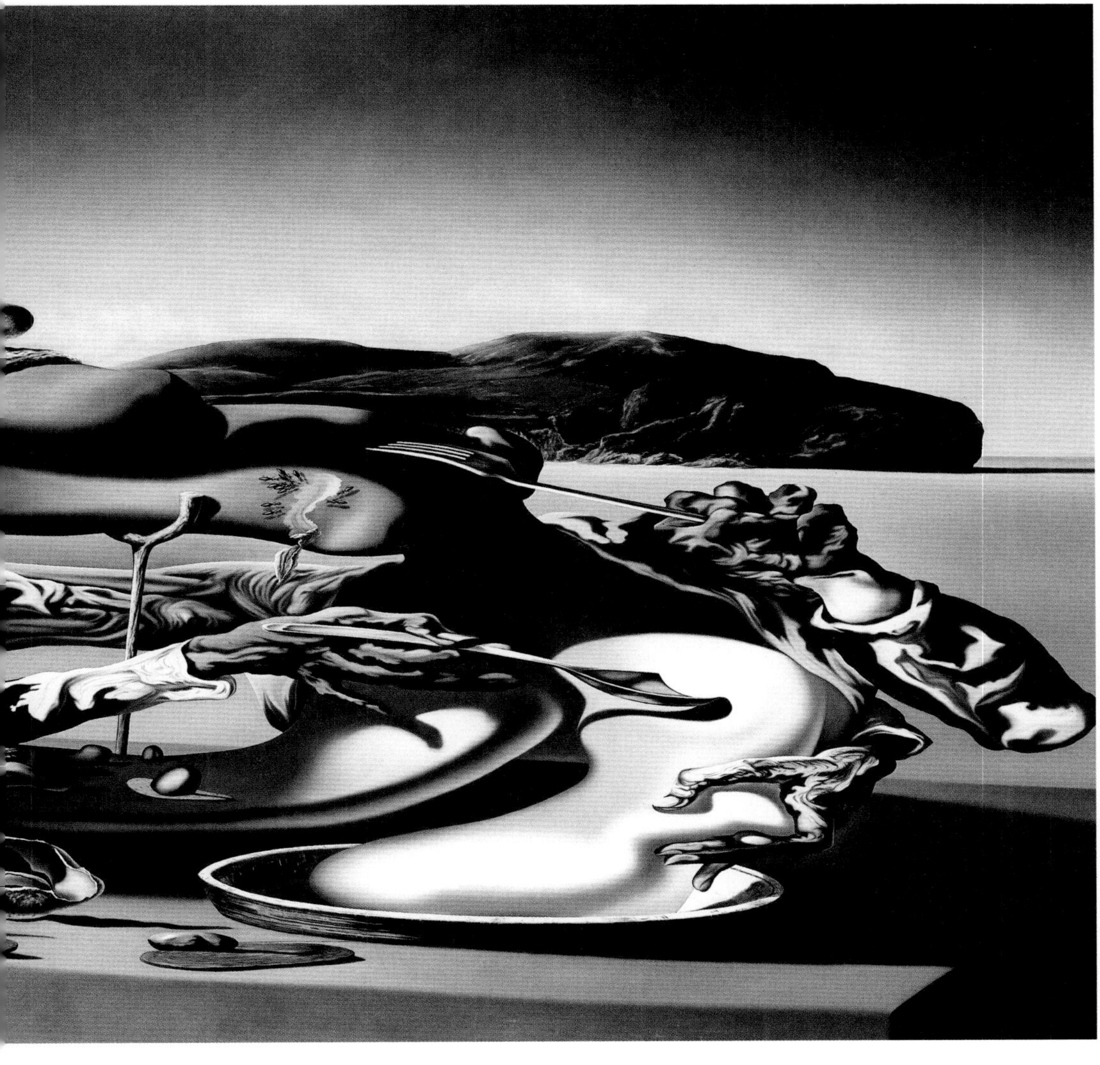

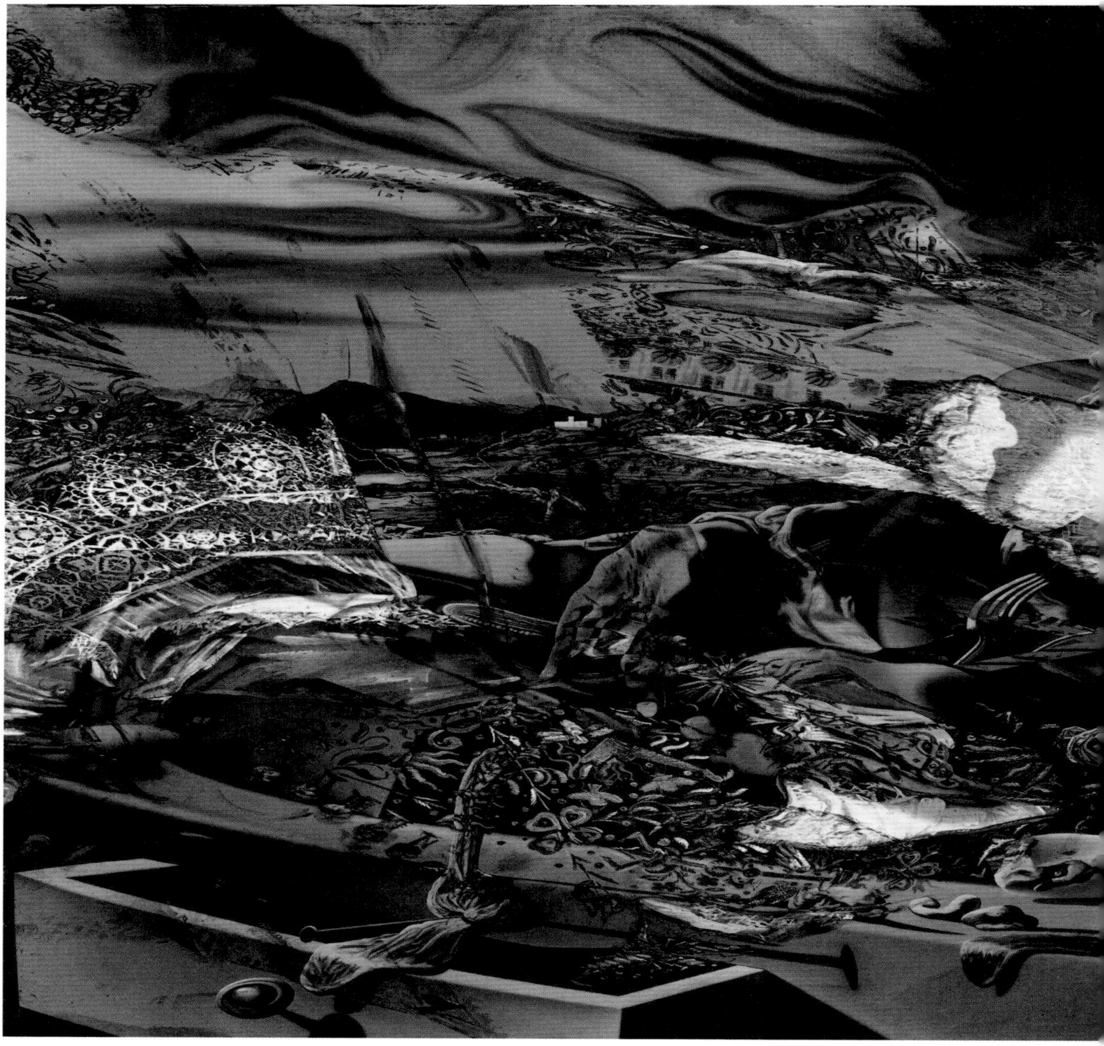

Glenn Brown,
*Two Personages in Love with a Woman (after "Autumnal Cannibalism", 1936 by Salvador Dalí, by kind permission of the Gala-Salvador Dalí Foundation) and (after "The Laughing Cavalier", 1624 by Frans Hals) for Phil King*, 2011

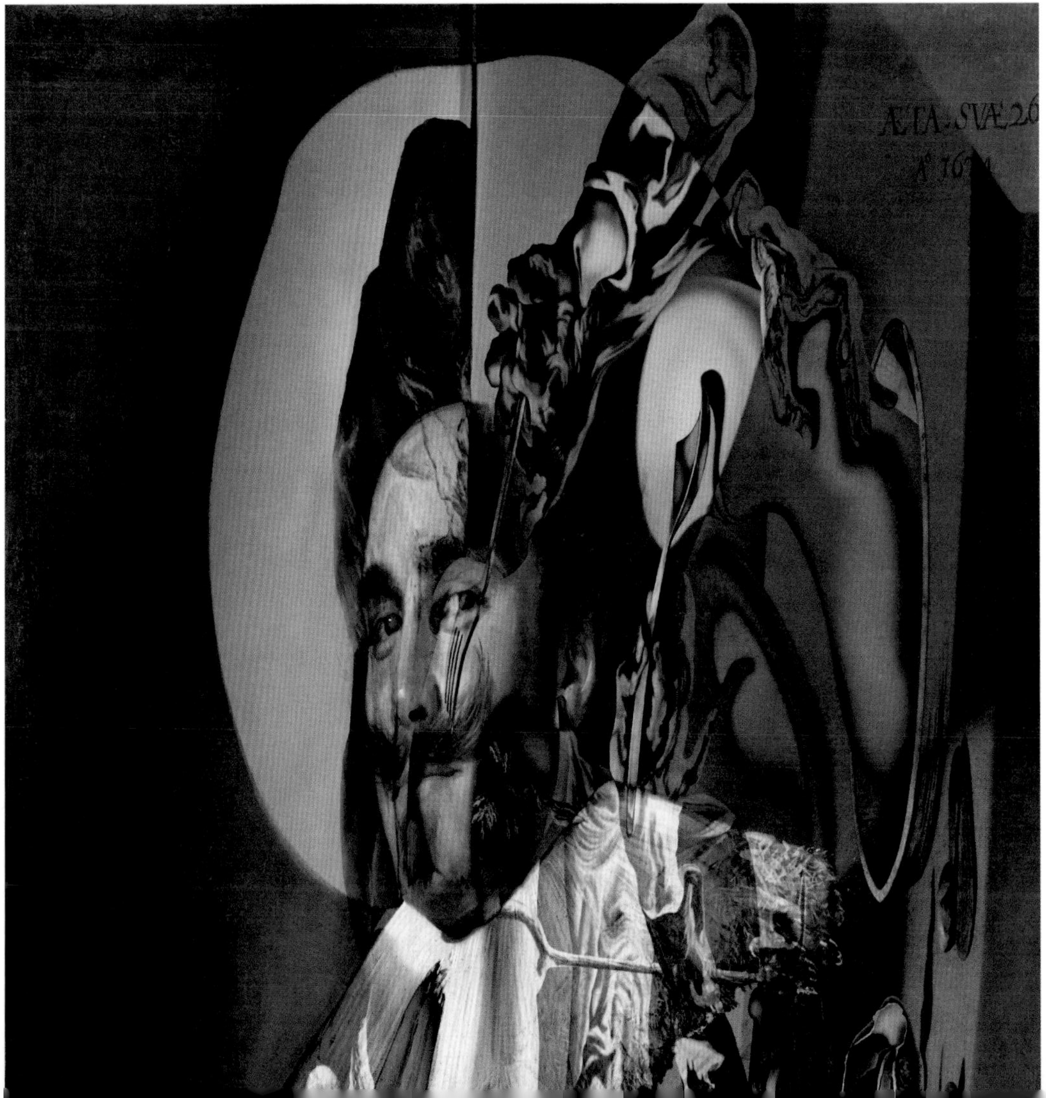
ÆTA: SVÆ 26
A° 16

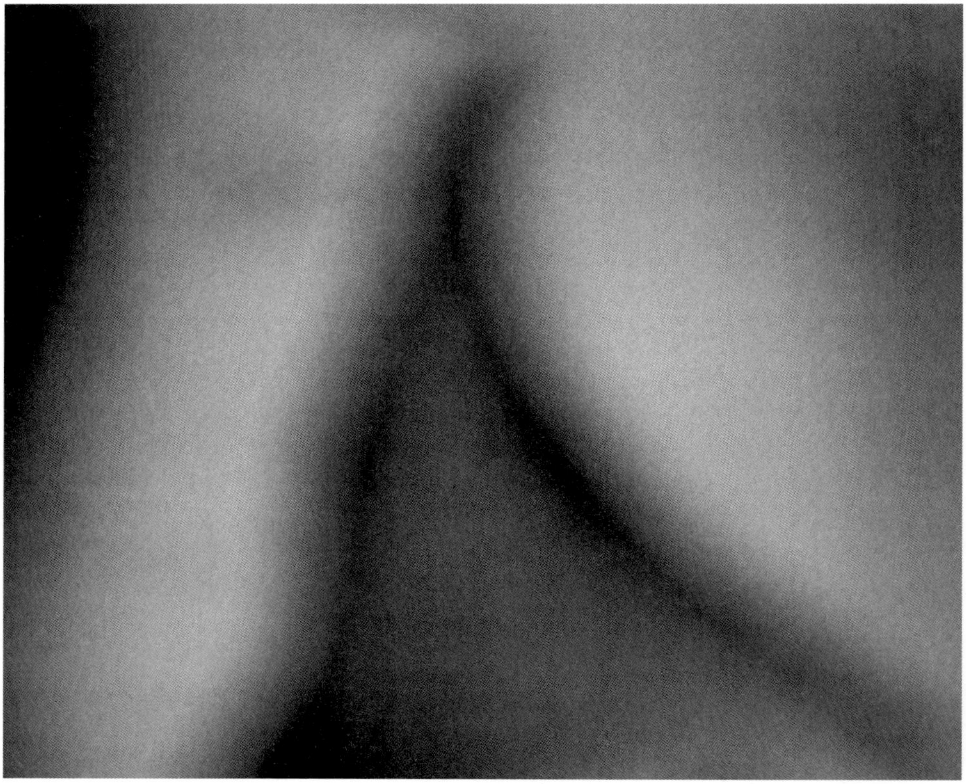

Glenn Brown,
*If God Exists Then Everything Is His Will II*, 2011

Glenn Brown,
*Love II*, 2011

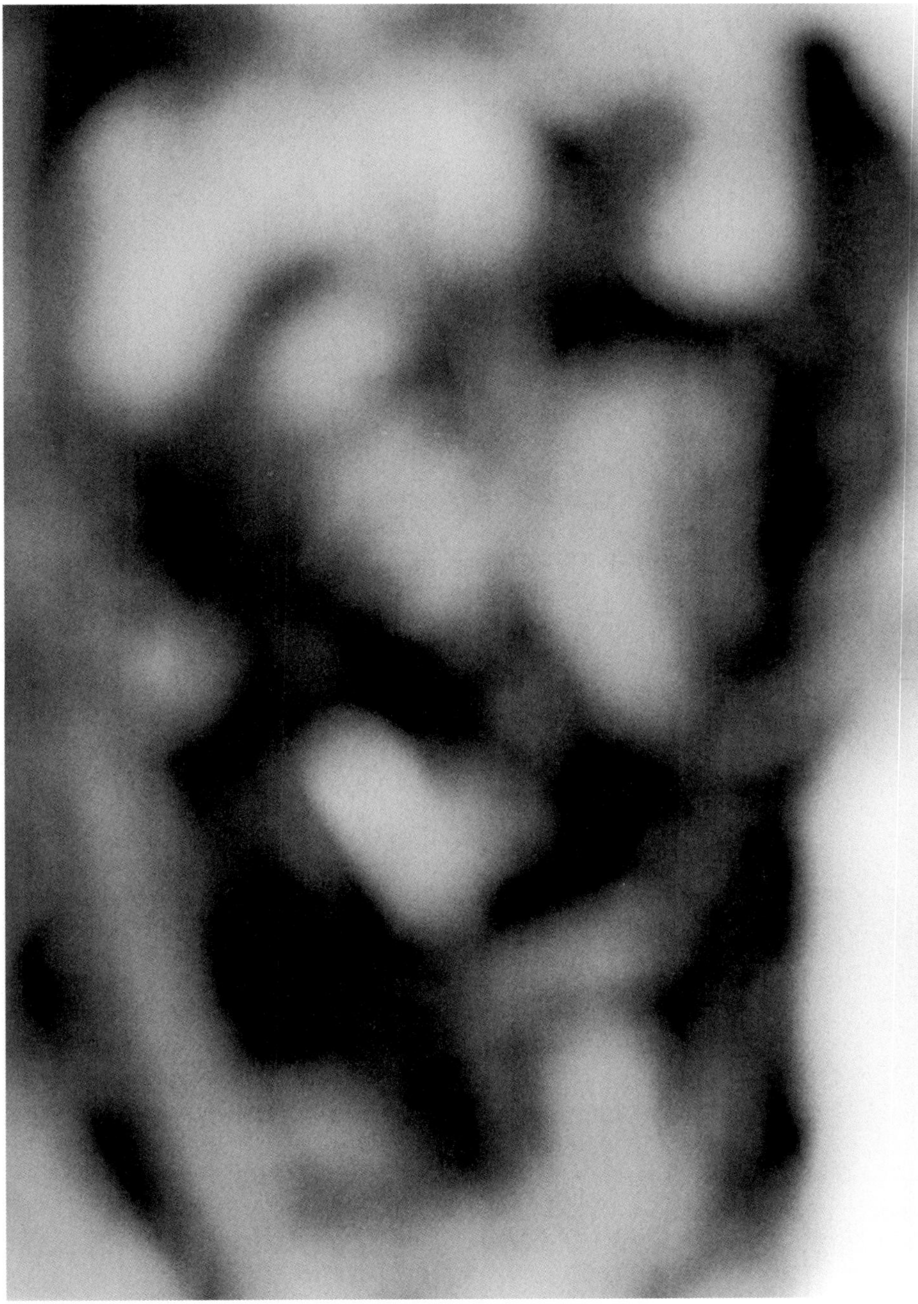

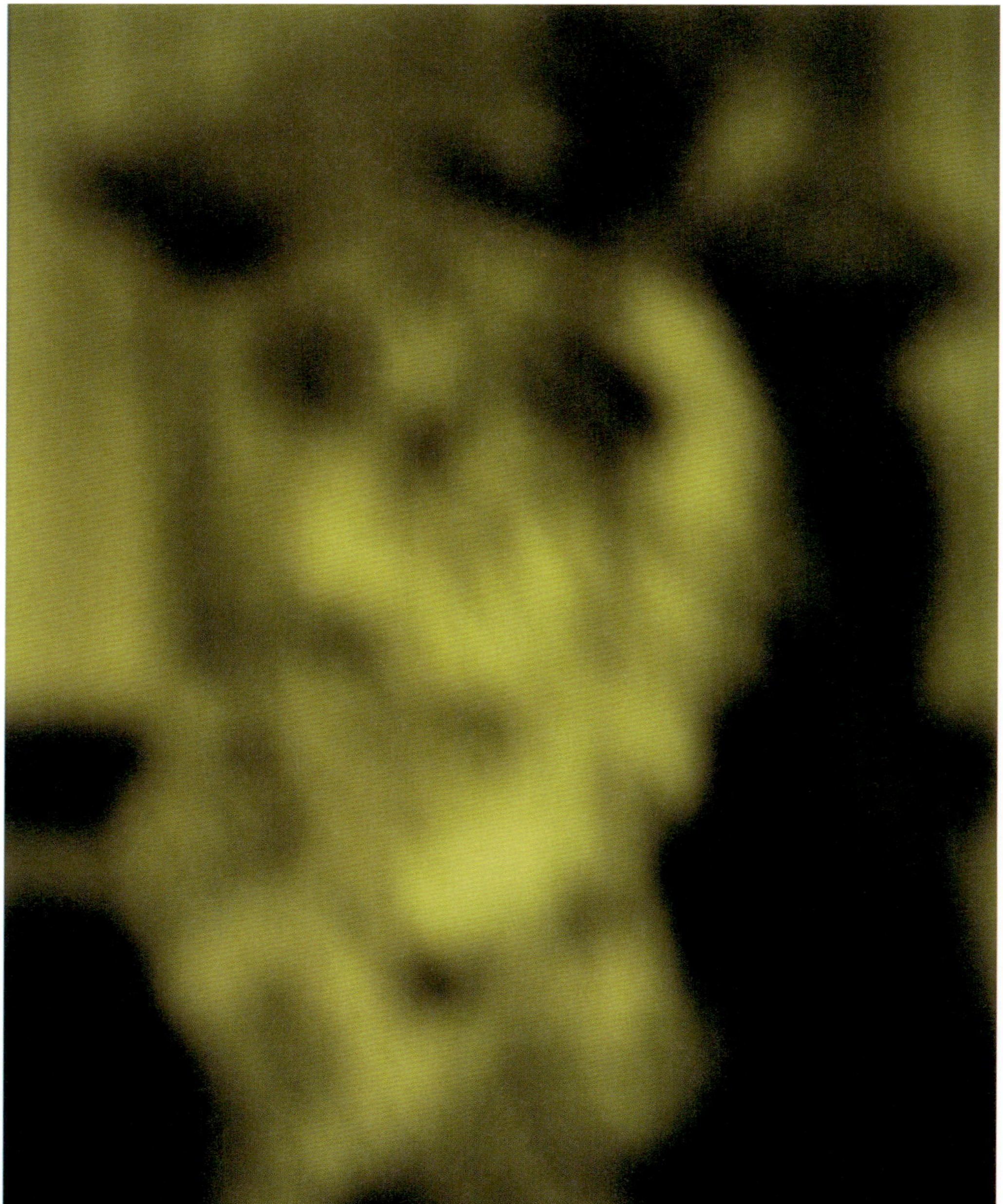

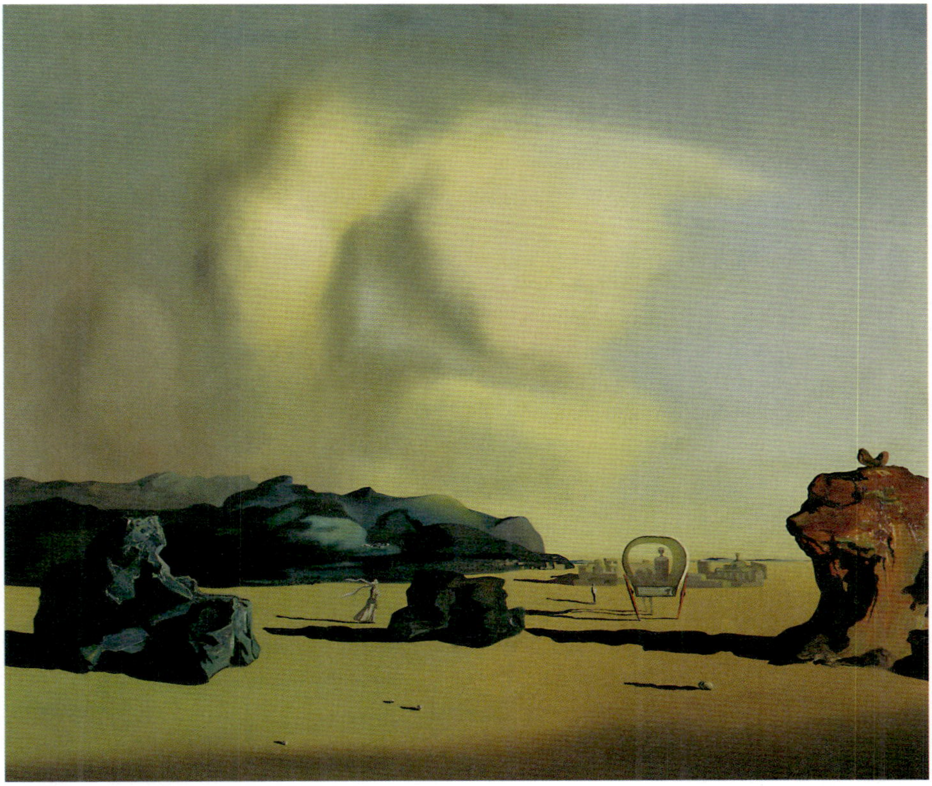

Glenn Brown,
*Paranoïac-Critical Method*, 1998

Salvador Dalí,
*Moment of Transition*, 1934

# David Lomas
# You Take My Place in this Showdown: Salvador Dalí und Glenn Brown

Die grundlegenden Ideen dieses Aufsatzes wurden bei der jährlichen Konferenz der UK Association of Art Historians im Jahr 2001 und einer Konferenz anlässlich der 100-Jahr-Feier von Salvador Dalí im Salvador Dalí Museum in St. Petersburg, Florida vorgestellt. Die Fortsetzung der Konferenz wurde als *New Critical Perspectives on Dalí at the Centennial* von William Jeffett et al. Bompiani 2004 herausgegeben.

Es gibt wenige große Künstler, die derart zwischen populärer Zustimmung und kritischer Geringschätzung schwanken, wie es bei Salvador Dalí immer schon der Fall war. Die Rezension der Ausstellung *Dalí's Optical Illusions* von Robert Hughes im *Time Magazine* vom März 2000 mit dem Titel „The Two Faces of Salvador Dalí" lässt die Kritik, die der Spanier „mit seinen treuherzig-fanatischen Augen" (Freud) nach wie vor anregt, erkennen. Dem Glanz von Dalís frühen Werdegang zum mutmaßlichen Betrug, Korruption und Fehlschlag der späteren Arbeiten widersprechend, bedient sich Hughes einer ergrauten, aber durchaus verlässlichen Kunstkritik. Seiner Kritik nach allerdings sei selbst der junge Dalí, ein hingebungsvoller Vertreter des täuschenden Illusionismus, des Tadels der „Zweigesichtigkeit" nicht enthoben:

> Nachdem viele Anstrengungen der modernen Malerei darauf angewendet wurden, die Illusion als Betrug, Lüge und Täuschung der tiefgründigeren Antriebe der Kunst zu verstoßen, versteht man, wie leicht Dalís Illusionismus als reine Gaunerei angegriffen werden konnte – eine Hochstapelei, die durch Dalís eklatante Bevorzugung Raffaels und sogar des erzakademischen Meissonier über Matisse oder Mondrian nur noch schlimmer wurde.



# David Lomas
# You Take My Place in this Showdown: Salvador Dalí with Glenn Brown

The main ideas in this essay were presented at the UK Association of Art Historians annual conference in 2001 and at a conference for the Salvador Dalí centennial in 2004 at The Salvador Dalí Museum, St. Petersburg, Florida. Proceedings of the latter were published as *New Critical Perspectives on Dalí at the Centennial*, ed. William Jeffett et al. (Bompiani, 2004).

There can be few major artists where such a glaring disparity exists between the level of popular acclaim and critical disdain, as has always been the case with Salvador Dalí. A review of the exhibition *Dalí's Optical Illusions* by Robert Hughes in *Time magazine* in March 2000 entitled "The Two Faces of Salvador Dalí" is indicative of the censure the Spaniard "with his candid, fanatical eyes" (Freud) still manages to inspire. Opposing the brilliance of Dalí's early career to the alleged fraudulence, corruption and failure of his later work, Hughes subscribes to a hoary but dependable trope of art criticism. Unpacking the terms of his critique, however, it would seem that not even early Dalí, as the devoted exponent of an eye-fooling illusionism, was above reproach for being "two-faced":

> Since a great deal of the effort of modernist painting was devoted to expelling illusion as a fraud, a lie and a cheat on the deeper impulses of art, one can easily see why Dalí's illusionism was so bitterly attacked as mere trickery – an imposture made even worse by Dalí's flagrant preference for Raphael and even the arch-academic Meissonier over Matisse or Mondrian.

Robert Hughes. "The Two Faces of Dalí," in *Time Magazine*, 20 March 2000, 58–60.

Robert Hughes, „The Two Faces of Dalí“, in: *Time Magazine*, 20. März 2000, S. 58–60.

Die Tricks und visuellen Pyrotechniken, die die Freier anziehen, haben ihn aber von jenen Verteidigern der heroischen Moderne entfernt, die ihn als einen verstehen, der Schindluder mit den Werten ihrer Tradition treibt. Die Beispiele der Schmähungen aufgrund Dalís Abtrünnigkeit vom Glauben gibt es zuhauf. Es ist daher erfrischend, dass die derzeitige Ausstellung Dalí in einem sympathischeren Licht zeichnet, indem sie einen Blick auf ihn durch die Augen zeitgenössischer Künstler erlaubt, die sich selbst von der Moderne entfernt haben, die mittlerweile zu großen Teilen als eine Strömung wahrgenommen wird, die ihren Verlauf bereits genommen hat. In diesem Aufsatz vertrete ich die Meinung, dass Dalí mehr als nur Wasser in der Mühle des aneignenden britischen Künstlers Glenn Brown ist. Das mühsame Kopieren ist eine Art der Hommage an einen Vorgänger mit dem Brown einiges gemeinsam hat. Mein Aufsatz beschäftigt sich mit dem Stellenwert des Modells, der Kopie und dem Vorrang, den wir dem Vergangenen geben. In diesem Fall, um auf Aspekte von Dalís Arbeitsweise hinzuweisen, die unserer Aufmerksamkeit bislang entgangen sein mögen: Die Kopie kommt auf das Original zurück und verändert unsere Wahrnehmung (und Bewertung). Indem ich den Titel meiner Arbeit einer von Browns Kopien von Dalís Arbeiten entlehne, werde ich im Zuge dessen erwägen, die beiden im Showdown der fortlaufenden Polemik zur Moderne in extremis auszutauschen.

Die eigentliche Quelle stammt vom Songtext *Heart and Soul* von Joy Division.

The tricks and visual pyrotechnics that draw in the punters have alienated him from the defenders of a heroic modernism, who see him as playing fast and loose with the values enshrined by that tradition. Many more examples could be cited of the opprobrium that is heaped on Dalí for his apostasy. Refreshingly, the current exhibition portrays Dalí in a more sympathetic light by allowing him to be seen through the eyes of contemporary artists, who have themselves taken leave from a modernism now widely viewed as having run its course. This essay will argue that Dalí is more than just grist to the appropriationist mill of the British artist, Glenn Brown. The act of laborious copying is a form of homage to a predecessor with whom Brown turns out to have quite a lot in common. My essay is concerned with the status of models and copies, and the priority we attribute to the former; in this case, by alerting us to aspects of Dalí's practice that may have eluded attention thus far, the copy rebounds on the original and alters our perception (and valuation) of it. Purloining my own title from one of Brown's copies of works by Dalí, I shall consider the two as trading places in the showdown and ongoing polemics over a modernism in *extremis*.

The actual source is the lyrics for *Heart and Soul* by Joy Division.

## Painting and the Simulacrum

In the run-up to the Turner Prize in 2000, it emerged that an entry by Brown, his *The Loves of Shepherds* (ill. 1), copied (more or less) a dust jacket illustration for a 1974 edition of *Double Star*, a novel by the cult science-fiction writer, Robert Heinlein (ill. 2). In the ensuing brouhaha,

Im Vorfeld des Turner Prizes im Jahr 2000 stellte sich heraus, dass der Beitrag Browns *The Loves of Shepherds* (Abb. 1) eine Illustration eines Schutzumschlags von der Novelle *Double Star* (Abb. 2) des Science-Fiction-Autors Robert Heinlein aus dem Jahr 1974 (mehr oder weniger) kopierte. Im daraus folgenden Tumult gabelten die Journalisten den Klappentext der Novelle auf: „Double, double – galactic trouble! Die Bühne für den größten Imitator ist bereit." Diese Details machten die Geschichte pikanter, schürten aber auch die Vermutung, dass die ganze Sache erfunden war. Manche mögen sagen, dass all das Teil des verlogenen Hypes des Turner Prizes ist und bis zu einem bestimmten Grad stimmt das auch. Aber der Verlauf der Geschichte brachte Aspekte auf, die für unser Thema von Bedeutung sind. Ein Artikel im *Daily Telegraph* etwa schrieb unverblümt, „die Diskussion, wann Inspiration aufhört und Plagiat beginnt, wurde wieder eröffnet." Ein Leitartikel in *The Times* vom 28. November, der die Geschichte aufdeckte, bemerkte zuversichtlich: „Kunst und Imitation sind alte Bettgenossen." Etwas ominöser war die Schlagzeile in derselben Zeitung am folgenden Tag: „Anwälte raten zur Kompensation." „Es handelt sich um einen eindeutigen Verstoß des Urheberrechts von 1988, da Roberts Arbeit von Brown reproduziert wurde", verlautbarte ein Anwalt. Ein anderer, der im Auftrag des Dalí Nachlasses schon einige Jahre zuvor in einem Disput mit Brown verhandelte, riet Tony Roberts, dem geschädigten Illustrator, das Werk „aushändigen und zerstören zu lassen" – eine etwas rachsüchtige Form der Wiedergutmachung, wie man meinen möchte – oder aber



journalists picked up on the blurb on the novel's back cover: "Double, double – galactic trouble! The stage was set for the greatest impersonation of all time." Such details added spice to the story but also a lingering suspicion that the whole thing had been cooked up. All part of the phoney hype that is the Turner Prize, you might say, and to some degree it was. But as the story ran, issues were aired that have a bearing upon our topic. As an article in the *Daily Telegraph* bluntly put it, "debate has re-opened about when inspiration ends and plagiarism begins." A leader article in *The Times* of November 28$^{th}$, which broke the story, sanguinely observed that: "Art and imitation have always been bedfellows." More ominous, however, was a headline in the same newspaper the next day: "Lawyers advise on a claim for compensation." "This is a clear infringement of the Copyright Designs Protection Act 1988 because the essence of Roberts's work has been reproduced in Brown," opined one lawyer. Another, who acted for the Dalí estate several years before in another dispute with Brown, advised that Tony Roberts, the aggrieved illustrator, could apply to have the offending work "delivered up and destroyed," a vindictive form of redress one might think, or else he could "seek an undertaking that no reproductions be made." The net effect of such a court order, redolent of archaic prohibitions against graven images, would have been to guarantee the uniqueness of a work that was deemed to be a derivative copy, doubly ironic given that the original in this case was a mass-reproduced image without any pretensions to high cultural status. One could go on, indeed the legal wrangling did. My point is that journalists, lawyers, and art world experts alike were exercised by

„eine Verpflichtungserklärung anzustreben, sodass keine Vervielfältigungen gemacht werden können." Das Endergebnis einer solchen Verfügung, die stark an archaische Verbote von Götzenbildern erinnert, wäre, die Einmaligkeit solcher Arbeiten zu garantieren, die als abgeleitete Kopie betrachtet wurden, was doppelt ironisch ist, nachdem das Original in diesem Falle ein massenproduziertes Bild ohne Anspruch auf hohe Kultur war. Man könnte das noch weiterspannen und der rechtliche Clinch tat das auch. Ich will damit sagen, dass die Journalisten, Anwälte und Kunstexperten in gleichem Maße durch die Störung der Mimesis, der Hierarchie von Modell und Kopie, die der westlichen Metaphysik zugrunde liegt, animiert wurden.

Das Konzept der Kopie *ohne* Original, das Konzept des Simulakrums, hat besonders in der Postmoderne an Aktualität gewonnen, und zwar ursprünglich im Rahmen einer Kritik der platonischen Repräsentation der französischen poststrukturalistischen Philosophen. Plato, der der Mimesis kritisch gegenüberstand, missbilligte die simulakre Kopie besonders. Den Platonismus zu überwinden bedeutete nach Gilles Deleuze, „dem Original der Kopie, dem Modell dem Bild gegenüber seine Vorrangstellung zu verweigern; die Herrschaft der Simulakren und der Spiegelung zu glorifizieren."

Gilles Deleuze, *Difference and Repetition*, übers. von Paul Patton, London 1994, S. 66.

Diese Ansicht wurde in Hinblick auf die Appropriation Art vielbeschworen. Theoretisch gesinnte Künstler, die mit diesem Trend assoziiert werden, nahmen sich hier Walter Ben-

a perturbation in the order of mimesis, that hierarchy of model and copy that underlies all of Western metaphysics.
The concept of a copy *without* an original, the concept of the simulacrum, has gained enormous currency within postmodernism. It did so initially in the context of a critique of Platonic representation by French poststructural philosophers. Plato, who was suspicious of mimesis in general, strongly disapproved of the simulacral copy. Overturning Platonism meant, in the words of Gilles Deleuze, "denying the primacy of original over copy, of model over image; glorifying the reign of simulacra and reflection."

Gilles Deleuze, *Difference and Repetition*, trans. Paul Patton, London, 1994, 66.

One situation where this notion has been subsequently invoked is in respect to appropriation art. The theoretically minded artists associated with this trend took their cue from Walter Benjamin's critique of the notions of originality and authorship in his famous essay *The Work of Art in the Age of its Technical Reproducibility*. Writing at the beginning of the 1980s, Douglas Crimp, a New York-based critic and curator, observed that:

> A group of young artists working with photography have addressed photography's claims to originality, showing those claims for the fictions they are, showing photographs to be always a representation, always-already-seen. Their images are purloined, confiscated, appropriated, stolen. In their work, the original cannot be located, is always deferred: even the self which might have generated an original is shown to be itself a copy.

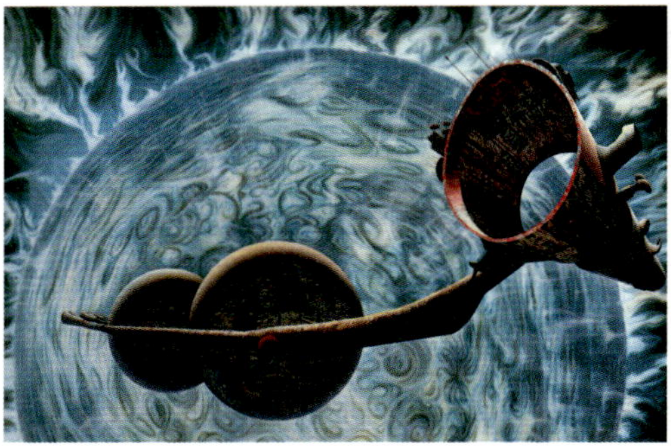

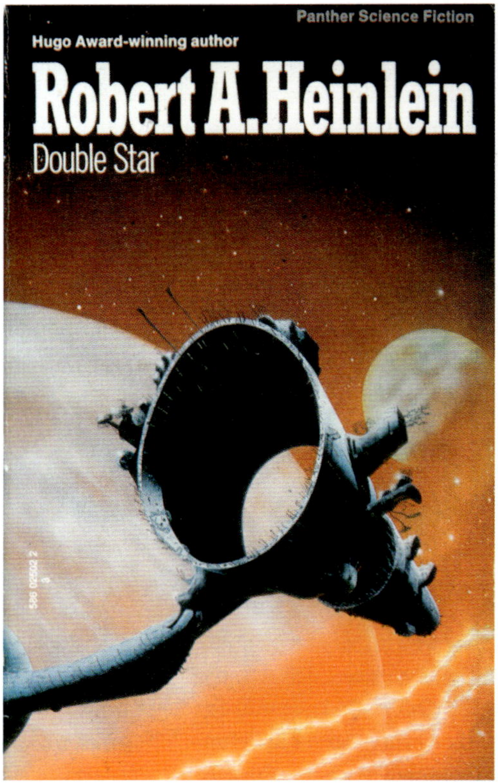


Abb./ill. 1: Glenn Brown,
*The Loves of Shepherd, after Tony Roberts*, 2000

Abb./ill. 2: Robert A. Heinlein,
*Double Star*, 1974

jamins Kritik an Originalität und Urheberschaft in seinem berühmten Aufsatz *Das Kunstwerk im Zeitalter seiner technischen Reproduzierbarkeit* zum Vorbild. Der New Yorker Kritiker und Kurator Douglas Crimp bemerkte Anfang der achtziger Jahre:

„Eine Gruppe junger Künstler, die mit Fotografie arbeiten, haben den Anspruch der Fotografie auf Originalität in Frage gestellt, indem sie sie als Fiktion entlarven und zeigen, dass die Fotografie immer eine Repräsentation von etwas bereits Gesehen-en ist. Die Bilder sind entwendet, konfis-ziert, zu eigen gemacht, gestohlen. In ihren Arbeiten kann das Original nicht ausfindig gemacht werden, sondern ist immer zurückgestellt: Selbst die treibende Kraft, die ein Original hätte produzieren können, erweist sich als Kopie."

Douglas Crimp, „The Photographic Activity of Postmodernism", in: *October* 15 (1980), S. 98.

Crimp war Mitherausgeber des Magazins *October*, das diese Gruppe von Künstlern (Sherrie Levine, Richard Prince u. a.) gefördert hat und war darüber hinaus sehr einflussreich, indem er für die Veröffentlichung der Übersetzungen einiger Schlüsseltexte von Deleuze, Derrida und Foucault verantwortlich zeichnete. Zu dieser Zeit stand *October* im Vorfeld der Neubewertung des Surrealismus, den sie im Dienste der Postmoderne wähnten. Glenn Brown ist ein junger Abkömmling dieser „pictures generation", wie sie von einer Ausstellung kürzlich getauft wurde, er unterscheidet sich aber von dieser in mehrfacher Hinsicht, nicht zuletzt in seiner Bezugnahme auf Dalí, einer Persönlichkeit, die von der älteren Generation von Künstlern und Autoren immer wieder gemieden wurde.

Douglas Crimp, "The Photographic Activity of Postmodernism," in *October* 15 (1980), 98.

Crimp was an editor of *October* magazine, which promoted this group of artists (Sherrie Levine, Richard Prince, et al.) and was, moreover, influential by virtue of publishing, in translation, a number of key texts by Deleuze, Derrida, and Foucault. During the same period, *October* was at the forefront of a re-assessment of surrealism that saw it placed in the service of postmodernism. Glenn Brown is a younger progeny of the "picture generation" as it has been anointed in a recent exhibition, but differs from them in a number of respects, not least in his receptiveness to the work of Dalí – a figure consistently shunned by this older generation of artists and writers.

See The *Pictures Generation, 1974–1984*, exh. cat., The Metropolitan Museum of Art, New York, 2009. Among the artists in this show were Jack Goldstein, Barbara Kruger, Louise Lawler, Sherrie Levine, Robert Longo, Allan McCollum, Richard Prince, David Salle, and Cindy Sherman.

It turns out that Dalí was actually remarkably prescient in introducing the simulacrum to surrealist discourse. He does so in the course of espousing the paranoïac-critical method whose superiority over the Bretonian surrealist orthodoxy of psychic automatism he would soon proclaim. Altogether, the words 'simulacra' and 'simulacral' recur more than a dozen times smattered throughout "The Rotting Donkey," the manifesto statement of his aesthetic credo, along with the other essays collected together and published as *La Femme visible* in 1930. Buried within "The Sanitary Goat," another of

Siehe *The Pictures Generation, 1974–1984*, Ausst.-Kat., The Metropolitan Museum of Art, New York 2009. Weitere Künstler waren Jack Goldstein, Barbara Kruger, Louise Lawler, Sherrie Levine, Robert Longo, Allan McCollum, Richard Prince, David Salle und Cindy Sherman.

So kann man sagen, dass Dalí ungemein vorausschauend war, was die Einführung des Simulakrum in den surrealistischen Diskurs angeht, indem er die paranoisch-kritische Methode unterstützte, die er bald der bretonischen surrealistischen Orthodoxie des psychischen Automatismus als überlegen voranstellen würde. Die Worte „Simulakrum“ und „simulakral“ kommen etwa ein Dutzend Mal verstreut im Manifest seines ästhetischen Credos „Der Eselskadaver“ vor, das gemeinsam mit anderen gesammelten Aufsätzen unter dem Titel *La Femme visible* 1930 veröffentlicht wurde.

Die deutsche Übersetzung von Dalís Schriften verwendet den Terminus „Wahnbild“. Der Deleuze'sche Begriff wird mit Trugbild übersetzt. (Anm. der Redaktion).

In „Die Sanitätsziege“ verbirgt sich ein bizarres Gedankenexperiment. Indem er einen nach seinen Angaben beliebigen Punkt veranschaulicht, bezieht sich Dalí auf eine „für gewöhnlich für velleitär gehaltene Geste eines Menschen, der auf einem Marmortisch den sicheren Fingersatz eines richtigen Pianisten (höchst vollkommen) nachahmt, obwohl er überhaupt nicht Klavier spielen kann, wobei er von der völligen Identität seiner Nachahmung überzeugt ist.“

Salvador Dalí, „Die Sanitätsziege“, in: Ders., *Unabhängigkeitserklärung der Phantasie und Erklärung*

the texts anthologised in the book, is a bizarre thought experiment. By way of illustrating what he calls a gratuitous point, Dalí refers to "the gesture, generally taken to be erratic, of a person who, without knowing how to play the piano, imitates (perfectly) on a marble table the confident fingering of a true pianist, convinced of the absolute similarity of his imitation." The gratuitous point, which we may suspect is a parody of Breton's 'point sublime,' Dalí continues: "would materialize precisely at the moment when the fake pianist would lose for a moment his absolute faith in his imitation, but would continue with it nonetheless with no less enthusiasm."

Salvador Dalí, *The Collected Writings of Salvador Dalí*, trans. Haim Finkelstein, Cambridge, 1998, 229.

Poised always on the cusp between truth and falsehood, the real and the imaginary, the sincere and the insincere, Dalí's entire project as an artist and individual is oriented toward this gratuitous point. Encapsulated in the celebrated dictum, "The only difference between myself and a madman is that I am not mad," this asymptotic point is a wellspring for Dalí's distinctive brand of humour as well as, more problematically, the resultant moral ambiguity that attends so much of what he does and says. The passage quoted above ends with a resounding affirmation: "Simulacra at the service of thought, reality at the service of simulacra – no longer could anything prevent those who still retain a faint idea of honesty from relying on the reality of the prodigious and identical imitation of the pianist."

Ibid.

*der Rechte des Menschen auf seine Verrücktheit.* *Gesammelte Schriften*, hg. von Axel Matthes und Tilbert Diego Stegemann. München 1974, S. 139.

Der beliebige Punkt, den man als eine Parodie auf Bretons „point sublime" verstehen kann, so Dalí weiter, würde: „in dem Augenblick konkret [...], wo der falsche Pianist momentan den absoluten Glauben an seine Nachahmung verlöre, sie aber fast genauso begeistert wie zuvor fortsetzte."

Ebd.

Immer an der Schwelle zwischen Wahrheit und Unwahrheit, dem Realen und dem Imaginären, aufrichtig und unaufrichtig, orientiert sich Dalís Projekt als Künstler und Individuum an diesem beliebigen Punkt, was in dem berühmten Spruch „der einzige Unterschied zwischen einem Verrückten und mir ist der, dass ich nicht verrückt bin" zum Ausdruck gebracht wird. Dieser asymptotische Punkt ist eine Quelle für Dalís charakteristischen Humor, so wie auch, etwas problematischer, die daraus resultierende moralische Ambiguität, die sein Handeln und seine Worte so oft begleiten. Der oben zitierte Absatz endet mit einer klangvollen Bekräftigung: „Die Wahnbilder im Dienst des Denkens, die Wirklichkeit im Dienst der Wahnbilder, nichts mehr wird künftige Leute, die noch einen schwachen Begriff von Ehrlichkeit haben, daran hindern können, mit der Wirklichkeit der *wunderbaren* und identischen Nachahmung des Pianisten zu rechnen [...]."

Ebd.

Dalí first applied the term 'simulacrum' to his reversing double and multiple images that were supposed to propagate according to the dictates of his desire independently of any external referent. He confidently predicts that such a visual demonstration would serve to discredit reality.

Salvador Dalí, "The Rotting Donkey" (1930), in *Collected Writings*, 223–226.

That the theme of the simulacrum continued to inform Dalí's preoccupation with optical illusions is evident in the latter part of the 1930s in a group of large paintings whose complex permutations of imagery André Breton somewhat unfairly dismissed as picture puzzles. Intriguingly, a new personage also makes his entrance in works such as *The Endless Enigma*: the figure of a reclining philosopher (Plato?) in the act of contemplating – as well he might, to judge from the mind-boggling title of one of the more resolved images from this period, *Transparent Simulacrum of a Feigned Illusion* (1938, ill. 3). As the exhibition *Dalí's Optical Illusions* showed, there is a consistent thread spanning Dalí's career, which led him eventually to the hologram as the realisation of his lifelong quest for a perfect simulacrum.

The motif of virtuality, and the power of visual illusions to deceive, are integral to the myth of Narcissus, the subject for one of Dalí's best-known paintings. Narcissus fell in love with a mere reflection, preferring it to the flesh and blood nymphs and youths who tried to seduce him. Here I wish to emphasise what Julia Kristeva aptly describes as "the concomitance of narcissism and the fake."

Dalí wendete den Terminus Simulakrum das erste Mal bei seinen Umkehrbildern an, die sich nach seinem Wunsche und unabhängig eines äußeren Bezugspunktes verbreiten sollten. Selbstbewusst sagt er voraus, dass diese visuelle Demonstration dazu diene, die Wirklichkeit anzuzweifeln.

Salvador Dalí, „Der Eselskadaver" (1930), in: Ders., *Gesammelte Schriften*, S. 131–135.

Dass das Thema des Simulakrum Dalís Auseinandersetzung mit optischen Illusionen weiterhin anregen sollte, erschließt sich gegen Ende der dreißiger Jahre in einer Anzahl großer Gemälde, deren komplexe Umsetzung von Symbolen von André Breton als Bilderpuzzle heruntergespielt wurde. Interessanterweise scheint eine neue Persönlichkeit in Werken wie *Das endlose Rätsel* auf: die Figur des liegenden Philosophen (Plato?) beim Denken – wie zu erwarten, wenn man den schwindelerregenden Titel eines seiner abgeklärteren Bilder der Zeit *Das durchsichtige Scheinbild* (1938, Abb. 3) bedenkt. Die Ausstellung *Dalí's Optical Illusions* zeigte, dass es einen roten Faden in Dalís Karriere gibt, der ihn schließlich zum Hologramm als Verwirklichung seiner lebenslangen Suche nach dem perfekten Simulakrum führte.

Das Sujet der Virtualität und die Täuschungskraft der visuellen Illusionen sind integrale Bestandteile des Mythos des Narziss, einem von Dalís berühmtesten Motiven. Narziss verliebte sich in sein Spiegelbild, das er dem Fleisch und Blut der Nymphen und Jünglinge, die ihn zu verführen suchten, bevorzugte. An dieser Stelle möchte ich betonen, was Julia Kristeva so treffend als „die Gleichzeitigkeit von Narzissmus und Fälschung"



Julia Kristeva, *Tales of Love*, trans. Leon S. Roudiez, New York, 1987, 126.

Dalí consistently prefers the 'false' to the 'true': recounting his past in *The Secret Life of Salvador Dalí* he affirms that, as with jewels, false memories are always more brilliant, more real, than true ones.

Salvador Dalí, *The Secret Life of Salvador Dalí*, trans. Haakon M Chevalier, London, 1981 [1942], 38.

One of the anecdotes he relates concerns the invention of a sort of decoy – a 'false phobia' – to thwart his school friends' malicious delight in provoking his very genuine fear of grasshoppers. "For a real terror," he writes, "I had thus succeeded in substituting its simulation."

Dalí, *The Secret Life*, 131.

*The Secret Life of Salvador Dalí* projects back to childhood views and enthusiasms held by Dalí when he wrote the book: though it was more than a decade after he had first joined the surrealists, it shows just how much the simulation problematic continued to dominate his self-perception. Haim Finkelstein elicits a thematics of falseness – false gold, false bronze, false shit, etc. – in Dalí's poem "The Great Masturbator" (1930), and which, in the same text, is termed a mimetic confounding.

Dalí, *Collected Writings*, 175.

Intriguingly, Brown has spoken about his art's positive alliance with the fake: "You don't quite know what you're looking at: you see brush marks, but they're not real brush marks – they're fake in one sense."

Julia Kristeva, *Tales of Love*, übers. von Leon S. Roudiez. New York 1987, S. 126.

beschreibt. Dalí favorisierte das „Falsche" gegenüber dem „Echten": In den Erzählungen aus seiner Vergangenheit in *Das geheime Leben des Salvador Dalí* bestätigt er, dass ähnlich wie bei Schmuck, unechte Erinnerungen immer besser und echter sind als die tatsächlichen.

Salvador Dalí, *Das geheime Leben des Salvador Dalí. Sonderausgabe zum 100. Geburtstag*. München 2004, S. 71.

Eine seiner Anekdoten handelt von der Erfindung einer Art von Köder – einer „falschen Phobie" –, um seine böswilligen Schulfreunde daran zu hindern, ihn mit seiner tatsächlichen Angst vor Grashüpfern zu quälen. „Den echten Schrecken", so schreibt er, „ersetzte ich mit einer Simulation."

Ebd., S. 223f.

*Das geheime Leben des Salvador Dalí* führt zurück zu Kindheitserinnerungen und -begeisterungen, die Dalí zur Zeit des Schreibens seines Buchs empfand: Auch wenn er den Surrealisten schon über ein Jahrzehnt beigetreten war, so zeigt es, wie sehr die Simulations-Problematik seine Selbstwahrnehmung beherrschte. Haim Finkelstein sieht in Dalís Gedicht „Der große Masturbator" (1930) die Thematik des Unechten – unechtes Gold, unechte Bronze, unechte Scheiße etc. – und das, was im selben Text mimetische Verwechslung genannt wird.

Salvador Dalí, *Gesammelte Schriften*, a.a.O., S. 141ff.

The absence of any distinction between model and copy in the double marks it as the supreme form of the simulacrum. The double is hence an impossible aporia for Platonic thought. Dalí considered himself to have been a simulacral replica of an elder brother also named Salvador who died just over nine months before he was born. In *The Secret Life of Salvador Dalí*, his mock confessional autobiography, Dalí says that he and his brother were indistinguishable, like two drops of water.

This comment, from *The Secret Life of Salvador Dalí* (p.2), echoes a passage from Breton's "Introduction to the Discourse on the Paucity of Reality": "[W]hatever may be written to the contrary, two leaves of the same tree are exactly alike. They are even the same leaf. I insist that if two drops of water have such a resemblance, it is because there is but one drop," in *What is Surrealism? Selected Writings*, ed. Franklin Rosemount, New York, 1978, 23.

Ian Gibson, in *The Shameful Life of Salvador Dalí*, scoffs at this suggestion, but in his dogged biographer's quest for the 'real' Dalí, I think that he misses the point. More in sympathy with Dalí's objectives in *Portrait of My Dead Brother* (1963, ill. 4), with its blow-up of the one extant photograph of the disappeared elder brother and its multiple references to processes of replication, including the double helix of their shared DNA, is a book by cultural historian Hillel Schwartz, *The Culture of the Copy: Striking Likenesses, Unreasonable Facsimiles*, an amazing compilation that chronicles the myriad ways in which living in a culture of the copy redefines our sense of self. Schwartz asks a question that is highly pertinent to Dalí: "Are we little else but

Interessanterweise hat sich Brown zum positiven Bündnis seiner Kunst mit dem Unechten geäußert: „Man weiß nicht genau, was man betrachtet: Man sieht Pinselstriche, aber es sind keine echten Pinselstriche – sie sind auf gewisse Art unecht."

Das zweifache Fehlen des Unterschieds zwischen Modell und Kopie mutiert er zu einer Höchstform des Simulakrum. Das Zweifache ist daher eine unmögliche Aporie des platonischen Gedankens. Dalí verstand sich selbst als eine simulakre Kopie seines älteren Bruders, der ebenso Salvador hieß und nur neun Monate vor seiner Geburt verstarb. In *Das geheime Leben des Salvador Dalí*, seiner Pseudo-Autobiografie, schreibt Dalí, dass er und sein Bruder nicht zu unterscheiden waren und sich wie ein Tropfen Wasser dem anderen glichen.



Das Zitat aus *Das geheime Leben des Salvador Dalí* (S. 219), gibt eine Passage aus Bretons „Introduction to the Discourse on the Paucity of Reality" wieder: „Was auch Gegensätzliches gesagt werden mag, zwei Blätter eines Baumes sind einander gleich. Sie sind gar dasselbe Blatt. Ich beharre darauf, dass zwei Tropfen einander so ähneln weil sie an sich derselbe sind.", in: *What is Surrealism? Selected Writings.*, hg. von Franklin Rosemount. New York 1978, S. 23.

In Ian Gibsons *The Shameful Life of Salvador Dalí* verspottet der Autor diese Theorie, aber auf der beharrlichen Suche des Biografen nach dem „echten" Dalí, hat er hier etwas Wesentliches nicht verstanden. Dichter an Dalís Ansatz in *Bildnis meines toten Bruders* (1963, Abb. 4), mit einer Vergrößerung einer erhaltenen Fotografie des verlorenen älteren Bruders und mehrfachen Hinweisen auf Replikationspro-

futile reenactments, or is reenactment the little enough that we can truly be about?"

Hillel Schwartz, *The Culture of the Copy: Striking Likenesses, Unreasonable Facsimiles*, New York, 1996, 377.

Unlike the ultimately rather tedious 1980s appropriation art, Brown does not simply replicate the pictures he copies: he manipulates, stretches, and warps them. The act of painting is also an occasion for Brown to free associate on his sources, hybridising pictures and titles. The logic of blending Dalí with appropriated sci-fi imagery owes in part to their lowbrow, populist appeal. "Fragonard is chocolate boxy, Dalí is archetypal adolescent surrealism, science fiction is sensationalist and utopian, appealing art for the masses," observes Brown.

Interview with Stephen Hepworth, 67.

But it is also justified by the fact that both these image categories conjure up an impossible, simulacral unreality using the pictorial devices of realism. Anxieties regarding an image world deprived of reference, a consequence of the increasing mediation of reality by photography, television, and now digital images – what Jean Baudrillard in a dystopic mood would term 'the desert of the real itself' – had begun to be registered by science fiction writers in the 1960s well before the simulacrum had become a hot topic in continental philosophy.

Jean Baudrillard, "Simulacra and Science Fiction" in *Simulacra and Simulation*, Ann Arbor, 1994, 121–127.

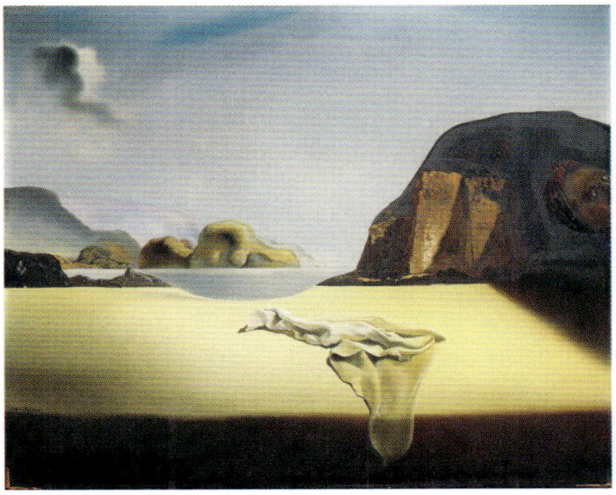

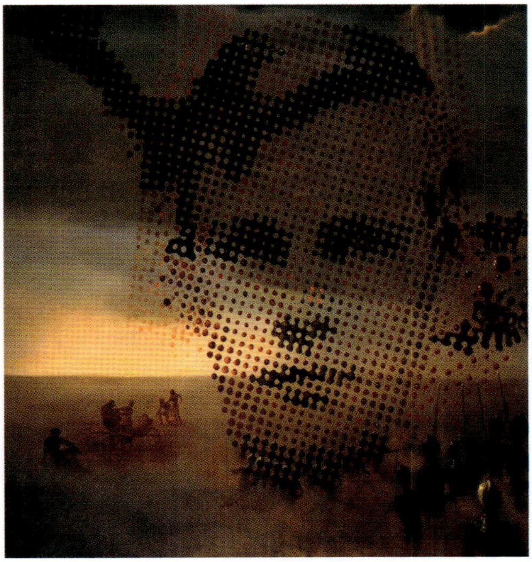

Abb./ill. 3: Salvador Dalí,
*Das durchsichtige Scheinbild des falschen Bildes/*
*Transparent Simulacrum of a Feigned Illusion*, 1938

Abb./ill. 4: Salvador Dalí,
*Bildnis meines toten Bruders/*
*Portrait of My Dead Brother*, 1963

zesse, einschließlich der Doppelhelix der gemeinsamen DNA, reicht da das Buch des Kulturhistorikers Hillel Schwartz *The Culture of the Copy: Striking Likenesses, Unreasonable Facsimiles* heran. Es handelt sich hierbei um eine verblüffende Sammlung von Berichten der unzähligen Arten, in der sich unser Selbstverständnis eines Lebens in einer Kultur der Kopie neu definiert. Schwartz stellt eine für Dalí höchst relevante Frage: „Sind wir kaum mehr als ein machtloses Nachahmen, oder ist Nachahmung das Wenige, das wir wirklich sein können?"

Hillel Schwartz, *The Culture of the Copy: Striking Likenesses, Unreasonable Facsimiles*. New York 1996, S. 377.



Anders als in der schlussendlich doch sehr peniblen Appropriation Art der achtziger Jahre, kopiert Brown nicht einfach Bilder, er manipuliert, dehnt und verzerrt sie. Das Malen an sich ist eine Gelegenheit für Brown anhand seiner Quellen frei zu assoziieren, Bilder und Titel zu hybridisieren. Die Idee Dalí mit Sci-Fi-Bildern zu vereinen, führt auf deren unprätentiösen, populären Reiz zurück. „Fragonard ist schokoladig, Dalí ist archetypischer, adoleszenter Surrealismus, Science-Fiction ist sensationslüstern und utopisch, die gefällige Kunst der Masse", bemerkt Brown.

Aus einem Interview mit Stephen Hepworth, S. 67.

Das wird auch durch den Umstand gerechtfertigt, dass beide Bildkategorien eine unmögliche, simulakrale Unwirklichkeit durch einen bildlichen Realismus heraufbeschwören. Die Ängste betreffend einer Bilderwelt ohne Bezugs-

As Brown seems also to have recognised, the strange deserted vistas and spatio-temporal disjunctures that derealise pictorial space in Dalí resonate with these later accounts of postmodernity. Dalí is a master of hyper-reality. It is notable that English author J.G. Ballard, who adapted the science fiction genre in order to chronicle the contemporary predicament, was a long-time champion of Dalí.

## Ersatz Modernism

It was amidst the highly polarised cultural landscape of the 1930s – a decade in which Dalí's reputation snowballed in the United States – that Clement Greenberg, the arch-defender of modernism, first came to prominence. His writing during that decade culminated with the publication of "Avant-Garde and Kitsch" in the journal *Partisan Review* in autumn 1939. The pivotal importance of that essay is undoubtedly because, as T.J. Clark writes, it sets out the main tenets of a theory of modernism that would persist largely unaltered in Greenberg's subsequent writings. Clark's concern is with the historical consciousness that he claims backs up the defence of modernism in these early texts but that is obscured by the later formalist apologias. It could be argued, however, that the attempt at historical justification only ever occurs *post facto* and even in these early texts serves to rationalise a prior discrimination that Greenberg makes between 'good' (morally and aesthetically superior) and 'bad' forms of imitation. Greenberg does not endorse a simple opposition between abstraction and illusion, as is sometimes erroneously thought, but rather follows Aristotle's *Poetics* in maintaining that all art is mimetic. Thus, modernism itself is a form punkte, einer Konsequenz der wachsenden Vermittlung von Wirklichkeit durch Fotografie, Fernsehen und jetzt auch dem digitalen Bild – was Jean Baudrillard in einer dystopischen Stimmung, die „Wüste des Wirklichen selbst" nennen würde –, wurden von Science-Fiction-Schriftstellern bereits in den Sechzigern, noch lange bevor das Simulakrum zu einem Bonmot der kontinentalen Philosophie wurde, bekundet.

Jean Baudrillard, „Simulacra and Science Fiction", in: *Simulacra and Simulation*. Ann Arbor 1994, S. 121–127.

Die seltsamen, verlassenen Landschaften und räumlich-zeitlichen Trennungen, die den bildlichen Raum bei Dalí entwirklichen, wie Brown auch zu erkennen scheint, schwingen in den späten Forderungen der Postmoderne mit. Dalí ist ein Meister der Hyperrealität. Es ist daher bemerkenswert, dass der englische Autor J. G. Ballard, der das Science-Fiction-Genre adaptierte, um das zeitgenössische Dilemma festzuhalten, ein langjähriger Verfechter von Dalí war.

Ersatzmoderne

Inmitten der stark polarisierten kulturellen Landschaft der dreißiger Jahre – ein Jahrzehnt, in dem sich Dalís Ruf in den Vereinigten Staaten zu verbreiten begann – erlangte der große Verteidiger der Moderne, Clement Greenberg, seine Berühmtheit. Seine Tätigkeit als Schriftsteller in dieser Zeit gipfelte in der Veröffentlichung von „Avantgarde und Kitsch" in der *Partisan Review* im Herbst 1939. Die zentrale Bedeutung dieses Aufsatzes liegt zweifellos darin, wie T. J. Clark schreibt,

of imitation – 'the imitation of imitating' is how Greenberg puts it:

> The non-representational or 'abstract,' if it is to have aesthetic validity, cannot be arbitrary and accidental, but must stem from obedience to some worthy constraint or original. This constraint, once the world of common, extraverted experience has been renounced, can only be found in the very processes or disciplines by which art and literature have already imitated the former.

Clement Greenberg, "Avant-Garde and Kitsch," in *Partisan Review* vol. VI, no. 5 (fall 1939), 34–49. In *Pollock and After. The Critical Debate*, ed. Francis Frascina, New York, 1985, 21–33.



The authority of modernism, its status as a well-founded claimant, results from its obedience to – its dutiful imitation of – the disciplines and processes of prior illusionistic art.

Over and against the avant-garde (the only true culture still remaining in Greenberg's estimation) stands a debased, meretricious and wholly insidious form of imitation to which in 1939 he attached the foreign German-sounding label of kitsch. Kitsch encompassed a variety of cultural forms which, at that apocalyptic moment, were viewed as threatening the elite culture that Greenberg, as a disciple of T.S. Eliot, felt duty-bound to defend: everything from Stalinist socialist realism to the home-grown menace of capitalist mass culture – "popular, commercial art and literature with their chromeotypes, magazine covers, illustrations, ads, slick and pulp fiction, comics, Tin Pan Alley music, tap dancing, Hollywood movies, etc., etc." (All these

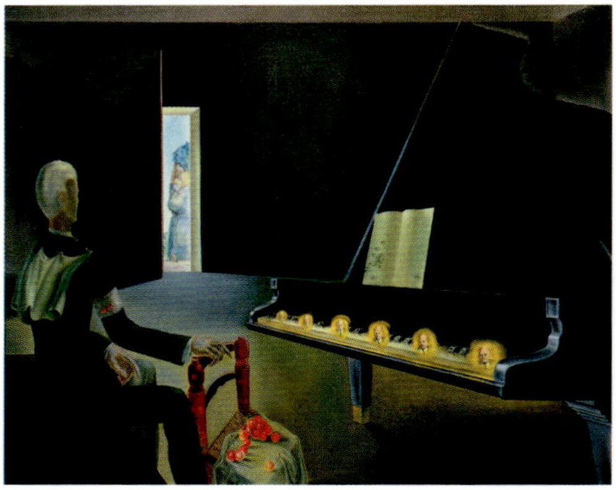

Abb./ill. 6: Salvador Dalí,
*Teilhalluzination: Sechs Erscheinungen von Lenin/ Partial Hallucination: Six Apparitions of Lenin on a Piano*, 1931

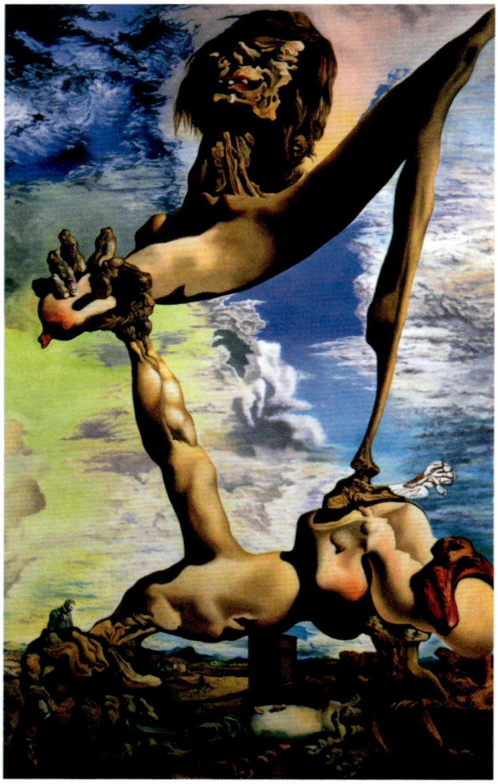

Abb./ill. 5: Glenn Brown,
*Dalí-Christ*, 1992

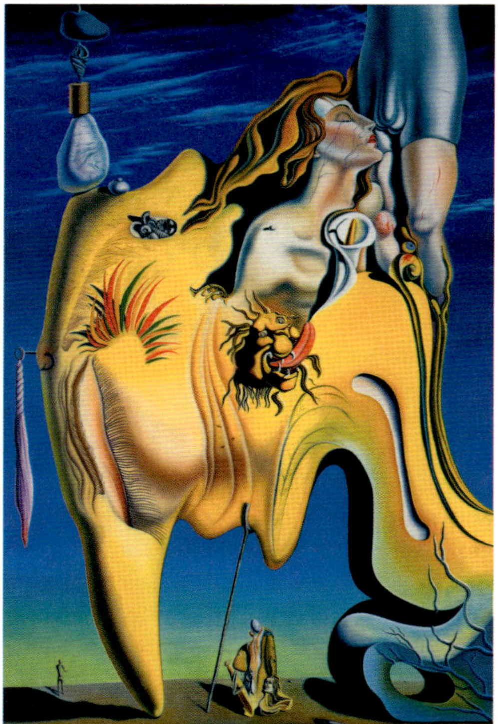

Abb./ill. 7: Glenn Brown,
*You Take My Place in this Showdown*, 1993

Grundsätze zur Theorie der Moderne abzustecken, die in Greenbergs weiterem Schaffen großteils unverändert bestehen bleiben. Clark konzentriert sich hier auf ein Geschichtsbewusstsein, von dem er behauptet, es bestätige die Verteidigungen der Moderne der frühen Texte, das aber von späteren formalistischen Rechtfertigungen verunklart wird. Es bleibe zu diskutieren, ob der Versuch der historischen Rechtfertigung immer erst *post facto* auftritt und selbst in den frühen Texten der Rationalisierung einer vorangegangenen Diskriminierung dient, die Greenberg zwischen „guter" (moralisch und ästhetisch überlegener) und „schlechter" Imitation unterscheiden lässt. Greenberg befürwortet keine einfache Opposition zwischen Abstraktion und Illusion, wie manchmal fälschlich angenommen wird. Er richtet sich eher nach Aristoteles' *Poetik*, in dem Glauben, dass jedwede Kunst mimetisch ist. Die Moderne selbst ist also Imitation – Greenberg nennt es das „imitieren des Imitierens":

„Das Gegenstandslose oder ‚Abstrakte' darf, wenn es ästhetische Geltung haben soll, nicht willkürlich oder zufällig sein, sondern muß aus der Unterordnung unter eine geeignete Beschränkung oder ein Vorbild erwachsen."

**Clement Greenberg, „Avantgarde und Kitsch" (1939), in: Ders., *Die Essenz der Moderne. Ausgewählte Kritiken und Essays*, hg. von Michael Glasmeier. Dresden 1997, S. 34.**

Die Autorität der Moderne, ihr Status als begründete Klägerin, stammt aus ihrer Gefügigkeit – ihrer pflichtgetreuen Imitation – zu den Disziplinen und Entwicklungen der vorangegangenen illusionistischen Kunst.

things consort promiscuously as reference points for Brown's painting.) Where Greenberg saw modernism as a last refuge of authenticity, kitsch on the other hand was inauthentic, ersatz culture: it uses for raw material "the debased and academicized simulacra of genuine culture" and yields only "vicarious experience and faked sensations." Kitsch is an illegitimate copy, offering a mere semblance of the true culture whose effects it conspires to replicate: "If the avant-garde imitates the processes of art, kitsch, we now see, imitates its effects." This Platonic dichotomy between an imitation that is faithful to the essence of painting, as opposed to a purely external imitation of effects, marks the gulf that separates "two such simultaneous cultural phenomena as the avant-garde and kitsch."

**Though it lies beyond the scope of this essay, there would be mileage in exploring the influence of Jewish religious prohibitions upon the terms in which Greenberg condemns kitsch as a promiscuous form of imitation.**

In a footnote to the essay "Avant-Garde and Kitsch," Greenberg claimed that surrealism, notwithstanding its radical politics, was a reactionary trend bent on restoring literary subject matter to art. The task of modernist painting, according to Greenberg, was to purge itself of alien elements, above all literature. He especially berates Dalí, an artist whose fault "is to represent the processes and concepts of his consciousness, not the processes of his medium." When Greenberg comes to write about surrealism some time later, in 1944, it is notable that by then he annexes the whole of surrealist art to his definition of kitsch, though plainly he still has in mind Dalí who was, by

Der einzigen – nach Greenberg – wahren Kultur steht die minderwertige, trügerische und tückische Imitation gegenüber, der er 1939 das Label Kitsch verleiht. Kitsch umfasst eine Reihe kultureller Formen, die, zu jenem apokalyptischen Moment, die Elite-Kultur zu bedrohen schien, die Greenberg, als treuer Anhänger von T. S. Eliot, so pflichtschuldig verteidigt: von stalinistischem, sozialistischem Realismus zur selbst gemachten Bedrohung der kapitalistischen Massenkultur – „populäre, kommerzielle Kunst und Literatur mit ihren Vierfarbendrucken, Zeitschriftenbildern, Illustrationen, Werbeanzeigen, Groschenromanen, Comics, Schlagermusik, Stepptanz, Hollywood-Filmen etc."

Ebd., S. 38.



(All diese Dinge verkehren frei miteinander als Bezugspunkte für Browns Arbeiten.) Wenn Greenberg die Moderne als letztes Refugium von Authentizität sah, so war Kitsch wiederum *nicht* authentisch: eine falsche Kultur, die sich die „entwerteten und akademisierten Simulakren der echten Kultur als sein Rohmaterial aneignet", die „Erfahrung aus zweiter Hand, vorgetäuschte Empfindung" hervorbringt.

Ebd., S. 40.

Kitsch ist eine illegitime Kopie, die allein den Anschein echter Kultur vermittelt, deren Effekte sie imitiert: „Wenn die Avantgarde die Verfahrensweisen der Kunst nachahmt, dann ahmt der Kitsch, wie wir nun sehen, ihre Wirkungen nach."

then, the most publicly visible face of surrealism in the United States:

> For the sake of hallucinatory vividness the surrealists have copied the effects of the calendar reproduction, postal card chromeotype and magazine illustration ... they prize the qualities of the popular reproduction because of its incongruously prosaic associations and because the reproduction heightens illusionistic effect by erasing paint texture and brushstroke.

Clement Greenberg, "Surrealist Painting" (1944), in *The Collected Essays and Criticism vol.1*, Chicago, 1986, 225–231; 229.

It must be said that this is quite a shrewd observation, though it may be that Greenberg was merely following Dalí's lead in characterising his art as hand-painted colour photography of the dream world. At any rate, it took an insider with his finger on the surrealist pulse to have discerned this trait previously. Louis Aragon, in the essay "The Challenge of Painting" (a catalogue preface for an exhibition of surrealist collage), drew attention to Dalí's perverse, anti-modernist adaptation of the collage medium in which painted passages strive to emulate the appearance of collaged fragments and vice versa, confounding the hand-painted with the mechanically reproduced.

Louis Aragon, "The Challenge to Painting," in Pontus Hultén ed., *The Surrealists Look at Art*, Venice, 1990, 69. The picture *The First Days of Spring* (1929) illustrates this peculiar use of the collage medium.

Ebd. S. 47.

Diese platonische Dichotomie zwischen einer Imitation, die dem Wesen der Malerei getreu ist statt einer rein äußerlichen Imitation der Effekte, markiert den Graben zwischen den beiden „zeitgleichen Kulturphänomenen, wie es die Avantgarde und der Kitsch sind".

Ebd. Wenngleich es den Rahmen dieses Aufsatzes sprengen würde, würde es sich lohnen, den Einfluss der jüdisch-religiösen Verbote zu untersuchen, aufgrund derer Greenberg Kitsch als promiskuitive Form der Imitation verdammte.

In einer Fußnote des Aufsatzes „Avantgarde und Kitsch" behauptet Greenberg, dass der Surrealismus, ungeachtet seiner radikalen Einstellungen, ein reaktionärer Trend mit dem Ziel war, literarische Themen zur Kunst zu machen. Die Aufgabe der modernen Malerei, nach Greenberg, war es, sich von fremden Elementen zu reinigen, vor allem aber von der Literatur. Insbesondere Dalí wirft er vor, ein Künstler zu sein, dessen Makel es ist „die Prozesse und Konzepte seines Bewusstseins darzustellen statt der Prozesse seines Mediums." Als Greenberg 1944 über den Surrealismus schreibt, ist es auffallend, dass er seine Definition von Kitsch der gesamten surrealistischen Kunst beilegt, wenngleich er schlicht an Dalí denkt, der zu diesem Zeitpunkt das bekannteste Gesicht des Surrealismus in den Vereinigten Staaten war:

„Wegen dieser halluzinatorischen Lebendigkeit haben die Surrealisten die Effekte von Kalenderreproduktionen, Farbpostkarten und Illustriertenbildern nachgeahmt. Allgemein schätzen

Less charitably, the newspaper critic Waldemar Januszczak has branded Dalí the poster king, observing that "his work is not so much eminently reproducible as a reproduction already."

Waldemar Januszczak, *The Guardian* (17 June 1980), 10.

Brown, who deploys the deceptions of *trompe l'oeil* with no less finesse than Dalí, poses similar conundrums for present day audiences. The Goldsmiths-trained practitioner is savvy about Gerhard Richter and has swotted up on Walter Benjamin, drawing upon a weighty body of postmodern theory interrogating the relationship of painting to photography. Those who expectantly awaited a return of painting in the Turner Prize were destined to have their hopes dashed: as Tate's curator of interpretation, Simon Wilson, hastened to point out, Brown "merely appropriates ideas" – that is to say, despite appearances, his work is conceptual rather than painterly. For an artist whose formation was in the 'eighties and early 'nineties, one imagines that the magazine *Modern Painters,* with its militant advocacy of the School of London and polemics against photographic-based practices, lies behind his wholly ironic engagement with the painterliness of Frank Auerbach, in which the airbrushed flatness of Brown's meticulous copy is a visual synonym for ironed-out expressive affect. On this point, the artist's long-time friend, Michael Stubbs, incisively remarks: "Brown offers us a flat simulacrum of the Expressionist work, a patiently copied version of the machismo gesture even though it's painted 'for real'."

sie die Eigenschaften der populären Reproduktionen wegen ihrer ausgefallenen prosaischen Assoziation, und weil die Reproduktion den illusionistischen Effekt noch erhöht, indem sie die Textur der Farbe und den Pinselstrich unsichtbar macht."

Clement Greenberg, „Surrealistische Malerei" (1944), in: Ders., *Die Essenz der Moderne*, S. 89.

Es soll hier angemerkt sein, dass das eine etwas durchtriebene Beobachtung ist, wenn es auch sein kann, dass Greenberg einfach nur Dalís Vorbild folgte, indem er seine Kunst als handkolorierte Fotografie einer Traumwelt charakterisierte. Wie dem auch sei, es bedurfte eines Insiders am Puls der surrealistischen Zeit, dieses Merkmal bereits zu unterscheiden. In seinem Aufsatz „Die Malerei in der Herausforderung" (ein Katalogvorwort zu einer Ausstellung surrealistischer Collagen) wies Louis Aragon auf Dalís perverse, anti-moderne Adaption der Collage hin, in der gezeichnete Passagen Collage-Charakter nachahmen und umgekehrt, und das Gemalte mit dem von mechanisch Produzierten verwechselt wird.

Louis Aragon, „The Challenge to Painting", in: *The Surrealists Look at Art*, hg. von Pontus Hultén. Venedig 1990, S. 69. Das Bild *Der erste Tag des Frühlings* (1929) illustriert diese spezifische Verwendung des Mediums Collage.

Weniger großzügig kennzeichnete der Kritiker Waldemar Januszczak Dalí als Poster-König, indem er anmerkte, dass „seine Arbeit nicht so sehr reproduzierbar sei als vielmehr bereits eine Reproduktion."

Michael Stubbs, "Glenn Brown: No Visible Means of Support," in *Glenn Brown*, exh. cat., Tate Liverpool, 2009, 105.

Brown's surfaces ambiguously resemble the much-vaunted flatness of the modernist picture plane while betraying the values of literalness and presence the latter was held to embody. Though he plainly has a firsthand acquaintance with many of the original artworks that occupy him – *Oscillate Wildly* (1999), a picture in his Turner Prize exhibition, reworked Dalí's *Autumn Cannibalism* (1936) in Tate's collection – it seems that he prefers to paint from reproductions and wilfully exploits the degradation of the image, the distortions of colour and other idiosyncrasies, that are an inevitable byproduct of reproductive technologies. *Oscillate Wildly* is like a black and white illustration of the original culled from an art history textbook that has been anamorphically stretched to the proportions of Picasso's *Guernica*. "I like the idea of working from reproductions," Brown says. "There's a purposeful impoverishment in living via second-hand information – in a world of videos, computers, film. I like the cheesy qualities of reproduction, especially when the colour goes way off and becomes acidic."

"Artificial Intelligence," Interview with Sarah Kent, *Time Out*, October 25, 2000.

When I spoke to Brown, he denied being attracted to Dalí on this score, notwithstanding the evidence of works such as *Dalí-Christ* (1992, ill. 5), which apparently responds to the overripe, artificially vivid hues of the original, *Soft Construction with Boiled Beans* (1936).

Waldemar Januszczak, *The Guardian.* 17. Juni 1980, S 10.

Brown, der die Täuschungen des *trompe l'œil* mit vergleichbarer Finesse wie Dalí anwendet, stellt ähnliche Rätsel für ein zeitgenössisches Publikum auf. Der Goldsmith-Absolvent ist Gerhard Richter bewandert, hat Walter Benjamin gebüffelt und stützt sich auf ein beachtliches Gewicht postmoderner Theorie, um die Beziehung von Malerei und Fotografie zu untersuchen. Wer die Rückkehr des Turner Prize zur Malerei erwartete, dessen Hoffnungen mussten zerschellen: Der Tate-Kurator der Interpretation Simon Wilson beeilte sich darauf hinzuweisen, Brown „ordne Ideen nur zu" – soll heißen, dass trotz ihrer Erscheinung seine Arbeit konzeptuell statt malerisch bleibt. Für einen Künstler, dessen formative Zeit die achtziger und neunziger Jahre waren, möchte man meinen, dass die Zeitschrift *Modern Painters* – die für ihre militante Fürsprache für die School of London bekannt ist, sowie für ihre Polemiken gegen foto-basierte Praktiken – hinter der ironischen Auseinandersetzung mit dem Malerischen von Frank Auerbach steht, in der die mit Airbrush gemalte Flachheit von Browns sorgfältigen Kopien ein visuelles Synonym eines ausgebügelten, expressiven Affekts ist. Hierzu bemerkt der langjährige Freund des Künstlers, Michael Stubbs: „Brown bietet uns ein flaches Simulakrum der expressionistischen Arbeiten an, eine geduldig kopierte Version der Macho-Geste, selbst wenn es ‚wirklich' gemalt wurde."

Michael Stubbs, „Glenn Brown: No Visible Means of Support", in: *Glenn Brown*, Ausst.-Kat., Tate Liverpool, 2009, S. 105.

The danger of the simulacrum, and the reason why for Greenberg it must be rejected beyond the pale of modern art, abjected one might say, is that it offends the very terms upon which the defence of modernism is based. We have reached a point where we can recognise that Dalí's and Brown's preparedness to side with the simulacral was yet another facet of a systematically elaborated anti-modernist stance that they both share. Taking up the cudgel from Greenberg, the critic Carter Ratcliffe in an essay entitled "Swallowing Dalí" (which has the merit of revealing the visceral basis of the intellectual operation of expulsion) would have us learn an object lesson about the perils of postmodernism, warning direly that it is Dalí's inauthenticity that matters most.

Carter Ratcliffe, "Swallowing Dalí," *Artforum* 21, no. 1 (September 1982), 33–40.

The Death of Painting

*"Dear Painter, paint me ..." – Painting the Figure Since Late Picabia*, an exhibition in 2002 at the Centre Georges Pompidou, showcased Glenn Brown together with a number of artists who collectively were held to demonstrate that figurative painting is alive and flourishing.

*"Dear Painter, paint me ..." – Painting the Figure Since Late Picabia*, curated by Alison Gingeras, exh. cat., Centre Georges Pompidou, Paris, 2002.

Its ostensible premise seemed to be to argue that the widely proclaimed death of painting was premature. In fact, much of the contemporary work included in the show could be said to engage conceptually with the condition of

Browns Oberflächen ähneln auf doppeldeutige Weise der viel gerühmten Flachheit der modernen Bildfläche, während sie daran festhält, die Werte der Buchstäblichkeit und Präsenz des Letzteren zu verkörpern. Wenngleich er viele der Originalwerke, die ihn beschäftigen, aus erster Hand kennt – *Oscillate Wildly* (1999), ein Bild in seiner Turner-Prize-Ausstellung, überarbeitete Dalís *Herbstlicher Kannibalismus* (1936) aus der Sammlung Tate – so scheint er es zu bevorzugen, von Reproduktionen abzumalen und nützt willentlich die kompromittierte Qualität des Bildes aus, die Verfälschungen der Farbe und andere Eigenheiten, die ein unvermeidliches Nebenprodukt der reproduktiven Technologien sind. *Oscillate Wildly* ist wie eine Schwarz-Weiß-Zeichnung des Originals aus einem kunsthistorischen Buch, das anamorph auf die Größe von Picassos *Guernica* ausgedehnt wurde. „Ich arbeite gerne nach Reproduktionen", sagt Brown. „Von Informationen aus zweiter Hand zu leben enthält eine entschlossene Verarmung – in einer Welt voller Videos, Computer und Film. Ich mag diese geschmacklose Qualität der Reproduktionen, vor allem wenn sich die Farbe komplett verändert und azidisch wird."

„Artificial Intelligence", Interview mit Sarah Kent, in: *Time Out*, 25. Oktober 2000.

Als ich mit Brown sprach, leugnete er, diesbezüglich von Dalí angezogen zu sein, ungeachtet solcher Arbeiten wie *Dalí-Christ* (1992, Abb. 5), das offensichtlich auf die überreifen, gekünstelt lebendigen Farbtöne des Originals *Weiche Konstruktion mit gekochten Bohnen* (1936) reagiert.



the death (or decline) of painting. A common feature was an un-ironic acceptance of trash contrasting with the high Modernist opposition of avant-garde art and kitsch. Brown, as we have seen, is even-handed in blending willy-nilly references to high and popular culture. In this regard, late Picabia was an apt reference point. By contrast, the inclusion of Bernard Buffet in the selection was anomalous, pointing to the problematic agenda behind the show.

In an essay entitled "The Death or Decline of Art" (1985), the philosopher Gianni Vattimo analyses the death of art under three aspects.

Gianni Vattimo, "The Death or Decline of Art," in Vattimo, *The End of Modernity: Nihilism and Hermeneutics in Post-Modern Culture*, trans. Jon R. Snyder, Cambridge, 1988.

Hegel's prediction of art's sublation by philosophy is realized, he says, albeit in caricatured form, in modernity. Vattimo speaks first of all of art's obsolescence at the hands of the mass media. Walter Benjamin described the withering away of the auratic properties of art in the age of technological reproduction.

Walter Benjamin, "The Work of Art in the Age of Mechanical Reproduction," in *Illuminations*, ed. Hannah Arendt, trans. Harry Zohn, New York, 1968, 217–251.

The aura, originally a function of the cultic value of the artwork within a fabric of tradition and ritual, came to be linked in the era of autonomous bourgeois art with the uniqueness of the original. (Its corollary, seen from the artist's point of view, Vattimo asserts, is the idea

Die Gefahr des Simulakrums und der Grund, warum es für Greenberg als völlig inakzeptabel abgelehnt werden muss, um nicht zu sagen *abjected*, ist, dass es gegen alle Regeln verstößt, auf denen die Verteidigung der Moderne aufbaut. An diesem Punkt erkennen wir, dass Dalís und Browns Bereitschaft, sich auf die Seite des Simulakrums zu schlagen, eine weitere Facette einer systematisch ausgearbeiteten, anti-modernen Haltung ist, die sie miteinander teilen. Der Kritiker Carter Ratcliffe schlägt in seinem Aufsatz „Swallowing Dalí" (mit dem Verdienst, dass er die instinktive Grundlage des gedanklichen Verfahrens der Ausschließung enthüllt) in Greenbergs Kerbe, in dem er uns nur zu gerne eine Lektion über die Gefahren der Postmoderne erteilen möchte, wenn er vor allem Dalís Nicht-Authentizität anprangert.

Carter Ratcliffe, „Swallowing Dalí", in: *Artforum* 21, Nr. 1, September 1982, S. 33–40.

Der Tod der Malerei

*„Lieber Maler, male mir ..." – Radikaler Realismus nach Picabia*, eine Ausstellung aus dem Jahre 2002, zeigte Arbeiten von Glenn Brown gemeinsam mit einer Reihe anderer Künstler, um zu zeigen, dass figurative Malerei wächst und gedeiht.

*„Lieber Maler, male mir ..." – Radikaler Realismus nach Picabia*. Centre Georges Pompidou, Paris, Kunsthalle Wien, Schirn Kunsthalle, Frankfurt a. M. 2002.

Die vordergründige Prämisse schien zu sein, dass das weitverbreitete Postulat des Todes der Malerei etwas voreilig war. Vielmehr aber

of genius.) The generalization of art as entertainment in the mass media is one of the forms of art's death; a second is the avant-garde ambition to bring about a utopian reintegration of art into life; a third is the path of high modernism, which sets an ever more restricted programme for art as a last ditch reaction to the encroachments of mass culture. The last-mentioned, in which authentic art literally paints itself into a corner – Adorno and Greenberg offer comparable versions of this modernist narrative – is a form of death by suicide. Vattimo states that the actual event of art's death, which ought to coincide with a cessation of art production, is indefinitely postponed; thus it is more accurate to speak of the decline of art. This paradoxical situation, in which art continues to be produced all the while contemplating its own death, 'constitutes the historical and ontological constellation in which we move.'

Vattimo, "The Death or Decline of Art," 52.

The philosopher Arthur Danto has observed that the end of art was "in the air" in the mid-1980s, a period that coincides with Brown's formation as a painter. Hans Belting's *The End of the History of Art?*, originally published in German in 1983, became available in English translation in 1987, while Danto's "The End of Art" was lead essay in a book titled *The Death of Art* (1984). Although Vattimo's prognosis for art is framed by his perspective on the death of metaphysics, as Danto notes, while his and Belting's analyses are internal to the art world, Vattimo does comment upon various artistic developments in the 1960s and 70s that heralded a rift with modernist autonomy: "earth-works, body art, street theater, and so on [in which] ließe sich sagen, dass die zeitgenössischen Arbeiten in der Ausstellung sich konzeptuell durchaus mit diesem Tod (oder Untergang) der Malerei auseinandersetzten. Ein gemeinsames Merkmal war die unironische Aufnahme von Schund, die der hohen modernen Opposition von Avantgarde-Kunst und Kitsch gegenüberstand. Brown, wie wir gesehen haben, vermischt unparteiisch planlose Referenzen der hohen und gefälligen Kunst. Diesbezüglich ist der späte Picabia ein passender Bezugspunkt. Im Gegensatz dazu steht die ungewöhnliche Aufnahme von Bernard Buffet, die die problematische Absicht der Ausstellung verdeutlicht.

In seinem Aufsatz mit dem Titel „Tod oder Untergang der Kunst" (1985) analysiert der Philosoph Gianni Vattimo den Tod der Kunst anhand dreier Aspekte.

Gianni Vattimo, „Tod oder Untergang der Kunst", in: Ders., *Das Ende der Moderne*, übers. von Rafael Capuro. Stuttgart 1990.

Hegels Prognose, dass die Kunst durch die Philosophie aufgehoben wird, sieht er in der Moderne bestätigt, wenngleich auf karikierte Weise. Vattimo spricht vor allem von der Veralterung der Kunst in den Händen der Massenmedien. Walter Benjamin beschrieb das Verblühen der Aura der Kunst im Zeitalter seiner technischen Reproduzierbarkeit.

Walter Benjamin, *Das Kunstwerk im Zeitalter seiner technischen Reproduzierbarkeit*. Frankfurt a. M. 1963.

Die Aura, die ursprünglich den kultischen Wert des Kunstwerks zwischen Tradition und Ritual



the status of the work becomes constitutively ambiguous." One of the consequences for Brown was that the status of painting became his abiding concern. This was not, as it was for Greenberg, a question of defining the essence of painting, but a question of how or whether painting was any longer possible. This is the case even when Brown makes a foray into sculpture: the three dimensional expressionist brush strokes that he displays in sealed Perspex vitrines like a museum display of some now extinct species have, as their true subject, painting, not sculpture. Among the artists Brown acknowledges as influencing his practice is Gerhard Richter whose trademark blur fills the background of several of Brown's more recent canvases. The invocation of Richter, an artist whose entire oeuvre is a reflection upon the condition of the end of painting, establishes a baseline from which Brown takes off. Brown's insistent references to the Old Masters – Rembrandt and El Greco are two of his favourites – express his belatedness in relation to a history of art that is ended. In this respect, they are less an affectionate homage than a parody, less like Picasso's reworkings of the same artists than René Magritte's mocking of the artistic canon in the pictures he produced in the 1940s under the German Occupation. (Another whole essay could be written about Brown's relation to Magritte, the most philosophical surrealist. The incongruous mismatch of title and image, which forces us back to painting as the real subject, is a trademark of Brown's work that insistently recalls Magritte.) Brown also plays havoc with the hierarchy of genres that govern traditional high art. An example of this is the series of flower-headed women, inspired once again by Dalí's example, that conflate still life with portraiture.

ausmachte, wurde in der Ära der autonomen bürgerlichen Kunst mit der Einmaligkeit des Originals verbunden. (Seine logische Folge, vom künstlerischen Standpunkt aus gesehen, bestätigt Vattimo, ist die Vorstellung von Genie.) Die Verallgemeinerung von Kunst als Unterhaltung in den Massenmedien ist eine der Formen des Todes der Kunst. Eine weitere ist das Streben der Avantgarde nach einer utopischen Wiedereingliederung von der Kunst in das Leben. Eine dritte ist jener Weg der Moderne, die ein noch restriktiveres Programm der Kunst als ein letztes Aufbäumen gegen die Übergriffe der Massenkultur erstellt. Letzteres, wo sich authentische Kunst in die Klemme bringt – Adorno und Greenberg bieten vergleichbare Versionen der modernen Erzählung an –, ist eine Form des Selbstmordes. Vattimo konstatiert, dass der Vorgang des Todes der Kunst, der mit dem Stillstand von Kunstproduktion zusammenfällt, auf unbestimmte Zeit verschoben ist. Daher ist es treffender, vom *Untergang* der Kunst zu sprechen. Diese paradoxe Situation, in der Kunst weiterhin produziert wird, während ihr eigener Tod erwogen wird, „stellt eine historische wie ontologische Konstellation dar, innerhalb derer wir uns bewegen."

Gianni Vattimo, „Tod oder Untergang der Kunst", S. 52.

Der Philosoph Arthur Danto bemerkte Mitte der achtziger Jahre, dass das Ende der Kunst „in der Luft" lag, jene Zeitspanne, in der sich Brown als Maler begann zu entwickeln. Hans Beltings *Das Ende der Kunstgeschichte*, ursprünglich 1983 auf Deutsch erschienen, wurde in englischer Übersetzung 1987 erhältlich, während Dantos „The End of Art" ein Leitartikel in dem Buch

Dalí, I would argue, evolved in a paradoxical relation of simultaneous recognition and disavowal of the death of art. "Instead of Reaction, or Revolution, RENAISSANCE!" he proclaims with false bravado.

Dalí, *The Secret Life*, 398.

Abandoning the revolutionary aspirations of the historical avant-garde – he declared surrealism finished – and suspicious of abstraction, Dalí tried to fill the resultant vacuum by a renewed emphasis on traditional painting skills. The vitriolic diatribes against modern art in such tracts as *Les Cocus du vieil art moderne [The Cuckolds of Antiquated Modern Art]* (1956) echo similar pronouncements by Giorgio de Chirico, who blamed the decadence of painting upon a pervasive deskilling.

See Giorgio de Chirico, "The Technique of Painting," in *The Memoirs of Giorgio de Chirico*, trans. Margaret Crosland, New York, 1994.

While purporting to deplore our "era of frightful mechanical progress and spiritual decadence," in Dalí's own words, it is striking that the practice of both artists was marked by the very conditions of reproducibility that are held responsible for the decay of art's aura. There is not the space here to examine in detail the myriad ways in which Dalí's painting was infiltrated by photographic technologies and associated modes of perception, but like de Chirico's practice of copying, which only gathered pace in the 1920s, it registered the very conditions that his reversion to a traditional painterly craft supposedly was reacting against.

*The Death of Art* (1984) war. Obwohl sich Vattimos Prognose für die Kunst auf der Perspektive des Todes der Metaphysik bildete, wie Danto anmerkt, während seine und Beltings Analyse aus der Kunstwelt stammen, so kommentiert Vattimo die verschiedenen künstlerischen Strömungen der sechziger und siebziger Jahre, die einen Bruch mit der modernen Autonomie ankündigen: „Land Art, Body Art, Straßentheater und so weiter, in denen der Stellenwert des Kunstwerks immer unklarer wird.“ Für Brown wurde eine der Konsequenzen daraus, dass der Stellenwert der Malerei zu seinem Anliegen wurde. Es ging ihm dabei nicht, wie Greenberg, um das Wesen der Malerei, sondern ob und wie Malerei nach wie vor bestehen kann. Das ist auch der Fall, wenn Brown Vorstöße in die Skulptur macht: Der dreidimensionale, expressionistische Pinselstrich, den er in einer versiegelten Perspex-Vitrine präsentiert wie in einem Museum, das eine ausgestorbene Spezies ausstellt, hat die Malerei und nicht die Skulptur zum Thema. Unter den Künstlern, die Brown zu seinen Einflüssen zählt, ist Gerhard Richter, zu dessen Markenzeichen die unscharfe Darstellung zählt und die in Browns neueren Leinwänden oft im Hintergrund zu finden ist. Der Bezug auf Richter, dessen gesamtes Œuvre eine Reflexion auf das Ende der Malerei ist, bildet eine Basis für Brown. Browns kontinuierliche Bezugnahmen auf alte Meister – Rembrandt und El Greco gehören zu seinen beiden Favoriten – drücken etwas hinsichtlich seiner Beziehung zu einer Kunstgeschichte aus, die es nicht mehr gibt. So gesehen sind sie weniger eine herzliche Hommage als vielmehr eine Parodie, nicht so sehr wie Picassos Bearbeitungen desselben Künstlers, als wie René Magrittes Gespött des künstlerischen Kanons in den



Suffice to note Dalí's definition of painting as: "'Photographie' à la main et en couleurs de l''irrationalité concrète' et du monde imaginatif en général.", in "Derniers modes d'excitation intellectuelle pour l'été 1934," *Documents 34* (June 1934), 33–5.

Putting a psychoanalytic gloss on the end-yet-continuation of painting, Yve-Alain Bois argues that the "task of mourning" that one might more naturally associate with postmodern art also fell to modernism at the beginning of the twentieth century.

Yve-Alain Bois, "Painting: The Task of Mourning," in *Endgame: Reference and Simulation in Recent Painting and Sculpture*, Boston, 1986, 29–49.

The end of modern art was foretold in its birth. The origins of abstraction, Bois notes, can be located in the liberation from mimesis brought about by the invention of photography with which it is historically co-terminus. At the same time, the crisis of art in industrial modernity, due to the appearance of photography, and mass reproduction, was understood as signaling the end of art. In a remark that underscores the unavoidable centrality of Marcel Duchamp to this rhetoric of the "end," Bois writes: "Mass production seemed to bode the end of painting through its most elaborate *mise-en-scène*, the invention of the readymade."

Ibid., 31. In a comment that bears upon Dalí's emulation of Ernest Meissonier's technique, Bois observes that traditional painterly finish and the mechanical come together and are fused in the slick surface of nineteenth-century academic painting – to which modernism, of course, arose in opposition.

Bildern, die er in den vierziger Jahren während der deutschen Besatzung schuf. (Man könnte einen ganzen Aufsatz über Browns Beziehung zu Magritte, dem philosophischsten Surrealisten, aufwenden. Die unvereinbaren Fehlpaarungen von Titel und Bild, die uns zurück zur Malerei als dem echten Thema führen, ist eines von Browns Kennzeichen, das beharrlich an Magritte erinnert.) Brown richtet auch in der Hierarchie der Gattungen in der traditionell hohen Kunst Verwüstung an. Ein Beispiel dafür wäre die Serie der Frauen mit Blumenköpfen, erneut von Dalí inspiriert, der Stillleben und Porträt verschmelzen ließ.

Dalí, so behaupte ich, entwickelte sich aus einer paradoxen Beziehung von Anerkennung und Nichtanerkennung des Todes der Kunst heraus. „Statt Reaktion oder Revolution, RENAISSANCE",

Salvador Dalí, *Das geheime Leben des Salvador Dalí*, S. 687.

verkündet er mit unaufrichtigem Wagemut. Die revolutionären Bestrebungen der historischen Avantgarde hinter sich lassend – er erklärte den Surrealismus als beendet – und der Abstraktion gegenüber suspekt, versuchte Dalí, das daraus resultierende Vakuum mit erneutem Nachdruck auf traditionelles malerisches Talent zu füllen. Die beißenden Hetzreden gegen die moderne Kunst in Abhandlungen wie *Les Cocus du vieil art moderne* (1956) geben ähnliche Erklärungen von Giorgio de Chirico wieder, der die Dekadenz der Malerei auf eine tiefgreifende Disqualifizierung zurückführte.

These same conditions also engender, by way of reaction, "the essentialist urge of modernist [abstract] painting" – to which, of course, Dalí was inveterately opposed. Although it would be foolhardy to apply a diagnostic label to Dalí, his response to what he understood as the decline of art bears the hallmarks of a manic defense, such as Bois discerns in appropriation art, more so than of mourning. Mania is a defensive operation equivalent to a denial and its behavioural and psychical correlates are over-activity, triumphalism, and oral cannibalism – all very familiar Dalínian traits.

Dalí's misfortune as a painter, and there can be no doubt that he was passionate about the craft of painting, was to have come after the "end" of art. Painting could only ever be for Dalí a simulacrum of painting. He repeatedly portrays painting itself as needing to be propped up perilously from within the picture frame – by one of his famous crutches in one instance, and by the lid of a grand piano in another. *Partial Hallucination: Six Apparitions of Lenin on a Piano* (1931, ill. 6) is like a textbook exercise in post-Renaissance single point perspective.

Dalí's library at the Fundació Gala-Salvador Dalí contains several classic treatises on perspective.

Note that the raised lid of the piano precisely touches the back edge of the ceiling in a simple box-shaped room. The edge runs strictly parallel to the upper border of the painting for which it serves as a proxy within the image. Thus, the piano lid, like the opened door at the back of the room, opens up a pictorial space that it supports, as it is in turn supported. In *Sleep* (c. 1937), a self-portrait head is held aloft by crutches,

Siehe Giorgio de Chirico, „The Technique of Painting", in: *The Memoirs of Giorgio de Chirico*, übers. von Margaret Crosland. New York 1994.

Unsere „Ära schrecklicher mechanischer Prozesse und spiritueller Dekadenz", so Dalís eigene Worte, missbilligend, so ist es doch erstaunlich, dass die Arbeit beider Künstler von den Bedingungen ihrer Reproduzierbarkeit geprägt ist, die für den Verfall der Aura der Kunst verantwortlich zeichnen. Es würde den Rahmen sprengen, die unzähligen Wege, in denen Dalís Gemälde von der Fotografie und ähnlichen Wahrnehmungsformen durchsetzt wurden, zu untersuchen, aber wie de Chiricos Vervielfältigungspraxis, die erst in den zwanziger Jahren in Schwung kam, kommen hier dieselben Bedingungen zu tragen, denen seine Rückkehr zum traditionellen malerischen Handwerk angeblich entgegenstand.

Es mag genügen, auf Dalís Definition der Malerei als: „‚Photographie' à la main et en couleurs de l'irrationalité concrète' et du monde imaginatif en général" hinzuweisen, aus: „Derniers modes d'excitation intellectuelle pour l'été 1934", in: *Documents*, 34, Juni 1934, S. 33-5.

Yve-Alain Bois verleiht der Debatte um das „Ende der Malerei, die dennoch weiterbesteht" psychoanalytischen Glanz, indem er die „Aufgabe des Trauerns", die man gemeinhin mit postmoderner Kunst assoziieren möchte, auch der Moderne am Beginn des 20. Jahrhunderts zuweist.

Yve-Alain Bois, „Painting: The Task of Mourning", in: *Endgame: Reference and Simulation in Recent Painting and Sculpture*. Boston 1986, S. 29–49.

as if to infer that the whole edifice of the dream world is liable to come crashing down at any instant, but one of the crutches has also been called upon to preserve the upper edge of the picture from toppling down like a shutter with it. Painting limps along, leaning on a prosthetic support. More than likely, Dalí was familiar with Freud's account of propping (anaclisis or *Anlehnung*) as a pervasive psychical operation, but he adapts it to comment wryly on the precarious condition of painting. *You Take My Place in this Showdown* (1993, ill. 7), Brown's remake of Dalí's picture *The Great Masturbator* (1929), rotates the work from a landscape format to a portrait one. The resultant lateral compression causes the central motif, a profile head (in fact, a self-portrait of Dalí), to buckle and droop like one of his famous soft watches so that Brown was forced to shove a crutch underneath it. Evidently, its function is to stop the whole pictorial image from sinking downwards.

Brown admits to drawing upon Dalí's obsession with the *putrefact*, and in an interview where he elaborates upon this matter, he relates the colours of putrefaction to the "decay" that is a by-product of the always-already-reproduced status of the postmodern image: "The subject was always the unhealthy, unreal world of books and illustrations. A world where the only air available was between the pages. Putrefaction seems to describe the colours of that world."

Where there is a whiff of decay, we naturally also look for a corpse. That corpse is painting.

Die Ursprünge der Abstraktion, so meint Bois, liegen in der Befreiung von der Mimesis durch die Erfindung der Fotografie, an die sie historisch grenzt. Gleichzeitig aber wurde die Krise der Kunst der industriellen Moderne wegen der Fotografie und der Massenproduktion so verstanden, als würden sie das Ende der Kunst signalisieren. In einer Bemerkung, die die unvermeidbare zentrale Position Marcel Duchamps in dieser Rhetorik des „Endes" unterstreicht, schreibt Bois: „Die Massenproduktion schien das Ende der Malerei anzukündigen durch ihr ausgeklügeltstes *mise-en-scène*, der Erfindung des Readymade."

Ebd., S. 31. In einer Bemerkung, die sich auf Dalís Nachahmung von Ernest Meissoniers Technik bezieht, bemerkt Bois, dass der traditionelle malerische Abschluss und das Mechanische zusammenkommen und sich in der glatten Oberfläche der akademischen Malerei des 19. Jahrhunderts vereinen – wogegen sich natürlich die Moderne erhob.

Dieselben Bedingungen verursachen als Reaktion „das unerlässliche Verlangen der modernen [abstrakten] Malerei" – dem Dalí natürlich unverbesserlicher entgegengestellt war. Auch wenn es töricht sein mag, Dalí ein diagnostisches Etikett zu verleihen, seine Reaktion auf das, was er als den Untergang der Kunst verstand, trägt eher das Kennzeichen einer fieberhaften Verteidigung, wie es Bois der Appropriation Art zuschreibt, als das des Trauerns. Die Manie ist eine Verteidigungsstrategie, die der Verleugnung gleicht, und Verhalten und Psyche entsprechen ihrer Über-Aktivität, dem Triumphalen und dem oralen Kannibalismus – lauter vertraute Merkmale Dalís.

"Last Night I Dreamt that Somebody Loved Me," Interview with Stephen Hepworth (London, May 2000), in: *Glenn Brown*, exh. cat., Centre d'art contemporain, Domaine de Kerguéhennec, 2000, 68.

Dalís Pech als Maler – und seine Leidenschaft für das Handwerk der Malerei kann nicht bezweifelt werden – war, dass er nach dem „Ende" der Kunst auftrat. Die Malerei konnte für Dalí nur noch das Simulakrum der Malerei sein. Er stellte die Malerei selbst vielfach als etwas dar, das innerhalb des Bildrahmens auf unsichere Art gestützt werden musste – wie etwa von seinen berühmten Krücken oder von einem Klavierdeckel. *Teilhalluzination: Sechs Erscheinungen von Lenin* (1931, Abb. 6) ist wie eine Lehrbuchaufgabe zur Zentralperspektive der Post-Renaissance.

**Dalís Bibliothek in der Fundació Gala-Salvador Dalí enthält einige Klassiker zur Perspektive.**



Man bemerke, wie der Klavierdeckel exakt an die Decke eines schachtelartigen Raumes stößt. Die Kante verläuft parallel zum oberen Rand des Gemäldes, das als Stellvertreter innerhalb des Bildes fungiert. Der Klavierdeckel und die offene Türe am Ende des Raums öffnen Bildräume, die sich gegenseitig stützen. *Der Schlaf* (ca. 1937) ist das Selbstporträt eines Kopfes, der von Krücken getragen wird. Es scheint, als könnte diese Traumwelt augenblicklich einstürzen. Eine der Krücken aber dient auch dazu, die obere Kante des Bildes vom Runterklappen zu bewahren. Die Malerei hinkt also nach und stützt sich auf. Es ist mehr als wahrscheinlich, dass Dalí mit Freuds Interpretationen zur „Anlehnung" als beherrschende, körperliche Handlung vertraut war, aber er wendet sie als trockenen Kommentar zur unsicheren Position der Malerei an. Browns *You Take My Place in this Showdown* von 1993 (Abb. 7), ein Remake von Dalís *Der große Masturbator* (1929), ist nicht mehr in horizontaler, sondern in vertikaler Ausrichtung. Die nunmehrige Querverdichtung resultiert in einem zentralen Motiv, einem Kopf im Profil (ein Selbstporträt Dalís), gewölbt und hängend wie eine seiner berühmten Uhren, sodass Brown gezwungen war, eine Krücke darunter zu schieben. Offensichtlich dient diese dazu, das Bild am Hinabsinken zu hindern.

Brown gibt zu, von Dalís Besessenheit mit der Verwesung zu schöpfen. In einem Interview äußert er sich dazu und verbindet die Farben der Verwesung mit dem „Verfall", der ein Nebenprodukt des postmodernen Bildes ist, das immer bereits reproduziert: „Das Thema war immer die ungesunde, unreale Welt der Bücher und Illustrationen. Eine Welt, in der die Luft nur zwischen den Seiten besteht. Die Verwesung beschreibt die Farben dieser Welt."

„Last Night I Dreamt that Somebody Loved Me", Interview mit Stephen Hepworth. London, Mai 2000, in: *Glenn Brown*, Ausst.-Kat., Centre d'art contemporain, Domaine de Kerguéhennec 2000, S. 68.

Wo es den Hauch der Verwesung gibt, suchen wir automatisch nach einer Leiche. Und diese Leiche ist die Malerei.

# Catherine Millet
# Dalí und ich

Vielleicht gehörte auch Dalí zu den Menschen, die aufgrund ihrer psychischen Veranlagung eines wenn auch imaginären Publikums bedürfen, um sich zu äußern, und so konnte eben auch Dalí nur schreiben, wenn er sich einen Gesprächspartner – und war der noch so fern, anonym oder hypothetisch – vorstellte und so tat, als würde er mit diesem sprechen.

„Der polymorph Perverse“

> **Als die Surrealisten einmal über Dalí „zu Gericht“ saßen, um seinen „angeblichen Hitlerismus“ zu befinden, schrieb der Künstler am 1. Mai 1952 in sein Tagebuch: „Der polymorphe Perverse, der ich in meiner Jugend gewesen war, erreichte einen hysterischen Höhepunkt: meine Kiefer zermalmten Gala, ich verliebte mich in die denkbar transzendental nach Ammoniak stinkenden verwesten Esel.“ Salvador Dalí, *Dalí sagt … Tagebuch eines Genies*, hg. von Michel Déon, übers. von Rolf und Hedda Soellner. München 1968, S. 29.**

Der Kunsthistoriker Ricard Mas Peinado hat in seinem Buch über das Leben und Werk Dalís angemerkt, dass diese Art der Kommunikation Dalí genauso wenig davon abhielt, von den Liebeserlebnissen seiner Kindheit zu erzählen, wie öffentlich über seine Sexualität zu sprechen. Er zitiert ein Interview mit dem Künstler, das 1976 im *Playboy* veröffentlicht wurde. Darin geht es um das Bild *Der große Masturbator* (Abb. 1): „Jedes Mal, wenn ich etwas Sperma verliere, bin ich überzeugt, es verschwendet zu haben. Ich habe immer Schuldgefühle.“ Und als müsse er eine allgemein bekannte Tatsache zurechtrücken, die er ein wenig übertrieben dargestellt hat, fügt er hinzu: „Um es vorweg zu sagen, ich bin sonst nicht so impotent.“



# Catherine Millet
# Dalí and me

Perhaps, because of a mental structure that means that some people cannot think without thinking of themselves in performance, Dalí could only write/speak to interlocutors, however distant, anonymous or hypothetical they may have been.

“Polymorphous pervert”

> **Describing his reactions during his “trial” by the Surrealists, Dalí writes *(Diary of a Genius)*, “the polymorphous pervert that I had been during my adolescence reached a peak of hysteria.”**

Ricard Mas Peinado notes that it never “bothered” Dalí to describe the romantic exploits of his childhood, any more than it did to talk about his sexuality in public. He cites an interview published in *Playboy* in 1976 in which Dalí talks about the picture *The Great Masturbator* (ill. 1): “Every time I lose a little sperm I'm convinced I've wasted it. I always feel guilty afterwards.” And, as though to rectify an aspect of his fame that might have been somewhat exaggerated, “To start with, I'm not as impotent as all that.”

> **Cited by Ricard Mas Peinado in *Dalí*; from the French translation Éditions Hazan, Vanves, 2003. Preface by Carlos Rojas.**

The same statement appears in interviews with Alain Bosquet published in 1966, but that isn't quite the same thing as making it in the pages of a popular magazine. The sexual inclinations, repulsions and complexes described in the writings are approached in a necessarily more schematic – and direct – manner in the interviews, including the books of interviews with Louis Pauwels, Alain Bosquet and André Parinaud

Zit. nach Richard Mas Peinado, in: *Dalí*, mit einem Vorwort von Carlos Rojas. Paris 2003.

Dieselbe Erklärung findet man in den 1966 mit Alain Bosquet geführten Gesprächen, aber in einer Zeitschrift erhält sie natürlich ein ganz anderes Gewicht. Die sexuellen Neigungen und Abneigungen sowie die Komplexe, an denen Dalí litt, wurden in seinen autobiografischen Schriften zwangsläufig schematischer dargestellt als etwa in einem Interview oder beispielsweise in den Gesprächen mit Louis Pauwels, Andre Parinaud und Alain Bosquet, die allesamt publiziert wurden. Diese Bücher verraten einem sogleich, dass man einen Mann vor sich hat, der, nachdem er einige Hemmungen überwunden hatte, nur eine einzige Frau liebte („Ich schwöre, dass ich nie eine andere Frau geliebt habe als Gala") und der eher Voyeur als Handelnder war („Gewöhnlich meide ich sexuelle Kontakte und lasse dem voyeuristischen Vergnügen ein wenig Masturbation folgen"). Dalí hat auch das Problem der Impotenz angeschnitten und versucht, die Notwendigkeit der Enthaltsamkeit bei großen Männern – Künstlern wie Diktatoren – rational zu erklären: „Die Männer, die einen schnellen Fick haben und sich ohne Schwierigkeit hingeben können, besitzen nur noch eine stark verminderte schöpferische Kraft [...]. Nehmen Sie Männer wie beispielsweise Leonardo da Vinci, Hitler, Napoleon, die ihre Zeit geprägt haben und so gut wie impotent waren."

Alain Bosquet, *Entretien avec Salvador Dalí*. Monaco 2000. – In *The Shameful Life of Salvador Dalí*, New York, London 1997, macht Ian Gibson auf ein Interview aufmerksam, das 1973 im britischen Fernsehen ausgestrahlt wurde und in dem Dalí dieselbe Theorie vertritt.

(this last known in English as *The Unspeakable Confessions of Salvador Dalí*). On opening these books we soon realise who we are dealing with: someone who, once he has got over his initial inhibitions, has had sexual relations with only one woman ("I swear I've only ever made love with Gala") and is more voyeuristic than active ("personally I avoid contact, accompanying the pleasures of voyeurism with a bit of masturbation"). Dalí takes on the problem of impotence and succeeds in rationalizing the need for abstinence in great men, artists and tyrants alike: "Men who fuck easily, and can give themselves without difficulty, have only a very diminished creative potency [...]. Look at Leonardo da Vinci, Hitler, Napoleon, they all left their mark on their times, and they were more or less impotent."

In *The Shameful Life of Salvador Dalí*, New York, London, WW Norton & Co., 1997, Ian Gibson mentions an interview in 1973 for a programme on British television in which Dalí advanced the same theory.

He does it so openly that this extreme honesty should perhaps be seen as one of those precipitate confessions in which you come to terms with a fault that is more feared than actually present, as when you hurriedly warn, "I'm clumsy" before picking up some fragile object that you do indeed run the risk of breaking, but which can also be moved from one place to another without damage.
Added to this is a pronounced liking for scatology, doubtless less dreadful than his surrealist friends might have feared when looking at the undeniably disturbing *Le Jeu lugubre* [The lugubrious game] (ill. 2), in which the figure in

Er äußerte sich dermaßen freimütig, dass man seine Worte beinahe als Geständnis eines Mannes auslegen muss, der sich mit einem Makel abgefunden hat, vor dem man sich mehr fürchtet, als dass er tatsächlich vorhanden ist. So als würde man gleichsam als Warnung vorausschicken: „Ich bin ungeschickt", bevor man einen zerbrechlichen Gegenstand in die Hand nimmt, den man kaputt machen, aber genauso gut unversehrt abstellen könnte. Auffallend ist ferner eine ausgesprochene Vorliebe für Fäkalien, die zweifellos weniger beunruhigend war, als die surrealistischen Freunde angesichts des Gemäldes *Das finstere Spiel* (Abb. 2) annahmen, auf dem die Gestalt im Vordergrund eine mit Kot beschmutzte Unterhose anhat – eine Vorliebe, die Dalí jedenfalls mit vielen teilt, die an Geschichten von Furzen und Exkrementen Gefallen fanden, und das waren nicht wenige.

Ian Gibson weist in *The Shameful Life of Salvador Dalí* darauf hin, dass der im Anhang des Tagebuchs veröffentlichte Text, der Auszug aus *L'Art de péter, ou Manuel de L'artilleur sournois* vom Grafen La Trompette in der amerikanischen Ausgabe entfallen ist.

Die Onanie wird vor allem durch den Titel eines seiner berühmtesten Bilder aus dem Jahr 1929 gepriesen, *Der große Masturbator*, das ihn übrigens 1930 zu einem Gedicht gleichen Titels inspirierte. Meines Wissens ist uns nicht annähernd so viel über die sexuellen Vorlieben von Matisse oder Picasso bekannt.
Ich räume ein, dass Dalí über die besondere Form analer Onanie, die er praktiziert zu haben scheint, nicht ins Detail geht. Aus einem Brief, den er während der Arbeit an dem Bild



the foreground is wearing stained underpants – a fondness in any case shared, at least in part, by all who delight in tales of farts and excrement, in other words quite a lot of people.

But not everyone. Ian Gibson, *op. cit.*, tells us that the piece published as an appendix to the French edition of the *Diary*, the extract from *L'Art de péter, ou Manuel de l'artilleur sournois*, by the Comte de La Trompette, was suppressed by the American publisher.

Onanism is particularly celebrated in the tide of *The Great Masturbator*, one of Dalí's most famous pictures, painted in 1929 – a title that was moreover borrowed in a poem of 1930.
As far as I know we do not have nearly as much information available on the sexual personalities of Matisse or Picasso.
I concede that Dalí gives no details on the particular form of anal onanism that he seems to have practised. A letter he wrote to a friend precisely while he was painting *Le Jeu lugubre*, cited by Ian Gibson in his very complete biography, in any case reveals that it was no secret to his close friends: "I would be delighted for you to come and I would have my fingers (as always) plunged into the famous hole, which is the arse hole and no other."

According to the account of the poet Rafael Alberti, on hearing of Dalí's relationship with Gala, García Lorca exclaimed, "That's impossible! He can only have an erection when someone sticks a finger up his arse." Gibson reproduces this quotation. We can surely suppose that, were "someone"'s finger not available, his own would do the job.

*Das finstere Spiel* an einen Freund schrieb und den Ian Gibson in seiner äußerst ausführlichen Biografie des Künstlers zitiert, geht jedenfalls hervor, dass diese Vorliebe im Kreis seiner Vertrauten kein Geheimnis war: „Ich wäre beglückt, wenn ihr kämet, und ich würde wie immer meine Finger in das berühmte Loch stecken, das nichts anderes als das Arschloch ist."

**Dem spanischen Dichter Rafael Alberti zufolge soll García Lorca, als er von der Liaison zwischen Gala und Dalí erfuhr, ausgerufen haben: „Das ist unmöglich! Er bekommt nur eine Erektion, wenn man ihm einen Finger in den Arsch steckt!" Zitiert bei Gibson, a.a.O. Kann man sich nicht vorstellen, dass er sich in Ermangelung des Fingers von „irgendjemand anderem" mit dem eigenen Finger beholfen hat?**

Auch im *Tagebuch eines Genies* findet man eine Anspielung darauf. Unter dem Datum des 2. September 1956 notierte Dalí „Ich erhielt ein Telegramm von der Fürstin P. Sie kündigt mir für morgen ihre Ankunft an. Ich vermute, dass sie mir die ‚chinesische Masturbationsvioline' überreichen will, die ihr Mann, der Fürst, mir als Geschenk von seiner letzten Chinareise mitzubringen versprach. Nach dem Abendessen träume ich unter einem Himmel, der sämtlichen Gemeinplätzen von kosmischen Ausmaßen Vorschub leistet, von der mit einem Vibratoransatzstück versehenen Violine. Dieses Ansatzstück ist dazu bestimmt, zunächst in den Anus eingeführt zu werden, danach und vor allem aber in das weibliche Geschlecht."

**Salvador Dalí, *Dalí sagt… Tagebuch eines Genies*, a.a.O., S. 158f.**

We also find an allusion in the *Diary*. Dalí receives a visit from Princess P, whose husband had promised him a gift of the "Chinese masturbatory violin." Instead of this she gives him a porcelain goose. "She claims that since I devised the famous swoon by vibrations in the anus, she has fears at the border and could not see herself easily explaining the use of this instrument to customs officials."

**Salvador Dalí, *Diary of a Genius*, Pan Books, London 1976, 146.**

It is unfair to claim that, while Dalí may have acknowledged his onanism and his paranoia, he was not prepared to admit to his homosexual inclinations. This view is expressed by Raphael Santos Torroella, a critic and friend of Dalí's, in words reported by Gibson. But in the sexual register surely everyone sees and hears what they want to – or can – see and hear. Pauwels records the following observation: "When Garcia Lorca wanted to possess me, I refused in horror. But as I grow older I'm a little more attracted to men. [...] On a very supple, almost feminine body, the sight of erect virility delights my eyes." Clues are scattered here and there, if only in *The Secret Life*. Perhaps precisely because the idea is placed in the chapter presented by its author as "False Childhood Memories" we should take seriously what Dalí said of his friend called Buchaques. "Buchaques appeared to me as beautiful as a little girl, yet his excessively chunky knees gave me a feeling of uneasiness, as did also his buttocks too tightly squeezed into pants that were too excruciatingly narrow."

Am folgenden Tag aber gab Dalí seiner Enttäuschung Ausdruck, dass die Fürstin ihm statt der chinesischen Analvioline eine Porzellangans gebracht hatte! „Sie gibt vor, seit ich die berühmte Lustohnmacht mittels Analvibrators erfunden habe, seien ihr Bedenken gekommen, und sie habe nicht recht gewusst, wie sie an der Grenze den Zöllnern den Verwendungszweck dieses Instruments erklären sollte.“

Ebd., S. 160.

Es ist ungerecht, Dalí vorzuwerfen, er habe zwar offen seinen Hang zur Selbstbefriedigung und seine Paranoia zugegeben, nicht aber seine Neigung zur Homosexualität. Gibson zitiert zum Beispiel einige diesbezügliche Äußerungen von Raphael Santos Torroella, eines Kritikers und Verwandten des Künstlers. Doch neigt auf sexuellem Gebiet nicht jeder dazu, nur das zu sehen und zu verstehen, was er selbst zu begreifen imstande ist? Pauwels hat beispielsweise in seinem Gespräch mit Dalí folgende Äußerung festgehalten: „Als Garcia Lorca mich besitzen wollte, verweigerte ich mich ihm voller Schrecken. Aber jetzt, da ich älter werde, fühle ich mich von den Männern ein wenig mehr angezogen. [...] Es ist ein erfreulicher Anblick für mich, wenn sich die Manneskraft über einem geschmeidigen, fast femininen Körper aufrichtet.“ Hier und dort finden sich verstreut diesbezügliche Hinweise, nicht zuletzt in *Das geheime Leben des Salvador Dalí*. Vielleicht sollte man Dalís Äußerungen über seinen Kameraden Buchaques im Kapitel „Falsche Kindheitserinnerungen“ doch ernst nehmen: „Buchaques kam mir so schön vor wie ein kleines Mädchen, doch seine übermäßig dicken Knie verursachten mir Unbehagen, ebenso sein



Salvador Dalí, *The Secret Life of Salvador Dalí*, translated by Haakon M. Chevalier, Vision Press, London 1976, 47.

Dalí had a predilection for buttocks, which he placed at the centre of major paintings such as *Young Virgin Auto-Sodomized by the Horns of Her Own Chastity*; it is tempting to correct his words to read "*above all* his buttocks too tightly squeezed into pants that were too excruciatingly narrow." Dalí openly cried, "I love Buchaques! I love Buchaques!"

Ibid., 48.

Most of the major writings cited here post-date the paintings in which Dalí reveals his emotional and sexual life, his desires and terrors. These are often very small in size, as required no doubt by their excessively detailed technical realisation, but perhaps also by the mental concentration that gave rise to them, and include *Le Jeu lugubre*, *The Great Masturbator*, *Portrait of Éluard*, *The Invisible Man* (1929), *The Old Age of William Tell* (1931) (ill. 3) and *The Enigma of William Tell* (1933), or the different variations on Millet's *Angelus*. Not only is Dalí history's "first painter of arses," but also one of the first painters of masturbation,

The phrase "first painter of arses" is Luis Romero's, published in French translation in *Dalí, tout Dalí en un visage*, Cercle d'Art, Paris, 1975 and 2003. Jean-Louis Gaillemin, in *Dalí, desirs inassouvis, du purisme au surréalisme* 1925–1935, Montreal, Le Passage, 2002, notes that Dalí was almost certainly the first "in the history of official painting" to use masturbation in the subject and title of a painting (140). However, Gaillemin is forgetting Egon Schiele.

Po, der viel zu fest in unerträglich enge Hosen gezwängt war."

Salvador Dalí, *Das geheime Leben des Salvador Dalí*, a.a.O., S. 85.

Dalí hatte eine Vorliebe für das Gesäß, das er in den Mittelpunkt seiner wichtigsten Bilder gerückt hat, beispielsweise in *Jugendliche Jungfrau, von der eigenen Keuschheit beschwult* (bekannt auch als: *Von den Hörnern ihrer eigenen Keuschheit autosodomisierte junge Jungfrau*). Daher möchte man seinen Kommentar über Buchaques richtigstellen: „*Vor allem sein Po, der in eine enge Hose gezwängt war*", müsste es heißen. Dalí erklärte geradeheraus: „Zweifellos war ich in ihn verliebt, denn anders war die Gefühlsverwirrung, in die seine Gegenwart mich versetzte, nicht zu rechtfertigen."

Ebd., S. 84.

Die meisten der hier zitierten Texte sind den Bildern vorausgegangen, die oft kleinformatig sind – was zweifellos in der äußerst sorgfältigen technischen Ausführung sowie in der geistigen Konzentration, aus der sie hervorgegangen sind, begründet ist. In ihnen hat Dalí sein Gefühls- und Sexualleben, seine Begierden und Ängste offenbart: *Das finstere Spiel* (1929), *Der große Masturbator* (1929), *Bildnis Paul Éluard* (1929), *Der unsichtbare Mann* (1930), *Das Greisenalter Wilhelm Tells* (1930) (Abb. 3) und *Das Rätsel des Wilhelm Tell* (1933), eine Serie von Bildern mit dem Thema des *Angelus von Millet*. Dalí ist in die Geschichte der Malerei nicht nur eingegangen als „der erste Maler von Hintern", sondern auch als einer der Ersten, in dessen Werken die Masturbation eine wichtige Rolle spielt.

to which it must be added that fellatio (as dreamed of by *The Great Masturbator*) and emasculation are not so commonly found on the walls of our museums and galleries, either. Small in size, intimate in content and very directly autobiographical, to the point of being almost contemporary, in some cases, with the events that inspired them, these pictures nevertheless had immense effect, first on the history of Surrealism and later on modernism. After his meetings with Federico García Lorca and Luis Buñuel in Madrid in 1922–1923, this period of the late 1920s and very early 1930s saw the main upheavals in both Salvador Dalí's adult life and in his work, from his arrival in Paris and participation in Surrealism to his meeting with Gala, then the wife of Paul Éluard, his break with his family and lean times, soon followed by his first contracts with galleries and beginnings of support from collectors (which matters).

Notably the group of connoisseurs called Le Zodiaque [the Zodiac], who made it their aim to support Dalí financially. Cf. Gaillemin, *op. cit.*

Lastly these were years in which he was developing his paranoiac-critical approach, which curiously would not be truly applied in the paintings until the second half of the 1930s – aside from the experimentation of *The Invisible Man* and *Paranoid Horse Woman* of 1930. Aged only twenty-five in 1929, Dalí first took on the monsters that occupied his fieldof vision, sometimes since childhood, creating a profusion of roaring lion's heads, portraits of grimacing old men – all with protruding eyes – locusts and ants. *The Metamorphosis of Narcissus* (1936—1937) (ill. 4) came only later. Dalí wrote,

Der Ausdruck „der erste Maler von Hintern" stammt von Luis Romero, in: *Todo Dalí en un rostro*. Barcelona 1975. Jean-Louis Gaillemin hebt in *Dalí, désirs inassouvis, du purisme au surréalisme, 1925–1935*. Paris 2002, hervor, dass Dalí zweifellos der Erste „in der Geschichte der offiziellen Malerei" war, der die Masturbation thematisierte und nach ihr ein Gemälde betitelte (siehe dort S. 140). Gaillemin lässt dabei jedoch Egon Schiele außer Acht.

Diese Bilder haben mit ihrem intimen, autobiografischen Kontext, der manchmal sogar von realen Ereignissen angeregt wurde, eine unermessliche Bedeutung für die Geschichte des Surrealismus und der Moderne überhaupt. Nachdem sich Dalí in den Jahren 1922 und 1923 mit Federico García Lorca und Luis Buñuel in Madrid angefreundet hatte, kam es Ende der zwanziger, Anfang der dreißiger Jahre zu grundlegenden Änderungen im Leben und in der Kunst von Salvador Dalí. Er reiste nach Paris, schloss sich den Surrealisten an, lernte Gala kennen, die damals mit Paul Éluard verheiratet war, und es kam zum Bruch mit dem Elternhaus. Es waren zwar auch magere Jahre, aber allmählich kamen die ersten Verträge mit Galerien und die ersten finanziellen Unterstützungen durch Sammler zustande, was sehr wichtig war.

Vor allem die in der Gruppe „Le Zodiaque" vereinten Kunstliebhaber hatten sich vorgenommen, Dalí finanziell zu unterstützen. Vgl. Jean-Louis Gaillemin, *Dalí, désirs inassouvis, du purisme au surréalisme*, a. a. O.

In jenen Jahren entwickelte er die paranoisch-kritische Methode, die – abgesehen von den



that it was "the first picture obtained entirely after the integral application of the paranoiac-critical method."

Salvador Dalí, *Oui, méthode paranoïaque-critique et autres texts*, Paris, Denoël, 1971, 6; nos. given are those of the short pieces (this has been published in English Boston MA 1998, but the excerpts quoted are translated anew from the original French).

It is the image of a young man squatting above a stretch of water, who becomes a hand holding an egg from which a narcissus is emerging. Then came *The Endless Enigma* (1938), the image of the body of a man lying down, which is also the body of a horse lying down, which is the body of a standing greyhound, which is a woman sitting next to a boat, the two of them simultaneously a bowl next to a mandolin, the seated woman-cum-bowl also being a face. Before calling up these "double-images" (and even triple or more, since he envisaged obtaining up to thirty images),

Ibid., 37.

whose surface holds the eye as a calm swell holds a boat, Dalí had to locate the threatening figures.
Of the iconic profusion of *Le Jeu lugubre*, we shall confine ourselves to noting here, in relation to the subject we embarked on earlier, a finger pointing to an anus, the statue's enlarged hand and of course the spattered underpants of the figure entering the picture from the bottom right corner, his feet still on the painter's – or observer's – own floor. On the right in *The Invisible Man*, a frightening group of three

Studien *Der unsichtbare Mann* und *Die Unsichtbaren: Schlafende, Pferd und Löwe* (1930) – sich erst in der zweiten Hälfte der dreißiger Jahre in seiner Malerei niederschlug. Letzteres Bild hat Dalí folgendermaßen erläutert: „Durch einen paranoischen Vorgang habe ich kürzlich das Bild einer Frau gemalt, die durch ihre Haltung, in Schatten wie in Gestalt, ohne jegliche Veränderung oder Entstellung ihres wirklichen Aussehens gleichzeitig ein Pferd darstellt."

Zitiert nach: Robert Descharnes, *Dalí. Die Eroberung des Irrationalen. Sein Werk – sein Leben*, übers. von Karin Hirschmann. Köln 1984, S. 100.

Zu Dalís neuer Verfahrensweise heißt es in seiner Schrift *Die sichtbare Frau*: „Durch einen eindeutig paranoischen Vorgang ist es möglich geworden, ein doppeltes Vorstellungsbild zu erhalten, das heißt die Darstellung eines Gegenstandes, die ohne die mindeste figürliche oder anatomische Veränderung gleichzeitig die Darstellung eines anderen, völlig verschiedenen Gegenstandes ist, auch sie frei von der irgendwie gearteten Verzerrung oder Anomalität, die auf ein Arrangement schließen ließe. Ein solch doppelgestaltiges Vorstellungsbild ist erreichbar geworden dank der Heftigkeit paranoischen Denkens."

Salvador Dalí, *Unabhängigkeitserklärung der Phantasie und Erklärung der Rechte des Menschen auf seine Verrücktheit. Gesammelte Schriften*, hg. von Axel Matthes und Tilbert Diego Stegmann, übers. von Brigitte Weidmann. München 1974, S. 132f.

Der im Jahr 1929 noch nicht einmal Fünfundzwanzigjährige schlug sich zunächst mit

adults and three youths confronts the viewer with the theme of emasculation (also identifiable in *Le Jeu lugubre*). It is hardly surprising that Dalí is at his least explicit in depicting the figure of the father. He does this by taking a detour through the figure of the Swiss hero William Tell, a father who placed his son in danger. The works whose tides feature Tell's name notably refer to the episode in which Dalí's father, a lawyer in Figuerés (although he was a free thinker), drove out and disinherited his son, who was sharing his live with a divorcee and whom he suspected of taking drugs.

Concrete and nothing but

During this period the images are as raw as the words, which Dalí never uses euphemistically. It was his way to retain the frank speech of his social origins and, anyway, if he was going to be the first painter of arses and the first to devote a piece of writing to pubic hair, it was better to express himself clearly: "It was necessary, entirely necessary, to come some day to the question of pubic hair. [...] It is not really possible to talk about it other than in a language stripped of euphemism, a natural language, clear and pared down, which means more or less that to speak this language it is preferable by a long way not to have too hairy a tongue."

Ibid., 59. We can appreciate the urgency with which Dalí presented this undertaking, all the more for its strong contrast with the approach of that hygienist and future reference-point for the avantgarde, Marcel Duchamp. Duchamp adorned his head with a star-shaped tonsure to meet the requirements of a photograph, abandoned paintbrush bristles and made a large, hairless nude (*Étant donnés: 1° la*

Ungeheuern herum, von denen einige bereits seit der Kindheit seine Fantasiewelt besetzten. Immer wieder malte er Köpfe brüllender Löwen und zu Fratzen verzogene Gesichter von Greisen – die einen wie die anderen mit aus den Augenhöhlen heraustretenden Augäpfeln – sowie Heuschrecken und Ameisen. Erst später malte er in dieser Technik die *Metamorphose des Narziss* (1936–1937, Abb. 4), indem er Motive verwendete, deren Formen sich ähneln und deren Bedeutung sich aus dem gegenseitigen Bezug ergibt, um so das Verhältnis zwischen Realität und Illusion darzustellen, das wiederum durch den Mythos des Narziss symbolisiert wird. Über dieses Gemälde schreibt Dalí, es sei „das erste Bild", das „nach uneingeschränkter Anwendung der paranoisch-kritischen Methode" entstanden sei.



Salvador Dalí, *Die Eroberung des Irrationalen. Essays*, a.a.O., S. 145.

Auf dem Bild ist eine Traumwelt mit einer Berglandschaft und einem See abgebildet, und in der linken Hälfte des Bildes erkennt man die Gestalt eines jungen Mannes, der sein Spiegelbild im Wasser anschaut. In der rechten Bildhälfte ist eine knochige Hand aus Stein zu sehen, die ein Ei, aus dem eine Narzisse blüht, in der Hand hält. 1938 malte Dalí *Das endlose Rätsel*, einen länglichen männlichen Körper, der zugleich der Körper eines liegenden Pferdes, eines im Gleichschritt gehenden Windhundes, einer neben einem Schiff sitzenden Frau sowie eine Obstschale neben einer Mandoline ist, wobei die sitzende Obstschalenfrau gleichzeitig ein Gesicht ist. Bevor Dalí diese „doppelten Vorstellungsbilder" schuf (die bisweilen drei- oder mehrgestaltig sind, denn Dalí strebte an, mittels der para-

*chute d'eau, 2° le gaz d'éclairage*). Cf. Didier Ottinger's demonstration, "des Nus, vite" in *Art Press* 154, January 1991.

However extraordinary, the stories Dalí tells us, with their characters, settings and props, are not offered as poetic transpositions, but as real people and proven facts. For similar reasons, the fauna and flora of the pictures should not be regarded as symbols. These elements are not dressed up to pander to the viewers sensibilities. Dalí stresses that, when he is painting, he does not himself understand the meaning of his pictures, many of which have titles containing the word "enigma." This "does not mean that these paintings have no meaning [...] on the contrary, their meaning is so profound, complex, coherent and involuntary that it escapes the simple analysis of logical intuition."

Ibid., 53.

To psychoanalysts both amateur and professional, I say please put your demystificatory arsenal away. While it was Dalí's ambition to paint "with the most imperialist rage for detail the images of concrete irrationality,"

Ibid., 53.

this was so that we would believe in them as strangely as he did. If, in the deceptive twilight darkness, a peasant man and woman in meditative contemplation turn into two lubricious and death-dealing monsters, and the painter, rather than taming them into insubstantial mirages, restores them to their full, petrified solidity, as tangible as the fear they inspire, who could or would dare take his place and reduce these monsters to handy symbols?

noisch-kritischen Methode sogar bis zu dreißig Bilder

Salvador Dalí, *Unabhängigkeitserklärung der Phantasie und Erklärung der Rechte des Menschen auf seine Verrücktheit. Gesammelte Schriften*, a.a.O., S. 24 („Moralische Position des Surrealismus").

in einem zu erzwingen!), bei denen das Prinzip des mehrdeutig lesbaren Vexierbildes zum Einsatz kommt und bei deren Betrachtung man den Eindruck von einer ruhigen, wogenden Bewegung gewinnt, musste er jedoch die bedrohlichen Objekte erst aufspüren.

Das Gemälde *Das finstere Spiel* verhalf Dalí zu einem aufsehenerregenden Entrée in den Kreis der Surrealisten: Ein Finger ist auf einen After gerichtet, die Hand der Statue ist übermäßig groß, und selbstverständlich trägt der Mann, der unten rechts im Bild eine andere Gestalt penetriert und mit den Füßen noch auf dem Holzaufbau desjenigen steht, der malt oder beobachtet, eine mit Fäkalien beschmutzte Unterhose. Auf der rechten Bildhälfte von *Der unsichtbare Mann* konfrontiert die erschreckend anmutende Gruppe – drei Erwachsene und drei Jugendliche – den Betrachter mit dem Kastrationsthema, das auch in *Das finstere Spiel* zu erkennen ist. Doch wen wundert's, dass Dalí sich vor einer eindeutigen Aussage drückte, wenn es um die Erinnerung an den Vater ging? Und sich dabei der Gestalt des Wilhelm Tell bediente, des Vaters, der seinen Sohn in Gefahr bringt? Die Gemälde mit dem Namen des Schweizer Volkshelden im Titel sind eine Anspielung auf Dalís Verstoßung und Enterbung durch seinen Vater. Der lebte als Notar in Figueres und konnte es, obgleich Freidenker, nicht hinnehmen, dass sein Sohn, den er

According to the new conception advanced at the same time by both Lacan and Dalí, paranoia is not an error of judgement on which irrational reasoning is built, but a phenomenon "consubstantial with fact."

Ibid., 44.

"The world is transformed [...] far more in its perception than in its interpretation," said Lacan. "The concrete nature of paranoid interpretation led Dalí to pay acute attention to the Surrealist objects known as "objects functioning symbolically," "object-poems" and "dreamlike objects." He gave them very detailed descriptions in an article that appeared in *Le Surréalisme au service de la Révolution* in 1931; he himself made a few striking examples (we shall see how apt this is), such as the *Retrospective Bust of a Woman* of 1933. These "delirious objects [are] intended to be put into circulation, in other words to intervene, to enter generally, daily into *collision* [my emphasis] with the others in life, in the full light of reality."

Ibid., 440.

The power Dalí gives to these objects he also gives to the images he materializes on canvas, which are neither displacements nor symbols substituted for reality, nor simulacra debilitated by a little common sense, nor bad dreams that the first event of the day casts back into the deepest depths of the unconscious. They too provoke collisions, and that can hurt! One can "really hurt oneself" with them, or at the least be seriously inconvenienced by them. As proof of this, *Le Jeu lugubre* certainly smelled no worse than any other painting on which the oil was not yet dry, yet some of the first people

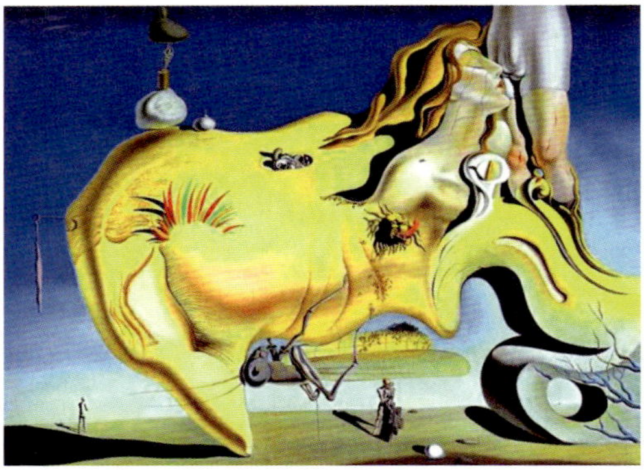

Abb./ill. 1: Salvador Dalí,
*Der große Masturbator/The Great Masturbator*, 1929

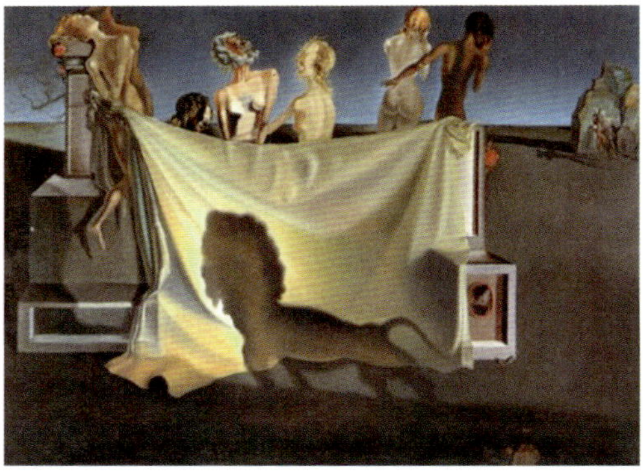

Abb./ill. 3: Salvador Dalí,
*Das Greisenalter Wilhelm Tells/The Old Age of William Tell*, 1931

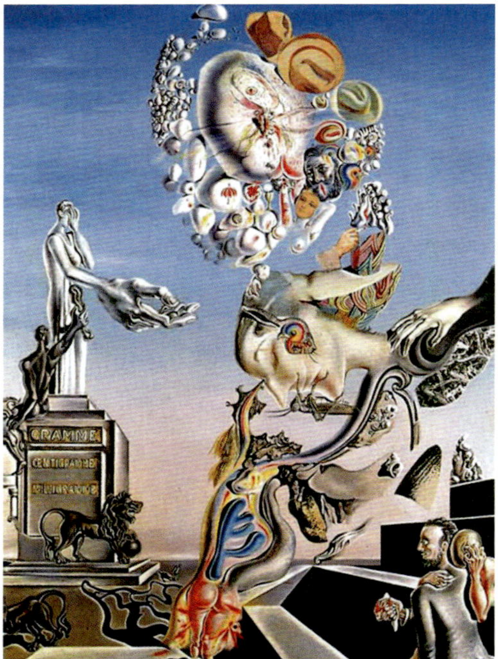

Abb./ill. 2: Salvador Dalí,
*Das finstere Spiel/The lugubrious game*, 1929

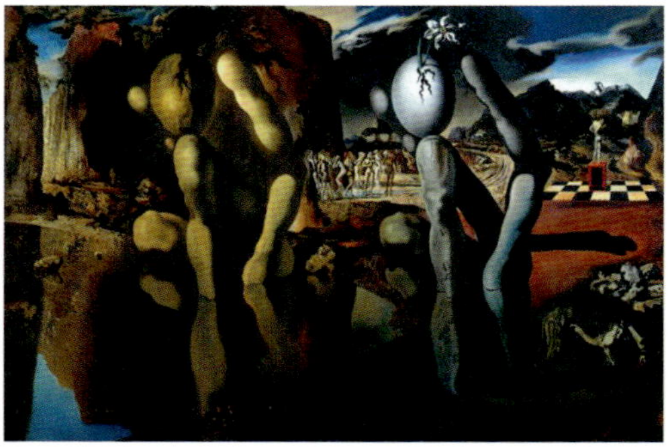

Abb./ill. 4: Salvador Dalí,
*Metamorphose des Narziss/*
*Metamorphosis of Narcissus*, 1937

überdies verdächtigte, Drogen zu nehmen, inzwischen mit einer geschiedenen Frau zusammenlebte.

Nichts anderes als konkrete Kunst

Dalís Malerei in dieser Zeit ist genauso schonungslos wie seine Schriften, da er Euphemismen grundsätzlich ablehnte. Das war seine Art, sich seiner Herkunft entsprechend keinen Zwang anzutun und so zum ersten Maler von Hintern zu werden und der Erste zu sein, der sich schriftlich über Schamhaare äußerte: „Doch es war nötig, war notwendig, ja unvermeidlich, über kurz oder lang bei dieser Behaarungsfrage zu landen [...]. Man kann kaum über sie sprechen außer in einer Sprache, die aller Euphemismen bar ist, in einer natürlichen, klaren und schmucklosen Sprache, was ungefähr besagen will, dass man gut dabei fährt, nicht zu viele Haare auf der Zunge zu haben, wenn man diese Sprache spricht."

Salvador Dalí, *Die Eroberung des Irrationalen. Essays*, a.a.O., S. 145.

Alle Geschichten, die uns seine Bilder vermitteln, sind mit ihren Figuren, ihrer Szenerie und ihrem Beiwerk – so außergewöhnlich sie auch sein mögen – nicht als poetische Umsetzungen, sondern als reale Gestalten und erwiesene Tatsachen zu verstehen. Aus ähnlichen Gründen dürfen die Tiere und Pflanzen auf den Bildern auch nicht als Symbole betrachtet werden, denn diese Elemente sollen keineswegs das Mitgefühl des Betrachters wecken. Der Künstler versteht in dem Augenblick, wo er malt, die Bedeutung seiner Bilder nicht – weshalb die Titel vieler seiner Bilder das Wort „Rätsel" enthalten. Das bedeutet aber nicht, so Dalí, „dass sie

to see it were really afraid of smelling shit. The episode is well known: on a visit to Cadaqués, the little port where Dalí had spent his holidays since his youth, the Surrealists started to worry and Gala decided to ask their new companion whether he indulged in scatological and indeed coprophagic practices. The account of the meeting in *The Secret Life* suggests that Dalí was initially tempted to say yes out of provocation, but decided against it faced with "the expression of [Gala's] face, exalted by the purity of an entire and lofty honesty."

Salvador Dalí, *The Secret Life of Salvador Dalí*, 231.

Perhaps it is because he recalled this incident that in 1930, in the emblematic piece *L'Âne pourri* [The Rotten Donkey], Dalí praises the paranoid power that "uses the external world to highlight the obsessional idea, with *the troubling particularity of making the reality of this idea valid for others*"

Salvador Dalí, *Oui, méthode paranoïaque-critique et autres texts*, 38.

(my emphasis). He was often to make this cheering observation. Is paranoid "madness" more easily shared than reason? This would explain why, a few years later, it was the most "delirious" of them all who captured the attention of the widest public.
Dalí replied differently to his visitors in Cadaqués in the long poem entitled, like the painting, *Le Grand Masturbateur*: "the man who eats/the incommensurable/turd/that the woman/shits/with love/into his mouth."

keine Bedeutung hätten: Im Gegenteil, ihre Bedeutung ist so unergründlich, komplex, zusammenhängend und unwillkürlich, dass sie der einfachen Analyse der logischen Anschauung entgeht".

Ebd., S. 12.

Amateur- und Berufspsychoanalytiker können also ihre entmystifizierenden Deutungen wieder einpacken. „Mein ganzer Ehrgeiz auf dem Gebiet der Malerei besteht darin, die Vorstellungsbilder der konkreten Irrationalität mit der herrischsten Genauigkeitswut sinnfällig zu machen",

Ebd., S. 12.

sagte Dalí im Jahr 1935. Wenn in der trügerischen Dunkelheit der Abenddämmerung ein Bauer und eine Bäuerin, beide in tiefe Andacht versunken, sich in zwei lüsterne, todbringende Ungeheuer verwandeln, und wenn der Maler, statt sie gefälliger zu gestalten, da sie halluzinatorische Trugbilder sind, sie als zu Stein erstarrte Masse ausarbeitet, die genauso greifbar ist wie das Grauen, das sie erregen – wer würde es wagen, an seine Stelle zu treten und diese Ungeheuer auf einfache Symbole zu reduzieren?

Entsprechend der neuen, von Lacan und Dalí gleichzeitig vertretenen Auffassung ist Paranoia das, was sich gegen den Verstand, die Vernunft richtet das Widervernünftige eben, der Wahnsinn, das Verrückte. Der Wahnsinn ist nicht in dem Sinn irrational, dass er keine immanente Logik besitzt und vollständig unbegründet ist – denn das Irrationale ist das Grundlose, das Abgründige. *Ratio* meint sowohl den Grund als auch die Vernunft. Das Vernünftige, Rationale



Ibid., 39.

We should note that in the meantime the woman who first came on reconnaissance had become the woman with whom he had established a relationship of love. But he gives another more theoretical answer when he starts to assert that the paranoiac-critical approach is an advance on the tried and tested Surrealist method of psychic automatism: "Surrealism in its early period offered specific methods to bring images closer to concrete irrationality. These methods, based on the exclusively passive and receptive role of the surrealist subject, are bankrupt and are giving way to new surrealist methods for the systematic exploration of the irrational. [...] The new delirious images of concrete irrationality suggest their physical, real 'possibility'; they go beyond the domain of psychoanalysable fantasies and 'virtual' representations." Further on he says, "Against the dream memory and impossible, virtual images of purely receptive states *that one can only recount* [Dalí's emphasis], the physical facts of 'objective' irrationality with which one can already hurt oneself."

Ibid., 53.

When one is hurt, one bleeds. "Bloody" is a recurrent word in Dalí's vocabulary, as in his homage to De Chirico's "bloody perspectives." Perhaps one can graze oneself on their sharp corners.

[...]

ist das Wohlbegründete. Doch nichts ist in sich so begründet und konsistent wie ein solider Wahn. Vor Lacan gingen die Psychiater davon aus, dass bei Persönlichkeiten mit einer „paranoischen Konstitution" der Wahn auf „Fehlurteilen" gegründet sei. In der paranoischen Interpretation wird versucht, den normalen, vernünftigen Mechanismen folgend, jedoch auf der Basis falscher Voraussetzungen, zu einem Urteil zu kommen. Auf diese „vernünftige" Weise werden aufgrund falscher Voraussetzungen falsche Urteile gefällt, die wahnhafte Bilder produzieren. Diese entziehen sich der logischen Interpretation und unterliegen einer „konkreten Irrationalität", wobei für Dalí der paranoische Vorgang ein „mit dem Tatsächlichen wesensgleiches Phänomen" ist.

Ebd., S. 28.

Lacan zeigt, dass die Interpretation ein Bestandteil der Wahnbilder ist, denn diese existieren bereits vor der Interpretation und werden lediglich offengelegt. Er schreibt: „Diese Phänomene, vor allem die Interpretationen, spielen sich im Bewusstsein ab, mit einer unmittelbaren, überzeugenden, auf Anhieb objektiven Bedeutung [...]. Sie sind niemals Früchte irgendeiner überlegenden Ableitung."

Jacques Lacan, *Über die paranoische Psychose und ihre Beziehung zur Persönlichkeit und frühe Schriften über die Paranoia*, übers. von Hans-Dieter Gondek. Wien 2002, S. 137f.

Infolge der konkreten Natur der paranoischen Interpretation richtete Dalí seine Aufmerksamkeit verstärkt auf surrealistische Objekte, „surreale Gegenstände mit symbolischer Funktion", „Gegenstandsgedichte" und „Traum-

The sex appeal of Narcissus

The care Dalí took in shaping his public persona, of which the revelation of some of his most personal habits is apart, makes him a predecessor of the avantgardists who claimed to have as much control over their lives as over their works. Although Warhol in his books is far meaner with confidences about his sexuality, he is rightly compared to Dalí. In a way, Dalí demonstrated a "Pop" intuition at a time when the artist who would later become its icon was still a student at the Carnegie Institute of Technology, and was a few years ahead of him in designing motifs for fabrics

**For amateurs and fetishists we can cite a motif of shoes designed by Dalí for ties in 1951, which is somewhat reminiscent of the shoe designs that earned Warhol his early successes.**



and occupying the pages of *Vogue* and *Harper's Bazaar*. Dalí also preceded Warhol in the film world, having understood the value of being photographed with the stars. Dalí began staging his public appearances and exploiting their echoes as soon as the media that made them possible came into being. By the time Warhol was predicting that everyone would be famous for fifteen minutes, Dalí had already managed to hold on a little longer, and on repeated occasions. "It is difficult to hold the world's interest for more than half an hour at a time. [...] I have been successful for twenty years, to the extent that papers publish the most incomprehensible news items of our time, sent by teletype [...] PARIS. Dalí gave lecture at Sorbonne on Vermeer's *Lacemaker* and the rhinoceros. [...] NEW YORK. Dalí landed in New York dressed in a golden space-suit."

objekte". Er beschreibt sie genau in einem 1931 in der Pariser Zeitschrift *Le Surréalisme au service de la Revolution* erschienenen Beitrag. Er selbst hat einige sehr bemerkenswerte surrealistische Objekte hergestellt wie beispielsweise die *Retrospektive Frauenbüste* (1933). „Ich war entschlossen, mein Schlagwort vom ‚surrealistischen Objekt' [...] in die Tat umzusetzen. [...] Das surrealistische Objekt ist ein vom praktischen und rationalen Standpunkt aus absolut nutzloser Gegenstand, einzig zu dem Zweck geschaffen, Wahnsinnsideen und -fantasien auf fetischistische Art mit einem Maximum an greifbarer Wirklichkeit zu materialisieren."

Salvador Dalí, *Das geheime Leben des Salvador Dalí*, a.a.O., S. 537.



Die Wirkung, die Dalí diesen Objekten zuschreibt, gesteht er auch den Gestalten zu, die er auf die Leinwand malt; sie sind weder Transpositionen noch Symbole, die an die Stelle der Realität treten, weder Trugbilder, die der gesunde Menschenverstand als Täuschung erkennt, noch schlechte Träume, die nach dem Erwachen gleich vom ersten Ereignis ins Unterbewusstsein zurückgedrängt werden. Genau wie die surrealistischen Objekte können auch die Bilder schmerzhafte Kollisionen verursachen. Man kann sich mit ihnen wirklich verletzen oder man kann sich zumindest durch sie belästigt fühlen. Das Gemälde *Das finstere Spiel* beispielsweise roch bestimmt nicht schlechter als irgendein anderes frisch mit Ölfarbe gemaltes Bild, doch die Ersten, die es in Augenschein nahmen, meinten tatsächlich, ein Kotgeruch wehe ihnen um die Nase. Aber Dalís surrealistische Freunde waren bei ihrem Besuch in Cadaqués, jenem kleinen Fischerort

Salvador Dalí, Diary of a Genius, 171–72.

And so on. While Dalí became interested very early in photography as a creative medium, as soon as he could he also became interested in it as a vector for celebrity. Just as Yves Klein had himself followed by the photographer Harry Shunk, so in 1941 Dalí began a long collaboration with Philippe Halsman. One could write a book about the very studied poses, the elegance – which we might describe as "offbeat" – of the suits, the extravagant disguises and repertoire of grimaces of the figure taking shape in front of cameras. In addition to Halsman, Dalí was photographed by Man Ray, Brassaï, Català-Roca, Eric Schaal, Platt Lynes and others. It was no coincidence that one of Dalí's friends, Robert Descharnes, who became an interpreter of and specialist on his work, started out as a photographer. As David Vilaseca rightly observes, "In the model of subjectivity proposed by Dalí, the self no longer pre-exists its representations, but is on the contrary constituted performatively through them, entirely externally on the surface; in a word, ex-centrically."

David Vilaseca, "Le réel de l'œuvre autobiographique de Salvador Dalí" in *Lire Dalí, op. cit.* note 6.

The media era was just beginning, but writing perhaps brought more weight to this work of constructing an image. *The Secret Life of Salvador Dalí*, first published in English in 1942, and *Diary of a Genius*, published in 1964, are dense books. Not published until 1963 but written in the first half of the 1930s, *Le Mythe tragique de l'Angélus de Millet* can be regarded as belonging to a new genre, the autobiographical essay. Dalí an der Costa Brava, wo der Künstler seit seiner Kindheit die Ferien zu verbringen pflegte, sichtlich konsterniert. Gala ging sogar so weit, sich bei ihrem neuen Lebensgefährten zu erkundigen, ob er nicht gar irgendwelchen skatologischen Praktiken nachging. In seiner Autobiografie *Das geheime Leben* schildert Dalí, wie das Bild aufgenommen wurde: „Die kotbeschmutzten Unterhosen waren mit solcher Selbstzufriedenheit bis in alle Einzelheiten realistisch gemalt, dass das ganze Surrealistengrüppchen von der Frage gequält wurde: Ist er nun ein Koprophage oder nicht? Die Möglichkeit, dass ich vielleicht einen Fall dieser abstoßenden Verirrung darstellte, erzeugte bei ihnen zunehmend ostentatives Unbehagen. Gala war es, die sich entschloss, diesen Zweifel auszuräumen. Sie nahm mich eines Tages beiseite und sagte, sie habe mit mir etwas sehr Ernstes zu besprechen, und bat mich, eine Zeit festzusetzen, zu der wir uns treffen und miteinander reden könnten."

Ebd., S. 396.

Offenbar erinnerte sich Dalí an diesen Vorfall, als er im Jahr 1930 in dem emblematischen Artikel *Der Eselskadaver* die Grundlagen seiner paranoisch-kritischen Methode verherrlichte, „die auf kritischer und systematischer Objektivierung wahnhafter Assoziationen und Interpretationen" beruht und „eine spontane Methode irrationaler Erkenntnis ist".

Salvador Dalí, *Unabhängigkeitserklärung der Phantasie und Erklärung der Rechte des Menschen auf seine Verrücktheit. Gesammelte Schriften,* a.a.O., S. 131.

became annoyed when, in 1962, the collector A. Reynolds Morse wanted to publish a notebook from his youth. He must have feared that those pages, which he had not revised, might damage the image he had so carefully refined in his other books. We should note, however, that he did give in, on condition that the publication would not be made commercially available. These notebooks, seven of which are now published under the tide *Journal d'un genie adolescent* [Diary of an adolescent genius], prove that at fifteen the budding genius displayed a stunning precocity in his capacities for observation and self-observation. And his fears were unfounded: it is amazing to find the seeds of so many obsessions that would be cultivated later.

All this material, in which we can include the other, extremely numerous publications that are not autobiographical but in which Dalí cannot resist being extremely present, did not discourage the insatiable hordes who came to his door with their note-pads and tape-recorders. As we can imagine, they were playing into Dalí's hands. Having told his own story once, Dalí told it again, like a painter who never stops retouching his painting. These conversations are structured around the same major themes (Gala, death, religion, eroticism and so on) and in them we reread – in slightly different versions – anecdotes we have already encountered in *The Secret Life* and the *Diary*. The greatest quantity of new material or new detail is to be found in accounts and thoughts of a sexual nature, which may be due simultaneously to the period, the oral character of the narration, encouragement from the interlocutors – and the maturity of the interviewee. The confidants are all well-known: Alain Bosquet (*Entretien avec*

Kann der „paranoische Wahn“ mehr mitteilen als die Vernunft? Das wäre eine Erklärung dafür, dass der Wahnsinnigste von allen einige Jahre später die Aufmerksamkeit der breiten Öffentlichkeit auf sich ziehen würde.
Seinen Besuchern in Cadaqués gab Dalí eine andere Antwort als in einem Gedicht, das – wie das Gemälde – *Der große Masturbator* betitelt ist: „Der Mann frisst / die unermessliche Scheiße / die ihm die Frau / liebevoll / in den Mund / scheißt“.

Salvador Dalí, *Die Eroberung des Irrationalen. Essays*, a.a.O., S. 92.

Festzuhalten ist, dass Dalí in der Zwischenzeit eine Liebesbeziehung mit der Frau eingegangen war, die den Zweifel ausräumen wollte. Aber seine Antwort bleibt immer noch eher theoretisch, als er die Vorteile der paranoisch-kritischen Methode im Vergleich zur surrealistischen hervorhebt: „Der Surrealismus wartet in seiner ersten Periode mit besonderen Methoden auf, um sich den Vorstellungsbildern der konkreten Irrationalität zu nähern. Diese Methoden, die auf der ausschließlich passiven und rezeptiven Rolle des surrealistischen Bildinhaltes beruhen, werden zugunsten neuer surrealistischer Methoden systematischer Erforschung des Irrationalen abgebaut. [...] Die neuen wahnhaften Vorstellungsbilder der konkreten Irrationalität streben ihrer körperlichen, wirklichen ‚Möglichkeit‘ entgegen; sie gehen über den Bereich ‚virtueller‘, der Psychoanalyse zugänglicher Phantasmen und Darstellungen hinaus.“ Und weiter heißt es: „Statt der Traumerinnerung und virtueller, unmöglicher Vorstellungsbilder rein rezeptiver Zustände, ‚die man nur erzählen kann‘, treten die körperlichen Tatsachen der



*Salvador Dalí*, 1966), Louis Pauwels (*Les Passions selon Dalí*, 1968) and André Parinaud (*Comment on devient Dalí, les aveux inauovables de Salvador Dalí*, 1973). The latter two books are written in the first person singular, which produces a bizarre effect when the style, which is moreover very pure, is that of Pauwels rather than Dalí. We are even treated to an interweaving of styles when we reach the appendix in which Dalí comments on what Pauwels has written, saying "I" in his place, and, to a lesser extent, with the quotations in bold that Parinaud includes throughout his book so that the reader can experience the master's "inimitable language." Were these interlocutors hoping to discover the truth of the human being behind the myth? Even when they ask impertinent questions, one suspects they did not believe there was one. Rather they wanted to find out if the myth definitively was the truth. In his preface Pauwels says that Dalí "does not distort reality, he [...] returns it to its initial ductility." Parinaud's foreword begins with the lines, "This book is a dalían novel and if the hero, Dalí, speaks in the first person, this is simply a stylistic stipulation. Dalí never says "*je*" [I], but "*jeux*" [games]." Many authors, possibly less shrewd than these two, have noted how hard it was to grasp the character even when he seemed to open himself up so willingly. But this is because it would be wrong to try to flush out the man hiding behind the appearance. Dalí must be looked at in the way that we look at his paintings from the 1930s. They contain several images that are not arranged one behind the other, like theatrical backdrops, but intertwined on a single surface.

Although it is an everyday phenomenon, we continue to be delighted, amused, scandalized

‚objektiven' Irrationalität, mit denen man sich immerhin wirklich verwunden kann."

Ebd., S. 13f.

„Verwunden" und „bluten" sind Ausdrücke, die bei Dalí häufig vorkommen. Er spricht beispielsweise von der „blutenden perspektivischen Malerei" von de Chirico, so als könne man sich an ihren scharfen Kanten wirklich verletzen.

[...]

Der Sex-Appeal des Narziss

Die Sorgfalt, die Dalí auf seine Darstellung in der Öffentlichkeit verwendete, wozu auch die Enthüllung einiger seiner intimsten Gewohnheiten gehörte, machte ihn zu einem Vorreiter der Avantgardisten, die sich in ihrem Lebenswerk zum eigenen Kunstprodukt stilisieren wollten. Obwohl Andy Warhol in seinen Schriften mit Vertraulichkeiten über sein Sexualleben geizte, hat man ihn zu Recht mit Dalí verglichen. In gewisser Hinsicht jedenfalls, immerhin schuf Dalí bereits intuitiv „Pop-Art", als Warhol, der die Pop-Ikone werden sollte, noch Gebrauchsgrafik am Carnegie Institute of Technology in Pittsburgh studierte. Mit einigen Jahren Vorsprung entwarf Dalí Stoffmotive

Für Liebhaber und Fetischisten sei hier auf ein Schuhmotiv hingewiesen, das Dalí 1951 für Krawatten entwarf und das sich nicht sehr von den Schuhentwürfen unterscheidet, die Warhol die ersten Erfolge einbrachten.

und publizierte in *Vogue* und *Harper's Bazaar*. Und schon früh wusste er den Vorteil des Films

or appalled, depending on our characters, that it should be the most narcissistic individuals, to the point in some cases of making it their job – actors, supermodels and the greatest harns among tennis and football players – who attract the most attention from those whom we hardly dare describe as their fellows. In every case we are amazed that people who are absorbed by selflove, and so, we think, least likely to regard the feeling of love as something to share, do not discourage the love that a great many others feel for them. Such love can sometimes entail seriously aggressive reactions, as when Valerie Solanas lodged two .22 bullets in Warhol's abdomen. "The Divine Dalí" was protected against such a thing by his good fortune (or by his seemingly more familiar exchanges with his flock?), but it is clear that his celebrity and the admiration of his fans were equalled only by the loathing with which he was viewed by another section of the public. The admiration and desire for identification that excellence in the practice of an art or any other discipline engenders are not enough to explain everything; we can see from our own private lives that a Narcissus can focus the attention of others without having displayed any merits at all. At the end of his study, cited above, carried out as an investigation, in other words without indulgence, Ricard Mas Peinado offers an explanation: "Exploring boundless egocentricity helps us to know ourselves a little better."
I would go further: exploring egocentricity like Dalí's helps us break down our own inhibitions. Going up close to a statue, even one partially self-erected, we are forced to measure the height of our own gaze against its size and to try to regain a piece of the space it disputes with us. While our ambivalent feelings towards Narcissus

für sich zu nutzen und ließ sich an der Seite von Stars fotografieren. Dalí hat seine Auftritte in der Öffentlichkeit inszeniert und sie in den Medien genutzt, sobald das technisch machbar war. Als Andy Warhol sagte, jedem stünde „seine Viertelstunde Berühmtheit" zu, hatte Dalí bereits mehr Zeit für sich „herausgeschlagen", wie er am 1. September 1958 notierte: „Es ist schwierig, die gespannte Aufmerksamkeit der Welt länger als eine halbe Stunde auf sich zu ziehen. Mir gelingt es, nun schon seit zwanzig Jahren, Tag für Tag. [...] Seit zwanzig Jahren bringe ich es fertig, dass die Zeitungen die unverständlichsten, durch Fernschreiber übermittelten Meldungen veröffentlichen: Paris: – Dalí hält an der Sorbonne einen Vortrag über Vermeers ‚Spitzenklöpplerin' und das Rhinozeros. [...] New York: – Dalí entsteigt in New York im goldenen Raumtaucheranzug dem berühmten ‚Ovociped', das er erfunden hat: eine durchsichtige Kugel, das neue Fortbewegungsmittel auf der Basis der in den innergebärlichen Paradiesen gezeugten Fantasiegebilde."

Salvador Dalí, *Dalí sagt... Tagebuch eines Genies*, a.a.O., S. 186 und S. 188.

Der Künstler interessierte sich schon früh für die Fotografie als schöpferisches und die Popularität beförderndes Mittel. So wie Yves Klein sich dem Fotografen Harry Shunk anschloss, arbeitete Dalí ab 1941 eng mit dem Fotografen Philippe Halsman zusammen, was bis zu dessen Tod im Jahr 1977 andauern sollte. Man könnte ein ganzes Buch schreiben über die gekünstelten Posen, die elegante Kleidung sowie über die extravaganten Verkleidungen und das Grimassenrepertoire der Gestalt, die



may include the desire to imitate him, part of that is the desire to imitate his autonomy. His attraction is due partly to the fact that he frees us from the duties that a shared love imposes and gives us access to the royal road of self-love. While ceaselessly watching over Dalí, Gala is also a model of very great freedom. We have the right to say to ourselves, let's dare to do as he does. Allowing oneself a little self-absorption soothes the need for aggression engendered by the other's self-absorption (it diverts reactions like that of Solanas).

"He was taking up too much space in my life" said Valerie Solanas to explain her action, although she was not a friend of the artist.

While Dalí's entourage seems to have included a few natural eccentrics, he undoubtedly encouraged them down that path by his own behaviour, and also provided them with a social space in which it was possible.
That the exhibition of oneself leads to self-revelation by others was something of which Dalí was well aware. However narcissistic he may have been, he would not have been the painter and writer we know had he settled for being the sole object of his own observations. We have to assume that he agreed to so many meetings and received importunate journalists as much to satisfy the voyeur that he was as for the happiness of being a focus of interest. But there was surely an even greater satisfaction in responding to both desires at the same time. Certain of having drawn his own portrait, as he understood it, in his autobiographies, Dalí could afford to be curious about the touches added to it by others and, simultaneously, oblige those others to appear in what then became a double portrait.

vor dem Objektiv der Fotografen Gebärden einstudierte. Denn außer Halsman lichteten ihn auch noch Man Ray ab, Brassaï, Francesco Català Roca, Eric Schaal, Platt Lynes ... Und es ist kein Zufall, dass der Surrealist Robert Descharnes, einer von Dalís engsten Freunden, der das Privileg genoss, hinter die für die Öffentlichkeit errichtete Fassade des Künstlers blicken zu dürfen, ehemals Fotograf war. David Vilaseca hat zu Recht bemerkt: „In dem Subjektivitätsmodell, das Dalí vorschlägt, existiert das Ich nicht vor seinen Darstellungen, sondern es formt sich im Gegenteil durch sie, in aller Äußerlichkeit, an der Oberfläche, kurzum exzentrisch."

David Vilaseca, „Le réel de l'œuvre autobiographique de Salvador Dalí", in: *Lire Dalí, Revue des Sciences humaines*, Nr. 262, Lille III, Charles-de-Gaulle-Universität. Lille 2001.

Es beginnt schon die Zeit der Mediatisierung, aber noch stützt sich Dalí bei der Stilisierung seiner selbst auf seine Schriften. Dalís Autobiografie *Das geheime Leben des Salvador Dalí*, die der Katalane 1942 in New York zuerst auf Englisch veröffentlichte, sowie *Das Tagebuch eines Genies*, 1964 erschienen, sind brillante Selbst- und Zeitanalysen. Der autobiografische Essay *Der tragische Mythos des Angelus von Millet*, 1933 entstanden, jedoch erst 1963 veröffentlicht, führt ein neues Genre ein. Als der amerikanische Sammler A. Reynolds 1962 ein Tagebuchheft des Künstlers unter dem Titel *A Dalí Journal 1920* zufällig bei einem Pariser Bouquinisten entdeckte und es herausbringen wollte, reagierte Dalí wütend. Zweifellos befürchtete er, dass diese Aufzeichnungen, die er nie korrigiert hatte, an seinem Image, an

At least he did not regard his interviewers as machines for asking questions, but as people whom he involved in the interview and whose questions he sometimes turned back on them. To the journalist Jacques Chancel, who felt duty bound to ask him about his appetite for acquiring wealth, Dalí retorted that this was indeed one difference between them, Dalí having to earn money to work while Chancel worked to earn money.

*Radioscopie*, 4 January 1971, on France Inter, released on CD by Radio France, 1999.

The portraits he creates in his writings are always sharp. (The portrait of Picasso is striking in its truth, Picasso who "will not be any taller but [who] will bear his flies in that imposing way that the author of *Faust* showed before him. [...] If he smiled at a wardrobe the smile came from his overcoat."

Salvador Dalí, *Oui, méthode paranoïaque-critique et autres texts*, 38.

The first chapters of *Hidden Faces* are largely a satire, entirely plausible sadly, on the aristocratic and bourgeois milieus of the immediately post-war period, who are shown as frivolous and thoughtless, their main concern being "to cuddle up" to avoid thinking about danger. Had Breton, who was so worried about Dalí's pseudo-Hitlerism during this period, actually read what was being published by Éditions Surréalistes itself? In *La Conquête de l'irrationnel Dalí* demonstrates a staggering lucidity: "Our contemporaries, systematically cretinized [...] by imaginative fasting, by famines of paternal affection and all sorts, vainly seek to bite into

dem er in den anderen Werken so penibel gefeilt hatte, kratzen könnten. Nur widerwillig stimmte er der Veröffentlichung zu, allerdings bloß unter der ausdrücklichen Bedingung, dass die Ausgabe nicht in den Handel kam. Diese Texte, in Schulhefte geschrieben, von denen sieben unter dem Titel *Aufzeichnungen eines werdenden Genies* gedruckt vorliegen, verraten eine für einen Fünfzehnjährigen erstaunliche Reife und ungewöhnliche Beobachtungs- und Selbstbeobachtungsgabe. Und dass seine Befürchtungen unbegründet waren, beweisen die Andeutungen bestimmter Obsessionen und erotischer Fantasien, die sein Leben und seine Bildwelt nachhaltig prägen sollten.
All diese Enthüllungen, zu denen noch zahlreiche andere nicht ausdrücklich autobiografische Veröffentlichungen hinzukommen, die jedoch allesamt autobiografischen Charakter haben, hinderten jedoch die besonders Unersättlichen nicht daran, ihn mit einem Notizblock oder einem Tonbandgerät aufzusuchen. Das mag durchaus ganz in Dalís Sinn gewesen sein. Nachdem er nämlich von sich selbst erzählt hatte, berichtete er noch einmal von sich als Maler, der nie aufhört, sein Gemälde zu überarbeiten. In seinen Gesprächen tauchten die immergleichen Themen auf – Gala, der Tod, die Religion, die Erotik –, und man begegnet in leicht veränderter Version Anekdoten wieder, die er bereits in *Das geheime Leben des Salvador Dalí* und in *Aufzeichnungen eines werdenden Genies* zum Besten gegeben hat.

In den Erzählungen und Reflexionen sexuellen Charakters findet man hingegen Unerhörtes oder neue Details, was vielleicht der Zeit, der mündlichen Erzählung, der Anregung der Gesprächspartner zu verdanken ist – und nicht



the senile, triumphal sweetness of the plump, atavistic, tender, militaristic and territorial back of a Hitlerian wet-nurse."

Ibid., 53. For more detail on the Surrealists' accusations against Dalí, see Ian Gibson, *op. cit.* note 3, 375–80, and Salvador Dalí, *Diary of a Genius*, for May 1952. The description Dalí gives of Hitler's "chubby flesh", soft and milky, comparable to that of a wet nurse, is a sexual diagnosis worth nothing. The comparison also figures in *Hidden Faces* in relation to a Nazi soldier whose chubby back is like that of a nurse. Showing a great deal perspicacity himself, Pierre Naville offers a fine analysis of all the aspects on which Breton and Dalí agreed in this area: "The down-to-earth maxims of historical materialism that Breton tried to acclimatize to ambiance of objective and more or less miraculous chance mattered little to him [Dalí]. He upended the relationship, so that social realities bent before the delirious requirements of the surreal. This made both Hitler and Stalin no more than fantastical dolls in an ironic game of history, of which Freud was the brilliant magician." See "Dalí, Dalí, Dalí!", *Le Temps surréel*, vol.I, *L'Espérance mathématique*, Paris, Galilée, 1977.

Among famous people there are those who "control" their image and those who play with it. The relationship to images of oneself circulating in the media does not depend on narcissism alone; it may depend as much, if not more, on a greater or lesser degree of intellectual maturity. Marie-José Mondzain observes that, contrary to what might be expected in a society that has grown used to the proliferation of images, there is "a fascinated, mute adhesion to everything we see, an infantile, magical gluttony of the eye."

zuletzt der Reife des Interviewten. Er vertraute sich lauter renommierten Personen an: Alain Bosquet (*Entretiens avec Salvador Dalí*, 1966; deutsch: *Hommage à Dalí mit den Gesprächen zwischen Alain Bosquet und Dalí*, 1974), Louis Pauwels (*Les Passions selon Dalí*, 1968; deutsch: *Meine Leidenschaften*, 1969, 1989), André Parinaud (*Comment on devient Dalí, les aveux inavouables de Salvador Dalí*, 1973; deutsch: *So wird man Dalí*, 1974, 1986). Hofften etwa seine Gesprächspartner, hinter dem Mythos die unverblümte Wahrheit über den Menschen Dalí zu finden? Selbst wenn sie dreiste Fragen stellten, glaubten sie offenbar selbst nicht daran. In seinem Vorwort schreibt Pauwels zu Recht über Dalí: „Er deformiert die Realität nicht, er transformiert sie, oder er gibt ihr vielmehr die ursprüngliche Dehnbarkeit wieder."

Salvador Dalí, *Meine Leidenschaften*, aufgezeichnet von Louis Pauwels, übers. von Jutta und Theodor Knust. München 1989, S. 26.

Das Vorwort von Parinaud beginnt mit folgenden Zeilen: „Dieses Buch ist ein Dalí-Roman. Wenn sein Held, Dalí, in der ersten Person spricht, so ist das nur ein stilistischer Kunstgriff. Dalí sagt nie *je*, sondern *jeux* [je – ich; jeux – Spiele]. Denn Dalí ist das Ja und das Nein, der Widerspruch selbst, die Herausforderung. Wenn Dalí ‚ich' sagt, so spricht nicht Dalí, sondern nur *ein* möglicher Dalí, den ich kenne und aus den tausend anderen, die er verkörpert, heraushöre."

Salvador Dalí, *So wird man Dalí*, zusammengestellt und präsentiert von André Parinaud, übers. von Franz Mayer. München, Zürich 1974, S. 7.

Marie-José Mondzain, "Image, sommes-nous propriétaires ou possedés", in *Art Press* no. 284, November 2002.

For her this evokes primitive practices and delirious behaviours, when a subject is incapable of telling the difference between himself and his reflection in a mirror or a photograph. In her view those who believe that they "own" their image are in fact "possessed" by it. From this point of view Dalí was not credulous and fooled still less. Nor was Warhol, fatalistically allowing himself to think that if he looked at himself in a mirror he would see nothing, because people claimed that he was himself a mirror and so logically, "if a mirror looks into another mirror, what is there for it to see?"

From Andy Warhol, *My Philosophy from A to B.*

In a mirror, as in everything that came before his eyes, Dalí was certainly able to see several images. He worked with photographers like a true actor, in costume, striking significant poses, exploiting his physiognomy: his habit of rolling his eyes, in the manner of Groucho and Harpo Marx whom he admired, is as much a part of his image as his moustaches. But he does not seem to have feared the cameras that captured images at random when he was part of a crowd. Indeed he behaved as though he completely accepted being multifaceted and as though splitting in two was one of his characteristics. In his writings Dalí often talks about himself in the third person and, in his novel, manages to refer to a "Dalínian maxim." This is not merely megalomania, it is also proof that the "I" had fully incorporated the "he" by which it was designated in the mouths of

Andere, vielleicht nicht so versierte Gesprächspartner haben betont, wie schwierig es war, Dalí zu fassen, selbst wenn er ein ausgesprochen starkes Mitteilungsbedürfnis zu haben schien. Doch etwas hinter dem äußeren Schein hervorzerren zu wollen, was sich dort verbarg, wäre sicherlich unklug gewesen. Dalí muss so wie seine Bilder aus den dreißiger Jahren betrachtet werden. Denn in ihnen sind mehrere Bilder enthalten, die wie die Kulissen einer Theaterdekoration nicht hintereinander stehen, sondern alle miteinander vermengt sind auf ein und derselben *Oberfläche*.

Man kann sich jeden Tag – je nach Veranlagung – an den Verhaltensweisen narzisstischer Menschen erfreuen oder verzweifeln, sich darüber lustig machen oder entrüsten; einige haben den Narzissmus sogar zu ihrem Beruf gemacht, Schauspieler beispielsweise, Topmodels oder herausragende Tennis- und Fußballstars. Jedenfalls wundert man sich, dass Menschen, die in ihre Selbstliebe versunken scheinen, durchaus empfänglich sind für die Liebe, die andere Menschen ihnen entgegenbringen. Allerdings kann eine solche Zuneigung auch in Aggressivität umschlagen, wie es bei Valerie Solanas der Fall war: Die junge Schauspielerin, eine eifrige Besucherin der Factory, Warhols New Yorker „Hauptquartier", und eine radikale Feministin, ging am 3. Juni 1968 hin und feuerte mit einer Pistole Kaliber 22 zwei Kugeln in Warhols Bauch ab. Das Schicksal – oder war es der vertraute Umgang mit seinen Getreuen? – bewahrte den „göttlichen" Dalí vor einem solchen Missgeschick, aber es ist nicht zu leugnen, dass der großen Bewunderung, die ihm seine Fans entgegenbrachten, eine ebenso heftige Abscheu gegenüberstand, die ein anderer Teil des Publikums hegte. Herausragende Leistungen



others. As if that were not enough, again in his novel Dalí suddenly intervenes, mingling with his characters and addressing one of them, "But I see you on your knees, Solange de Cléda, in your room when you are alone..." This direct address appears on a page that deals with the fact that "Solange de Cleda offers psychiatry a truly singular case. [...] Splitting more and more every day"!

In 1966, in a collection entitled "Lettre ouverte" [Open letter], Dalí published an open letter to ... Salvador Dalí. The exchange of letters between the "anarchistic" or "surrealist" Dalí and "Dalí Avida Dollars," who call each other "excellentissimo" and "beloved," but who sometimes also do not agree, is an artifice intended to comment on opinions circulating on Dalí, and indeed to respond to attacks addressed to him, or to his double, adopting and retouching the image that others have of him. You have to live with this other self that society assigns to you like a Siamese twin, particularly if you are a public figure. In the short piece *Borges and I*, Borges summed up the situation very well: "I know of Borges from the mail and see his name on a list of professors or in a biographic dictionary, I like hourglasses, maps, eighteenth-century typography [...] he, shares these preferences, but in a vain way that turns them into the attributes of an actor." Borges ends with a question: "I do not know which of us has written this page."

Jorge-Luis Borges, "L'Auteur" in *Œuvres complètes II*, "Bibliothèque de la Pleïade," Gallimard 1999.

At the end of *Lettre ouverte à SalvadorDalí*, one gets a bit lost and it is hard to tell which Dalí is

in der Kunst, in der Wissenschaft oder im Sport rufen zwar Bewunderung und Identifikationswünsche hervor, aber sie erklären nicht alles. Im Privatleben stellt man oft fest, dass ein Narziss die Blicke der anderen auf sich konzentriert, ohne sich darüber im Klaren zu sein, ob es ihnen überhaupt etwas brachte.
Am Ende seiner bereits erwähnten Untersuchung, die sich wie eine nüchterne Ermittlung liest, bietet Ricard Mas Peinado die folgende Erklärung: „Es hilft uns, uns ein wenig besser kennenzulernen, wenn wir die grenzenlose Ichbezogenheit eines Individuums erforschen."
Ich würde einen Schritt weitergehen: Die Erforschung einer solchen Ichbezogenheit hilft uns, unsere eigenen Hemmungen zu überwinden. Wenn wir uns einer großen Statue nähern, sind wir genötigt, unseren Blick an ihrer Höhe auszurichten und zu versuchen, einen kleinen Teil des Raumes zurückzugewinnen, den sie uns streitig macht. Wenn sich zu dem ambivalenten Gefühl, das uns beim Anblick des Narziss beschleicht, der Wunsch gesellt, ihn nachzuahmen, ist es auch berechtigt, seine Autonomie zu übernehmen. Seine Anziehungskraft rührt nämlich teilweise daher, dass er uns von den Pflichten der geteilten Liebe entbindet und uns den Königsweg der Selbstliebe zeigt. Und ist nicht Gala, die sich ununterbrochen um Dalí gekümmert hat, zugleich ein leuchtendes Beispiel für große innere Freiheit? Wagen wir, was der Narziss wagt, können wir uns zu Recht fragen. Wenn man sich selbst ein wenig Nabelschau gestattet, beschwichtigt man damit nötigenfalls die Aggressivität, die jeweils die Nabelschau des anderen hervorruft – was von Reaktionen wie der von Valerie Solanas abhält.

addressing the other. However, one of them notes the transcription errors made by Alain Bosquet in the interviews published shortly before and dryly criticizes the writer's work as "based on surrealist banalities and commonplaces." Yet – and let us salute this rhetorical detour – "the plebeian word 'bastard' will never leave or fall from the lips or pen of Dalí." Of which Dalí? It's a cunning manoeuvre. Those who have taken Dalí on, or betrayed him, meet with responses from several Dalís. So who exactly was their target? Where is he? It is quite possible that he is primarily in their own heads. One more Dalí! One among many ....

Excerpts from: *Catherine Millet, Dalí and Me*. Translated by Trista Selou. Scheidegger & Spiess. Zurich 2008, 14-23 and 31-37.

„Er nahm zuviel Raum in meinem Leben ein", erklärte Solanas, um ihre Tat zu rechtfertigen, obwohl sie ja nicht einmal eine Geliebte des Künstlers war. Zitiert von David Bourdon, in: *Andy Warhol*. Ostfildern-Ruit 1989.

Wenn es in der Gefolgschaft Dalís einige Exzentriker gab, hatte er sie womöglich durch sein eigenes Verhalten dazu ermutigt? Zumal er ihnen den gesellschaftlichen Rahmen bot, in dem dies möglich war?
Dalí wusste durchaus, dass immer, wenn einer sich zur Schau stellte, bald andere seinem Beispiel folgten. So narzisstisch er auch war, er hätte jedoch nicht der Maler oder der Schriftsteller sein können, den wir kennen, wenn er sich damit begnügt hätte, der einzige Gegenstand seiner Betrachtungen zu sein. Vermutlich traf er Verabredungen oder empfing lästige Journalisten, um seinen Voyeurismus zu befriedigen, aber andererseits bereitete es ihm auch Freude, im Mittelpunkt des Interesses zu stehen, und mit noch größerer Zufriedenheit erfüllte es ihn, wenn er beide Neigungen zugleich befriedigen konnte. Auch war Dalí gemäß den Selbstporträts in seinen autobiografischen Schriften neugierig auf die Farbtupfer, die andere hinzufügten, und überzeichnete sie, um nun in einem Doppelporträt in Erscheinung zu treten. Zumindest betrachtete er seine Interviewpartner nicht als Fragen produzierende Maschinen, sondern als Menschen, die er in das Gespräch einbezog und denen er zuweilen selbst Fragen stellte. Dem Journalisten Jacques Chancel, der sich bemüßigt fühlte, ihn über seine Geldgier zu befragen, entgegnete Dalí, dass es tatsächlich einen großen Unterschied zwischen ihnen beiden gebe: Er müsse Geld verdienen, um zu arbeiten, während Chancel arbeite, um Geld zu verdienen.

Vgl. *Röntgenoskopie*, gesendet am 4. Januar 1971 von France Inter, als CD veröffentlicht von Radio France, 1999.

Die Porträts der Zeitgenossen, die er in seinen Schriften skizziert, sind alle immer sehr pointiert. Picassos Beschreibung beispielsweise besticht durch seine Schonungslosigkeit: „Wenn Picasso zufällig und sehr spät nachts für einen Augenblick griechisch drapiert auf seinem Balkon erscheint, wenn sein herrlicher Arbeitshelm auf die Rue la Boétie jene Lichtwellen wirft, die den Vorübergehenden kundtun, dass sein Genie soeben Figuren von erdrückender Hässlichkeit und übermenschlicher Nichtswürdigkeit erfunden hat, wird Picasso augenblicklich die Wanderherzen und -nieren der Nachtschwärmer erobern wie kein anderer Künstler vor ihm. [...] Picasso wird nicht größer sein, doch seinen Hosenschlitz so imposant tragen wie vor ihm der Verfasser des *Faust*, was ihn aztekischer macht, als er in Wirklichkeit ist. [...] Wenn er einem Schrank zulächelte, kam dieses Lächeln aus seinem Überzieher, und wenn er sich an dem Schrank berauschen wollte, wünschte er auch, dass sein Überzieher von ganzer Seele, von ganzem Stoffe glücklich sei."

Salvador Dalí, *Die Eroberung des Irrationalen. Essays*, a.a.O., S. 135f.

Die ersten Kapitel seines Romans *Verborgene Gesichter* sind größtenteils eine Satire auf die frivolen aristokratischen und bürgerlichen Gesellschaftskreise in der unmittelbaren Vorkriegszeit, die zudem den Kopf in den Sand steckten oder „sich einzurollen" versuchten, wie Dalí es ausdrückt, um nicht über die heraufziehende Gefahr nachdenken zu müssen. Hatte Breton, der sich zu dieser Zeit über Dalís Pseudo-Hitlerismus so sehr aufregte, überhaupt gelesen, was im Verlag der Surrealisten erschienen war? Mit verblüffender Klarsicht kommentierte Dalí in *Die Eroberung des Irrationalen* den Zeitgeist: „Bei dieser kulturellen Lage unternehmen unsere Zeitgenossen, die durch Technik und Architektur der Selbstbestrafung, bürokratisch-psychologische Glückwünsche, ideologische Verwirrung und imaginatives Fasten, väterlichen und anderen Gefühlshunger systematisch verdummt werden, umsonst den Versuch, in die vertrottelte, triumphale Süße des fleischigen, atavistischen, zärtlichen, militaristisch-territorialen Rückens einer hitlerischen Amme zu beißen, um endlich auf irgendeine Weise mit der geweihten totemistischen Hostie zu kommunizieren, die man ihnen kürzlich vor der Nase weggeschnappt hatte und die bekanntlich gerade jene symbolisch-geistige Nahrung war, die der Katholizismus zur Besänftigung der kannibalischen Raserei moralischen und irrationalen Hungers jahrhundertelang aufgetischt hatte."

Ebd., S. 9f. Details über Dalís „Hiterlismus" und die Reaktion der Surrealisten bieten: Ian Gibson, a.a.O., S. 375–380 und Salvador Dalí in: *Das Tagebuch eines Genies* (Mai 1952), S. 25ff. Die Faszination ging für ihn aus „von Hitlers weichem und fleischigem Rücken, der immer so prall in seine Uniform geschnürt war. So oft ich begann, den Lederriemen zu malen, der sich von seinem Gürtel schräg über die Schulter zog, versetzte die Weichheit dieses unter dem Waffenrock komprimierten Hitlerfleisches mich in eine schmack-, nahr- und wagnerhafte Ekstase, die mein Herz heftig schlagen ließ, eine höchst seltene Erregung, die ich nicht einmal beim Liebesakt empfand. Hitlers pralles Fleisch, das ich mir wie das göttlichste Fleisch einer sehr weißhäutigen Frau vorstellte, faszinierte mich" (S. 25f.). Diese Beschreibung ist zweifellos ein beachtenswerter psycho-pathologischer Hinweis. Der Vergleich kommt auch in *Verborgene Gesichter* in Bezug auf den Rücken eines Nazi-Soldaten vor. Pierre Naville hat den Antagonismus von Breton und Dalí auf diesem Gebiet genau analysiert, siehe dazu: „Dalí, Dalí, Dalí!", in: *Le Temps du surréel, Band I, L'Espérance mathématique*. Paris 1977.

Unter berühmten Menschen gibt es solche, die ihr Äußeres „unter Kontrolle haben", und andere, die weniger Wert darauf legen. Das Verhältnis eines Individuums zu seinem von den Medien propagierten Bild hängt nicht nur vom Grad seines Narzissmus ab, sondern mehr noch von der intellektuellen Reife des Betreffenden. Marie-José Mondzain hat festgestellt, dass in einer Gesellschaft, die eine Überflutung mit Bildern gewohnt ist, „all das, was man sieht, eine unwiderstehliche, stillschweigende und stumme Zustimmung findet, und eine kindliche, magische Gier des Blickes existiert".

Marie-José Mondzain, „Image, sommes-nous propriétaires ou possédés", in: *Art Press*, Nr. 284, November 2002.

Obwohl man es ja eigentlich anders erwarten würde. Diese Erkenntnis erinnert sie an primitive oder wahnhafte Verhaltensweisen, wenn ein Individuum nicht in der Lage ist, zwischen sich selbst und seinem Spiegelbild oder einem Foto zu unterscheiden. Mondzain zufolge ist derjenige, der glaubt, der „Besitzer" seines Bildes zu sein, in der Tat von diesem Bild „besessen".

Dalí durchschaute diesen Mechanismus genauso wie Andy Warhol, der sogar zu äußern wagte, er werde nichts sehen, wenn er sich im Spiegel betrachten würde, weil die Leute behaupteten, er selbst sei ein Spiegel, denn „wenn ein Spiegel in einen anderen Spiegel schaut, was kann er denn schon sehen?".

Andy Warhol, *Die Philosophie des Andy Warhol von A nach B und zurück*, übers. von Regine Reimers. Frankfurt a. M. 2006.

Dalí hingegen war sicher imstande, in einem Spiegel, wie in allem, was sich seinem Blick bot, mehrere Bilder zu sehen. Mit den Fotografen arbeitete er wie ein echter Schauspieler; er trug Kostüme, nahm extravagante Posen ein, beschäftigte sich intensiv mit seinem physiognomischen Ausdruck: Sein Augenrollen, das ihm die amerikanischen Schauspieler und Entertainer Harpo und Groucho Marx vormachten, die er bewunderte, war ebenso eines seiner charakteristischen Merkmale wie sein Schnurrbart. Aber er hat auch nicht die Kameras gescheut, die auf ihn gerichtet wurden, während er ein Bad in der Menge nahm, und Schnappschüsse von ihm machten. In der Tat räumte er ohne Weiteres ein, dass er verschiedene Facetten habe, und es scheint, als sei auch die Persönlichkeitsspaltung eine seiner Charakteristiken gewesen. In seinen Schriften hat Dalí oft von sich in der dritten Person gesprochen, und dies in seinem Roman *Verborgene Gesichter* sogar zu seinem „Grundsatz" erklärt. Das ist keineswegs nur Größenwahn, sondern auch ein Beweis dafür, dass das „Ich" das „Er", die Perspektive der anderen also, vollkommen integriert hatte. Als sei dies immer noch nicht genug, schaltete Dalí sich in seinen Roman direkt ein, mischte sich unter die handelnden Personen und sprach sie unmittelbar an. „Aber, Solange de Cleda, ich sehe Sie doch in Ihrem Zimmer knien, wenn Sie allein sind.“ Diese Anrede beruht auf der Tatsache, dass „Solange de Cleda ein ganz und gar einzigartiger Fall für die Psychiatrie ist. [...] Sie spaltet sich jeden Tag mehr!“

1966 veröffentlichte Dalí in *Lettre ouverte* einen „Offenen Brief an ... Salvador Dalí“. Der fingierte Briefwechsel zwischen Dalí, dem „Anarchisten“ oder „Surrealisten“, und Dalí, dem „Geldgierigen“ („avida dollars“), in dem die verschiedenen Persönlichkeiten sich mit „Exzellenz“ und „Inniggeliebter“ anreden und sich dabei manchmal nicht einig sind, war ein Kunstgriff. Damit kommentierte Dalí die unterschiedlichen Meinungen, die über ihn in Umlauf waren, und wirkte der Kritik entgegen, die an ihm oder seinem Double geübt wurde. Gleichzeitig konnte er sich das Bild, das die anderen von ihm hatten, aneignen oder es zurechtrücken. Es ging ihm darum, sich mit diesem anderen Selbst einzurichten, das die Gesellschaft einem bisweilen wie einen siamesischen Zwilling zuschreibt, vor allem wenn man eine Person des öffentlichen Lebens ist. Der argentinische Schriftsteller Jorge Luis Borges hat in dem kurzen Text *Borges und ich* recht klarsichtig diese Situation beschrieben: „Von Borges erhalte ich Nachrichten durch die Post und lese seinen Namen in einem Professorenkolleg oder in einem biografischen Lexikon. Ich mag Sanduhren, Landkarten, die Typografie des 18. Jahrhunderts, Etymologien, das Aroma von Kaffee und Stevensons Prosa; der andere teilt zwar diese Vorlieben, aber in aufdringlicher Art, die sie zu Attributen eines Schauspielers macht.“ Der Schluss bleibt bezeichnenderweise bei Borges offen: „Ich weiß nicht, wer von beiden diese Seite schreibt.“

Jorge Luis Borges, *Borges und ich. Gedichte und Prosa*, übers. von Karl August Horst und Gisbert Haefs. Frankfurt a. M. 1993, S. 46f.

Am Ende von „Offener Brief an Salvador Dalí“ hat man Mühe herauszufinden, welcher Dalí sich an welchen wendet. Es geht jedoch immer darum, dass einer der Dalís die Fehler aufdeckt, die Alain Bosquet bei der Transkription der kurz zuvor erschienenen Gespräche (1966) unterlaufen sind, in denen er barsch über die literarischen Schriften und die Gedichte Dalís urteilt. Sie seien „eine ununterbrochene Folge von Bildern aus Wortspielen und ähnlich klingenden Wörtern. Es sind reine und einfache Lautverwechslungen, die dem ähneln, was in der surrealistischen Epoche Robert Desnos und Benjamin Péret machten“.



*Hommage à Dalí mit den Gesprächen zwischen Alain Bosquet und Dalí*, hg. von Richard P. Hartmann, übers. von K. Schulte. München 1974, S. 90f.

Von welchem Dalí ist hier die Rede? Es ist wie gesagt ein Kunstgriff. Seinen Widersachern und Kritikern antworten gleich mehrere Dalís. Wer aber ist der, den sie im Visier zu haben glauben? Wo ist er? Womöglich befindet er sich zunächst nur in ihrem Kopf. Noch ein Dalí mehr! Einer von vielen ...

Auszüge aus: *Catherine Millet, Dalí und ich*, übers. von Annalisa Viviani, Zürich: Scheidegger & Spiess, 2008, S. 15–26 und S. 36–44.

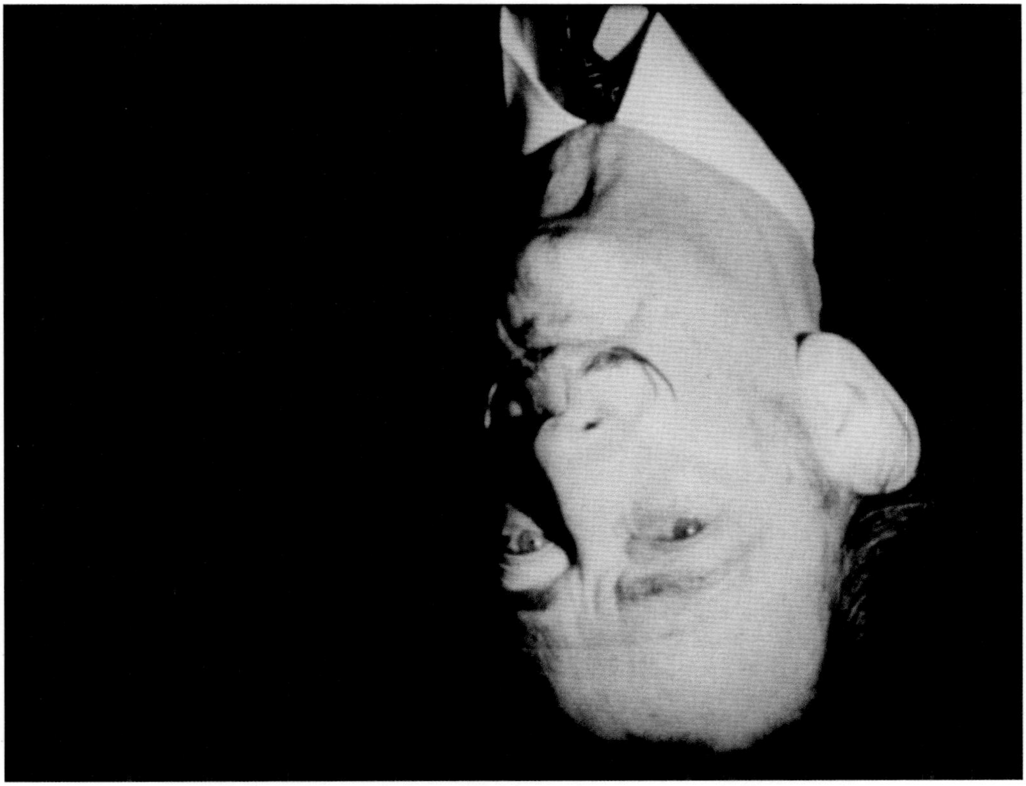



Andy Warhol,
*Screen Test: Salvador Dalí*, 1966

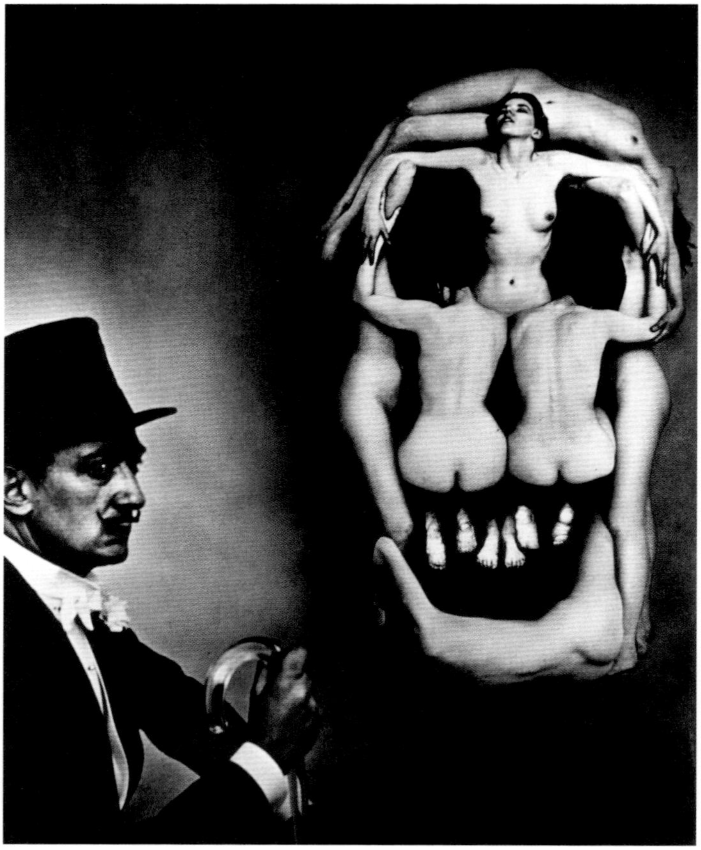

Salvador Dalí & Phillippe Halsman,
*Dalí Skull*, New York, 1951

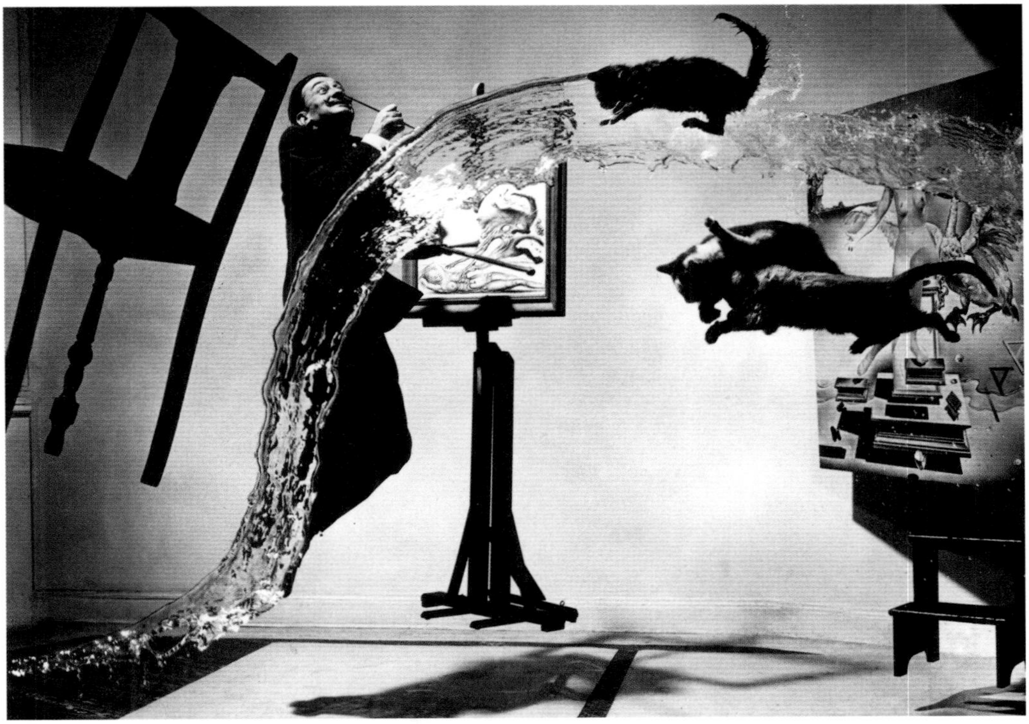

Salvador Dalí & Phillippe Halsman,
*Dalí Atomicus*, New York, 1948

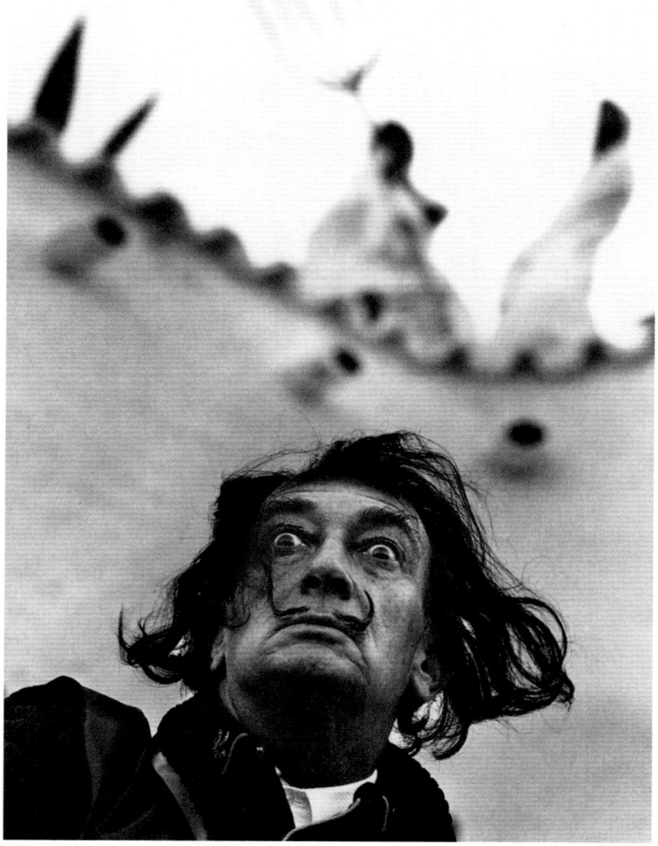

Salvador Dalí & Phillippe Halsman,
*Dalí in Port Lligat*, 1964

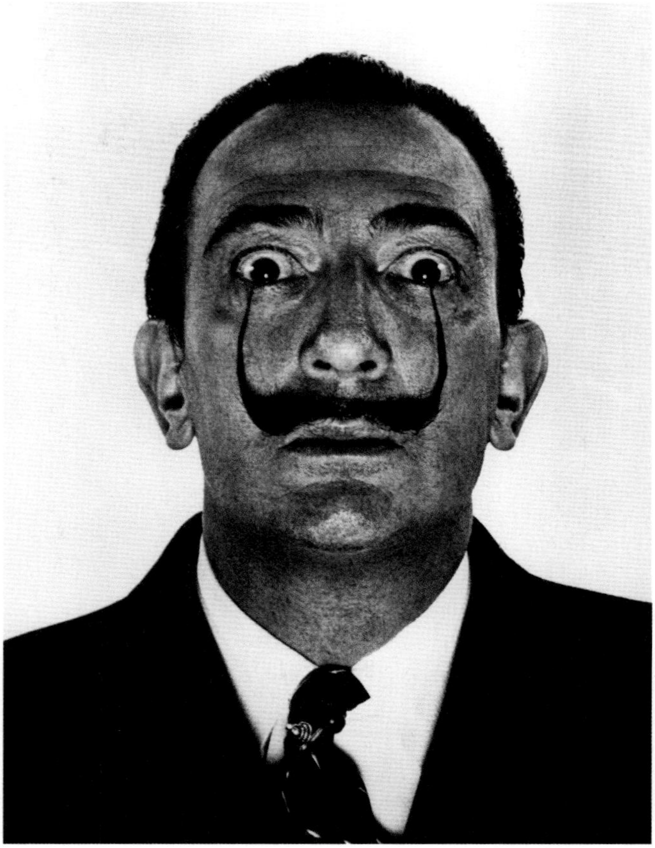

Salvador Dalí & Phillippe Halsman,
*Dalí's Mustache*, New York, 1953

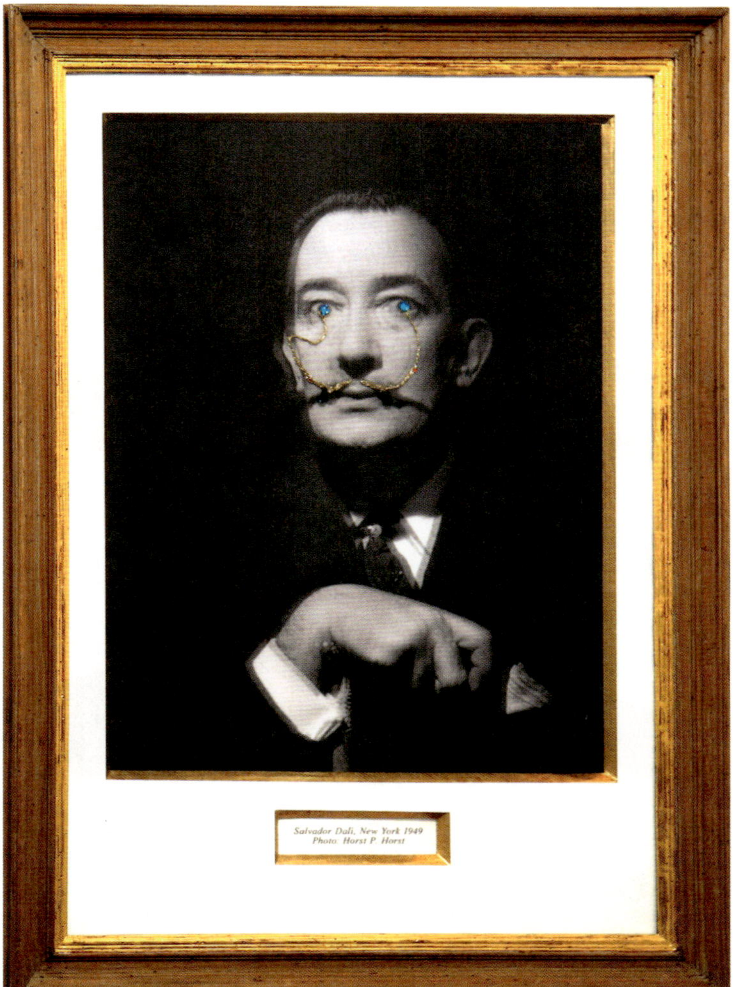


Francesco Vezzoli,
*Le Surréalisme, c'est moi! (Portrait of Salvador Dalí with Jewels and Tears, After Horst)*, 2009

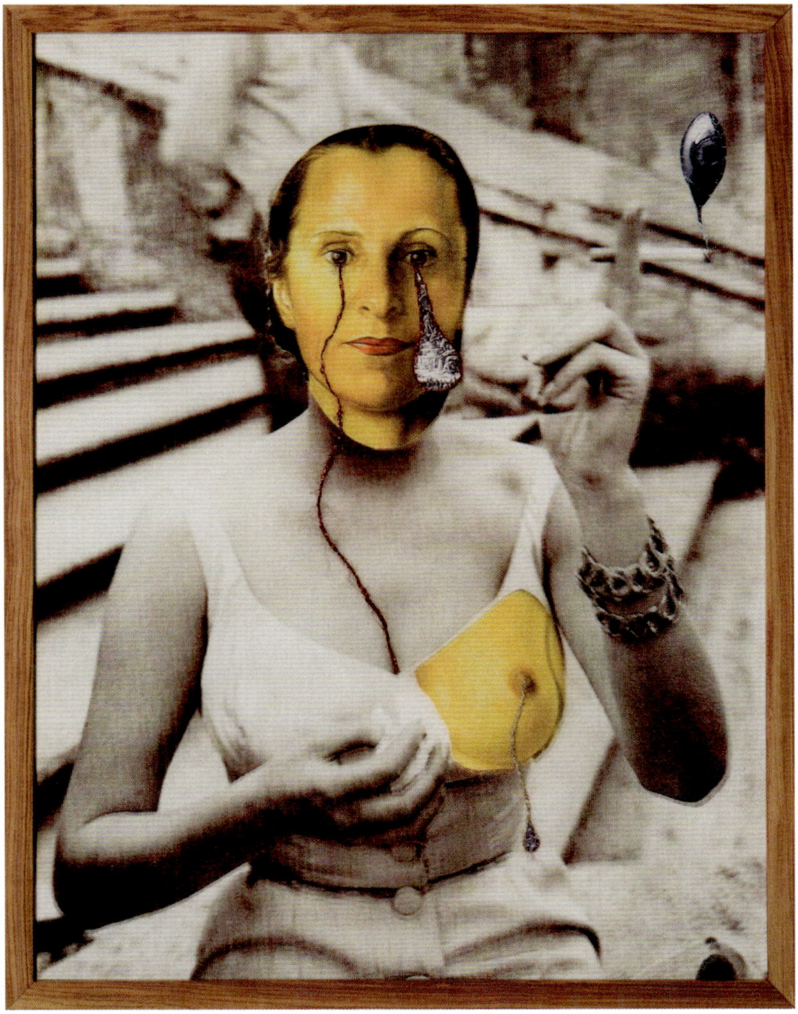

Francesco Vezzoli,
*Gala as Sylvia in La Dolce Vita*, 2008

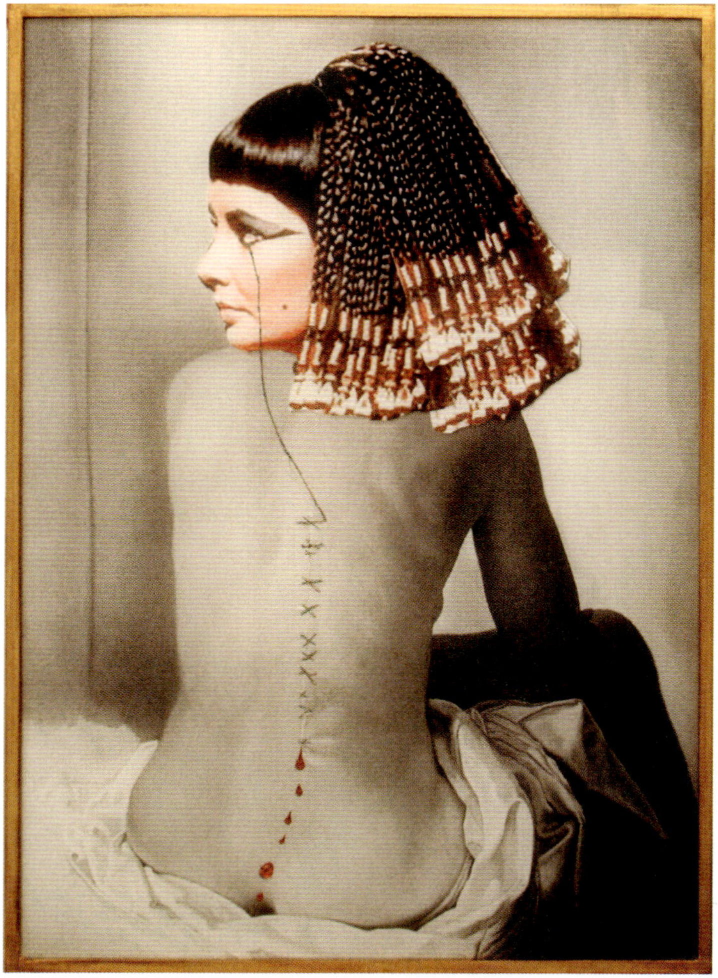

Francesco Vezzoli,
*Surrealiz (Lucio Fontana as Marco Antonio)*, 2008

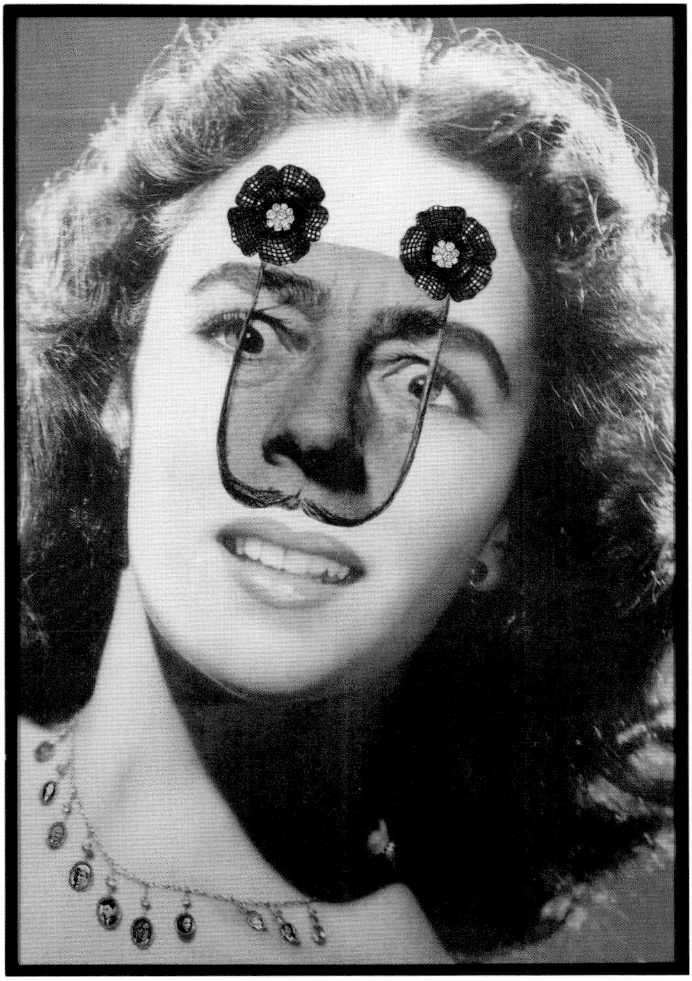

Francesco Vezzoli,
*Surrealiz (Who's afraid of Salvador Dalí?)*, 2008

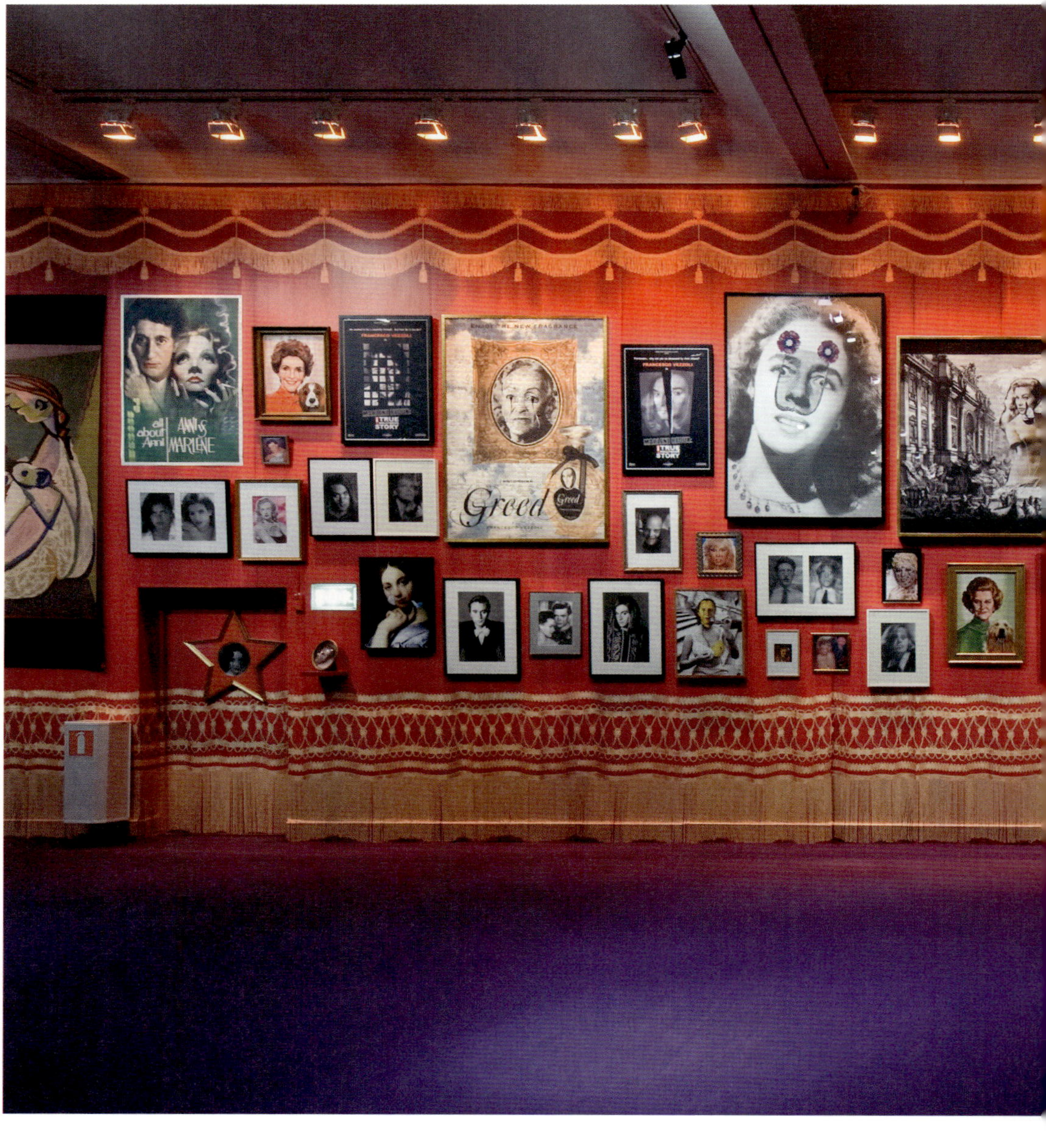


Installationsansicht/installation view:
Francesco Vezzoli,
*Dalí Dalí featuring Francesco Vezzoli*,
Moderna Museet, Stockholm, 2009

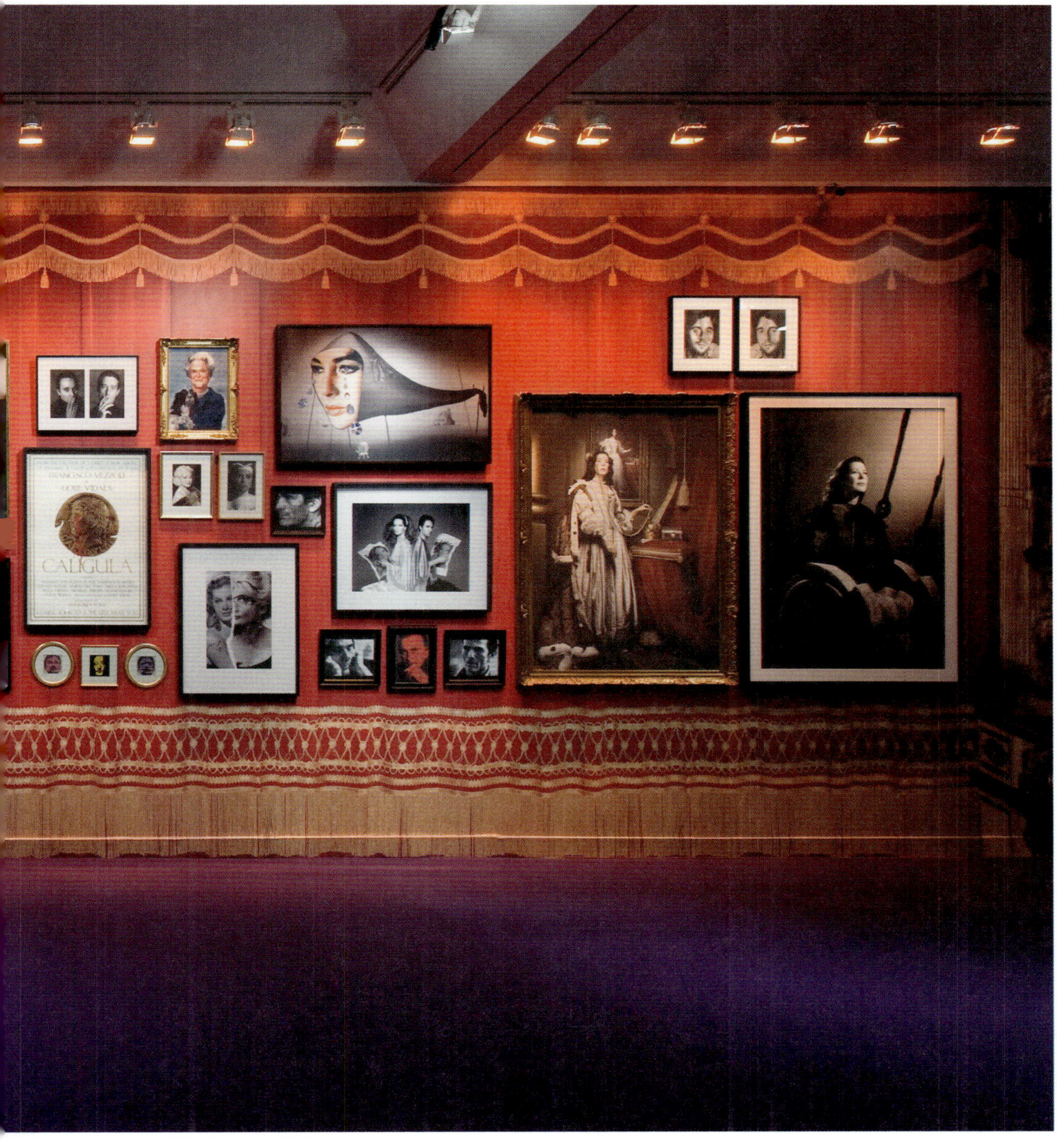
CALIGULA

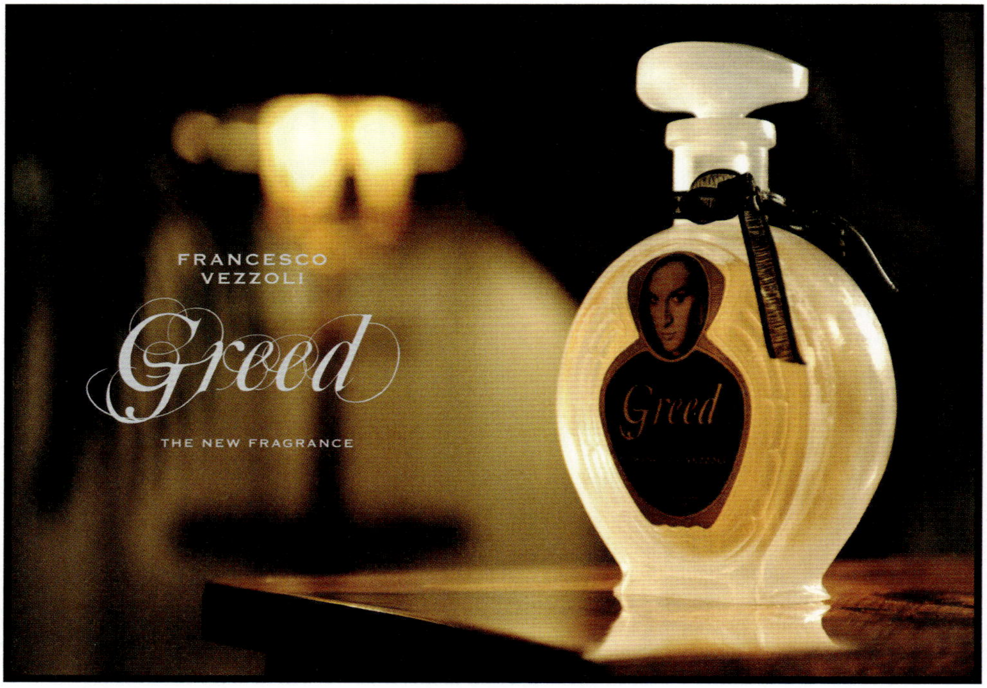


Francesco Vezzoli,
*Greed*, 2009

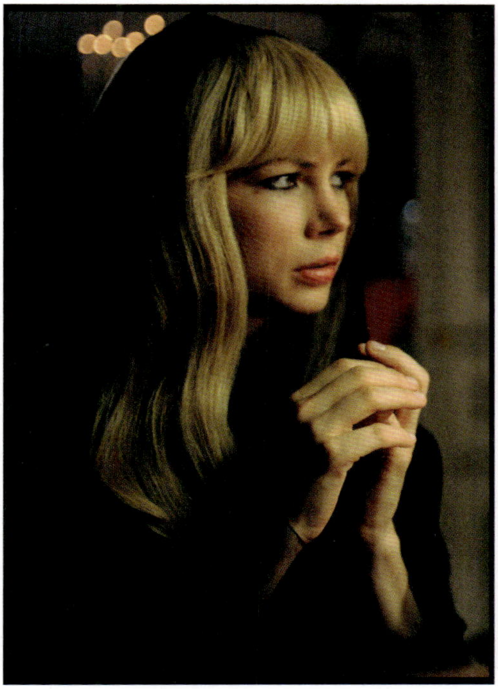

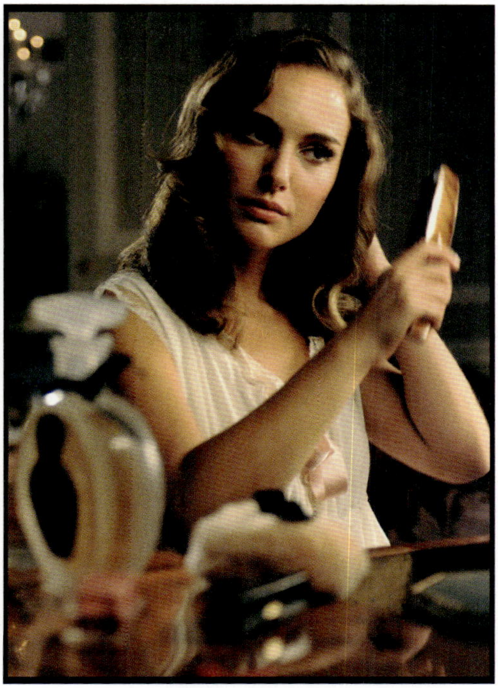

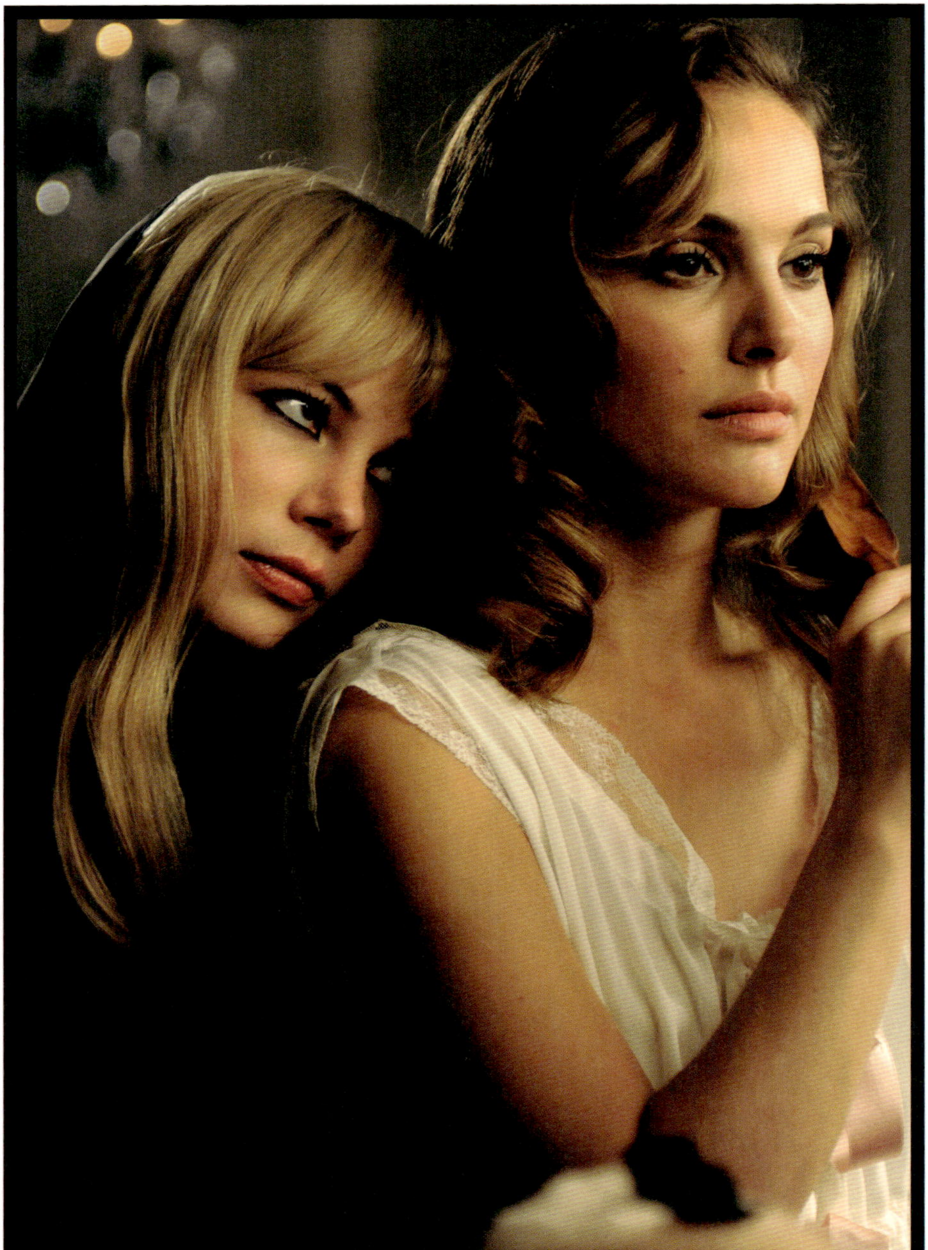

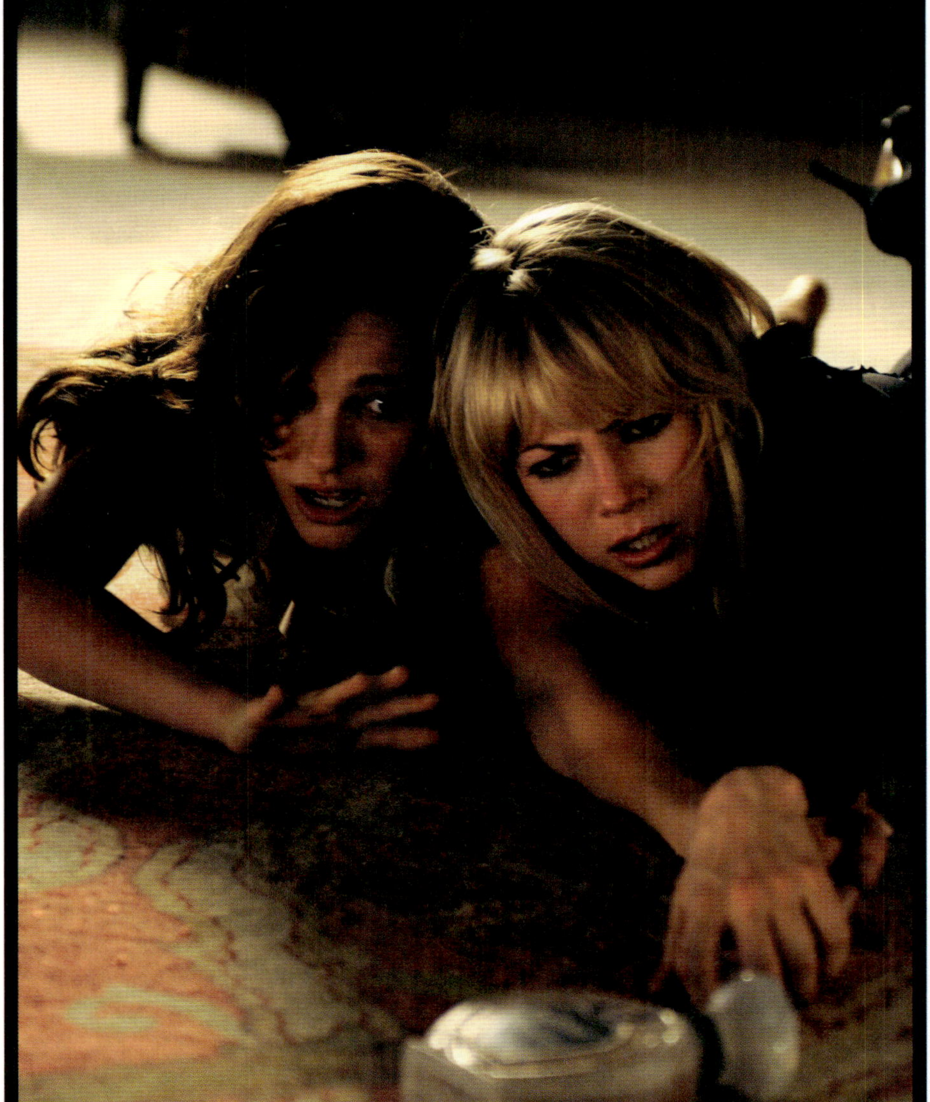

# Wolfgang Fetz
# Dalí – Warhol

*Dalí Kissing Andy*: Die später in Auflage publizierte Fotografie von Christopher Makos (der Warhol angeblich mit den Subtilitäten des Polaroids bekannt gemacht hatte) stammt aus dem Jahr 1978 (Abb. 1). Salvador Dalí ist zu diesem Zeitpunkt 74, Andy Warhol 50. Zwei Künstler, die ihre relevanten Beiträge zur Kunstgeschichte des 20. Jahrhunderts längst geleistet hatten, der eine in den dreißiger, der andere in den sechziger Jahren. Dennoch, zwei Künstler, die im erhabenen wie komfortablen Zenit ihres Nachruhms standen. Das Centre Georges Pompidou war eben dabei, Dalí eine große Retrospektive auszurichten, das Teatro-Museo Dalí, Adorationsaggregat des Großmeisters und meistbesuchtes Museum Spaniens nach dem Prado, war wenige Jahre zuvor in Figueres, seinem Geburtsort, eröffnet worden. Warhol hatte *THE Philosophy of Andy Warhol* veröffentlicht, ein Steinbruch für Zitierwütige und ultimatives Vademecum für Dandys, er pflegte das Showbusiness und hielt weiterhin das Fließband seiner Prominentenporträts auf Hochbetrieb.

*Dalí Kissing Andy* ist nicht weiter bedeutsam. Einer unter jenen nicht wenigen Schnappschüssen, die Warhol auf Kussjagd zeigen. Freilich, diese Fotografie fixiert eine Konstellation, die über die schiere Koinzidenz des Anlasses hinaus von weitergehendem Interesse ist. Hier treffen, in freundlicher Überblendung und ohne förmlich deklarierte Absicht, zwei Welten aufeinander, deren Unvereinbarkeit, ja Rivalität von einem unerwarteten Magnetismus überwölbt wird.

Zwischen Dalí, diesem wie mondsüchtig nach Erfolg schielendem Exzentriker, und Warhol, der besessen die Attitüde des Superstars kultivierte, liegt knapp eine Generation. Zu au-

*Dalí Kissing Andy*: The photograph of Christopher Makos (ill. 1), later published as an edition and which Warhol is said to have made public with all the subtlety of Polaroid, dates from 1978. At that time, Salvador Dalí was 74, Andy Warhol 50: two artists who had already made their relevant contributions to twentieth century art history, respectively, long before: the former in the thirties, the latter in the sixties. Nevertheless, two artists standing at the sublime yet comfortable zenith of their late fame. The Centre Georges Pompidou was in the act of installing a great retrospective for Dalí; the Teatro-Museo Dalí, an aggregation of adoration for the great master and the most visited museum in Spain after the Prado had been opened a few years earlier in Figueres, his birthplace. Warhol had published *THE Philosophy of Andy Warhol*, a quarry for those thirsting for quotations and an ultimate vademecum for dandies, cultivating show business and continuing to maintain the conveyor belt of his celebrity portrait at high speed.

*Dalí Kissing Andy* is of no more significance than this: one of the quite numerous snapshots showing Warhol hunting for kisses. Admittedly, this photograph is of greater interest than the mere coincidence of its occasion. Here, in a friendly cross-fade and without a formal declaration of intention, two worlds encounter one another, whose incompatibility, even rivalry, is overarched by an unexpected magnetism. Between Dalí, this eccentric squinting for success as if moonstruck, and Warhol, who obsessively cultivated the attitude of a superstar, there is a short generation. The leap is too obvious to make one speculate on overlaps in their individual artistic development. The former grew up in the boiling room of the Parisian Surrealists.

genfällig der Sprung, als dass man sich Spekulationen über Schnittmengen in ihren künstlerischen Entwicklungsgängen hingeben wollte. Ersterer war im Hitzekessel der Pariser Surrealisten groß geworden. Dort mochte André Bretons – ja, man mag es nicht anders nennen: spießbürgerliche – Fantasie, „mit Revolvern in den Fäusten auf die Straße zu gehen und blindlings, so lange man kann, in die Menge zu schießen",

André Breton, „Zweites Manifest des Surrealismus" (1930), in: Ders., *Die Manifeste des Surrealismus*, Reinbek bei Hamburg 1977, S. 56.

noch als probate Provokation durchgehen. Der zweite hatte sein Curriculum als Gebrauchskünstler im boomenden New York der fünfziger Jahre gestartet. Mit Entwürfen für Schuhmodeanzeigen, deren unwiderstehlicher Charme für nicht wenige bis in unser Heute strahlt. Und doch verband die beiden mehr, als es jene äußerlichen Accessoires oder Insignien vielleicht vermuten ließen, die in den Siebzigern längst schon Logo-Status erlangt hatten: D&W – hochgezwirbelte Velázquez-Schnauzhaare und Knaufstock hier, Perücke und Kamera dort.
Man müsste auf einem sehr hohen abstrakten Niveau argumentieren, um substanzielle Verbindungslinien zwischen deren Œuvres zu definieren. Und ihr Habitus ist in vielem augenscheinlich konträr. Und doch gibt es Parallelen, die einen ebenso zwingenden wie simplen Grad an Signifikanz aufweisen. Beide, Dalí wie Warhol, sind Fassungen eines spezifischen Künstlertypus', der zuallererst mit ihnen gleichsam prototypisch wurde. Es ist mit Sicherheit keine grobe Entstellung, wenn

There, André Breton's fantasy – one can only call it philistine – of "going into the street with revolvers in your fist and shooting blindly into the crowd as much as possible,"

André Breton, "Second Manifesto of Surrealism" (1929).

may still have been acceptable as an effective provocation. The latter started his course as an industrial artist in booming 1950s New York with sketches for shoe fashion advertisements, whose irresistible charm still radiates into our present day, not only for a few. And yet the two are connected by more than certain external accessories or insignia (which had achieved the status of logos long before the seventies) might perhaps suggest: D&W: Velázquez mustachios twisted up high and a cane in the one case, a wig and a camera in the other.
One would have to find arguments at an extremely high level of abstraction to define substantial lines of association between their oeuvres. And their environments seem to contradict each other in many ways. And yet, there are parallels that demonstrate a degree of significance both convincing and simple. Both Dalí and Warhol are versions of a specific type of artist that first began as something like a prototype in these two. No doubt it is a gross distortion if I view D&W as asymptotic twins in this regard. What each of them staged with a high degree of intelligence and consistency goes far beyond what, for example, Ernst Kris and Otto Kurz had already reconstructed at the beginning of the thirties in their "historical experiment" on the "legend of the artist": the legends and anecdotal attributions with which artists' biographies are finely chiselled. Forms of both retrospective

ich D&W in dieser Hinsicht als asymptotische Zwillinge betrachte. Was jeder für sich mit einem hohen Maß an Intelligenz und Konsequenz in Szene gesetzt hat, geht weit über das hinaus, was etwa Ernst Kris und Otto Kurz bereits zu Beginn der dreißiger Jahre in ihrem „geschichtlichen Versuch" über die „Legende vom Künstler" rekonstruiert hatten: die Legenden und anekdotischen Zuschreibungen, mit denen Künstlerbiografien ziseliert werden. Formen retrospektiver, aber auch zeitgenössischer Nobilitierung und Mythenbildung, die von Dalí und Warhol systematisch zu einem Instrument der Selbstvermarktung radikalisiert wurden. Das war nicht unbedingt etwas gänzlich Neues. Auch Tizian und Tintoretto hatten, in ihrem kleinen Venedig, präzise Einsichten, was den Markt betraf. Und Geschäftigkeit und Ruhmsucht waren dem ausgebildeten Kunstsystem stets schon inhärent. Neu war vielleicht die Weise, in der das Werk und die Vermarktung des „Autors" sich aus einer kohärenten inneren Dynamik heraus speisen ließen.
Es gibt zweifellos Gleichklänge, die sich bis ins Biografische hineinverfolgen ließen. So etwa ihr ambivalenter Zugang zur Sexualität, der wohl eher, ich spekuliere, auf Formen „halluzinatorischen Lustgewinns", denn auf „Vollzug" gerichtet war, im künstlerischen Werk jedoch eine zumindest zeitweilig ungeschminkte, „pornografische" Direktheit entfaltete. Warhol: „Sex ist ohnehin auf dem Bildschirm und dem Papier erregender als unter der Bettdecke."

Andy Warhol, *Die Philosophie des Andy Warhol von A bis B und zurück* (1975), München 1991, S. 45.

Dabei mag es sich um eine Marginalie handeln. Weitaus entscheidender sind die Korrespon-



and contemporary ennoblement and mythologizing were systematically radicalised by Dalí and Warhol into an instrument for self-marketing. That was not entirely new. In their little towns of Venice, Titian and Tintoretto, they had accurate insights into whatever affected the market. And bustling and yearning for fame had always been an inherent part of the fully developed art system. New, perhaps, was the way in which both the work and the marketing of its "authors" were fed from a coherent inner dynamism.
There are doubtless consonances that can be pursued into biographical features. For example, their ambivalent attitude to sexuality, aimed, I would suggest, more at forms of "hallucinatory lust fulfilment" than at "performance," but developing at times into an undisguised "pornographic" directness. Warhol: "Sex is more exciting on the screen and between the pages than between the sheets."

Andy Warhol, *THE Philosophy of Andy Warhol (From A to B and Back Again)*, 1975.

But this may be merely a note in the margin. Much more significant are correspondences of self-staging and strategies for generating attention. This is where they come together, though without creating identical models. In a fluid process they produce environments where art and life, fiction and reality melt together into sometimes dazzlingly garish echo rooms. They come together, but do not form identical models. Their kinship, both explicit and fragile as it is, is based on the comprehensive dimension of their intentions, the tendency to view the world as a kaleidoscope that one denzen der Inszenierung und die Strategien, Aufmerksamkeit zu generieren. Hier treffen sie sich, ohne indes identische Muster zu bilden. Sie produzieren in einem flutenden Prozess Environments, in denen Kunst und Leben, Fiktion und Wirklichkeit zu mitunter grell glitzernden Echoräumen verschmelzen. Es ist das Flächendeckende des Anspruchs, die Neigung, die Welt als Kaleidoskop zu betrachten, an dem man nur ausdauernd genug drehen muss, um ein permanentes Bild seiner selbst gespiegelt zu erhalten, das die so explizite wie brüchige Verwandtschaft der beiden Künstler begründet. Auf einen warholschen Nenner gebracht: „Öffentliche Aufmerksamkeit zu bekommen, ist wie Erdnüsse knabbern. Hat man erst einmal angefangen, kann man nicht mehr aufhören."

Andy Warhol und Bob Colacello, *Andy Warhol's Exposures*. New York 1980, S. 176.

Am 1. Juli 1936 beabsichtigte Dalí, in den Londoner New Burlington Galleries im Rahmen der *International Surrealist Exhibition* einen Vortrag über seine paranoisch-kritische Methode zu halten, „in einem Taucheranzug, um das Unterbewußtsein zu versinnbildlichen". Das Ganze war selbstredend als Performance gedacht, mit der „er sich vor internationalem Publikum als zentrale Figur der surrealistischen Bewegung inszenieren wollte".

Sebastian Neußer, *Die verborgene Präsenz des Künstlers. Inszenierungen der Abwesenheit bei Salvador Dalí, Joseph Beuys, Robert Morris und Vito Acconci*. Bielefeld 2011, S. 32.

need only turn persistently enough to obtain a permanent image of oneself as a reflection. Reduced to a Warhol denominator: "Getting public attention is like nibbling nuts. Once you start you can't stop."

Andy Warhol and Bob Colacello, *Andy Warhol's Exposures*, New York, 1980, 176.

On July 1st, 1936, Dalí intended to give a talk on the subject of his paranoïac-critical method in London's New Burlington Galleries as part of the *International Surrealist Exhibition*, "wearing a diving suit to symbolise the subconscious." Of course the whole thing was planned as a performance with which "he wanted to put himself on stage in front of an international audience as a central figure of the Surrealist movement."

Sebastian Neußer, *Die verborgene Präsenz des Künstlers. Inszenierungen der Abwesenheit bei Salvador Dalí, Joseph Beuys, Robert Morris und Vito Acconci*, Bielefeld, 2011, 32.

Realistically, the waterproof diver's helmet would not have permitted a speech to take place. In his hypertrophic "autobiographical" essay, *The Secret Life of Salvador Dalí*, which came out six years later, he stylised this performance as a catastrophic event that he survived only because of a great deal of luck. Because of a technical defect, he was within a whisker of being suffocated. With a certain instinct, Dalí had found a way to attract the highest degree of attention to himself. At the same time, he transformed the incident into a biographical event, which "has become a fixed component in artist self-mythologizing."

Der wasserdichte Taucherhelm hätte eine Rede naturgemäß nicht zugelassen. In seinem hypertrophen „autobiografischen“ Abriss, *Das geheime Leben des Salvador Dalí*, der sechs Jahre später erscheinen sollte, stilisiert er den Auftritt zu einem katastrophischen Ereignis, das er nur mit viel Glück überlebte. Aufgrund eines technischen Defekts wäre er um ein Haar erstickt. Mit sicherem Instinkt hatte Dalí einen Modus gefunden, ein Höchstmaß an Aufmerksamkeit auf sich zu ziehen. Gleichzeitig transformierte er den Vorfall zu einem biografischen Ereignis, das „zum festen Bestandteil anekdotischer Künstlermythologisierung geworden ist“.

Ebd., S. 32.



Damit stellt er sich einerseits in den Zusammenhang des „Bürgerverblüffens“, wie es Peter Sloterdijk nannte, der bereits von den Dadaisten ab 1916 und in der Folge von den Surrealisten in alle Richtungen durchdekliniert worden war.
Was dort noch als Provokation, als radikale politische Geste, als Ausstieg aus dem Gesellschaftsvertrag gedacht war, wird bei Dalí zum Marketinginstrument, Remedium der Selbstinszenierung. 1939 erhielt er vom New Yorker Kaufhaus Bonwit Teller das Angebot, zwei Schaufenster zu dekorieren. Als es mit der Geschäftsleitung, die ohne Rücksprache mit dem Künstler Teile der Schaufensterinstallation entfernen hatte lassen, zum Streit kam, entschloss sich Dalí zum Aktionismus. Er stieg in eines der Fenster, um eine „mit Astrachan ausgeschlagene ‚haarige‘ Badewanne, die bis zum Rand mit Wasser gefüllt war“,

In doing so, he situated himself in the context of “astonishing the bourgeoisie” (*Bürgerverblüffen*), as Peter Sloterdijk called it, which had gone through all possible declensions from the Dadaists of 1916 to the Surrealists.
In that tradition, it had still been intended as a provocation, a radical political gesture, an exit from the social contract, but in Dalí it became a marketing instrument, a panacea for self-presentation. In 1939, he was commissioned by the New York department store Bonwit Teller to decorate two display windows. When a dispute arose with the management, who had had part of the display removed without consulting the artist, Dalí chose Actionism as his strategy. He climbed into the window to remove a “hairy bathtub lined with Astrakhan. It was filled with water up to the edge”:

Salvador Dalí, *The Secret Life of Salvador Dalí*, New York, 1993, 372.

“[...] my apparition in the window, for a large crowd gathered to watch me. [...] I took hold of the bathtub with both hands, and tried to lift it so as to turn it over. I felt like the Biblical Samson between the pillars of the temple. The bath-tub was much heavier than I had calculated, and before I could raise one side, it slipped right up against the window so that, at the moment when, with a supreme effort, I finally succeeded in turning it over, it crashed into the plate glass, shattering it into a thousand pieces. [...] Then I coolly appraised the situation and judged it much more reasonable to leave by the hole in the window bristling with the stalactites and the stalagmites of my anger than to go back to through the door in the rear of the shop window.”

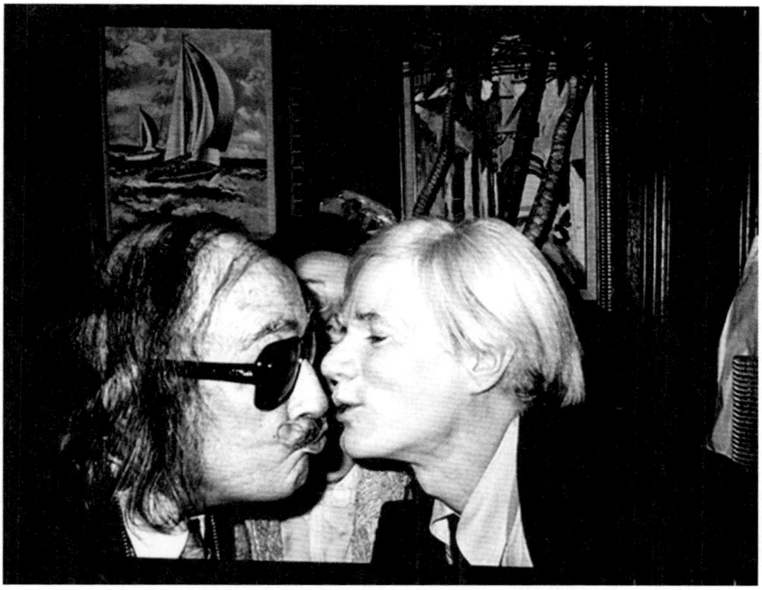

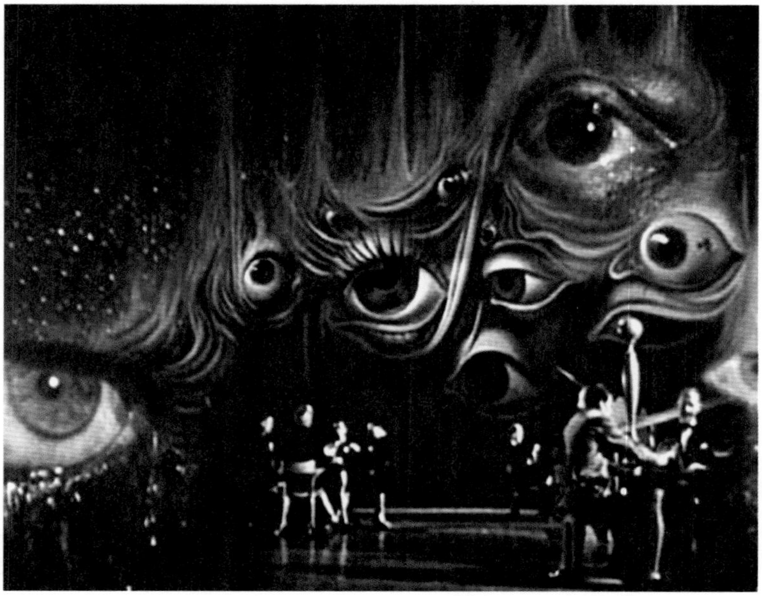



Abb./ill. 1: Christopher Makos, *Dalí Kissing Andy*, 1979

Abb./ill. 2: Still aus/still from Alfred Hitchcock, *Spellbound*, 1945, Traumszene von/dream sequence by Salvador Dalí

Salvador Dalí, *Das geheime Leben des Salvador Dalí*. München 2004, S. 642.

zu beseitigen. „Mein Auftauchen im Fenster muss irgendwie sehr ungewöhnlich gewirkt haben, denn es sammelte sich sofort eine große Menschenmenge, um mich zu beobachten. [...] Ich packte die Badewanne [...] und versuchte sie hochzuheben und umzukippen. Die Badewanne war viel schwerer als angenommen, und bevor ich sie hochheben konnte, rutschte sie direkt zum Fenster, so dass sie in dem Moment, als ich es schließlich mit äußerster Anstrengung schaffte, sie auszuleeren, in die Scheibe krachte, die in tausend Stücke zerbarst. [...] In kühler Einschätzung der Lage kam ich dann zu dem Schluss, es sei viel vernünftiger, das Geschäft durch das von den Stalaktiten und Stalagmiten meiner Wut starrende Fenster zu verlassen, als durch die Tür im hinteren Teil der Auslage zurückzugehen."

Ebd., S. 645.

Dieses Spektakel, in dem wiederum das „Katastrophische" den Grundtenor ausmacht (und das ihm ordentliche Publicity einbrachte), ist eine Art Reinzeichnung der habituellen Hyperventilation, die Dalí zeitlebens als Markenzeichen vor sich herträgt. (Wirkliches Leben: Das Schussattentat von Valerie Solanas auf Warhol, 1968, das ihn auf die Titelseiten brachte.) Das Erhitzt-Superlativische, die Neigung zur Verblüffungspose sind die zweite Natur des katalanischen „Erlösers der modernen Malerei". Sie durchziehen Werk wie Leben. Man kann leicht den Eindruck gewinnen, der „öffentliche" Dalí befände sich in einem Zustand permanenter Rushhour, das



Ibid., 374–375.

This spectacle, where the "catastrophic" is again responsible for the dominant tone (and which brought him a nice amount of publicity), is a kind of fair drawing of the hyperventilation that Dalí habitually carried around with him all his life as a trademark. (Real life: the gun fired at Warhol by Valerie Solanas in 1968, which put him on the front page.) The overheated superlatives, the tendency to pose as a bluff, were second nature to the Catalan "Saviour of modern painting." They run through both his work and his life. It is easy to get the impression that the "public" Dalí was in a state of permanent rush hour, and it sometimes reached the point of involuntary self-parody. By comparison, Warhol seems undercooled. If one grants him a kind of dandyism, then it's surely in a form that cultivates distance, a certain indifference. While Dalí, compulsively outré, represents the classical type of the aging enfant terrible as dandy, Warhol is more like the summation of what Susan Sontag described in her "Notes on 'Camp'" (1964). She sees "camp" as a kind of "Dandyism in the age of mass culture," which "makes no distinction between the unique object and the mass-produced object. Camp taste transcends the nausea of the replica."

Susan Sontag, "Notes on 'Camp'" (1964), 11. www.math.utah.edu/~lars/Sontag::Notes%20on%20camp.pdf

And she sums up: "Here, one may compare Camp with much Pop Art, which – when it is not just Camp – embodies an attitude that is related, but still very different. Pop Art is more flat and dry, more serious, more detached, ultimately nihilistic."

geht mitunter bis zur unfreiwilligen Selbstparodie. Im Vergleich dazu wirkt Warhol unterkühlt. Unterstellte man ihm einen Hang zum Dandyismus, dann sicherlich in einer Form, die die Distanz, eine gewisse Indifferenz pflegt. Während Dalí zwanghaft outrierend den klassischen Typus des Bürgerschreck-Dandys repräsentiert, trifft auf Warhol eher das zu, was Susan Sontag 1964 in ihren *Anmerkungen zu „Camp“* notiert. Sie betrachtet „Camp“ als eine Form des „Dandyismus im Zeitalter der Massenkultur“, die „keinen Unterschied zwischen dem einzigartigen Gegenstand und dem Massengut“

Susan Sontag, „Anmerkungen zu ‚Camp‘“ (1964), in: *Kunst und Antikunst. Essays*. München, Wien 1980, S. 337.

macht. „Der Camp-Geschmack lässt die Übelkeit unter sich, die die Reproduktion bewirkt.“

Ebd., S. 337.

Und sie resümiert: „An dieser Stelle könnte man Camp mit einem Großteil der Pop Art vergleichen, die – wenn sie nicht einfach Camp ist – eine Haltung zum Ausdruck bringt, die verwandt, aber dennoch ganz anders ist. Pop Art ist fader und trockener, ernster und gleichgültiger, letztlich nihilistisch.“

Ebd., S. 340.

Für den Surrealisten Dalí findet die Essayistin gerade noch einen Nebensatz: „Im öden Grenzgebiet des Camp gibt es eine Menge hübscher Dinge: die aalglatten Phantasien Dalís [...] “

Ebd., S. 332.

Ibid., 13.

In her essay, she finds a subordinate clause for the Surrealist Dalí: “On the barren edge of Camp lie a number of attractive things: the sleek fantasies of Dalí ...”

Ibid., 7.

Among the dense wills-o’-the-wisp of consumerism, entertainment, the culture industry and art, Warhol and Dalí run at noticeably different operating temperatures.

Dalí’s approach to art is marked by a genius aesthetic commercially reduced to a trivial topos, whose phenotype had its first major appearance in the Renaissance. The artist acts as an all-round man, juggling with exalted, Vinci-like gestures. Dalí behaves like a powerful headlight that penetrates and illuminates every scratch, no matter how insignificant. In his “autobiography” (autofiction would be more accurate), he quotes the formula all too well known since Augustine and Rousseau: “Never before had anyone exposed himself in such a way in the innermost parts and depth of his being,”

Salvador Dalí, So *wird man Dalí*, München, Zürich, 1974, 227.

and, in the same breath, covers over everything that comes into his hands or before his eyes with this same innermost being, an exhilarating presumptuousness. He takes things over with the gesture of triumph. His paranoïac-critical method, which even the idiosyncratic Breton (who, after hesitating for a long while, shipped

Im dichten Irrlichtern der Welt des Konsums, der Unterhaltung, der Kulturindustrie und der Kunst laufen Warhol und Dalí auf erkennbar unterschiedlicher Betriebstemperatur.

Dalís Zugang zur Kunst ist geprägt von einer zum Trivialtopos herabgewirtschafteten Genieästhetik, deren Phänotyp in der Renaissance seinen ersten Großauftritt hatte. Der Künstler agiert als Alleskönner, er jongliert mit erhabener, leonardoesker Geste in die Breite. Dalí verhält sich wie ein gewaltiger Scheinwerfer, der jede noch so unbedeutende Ritze durch- und erleuchtet. Wenn er in seiner „Autobiografie" (präziser wäre „Autofiktion") die seit Augustinus und Rousseau sattsam bekannte Formel herbeizitiert: „Noch nie hatte sich ein Mensch in seinem Innersten und in der Tiefe des Seins so preisgegeben",



Salvador Dalí, *So wird man Dalí*, Wien. München, Zürich 1974, S. 227.

dann stülpt er im gleichen Atemzug dieses Innerste als beglückende Zumutung über alles, was ihm in die Hände oder vor Augen gerät. Er nimmt sich der Dinge mit der Geste des Triumphators an. Seine „paranoisch-kritische Methode", die selbst der idiosynkratische Breton, der Dalí nach langem Zögern aus dem Kreis der Surrealisten expediert hatte, zu den höheren surrealistischen Errungenschaften rechnete, funktioniert wie eine Trickmaschine. Sie erlaubt es, sämtliche Genres mit gleichsam imperialem Anspruch zu durchdringen. Sie ist aktive Projektion. „Paranoisch-kritische Aktivität bedeutet: spontane Methode irrationaler Erkenntnis, die auf der kritisch-interpretierenden Assoziation wahnhafter Phänomene beruht."

Dalí out of the circle of the Surrealists) still counted as one of the higher achievements of Surrealism, functioned something like a trick appliance. The method makes it possible to penetrate all genres with the same imperial assertiveness. It is active projection. "paranoïac-critical activity means a spontaneous method of irrational perception based on the critical-interpretative association of manic phenomena."

Salvador Dalí, "Die Eroberung des Irrationalen [The Conquest of the Irrational]" (1935), in *Unabhängigkeitserklärung der Phantasie und Erklärung der Rechte des Menschen auf seine Verrücktheit. Gesammelte Schriften*, ed. by Axel Matthes and Tilbert Diego Stegmann, München, 1974.

That is the lever, the magnifying glass with which the paranoid-critical artist submits himself to every aspect of "reality." (He is distinguished from the merely delirious by his degree of objectification, the specification of "work.") "America" offered him the ideal soil for this purpose. His approach takes on a quality of ubiquity and he really does become the "polyfacetic" Dalí he likes to call himself: he supplies artwork for the cover pages of fashion journals (*Vogue, Harper's Bazaar*), designs advertising materials, ties, swimsuits, rugs, jewellery: "Ah, I like advertising in all its forms. I am an exhibitionist."

Salvador Dalí, quoted by Ricardo Mas Peinado, in *Dalí*, Petersberg, 2004, 259.

(Warhol: "I will use my name to advertise clothing, cigarettes, audio tapes, audio materials, rock-'n-roll records, films and film materials, food, helium, whips, money.")

Salvador Dalí, „Die Eroberung des Irrationalen" (1935). In: Ders., *Unabhängigkeitserklärung der Phantasie und Erklärung der Rechte des Menschen auf seine Verrücktheit. Gesammelte Schriften,* hg. v. Axel Matthes und Tilbert Diego Stegmann. München 1974.

Das ist der Hebel, das Brennglas, mit dem der kritische Paranoiker sich jeden Aspekt von „Wirklichkeit" zu unterwerfen vermag. (Vom bloß Delirierenden unterscheidet er sich durch den Grad der Objektivierung, der Konkretisierung als „Werk".)
„America" bot ihm dafür den idealen Boden. Sein Zugriff nimmt ubiquitäres Ausmaß an, er wird tatsächlich zum „polyfacetic" Dalí, als den er sich gerne bezeichnet: Er liefert Vorlagen für Titelseiten von Modezeitschriften (*Vogue, Harper's Bazaar*), entwirft Werbeanzeigen, Krawatten, Badeanzüge, Teppiche, Schmuck: „Ah, mir gefällt Werbung in allen Formen. Ich bin ein Exhibitionist."

Zit. nach Ricardo Mas Peinado in: *Dalí.* Petersberg 2004, S. 259.

(Warhol: „Ich werde mit meinem Namen werben für: Kleider, Zigaretten, Tonbänder, Tonmaterial, Rock 'n' Roll-Platten, Filme und Filmmaterial, Speisen, Helium, Peitschen, Geld.")

Andy Warhol und Pat Hackett, *POPism. The Warhol '60*. New York 1980, S. 152.

Mitte der dreißiger Jahre entstand die Gouache *Gesicht der Mae West, das als Wohnung benutzt werden kann.* Die Lippen des charismatischen Hollywoodstars waren als Sofa dargestellt. Wenig später wurden sie als Möbelstück nach-

Andy Warhol and Pat Hackett, *POPism. The Warhol '60*, New York, 1980, 152.

His first gouache was made in the mid thirties: *The Face of Mae West (Usable as a Surrealist Apartment)*. The lips of the charismatic Hollywood star were presented as a sofa. Not long afterwards they were imitated as an item of furniture. The first version was in satin and was "shocking pink." That is the colour of a lipstick by Mae West. Did Warhol think of that in 1962 when he pressed Marilyn Monroe's lips through his screen printer?
Dalí continued to work for and with the fashion designer Elsa Schiaparelli, the crazy counterpart to Coco Chanel. For example, in 1945 he designed a splendid crystal flacon for her luxury perfume *Le Roy Soleil*. Later he designed flacons for a wide range of firms. He produced designs for stage sets, he directed at the Metropolitan Opera. In 1945, he arrived in Hollywood. He worked with Hitchcock (*Spellbound*, ill. 2). A work planned with Walt Disney (*Destino*) was never carried through. Dalí's Hollywood liaison did not run especially well in any case. Warhol as well (both were prepared to be convinced that Hollywood represented the real artistic upper class), who had a comparably low level of success in this environment twenty years later. His *Frankenstein* and *Dracula* remained casual, as they were, and remained, in spite of the participation of producer giants like Carlo Ponti, insignificant islands in a big stream – definitely side issues. For Dalí, that was hardly a disaster. His commercial empire expanded from the beginning of the sixties in such a way that he employed John Peter Moore as managing director, who was an Irish officer and a member of the Vati-

gebaut. Die erste Version in Satin und in „shocking pink“. Nach der Farbe eines Lippenstifts von Mae West. Ob Warhol daran gedacht hat, als er 1962 Marilyn Monroes Lippen durch seine Siebdruckmaschinerie gejagt hat?
Dalí arbeitet weiterhin für und mit der Modeschöpferin Elsa Schiaparelli, diesem verrückten Counterpart zu Coco Chanel. So gestaltete er 1945 einen prächtigen Kristall-Flakon für ihr Luxusparfüm *Le Roy Soleil*. In der Folge lieferte er Flakonentwürfe für verschiedenste Häuser. Er produziert Bühnenbildentwürfe und inszeniert an der Metropolitan Opera. 1945 ist er in Hollywood angekommen. Er arbeitet mit Hitchcock (*Spellbound*, Abb. 2). Ein geplantes Projekt mit Walt Disney (*Destino*) wird nicht realisiert. Dalís Hollywood-Liaison verläuft jedenfalls nicht besonders großartig. Auch Warhol, beide waren bereit, sich einzureden, dass Hollywood die eigentliche artistische Upperclass darstellte, hatte, zwanzig Jahre später, vergleichbar geringen Erfolg auf diesem Boden. Seine Filme *Frankenstein* und *Dracula* blieben, beiläufig wie sie waren und trotz Beteiligung von Produzentengrößen wie Carlo Ponti, unbedeutende Inseln in einem großen Strom, definitive Nebensächlichkeiten.
Das war für Dalí kaum desaströs. Sein Kommerzbereich expandierte ab Beginn der sechziger Jahre in einer Weise, dass er sich mit dem irischen Offizier und Mitglied der vatikanischen Propagandaabteilung John Peter Moore einen Geschäftsführer engagiert, unbekümmert um alle Grenzen zwischen Kitsch, Trivialität und künstlerischem „Ethos“.
Kein Zweifel: Dalí, der es bereits 1936 auf die Titelseite der *Time* gebracht hatte, hatte die große Bresche geschlagen: In der Erzeugung von neuen, kommerziell verwertbaren Reizmustern war er – der Künstlerfürst unter



can's department for propaganda, untroubled by any borders between kitsch, triviality and artistic "ethos."

Without a doubt: Dalí, who had already made it onto the cover of *Time* in 1936, had made his great break-through: in the production of new, commercially viable optical stimuli he was – as the prince of artists among artists – unbeatable. And by return of post he received the disdain of the avant-garde, who were unable to reconcile such "slapstick" with their "sacred" principles. It was not by chance either that he was banned by André Breton, who threw the anagram "Avida Dollars" ("greedy for dollars") at him. The pathos, indeed frequently the sugariness and artificiality of his art, was taken up without question in a market that had increasingly begun to blur the borders between High Art and Low Art. His kind of "genius" was nicely compatible with the levels of expectation in a rapidly developing entertainment and adventure society.
As far as marketing routines were concerned in the optimisation of value of the older artist, Warhol could have joined in seamlessly. But the "Warhol" system developed along different tracks: it was fed from diverging conditions and made use of registers of a completely different kind. On the one hand, on the basis of his many years of successful work as a commercial artist in the fifties, he had acquired with certainty a more specific, at least "more contemporary," "feeling" for certain subtleties in the market; On the other, he moved, with regard to his acculturation and the modulations of his instinct, in a mental setting which would ultimately have to exclude a Dalí galaxy. That was perforce to lead him to other strategies and

den Künstlern – unschlagbar. Was ihm postwendend die Verachtung der Avantgarde einbrachte, die derartigen „Klamauk“ keineswegs mit ihren „heiligen“ Prinzipien vereinbaren konnte. Nicht umsonst auch traf ihn der Bannfluch André Bretons, der ihm das anagrammatische „Avida Dollars“ („gierig nach Dollars“) nachwarf. Das Pathetische, ja nicht selten Zuckrige und Aufgesetzte seiner Kunst ließ sich problemlos in einen Markt hinein verlängern, der die Grenzen zwischen High und Low zunehmend zu verwischen begann. Seine Form von „genialisch“ inszeniertem Kunsthandwerk bediente in schönster Kongruenz die Erwartungshorizonte einer sich rasant entwickelnden Unterhaltungs- und Erlebnisgesellschaft.
Warhol hätte (was die Marketingroutinen, die Verwertungsoptimierungen des Älteren angeht) nahtlos daran anknüpfen können. Doch das System „Warhol“ entwickelte sich auf Schienen abseits davon, es speiste sich aus divergenten Voraussetzungen und bediente völlig andersgeartete Register. Einerseits hatte er aufgrund seiner langjährigen und erfolgreichen Tätigkeit als Gebrauchskünstler während der fünfziger Jahre mit Sicherheit ein spezifischeres, zumindest „zeitgenössischer“ gestimmtes „Feeling“ für gewisse Subtilitäten des Marktes ausgebildet. Andererseits bewegte er sich von seiner Kulturalisation und den Modulationen seines Instinkts her gesehen in einem Mental-Setting, dem eine Dalí-Galaxie letztlich äußerlich bleiben musste. Das sollte ihn zwangsläufig zu anderen Strategien und Allianzbildungen führen. Ich erwähnte bereits die unterschiedliche „Betriebstemperatur“ der beiden. Keine Frage, man sollte mit Metaphorisierungen wie „kalt – heiß“ (Moderne vs.

other allies. I have already mentioned the different “operating temperatures” of the two artists. Certainly, one should use metaphors like “cold-hot” (Modern vs. Postmodern, for example) with caution. But Warhol’s “coolness” (no less than Dalí’s “heat”) is significant: it embraces both the “public” persona, the presentation of self, and his work. The distanced opaqueness of his understatement, the suspension of the emotional, the “coolness” with which he utters platitudes (the number of real aperçus is comparatively limited), and also the persistent celebration of trivial, affirmative surfaces, drives Warhol towards the tipping point of ennui or, if one will, nirvana. What in Dalí is a paranoïac-critical method is in Warhol the serial, the untempered uniformity, the long unimpassioned gaze of the camera, the monotony of social gossip, an on and on and on: surfaces that conceal nothing, that resist any “depth.” The surface as fetish, as a form of indifference. Everything is good and pretty as long as the “machine” can be kept running. In an interview in 1963, he postulated: “I think everyone should be a machine. I think that everyone should act like Everyman. Is that what Pop Art is about? Yes, it means liking things. And is liking things like being a machine? Yes, because you do the same thing every time. You do it again and again.”

Andy Warhol, “Interview” (1963), quoted from *Riten der Selbstauflösung*, ed. by Oswald Wiener and Verena von der Heyden-Rynsch, Munich, 1982, 296.

And elsewhere he makes his point even stronger: “When Picasso died I read in the paper that he had made 4000 masterpieces in his lifetime.

Postmoderne beispielsweise) zurückhaltend umgehen. Aber die „Kälte" Warhols (wie umgekehrt die „Hitze" Dalís) ist signifikant, in ihr schließt sich die „öffentliche" Person, die Selbstinszenierung, mit seinem Werk zusammen. Das distanziert-undurchsichtige seines Understatements, die Suspension des Emotionalen, die „coolness", mit der er Plattitüden von sich gibt (die Zahl der wirklichen Aperçus hält sich in Grenzen), ja, und dann dieses hartnäckige Zelebrieren von trivialen, affirmativen Oberflächen, das er bis zum Kippen in den Ennui oder, wenn man so will, in ein göttliches Nirwana hintreibt. Was für Dalí die paranoisch-kritische Methode ist, ist für Warhol das Serielle, die untertemperierte Gleichförmigkeit, der lange, unbeteiligte Blick der Kamera, die Monotonie des Gesellschaftsklatsches, ein on and on and on: Oberflächen, die nichts verbergen, die sich jedem „Dahinter" verweigern. Die Oberfläche als Fetisch, als Form der Indifferenz.

Alles ist gut und pretty, solange die „Maschine" am Laufen gehalten werden kann. In einem Interview von 1963 postuliert er: „Ich glaube, dass jeder eine Maschine sein sollte. Ich glaube, dass jeder wie jedermann handeln sollte. Ist es das, worum es bei der Pop-Art geht? Ja, es bedeutet, die Dinge zu mögen. Und die Dinge zu mögen, ist wie eine Maschine sein? Ja, weil man jedes Mal dasselbe tut. Man tut es immer wieder."

Andy Warhol, „Interview" (1963), zit. n.: *Riten der Selbstauflösung*, hg. von Oswald Wiener und Verena von der Heyden-Rynsch. München 1982, S. 296.



I thought, 'So what? I can do that in one day.' In my way, using my technique, four thousand a day. And they would all be masterpieces, because all of them would be the same painting."

Andy Warhol, quoted from Rainer Crone, *Andy Warhol. Die frühen Werke 1942–1962*, Stuttgart, 1987, 22

The desire for no distinction and the highest possible reduction of difference is inherent in his urge to produce. With the same insistence he used in making his Campbell's soup cans, endless and unaltered, he later turned out his portraits of stars: Liz Taylor, Mao, the Shah of Persia, Goethe, Beuys, Agnelli, Mona Lisa, Mick Jagger. Emptying out meaning through equalisation: "Warhol's art is ... an extended, merciless exercise in entropic banality,"

Donald Kuspit, *Der Kult vom Avantgarde-Künstler*, Klagenfurt, 1995, 137.

wrote Donald Kuspit. It signalises "the end of faith in the healing power of art. It exists to make us disillusioned about art, and is, therefore, an art of disillusionment. As such, it is the first genuinely postmodern art."

Ibid., 138.

That may well be right in its way. However, "faith in the healing power of art," which cannot disguise its origins in a religious context, is replaced by a secular form of the religious: capitalism – if one accepts the assumptions of Walter Benjamin, who describes capitalism as an "essentially religious phenomenon" in a fragment from 1921. Warhol is the high priest without qualities in this radical "displacement,"

Und an anderer Stelle spitzt er seinen Standpunkt noch zu: „Als Picasso starb, las ich in der Zeitung, er hat 4000 Meisterwerke hergestellt in seinem Leben. Ich dachte, ‚Geh, das kann ich an einem Tag.' Auf meine Weise, in meiner Technik, viertausend am Tag. Und sie wären alle Meisterwerke, weil sie alle das gleiche Gemälde wären."

Zit. n. Rainer Crone, *Andy Warhol. Die frühen Werke* 1942–1962. Stuttgart 1987, S. 22.

Das Verlangen nach Unterschiedslosigkeit und höchstmöglicher Differenzreduktion sind seinem Produktionsehrgeiz inhärent. Mit der gleichen Insistenz, mit der er seine Campbell's Suppendosen endlos und ungerührt addiert, speit er später seine Star-Porträts aus: Liz Taylor, Mao, der Schah von Persien, Goethe, Beuys, Agnelli, Mona Lisa, Mick Jagger. Bedeutungsentleerung durch Egalisation: „Warhols Kunst ist [...] eine ausgedehnte, erbarmungslose Übung in entropischer Banalisierung",

Donald Kuspit, *Der Kult vom Avantgarde-Künstler* (1993). Klagenfurt 1995, S. 137.

schrieb Donald Kuspit. Sie signalisiere „das Ende des Glaubens an die Heilkraft der Kunst. Sie existiert, um uns bezüglich der Kunst zu desillusionieren, und ist somit eine Kunst der Desillusionierung. Als solche ist sie die erste wirklich postmoderne Kunst."

Ebd., S. 138.

Das mag zweifellos seine Richtigkeit haben. Allerdings tritt an die Stelle „des Glaubens an die Heilkraft der Kunst", der seine Abkunft

See Walter Benjamin, "Kapitalismus als Religion" (um 1921), in *Walter Benjamin, Gesammelte Schriften*, ed. by Rolf Tiedemann and Hermann Schweppenhäuser, VI, Franfurt a. M., 1985, 100-103.

this new promise of salvation: fame and wealth. In this, he is much closer to the sacred prose of the present than Dalí. In contrast to the latter, who tried to soak the market in a pre-modern idea of genius, Warhol took his mottos and his material from the unfettered market itself. Of course, this escalation of value could also not manage without capitalist-style serial production. He is said – and this has its own beautiful irony – to have signed between forty and sixty thousand blank sheets of drawing paper, and in the eighties he advanced to being the most frequently faked artist of all times.

The core of the "Warhol System" was the Factory, that "comical orphanage for wannabe talents," as Truman Capote once remarked. The "shy" demiurge Warhol turned himself into a magnate. As a dandy who submitted to a domesticated American form of "désinvolture," he sat on his throne in the midst of "cultural space garbage," "hovering fragments from various subcultures of the sixties,"

Robert Hughes, *Denn ich bin nichts, wenn ich nicht lästern darf. Kritische Anmerkungen zu Kunst, Künstlern und Kunstmarkt*, Munich, 1995 [1982], 323.

as Robert Hughes said acidly. The Factory, at first just a studio, grew rapidly into a showroom for a permanent performance, developing into the control station of "Andy-Warhol-aus einem religiösen Kontext nicht verbergen kann, eine säkularisierte Form des Religiösen: der Kapitalismus – folgt man der Mutmaßung Walter Benjamins, der in einem Fragment von 1921 den Kapitalismus als „essentiell religiöse Erscheinung" beschreibt. Warhol ist der „eigenschaftslose" Hohepriester dieser radikalen „Verschiebung",

Walter Benjamin, „Kapitalismus als Religion" (um 1921), in: Walter Benjamin, *Gesammelte Schriften*, hg. von Rolf Tiedemann und Hermann Schweppenhäuser, Bd. VI. Frankfurt a. M. 1985, S. 100–103.

der neuen Heilsversprechung: Ruhm und Reichtum. Darin ist er weit näher an der heiligen Prosa der Gegenwart als Dalí. Im Unterschied zu diesem, der den Markt mit einem vormodernen Geniekonzept zu durchdringen versuchte, bezog Warhol seine Maximen, seinen Stoff aus dem entfesselten Markt selbst. Natürlich kam auch letzterer, dieser Verwertungseskalateur, nicht um das Kapitalistisch-Serielle herum. Er soll, und das hat seine eigene, schöne Ironie, zwischen 40–60.000 Grafikbögen blanko signiert haben, und in den achtziger Jahren avancierte er zum meistgefälschten Künstler aller Zeiten.

Kernzelle des „Systems Warhol" war die Factory, dieses „komische Waisenhaus für Möchtegerntalente", wie Truman Capote einmal notierte. Der „scheue" Demiurg Warhol machte sich zum

Robert Hughes, *Denn ich bin nichts, wenn ich nicht lästern darf. Kritische Anmerkungen zu Kunst, Künstlern und Kunstmarkt*. München 1995 (1982), S. 323.



Enterprises," which, fitted out with a number of managing directors, managed the marketing aspect of the "Warhol Look." It became a parade ground for rising "superstars," a term that Warhol first made current. "My superstars." At this time, Hollywood knew only "stars." Among those who took part was Isabelle Dufresne, who had earlier served at Dalí's court as a model and companion. Under the name Ultra Violet she became a member and a "superstar" of the Factory, as did Jane Holzer and Joe Dallesandro. Jonas Mekas, an avantgarde film-maker, originally from Lithuania, who also filmed Dalí happenings in New York in 1963/64, wrote a concise sketch of this shimmering scene: "And there he was, Saint Andy, and he let everyone come into his world, his quarter. Effortlessly and painlessly, he moved them around, coordinated them, used the energy and power that was streaming there, balanced them, pushed them together – a very subtle manipulation of the most extreme temperaments ..."

Jonas Mekas, "Notes after Reseeing the Movies of Andy Warhol," in John Coplans, *Andy Warhol*, New York, 1971, 140.

Even though it had something of the aura of a sect, a microcosm arose, which was without precedent in respect to its form of production and the manner of its ostentatious, noisy marketing. The Factory mutated into a myth, became itself a "superstar," and Andy Warhol became the prototype of a new kind of artist. A kind that was to determine the field, at least the cliché of what we understand as an "artist" in the "hot" art industry beginning in the nineties. Dalí and Warhol provided the perfect blueprints for it.

Magneten. Als Dandy, der sich einer amerikanisch domestizierten Form von „Désinvolture“ hingab, thronte er inmitten von „kulturellem Weltraumschrott“, „schwebenden Bruchstücken aus diversen Subkulturen der sechziger Jahre“, wie Robert Hughes ätzte. Die Factory, ursprünglich ein simples Studio, Atelier, wuchs sich in kürzester Zeit zum Schauplatz einer permanenten Performance aus, entwickelte sich zur Schaltstelle von „Andy-Warhol-Enterprises“, die, mit mehreren Geschäftsführern bestückt, die Vermarktung des „Warhol Looks“ betrieb. Sie wurde zum Übungsplatz für angehende „Superstars“, ein Begriff, den erst Warhol als solchen gängig machte: „Meine Superstars“. Hollywood kannte zu dieser Zeit schließlich nur den „Star“. Unter anderem verkehrte dort auch Isabelle Dufresne, die zuvor als Modell und Wegbegleiterin zu Dalís Hofstaat gehört hatte. Unter dem Namen Ultra Violet wurde sie Mitglied und „Superstar“ der Factory, wie Jane Holzer oder Joe Dallesandro. Jonas Mekas, ein ursprünglich aus Litauen stammender Avantgardefilmer, der 1963/64 auch Dalí-Happenings in New York filmte, skizziert ein konzises Bild jener schillernden Szenerie: „Und da war er, der Heilige Andy, und ließ sie alle rein in seine Welt, in sein Quartier. Anstrengungslos und schmerzlos bewegte er sie herum, koordinierte sie, benutzte die Energien und Kräfte, die hineinströmten, balancierte sie aus, stieß sie zusammen – ein sehr subtiles Manövrieren der extremsten Temperamente [...] “

Jonas Mekas, zit. nach Klaus Theweleit, *Buch der Könige, Bd. 2, Recording angels' mysteries, Basel*, Frankfurt a. M. 1994, S. 477. [Original: Jonas Mekas, „Notes after Reseeing the Movies of

In addition: Everything is good and pretty as long as the "machine" can be kept running. Meanwhile, a "macrocosm," whose design and operating principle is (has become) almost congruent with the "free market," runs this machine accordingly in "synergy." Parallels to the "big market" are also seen in the very same field that Andy Warhol delivered a "blueprint" for: "The art world has become such a self-promotional universe that I've basically grown obsessed with deconstructing the very means of promotion," says Francesco Vezzoli.

Scott Rothkoph, "1000 Words: Francesco Vezzoli talks about Democrazy," in *Artforum*, Sommer 2007, S. 449.

Vezzoli's art is above all about the promotion of art and artists in relation to a (mass) media production and marketing system .

Andy Warhol" in: John Coplans, *Andy Warhol*. New York 1971, S. 140 f.

Mit der Factory entstand, auch wenn sie den gewissen „goût" des Sektenhaften ausstrahlen mochte, ein Mikrokosmos, der sowohl in seiner Produktionsform als auch in der Weise seiner ostentativen, lauten Vermarktung ohne Vorbild war. Die Factory mutierte selbst zum Mythos, wurde „Superstar" und Andy Warhol zur Leitfigur eines neuen Künstlertypus. Ein Typus, der im sich „heiß" laufenden Kunstbetrieb ab den neunziger Jahren zunehmend das Feld, zumindest das Klischee dessen, was wir unter „Künstler" zu verstehen haben, bestimmen sollte. Dalí und Warhol hatten den perfekten Blueprint dazu abgeliefert.



Der 1971 geborene Vezzoli geht der Promotion von Kunst und Künstlern nach, wobei er vor allem deren (massen-)mediale Inszenierung und Vermarktung analysiert. Weiterhin gilt: Alles ist gut und pretty, solange die „Maschine" am Laufen gehalten werden kann. Mittlerweile ein „Makrokosmos", dessen Konstruktions- und Funktionsprinzip mit dem der „freien Marktwirtschaft" nahezu kongruent (geworden) ist, läuft diese Maschine dementsprechend „synergetisch". Parallelen zum „großen Markt" werden auch in jenem Bereich gesichtet, für den schon Andy Warhol einen „Blueprint" abgeliefert hatte: „The art world has become such a self-promotional universe that I've basically grown obsessed with deconstructing the very means of promotion", sagt Francesco Vezzoli.

Scott Rothkoph, "1000 Words: Francesco Vezzoli talks about Democrazy", in: *Artforum*, Sommer 2007, S. 449.

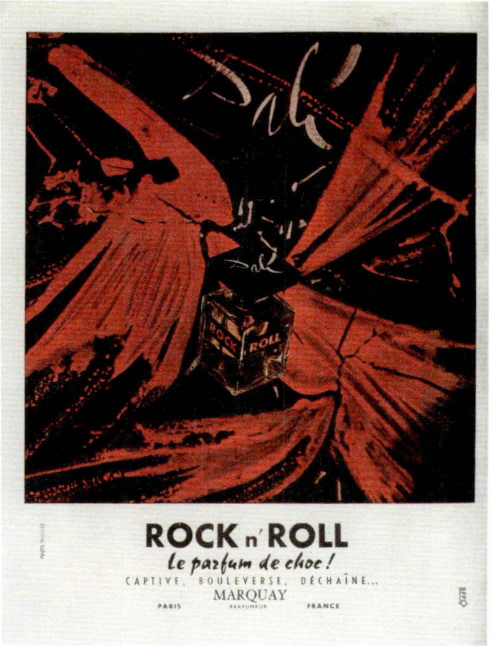


*Rock'n Roll, le parfum de chock!, United States Lines*, 1957

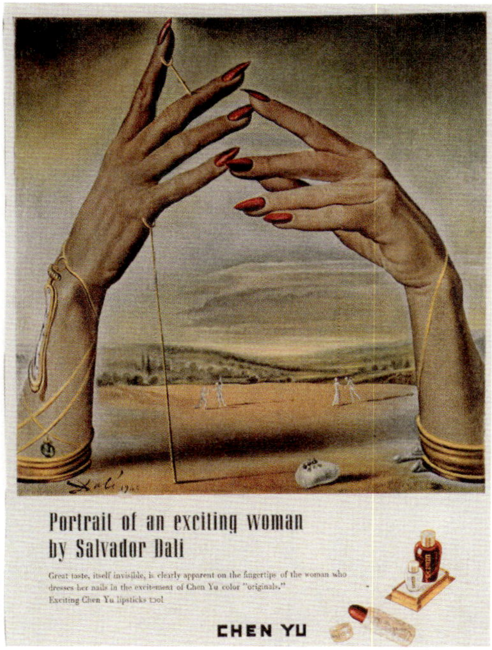


*Chen Yu, Vogue*, 01/09/1945



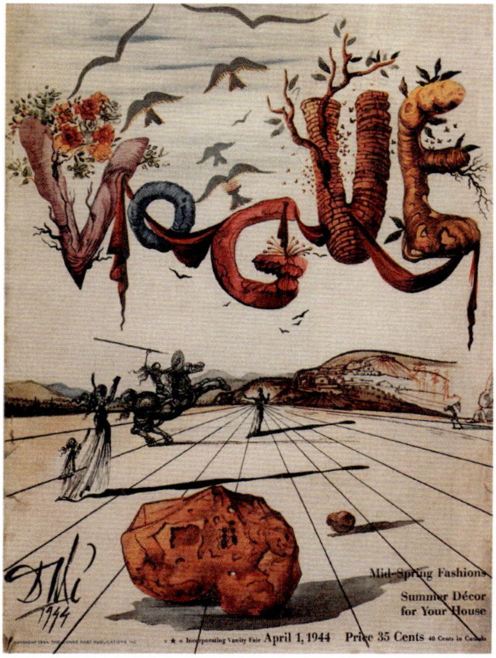


*Vogue*, 01/04/1945

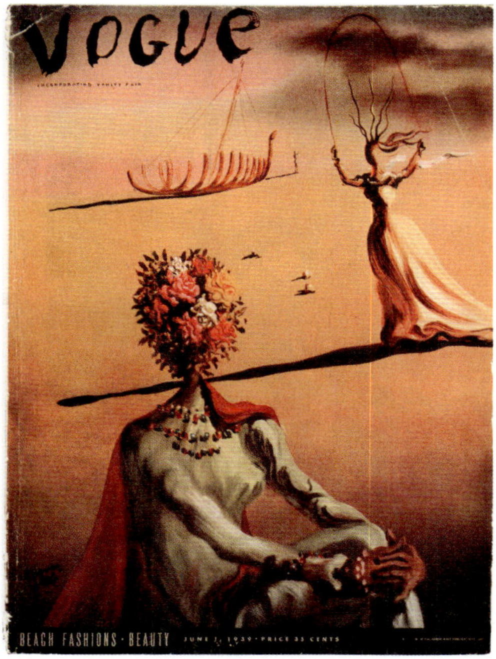


*Vogue*, 01/06/1939

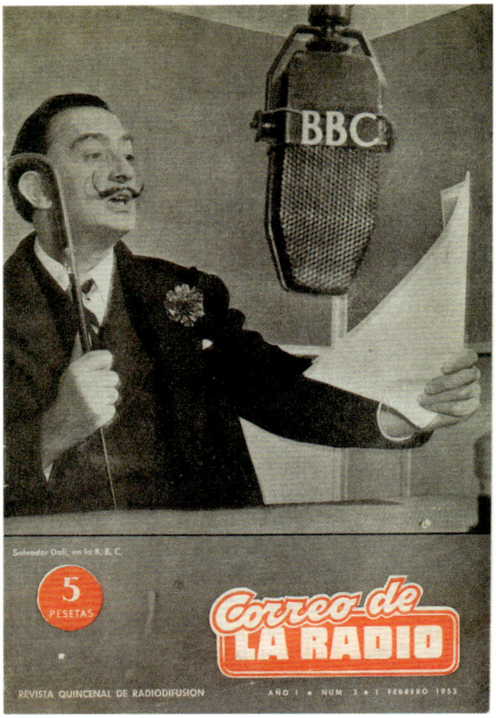


*Correo de la radio*, 01/02/1953

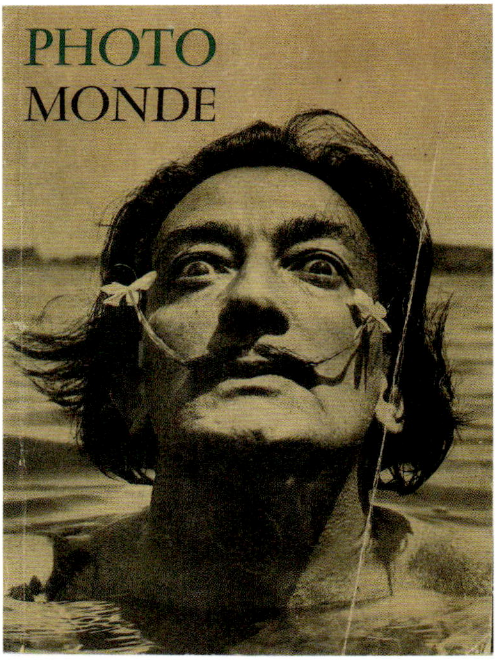


*Photo Monde*, 02/1954

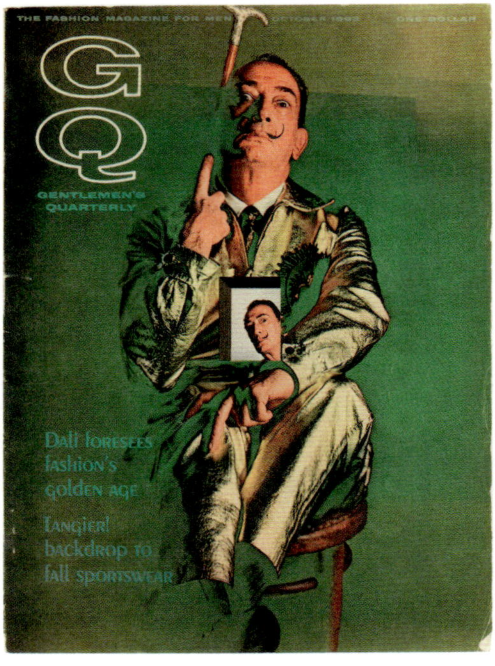


*Gentlemen's Quaterly*, 10/1963

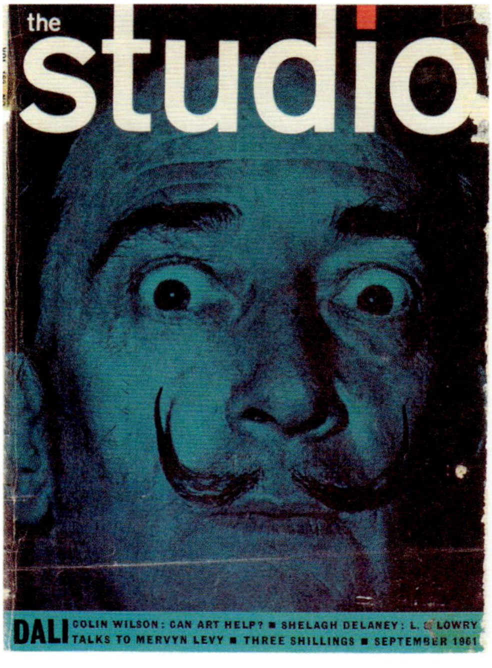


*The Studio*, 09/1961

# Schuldige Augen
# Glenn Brown im Gespräch mit Gerald A. Matt und Katarzyna Uszynska

**Gerald A. Matt und Katarzyna Uszynska** Gustav René Hocke hat in seinem Buch *Die Welt als Labyrinth* die Kunstgeschichte als bipolares System aus Klassischem und Manieristischem begriffen und den Manierismus als wiederkehrende Haltung definiert, die im Surrealismus eine Art Reinkarnation erlebt, ein Gedanke, den Umberto Eco neu akzentuierte, indem er den Manierismus in Zusammenhang mit der Postmoderne gebracht hat. Er war der Meinung, dass die „Postmoderne keine zeitlich begrenzte Strömung ist, sondern eine Geisteshaltung oder, genauer gesagt, eine Vorgehensweise, ein Kunstwollen. Man könnte geradezu sagen, dass jede Epoche ihre eigene Postmoderne hat, so wie man gesagt hat, jede Epoche habe ihren eigenen Manierismus (und vielleicht, ich frage es mich, ist Postmoderne der moderne Name für Manierismus als metahistorische Kategorie)."

Umberto Eco, Nachschrift zu *Der Name der Rose*. München, Wien 1984, S. 77.

Fühlst du dich jener Geisteshaltung, jenem Kunstwollen, das Eco hier beschreibt, zugehörig?

**Glenn Brown** Für mich sind sowohl Klassizismus als auch Modernismus politisch motivierte Puristenideologien. Sie hängen von einem religiösen Verständnis von Recht und Unrecht, einem Ideal, ab. Ich wurde von jenen gelehrt, die als alte Schule modernistischer Künstler bezeichnet werden könnten. Ihre Klassen waren wie Predigten, wo man über die Doktrin der abstrakten Kunst informiert und dazu

# Guilty Eyes
# Glenn Brown in Conversation with Gerald A. Matt and Katarzyna Uszynska

**Gerald A. Matt and Katarzyna Uszynska** In his book *Die Welt als Labyrinth* [*The World as a Labyrinth*], Gustav René Hocke understands art history as a bipolar system of classical and Mannerist elements, and defines Mannerism as a recurrent attitude, reappearing in Surrealism – an idea which Umberto Eco accentuated by relating it to Postmodernism: for him, "Postmodernism is not a trend to be chronologically defined, but, rather, an ideal category – or, better still, a *Kunstwollen*, a way of operating. We could say that every period has its own Postmodernism, just as every period would have its own Mannerism (and, in fact, I wonder if Postmodernism is not the modern name for Mannerism as metahistorical category)."

Umberto Eco, Postscript to *The Name of the Rose*, Orlando, Florida, 1984, 66.

Do you feel close to the attitude described by Eco, to this kind of *Kunstwollen*?

**Glenn Brown** For me, both Classicism and Modernism are politically motivated purist ideologies. They rely on a religious sense of right and wrong, an ideal. I was taught by some, what could be termed, old school Modernist artists. Their classes were a little like a sermon in that you were informed of the doctrines of abstract art, and asked to reach deep inside yourself and push your work still further to an abstract nirvana. My eventual reaction was to find this comic, but only after being affected by it. I can't say that I think Postmodernism is an ideal position for me, in so much as war is not an ideal state. Postmodernism and Mannerism are reactions to something, a tearing away from angehalten wurde, in das tiefste innere Selbst vorzudringen, um die Arbeit zu einem immer noch abstrakteren Nirwana hinzutreiben. Meine Reaktion darauf war schließlich, es komisch zu finden, aber erst nachdem ich sehr davon geprägt wurde. Ich kann nicht sagen, dass Postmodernismus eine ideale Position für mich ist, so wie Krieg kein idealer Zustand ist. Postmodernismus und Manierismus sind Reaktionen auf etwas, ein sich Losreißen von der Meisterdoktrin, sie sind ein konstanter traumatischer Zustand, ein virtuelles Schlachtfeld. Ich will dieses Trauma nicht repräsentieren, dieses beständige unbehagliche Fragezeichen und den Mangel an Vertrauen. Aber ich tue es dennoch, weil ich keine Alternative weiß, ich habe nicht „die" Antwort. Ich neige aber dazu, eine Antwort irgendeiner Art zu wollen. Wenn Manierismus eine Verzerrung der klassischen Wahrheit darstellt, dann ist es auch ein vom Ideal abweichender Bruch.

Katarzyna Uszynska Die Kunst des Manierismus enthüllt die der äußeren Wirklichkeit immanente Täuschung. Ein wesentliches Anliegen der Manieristen war es, die Dinge in ihrer Widersprüchlichkeit und Komplexität zu erfassen, den Dingen damit auf den Grund zu gehen und die Doppelbödigkeit der Wahrheit aufzuzeigen. Desillusionierung durch Illusion gewissermaßen. Entspricht dies auch deiner Einstellung?

Glenn Brown Ich habe Kunst nie als Darstellung der Wirklichkeit empfunden. Es geht immer darum, ein inneres Verständnis der Wirklichkeit zu erzielen. Ich benütze Bilder als Sprache, die mir in ihrer Anwendung und Formulierung hilft, meine Weltsicht zu erläutern. Ich musste



the master doctrine, they are a constant traumatic state of being, a virtual battlefield. I don't want to represent this trauma, this continual uneasy question mark and lack of faith, but I do because I don't know the alternative, I don't have 'the' answer, but I am inclined to want an answer of some sort. If Mannerism represents a distortion of the classical truth then it is also a fault line away from the ideal.

Katarzyna Uszynska The art of Mannerism unmasks the deception that is inherent in external reality. It was important to the Mannerists to grasp things in their inconsistency and complexity, to explore the fundamental qualities of things, and thus to reveal the ambiguity of truth – in a sense, to use illusion as a means of bringing about disillusionment. Does that approach seem close to your own?

Glenn Brown Art, to me, has never felt like a depiction of reality. It is always about developing any number of understandings of reality. I view all paintings as a language to be used and shaped to help comment on what I feel about the world. I am learning how to construct all these artificial devices together to form a coherent and interesting image. We each have our individual view of the world, so what becomes interesting is when an artist manages to communicate their own perspective, in a manner that seems both real, familiar and articulate, yet alien at the same time.

Katarzyna Uszynska The Mannerists perplexed their viewers with inversion and trompe-l'œil effects, with unusual metaphors and bizarre humor. Inversion, breaking the rules malen lernen und lerne es noch immer. Ich lerne, wie ich all diese artifiziellen Kunstgriffe miteinander verbinde, damit ein kohärentes und bemerkenswertes Bild entsteht. Wir haben alle unser individuelles Weltbild. Deshalb wird es interessant, wenn es einem Künstler gelingt, seinen eigenen Standpunkt in einer Weise zu vermitteln, die zugleich vertraut und fremdartig erscheint.

Katarzyna Uszynska Mit Umkehrung und Trompe-l'œil-Effekten, mit ungewohnten Metaphern und skurrilem Humor verwirrten die Manieristen die Betrachter ihrer Werke. Auch Arcimboldos Bilder erstaunen, machen perplex, überraschen und unterhalten. Die Inversion, das „Sich-gegen-die-Regeln-Wenden" oder einfach das „Auf-den-Kopf-Stellen" sind auch die Mittel, die du in deiner Arbeit gerne anwendest. Macht es dir Spaß, den Betrachter zu verwirren?

Glenn Brown Wie das Sprichwort sagt: „Reisen erweitert den Horizont". Das bedeutet: Eine nicht vertraute Umgebung bringt dich dazu, auf unterschiedliche und neue Arten zu denken. Auf Arten, die einer anderen Kultur ähnlicher sind als der eigenen. Ich bin oft aufgewühlt, wenn ich meine Bilder betrachte. Ich bin mir nicht sicher, worauf ich mein Augenmerk lenken soll. Soll ich mich auf die glatte Beschaffenheit der Oberfläche konzentrieren, die die Farbe hinterlässt? Oder soll ich dem Weg der Komposition folgen, der das Auge über die Oberfläche führt, von Farbe zu Farbe, von der Form zur Linie und wieder zur Form? Wenn ich mit kunstvollen Pinselstrichen arbeite, die sich illusionistisch um den dargestellten Gegenstand schlängeln, dann erscheinen sie

and simply turning things upside down are techniques that you like to use in your work. Do you like to perplex the viewer?

Glenn Brown As the saying goes: travel broadens the mind. That is to say that having one's feet off familiar ground makes one think in different or alternative ways, ways that are more similar to another culture than one's own. I often feel troubled looking at my paintings; I am not sure what I should be looking at. Do I concentrate on the smooth surface finish that the paint makes on its surface or the flat compositional way that one's eye moves over the surface from color to color, from shape to line to shape? Do I develop the artificial brush marks as they curl illusionistically around the perceived object, so these fake brush marks appear real and luscious? Or do I work up the paintings main object so that it has mastery of the illusion of space around it and becomes almost real? I try to worry over all these things at once, and hope that the viewer will somehow come along with me and be happy to worry about these conflicts too. I find it hard to think of other people enjoying the results if I am not perplexed by what I have made.

Gerald A. Matt Your sources of inspiration include pictures by various painters, however, ranging from the old masters like Rembrandt, El Greco and Jean-Honoré Fragonard, and the Symbolists William Blake and Henry Fuseli to Surrealists such as Salvador Dalí. What do you find so fascinating about the different epochs and styles? How do you choose your models, what does the selection process look like?

lebensnah zu sein und sprechen die Sinne an. Oder ich entwickle das zentrale Motiv des Bildes aus dem umgebenden Raum heraus, sodass es diesen dominiert und zu seinem Thema wird. So versuche ich, mir über all diese Dinge gleichzeitig klar zu werden, und hoffe, dass der Betrachter mich irgendwie begleitet und sich über diese Gegensätze auch gerne den Kopf zerbricht. Wenn das, was ich gemacht habe, mich nicht verblüfft, kann ich mir nur schwer vorstellen, dass andere Leute an den Ergebnissen Gefallen finden.

Gerald A. Matt Deine Inspirationsquellen sind Bilder aus einer breiten Palette von Malern, beginnend mit den großen Meistern wie Rembrandt, El Greco, Jean-Honoré Fragonard über die Symbolisten wie William Blake oder Johann Heinrich Füssli, die Surrealisten wie Salvador Dalí bis hin zu den fantastischen Malereien von John Martin. Was reizt dich so an den unterschiedlichen Epochen und Stilrichtungen? Wie wählst du deine Vorlagen aus, wie findet der Selektionsprozess statt?

Glenn Brown Ich ordne meine Bibliothek von Kunstabbildungen nicht chronologisch. Bücher und Bilder sind absichtlich tragbare Objekte. Sogar Gemälde für spezifische Umgebungen können bewegt werden und werden es auch. Bücher haben keine Achtung vor Zeit und Ort, sodass zum Beispiel die Abbildung eines Albert Oehlen Bildes neben einem El Greco Bild auftauchen kann und ihre Ähnlichkeiten offensichtlich werden. Mein Verständnis der Kunstgeschichte ist natürlich historisch geordnet, aber ich versuche mein Bestes, jeden Sinn für Fortschritt zu brechen, durch die Art, wie die



Glenn Brown I do not arrange my library of art images chronologically. Books and paintings are purposefully portable objects. Even paintings made for particular settings can and do get moved. Books have no respect for time and place, so, for instance, an image of an Albert Oehlen painting can turn up next to an El Greco painting and their similarities can become apparent. My understanding of art history is of course historically ordered, but I try my best to break any sense of progression by the way the books lay open on my table and floor, and the way the files of images are arranged on my computer. I encourage the images to converse as I dream of how they will change. Images sit around for months or years until they have fermented and metamorphosised into something belonging to me; only then will I start to paint them.

Gerald A. Matt Though your pictures frequently have a striking resemblance to their models at first sight, they present themselves differently upon closer inspection. The abstract Auerbach portraits' impasto turns out to be an illusion, a trompe l'oeil; Pierre-Auguste Renoir's *Bouquet of Roses* sees different color variants, and Jean Honoré Fragonard's *Fair-Haired Child* is turned upside down – the silhouette of *Song to the Sirene* in our Dalí exhibition becomes mammoth. You seem to make these painters' originality your subject and question it at the same time.

Glenn Brown The originality of Auerbach, Renoir and Fragonard is their subject. The woman, the flowers and the child are all fleeting subjects – once the paintings were finished, the subjects

Bücher offen auf meinem Tisch und Boden liegen und die Art, wie ich Bildordner auf meinem Computer anlege. Ich ermutige die Abbildungen dazu, sich zu unterhalten; ich träume davon, wie sie sich verändern werden. Abbildungen sitzen für Monate oder Jahre herum, bis sie gegoren sind und sich zu etwas metamorphisiert haben, das mir gehört; erst dann beginne ich, sie zu malen.

**Gerald A. Matt** So täuschend die Bilder von dir auf den ersten Blick ihren Vorlagen ähneln, so unterschiedlich sind sie jedoch bei näherer Betrachtung. Der pastose Pinselstrich der abstrakten Porträts nach Auerbach entpuppt sich nur als eine Illusion, ein Trompe-l'œil-Trick; Pierre-August Renoirs *Bouquet of Roses* entsteht in verschiedenen Farbvariationen, Jean Honoré Fragonards *Blondes Kind* stellst du auf den Kopf, die Silhouette von *Song to the Siren* in unserer Dalí-Ausstellung wächst ins Riesenhafte. Du scheinst einerseits die Originalität dieser Maler zu thematisieren und gleichzeitig zu hinterfragen.

**Glenn Brown** Die Originalität von Auerbach, Renoir und Fragonard ist ihr Gegenstand. Die Frau, die Blumen und das Kind sind flüchtige Motive, sobald die Bilder fertig waren, änderten sie sich und verschwanden. Es ist dieser Vorgang, den lebendigen Moment darzustellen, der im Grunde genommen originell ist und nicht wiederholt oder kopiert werden kann. Das ist das Thema meiner Bilder: meine Unfähigkeit, die Zeit anzuhalten und daher den Tod zu vermeiden. Ihre Motive waren lebendige Entitäten. Fragonards *Blondes Kind* (sein Sohn) ist jetzt wahrscheinlich nicht mehr als ein wenig

changed and were gone. It is that act of representing the living moment that is essentially original and cannot be repeated or copied. That is the subject of my paintings, my inability to stop time and therefore avoid death. Their subjects were living entities. Fragonard's *Fair-Haired Child* (his son) is now probably little more than soil. I find that fascinating and beautiful and I am trying to get my head around it. My paintings do, in some sense, attempt to be avatars. They bring a failed attempt closer in appearance to the original moment of conception.

**Gerald A. Matt** Your conceptual approach and eclectic manner suggest that your work is close to postmodern appropriation art. Despite all those models you draw on, your nearly ritual-like brushwork reveals how you solemnize the act of painting, which makes you achieve an unmistakable originality. Is this a deliberate trick or another cliché you employ in order to reject it? What is the purpose of this contradictory procedure?

**Glenn Brown** I remember quite some time ago trying to make paintings like Georg Baselitz. It did not take me long to realize that the painterly gesture is a fraudulent act. Painting is acting, or rather it is the trace left after an act of acting the part of a painter. Baselitz acts like Baselitz because the audience likes him to. His big beefy paintings are what are left behind after he has acted his part. I don't claim that he is not being in some part himself 'original' when painting, just that I think he could act differently if he wanted, if the audience would like it better, perhaps. Being self-aware, he knew

Erde. Ich finde das faszinierend und schön, und ich versuche es zu begreifen. Meine Bilder wollen in gewisser Hinsicht Avatare sein. Sie sind ein fehlgeschlagenes Experiment, der Erscheinung im Moment ihrer Entstehung nahe zu sein.

**Gerald A. Matt** Der konzeptuelle Gedanke und die eklektische Manier in deinen Arbeiten könnte man in die Nähe einer postmodernen Appropriation Art rücken. Bei all diesen vielen Vorlagen und Vorbildern lässt sich in deiner ritualhaften Pinselführung jedoch ein Zelebrieren des Malaktes beobachten, die eine eigene unverwechselbare, unverkennbare Originalität erreicht. Ein Charakteristikum, das gerade einem Vertreter der Moderne eigen ist. Sind das überlegte Kunstgriffe, ist es ein weiteres Klischee, das du bewusst aufgreifst, um es wieder zu verwerfen? Zu welchem Zweck verwendest du diese Widersprüche?

**Glenn Brown** Ich erinnere mich daran, dass ich vor ziemlich langer Zeit einmal versucht habe, Bilder wie Georg Baselitz zu machen. Ich brauchte nicht lang, um zu bemerken, dass die künstlerische Geste ein betrügerischer Akt ist. Malen ist Schauspielern, oder, besser, die hinterlassene Spur des Malers nach der Darbietung. Baselitz tritt wie Baselitz auf, weil es das Publikum mag. Seine großen fleischigen Bilder sind das, was er zurückgelassen hat, nachdem er seinen Part gespielt hat. Ich behaupte nicht, dass er nicht in irgendeiner Weise er selbst ist und „originell", wenn er malt. Ich denke nur, dass er sich anders verhalten könnte, wenn er wollte, wenn es das Publikum vielleicht gerne hätte. Es war ihm bewusst, dass



that he could alter his performance. Just as a regional accent is adopted so one's peers can better understand the speaker, it could be otherwise: one could adopt other accents or figures of speech, perhaps for comic affect. This petit fraud fascinated me because I could never tell whether or not I was being myself when I painted. I tried being myself, but it always looked like someone else. Originality is so hard to find. I thought the best option was to study another artist's acted gestures, without trying to act their part so that I might discover which role I best suited. I am still looking for the perfect role, but I don't expect to find it soon.

**Gerald A. Matt and Katarzyna Uszynska** The hyperreal world of your landscapes, in which familiar proportions are abandoned and larger-than-life details abound – an approach combining atomization and monumentalization – makes us also think of the Surrealists, of Salvador Dalí and his dream visions, for example. You confront us with Dalí's *Autumnal Cannibalism* from 1936 in a distorting mirror. Is this a dream within a dream? Why are you so fascinated with Dalí's Surrealism?

**Glenn Brown** I was interested in Dalí's work for film, especially Alfred Hitchcock's *Spellbound*. The film is in Black and White, and Dalí also works to the proportions of a cinema screen. When I realized that the other great painting of the Spanish civil war, Picasso's *Guernica*, had the same proportions and scale as a Cinemascope screen, I wanted to join the two great paintings together. *Oscillate Wildly* tries to be my dream of Picasso and Dalí together in a film clip. I read that children, like myself, brought up er die Möglichkeit hätte, seine Performance zu ändern. Genauso wie ein regionaler Akzent angenommen wird, damit die Kollegen den Sprecher besser verstehen, könnte es auch anders sein; man könnte andere Akzente oder Redewendungen ob der komischen Wirkung übernehmen. Dieser geringfügige Betrug faszinierte mich, weil ich nie sagen konnte, ob ich ich selbst war, wenn ich malte. Ich versuchte, ich selbst zu sein, aber es sah immer wie jemand anderes aus. Originalität ist so schwer zu finden. Ich dachte, es sei die beste Option, die gespielten Gesten eines anderen Künstlers zu studieren, ohne zu versuchen, ihn darzustellen, so dass ich entdecken könnte, welche Rolle am besten zu mir passt. Ich suche noch immer nach der perfekten Rolle, aber erwarte nicht, sie bald zu finden.

> **Gerald A. Matt und Katarzyna Uszynska** Die hyperreale Welt deiner Landschaften, eine Welt zwischen Traum und Wirklichkeit, in der die Größenverhältnisse verschoben werden und Details überdimensionale Maße erhalten – eine Atomisierung des Details bei gleichzeitiger Monumentalisierung des Dargestellten – lässt auch an die surreale Welt, an die Traumbilder von Salvador Dalí denken. Die Arbeit Dalís *Autumnal Cannibalism* aus dem Jahr 1936 zeigst du nochmals in einem „verzerrten Spiegel". Ein Traum in einem Traum? Was fasziniert dich so sehr an dem Surrealismus Dalís?

**Glenn Brown** Ich war an Dalís Mitarbeit an Filmen interessiert, besonders Alfred Hitchcocks *Spellbound*. Der Film ist Schwarz-Weiß und Dalí arbeitete nach den Proportionen einer

watching black and white television have a tendency to have black and white dreams. In other words, if I am to analyze my unconscious, I must consider my dreams to be television/cinema productions that are directed, produced and lit by others.

> **Gerald A. Matt** You value perfection and technique very highly in your painting. In addition to that, you are also interested in the history of painting. Do you see certain affinities between yourself and Dalí?

**Glenn Brown** Returning to my studio with a friend (Nick Fudge) after seeing *Surrealism: Desire Unbound* at Tate Modern in 2001 was a depressing moment. It was clear to both of us that my paintings looked woolly, blurry and plain. Dalí's paintings had opened our eyes and sharpened our senses. I said, "but what about Richter, photography and the materiality of paint?" Nick scoffed at Richter, who was only a usable model if one did not want to paint, which I plainly did. The problem was, we had both seen the Dalís: the beautiful, intense genius of Dalí that makes photography redundant. It was the sheer clarity of his paintings and drawings that was undeniable. No photograph can be as sharply and aggressively in focus. You don't just see, you feel and smell and recollect his paintings like you have put glasses on for the first time after years of blurry, watery sight. They are sharp, accurate renditions of things you know but have never seen before, as they only existed in your, and Dalí's, mind. Paint and ink become precision materials for a forensic surgical examination of the human condition. From that day on, my paintings changed. They became sharper, harder, more cruel, more hyper-super-surreal,

Kinoleinwand. Als ich realisierte, dass Picassos *Guernica*, das großartige Gemälde des Spanischen Bürgerkriegs, dieselben Proportionen und denselben Maßstab hat wie eine Cinemascopeleinwand, wollte ich die beiden großen Bilder miteinander verbinden. *Oscillate Wildly* ist der Versuch, meinen Traum von Picasso und Dalí in einem Filmclip zu vereinen. Ich habe gelesen, dass Kinder, die, wie ich selbst, mit schwarz-weißem Fernsehen aufgewachsen sind, die Tendenz haben, in Schwarz und Weiß zu träumen. Mit anderen Worten, wenn ich mein Unbewusstes analysieren soll, muss ich annehmen, dass meine Träume von anderen inszenierte, produzierte und beleuchtete Fernseh- bzw. Kinoproduktionen sind.

**Gerald A. Matt** Du legst großen Wert auf Perfektion und Technik in deiner Malerei. Darüber hinaus interessierst du dich auch für die Geschichte der Malerei. Siehst du auch hier gewisse Affinitäten zwischen dir und Dalí?



**Glenn Brown** Es war ein deprimierender Augenblick, als ich mit einem Freund (Nick Fudge) in mein Studio zurückkam, nachdem wir uns die Ausstellung *Surrealism: Desire Unbound* in der Tate Modern 2001 angeschaut hatten. Uns war klar, dass meine Bilder verschwommen, unklar und platt aussahen. Dalís Gemälde hatten uns die Augen geöffnet und unsere Sinne geschärft. Ich sagte: „Aber was ist mit Richter, der Fotografie und der Materialität von Farbe?" Nick spottete über Richter, der nur ein brauchbares Modell war, wenn man nicht malen wollte, was ich einfach tat. Das Problem war, wir beide hatten Dalí gesehen: den schönen, intensiven Genius von Dalí, der die Fotografie

less soft and blurry and with less Richter blurry bullshit – altogether more Dalí. In other words, they engage the eye in a conversation with paint that relies on sophistication, not faux stupidity.

**Gerald A. Matt** Many titles of your works such as *Dalí-Christ* (1992, after *Dalí's Soft Construction with Boiled Beans: Premonition of Civil War* from 1936) point towards your models. Which impressions and tensions might result from juxtaposing the two works?

**Glenn Brown** I painted *Dalí-Christ* 18 years ago while I was a student, so its relevance to me now is somewhat limited. Though I think it was a very important painting for me to do. I did however have the chance, whilst exhibiting at the Tate in Liverpool, to see *Oscillate Wildly* in close proximity to *Autumnal Cannibalism*, its source. I was shocked and dismayed to discover that after years of hailing Dalí as the 'second coming,' my painting looked better in some ways than the original, which was rather small and dull brown. I found this discovery very melancholic and sad.

**Gerald A. Matt** There are other works – one might even say a series of works – that relate directly to works by Dalí. Would you comment on that?

**Glenn Brown** Dalí was such a great borrower of styles. To think of his work without Yves Tanguy, De Chirico, and Max Ernst who all preceded him is unthinkable. I borrow tricks from paintings such as *International Velvet* (2004), *Seventeen Seconds* (2005), *Debaser* (2009) and *Christ Returns to the Womb* (2009), but most überflüssig macht. Es war die reine Klarheit seiner Bilder und Zeichnungen, die unbestreitbar waren. Keine Fotografie kann so scharf und aggressiv im Fokus sein. Man sieht, fühlt, riecht und erinnert sich einfach an seine Bilder, als hätte man nach Jahren verschwommener, wässeriger Sicht zum ersten Mal eine Brille aufgesetzt. Sie zeigen die scharfe und präzise Wiedergabe von Dingen, die man kennt, jedoch nie zuvor gesehen hat, weil sie nur in Dalís und der eigenen Vorstellung existieren. Farbe und Tinte werden zu Genauigkeitsmaterialien für eine forensische chirurgische Untersuchung des Menschseins. Seit diesem Tag haben sich meine Bilder verändert. Sie wurden schärfer, härter, grausamer, hyper-super-surreal, weniger weich und verschwommen mit weniger verschwommenem Richter-Scheiß, insgesamt mehr Dalí. Mit anderen Worten, sie verwickeln das Auge in ein Gespräch mit der Farbe, das von hoher Kultiviertheit ist, nicht von falscher Dummheit.

Gerald A. Matt Der Titel *Dalí-Christ (after „Soft-Construction with Boiled Beans: Premonition of Civil War" 1936 by Salvador Dalí)*, 1992, wie auch viele andere Titel deiner Arbeiten, verweist auf die von dir verwendete Vorlage. Welche Eindrücke, welche Spannungen könnten sich aus einer Gegenüberstellung der beiden Werke ergeben?

Glenn Brown Ich habe *Dalí-Christ* vor 18 Jahren als Student gemalt, daher ist die Bedeutung dieses Bildes für mich begrenzt. Obwohl ich denke, dass es sehr wichtig für mich war, dieses Bild zu malen. Ich hatte allerdings einmal das Glück, meine Arbeit *Oscillate Wildly* bei einer

especially from Dalí. Psychoanalysis developed a language for us to dream in and thus to produce paintings in – in the style of the Surreal.

Gerald A. Matt One of your works shows flowers in the place of a head. Is this a head that turned into flowers or are we looking at flowers that will turn into a head? By the way, this is a motif we can find in Dalí – included in the Vienna exhibition.

Glenn Brown The flowers will not turn into a head nor will the head turn into flowers. The flowers do not replace a head, nor the shoulders replace a vase. Yet we are looking at a portrait. Like Dalí's *Flores Surrealistas* (1938), my works *Architecture and Morality* (2004) and *Debaser* (2009) are portraits of a figure with flowers as a head. That is how they are, and will stay. It is not a trick of light transformation, though it is monstrous. Dalí painted a woman in this happy condition, while my figures are more androgynous. They are not thinking, or looking like flowers – they are thinking and acting and feeling like flowers think, feel and act, because that is all they can do. It is perhaps a sad, stupid, idiotic state or it may be a euphoric ecstatic state of heightened clarity. It depends on how you look at it. Surrealism makes the subconscious real and tactile, not transient as smoke, where even metamorphosis becomes a physical reality. To believe otherwise would diminish its power.

Gerald A. Matt The mutated female body in your work *Misogyny* (2006) reminds us of Surrealist depictions of women as limbless, prostheses-like beings. These manipulated and disfigured bodies have been interpreted

Ausstellung in der Tate Liverpool in der Nähe von Dalís *Autumnal Cannibalism* zu sehen, dem Ausgangspunkt. Ich war geschockt und bestürzt, als ich feststellte – nachdem ich Dalí jahrelang als „zweiten Messias" begrüßt hatte –, dass mein eigenes Gemälde in mancher Hinsicht besser aussah als das Original, das eher klein und matt braun wirkte. Diese Entdeckung stimmte mich sehr melancholisch und traurig.

**Gerald A. Matt** Es gibt mehrere Werke, man könnte fast sagen eine Serie, die sich direkt auf Arbeiten von Dalí beziehen. Kannst du etwas darüber sagen?

**Glenn Brown** Dalí war solch ein großer Entlehner von Stilen. Seine Arbeiten sind undenkbar ohne den Einfluss seiner Vorgänger Yves Tanguy, de Chirico und Max Ernst. In Bildern wie *International Velvet* (2004), *Seventeen Seconds* (2005), *Debaser* (2009) und *Christ Returns to the Womb* (2009) leihe ich mir Kunstgriffe von allen vorher genannten, aber im Besonderen von Dalí. Die Psychoanalyse hat eine Sprache entwickelt, in der wir träumen und auf diese Art Bilder im Stil des Surrealen produzieren können.

**Gerald A. Matt** Eine deiner Arbeiten zeigt statt eines Kopfes Blumen. Ist es ein Kopf, der zu Blumen wurde, oder sehen wir Blumen, aus denen ein Kopf werden wird? Im Übrigen ein Motiv, das wir bei Dalí finden und auch in einem Bild in der Wiener Ausstellung.

**Glenn Brown** Die Blumen verwandeln sich nicht in einen Kopf, noch verwandelt sich der Kopf in Blumen. Die Blumen ersetzen keinen Kopf,



as projection surfaces for a Surrealist artist's fears and desires. Are fear, desire, or emotions in general reflected in your work at all?

**Glenn Brown** I have been accused of making expressionless paintings without real emotion. There is a tendency to consider Expressionism as the only carrier of true emotion; I would refute this. If my paintings are cold and lifeless, then I feel this absolutely, with strong emotion. I can't help throwing in a little black humour, which means I paint emotions that perhaps I don't feel but that I can imagine feeling. Or perhaps I do feel but don't want to. I see the figure in *Misogyny* as a god, a colossal icon of power, not a helpless limbless thing. Both women and men are treated to all sorts of humiliation in my paintings, and often the figure is androgynous, which perhaps is a humiliation too.

**Gerald A. Matt** The viewer standing in front of one of your pictures has a riddle to solve. You emphasized in various interviews that the solution depends on the beholder's knowledge and conscience: people have to fall back on their understanding of the cultural milieu, on what is familiar to them and on what they have learned. To what extent do you address the viewer's unconscious?

**Glenn Brown** The viewer's unconscious memory is as learned as their conscious memory. To what extent the viewer has a knowledge of art history is perhaps a salient point, but even then I have seen hundreds of thousands of paintings in my life, not many of which I can consciously recall, but most of which have ended up in the soup of knowledge that I call my mind. For a noch ersetzen die Schultern eine Vase. Doch wir sehen ein Porträt. *Flores Surrealistas* (1938), meine Arbeiten *Architecture and Morality* (2004) und *Debaser* (2009) sind Porträts von einer Figur mit Blumen als Kopf. So sind sie und so bleiben sie. Es ist nicht der Kunstgriff einer seichten Transformation, obwohl es monströs ist. Dalí malte eine Frau in diesem glücklichen Zustand, während meine Figuren androgyner sind. Sie denken nicht an Blumen oder sehen so aus, sie denken, fühlen, agieren, wie Blumen denken, fühlen und agieren, weil das alles ist, was sie tun können. Es ist vielleicht ein trauriger, dummer, idiotischer oder vielleicht ein euphorischer, ekstatischer Zustand erhöhter Klarheit. Es kommt darauf an, wie man es betrachtet. Der Surrealismus macht das Unterbewusste real und fühlbar, keinen vorübergehenden Rauch, sogar Metamorphose wird hier eine physische Realität, anderes zu glauben, würde seine Kraft mindern.

Gerald A. Matt In deiner Arbeit *Misogyny* (2006) könnte der mutierte Frauenkörper mit den surrealistischen Frauendarstellungen als gliederlose, prothesenähnliche Wesen in Zusammenhang gebracht werden. Dieser manipulierte und entstellte weibliche Körper wurde als Projektionsfläche von Ängsten oder lustvollen Wünschen des surrealistischen Künstlers interpretiert. Sind Angst, Lust und Gefühle überhaupt Kategorien in deiner Arbeit?

Glenn Brown Mir wurde vorgeworfen, ausdruckslose Bilder ohne wirkliche Emotion zu machen. Es gibt eine Tendenz, den Expressionismus als den einzigen Träger wahrer Emotion zu betrachten. Ich würde dies anfechten. Wenn meine

viewer not to have experienced painting's rich and exotic history, even if they cannot recall a single work, would be a pity. Then again, perhaps life itself is potentially such a rich visual experience that painting's addition to reality is relatively unimportant. Whichever it is, the viewer must bring his or her imagination to cast its shadow over my work, in order to make sense of the nonsensical creations I try to create.

Gerald A. Matt and Katarzyna Uszynska Your picture *The Tragic Conversion of Salvador Dalí (after John Martin)* from 1998 definitely has an apocalyptic impact. How would you describe the relationship between the two painters and its reflection in your work? Monumental science fiction landscapes and hyperrealistic representations meticulously rendered to the last detail endow your pictures with a filmic atmosphere. Viewers become immersed in them as if they were confronted with a movie on a screen. What do you find so fascinating about the utopian fantasy pictures by painters such as Chris Foss or Adolf Schaller?

Glenn Brown That was my big problem: how can one make science fiction paintings in an age of film? But how can science fiction films survive in an age of video games? The illustrators that I referred to in my paintings have all, it appears, disappeared. Their extraordinary inventiveness seems no longer to be useful in the computer age. So what was the point in my work? Looking at a painting is not the same as looking at an illustration or a film; it is not a fleeting moment. The eye must work a little longer and in a different way. One studies a painting, not slowly neces-

Bilder kalt und leblos sind, dann empfinde ich das absolut mit starker Emotion. Ich kann nicht anders, als etwas schwarzen Humor hinein zu streuen, was bedeutet, dass ich vielleicht Emotionen male, die ich nicht empfinde, mir aber vorstellen kann. Oder vielleicht fühle ich so, will es aber nicht, was auch immer. Ich betrachte die Figur in *Misogyny* als einen Gott, eine kolossale Ikone der Macht, nicht als ein hilfloses Ding ohne Arme und Beine. Sowohl Frauen als auch Männer werden in meinen Bildern allen Arten der Erniedrigung ausgesetzt, und oftmals sind die Figuren androgyn, was vielleicht auch eine Demütigung ist.

**Gerald A. Matt** Wenn ein Betrachter vor einem deiner Bilder steht, hat er ein Rätsel zu lösen – du hast mehrmals in deinen Interviews betont, dass die Lösung vom Wissen und Gewissen des Betrachtenden abhängt, weil der Betrachter auf den persönlichen Wissensbestand seines kulturellen Umfeldes zurückgreifen muss, auf das für ihn Bekannte und Erlernte. Inwieweit sprichst du das Unbewusste des Betrachters an?

**Glenn Brown** Das unbewusste Gedächtnis des Betrachters ist ebenso erlernt wie die bewusste Erinnerung. Bis zu welchem Grad der Betrachter Kenntnisse der Kunstgeschichte hat, ist vielleicht ein springender Punkt, aber selbst dann habe ich in meinem Leben Hunderttausende von Bildern gesehen. Nur an wenige kann ich mich bewusst erinnern, aber die meisten von ihnen sind in der Suppe meines Wissens gelandet, die ich meinen Verstand nenne. Es wäre schade für den Betrachter, die reiche und exotische Geschichte der Bilder nicht zu erfahren, auch wenn er sich an keine einzige Arbeit erin-



sarily, because our eyes and brains can work at such great speed, but long enough to take in the view. The composition is all-important, and unforgiving. The scale is in relation to the human body, unlike film and illustration that have no correct scale. Painting is such a precise technology. Try printing or reproducing a painting mechanically and you realize all precision is lost; its copy is a pathetic, dead thing. The color, glazed or flat, is lost. Razor sharp edges become a blur, and beautiful gradations of colour become monochrome. Painting cannot easily be replaced and can still be an extraordinary spectacle if viewed in the flesh. I always think of Kandinsky's large paintings, or De Koonings best *Women* paintings as science fiction – escapes from the real into gravity-less unreal worlds of high drama.

**Gerald A. Matt** You are known as a painter, and now you are working with photography as well. As a result, photographic works can be seen in the exhibition *Le Surréalisme, c'est moi!* whose unclear contours and blurrings resulting from enlargement evoke a world of images somewhere between abstraction and dream, pictures that are being shown in direct proximity to Dalí's dream set for Hitchcock's *Spellbound* and his painting *The Eye*. Do you feel comfortable in that proximity?

**Glenn Brown** I like the discomfort of the proximity. How can one ignore film and photography. As I have said, I find painting in many ways to be a superior, more direct medium, but photography is undeniably powerful. The recent photographs I have made have been black and white. Indeed, *Oscillate Wildly* 1999 is black and white because of early film, and its shape nert. Andererseits ist das Leben selbst vielleicht potenziell solch eine reiche visuelle Erfahrung, dass zusätzliche Bilder relativ unwichtig sind. Wie dem auch sei, die Fantasie des Betrachters muss einen Schatten über meine Arbeit werfen, um die unsinnigen Schöpfungen zu verstehen, die ich zu kreieren versuche.

**Gerald A. Matt und Katarzyna Uszynska** Das Gemälde *The Tragic Conversion of Salvador Dalí (after John Martin)* von 1998 ist eine apokalyptische Darstellung. In welchem Verhältnis stehen die beiden Maler in deinem Werk zueinander? Die monumentalen Science-Fiction-Landschaften – hyperrealistische Darstellungen voller Akribie und detailhafter Präzision – verleihen deinen Bildern eine filmische Atmosphäre. Man taucht förmlich in diese ein, als befinde man sich vor einer Kinoleinwand. Was fasziniert dich an den utopischen Fantasiebildern eines Chris Foss oder Adolf Schaller?

**Glenn Brown** Das war mein großes Problem: Wie kann man im Filmzeitalter Science-Fiction-Bilder machen? Und wie können Science-Fiction-Filme im Zeitalter der Videospiele erhalten bleiben? Die Illustratoren, auf die ich mich in meinen Bildern beziehe, scheinen alle verschwunden zu sein. Ihr außergewöhnlicher Einfallsreichtum scheint im Computerzeitalter nicht mehr nützlich zu sein. Was also war der Sinn meiner Arbeit? Sich ein Bild anzusehen, ist nicht das Gleiche, wie eine Illustration oder einen Film; es ist kein flüchtiger Moment. Das Auge muss etwas länger funktionieren und auf eine andere Weise. Man studiert ein Bild nicht unbedingt langsam, weil unsere Augen und unser Gehirn mit hoher Geschwindigkeit

is that of 'Cinemascope'. It is Dalí for the 'big screen.' The blurred images *Love II* and *If God Exists then Everything is His Will II*, both 2011, are less influenced by Dalí than depictions of parts of his work. They are the antithesis of his acute painting method, but that is why they aren't paintings. They are woolly and colourless because that is what photographs do best. You must look at them from Dalí's paranoïac-critical method even if they are not made using it. They are Rorschach test images in that you see what you want, there is no right or wrong interpretation, which is very un-Dalí. *Two Personages in Love with a Woman* (2011) is again colourless because it uses photographic methods. We tried printing it as a photograph, but it became too soft. It is an inkjet print. Tiny jets spray ink onto the paper. The ink sits on the surface of the paper, the lines are sharp and the black is hard and dense. The image had to look cruel, not soft, this was important. The print is an amalgamation of Dalí, Picasso and Miro's great works on the Spanish Civil War, with Frans Hals' depiction of Dalí, the caballero overseeing the tragedy.

**Katarzyna Uszynska** Your amorphous figures, which are part of various realities, have been stretched, shifted or enlarged until they have lost their iconographic identity, and thus seem to be timeless and allusionless in their apparently empty environment. Your unidentifiable science fiction conglomerations create a feeling of being in a no-man's-land, and the empty backgrounds of your portraits leave the impression of a faceless, undefined space. Where are the figures and places of your works located? What time period can be assigned to them?

arbeiten können, aber lange genug, um die Ansicht aufzunehmen. Die Komposition ist entscheidend und unversöhnlich. Der Maßstab stellt den Bezug zum menschlichen Körper her, bei Film und Illustration ist dieser nicht korrekt. Malerei ist eine sehr präzise Technologie. Wenn Sie versuchen, ein Bild zu drucken oder mechanisch zu reproduzieren, merken Sie, dass alle Genauigkeit verloren geht; die Kopie ist ein mitleiderregendes totes Ding. Farbe, Glasur oder Ebene gehen verloren. Rasiermesserscharfe Kanten verschwimmen und schöne Farbabstufungen werden monochrom. Malerei kann nicht leicht ersetzt werden und kann im Original betrachtet, immer noch ein außergewöhnliches Spektakel sein. Ich stelle mir Kandinskys großformatige Gemälde oder de Koonings Frauenbilder immer als Science-Fiction vor, als Flucht vor dem Realen in die schwerelose, unwirkliche Welt eines großen Dramas.



Gerald A. Matt Für Dalí ist das Auge von zentraler Bedeutung. In *The Eye* wird es gar zu einer Art Raumschiff. Szenarien von Raumschiffen und außerirdischen Welten spielen auch bei dir eine Rolle, aber auch Augen scheinen sich in deinen Arbeiten förmlich in Bewegung zu befinden.

Glenn Brown Ich beschreibe das Auge gerne, aber manchmal wird seine Antidarstellung notwendig. Meine Augen sind gestoßen, erblindet und krank, sodass der Betrachter schauen kann, ohne selbst angeschaut zu werden. Das ist ein sehr egoistisches, böses und frauenfeindliches Spiel von Picasso und ganz und gar nicht die Großzügigkeit von Dalí, der gerne gesehen wurde, um zu sehen. Er mochte nichts lieber, als seine Liebhaber zu beobachten, ohne selbst geliebt zu werden.

Glenn Brown I love the idea of painting as a form of time travel. To look at a Vermeer is to be taken back in time. Unlike literature, one has the actual object that has traveled through time to look at. We see the hand of the artist in the painted surface all but unchanged by time, whilst the subject is dead and gone, destroyed by time. This is why I liked my science fiction paintings to have a timeworn feeling. I used a palette of colors that was more redolent of the seventeenth and eighteenth centuries than the future. In that sense, they represent time warps. The feeling I wanted to capture whilst painting the Pope upside down had less to do with the seventeenth century and more to do with 1950s pulp sci-fi illustrations. Reading a painting of mine is a very subjective thing, it all depends on what historical baggage the viewers have at their disposal.

Katarzyna Uszynska The practice of changing perspective and an emphasis that is shifted to the fragment is something found in the Mannerist period but also again in modern and contemporary art, as can be seen in Gerhard Richter's work *Nose* from 1963, in which an enlarged facial detail achieves an astonishingly disconcerting value in its own right. In your piece *work in progress*, the apples become giants on a superhuman scale – the "ordinary" still life turns out to be a landscape. The fragment, a detail of the picture, repeatedly serves as a model for your paintings – a body part such as a foot or a fist becomes independent. Why are you interested in the fragmentary, in the disintegration and deconstruction of images?

Für mich sind alle Körperöffnungen ziemlich gleich, ob sie hören, scheißen, essen, pissen oder sehen. Wir kommen hilflos in einem Durcheinander von Körperflüssigkeiten und Feststoffen auf die Welt und verlassen sie auf ziemlich dieselbe Art und Weise. Ich verweise das Auge auf einen niedrigeren Status zurück als Dalí, obwohl es eindeutig von großem Nutzen ist. Ich versuche das Auge der Betrachter so viel wie möglich zu beanspruchen, um es am Bild zu halten. Ich fürchte, wenn sie bemerken würden, dass sie beobachtet werden, während sie durch meine verschiedenen Löcher spähen, wäre alles verloren. Armer scheuer Betrachter. Ich habe Wochen meines Lebens damit verbracht, Fenster zu malen. Die Raumschiffe und schwimmenden Städte, die ich gemalt habe, sind mit Zehntausenden bedeckt. Tausende von winzigen Fenstern, die im Weltraum hängen mit Tausenden von winzigen Augen. Alle schauen, suchen, beobachten, was draußen liegt. Aber sie werden nie gesehen. Meine Raumschiffe haben Augen, schuldige Augen, sehend, aber unbemerkt.

Katarzyna Uszynska Deine amorphen Figuren, die sich aus Teilen verschiedener Realitäten bilden, haben nach dem Dehnen, Verschieben, Vergrößern etc. und auch durch das leer wirkende Umfeld ihre ikonografische Zugehörigkeit verloren und wirken dadurch zeit- und bezugslos. Durch deine unidentifizierbaren Science-Fiction-Konglomerationen fühlt man sich in ein Niemandsland versetzt. Auch die leeren Hintergründe deiner Porträts hinterlassen den Eindruck eines geschichtslosen, undefinierten Raumes. Wo befinden sich die Figuren und die Orte deiner Arbeiten? Welcher Zeit gehören deine Arbeiten an?

Glenn Brown On certain occasions, such as suffering from the delirious effects of a bad case of the flu, I have had a sort of dream. It is very delirious in nature, a sort of spicy semi-conscious form of dreaming. I always have the same thing happen. It is half vision, half feeling, half premonition, and 150% real. I see and feel large spheres with a texture akin to rubberized sandpaper. I always feel this is very important even when well again, though I cannot explain why. I asked other people about similar experiences and concluded that there was something shared and fundamental occurring. One person described a giant ball of mud that constantly moved, the feeling of being run over by giant car tires. One's sense of scale goes awry. As if the whole experience was taking place at the level of atoms, while strangely being on a planetary scale also. I do realize how boring stories of other people's dreams become, but, as I said, I feel this is quite a fundamental thing. So if my apples have an odd sense of scale, an overly developed texture, and an odd, unnatural color, it may have something to do with this.

Katarzyna Uszynska Your heads shift between real and abstract shapes, which have often already lost their features and contours and are transformed into pure color. What is it about these intermediate conditions that so stimulates you?

Glenn Brown That no-man's-land between figuration and abstraction has always been the place I want to reside in. To be between states, in flux, subject to change, animated, is to be in a constantly excited moment. The figures are very often of indeterminate sex. They appear as

**Glenn Brown** Mir gefällt die Idee von der Malerei als einer Art Zeitreise. Einen Vermeer anzusehen, bedeutet, in eine frühere Zeit versetzt zu werden. Im Gegensatz zur Literatur kann man das reale Objekt, das durch die Zeit gereist ist, betrachten. Die Handschrift des Künstlers auf der gemalten Oberfläche wird durch die Zeit praktisch nicht verändert, während das Modell tot und gegangen ist, zerstört durch die Zeit. Aus diesem Grund wollte ich, dass meine Science-Fiction-Bilder den Eindruck des Gealtertseins erwecken. Ich habe eine Farbpalette verwendet, die stärker an das 17. oder 18. Jahrhundert erinnert als an die Zukunft. In diesem Sinne repräsentieren meine Bilder Zeitschleifen. Die Stimmung, die ich einfangen wollte, als ich den Papst auf den Kopf gestellt gemalt habe, hat weniger mit dem 17. Jahrhundert zu tun als vielmehr mit den Illustrationen zur Schundliteratur im Bereich der Science-Fiction der fünfziger Jahre. Eines meiner Bilder zu lesen, ist eine sehr subjektive Sache. Das Resultat hängt ganz davon ab, über welches historische Wissen der Betrachter verfügt.

**Katarzyna Uszynska** Die Praktiken der wechselnden Perspektive oder der Verlagerung des Schwerpunkts auf das Fragment findet man seit der Zeit des Manierismus auch in der modernen und in der zeitgenössischen Kunst wieder, wie zum Beispiel in Gerhard Richters Arbeit *Nase* von 1963, wo das vergrößerte Gesichtsdetail einen befremdenden, erstaunlichen Eigenwert erreicht. In deiner Arbeit, einem work in progress, werden die Äpfel zu Giganten, die eine übermenschliche Größe erreichen. Das gewöhnliche Stillleben entpuppt sich als Landschaft. Das Fragment, ein Bild-



children but have the skin and attitude of someone ancient. The paintings appear to be constructed of large and lavish brush marks while still having no apparent brush marks at all. Some refer to particular paintings as "beautiful and good enough to eat," others may find them repellent and difficult to look at. If one is to present paintings that are a mass of contradictions, I find it takes time to balance these contradictions. The aim is to do this as precisely as one can.

**Katarzyna Uszynska** Your figures often remind me of bodies in the process of decomposition. In your work, you repeatedly make reference to literary sources, such as *The Picture of Dorian Gray* by Oscar Wilde. While Dorian Gray's person remains untouched by his excesses and dissolute life, his face in the painting becomes grotesquely ugly over the years. The confrontation with it leads to catastrophe. Have your figures put catastrophe behind them?

**Glenn Brown** The American artist Ivan Albright painted the picture of Dorian Gray for the 1944 film adaptation of Wilde's book. Like many of the British Pre-Raphaelite painters, he had an over-anxious zeal for detail, very often at the expense of a painting's overall compositional success. Albright's figure is grotesque and ugly, but so is his painting method. The detailed squirms of paint that cover every centimetre of the man and the room around him seem to be a gross misunderstanding of what it is to make a good painting. Such an ugly vision could only have been created by an artist who, through naivety and obsession, seemed not to be overly aware of how difficult it was for anybody other detail, dient immer wieder als Vorlage für deine Malereien. Ein Körperteil, wie ein Fuß oder eine Faust, verselbstständigt sich. Was interessiert dich am Fragmentarischen, an der Zersetzung und Dekonstruktion von Bildern?

Glenn Brown Bei bestimmten Gelegenheiten, zum Beispiel im Fieberwahn als Folgeerscheinung einer starken Grippe, hatte ich eine Art von Traum. Er ist wie ein Delirium, eine witzige, halb bewusste Art des Träumens. Es passiert immer dasselbe. Es ist zur Hälfte Vision, zur Hälfte Gefühl, zur Hälfte Vorahnung und zu 150 Prozent real. Ich sehe und fühle große Kugeln mit einer Oberflächenstruktur, die gummiertem Schmirgelpapier sehr ähnelt. Ich spüre immer, dass das sehr wichtig ist – auch wenn es mir wieder gut geht –, aber ich kann nicht erklären warum. Ich habe andere Leute nach ähnlichen Erfahrungen gefragt und bin zu dem Schluss gekommen, dass da etwas Gleichartiges und Elementares geschieht. Eine Person hat einen riesigen Ball aus Schlamm beschrieben, der sich ständig bewegte, eine andere hatte das Gefühl, von riesigen Autoreifen überrollt zu werden. Das eigene Gefühl für eine Größenordnung verliert sich, so als ob das ganze Erlebnis im atomaren Bereich stattfände, während man sich seltsamerweise auch in der Größenordnung von Planeten bewegt. Mir ist klar, wie langweilig Geschichten über die Träume anderer Leute sind, aber ich glaube – wie bereits gesagt –, dass das eine sehr elementare Angelegenheit ist. Wenn meine Äpfel also einen eigenartigen Maßstab haben und eine übermäßig entwickelte Textur und eine seltsame Farbe, dann hat das möglicherweise damit zu tun.

than himself to look at one of his paintings. Of course, I do not mean to ignore the book, which is probably the closest literary description of what I wish to depict. After all, it is Dorian's mind that is said to be on display in the final hidden painting, and not his outward appearance, and to me that is the sign of a great portrait. Frank Auerbach and Willem de Kooning's "Women" paintings come to mind.

Katarzyna Uszynska As much as you love color and the act of painting itself, your compositions and the whole idea of your representations have been given a lot of thought. How do your concepts develop, and how do you implement them? How does *Roses in a Bowl* by Henri Fantin-Latour become *The Angel of Mons?*

Glenn Brown One of the interesting things about reproductions of paintings in books is that one tends to look at them horizontally rather than vertically. As I often leave books open so I can look at a painting for a while, the correct orientation of the reproduction becomes less important. The image is easily observed from any angle. Such was the case with *The Angel of Mons*. I liked the roses on their side so that the bowl of roses looked more like a wreath. The security of the table on which the roses sat was also discarded in favor of the Velázquez-like infinite ground. It seemed to me that the roses should be painted on a scale that gave them more of an overblown sense of threat. As flowers, along with children and rural landscapes, are thought to be the most accessible subjects for paintings, I thought it was a good idea to make the painting virtually all green. Green paintings are always the most difficult to

**Katarzyna Uszynska** Deine Köpfe changieren zwischen realen und abstrakten Formen, die ihre Züge und Konturen oft bereits verloren haben und in reine Farbe übergehen. Was reizt dich so an diesen Zwischenzuständen?

**Glenn Brown** Dieses Niemandsland zwischen figürlicher Darstellung und Abstraktion war immer genau der Ort, wo ich hin wollte. Ist man in Zwischenstadien, im Wandel begriffen, so bleibt eine Änderung möglich, bleibt man lebendig, dann ist man ständig in einem Zustand des Angeregtseins. Die Figuren sind sehr oft unbestimmten Geschlechts. Sie wirken wie Kinder, haben aber die Haut und die Haltung alter Leute. Die Bilder scheinen aus großen und freizügigen Pinselstrichen konstruiert zu sein, tragen jedoch zugleich überhaupt keine sichtbaren Pinselstriche. Manche sagen von bestimmten Bildern, sie seien „schön und zum Anbeißen", andere finden sie möglicherweise abstoßend und schwierig. Wenn jemand Bilder vorlegt, die sehr widersprüchlich sind, dann braucht es meiner Meinung nach Zeit, diese Widersprüche auszugleichen. Das Ziel ist, sie so präzise zwischen den beiden widersprüchlichen Stadien anzusiedeln, wie man kann.

**Katarzyna Uszynska** Deine Figuren erinnern mich oft an im Verfall befindliche Körper. Immer wieder sprichst du die literarischen Bezüge deiner Arbeit an, wie zum Beispiel *Das Bildnis des Dorian Gray* von Oscar Wilde. Während Dorian Gray als Person von den Folgen seiner Ausschweifungen und seines exzessiven Lebenswandel verschont bleibt, verzerrt sich sein gemaltes Abbild im Laufe der Jahre zur hässlichen Fratze.



sell, so I am told, especially when the green is of a deliberately unpleasant acid hue. When one takes a closer look at the painting, things other than flowers start to emerge. The painting took months to paint because I kept changing it, adding color or leaves only to take them off again. Like with all my paintings, I did not have a clear idea of how it would end when I started. I hopefully have a feeling that I want the painting to capture, but often that goes for a walk too, and only when I feel the painting has a personality all its own, and often one that I feel is a bit of a stranger to me, do I conclude that the painting is finished.

**Gerald A. Matt** For Dalí, the eye is of central importance. In *The Eye* it even becomes a kind of space ship. Scenarios involving space ships and extraterrestrial worlds also play a role in your work, and eyes also seem to be in motion there.

**Glenn Brown** I like to depict the eye, but sometimes its anti-depiction becomes necessary. Eyes are poked, blinded and diseased, so that the viewer is able to gaze without being gazed upon. This is a very selfish, nasty and misogynous game of Picasso's, and not at all like the generosity of Dalí, who liked to be seen to see. He liked nothing better than to watch his lovers without being loved himself.
To me, all orifices are much the same, whether they hear, shit, eat, piss or see. We come into this world helpless, in a mess of bodily fluids and solids, and leave it much the same way.
I relegate the eye to a lower status than Dalí, though it is clearly of great use. I try to engage the viewers' eyes as much as possible to best hold them to the painting. I fear that if they

Die Konfrontation mit dem Bild Grays führt zur Katastrophe. Haben deine Figuren die Katastrophe hinter sich?

Glenn Brown Der amerikanische Künstler Ivan Albright malte das Bild von Dorian Gray für die Verfilmung von Wildes Buch aus dem Jahre 1944. Ivan Albright hatte wie viele der britischen präraffaelitischen Maler eine ausgeprägte, übermäßige Vorliebe für das Detail, die sehr oft auf Kosten des Gelingens der Gesamtkomposition eines Bildes ging. Albrights Bild ist grotesk und hässlich, aber das resultiert aus seiner Malweise. Die detailreichen Windungen der Farbe, die jeden Zentimeter des Mannes und des Raumes um ihn herum bedecken, wirken wie ein grobes Missverständnis dessen, was es bedeutet, ein gutes Bild zu machen. Ein derart hässliches Gesicht hat offensichtlich nur ein Maler erschaffen können, der infolge von Naivität und Besessenheit kaum erkannt hat, wie schwer es jedem anderen außer ihm selbst fallen wird, eines seiner Bilder zu betrachten. Ich habe natürlich nicht vor, das Buch zu ignorieren. Es ist vermutlich die literarische Beschreibung, die dem, was ich darstellen möchte, am nächsten kommt. Schließlich ist es Dorians Psyche, die im endgültigen versteckten Bild gezeigt werden soll, und nicht seine äußere Erscheinung. Für mich ist das das Kennzeichen eines großartigen Porträts. In diesem Zusammenhang fallen mir Frank Auerbach und Willem de Koonings *Women*-Bilder ein.

Katarzyna Uszynska Bei aller Liebe zur Farbe und zum Akt des Malens selbst sind deine Bildkompositionen und die gesamte Idee der Darstellung sehr genau überlegt. Wie entwickeln sich deine Konzepte und wie

noticed they were being watched while peeping at my various holes, all might be lost. Poor timid viewer. I have spent weeks of my life painting windows. The space ships and floating cities I have painted are covered with tens of thousands of them. Thousands of tiny windows hanging in space, each filled with thousands of tiny eyes. All looking, searching, observing what lies outside. But they are never seen. My spaceships have eyes, guilty eyes, seeing but unseen.

Gerald A. Matt Your pictures are characterized by great precision, a remarkable painterly expertise, and an enormous meticulousness. It often takes you quite long to finish a work. Could you tell us something about your working method? Friedrich Nietzsche maintained that "our historical education leads to the death of every culture."

Friedrich Nietzsche, *Kritische Gesamtausgabe*, ed. by Giorgio Colli and Mazzino Montinari, Berlin and New York 1967.

Past, present and future directly collide in your pictures, their chronological and historical connections being confused and blurred. Ultimately, they end in chaos and are not recognizable to the viewer anymore. Are you telling the viewers that they had better get rid of historical modes of reception, and offering them a new way of looking at pictures?

Glenn Brown A culture is made of its history, it reacts in accordance with its past experiences. I see that an historical education, or perhaps more to the point a multi-cultural historical setzt du sie um? Wie werden die Rosen in einer Schüssel von Henri Fantin-Latour zu *The Angel of Mons*?

**Glenn Brown** Ein interessanter Aspekt der Reproduktionen von Gemälden in Büchern besteht darin, dass man sie tendenziell eher horizontal als vertikal ansieht. Da ich Bücher vielfach offen lasse, damit ich ein Bild eine Zeit lang ansehen kann, wird die korrekte Ausrichtung der Abbildung weniger wichtig. Das Bild kann leicht von jedem Blickwinkel aus betrachtet werden. So war es bei *The Angel of Mons*. Ich mochte die Rosen, wenn ich sie von der Seite ansah. Die Schale mit Rosen wirkte dadurch eher wie ein Kranz. Die vom Tisch mit den Rosen vermittelte Statik und Sicherheit wurde dabei ebenso verworfen wie die Funktion des Hintergrundes bei Velázquez, der sich in der Unendlichkeit verliert. Es schien mir, dass die Rosen in einem Maßstab gemalt werden sollten, der ihnen eher eine bedrohliche, schwülstige Wirkung verlieh. Da Blumen zusammen mit Kindern und ländlichen Gefilden als die am leichtesten zugänglichen Themen bei Bildern gelten, habe ich es für eine gute Idee gehalten, das Bild fast zur Gänze in Grün zu halten. Grüne Bilder sind immer sehr schwierig zu verkaufen, wie mir erzählt wird, besonders wenn das Grün mit Absicht einen unangenehmen, scharfen Ton erhält. Wenn jemand das Bild näher betrachtet, tauchen andere Dinge als Blumen auf. Es hat Monate gedauert, das Bild zu malen, weil ich es immer wieder verändert habe. Ich habe Farbe oder Blätter hinzugefügt, nur um sie wieder zu entfernen. Wie bei allen meinen Bildern hatte ich zu Beginn keine klare Idee, wie es enden wird. Ich hoffe, bei meiner Arbeit ein Gefühl zu spüren, das im Bild einge-



education challenges the here and now of culture, and that is the excitement, destruction and rebuilding of it. Defining a culture is rather like describing clouds; it is the continual movement that is its greatest value. Nietzsche was no postmodernist. I have put myself in Plato's cave, only able to view the world from the shadows cast on the wall. This is history and it is all I have, I am only able to make a judgment after the event. But I can say for certain that the shadows will change and that I will never fully understand what they represent. I know that history is written by its victors, and is by definition always wrong, and this is perhaps Nietzsche's point. If culture is defined by its history and history is an impossibly moving target, then change and misunderstanding are its defining creations. I feel like I have talked my self out of the activity of painting, because in the end it lacks animation. Perhaps I want the paint to stay wet forever, and to never actually finish.

This interview is based on two conversations between Katarzyna Uszynska and Glenn Brown in the context of the exhibition in the Kunsthistorisches Museum, April 22 to June 1, 2008 (quoted from: *Glenn Brown*, ed. by Wilfried Seipel, exh. cat., Kunsthistorisches Museum, Vienna 2008), and a conversation between Gerald A. Matt and Katarzyna Uszynska with Glenn Brown, December 2009, extended in May 2011.

fangen werden soll – doch vergeht das oft auch wieder. Nur wenn ich meine, dass das Bild eine eigene Persönlichkeit besitzt – und oft ist es eine, die mir ein wenig fremd vorkommt –, entscheide ich, dass das Bild fertig ist.

**Gerald A. Matt** Du bist als Maler bekannt. Und nun arbeitest du auch mit Fotografie. So sind in der Ausstellung *Le Surréalisme, c'est moi!* Fotoarbeiten zu sehen, deren unscharfe Konturen und durch Vergrößerung entstandene Verwischungen eine Bildwelt zwischen Abstraktion und Traum evozieren, Bilder, die in unmittelbarer Nähe zu Dalís Traumdekor von Hitchcocks *Spellbound* und seinem Gemälde *The Eye* gezeigt werden. Eine Nachbarschaft, in der du dich wohlfühlst?

**Glenn Brown** Ich mag das Unbehagen von Nähe. Wie kann man Film und Fotografie ignorieren? Wie schon gesagt, halte ich Malerei in vielerlei Hinsicht für ein überlegenes, direktes Medium, aber Fotografie ist unbestreitbar mächtig. Die neuen Fotografien, die ich gemacht habe, sind schwarz und weiß. In der Tat ist *Oscillate Wildly* (1999) schwarz-weiß wegen des frühen Films, die Form ist Cinemascope. Es ist Dalí für den „großen Bildschirm". Die verschwommenen Abbildungen *Love II* und *If God Exists then Everything is His Will II*, beide 2011, sind weniger von Dalí beeinflusst als vielmehr Darstellungen von Teilen seines Werks. Sie sind die Antithese seiner akkuraten Malmethode, aber darum sind es keine Gemälde. Sie sind verschwommen und farblos, weil es das ist, was Fotografien am besten können. Man muss sie von Dalís paranoisch-kritischer Methode her denken, selbst wenn sie nicht mithilfe dieser

Methode gemacht wurden. Es sind Rorschachtest-Abbildungen in dem Sinne, dass man darin sehen kann, was man will. Es gibt keine richtige oder falsche Interpretation, was eigentlich Dalí ist. *Two Personages in Love with a Woman* (2011) wiederum ist farblos, weil dafür fotografische Methoden verwendet wurden. Wir haben versucht, es als Fotografie zu drucken, aber es wurde zu weich. Es ist ein Tintenstrahldruck. Winzige Strahlen sprühen Tinte auf Papier. Die Tinte sitzt auf der Oberfläche des Papiers, die Linien sind scharf und das Schwarz ist hart und dicht. Die Abbildung musste grausam, nicht weich aussehen, das war wichtig. Der Print ist ein Amalgam aus Dalís, Picassos und Miros großartigen Arbeiten über den Spanischen Bürgerkrieg. Mit Frans Hals' Darstellungen von Dalí, dem Caballero, der die Tragödie überblickt.



Gerald A. Matt Friedrich Nietzsche sagte: „Unsere historische Bildung geht auf den Tod jeder Kultur."

Friedrich Nietzsche, *Kritische Gesamtausgabe, KGW*, hg. von Giorgio Colli und Mazzino Montinari. Berlin, New York 1967.

Vergangenheit, Gegenwart und Zukunft treffen in deinen Bildern unmittelbar aneinander, wobei ihre letztlich chronologischen und geschichtlichen Zusammenhänge verwirrt und verwischt werden, letztlich im Chaos enden und für den Betrachter nicht mehr erkennbar sind. Möchtest du dem Betrachter sagen, er soll sich von der historischen Bildrezeption befreien und ihm eine neue Weise der Bildbetrachtung anbieten?

**Glenn Brown** Eine Kultur wird von ihrer Geschichte gemacht, sie reagiert ihren vergangenen Erfahrungen entsprechend. Ich sehe, dass eine historische Bildung oder vielleicht eher eine multikulturelle historische Bildung das Hier und Jetzt der Kultur herausfordert, aber das ist die Spannung von Zerstörung und Wiederaufbau. Eine Kultur zu definieren, entspricht eher der Beschreibung von Wolken; die beständige Bewegung ist ihr größter Wert. Nietzsche war kein Postmodernist. Ich habe mich in Platos Höhle begeben, um die Welt als Schatten an der Wand zu betrachten. Das ist Geschichte und es ist alles, was ich habe. Ich kann nur etwas nach einem Ereignis beurteilen. Aber ich kann mit Sicherheit sagen, dass sich die Schatten ändern und dass ich nie vollständig verstehen werde, was sie darstellen. Ich weiß, dass die Geschichte von Siegern geschrieben wird und per definitionem immer falsch ist. Und das ist vielleicht Nietzsches Punkt. Wenn Kultur von ihrer Geschichte definiert wird, aber Geschichte eine sich bewegende Zielscheibe ist, dann sind Veränderung und Missverständnis ihre definitionsgebende Schöpfung. Ich habe das Gefühl, dass ich mir die Aktivität des Malens ausgeredet habe, weil es ihr am Ende an Lebhaftigkeit fehlt. Vielleicht möchte ich, dass die Farbe für immer nass bleibt, und beende ein Bild nie.

Dieses Interview basiert auf zwei Gesprächen zwischen Katarzyna Uszynska und Glenn Brown, die im Rahmen der Ausstellung im Kunsthistorischen Museum vom 22. April bis 1. Juni 2008 stattfanden (zit. aus: *Glenn Brown*, hg. von Wilfried Seipel, Ausst.-Kat., Kunsthistorisches Museum, Wien 2008.), und einem Gespräch zwischen Gerald A. Matt und Katarzyna Uszynska mit Glenn Brown im Dezember 2009, das im Mai 2011 erweitert wurde.

# Stummfilm Aquarium Markus Schinwald im Gespräch mit Lucas Gehrmann

**Lucas Gehrmann** Für die Ausstellung *Le Surréalisme, c'est moi!* entwickelst du gerade eine Installation in einem abgedunkelten Raum, in dem ein Aquarium mit einem dahinter befindlichen Bühnenbild oder jedenfalls eine „Szene" in irgendeiner Form zu sehen sein wird. Soweit ich weiß, referierst du dabei auf den Pavillon, den Salvador Dalí 1939 für die World Fair in New York gemacht hat, von dem noch Fotografien erhalten sind, die in der Ausstellung auch zu sehen sein werden. Innen gab es dort eine Art Aquarium in der Form eines gläsernen Pools, in den als „Meerjungfern" kostümierte Frauen hineinsprangen und in dem auch einige Unterwasser-Puppen schwammen, eine hieß „Zebralady". Außerdem bot sich in diesem Pavillon eine Situation, wo die Besucher passagenweise hindurchgehen mussten, und wenn ich an dein Projekt für den Pavillon der diesjährigen Biennale von Venedig denke, scheint es hier wie dort einige Parallelen zu geben. Bei Dalí und bei dir gibt es den Gedanken, sich durch verschiedene Orte oder Situationen des sozusagen nicht nur Sichtbaren hindurch zu bewegen …

**Markus Schinwald** Ja, vor der Arbeit an meinem Aquarium habe ich mir diese Dalí-Arbeiten angeschaut, wobei mich Dalí ja als Großes und Ganzes nicht so sehr interessiert, also seine abgeschlossenen Werke. Aber ich habe mir Teile herausgenommen oder, wenn man so will, Dalí filetiert und mir dann einzelne Punkte rausgeholt und dabei auch viele Momente, die es bei Dalí gibt, sogar entschärft. Dalí hat in dem New Yorker Pavillon ja sehr spektakulär gearbeitet, was bei meinem Aquarium überhaupt



# Silent movie: Aquarium Markus Schinwald in Conversation with Lucas Gehrmann

**Lucas Gehrmann** You are currently developing an installation in a darkened room for the show *Le Surréalisme c'est moi!* – in which there's to be an aquarium with a stage set, or at least a kind of 'scene' visible behind it. As far as I know, you are referencing the pavilion Salvador Dalí made in 1939 for the World Fair in New York, of which some photographs have survived – some surviving photographs of it will be on display in the exhibition. Inside, there was a kind of aquarium in the shape of a glass pool, into which women dressed up as 'mermaids' dived, and a few underwater dolls also floated around, including one called Zebra-lady. Moreover, the pavilion featured a setting wherein visitors had to walk through a passageway. Now, there again seems to be some parallels to the idea that we are moving through different places or situations of the not-only-visible, as it were …

**Markus Schinwald** Yes, prior to the work on my aquarium I studied those Dalí pieces, although by and large I am not that interested in Dalí in regards to his finished works. What I did do was take parts of them, filleting Dalí so to speak, and then extracted individual points and actually took the sting out of many of the elements to be found in Dalí. Dalí's piece in the pavilion in New York had a very spectacular vein, and that is definitely not the case with the aquarium, meaning that its thrust is in the opposite direction.

**Lucas Gehrmann** Back then, the original plan was for the gallerist, Levy, to host a Surrealism exhibition at the World Fair with several artists, and then the organizers said they wanted to have something with a celebrity nicht der Fall ist, also das läuft eigentlich in die Gegenrichtung.

**Lucas Gehrmann** Damals war ursprünglich vorgesehen, dass der Galerist Levy für die World Fair mit mehreren Künstlern eine Surrealismus-Ausstellung macht, und dann haben die Veranstalter gesagt, sie möchten etwas Prominentes und Spektakuläres haben, das vor allem dem amerikanischen Publikumsgeschmack entsprechen sollte, das heißt, es sollte durchaus auch populär sein. Wie „populär" ist dein Aquarium?

**Markus Schinwald** Das Populäre hat mich schon interessiert, aber nicht, um für das Publikum etwas Populäres zu schaffen, sondern umgekehrt, um etwas zu machen, was das Publikum selber schon tut. Also das Aquarium und der Aquariumsbau sind etwas, das eigentlich überall vorkommt, außer in der Kunst. Es geht mir vor allem darum, das Interesse quasi von den Besuchern zu holen und etwas mit den Versatzstücken Dalís zu bauen.

**Lucas Gehrmann** Also eine Art Alltagsobjekt als Ausgangssituation ...

**Markus Schinwald** Ja, es gibt eigentlich relativ wenige kreative Bereiche, wo sich jemand betätigt, der mit Kunst überhaupt nichts zu tun hat. Und das Aquarium ist sicher einer davon, das interessiert mich sehr. Ein anderer kreativer Bereich wäre zum Beispiel das Schreiben von Gedichten, das hört aber mit einem bestimmten Alter auf, denn meistens schreibt man Gedichte nur, wenn man verliebt ist.

**Lucas Gehrmann** In einem Aquarium bewegt sich ja auch meistens etwas ...

edge, something spectacular that would primarily be in line with American tastes, meaning that it should clearly be popular. How "popular" is your aquarium?

**Markus Schinwald** I've always been interested in what is popular, not in the sense of wanting to make something popular for the viewers but, conversely, of making something that the viewers themselves already do. The aquarium and the aquarium building are things to be encountered everywhere – other than in art. My focus is more or less on grabbing what the viewers find interesting and building something with certain elements culled from Dalí.

**Lucas Gehrmann** So a kind of everyday object as the launch pad ...

**Markus Schinwald** That's right, because there are really very few creative spaces for someone to engage with that have little to do with art. The aquarium is one of those spaces, and that makes it interesting for me. Another creative sphere would be writing poems, for example, but that stops at a certain age, because most people only write poems when they are in love.

**Lucas Gehrmann** Things tend to move around in an aquarium ...

**Markus Schinwald** Yes, there is always movement going on, and I wanted to see how this compares to the way I watch movies. I cannot take a boring movie for very long, but I don't mind sitting in front of an aquarium for hours – because I know that nothing is going to happen, there is no development or progress. To me, the aquarium has the feel of a pleasantly boring movie.

**Markus Schinwald** Da bewegt sich etwas und daran hat mich der Vergleich mit meinem eigenen Betrachten von Filmen interessiert. Einen langweiligen Film halte ich nicht lange aus, es macht mir aber überhaupt nichts aus, stundenlang vor einem Aquarium zu sitzen – wo ich ja weiß, dass da nichts passieren wird oder nichts rauskommt. Das Aquarium hat etwas von einem angenehm langweiligen Kino, finde ich.

**Lucas Gehrmann** Wobei deine Filme zwar nicht „langweilig" sind, aber viele Passagen haben, in denen es sehr gemächlich vorangeht.

**Markus Schinwald** Ja, aber bei meinen Filmen will ich schon, dass immer auch so ein Slapstick-Moment vorkommt. Dabei versuche ich aber, die Zeit rauszunehmen, also dass Bewegungen oder das Wenige, was passiert, möglichst gediegen abläuft und nicht aufgeregt und hysterisch.

**Lucas Gehrmann** Es könnte das Ganze theoretisch auch weitergehen.

**Markus Schinwald** Es könnte weitergehen, aber das Ganze, das bei mir zehn Minuten dauert, könnte man problemlos auch in einer Minute abhandeln.

**Lucas Gehrmann** Nochmals zurück zu deinem Aquarium: Weißt du schon, was du dahinter aufbauen oder zeigen wirst?

**Markus Schinwald** Bei Dalí interessieren mich seine langen Perspektiven, wo nichts passiert. Und wenn das in dem Aquarium selber nicht gelingt, dann werde ich dahinter



**Lucas Gehrmann** I wouldn't call your films "boring" at all, but there are many passages where the pace slows right down.

**Markus Schinwald** Right, but I do always want my films to include a kind of slapstick moment. And in that time I try to slow down the pace so that movements or the little that does happen unfolds as unhurriedly as possible and does not come across as agitated or hysterical.

**Lucas Gehrmann** Theoretically speaking, the whole thing could just continue endlessly.

**Markus Schinwald** Yes, it could, and the passage in my film that takes ten minutes to unfold could equally be over in just a minute.

**Lucas Gehrmann** Let's go back to your aquarium once more: do you have any idea yet what you are going to install or show behind it?

**Markus Schinwald** What interests me in Dalí are his long passages where nothing happens. And if this proves difficult to achieve in the aquarium itself, then I will set up a small moving stage behind it whose function it is to extend the perspective. In other words, to create a space that is dedicated to emptiness.

**Lucas Gehrmann** You gaze into the aquarium and see the fish there ...

**Markus Schinwald** ... moving like actors ...

**Lucas Gehrmann** ... and behind it you encounter this vanishing perspective. Which is very much commensurate with Classical theater, einfach eine kleine Zugbühne setzen, die eigentlich die Funktion hat, so eine Perspektive zu verlängern. Also einen Raum zu bilden, dem die Leere gewidmet ist.

Lucas Gehrmann Man blickt in das Aquarium hinein, sieht dort die Fische ...

Markus Schinwald ... die sich wie Schauspieler bewegen ...

Lucas Gehrmann ... und dahinter gibt es dann diese Fluchtperspektive. Was ja dem klassischen Theater entspricht, dem Barocktheater oder auch schon dem römischen Theater.

Markus Schinwald Ja.

Lucas Gehrmann Und bei Dalí dürfte dich doch auch seine Darstellung oder Thematisierung der Veränderung der Dinge in einem Zusammenhang interessieren; das war jedenfalls eine Annahme, weswegen wir dich auch gefragt haben, ob du bei dieser Ausstellung mitmachen möchtest. Also ich spiele auf Dalís „paranoisch-kritische" Methode an, bei der in einem Ding mehrere Interpretationsansätze oder Sehweisen möglich gemacht werden. Vergleichbares gibt es ja in deinen Arbeiten auch immer wieder.

Markus Schinwald Es gibt in meinen Arbeiten zum Surrealismus mehrere wichtige Überschneidungspunkte. René Magritte ist zum Beispiel eine Person, die mir näher ist als Dalí. Gleichzeitig ist die Einladung der Kunsthalle besonders interessant für mich, ein Anlass, mich

Baroque theater or even Roman theater before it.

Markus Schinwald Yes, that's right.

Lucas Gehrmann And in Dalí what should still be interesting to you is how he depicted or presented the issue of how things change in a certain context; at least this is how we saw it, and it's one of the reasons we asked you to take part in this exhibition. Likewise, Dalí's "paranoïac critical" method, by which each thing can be interpreted or visualized in a variety of different ways, gives us several methods of viewing. This is a recurrent theme also in your work.

Markus Schinwald There are several important points where my work overlaps with Surrealism. René Magritte, for example, is closer to me as a person than is Dalí. At the same time, being invited by Kunsthalle to participate in an exhibition on an artistic figure whom I would not normally study in so much detail is quite inspiring. What I'm saying is that my contribution to a Magritte exhibition would probably be less exciting than one I did for Dalí; in other words, I would probably pay Magritte too much respect. But being invited to this exhibition made me see Dalí from a different perspective. Usually exhibition titles tend to be very general, such as "On nature" or whatever, which gives you a lot of leeway. But in the case of Dalí, it's a kind of closed cosmos, where you actually do need to find loopholes. So how can I worm my way into the Dalí universe, or what can I do to get something out of it? This was a very exciting process. Which also sparked some ideas for other works.

mit einer Person, mit der ich mich gar nicht so sehr auseinander gesetzt habe, zu beschäftigen. Also ein Beitrag zu einer Magritteausstellung würde für mich wahrscheinlich langweiliger ausfallen als zu Dalí, das heißt mit Magritte würde ich bestimmt zu respektvoll umgehen. Dalí habe ich mir durch die Ausstellungseinladung aber auch anders angeschaut. Sonst bekommt man ja bei Ausstellungen nur generelle Titel geliefert, so wie „Über die Natur" oder weiß der Kuckuck was, die einem sehr vieles offen lassen. Aber Dalí, das ist schon so ein abgeschlossener Kosmos, bei dem man Schlupflöcher tatsächlich finden muss. Wie also kann ich mich in den Kosmos Dalí irgendwie hineinbiegen oder was kann ich mir aus Dalí rausklauben? Das war recht spannend. Und es fallen da auch ein paar Nebenarbeiten gleich mit ab.

Lucas Gehrmann Zum Beispiel?

Markus Schinwald Na ja, das ist noch gar nicht so konkret, aber wenn ich jetzt Filme andenke, dann liegt eine Gedankensammlung immer ein bisschen am Tisch bei mir und wenn ich sie brauche, nehme ich sie mir.

Lucas Gehrmann Hast du dich über deine neue Beschäftigung mit Dalí auch mit der Theorie des Surrealismus näher beschäftigt?

Markus Schinwald Ein bisschen, aber in den Surrealismus im Großen und Ganzen wollte ich nicht komplett eintauchen, sein Begriff war mir immer zu stark ganzheitlich – also immer diese großen Fragen, und auch immer der direkte Weg zur Psyche. Mich interessiert eher ein kurviger Weg dahin.



Lucas Gehrmann Can you give an example?

Markus Schinwald Well, it's all still very much up in the air, but when I start thinking about a new movie now there's a collection of thoughts on my desk ready to grab.

Lucas Gehrmann When you studied Dalí for this exhibition did you also include the theory of Surrealism?

Markus Schinwald A little, yes, but I didn't want to immerse myself completely in Surrealism by and large; to me the concept always felt a touch too holistic – always broaching all the big questions, and always aiming straight for the mind. I am more interested in getting there in a roundabout way.

Lucas Gehrmann Well, times have changed since, but some of the ideas in Surrealism are still very much alive today ...

Markus Schinwald In art, there are always phases where you have a special interest in one thing or another and I believe that, compared to the art produced in the 1990s for example, which was somewhat juiceless, there is a growing wish for pathos today, such as is always inherent in Surrealism. Which I find rather curious. I think it needs to be broken somehow!

Lucas Gehrmann And it was in the 1990s, if not before, that our idea of this world as a world of multiple realities began to unfold, including new possibilities created in media-technology to generate new worlds or "realities."

**Lucas Gehrmann** Wir leben ja auch in einer anderen Zeit; wobei es ja schon Gedanken gibt im Surrealismus, die heute noch immer virulent sind ...

**Markus Schinwald** Es gibt ja in der Kunst so Phasen, in denen einen bestimmte Sachen interessieren oder auch nicht, und ich glaube, dass im Unterschied zu den neunziger Jahren zum Beispiel, als die Kunst eher trocken ausgefallen ist, heute ein Wunsch nach solch einem Pathos gewachsen ist, das der Surrealismus immer impliziert. Und das ist gerade spannend, ich meine, man muss dieses Pathos irgendwie brechen!

**Lucas Gehrmann** Und spätestens in den Neunzigern ist ja auch die Vorstellung von dieser Welt als einer Welt mit vielen Wirklichkeiten aufgebrochen, einschließlich der neuen medientechnologischen Möglichkeiten der Generierung neuer Welten bzw. „Wirklichkeiten".

**Markus Schinwald** Ja, und auch das Bewusstsein, dass man das, was man tut, nicht immer ganz und gar glauben muss.

**Lucas Gehrmann** Genau, und diese Relativierbarkeit des „Realen" haben die Surrealisten durchaus vorweggenommen. Und auch der Aspekt, den du erwähnst, wenn du sagst, dass dich der Betrachter interessiert als ein von außen kommender beziehungsweise jemand, der nicht so stark im kunstimmanenten System steckt und von der Theorie nicht viel weiß oder unbedingt wissen muss, der wird ja im Surrealismus auch oft mitgedacht als eine Position, die das Bild mit verändert. Also Bild und Betrachter sind

**Markus Schinwald** Yes, and with it the realization that you don't always have to believe fully in what you do.

**Lucas Gehrmann** Precisely, and the Surrealists prefigured that the notion of "reality" can in fact be relativized. Along with the aspect you mentioned earlier, saying that you are interested in the viewer as someone from outside or someone who is not quite as immanently caught up within the art system or is not so well-versed in the theory of it, and neither does he have to be. In Surrealism, such viewers are included as an aspect that causes the image to change. Meaning that image and beholder are interacting on a kind of virtual level. Dalí also wrote about this when he sought to determine his own position in relation to the outside world, as well as to the world depicted in his images. An issue that still carries a lot of relevance today.

**Markus Schinwald** Yes, absolutely!

**Lucas Gehrmann** Even before you immersed yourself in Dalí's work for the current show, you were already working on making a number of different positions and worlds perceptible, including the uncanny, which, according to Freud, is unleashed from things we know and trust when these things leave their "logical" places as it were ...

**Markus Schinwald** ... the invisible; yes, it happens. I worked with curtains for a while, and there is no way of getting around Surrealism here, you simply cannot ignore it. Again, Magritte would be a prime example of an artist who works with curtains! That said, I never referenced Surrealism directly.

da sozusagen virtuell interaktiv. Dalí hat sich dazu ja auch schriftlich geäußert, wenn er sich gefragt hat, wo seine eigene Position ist in Relation sowohl zur äußeren Welt als auch zu der Welt in den Bildern. Und das ist eine Frage, die nach wie vor aktuell ist.

**Markus Schinwald** Ja, absolut!

**Lucas Gehrmann** Du hast schon früher, bevor du dich jetzt aktuell mit Dalí beschäftigt hast, mehrere Standpunkte und Welten parallel wahrnehmbar gemacht, dabei auch das Unheimliche, das laut Freud aus dem Vertrauten und Altbekannten sozusagen herauskippt, wenn dieses seinen „logischen" Standort verlässt ...



**Markus Schinwald** ... das nicht Sichtbare; ja, das kommt vor. Ich habe eine Zeit lang viel mit Vorhängen gearbeitet, da kommt man um den Surrealismus auch nicht herum, also das kann man einfach nicht ignorieren, Magritte wäre da wieder ein Beispiel, der Vorhangkünstler schlechthin! Aber ich habe mich nie direkt auf den Surrealismus bezogen.

**Lucas Gehrmann** Den Vorhang gibt es als Bühnenvorhang, und dann gab es in der Antike auch den Vorhang vor dem Bild, um es zu schützen ... Welche Rolle spielt bei dir der Vorhang?

**Markus Schinwald** Ich bin eigentlich über einen kleinen Umweg zum Vorhang gekommen – über die Kleidung. An der Kleidung hat mich der Aspekt ihrer architektonischen Funktion interessiert, wo also Kleidung den Körper „verrückt" oder ihn verformt, verändert, wie

**Lucas Gehrmann** A curtain can be a stage curtain, while in the Ancient World it was placed before the artwork to protect it ... What is the role of the curtain in your work?

**Markus Schinwald** I actually arrived at the idea of the curtain in kind of a roundabout way – through clothes. What interested me in clothes was the aspect of their architectural function; in other words, how clothes can be used to shift and 'madden' the contours of the body, change it or give it a different shape, just like high heels will lift it, and in that sense do something to the body. And I perceived the curtain as an architectural means that precisely does *not* do this. In this regard, the curtain has no tectonic function – all it does is stop the gaze, it does not divide the space, it's something of a liquid wall.

**Lucas Gehrmann** But when it's in the window it separates the inside from the outside space?

**Markus Schinwald** It only stops the gaze, it does not separate the space. But it can take on a dramatic function, such as the curtain in Alfred Hitchcock movies...

**Lucas Gehrmann** ... because it moves.

**Markus Schinwald** That's right.

**Lucas Gehrmann** Strictly speaking, such dramaturgic effects would traditionally also have a soundtrack. Whereas in your films, the music and the scripts are never directly related to the "action," but ...

auch ein Stöckelschuh ihn hebt, also etwas mit dem Körper tut. Und den Vorhang habe ich als architektonisches Moment begriffen, das genau das nicht tut. Der Vorhang hat in diesem Sinne keine tektonische Funktion – er trennt nur den Blick, nicht den Raum, und ist so etwas wie eine flüssige Wand.

Lucas Gehrmann Aber wenn er im Fenster hängt, trennt er doch den Innen- vom Außenraum!?

Markus Schinwald Er trennt nur die Sicht und nicht den Raum! Er kann dabei aber auch eine dramaturgische Funktion haben wie zum Beispiel der Vorhang bei Alfred Hitchcock ...

Lucas Gehrmann ... indem er sich bewegt.

Markus Schinwald Ja.

Lucas Gehrmann Wobei zu solcher Dramaturgie klassischerweise noch die Filmmusik gehört. Bei deinen Filmen dagegen haben die Musik und auch die Texte ja nie direkt mit der „Handlung" zu tun, sondern ...

Markus Schinwald ... sie liegen immer drüber. Ich benutze auch so gut wie keine Originaltöne, und wenn ich bestimmte Bewegungen mit einem Ton hinterlege, dann sind das gelogene Töne, das ist nie das, was man gehört hat.

Lucas Gehrmann In dem Raum mit deinem Aquarium wird es keinen Sound geben, oder?

Markus Schinwald Nein, das wird ganz ohne Ton sein.

Markus Schinwald ... they are superimposed. Also, I tend to hardly use the original sound, and if I add sound to particular movements then it's always fake sound, never what you would have heard originally.

Lucas Gehrmann Is it true that there will not be any sound in the room with your aquarium?

Markus Schinwald Yes, correct, there will not be any sound at all.

Lucas Gehrmann A silent movie as it were.

Markus Schinwald Yes.

Lucas Gehrmann Well, the fish don't really speak, do they.

Markus Schinwald (laughs) The fish are perhaps simply silently thinking of beautiful things.

Lucas Gehrmann I'm not really sure whether or not there was music in Dalí's pavilion, I will have to read up on it.

Markus Schinwald Me neither, but my guess would be: yes. Dalí always went all the way.

Lucas Gehrmann At least the mermaids splashing into the water would have created some kind of noise.

Markus Schinwald I'd say Dalí would not have been happy with my aquarium. For him, it would surely have been too calm, too unexciting.

**Lucas Gehrmann** Stummfilm sozusagen.

**Markus Schinwald** Ja.

**Lucas Gehrmann** Die Fische sprechen ja auch nicht.

**Markus Schinwald** (lacht) Die Fische denken vielleicht still an etwas Schönes.

**Lucas Gehrmann** Ich weiß jetzt gar nicht, ob es in Dalís Pavillon Musik gab oder nicht, da muss ich mal nachlesen.

**Markus Schinwald** Das weiß ich auch nicht, aber ich würde vermuten: ja. Er hat nichts ausgelassen, der Dalí.

**Lucas Gehrmann** Zumindest das Springen der Meeresjungfrauen ins Wasser wird man gehört haben.

**Markus Schinwald** Dalí wäre wahrscheinlich nicht einverstanden gewesen mit meinem Aquarium. Das wäre ihm bestimmt zu ruhig, zu unaufgeregt gewesen.

**Lucas Gehrmann** Wobei er sich da ja offenbar den amerikanischen Seh- und Unterhaltungsgewohnheiten angepasst hat.

**Markus Schinwald** Die ja auch alles andere als ruhig und unaufgeregt sind. Ich glaube, er hat populäre Sehmuster komplett verinnerlicht. Ich habe mir ein paar Werbespots angeschaut, in denen er auftritt, und er konnte einfach nicht nichts tun. Sobald die Kamera an war, musste er zumindest mit den Augenbrauen spielen, also damit alles irgendwie mit Bewegung gefüllt wird.

**Lucas Gehrmann** Yes, although he quite manifestly adapted to the American way of perception and entertainment.

**Markus Schinwald** Which is anything but calm and unexciting. I believe he completely internalized popular patterns of seeing. I watched a few ads in which he appeared; it's like he could not simply do nothing. As soon as the camera was on him, he had to at least mess around with his eyebrows so as to create some kind of movement.

**Lucas Gehrmann** No doubt he was a great show-off.

**Markus Schinwald** Very much so!

**Lucas Gehrmann** Which you are not, in the sense that you don't feature in your own works. Which is one side to Dalí that other artists in the exhibition ...

**Markus Schinwald** ... take care of.

**Lucas Gehrmann** Yes, take care of (laughs), at least to a certain degree. That said, we were curious about one aspect that could have been implemented very differently in your work; namely, the crux of the subject. In other words, the fact that every human being is always at the center of his own universe while at the same time denying this, because we like to pretend or believe that we perceive the world objectively, and, for the sake of politeness, tend not to put ourselves in the limelight, at least not to the same extent that Dalí did in an almost provocative sense.

**Lucas Gehrmann** Er war unbedingt ein großer Selbstdarsteller.

**Markus Schinwald** Ja, ja!

**Lucas Gehrmann** Was du ja in diesem Sinne nicht bist, also in deinen eigenen Arbeiten kommst du ja nicht vor. Das ist ein Dalí-Aspekt, den wir in der Ausstellung daher mit anderen Künstlern ...

**Markus Schinwald** ... abdecken.

**Lucas Gehrmann** Ja, abdecken (lacht), anreißen zumindest. Wobei uns etwas schon auch interessiert hat, was in deiner Arbeit ganz woanders angesiedelt sein könnte, nämlich die Crux mit dem Subjekt, dass also jeder Mensch immer auch Mittelpunkt der Welt ist und das zugleich verleugnet, weil wir ja lieber vorgeben oder glauben möchten, die Welt objektiv zu begreifen und uns anstandshalber zumindest nicht so ins Zentrum setzen, wie Dalí das geradezu provokativ gemacht hat.

**Markus Schinwald** Ganz aus kommt man da eh nicht, aber ich habe schon immer versucht, eine gewisse Distanz zu den Arbeiten einzuhalten, aus der heraus man auch einen Schritt zurück machen kann und dann sieht, dass das eine oder andere schief gelaufen ist. Ich habe mir schon beigebracht, die Option des Scheiterns irgendwie zu bewahren.

**Lucas Gehrmann** Bei deinen Filmen – wir haben ja gerade deinen neuesten Film für Venedig gesehen – gibt es meistens Kamerafahrten per Kran oder auf der Schiene,

**Markus Schinwald** But you cannot stay out of it altogether, as you always have to try and keep a certain distance from the work so as to be able to take a step back and realize that one thing or another went wrong. I have definitely had to teach myself to preserve the option of failure.

**Lucas Gehrmann** In your films – we have just seen your latest film for Venice – the camera tends to move along on a crane or track, meaning that the camera is seldom stable and rarely a "subjective camera," but rather one that moves along slowly ...

**Markus Schinwald** It is often the case that the camera moves about a great deal more than what it actually depicts.

**Lucas Gehrmann** Which means it takes on lots of different perspectives ...

**Markus Schinwald** Yes, which I sometimes understand to be like some kind of sensing, some sounding out of the details. And then you magnify even very small movements.

**Lucas Gehrmann** Just like in your current film with the double bottom and the tangled cables, in which a step dancer appears, does his dance performance, and leaves the stage again ...

**Markus Schinwald** Yes, exactly.

**Lucas Gehrmann** And in the exhibition, the viewers or spectators can choose their vantage point in front of the aquarium, either by keeping their distance or gazing into it from up close, and when they turn around das heißt die Kamera ist selten stabil oder ist auch selten eine „subjektive Kamera", sondern sie fährt langsam dahin ...

**Markus Schinwald** Oft ist es so, dass sich die Kamera mehr bewegt als das, was sie abbildet.

**Lucas Gehrmann** Wodurch sie eben viele unterschiedliche Standpunkte einnimmt ...

**Markus Schinwald** Ja, manchmal habe ich das begriffen wie eine Art Abtasten, ein Ausloten von Kleinigkeiten. Man setzt da quasi die Lupe auf ganz kleine Bewegungen.

**Lucas Gehrmann** Wie gerade hier in deinem Film mit diesem doppelten Boden und dem Kabelsalat, wo ein Stepptänzer auftaucht, seinen Tanz absolviert und dann wieder abgeht ...

**Markus Schinwald** Ja, ja.

**Lucas Gehrmann** Und in der Ausstellung können die Betrachter bzw. Zuschauer ja ihren Punkt einnehmen vor dem Aquarium und entweder mit Abstand oder ganz aus der Nähe hineinschauen, und wenn sie sich umdrehen, sehen sie gleichzeitig Fotos von Dalís Pavillon von 1939.

**Markus Schinwald** Mein Aquarium ist quasi durch die Fische animiert und von dem Pavillon wird es nur die Fotos geben, so dass man auch unabhängig von den beiden Medien irgendwie einen Tempowechsel spürt.

**Lucas Gehrmann** Das heißt auch über das Tempo des Taktens beim Ablauf der Bilder.



they also come face to face with photographs of Dalí's 1939 pavilion.

**Markus Schinwald** My aquarium is animated by the fish, so to speak, while the pavilion will only be present in the photographs, so that even irrespective of the two media used, we somehow experience a change in pace.

**Lucas Gehrmann** And this includes the pace at which the image sequence is timed.

**Markus Schinwald** Yes, it's going to be very slow. It's not quite finalized though, because I'm not going to be the one to decide on the pace; rather, it depends on how the viewers are conditioned, how much they can remove the pace and allow themselves to linger. Either they pause and gaze for a while or they simply move on.

**Lucas Gehrmann** I also think that aquariums are about contemplation. You sit in front of them and gaze at the movement of the fish and how they change with the light, we are all familiar with that. I don't know in what way the situation is going to change with a big audience ushered through like in the zoo, for example. Perhaps this will speed things up somewhat. The exhibition would present a good opportunity to study this, don't you think? I mean, how the audience behaves in such a context. Would you be interested in observing the observers?

**Markus Schinwald** I will certainly have a look at how things work out in relation to one another. With pictures or films, you tend to have a certain idea, and things are not really that different in my exhibitions.

**Markus Schinwald** Ja, das wird sehr langsam laufen. Das weiß ich noch nicht genau, das hängt auch nicht unbedingt von mir ab, sondern davon, wie ein Zuseher konditioniert ist, wie sehr er das Tempo rausnehmen und verweilen kann. Er schaut eine Weile dort rein oder er läuft durch.

**Lucas Gehrmann** Ich denke auch, dass Aquarien etwas Kontemplatives haben. Wo man also davor sitzt und einfach der Bewegung der Fische zuschaut und wie sie sich verändern im Licht, das kennen wir wirklich alle. Ich weiß nicht, wie es in Situationen mit viel Publikum ist, das durchgeschleust wird wie zum Beispiel in einem Zoo, da geht vielleicht alles schneller. Das könnte man eigentlich beobachten lassen in der Ausstellung, also das Verhalten des Publikums, oder? Wäre eine solche Betrachtung der Betrachter interessant für dich?

**Markus Schinwald** Ich werde mir das sicher mal so anschauen, wie das im Verhältnis ist. Bei Bildern oder auch bei Filmen weiß man das ungefähr, und in meinen Ausstellungen ändert sich das auch nicht so sehr.

**Lucas Gehrmann** Also die Leute bleiben?

**Markus Schinwald** Und wie die Leute bleiben!

**Lucas Gehrmann** Wobei es bei Gruppenausstellungen nicht immer so ganz einfach ist, alles anzuschauen. Gerade bei Film und Video braucht man viel Zeit und oft auch Geduld, wenn sehr vieles läuft.

**Markus Schinwald** Ja, und wenn ich selber an einer Einzelausstellung arbeite, dann ist das fast

**Lucas Gehrmann** So people pause and linger?

**Markus Schinwald** Yes, you'd be surprised *how long* they linger!

**Lucas Gehrmann** Sure, but with group exhibitions it is not always that easy to see everything. Film and video in particular are very time-consuming and test people's patience when there's a lot going on.

**Markus Schinwald** Yes, and when I have a solo exhibition now, it's almost like editing film, in the sense of: when do you need to say stop? Where do you add something new, so as to best enable an exhibition that has a dramaturgical structure? And this is seldom possible with group exhibitions; there are too many factors to juggle.

**Lucas Gehrmann** *Le Surréalisme, c'est moi!* has a kind of continuous dramaturgical structure, it's a circuit at least, so it could work here.

**Markus Schinwald** Yes, I agree. And the number of artists exhibiting is limited.

**Lucas Gehrmann** And in Venice you will create the kind of situation you need yourself. Before Venice, did you ever get the opportunity to make an installation this big?

**Markus Schinwald** Venice is actually a small installation by comparison, its footprint isn't really that large. Two years ago at Budapest Art Hall I did an installation spanning 2,500 square meters; the pavilion in Venice is only a fraction of that. And there have been very large wie Filmschneiden. Also eine Ausstellung dramaturgisch anzudenken – wo muss man stopp sagen und wo etwas Neues reinkommt. Und das ist bei Gruppenausstellungen eben selten möglich, da sind zu viele Faktoren unter einen Hut zu bringen.

Lucas Gehrmann Im Fall von *Le Surréalisme, c'est moi!* gibt es ja eine Art durchgehende Dramaturgie, einen Parcours zumindest, da könnte es also schon funktionieren.

Markus Schinwald Ja, das glaube ich auch. Da ist auch die Künstleranzahl überschaubar.

Lucas Gehrmann Und in Venedig schaffst du dir sowieso eine Situation, wie du sie magst, selber. Konntest du früher schon eine so große Installation machen wie jetzt die für Venedig?

Markus Schinwald Eigentlich ist das eine kleine Installation, denn von den Quadratmetern her ist das gar nicht viel in Venedig. Vor zwei Jahren habe ich die Kunsthalle Budapest gemacht mit 2500 m, dagegen ist der Pavillon in Venedig nur ein Bruchteil. Oder auch im migros museum in Zürich hat es sehr große Installationen gegeben. Venedig ist, wenn man beim Film bleibt, ein Kurzfilm!

Lucas Gehrmann Was ja auch in den Kontext einer Biennale passt, wo es ohnehin eine Menge an Stationen gibt wie in einer Gruppenausstellung mit ganz verschiedenen Subthemen.
Zum Schluss dieses kleinen Gesprächs noch die übliche Frage: Was hast du als Nächstes vor, gibt es schon Projekte für die weitere Zukunft?



installations at Zurich's Migros Museum. Staying with the movies theme, Venice is therefore only a short film!

Lucas Gehrmann Which fits into the context of a Biennial, which itself is structured into a lot of different stages, much like a group exhibition features a variety of different subthemes. To round off our short conversation, let me ask you the usual question: what are you going to do next? Are there any projects planned for the near future?

Markus Schinwald The day before or after the opening of the Dalí exhibition, I am doing a performance in Prague, together with the Russian choreographer Oleg Soulimenko.
In this performance, the stage will be suspended from the ceiling upside down or, rather, it will float six meters above your head. In terms of gravity there are some parallels with the installation I did for Kunsthalle; in fact, it is a box with countless flaps where the pace has been slowed right down. But because it floats above the audience, it is spectacular in itself.
We did the same in Belgium before: there is a dancer inside a kind of box and you only get to see individual body parts sticking out before he leaves the box completely – then the flap turns into a chair, the platform into a table, and right at the end the leg of the table, or a table pole, so it seems, extends up to six meters long before descending very slowly to the ground. Then comes the Belgian world champion in pole dancing. The thing in itself has a lurid and sensational feel to it, but the elongated time scale gives it a very peculiar edge. The aim was to transform something spectacular into something dull.

Markus Schinwald Einen Tag vor oder einen Tag nach der Dalí-Eröffnung mache ich in Prag eine Performance, die ich gemeinsam mit dem russischen Choreographen Oleg Soulimenko entwickelt habe, wo die Bühne umgedreht an der Decke klebt oder eigentlich sechs Meter über dem Kopf schwebt. In Bezug auf die Schwerkraft gibt es auch Parallelen zur Arbeit für die Kunsthalle. Eigentlich ist es ein Kasten mit vielen Klappen drinnen, das Tempo ganz rausgenommen. Aber durch dieses Schweben über dem Kopf ist es irgendwie schon spektakulär. Wir haben das schon einmal in Belgien gezeigt; da gibt es einen Tänzer in einer Art Schachtel, wobei man erst nur einzelne Körperteile sieht, die herauskommen, bis er ganz rausschlüpft – und aus der Klappe wird ein Stuhl, aus einer Plattform ein Tisch und ganz am Schluss wird das Tischbein bzw. diese Tischstange sechs Meter lang, kommt als Stange ganz langsam zum Boden herunter und zuletzt kommt die belgische Weltmeisterin im Pole Dance. Das ganze Ding an sich ist reißerisch und spektakulär, doch durch die zeitliche Ausdehnung kriegt es etwas ganz Merkwürdiges. Der Versuch war, aus etwas sehr Spektakulärem etwas Fades zu machen.

Lucas Gehrmann Und etwas Langsames; es ist also auch eine Arbeit gegen die Schnelligkeit und den medialen Action-Overkill, die Sehgewohnheiten unserer Zeit?

Markus Schinwald Eigentlich sind Performances immer wie Aquarien anzuschauen.

Lucas Gehrmann Auch in deinen Filmen schweben die Figuren oft ganz langsam weg ...

Lucas Gehrmann And something slow; after all, the piece is also meant to comment on our fast lifestyles and the action overkill in the media – the way we nowadays perceive the world around us, am I right?

Markus Schinwald Strictly speaking, all performances should be viewed like aquariums.

Lucas Gehrmann In your films, the characters also tend to float away very slowly ...

Markus Schinwald ... yes, but you don't wait around to see the end of it. It simply starts again from the beginning ...

Lucas Gehrmann ... and suddenly there they are again. You mentioned transformation, which likewise plays a role, in that a table morphs into a platform or certain objects are assigned extraordinary functions.

Markus Schinwald It's a mix of amusement park, magic and yoga. At the end of August, I will be doing an exhibition at Kunstverein Hannover, where I would like to work with aquariums once again; over the years, I've accumulated a number of architectural models from my own exhibitions and I quite like them, but in order to work, they will need to be placed in specific contexts, which is why I am going to install some of these models in aquariums.

Lucas Gehrmann One aquarium for each model. Does this mean you can walk around the aquariums?

Markus Schinwald Yes, viewers will be able to walk around the aquariums, just like small exhibits

**Markus Schinwald** ... wo man auch nicht wartet, wie das ausgeht. Das fängt wieder von vorn an ...

**Lucas Gehrmann** ... und sie sind plötzlich wieder da. Und das Transformieren, wie du gesagt hast, spielt dabei auch eine Rolle, aus einem Tisch wird eine Plattform oder bestimmte Gegenstände erhalten andere Funktionen.

**Markus Schinwald** Es ist so eine Mischung aus Jahrmarkt, Zauberei und Yoga. Ende August mache ich dann eine Ausstellung im Kunstverein Hannover und da möchte ich noch einmal mit den Aquarien arbeiten. Ich habe im Laufe der Jahre einige Architekturmodelle meiner eigenen Ausstellungen angesammelt und ich mag die ganz gern, aber ohne die Bespielung funktionieren sie als Modelle nicht ganz, und daher werde ich einige dieser Modelle in Aquarien einbauen.

**Lucas Gehrmann** Pro Modell ein Aquarium; kann man da um die Aquarien herumgehen?

**Markus Schinwald** Da wird man um die Aquarien herumgehen können, wie um kleine Ausstellungen in der Schwerelosigkeit. Was ich bei Aquarien auch mag, ist, dass eben nichts so direkt an den Boden gebunden ist und die Lebewesen schwimmen oder schweben.

**Das Gespräch mit Markus Schinwald führte Lucas Gehrmann im Mai 2011.**



in zero gravity. What I also like about aquariums is that you are not directly bound to the ground; rather, the animals swim or float.

**Lucas Gehrmann spoke with Markus Schinwald in May 2011.**

## Dalí gegenüber sterbe ich sprichwörtlich vor Neid Francesco Vezzoli im Gespräch mit Caroline Corbetta

**Caroline Corbetta** Das letzte Mal begegneten wir uns am Set für einen Beitrag der Spezialausgabe der *Uomo Vogue* anlässlich der Biennale von Venedig, in dem du Dalí in der berühmten Fotoserie von Philippe Halsman dargestellt hast. Dreizehn Jahre liegen zwischen dieser unterhaltsamen Hommage und jener Stickarbeit, auf der du das Gesicht Salvador Dalís mit kleinen Stichen porträtiert hast. Seither hast du dich in deiner künstlerischen Praxis mehrfach auf Dalí bezogen, obwohl der katalanische Künstler in Künstlerkreisen noch bis vor wenigen Jahren als ein „Unberührbarer“ galt. Nun kann man nicht behaupten, dass diese Diskussionen beendet wären, aber Ausstellungen wie die aktuelle tragen dazu bei, ein noch ungehobenes Erbe zu erforschen und Dalí seine Rolle als Erneuerer zuzuerkennen. Er war tatsächlich der Erste, der sich mit seiner *Persona* als künstlerisches Instrument beschäftigt hat, wobei er die Grenzen der Kunst zu überwinden suchte und in den Bereichen Mode, Design, Werbung usw. experimentierte. Diese Haltung ist heute allgemein verbreitet und erregt dennoch nach wie vor den Unmut der allzu gestrengen Kritiker, obgleich sich das von Dalí vorgelebte Szenario ja gewissermaßen bewahrheitet hat. Ich denke, du warst dir dieser Problematik und der Folgen bewusst, als du im Jahr 1998 sein Gesicht gestickt hast. Das war bereits ein deutliches künstlerisches Statement, provozierend und ungewöhnlich nicht nur in der damaligen italienischen Kunstszene. War es tatsächlich so?

## In front of Dalí I am literally sick with envy Francesco Vezzoli in conversation with Caroline Corbetta

**Caroline Corbetta** The last time we met was on the set of a photo-shoot for the special issue of *Uomo Vogue*, dedicated to the 2011 Venice Biennale, where you decided to reincarnate Dalí in those famous pictures taken by Philippe Halsman. Thirteen years have passed between this contemporary amusing tribute and the embroidery portrait you made of Salvador Dalí (1998). Over the years you have repeatedly made reference to his figure in your artistic practice, even though the Catalan artist was considered a true “untouchable” in the artistic circle until recently. We cannot really say he has been fully rehabilitated, but exhibitions like this one help to investigate a legacy still to be explored, and to acknowledge Dalí's role as an innovator. Indeed, he was the first to work with his *persona* as a proper artistic tool and to overcome the boundaries of art in order to experiment in the fields of fashion, design, advertising ... This attitude is rather common today but it continues to raise eyebrows among the most intransigent critics, despite the fact that somehow the scenario that Dalí had envisioned has become true. I do not think you were unaware of all these implications when you stitched his face back in 1998. From my point of view, that was already a sharp artistic statement. Provocative and heterodox, especially if compared to the art scene of the moment, in Italy and elsewhere.

**Francesco Vezzoli** Not to minimize that statement, but rather to contextualize it, I would like to point out that I not only stitched a portrait of Dalí at the time, but also those of other decadent figures, such as Mario Praz, Luchino

**Francesco Vezzoli** Nicht um dieses Statement kleinzureden, sondern um es in einen Kontext zu stellen, möchte ich darauf verweisen, dass ich zu jener Zeit nicht nur ein Porträt Dalís, sondern auch weiterer „dekadenter" Persönlichkeiten wie Mario Praz, Luchino Visconti, Giò Ponti gestickt habe ... Bei all diesen Leuten handelt es sich um Ikonen, die zumindest mit Misstrauen betrachtet wurden. Sie galten als unberührbare Intellektuelle, weil sie in ihren Arbeiten als zu dekorativ oder kommerziell oder in ihrer ideologischen Positionierung als zu wenig links stehend angesehen wurden. Mir hingegen bereitete es Vergnügen, als Spross einer gemäßigt linken Familie und nach einer ziemlich radikalen künstlerischen Ausbildung in London gerade diesen Personen zu huldigen, denen gegenüber ich eine starke emotionale und ästhetische Affinität empfand, die ich mir allerdings nicht am Cover von *Frieze* oder *Flash Art* vorstellen konnte. Meine Stickereiarbeiten mit kleinen Stichen – ich lege hier Wert auf den genauen sprachlichen Ausdruck – stellten für mich eine bewusst provokante und zugleich für meine künstlerischen Wurzeln bedeutsame Geste dar. Sie führten die *political correctness* und die Welt der Filmclubs meiner Eltern mit der bürgerlichen Vorstellung meiner Großmütter zusammen, in deren Wohnzimmern ich die Shows im Fernsehen gesehen hatte.
Ich erinnere mich, dass ich gegen Ende der neunziger Jahre sehr häufig an das Werk von Sarah Lucas dachte, das ich damals sehr stark fand, und ich verstand, dass sie ihre Kraft aus der radikalen Darstellung der eigenen sozialen Herkunft aus der Arbeiterklasse bezog. Ich, der ich mich wie jemand aus der Provinz mit zu großen Ansprüchen und Ambitionen fühlte, liebte Luchino Visconti mit all seinen Snobis-



Visconti, Giò Ponti ... All icons that had been handled with suspicion, to say the least. These intellectuals were untouchable because they were considered too decorative or too commercial, or not enough left-oriented in their ideological positionings. And despite the fact that I am coming from a politically left-moderate Italian family and had a pretty radical artistic education in London, I wanted to celebrate these figures because I used to feel a deep emotional as well as aesthetical involvement towards them, although I wasn't seeing them on the altars of covers such as *Frieze* or *Flash Art*. And my choice of embroidering them with the technique of needlework – I would like to emphasize the choice of language – was a deliberately provocative act but, at the same time, one that revealed my cultural roots, in which the "politically correct" and all the arthouse film imagery, coming from my parents, was juxtaposed to the bourgeois vision of my grandmothers in whose living room I used to watch variety shows on television. At the time, around the late nineties, I remember thinking quite often about the work of Sarah Lucas, which I considered very strong, and I knew that her strength came from representing certain features of her social background – the working class – from a radical position. Feeling like a provincial with too-high pretensions and aspirations, I celebrated Luchino Visconti, with his snobbery and all his intellectual references, as well as the pretentiousness of Mario Praz, who had built an empire-style maisonette in the heart of Rome ...

The house-museum of Mario Praz was the set of Francesco Vezzoli's first video *Ok, the Praz is right! (An Embroidered Trilogy)*, 1997 men und intellektualistischen Bezügen, wie auch die Anmaßung eines Mario Praz, der sich im Herzen Roms eine *maisonette* im kaiserlichen Stil errichten ließ

Die inzwischen als Museum genutzten Räume des ehemaligen Wohnhauses von Mario Praz bildeten den Schauplatz für das erste Video von Francesco Vezzoli *Ok, the Praz is right! [An Embroidered Trilogy]*, 1997.

... und schließlich auch Dalí ... Sie alle waren Personen, denen es gelungen war, ihren politisch wenig korrekten Traum zu realisieren.

Caroline Corbetta In jedem Fall stellten die gestickten Porträts sowohl von der Technik als auch von den Motiven her einen Bruch mit der damaligen künstlerischen Praxis, insbesondere in Italien, dar ...

Francesco Vezzoli Ich beobachtete das soziale Panorama insgesamt. In meinem Land fielen mir gewisse Phänomene im Bereich des Fernsehens und der Politik auf, die absolut nicht dem entsprachen, was mir die Medien zur Verbreitung von Kunst anboten, nämlich eine anspruchsvolle, bisweilen auch sehr essenzielle Kunst. Dagegen nahm ich um mich herum eine Art von ästhetischer und ideologischer Restauration wahr, die leider bis heute spürbar andauert. Ich entschied mich dafür, mit meiner Kunst darüber zu sprechen.

Caroline Corbetta Ich betrachte deine Arbeit in der Tat als ambitioniertes soziales Fresko über die Rolle des Künstlers in der zeitgenössischen Gesellschaft. Der Künstler, der mit seiner poetischen Chronik über die

... and even Dalí ... To sum up, these were all people who had managed to make their (a little politically incorrect) dreams come true.

Caroline Corbetta But those embroidered portraits, both in technique and subject matter, represented a break with the art scene of the time, especially the Italian one ...

Francesco Vezzoli I was interested in the social scene more in general. And in my country, I could see some mediatic and political phenomena that were incredibly distant from what the art magazines were offering; namely, an art that was very sophisticated, sometimes very essential. Meanwhile, I could see around me a sort of ideological and aesthetic restoration that is still, unfortunately, deeply in progress. And I decided to use my art to talk about this.

Caroline Corbetta I consider your work to be like an ambitious social fresco that revolves around the role of the artist in contemporary society. The artist that speaks, through a poetic chronicle, about the world he lives in. A world in which he wants to have an active role. Do you fit this definition?

Francesco Vezzoli In answer to this question, I want to tell you about a discussion I had just yesterday with an old friend, who has made choices which are very different from my own. I was trying to tell him about my vision of the world, my attempts in understanding which direction the world is going in; the fact I use my artistic identity as a platform to meet and confront contemporary intellectuals, architects,

Welt erzählt, in der er lebt und in der er etwas bedeuten möchte. Erkennst du dich in dieser Definition wieder?

Francesco Vezzoli Zu diesem Thema möchte ich dir von einer Diskussion mit einem alten Studienkollegen berichten, der einen ganz anderen Weg als ich eingeschlagen hat. Ich versuchte, ihm meine Weltsicht zu erklären, meine Versuche durch Begegnungen mit Intellektuellen, Architekten und Politikern zu verstehen, in welche Richtung sich das Denken entwickeln wird. Dabei nutze ich meine Identität als Künstler als Plattform, um diese Begegnungen zu ermöglichen. Mein Freund bedrängte mich mit der Aussage, er sei an jenen Menschen interessiert, die vor dem Haus von Philippe Green, dem Gründer der Bekleidungskette Top Shop, protestieren, weil dieser in England keine Steuern bezahlen möchte. Ich hingegen bin mehr daran interessiert, wie viele Menschen bei Topshop die neueste von Kate Moss gestaltete Kollektion kaufen werden. Ich möchte verstehen, in welche Richtung sich die Welt bewegt. Ich möchte wissen, welche Stiftung oder welches Museum eines Tages von Philippe Green finanziert werden wird und um welche Art von „Finanzkunst" es sich dabei handeln wird. Tatsächlich wollte ich als Kind Journalist werden. Und wenn ich daran denke, welche Rezension mir am meisten Freude bereitet hat, so ist es jene von Giorgio Verzotti in *Artforum*.

„Francesco Vezzoli: Gagosian Rome", in: *Artforum*, Heft 47, April 2009.

Er hat mich mit Honoré de Balzac verglichen, der ein großartiger Beobachter der Gesellschaft und Erzähler war.



politicians ... He replied saying he is more interested in those who are standing outside the house of Philip Green, the founder of the clothing chain Topshop, and protesting against him because he is not paying taxes in England. On the contrary, I am more curious to know how many of us will go to Topshop to buy yet another edition of clothing designed by Kate Moss. I want to understand what direction the world is moving in. I want to know which foundation or museum will be financed by Philip Green tomorrow, what kind of art he will fund and why. I try to foresee which scenarios will take place in the next ten years. In fact, I wanted to be a journalist as a child. And if I think of a review that I enjoyed the most, it was the one by Giorgio Verzotti in *Artforum*,

"Francesco Vezzoli: Gagosian Rome," in *Artforum* vol. 47, April 2009.

in which he compared me to Honoré de Balzac, a great observer and narrator of society. By the way, my mother recently said (with her eyes veiled by melancholy) that the world has become exactly the opposite of what she and her friends had dreamed of. Their values and their aesthetic parameters have been refuted. All of them. I was educated to think in a "politically correct" way and to have a true understanding of the rights of others, and yet today I find an exasperated and corrupt conservative party, a confused left wing party and a general political situation which is violent and contradictory ... I want my work to be a mirror of all of this.
Returning to Dalí, he was an artist who was ready in advance for the art industry; and after his appearance, the art-world evolved from

Mit Bezug auf unsere Gesellschaft, in der wir leben, meinte kürzlich meine Mutter mit melancholisch verklärten Augen, dass die Welt heute das exakte Gegenteil von dem geworden sei, wie sie und ihre Freunde sie sich einst erträumt hatten. All ihre Werte und ästhetischen Parameter wurden widerlegt. Ich, der ich zu politischer Korrektheit, einem gemäßigt linken Denken und einem Verständnis für die Rechte der anderen erzogen wurde, finde mich heute einer aufgebrachten und korrupten Rechten, einer orientierungslosen Linken und einer allgemein sehr gewalttätigen und widersprüchlichen politischen Situation gegenüber ... Mit meiner Arbeit versuche ich, all dies zu dokumentieren.
Dalí war ein Künstler, der damals schon bereit war für die Kunstindustrie, wobei sich die Kunst seiner Zeit sozusagen aus ihrer handwerklichen Nische auf ein industrielles Level hin entwickelte. Künstler wie Dalí bewiesen dabei Weitblick – im Guten wie im Bösen. Auch wenn man sie als Kritiker nicht als die allerbesten Künstler bezeichnen kann, so waren sie dennoch ohne Zweifel die scharfsinnigsten, zumal sie ihre Kunst in sehr professioneller Weise erst als Schöpfung der Kreativität und anschließend als Gestaltung eines Produkts konzipiert haben. In diesem Sinne setzten sie sich kreativ mit der öffentlichen Gestaltung der eigenen künstlerischen Identität auseinander. Abschließend möchte ich dazu sagen, dass es zu Zeiten von Dalí einen Teil der Kunstwelt gab, der bis heute besteht und einen intellektuell sehr kultivierten und zugleich kommunikativ schizophrenen Diskurs verfolgt, den ich mit Bewunderung und Respekt betrachte. Jedoch ist dieser Diskurs recht weit entfernt von der Wirklichkeit, die sich immer vielfältiger und komplexer gestaltet.

the level of handcraft and niche production to the level of industry. Artists as Dalí, for better or for worse, were much more far-sighted. A critic may claim they were not the best, but they were certainly the most insightful, because they had structured their art professionally as the creation of an identity, and subsequently as the construction of a product. In this sense, they were creatively directed by a very public management of their artistic identity. In the end, there is a part of the art world that existed already at the time of Dalí, which still exists and continues a discourse which is very intellectually refined, although schizophrenic towards the aspects of communication. I admire and respect them. But sometimes it is very far from representing a reality that is increasingly more diverse and complex.

Caroline Corbetta The problem is that, for many, the artist's role should be to move away or even to oppose the process of aesthetic and political restoration that is taking place in society. Instead, discussing of, and even exploiting, certain mechanisms as a mean of artistic strategy, as Dalí did and as you do too, is considered an act of complicity. As a matter of fact, you enjoy a bad reputation, not unlike that of Dalí. Because if it is true that on one hand you have the exhibitions in important museums and the support of well-known intellectuals, on the other, you suffer a violent ostracism by those who consider you an accomplice of the system, the prototype of the fame-hungry and over ambitious artist.

Francesco Vezzoli The concept of resistance is very clear to me and I highly respect those

**Caroline Corbetta** Es geht hier darum, dass für viele die Rolle des Künstlers in einer distanzierten, wenn nicht gar oppositionellen Haltung gegenüber Prozessen der ästhetischen und politischen Restauration bestehen müsste, von der die Gesellschaft gegenwärtig erfasst ist. Diese Mechanismen als Instrumente einer künstlerischen Strategie auszunutzen und darüber zu erzählen, wie ihr beide, Dalí und du, es gemacht habt, wird heute geradezu als ein Akt der Komplizenschaft betrachtet. Tatsächlich genießt du – ähnlich wie Dalí – einen schlechten Ruf: Einerseits hast du Ausstellungen in den wichtigen Museen und wirst von bekannten Intellektuellen unterstützt – andererseits jedoch erfährst du eine heftige Ablehnung von einigen, die dich als zweifelhaften Archetyp des Künstlers als Komplizen und Emporkömmling sehen.



**Francesco Vezzoli** Das Konzept des Widerstands ist mir sehr bewusst und ich respektiere absolut jene Künstler, die sich dafür entscheiden, bestimmte Erwartungen unserer Zeit zu ignorieren oder sich diesen sogar entgegenzusetzen. Dabei handelt es sich um eine intellektuell nicht angreifbare Position. Zugleich frage ich mich jedoch auch, welche Sichtbarkeit und damit soziale Relevanz ihre Sicht der Dinge haben kann. Im vergangenen Jahr nahm ich an einer Tagung in der Garage CCC in Moskau teil, wo ich mit unterschiedlichen Künstlern am Podium saß. Viele der Teilnehmer brachten eine ganze Reihe von allgemeinen Bedenken gegen das heutige Kunstsystem vor. Ich denke, heute macht es für die Künstler weniger Sinn als in der Vergangenheit, eine radikale Position zu äußern, gerade weil sie alle Teil des Systems

artists who choose to ignore or even oppose these aspects of our contemporary world. Their position is intellectually unassailable, but I also wonder what kind of visibility and therefore social impact their vision can have. Last year, I was at a conference at Moscow's Garage CCC and I was on stage with various artists and many of them were gasping out a whole series of vague protests against today's art system. I think that it makes less sense today than in the past for artists to express a radical position, because they are part of this system. Let me explain: an artist is a privileged person who is part of an industry of luxury – to use a provocative definition of the art system – which is supported by the brands that make our lives seem more luxurious. So I think the concept of resistance, which is not distant from my thinking, should be radically reconfigured. Many have seen, in my relation to celebrities, a metaphor of my complicity with the star-system. As I have said many times before, I have no friends among celebrities. Not because I do not like them, but because I feel a kind of admiration and a desire to keep their mystery at a distance. I should also reiterate that in my work I have never tried to deconstruct the Hollywood star-system, I do not have this ambition. I have only questioned the art system in contemporary society. And I have always and exclusively made art. I did not make the trailer for the fake remake of *Caligula* because I wanted to make a movie. I did not make *Greed*, the perfume that does not exist, because I wanted to shoot a commercial. I have always and exclusively done art that functions in dialogue with the art system in contemporary society. I wanted to create a kind of reflecting mirror, albeit

sind. Lass mich das genauer erklären: Ein Künstler ist eine privilegierte Person, die Teil einer Luxusindustrie ist – um eine provokante Definition des Kunstsystems zu verwenden –, die von den Marken gestützt wird, die unser Leben scheinbar luxuriöser gestalten. Daher glaube ich, dass das Konzept des Widerstands, das meinem Denken ganz und gar nicht fremd ist, radikal erneuert werden müsste. Viele haben in meiner Beziehung zu Berühmtheiten die Metapher für meine Komplizenschaft mit dem System gesehen, wobei sie betonten, dass ich – zumal ich das Starsystem in Frage stellte – dasselbe nicht mehr in meinen Arbeiten darstellen dürfte. Abgesehen davon habe ich, wie ich bereits mehrfach gesagt habe, keine Freunde unter den Stars. Nicht, weil sie mir nicht gefallen würden, sondern weil ich zwar eine Art von Bewunderung empfinde, zugleich aber das Bedürfnis nach Distanz ihrem Geheimnis gegenüber.
Zudem möchte ich betonen, dass ich in meinen Arbeiten nie versucht habe, das Starsystem Hollywoods zu dekonstruieren, dies ist nicht meine Absicht. Ich habe immer und ausschließlich vom System der Kunst in der zeitgenössischen Gesellschaft gesprochen. Und ich habe nie etwas anderes als Kunst gemacht. Der Trailer des fingierten Remakes von *Caligula* ist nicht entstanden, weil ich einen Film drehen wollte. Ich entwarf das nicht existierende Parfum *Greed* nicht deswegen, weil ich einen Werbespot drehen wollte. Ich habe ausschließlich Kunst gemacht, die im übertragenen Sinn davon spricht, wohin sich das System der Kunst heutzutage bewegt. Ich wollte dies reflektieren, einen – wenn auch etwas deformierten – Spiegel schaffen. Dennoch gibt es immer noch Leute, die lieber glauben, dass es mir an einer Kritik des

distorted. There are still those who prefer to think that I should make a critique of the celebrity system, while what I'm tackling are purely artistic issues. Rather than reclaim my integrity, I want to highlight the fact that mine is an artistic discourse. I put my *Caligula* alongside a *Homage to the Square by Joseph Albers*. It is, of course, clear that in my work there is a tendency towards redundancy, towards the kitsch, but I'm engaging in intellectual provocation, I am reflecting on the dominant imaginary proposed by the media, on the re-establishment of the aesthetic standards, while there's some kind of artistic culture denying or refusing to confront with this type of social transformation. In a Surrealist artistic identity such as Dalì's, the problem of the social role of the artist was already resolved. For example, he had transformed the artist's relationship with the media, into a big, artistic game.

**Caroline Corbetta** Speaking of the artist's relationship with the media, Dalí cleverly constructed his public persona and exploited it also outside the boundaries of art – as Andy Warhol would eventually do as well later on. Unlike those two, who made the most of their respective artistic persona and turned it into a marketable commodity outside of the golden fence of art, you act only within the art system, as you have reiterated earlier on. As a matter of fact, you have never made an advertisement or signed a piece of furniture or a bag ...

**Francesco Vezzoli** It's my act of resistance. In fact, today's art world offers such broad interactive possibilities that artists do not need to

Starsystems gelegen ist, während es mir doch vielmehr um einen exklusiv künstlerischen Diskurs geht. Dabei möchte ich weniger meine Integrität betonen, als vielmehr die Tatsache aufzeigen, dass es sich hier um einen künstlerischen Diskurs handelt. Ich stelle meinen *Caligula* neben eine *Homage to the Square by Joseph Albers* von Joseph Albers. Dahinter steht dieselbe Art der Überlegung.
Außerdem ist offensichtlich, dass sich meine Arbeit durch eine Vorliebe für das Überflüssige und den Kitsch auszeichnet, dennoch geht es mir auch um eine intellektuelle Provokation. Ich reflektiere über die dominierenden Vorstellungswelten, die uns die Medien präsentieren, über die Restauration des Geschmacks und der vorherrschenden Themen, während ein großer Teil der künstlerischen Kultur diese soziale Transformation ignoriert oder sich erst gar nicht damit auseinandersetzt. In einer surrealistischen Identität wie jener von Dalí schien die Problematik der sozialen Rolle des Künstlers bereits gelöst. Er gestaltete seine Beziehung zu den Medien als großes künstlerisches Spiel.



**Caroline Corbetta** Das mediale Bild seiner Person in der Öffentlichkeit hatte Dalí sorgfältig konstruiert und profitierte davon auch außerhalb der Grenzen des Kunstbetriebs. So wie es in der Folge auch Warhol tat, der von Dalí diesbezüglich einiges gelernt hatte. Im Gegensatz zu diesen beiden, die ihre eigene künstlerische *Persona* maximal ausnutzten, bis hin zu ihrer Transformation in ein handelbares Gut jenseits des goldenen Zauns der Kunst, agierst du ausschließlich innerhalb des künstlerischen Systems, wie du es eben selbst ausführlich geschildert hast. Niemals hast du eine Werbung oder ein Mobiltelefon oder eine Tasche gestaltet.

do as Dalí and Warhol did to be able to express themselves. At that time, the art system was not an industry, it was a highly limited and elitist context. But today it is a huge system – an artist is somehow forced into collaborations with museums, foundations, opera theatres, private and public companies ... You have to relate to different brands which have complex and totally distinct aesthetic as well as productive aims. And every time it's a very exciting challenge, in terms of roles and identity, but you can always preserve your external and privileged role as an artist.

**Caroline Corbetta** In your artistic trajectory, that consciously draws several points of reference from Dalí, a very important step was the exhibition at the Moderna Museet *Dalí Dalí featuring Francesco Vezzoli.*

*Dalí Dalí featuring Francesco Vezzoli* at Moderna Museet, Stockholm, 19 September 2009 – 17 January 2010, curated by John Peter Nilsson and Caroline Corbetta

Together, we designed your work as a theater, a two-dimensional stage space, crowded by your characters and self-portraits. A glittering and kitschy surface behind which was, unexpectedly, a dark room with some of your most important videos. All this was happening in front of some of Dalí's most important paintings, his experiments in fashion,advertising, design ... Even in Vienna, you are once again put in direct relation to his art: how did and how do you live out this confrontation?

**Francesco Vezzoli** Dies ist meine Art des Widerstands. Tatsächlich bietet die Welt der Kunst heutzutage dermaßen vielfältige interaktive Möglichkeiten, dass ein Künstler nicht mehr wie Dalí oder Warhol vorgehen muss, um sich entsprechend auszudrücken. Damals war das System der Kunst noch keine Industrie, sondern bewegte sich vielmehr in einem sehr beschränkten und elitären Kontext. Heute hingegen handelt es sich um ein gewaltiges System. Als zeitgenössischer Künstler ist man gewissermaßen zur Kooperation mit Museen, Stiftungen, Theatern und Unternehmen gezwungen. Ein Künstler muss sich heute mit verschiedensten Marken auseinandersetzen, mit komplexen und unterschiedlichen ästhetischen sowie produktiven Zielen. Und jedes Mal handelt es sich um eine sehr stimulierende Herausforderung für verschiedene Rollen und Identitäten, als Künstler jedoch bewahrt man stets seine privilegierte Rolle als einer, der von außen kommt.

**Caroline Corbetta** In deinem Werdegang als Künstler, in dem du bewusst bestimmte Anregungen etwa von Dalí erhalten hast, war die Ausstellung im Moderna Museet *Dalí Dalí featuring Francesco Vezzoli* eine sehr wichtige Etappe.

*Dalí Dalí featuring Francesco Vezzoli*, Moderna Museet, Stockholm, vom 19. September 2009 bis 17. Januar 2010, kuratiert von John Peter Nilsson und Caroline Corbetta.

Dort haben wir gemeinsam deinen Beitrag als ein Theater, als einen zweidimensionalen szenischen Raum konzipiert, der angefüllt war mit deinen Figuren und Selbstporträts. Eine glitzernde und kitschige Oberfläche,

**Francesco Vezzoli** For me to be compared with the work of Dalí is very complex and painful: I live it with extreme distress and with a sense of inferiority because he had such impressive painting skills. In Vienna, I am somehow relieved because I am surrounded by jewelry designed by him... So I thought to exhibit my *Surrealiz* series, composed by three embroidered portraits of Elizabeth Taylor. By the way, she loved jewelry! Even if I am allowed to believe that I have some clarity and courage in my analysis of certain social mechanisms inrelation to the art system, then – in front of Dalì's skills – I am literally sick with envy. He was a great painter. And maybe he would have been glad to know that we are finishing this interview on that note.

Caroline Corbetta spoke with Francesco Vezzoli in May 2011.

hinter der sich überraschenderweise ein Dark Room befand, in dem einige deiner wichtigsten Videos liefen. All dies passierte neben den bedeutendsten malerischen Werken Dalís, als auch seinen Experimenten im Bereich der Mode, der Werbung, des Designs ... Auch in Wien befindest du dich mit deinen Arbeiten einmal mehr in einer direkten Beziehung zur Kunst Dalís.
Wie erlebst du diese Gegenüberstellung?

**Francesco Vezzoli** Ich empfinde diese Gegenüberstellung mit den Werken Dalís auf einem physischem Level als sehr komplex und schmerzhaft: Sie bereitet mir große Qualen und gibt mir ein Gefühl der Minderwertigkeit, angesichts der beeindruckenden malerischen Fähigkeiten Dalís. In Wien fällt es mir ein wenig leichter, denn hier bin ich umgeben von Schmuckstücken, die er gestaltet hat. Diesen wollte ich meine gestickten Porträts aus der Serie *Surrealiz* gegenüberstellen.
Liz Taylor liebte Schmuck übrigens sehr! Wenn ich glauben darf, einen gewissen Scharfblick und Mut bei der Analyse und dem Miteinander-in-Beziehung-Setzen einiger sozialer Mechanismen und der Funktionsweise des Systems der Kunst bewiesen zu haben, so sterbe ich sprichwörtlich vor Neid. Dalí war ein großartiger Maler! Und vielleicht hätte es ihn gefreut zu hören, dass dieses Interview so endet.

Das Gespräch führte Caroline Corbetta mit Francesco Vezzoli im Mai 2011.

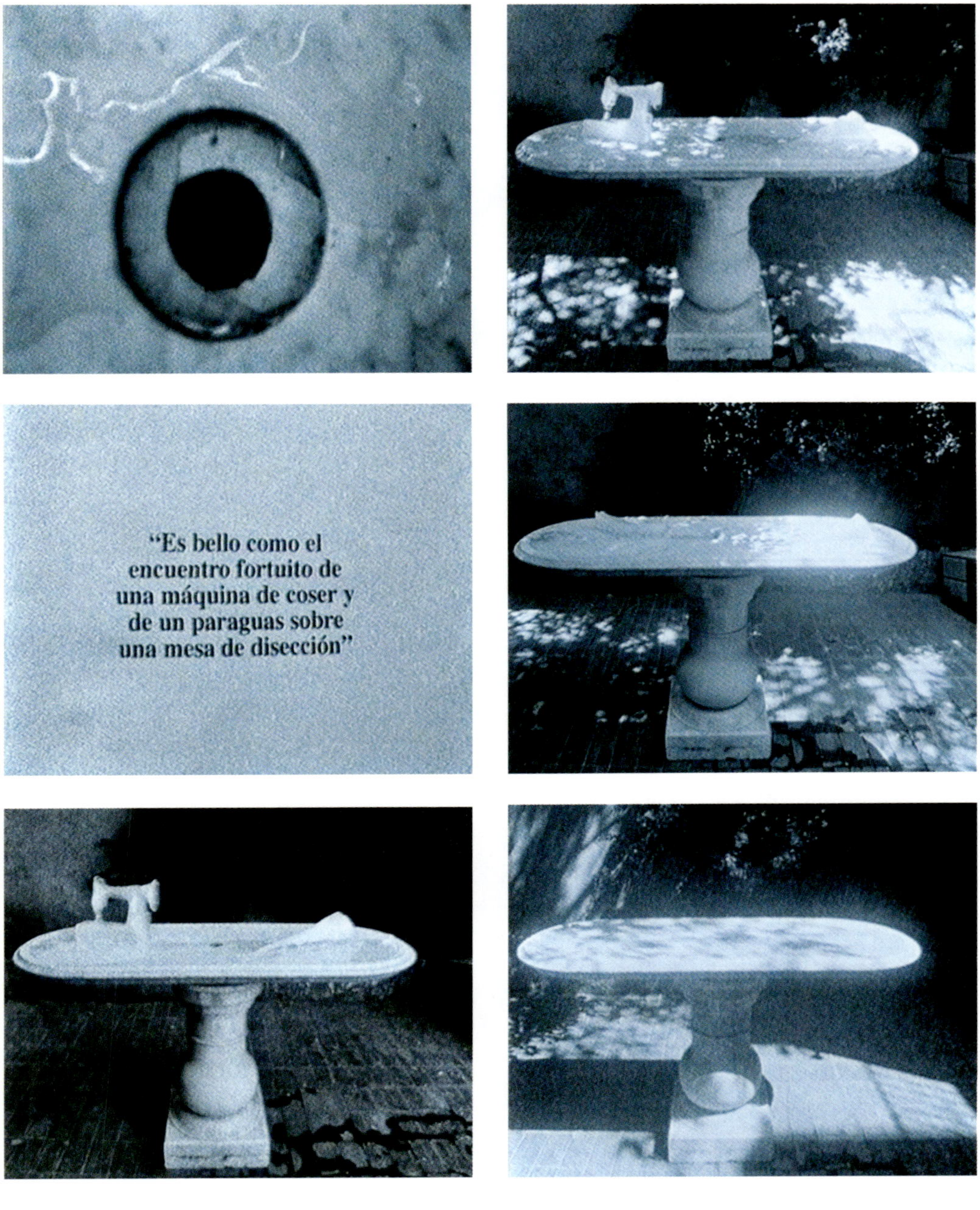


Jean-Michel Othoniel,
*Es bello como el encuentro fortuito entre un paraguas y una máquina de coser*, 1993

# Synne Genzmer
# Hommage

„Durch einen eindeutig paranoischen Vorgang ist es möglich geworden, ein doppeltes Vorstellungsbild zu erhalten: das heißt die Darstellung eines Gegenstandes, die ohne die mindeste figürliche oder anatomische Veränderung gleichzeitig die Darstellung eines anderen, völlig verschiedenen Gegenstandes ist, auch sie frei von jeder irgendwie gearteten Verzerrung oder Anomalität, die auf Arrangement schließen ließe." Ein Augapfel – oder ein Abfluss? Tränenflüssigkeit, die den Blick verschleiert. Wie langsam in den kreisförmigen Ausguss rinnendes Wasser. „Ich suchte eine Seele, die mir ähnlich wäre und konnte sie nicht finden. Ich durchsuchte die verborgensten Winkel der Erde; meine Ausdauer war vergeblich. Allein konnte ich jedoch nicht bleiben. Ich brauchte jemanden, der meinen Charakter bejahte; ich brauchte jemanden, der ebenso dachte wie ich. Es war am Morgen; die Sonne erhob sich in ihrer ganzen Herrlichkeit am Horizont, da erhob sich auch vor meinen Augen ein Jüngling, unter dessen Schritten Blumen hervorsprossen." Ein weißer Marmortisch, vielleicht in einem Hinterhof. Sonnenstrahlen, die durch das Blattwerk fallen. Schattenspiele. Auf der weißen Tischplatte ein weißer Regenschirm und eine weiße Nähmaschine. Glatt. Ohne Strukturen. Wachs. Oder Eis. „Er ist sechzehn Jahre und vier Monate alt. Er ist so schön wie die Einziehbarkeit der Raubvogelkrallen; oder auch wie die Unschlüssigkeit der Muskelbewegungen in den Wunden der Weichteile der hinteren Genicksgegend; oder vielmehr wie jene perpetuelle Rattenfalle, die von dem gefangenen Tier selbst immer von neuem gespannt, allein und unaufhörlich Nagetiere fangen kann und die sogar unter Stroh versteckt arbeitet; und vor allem wie die unvermutete Begegnung



# Synne Genzmer
# Homage

"It is a clearly paranoid process that has made it possible to achieve a double image -that is, a representation of an object which becomes, without the slightest figurative or anatomical modification, the representation of another, absolutely different object, it too devoid of any distortion or abnormality that could indicate some sort of manipulation." An eyeball – or a drain? Tears that obscure the view. Like water, running slowly into a circular sink. "I sought a soul that might resemble mine and I could not find it. I rummaged in all the corners of the earth: my perseverance was useless. Yet I could not remain alone. There must be someone who approved of my character; there must be someone who had the same ideas as myself. It was morning. The sun rose in its magnificence at the horizon and behold! A young man also appeared, at whose presence flowers sprang up in his path." A white marble table, perhaps in a backyard. Sunlight falling through the foliage. Shadow. On the white table top, a white umbrella and a white sewing machine. Smooth. Without structures. Wax. Or ice. "He is sixteen years and four months old! He is as handsome as the retractability of the claws of birds of prey; or again, as the uncertainty of the muscular movements of wounds in the soft parts of the posterior cervical region; or rather as the perpetual rat trap, re-set each time by the trapped animal, that can catch rodents indefinitely and works even when hidden beneath straw; and especially as the fortuitous encounter upon a dissecting table of a sewing-machine and an umbrella!" Water runs through a hole in the middle of the stone table, is making its way along the joints of the paved floor, seeps into the cracks of the earth. Melt in the sun. To become water.

einer Nähmaschine und eines Regenschirms auf einem Seziertisch!“ Wasser läuft durch eine Öffnung in der Mitte des steinernen Tisches, bahnt sich seinen Weg entlang der Fugen des gepflasterten Bodens, versickert in den Ritzen der Erde. In der Sonne schmelzen. Zu Wasser werden. Formlos. „Es ist halb neun, und er hofft, um neun Uhr zu Hause zu sein; es ist sehr anmaßend von ihm, so zu tun, als wäre er sicher, die Zukunft zu kennen. Könnte nicht irgendein unvorhergesehenes Hindernis sich ihm in den Weg stellen? Und wäre ein solcher Umstand so selten, daß er es verantworten könnte, ihn als Ausnahme gelten zu lassen? Warum betrachtet er es nicht vielmehr als eine anormale Tatsache, daß es ihm jetzt möglich war, sich frei von Unruhe und sozusagen glücklich zu fühlen? Tatsächlich, mit welchem Recht könnte er behaupten, seine Wohnung ohne Schaden zu erreichen, wenn jemand ihn belauert und ihm von hinten folgt, als wäre er seine künftige Beute?“ Senkrecht durchschneidet die Nadel der Nähmaschine das Bild des Auges. Ein Auge sieht uns an. Unverletzt. Ein Regenschirm hängt an einem Band herab, an der Wand sein Schatten, gegenüber wie auf einem Kleiderhaken ein Skelett. Beckenknochen Rippenbögen. Elegant geschwungen. Fleischlos. Leblos. „Warum dreht er sich nicht um? Er würde alles begreifen. Denkt man je an die einfachsten Mittel, einem beunruhigenden Zustand ein Ende zu setzen? Wenn ein Landstreicher, der jenseits der Stadtgrenze durch einen Vorort zieht, eine Salatschüssel voll Weißwein in der Kehle, und das Wams in Fetzen, an einem Grenzstein einen alten muskulösen Kater sitzen sieht, Zeitgenossen der Revolution, denen unsere Väter beigewohnt

Formless. “It is half past eight and he hopes to arrive home by nine o’clock. It is a great presumption on his part to claim to be certain of knowing the future. Could not some unforeseen obstacle impede his progress? And would that circumstance occur so infrequently that he should take it upon himself to consider it an exception? Should he not rather consider it abnormal that he has had reason hitherto to feel devoid of anxiety and, so to speak, happy? By what right indeed does he assume that he will reach home sage and sound, when behind him someone watches and follows him as future prey?” Vertical cuts the needle of the sewing machine through the image of the eye. An eye looks at us. Uninjured. An umbrella is hanging down by a strip, his shadow on the wall, on the other side, a skeleton, like on a coat hanger. Pelvic bones. Ribs. Elegantly curved. Meatless. Lifeless. “Why does he not turn around? He would understand everything. Does one never think of the simplest means of putting an end to a state of alarm? When a prowler crosses an alley in the slums with a bottle of white wine in his belly and his shirt in tatters; if in a corner he spies an old sinewy cat, contemporary to the revolutions in which our fathers took part, contemplating in melancholy the moonbeams pouring down upon the slumbering plain; he approaches tortuously in a curved line and signals to a bow-legged dog, which leaps forward. The noble animal of the feline race awaits her adversary with courage and sells her life dearly. Why did she not run away? It would have been so easy.” An unexpected encounter. Who meets whom? Who sees? The iron ring of the running knot, gleaming in the sunlight, itself helps to complete the illusion. In the course of his parabola, the condemned haben, der melancholisch die Mondstrahlen, die auf die schlafende Ebene fallen, betrachtet, dann schlängelt er sich in ungerader Linie heran und macht einem krummbeinigen Hund ein Zeichen, der sofort herbeistürzt. Das edle Tier aus dem Katzengeschlecht erwartet mutig seinen Gegner und ringt teuer um sein Leben. Warum ergriff er denn nicht die Flucht? Es wäre so leicht gewesen.“ Eine unvermutete Begegnung. Wer begegnet wem? Wer sieht? „Der eiserne Ring der Schlinge, der in den Strahlen der Sonne blinkt, verpflichtet dazu, das Trugbild selbst zu vervollständigen. In der Beschreibung seiner Parabel durchschneidet der zum Tode Verurteilte die Atmosphäre bis zum linken Ufer, geht dank der Stoßkraft, die ich für unendlich halte, darüber hinaus, und sein Körper schlägt gegen die Kuppel des Panthéon, während das Seil mit seinen Windungen teilweise die obere Decke der ungeheuren Wölbung umschlingt. Auf seiner kugelförmigen und konvexen Oberfläche, die nur in der Form an eine Orange erinnert, sieht man zu jeder Stund des Tages ein verdorrtes Skelett, das dort hängengeblieben ist.“ Ein Stillleben. Bei Salvador Dalí die mit Tusche gezeichneten Gegenstände der berühmtesten Metapher des Surrealismus. Disparat auf derselben Realitätsebene, montiert (*Homenaje a Lautréamont*, ca. 1945, Abb. S. 13). Bei Jean-Michel Othoniel ein Ensemble, das vor dem Kameraauge seinen Zustand verändert, sich verflüssigt, verschwindet (*Es bello como el encuentro fortuito entre un paraguas y una máquina de coser*, 1993, Abb. S. 287) Den Jüngling sehen wir nicht. Nur ein Gerippe. Nur ein Fluides. Ein codiertes Bild. Wo ist das Subjekt? Wer ist das Subjekt? Berichten seines Verlegers zufolge dichtete Isidore Lucien Ducasse sein schwarzromantisches Inferno nachts am Klavier,



youth cleaves the atmosphere right to the left bank, passes it by virtue of the driving force which I suppose to be infinite, and his body hits the dome of the Pantheon, while the rope partly coils around the upper wall of the immense cupola. There upon its spherical and convex surface area, which resembles an orange only in shape, a wasted skeleton may be seen at any hour of the day , stuck hanging.” A still life. With Salvador Dalí, the objects of the most famous metaphor of surrealism drawn with ink. Disparate yet on the same level of reality, mounted (*Homenaje a Lautréamont*, ca. 1945, ill. p. 13). With Jean-Michel Othoniel, an ensemble that changes its state before the camera eye, becomes liquid and disappears (*Es bello como el encuentro fortuito entre un paraguas y una máquina de coser*, 1993, ill. p. 287) The youth we do not see. Only a skeleton. Only a fluid. A coded image. Where is the subject? Who is the subject? According his publisher, Isidore Lucien Ducasse fabled his gothic-romantic inferno on a piano at night, “where he loudly declaimed, wildly stuck the keys, and, to these sounds, hammered out ever new verses.” He died on November 24th, 1870 in Paris at the age of 24 under mysterious, unexplained circumstances. His biography has remained enigmatic. Post mortem in 1874, *The Songs of Maldoror* was published under the pseudonym Comte de Lautréamont. In fact, Mervyn, Maldoror’s evil blasphemic Ego, has done nothing to the unknown young man. He was tempted. To incorporate the opponent by murder, to appropriate, to own. Shortly before his death, Ducasse wrote a preface to his *Songs of the Good*, the *Poésis* remained in fragments. “Death, you are not one of my personal acquaintances, but you’re my deepest ignorance, and the desire to know consumes me.”

„wo er laut deklamierte, wild in die Tasten schlug und zu den Klängen immer neue Verse heraus hämmerte." Er starb am 24. November 1870 in Paris im Alter von 24 Jahren unter mysteriösen, ungeklärten Umständen. Seine Biografie ist bis heute rätselhaft geblieben. Post mortem erschienen im Jahre 1874 *Die Gesänge des Maldoror* unter dem Pseudonym Comte de Lautréamont. Tatsächlich hat Mervyn, das böse blasphemische Ich des Maldoror, dem unbekannten Jüngling nichts getan. Er war in Versuchung. Sich das Gegenüber durch Morden einzuverleiben, anzueignen, zu besitzen. Kurz vor seinem Ableben hat Ducasse ein Vorwort zu seinen *Gesängen des Guten* verfasst, die *Poésies* blieben jedoch Fragment. „Tod, du gehörst nicht zu meinen persönlichen Bekanntschaften; du bist vielmehr meine tiefste Unbekanntschaft, und die Lust zu wissen verzehrt mich."


Zitate aus:

Salvador Dalí, „Der Eselskadaver", in: Ders., *Unabhängigkeitserklärung der Phantasie und Erklärung der Rechte des Menschen auf seine Verrücktheit. Gesammelte Schriften*, hg. von Axel Matthes und Tilbert Diego Stegman. München 1974.

Lautréamont, *Das Gesamtwerk*. Reinbek bei Hamburg 2009.

Salvador Dalí, in: „Der Ruhm", in: Ders., *Meine Leidenschaften*, aufgezeichnet von Louis Pauwels. München 1989.

Quotes from:

Salvador Dalí, "The Rotting Donkey" [1930], in *The Collected Writings of Salvador Dalí*, ed. Haim Finkelstein, Cambridge, 1998.

Comte de Lautréamont, *Les Chants de Maldoror*, New York, 1966.

*Salvador Dalí, "Der Ruhm" in Salvador Dalí, Meine Leidenschaften*, recorded by Louis Pauwels, Munich, 1989.

# Angst zersplittert einen Louise Bourgeois im Gespräch mit Gerald A. Matt

Gerald A. Matt Ihr Leben und Ihr Werk stehen seit Anbeginn Ihrer künstlerischen Praxis in einem sehr engen Verhältnis zueinander. Sie erweitern das Feld der Psychoanalyse, indem Sie der Konzentration auf das Wort die Bildlichkeit hinzufügen. Und Sie beschreiten im Bereich der Kunst ein Feld, das zur Sinnerschließung auf die Autobiografie und hermeneutische Modelle wie die Psychoanalyse zurückgreift. Leben und Kunst werden enggeführt. Inwieweit kann, darf oder gar muss Kunst authentischer Ausdruck der seelischen Befindlichkeit sein?

Louis Bourgeois Ich interessiere mich ausschließlich für Form. Bewusst oder unbewusst – es besteht eine Verbindung zwischen dem Erfinden der Form und meiner spezifischen Pathologie.

Gerald A. Matt Es werden die Medien Zeichnung und Skulptur gegenübergestellt. Die Zeichnungen stehen in ihrer Flüchtigkeit und Leichtigkeit der Körperlichkeit und Präsenz der skulpturalen Arbeiten diametral entgegen. In welchem Verhältnis stehen in Ihrem Œuvre Zeichnung und Skulptur? Sind beide Medien als gleichwertig zu betrachten?

Louis Bourgeois Ich gebe weder einem bestimmten Medium noch einer bestimmten Technik den Vorzug. Jedes Material bietet gewisse Möglichkeiten, und ich will alle Möglichkeiten ausloten. Ich habe es mit einem Gefühl zu tun, dem ich Form geben will. Skulpturen erlauben mir ein Verhältnis zu meinem Körper, das mir das Zeichnen nicht gestattet. Ich brauche Distanz. Ich muss im wirklichen Raum agieren können. In diesem Sinn sind die Zeichnungen eher geistige Notate als körperliche, eher Denken



# Fear fragments you Louise Bourgeois in Conversation with Gerald A. Matt

Gerald A. Matt Your life and your work have, from the very outset of your career as an artist, stood in a very close relationship to one another. You have extended the field of psychoanalysis by adding to its concentration on words a pictorial dimension. And you describe within the sphere of art an area which, to reveal its inner meaning, requires one to take recourse to your autobiography and hermeneutic models like psychoanalysis. Life and art run in close parallelism. To what extent can or may or perhaps even must art be an authentic expression of ones psychological state of being?

Louis Bourgeois I am exclusively interested in form. Consciously or unconsciously, the invention of form connects to my pathology.

Gerald A. Matt The media of drawing and sculpture face each other, the drawings, with their lightness and swiftness on the one side, and the corporeality and heavy presence of the sculptures as diametrical opposites. What is the relationship between the drawings and the sculptures in your work? Are both media to be viewed as equivalents?

Louis Bourgeois I am not interested in privileging any particular medium or technique. Each material offers possibilities and I want to explore them all. I am dealing with an emotion that I want to give a form. Sculpture allows me a relationship to my body that drawing does not. I need distance. I need to act out in real space. In this sense, the drawings are somehow more mental notations than physical, more thinking than actually doing. More and more I am giving als tatsächliches Tun. Die Zeichnungen bekommen zusehends etwas Körperliches: Auf beiden Seiten zeichnen, die Oberfläche durchstoßen sowie Zeichnungen aus Stoff machen und nähen, das gibt der zweidimensionalen Oberfläche Körper.

**Gerald A. Matt** Susan Sontag hat einmal den Künstler „als exemplarisch Leidenden" beschrieben. Ihr Beitrag der *Sainte Sébastienne* übersetzt die männlich androgyne Figur des heiligen Sebastian in eine weibliche und unterstreicht damit noch einmal mehr den geschlechtlich indifferenten Charakter der Figur. Identifizieren Sie sich selbst als „Sainte Sébastienne"?

**Louis Bourgeois** Ich habe nicht das Gefühl, dass die Leute gegen mich sind. Ich übernehme für meine Probleme die Verantwortung. Was bringt es, anderen die Schuld zu geben? Meine Qual liegt darin, eine Situation oder ein Problem nicht zu begreifen. Nicht verführen zu können. Es nicht zu schaffen, dass ich geliebt werde. Ich gebe nicht auf. Vielleicht wissen Sie das nicht, aber die Heftigkeit in meiner Arbeit rührt daher, dass ich immer etwas besser zu machen versuche. Ich bin ein optimistischer Mensch.

**Gerald A. Matt** Viele der in der Ausstellung *Aller-Retour* gezeigten Arbeiten sind Kombinationen von Bild und Text. Ihr Spätwerk hat in seiner Skizzenhaftigkeit Ähnlichkeit mit einem Tagebuch. Sie geben dem Tagebuch den Rang eines eigenständigen künstlerischen Mediums, das in seiner Unmittelbarkeit und seinem direkten Ausdruck als konsequente Fortführung Ihres bisherigen Œuvres steht. Wie sehen Sie Ihre Rolle als Künstlerin?

the drawings a physicality. Drawing on both sides, piercing the surface, and constructing drawings out of fabric and sewing gives a physicality to the two dimensional surface.

**Gerald A. Matt** Susan Sontag once described the artist as an "exemplary sufferer." Your contribution, entitled *Sainte Sébastienne* cast the male/androgynous figure of the saint into female shape, thus underscoring even more the character's indifference to gender differences. Do you yourself identify with "Sainte Sébastienne"?

**Louis Bourgeois** I don't feel people are against me. I take responsibility for my problems. What is the use of blaming others? My inability to understand the situation or the problem is my torment. It's my inability to seduce. It's my inability to make myself loved. I don't give up. You might not know it but the ferociousness in the work is my attempt to try and try again to make things better. I am an optimistic person.

**Gerald A. Matt** Many of the works exhibited in the exhibition *Aller-Retour* are works in a combination of images and texts. Your latter work, in its sketchiness, invites comparisons with a diary. You bestow upon the diary a rank as being artistic medium in its own right. One that in its immediateness and its direct expression stands as a logical continuation of your oeuvre so far. How do you see your own role as an artist?

**Louis Bourgeois** The artist has access to his unconscious and the gift of sublimation. This process and connection is complicated electronics. I am almost passive in this creative process. It's a mystery, but if there is magic

**Louis Bourgeois** Künstler haben Zugang zu ihrem Unbewussten und die Gabe der Sublimierung. Die Elektronik dieses Prozesses und dieser Verbindung ist kompliziert. Ich bin bei diesem kreativen Prozess beinahe passiv. Es ist mir ein Rätsel, aber wenn die Produktion etwas Magisches hat, gilt das auch für das Betrachten. Meine Erinnerungen sind, wie ich immer gesagt habe, Dokumente, aber man muss, wenn es um Kunst geht, vorsichtig sein und unterscheiden, was ich als Produzentin von Kunst sage. Das Einzige, was zählt, ist die Form, nicht meine Biografie. Die Form muss überzeugend sein. Wenn nun ein Betrachter nicht überzeugt ist oder keinen Bezug zu der Arbeit herstellen kann, ist das nicht mein Problem. Kommunikation interessiert mich nicht. Mir geht es darum, mich auszudrücken. Ich bin niemandem etwas schuldig.



**Gerald A. Matt** Was würden Sie noch gerne machen?

**Louis Bourgeois** Ich hatte immer Angst, ausgeschlossen und allein gelassen zu werden. Durch das Nähen versuche ich, die Dinge zusammenzuhalten oder wieder ganz zu machen. Angst zersplittert einen. Das Gegenmittel heißt Vertrauen. Je mehr man weiß, desto mehr vertraut man. Ich möchte mit mir und allen anderen Frieden schließen. Meinem Gefühl nach habe ich das noch immer nicht getan.

**Aus einem Gespräch zwischen Louise Bourgeois und Gerald A. Matt anlässlich der Ausstellung *Louise Bourgeois. Aller-Retour* der Kunsthalle Wien 2005.**

in the making, there is magic in the viewing. As I always stated, my memories are my documents, but you have to be careful when talking about art and differentiate what I say as the maker. The only thing that counts is the form, not my biography. The form must be convincing. Now, if the viewer is not convinced or does not connect to the work, it's not my problem. I am not interested in communication. I am interested in self expression. I don't owe anything to anybody.

**Gerald A. Matt** And finally, what would you like yet to accomplish?

**Louis Bourgeois** I have always had the fear of being separated and abandoned. The sewing is my attempt to keep things together and make things whole. Fear fragments you. Trust is the remedy. The more you know, the more you trust. I want to make peace with myself and with everyone else. I still feel I am trying to get there.

**From a conversation between Louise Bourgeois and Gerald A. Matt on the occasion of the exhibition *Louise Bourgeois. Aller-Retour* at Kunsthalle Wien in 2005.**

**Biografien/Biographies**

**Salvador Dalí**

1904
Salvador Felipe Jacinto Dalí Domènech wird am 11. Mai als zweites Kind von Salvador Dalí Cusi und Felipa Domènech Ferrés in Figueres, Katalonien, geboren. Er erhält den Namen seines neun Monate zuvor verstorbenen Bruders Salvador I./Salvador Felipe Jacinto Dalí Domènech is born on May 11th as the second child of Salvador Dalí Cusi and Felipa Domènech Ferrés in Figueres, Catalonia. He is named after his brother Salvador I., who passes away nine months before his birth.

1922
Dalí zieht nach Madrid und lernt dort Federico García Lorca kennen, mit dem er zeitweise das Zimmer teilt und eine enge Freundschaft aufbaut. Einer sexuellen Beziehung entzieht Dalí sich jedoch. Dalí besucht die Real Academia de Bellas Artes de San Fernando, wo er die altmeisterlichen Techniken erlernt. Im Oktober 1926 wird er der Akademie verwiesen, weil er die Abschlussprüfung verweigert. In dieser Zeit beginnt Dalí, sich intensiv mit den psychoanalytischen Schriften Sigmund Freuds zu beschäftigen./Dalí moves to Madrid and becomes acquainted with Federico García Lorca, with whom he sometimes shares a room and builds up a close friendship; however, Dalí turns down a sexual connection with Lorca. Dalí attends the Real Academia de Bellas Artes de San Fernando, where he learns the techniques of the masters. He is expelled from the academy in October 1926 when he refuses to take the final examination. At this time, Dalí starts to occupy himself intensively with the psychoanalytical writings of Sigmund Freud.

1929
Luis Buñuel und Dalí arbeiten gemeinsam an dem Film *Un chien andalou* (Der andalusische Hund), der im selben Jahr in Paris uraufgeführt wird und als Meisterwerk des surrealistischen Films gilt. Über Joan Miró macht Dalí in Paris die Bekanntschaft der Gruppe der Surrealisten und verbringt den Sommer u. a. mit René Magritte, Paul Éluard und dessen Frau Helena, genannt Gala, im katalonischen Cadaqués. Dalí verliebt sich in die zehn Jahre ältere, aus Russland emigrierte Gala Dalí's Worte auf einer Zeichnung „Manchmal spucke ich mit Vergnügen auf das Porträt meiner Mutter“ führen zum Bruch zwischen Dalí und seinem Vater./Luis Buñuel and Dalí work together on the film *Un chien andalou* (An Andalusian Dog), which premiers in Paris the same year and is regarded as a masterpiece of surrealistic film. Through Joan Miró, Dalí makes the acquaintance of a group of Surrealists in Paris and spends the summer with, amongst others, René Magritte, Paul Éluard and his wife Helena, better known as Gala in the Catalonian Cadaqués. Dalí falls in love with the ten-years-older Gala, who emigrated from Russia. Dalí's words on a drawing, "Sometimes I spit with pleasure on the portrait of my mother," lead to the break between Dalí and his father.

1930
In der Zeitschrift *Le Surrealisme au service de la Revolution* erscheint der Aufsatz „L'Âne pourri“ (Der Eselskadaver). Darin legt Dalí seine auf Doppelbildern basierende paranoisch-kritische Methode dar und bringt Surrealismus und Wahnsinn in einen produktiven Zusammenhang. Dalí und Gala kaufen ein kleines Fischerhaus in Port Lligat, wo sie fortan viel Zeit verbringen. Gala ist nicht nur Dalís Muse, sondern auch seine Managerin, die Ausstellungen organisiert und für den Verkauf seiner Objekte sorgt./Dalí publishes the essay "L'Âne pourri" (The Rotten Donkey) in the magazine *Le Surrealisme au service de la Revolution.* Dalí writes about his paranoïac-critical method, based on double images, and makes a productive connection between surrealism and insanity. Dalí and Gala buy a little fisherman's house in Port Lligat where they spend a lot of their time. Gala not only becomes Dalí's muse but also his manager, organizing exhibitions and taking care of sales.

1932

In der Julien Levy Gallery in New York wird u. a. das Gemälde *La persistencia de la memoria* (Die Beständigkeit der Erinnerung) ausgestellt, das die ersten schmelzenden Uhren zeigt und Dalís Bekanntheit in Amerika begründet./ Julien Levy Gallery presents, amongst others, the painting *La persistencia de la memoria* (The persistance of memory), which features Dalí's first melting watches and establishes his fame in America.

1934

Dalí und Gala heiraten. Seine enge Verbundenheit demonstriert Dalí, indem er eine Zeit lang seine Werke mit „Gala-Dalí" signiert./Dalí stellt die umfangreichen Illustrationen zum Kultbuch der Surrealisten, Lautréamonts *Gesänge des Maldoror* fertig, die als seine wichtigste grafische Arbeit gelten. Dalí and Gala get married. Dalí shows his close attachment to his wife by signing his works with "Gala-Dalí"" for a while. Dalí finishes his extensive illustrations for the Surrealist cult book, Lautréamont's *Chants des Maldoror*, which are considered his most important graphical works.

1936

Im Rahmen der *International Surrealist Exhibition* in London hält Dalí eine Lesung im Taucheranzug, um den Eintritt seines Werks in die Tiefen des Unterbewusstseins zu veranschaulichen. Dalí erscheint in einer Fotografie von Man Ray auf dem Cover des *Time Magazine*, was als der Beginn seiner internationalen Kariere als Künstlerstar gewertet wird./As part of the *International Surrealist Exhibition* in London, Dalí holds a reading in a diving suit in order to illustrate the entry of his work into the depths of the subconscious. Dalí appears in a photograph by Man Ray on the cover of *Time Magazine*, considered to signal the beginning of his international career as a star-artist.



1938

Die *Exposition Internationale du Surréalisme* in Paris zeigt Dalís legendäres *Taxi pluvieux* (Regentaxi), ein efeuumranktes, von innen mit Wasser berieseltes Automobil mit einer weiblichen Schaufensterpuppe in Abendrobe und einer Nähmaschine auf dem Rücksitz. Dalí besucht Sigmund Freud in London, der durch die Begegnung mit „dem jungen Spanier mit den treuherzig-fanatischen Augen" seine Geringschätzung des Surrealismus revidiert./The *Exposition Internationale du Surrealism* in Paris features Dalí's legendary *Taxi pluvieux* (Rainy Taxi), an ivy-covered car sprinkled in water from the inside, holding, in the back seat, a sewing machine and a female mannequin in an evening dress. Dalí visits Sigmund Freud in London, who, after encountering "the young Spaniard with the candid, fanatical eyes" revises his contempt of Surrealism.

1939

Für die New Yorker Weltausstellung entwirft Dalí den *Dream of Venus*-Pavillon. Auf das Verbot des Komitees, eine Reproduktion von Botticelli's *Geburt der Venus* mit Fischkopf an der Außenfassade anzubringen, reagiert er mit der Veröffentlichung der *Unabhängigkeitserklärung der Phantasie und Erklärung der Rechte des Menschen auf seine Verrücktheit*. Es kommt zum endgültigen Bruch mit der Gruppe der Surrealisten. André Breton wirft Dalí Geldgier, Erfolgssucht, Faschismus und Rückwärtsgewandtheit vor und erfindet das Anagramm „Avida Dollars", das soviel wie „Gier nach Dollars" bedeutet. Dalí widmet sich in den folgenden Jahren zunehmend auch dem Schmuck-, Werbe- und Bühnenbilddesign./For the New York World Fair, Dalí designs the *Dream of Venus* pavilion. In reaction to the committee's ban of his reproduction of Botticelli's *Birth of Venus*, with a fish head on its façade, he responds with the publication of the *Declaration of the Independence of the Imagination and of the Rights of Man to His Own Madness*. It marks his final break with the Surrealist group. André Breton accuses Dalí of mammonism, success addiction, fascism and backwardness, and invents the anagram "Avida Dollars," meaning "greed for dollars." Dalí increasingly devotes himself to jewelry, advertising and stage design in the following years.

1940
Aufgrund der Besetzung Frankreichs durch deutsche Truppen reisen Dalí und Gala in die USA, wo sie bis 1948 im Exil leben./Due to the occupation of France by German troops, Dalí and Gala travel to the U.S., where they live in exile until 1948.

1942
In New York erscheint Dalís halbfiktive Autobiografie *The Secret Life of Salvador Dalí*, die mit dem Satz beginnt: „Im Alter von sechs Jahren wollte ich Koch werden. Mit sieben wollte ich Napoleon sein. Und mein Ehrgeiz ist seither stetig gewachsen."/ Dalì s semi-fictional autobiography *The Secret Life of Salvador* appears in New York, beginning with the sentence: "At the age of six I wanted to become a cook. At seven I wanted to be Napoleon. And my ambition has grown steadily since then."

1945
Auf Einladung von Alfred Hitchcock arbeitet Dalí am Film *Spellbound* (Ich kämpfe um dich) mit, einer der ersten Hollywood-Produktionen, die sich mit Freuds Psychoanalyse beschäftigt./At the invitation of Alfred Hitchcock, Dalí works on the film *Spellbound*, one of the first Hollywood productions dealing with Freud's psychoanalysis.

1948
Dalí und Gala kehren nach Port Lligat zurück./Dalí and Gala return to Port Lligat.

1951
Dalí veröffentlicht das *Mystische Manifest*, das den Beginn seiner korpuskularen Periode markiert. Unter dem Eindruck der Atomphysik stellte er in dieser Zeit Bildelemente in dreidimensionalen Bruchstücken dar.
Dalí publishes the *Mystical Manifesto*, marking the beginning of his corpuscular period. Influenced by atomic physics, he begins representing elements in three-dimensional image fragments.



1955
Dalí hält einen Vortrag an der Sorbonne über *Die phänomenologischen Aspekte der paranoisch-kritischen Methode*. Seinen Auftritt inszeniert er medienwirksam, indem er in einem mit Blumenkohl gefüllten, weißen Rolls-Royce vorfährt./Dalí gives a lecture at the Sorbonne on *The Phenomenological Aspects of the Paranoïac-Critical Method*. His appearance is clearly staged for media coverage, as he drives up in a white Rolls-Royce filled with cauliflowers.

1964
Dalí wird mit der höchsten spanischen Ehrung, dem *Gran Cruz de Isabel la Católica*, ausgezeichnet.
Dalí is awarded the *Gran Cruz de Isabel la Católica*, the highest Spanish honor.

1965
Dalí besucht Andy Warhols Factory. Bei diesem Anlass entsteht ein *Screentest* von Dalí. Während Dalí und Gala sich zunehmend voneinander distanzieren, lernt Dalí die vermutlich transsexuelle Amanda Lear kennen, die seine neue Muse wird./Um 1965 beginnt Dalí damit, zehntausende Papierbogen blanko zu signieren, was 1981 zu einem internationalen Skandal führt. 40.000 gefälschte Druckgrafiken konnten bisher sichergestellt werden./
Dalí visits Andy Warhol's Factory. This results in a *Screentest* of Dalí. While Dalí and Gala increasingly distance themselves from each other, Dalí meets the presumable transsexual Amanda Lear, who becomes his new muse.
In 1965, Dalí begins to sign thousands of blank sheets of paper, leading to an international scandal in 1981. 40,000 fake prints have so far been secured.

1969
Dalí erwirbt ein Schloss in Púbol, das er Gala schenkt./Dalí buys a castle in Púbol as a present for Gala.

1974
Das Teatre-Museu Dalí, ein surreales Gesamtkunstwerk, wird in Figueres eröffnet. Es ist das größte surrealistische Objekt der Welt und nach dem Prado das am meisten besuchte Museum Spaniens./The Teatre-Museu Dalí, a surreal work of art, opens in Figueres. It is the largest surrealistic object in the world and, after the Prado, the most visited museum in Spain.

1982
In St. Petersburg, Florida, eröffnet das Salvador Dalí Museum. Am 10. Juni stirbt Gala. Ihr Grab befindet sich in der Krypta von Schloss Púbol. Spaniens König Juan Carlos I verleiht Dalí den Titel Marquis de Púbol./The Salvador Dalí Museum opens in St. Petersburg, Florida. On the $10^{th}$ of June, Gala dies. Her grave is located in the crypt of Castle Púbol. Dalí is given the title Marquis de Púbol by the Spanish King, Juan Carlos I.

1983
Dalí vollendet sein letztes Ölgemälde. In Madrid, Barcelona und Figueres findet die erste große Retrospektive seines Werkes in Spanien statt./Dalí completes his last oil painting. The first major retrospective of his work in Spain is shown in Madrid, Barcelona and Figueres.

1989
Dalí stirbt am 23. Januar an Herzversagen und wird unter der Kuppel des Teatre-Museu beigesetzt./
Dalí dies on the $23^{rd}$ January of heart failure and is buried under the dome of the Teatre-Museu.



**Louise Bourgeois**

| | |
|---|---|
| 1911 | geboren in Paris, gestorben 2010 in New York |
| 1932–1935 | Studium der Mathematik an der Sorbonne in Paris |
| 1936–1938 | Studium an der Ècole du Louvre, an der Académie de la Grande Chaumière, an der Académie d'Espagnat sowie an der Académie Julian in Paris |
| 1938–2010 | lebte und arbeitete in New York |

| | |
|---|---|
| 1911 | born in Paris, died 2010 in New York |
| 1932–1935 | Studies Mathematics at the Sorbonne, Paris |
| 1936–1938 | Studies at the Ècole du Louvre, at the Académie de la Grande Chaumière, at the Académie d'Espagnat and at the Académie Julian, Paris |
| 1938–2010 | lived and worked in New York |

Einzelausstellungen/Solo Exhibitions (Auswahl/Selection)

| | |
|---|---|
| 2011 | *Louise Bourgeois, El Retorno do lo Reprimido*, Fundación Proa, Buenos Aires |
| | *Louise Bourgeois,* National Gallery of Iceland, Reykjavik |
| | *Alex Van Gelder – Louise Bourgeois ARMED FORCES*, Hauser & Wirth, Zürich/Zurich |
| | *Louise Bourgeois: Mother and Child*, Kunstforeningen GL Strand, Kopenhagen/Copenhagen |
| 2010 | *Louise Bourgeois*. Museum of Cycladic Art, Athen/Athens |

*Louise Bourgeois: Les Fleurs*, Kukje Gallery, Seoul
*Louise Bourgeois: Moi*, Eugénie Grandet Maison de Balzac, Paris

2009 *Louise Bourgeois: Retrospective*, The Hirshhorn Museum, Washington DC

2008 *Louise Bourgeois*, Museo Nazionale di Capodimonte, Neapel/Naples
*La Rivière Gentille*, Hauser & Wirth, Zürich/Zurich
*Recent Drawings*, Inverleith House, Edinburgh
*Louise Bourgeois*, Solomon R. Guggenheim Museum, New York

2007 *Louise Bourgeois. Hours of the Day*, Carolina Nitsch Project Room, New York
*Bourgeois in Boston*, Institute of Contemporary Arts, Boston
*Louise Bourgeois: Quarantania 1947/1990*, Christine König Galerie, Wien/Vienna
*Louise Bourgeois: Crouching Spider*, Philadelphia Museum of Art, Philadelphia
*Louise Bourgeois: The Woven Child*, Worcester Art Museum, Worcester
*Fugue*, Kunstmuseum Bern, Bern

2006 *Louise Bourgeois – Scultura e Opere Grafiche*, Christine Bader, Lugano
*Louise Bourgeois – Estampes et porcelaines 1996–2005*, Galerie Lelong, Paris
*Louise Bourgeois. La famille*, Kunsthalle Bielefeld, Bielefeld

2005 *Louise Bourgeois. Aller-Retour*, Kunsthalle Wien, Wien/Vienna
*Louise Bourgeois. Works on Paper and Cloth*, Gallery Paule Anglim, San Francisco
*Louise Bourgeois. La Sage Femme*, Neue Galerie im Höhmannhaus, Augsburg

2004 *Louise Bourgeois – Prints*, Karsten Greve, Paris
*The Reticent Child*, Cheim & Read Gallery, New York
*Louise Bourgeois: Stitches in Time*, CAC – Centro de Arte Contemporàneo, Malaga

2003 *A View from the Outside, Louise Bourgeois. The Reticent Child*, Sigmund Freud Museum, Wien/Vienna
*Louise Bourgeois. The Early Work*, Aspen Art Museum, Aspen
*Louise Bourgeois. Intimate Abstractions*, Akademie der Künste, Berlin
*Louise Bourgeois*. Louisiana Museum for Moderne Kunst, Humlebaek, Dänemark/Denmark
*Spiders. Louise Bourgeois*, Shiraishi Contemporary Art, Tokyo
*Louise Bourgeois. The Insomnia Drawings*, The Whitney Museum of American Art, New York
*Louise Bourgeois*, White Cube Gallery, London

2002 *Louise Bourgeois*, Helsinki City Art Museum, Helsinki
*Louise Bourgeois. Le Jour La Nuit Le Jour (film and sound installation)*, Palais de Tokyo, Paris
*Louise Bourgeois*, Museet for Samtidskunst, Oslo
*Louise Bourgeois. Works in Marble*, Hauser & Wirth, Zürich/Zurich

2001 *Louise Bourgeois*, Solomon R. Guggenheim Museum Bilbao, Bilbao
*Louise Bourgeois. Reconstruction of the Past*, Akademie der bildenden Künste, Wien/Vienna
*Louise Bourgeois. Passage Dangereux*, Kunstraum Innsbruck, Innsbruck, Österreich/Austria

2000 *Louise Bourgeois (retrospective and installation)*, Tate Modern, London; Grafiska Sallskapet, Stockholm; Göteborg Museum of Art, Göteborg
*Installation of The Welcoming Hands by Louise Bourgeois*, Jardin des Tuileries, Paris

1999 *Louise Bourgeois. Prints 1989–1998*, Minneapolis Institute of Arts, Minneapolis
*Louise Bourgeois. Memoria y arquitectura*, Museo Nacional, Centro de Arte Reina Sofìa, Madrid
*Louise Bourgeois*, Ernst-Museum, Budapest

1998 *Louise Bourgeois. Recent Work*, Serpentine Gallery, London
*Louise Bourgeois: Topiary*, The Whitney Museum of American Art, New York

1997 *Louise Bourgeois: Blue Days and Pink Days*, Prada Foundation, Mailand/Milan
*Louise Bourgeois. Hamlet and Ophelia*, Brooklyn Academy of Music, Brooklyn; Robert Miller Gallery, New York

*Louise Bourgeois. Homesickness*, Yokohama Museum of Art, Yokohama
1996 *Red Room*, Hauser & Wirth, Zürich/Zurich
*Louise Bourgeois. Drawings*, University Art Museum, University of California, Berkeley; The Drawing Center, New York; The List Visual Art Center, Cambridge
*Louise Bourgeois. Der Ort des Gedächtnisses. Skulpturen, Environments und Zeichnungen. 1946–1995*, Deichtorhallen Hamburg, Hamburg
*Louise Bourgeois. Skulpturen und Objekte*, Rupertinum, Salzburg
*Louise Bourgeois*, Museo Rufina Tamayo, Mexico City, Mexico
*The Prints of Louise Bourgeois*, Bonnefanten Museum, Maastricht
1995 *Louise Bourgeois.* MARCO – Museo de Arte Contemporaneo, Monterrey
*Louise Bourgeois.* The Prints of Louise Bourgeois, Museum of Modern Art, Oxford
*20th Century Master Drawings*, Barbara Mathes Gallery, New York
*Louise Bourgeois*, Museum of Contemporary Art, Sydney
*The Locus of Memory*, Galeria Rudolfinum, Prag/Prague
*Louise Bourgeois. Pensées-Plumes*, Centre Georges Pompidou, Paris
*Louise Bourgeois. Sculptures, environnements, dessins. 1938–1995*, Musée d'Art moderne de la Ville de Paris, Paris
1994 *The Prints of Louise Bourgeois*, MoMA - Museum of Modern Art, New York
1993 *Louise Bourgeois. Personnages, 1940s, Installations, 1990s*, Laura Carpenter Fine Art, Santa Fe
1992 *Installation of recent acquisitions*, National Gallery of Art, Washington
*Louise Bourgeois. Drawings*, Second Floor, Reykjavik
*Currents 21: Louise Bourgeois*, Milwaukee Art Museum, Milwaukee
1991 *Louise Bourgeois. A Retrospective Exhibition*, Kunstmuseum Bern, Bern; Kröller-Müller Museum, Otterlo, Niederlande/Netherlands
1990 *Louise Bourgeois. 1939–89. Skulpturen und Zeichnungen*, Galerie Krinzinger, Wien/Vienna
1989 *Louise Bourgeois: Legs*, Ydessa Art Foundation, Toronto
*Louise Bourgeois. 100 Zeichnungen*, Galerie Lelong, Zürich/Zurich
*Louise Bourgeois. Works from the Sixties*, Dia Art Foundation, Bridgehampton, New York State
1988 *Louise Bourgeois. Works On Paper*, Museum Overholland, Amsterdam
1987 *Louise Bourgeois.* Everson Museum of Art, Syracuse, New York State
*Sculpture 1947–1955*, Gallery Paul Anglim, San Francisco
1986 *Louise Bourgeois. Sculptures and Drawings*, Texas Gallery, Houston
*Eyes*, The Doris Feldmann Plaza, New York
1985 *Louise Bourgeois*, Serpentine Gallery, London
1984 *Louise Bourgeois. Sculpture*, Robert Miller Gallery, New York
1983 *Louise Bourgeois. Retrospective*, Contemporary Arts Museum, Houston; Museum of Contemporary Art, Chicago; Akron Art Museum, Akron, Ohio
1982 *Louise Bourgeois: Retrospective*, MoMA – Museum of Modern Art, New York
1981 *Louise Bourgeois. Femme Maison*, Renaissance Society, University of Chicago, Chicago
1980 *The Iconography of Louise Bourgeois*, Max Hutchinson Gallery, New York
1979 *Louise Bourgeois. Sculpture 1941–1953. Plus One New Piece*, Xavier Fourcade Gallery, New York
1978 *Triangles. New Sculpture and Drawings*, Xavier Fourcade Gallery, New York
1974 *Sculpture 1970–1974*, 112 Greene Street Gallery, New York
1964 *Louise Bourgeois. Recent Sculpture*, Stable Gallery, New York
1959 *Sculpture by Louise Bourgeois*, Andrew D. White Art Museum, Cornell University Ithaca, New York State

1953 *Louise Bourgeois. Drawings for Sculpture and Sculpture*, Peridot Gallery, New York Allan Frumkin Gallery, Chicago

1950 *Sculptures*, Peridot Gallery, New York

1949 *Late Work. 1947–1949: Standing Figures*, Peridot Gallery, New York

1945 *Paintings by Louise Bourgeois*, Bertha Schaefer Gallery, New York

Bibliografie/Bibliography (Auswahl/Selection)


- Anne Coxon, *Tate Modern Artists: Louise Bourgeois*. London 2010.
- Germano Celant, *Louise Bourgeois. The Fabric Works*. Mailand 2010.
- Mark Welzel (Hg./ed.), *200 Artworks. 25 Years Artist's Editions for Parkett*. Zürich/Zurich 2009.
- Hauser & Wirth (Hg./ed.), *Louise Bourgeois. Nothing to Remember*. Göttingen 2009.
- Christian Rattemeyer (Hg./ed.), *Compass in Hand*, Ausst.-Kat./Exh. cat., MoMA – Museum of Modern Art, New York. New York 2009.
- *Louise Bourgeois*, mit Texten von/with texts by Marie-Laure Bernadac und/and Jonas Storsve, Ausst.-Kat./Exh. cat., Centre Georges Pompidou, Paris. Paris 2008.
- Frances Morris (Hg./ed.), *Louise Bourgeois*, Ausst.-Kat./Exh. cat., Tate Modern, London. London 2007.
- Mark Lisa, Gabrielle Lisa, Elizabeth Hamilton (Hg./ed.), *WACK! Art and the feminist Revolution*, Ausst.-Kat./Exh. cat., MoCA Los Angeles. London 2007.
- Louise Bourgeois, *Louise Bourgeois. Recent prints on cloth and paper*. London 2007.
- Louise Bourgeois, *Louise Bourgeois*. Zürich/Zurich 2006.
- Marie-Laure Bernadac, *Louise Bourgeois*. Paris 2006.
- Christine Bader (Hg./ed.), *Louise Bourgeois. Scultura e Opere Grafiche*. Lugano 2006.
- *Louise Bourgeois. La Famille*, mit Texten von/with texts by Thomas Kellein und/and Louise Bourgeois. Köln/Cologne 2006.
- Gerald A. Matt, Peter Weiermair (Hg./eds.), *Louise Bourgeois. Aller-Retour*, Ausst.-Kat./Exh. cat., Kunsthalle Wien, Wien. Nürnberg/Nuremberg 2005.
- Eva Keller, Regula Malin (Hg./ed.), *Louise Bourgeois. Emotions Abstracted. Werke 1941–2000*, Ausst.-Kat./Exh. cat., Daros Museum, Zürich. Zürich/Zurich 2004.
- Frances Morris (Hg./ed.), *Louise Bourgeois. Stiches in Time*, Ausst.-Kat./Exh. cat., Irish Museum of Modern Art, Dublin. Dublin 2003.
- *Louise Bourgeois. Life as Art*. Ausst.-Kat./Exh. cat., Louisiana Museum of Modern Art, Louisiana. Humblebaek 2003.
- Beatrice Stammer (Hg./ed.), *Louise Bourgeois: Intime Abstraktionen*, Ausst.-Kat./exh. cat., Akademie der Künste, Berlin. Berlin 2003.
- Robert Storr, Paulo Herkenhoff, Allan Schwartzman, *Louise Bourgeois*. London 2003.
- Jan Greenberg, Sandra Jordan, *Runaway Girl: The Artist Louise Bourgeois*. New York 2003.
- Gerald A. Matt (Hg./ed.), *Heiliger Sebastian. A Splendid Readiness for Death*, Ausst.-Kat./Exh. cat., Kunsthalle Wien, Wien. Bielefeld 2003.
- Michaela Unterdörfer, *Louise Bourgeois. Works in Marble*. München/Munich 2002.
- Juan Vicente Aliaga, *Louise Bourgeois*, Ausst.-Kat./Exh. cat., Galeria Soledad Lorenzo. Madrid 2002.
- Eckhard Schneider, *Louise Bourgeois*, Ausst.-Kat./Exh. cat., Kunsthaus Bregenz. Bregenz 2002.
- *Louise Bourgois*, Ausst.-Kat./Exh. cat., Tate Gallery, London. London 2000.
- *Louise Bourgeois, Memory and Architecture*, Ausst.-Kat./Exh. cat., Museo National Centro de Arte Reina Sofía. Madrid 1999.

- Ian Cole (Hg./ed.), *Louise Bourgeois*, Ausst.-Kat./Exh. cat., Museum of Modern Art. Oxford 1996.
- *Louise Bourgeois: Sculptures, environnements, dessins 1938–1995*, Ausst.-Kat./Exh. cat., Musée d'Art moderne de la Ville de Paris. Paris 1995.
- Marie-Laure Bernadac, *Louise Bourgeois Pensées-plumes*, Ausst.-Kat./Exh. cat., Centre Georges Pompidou. Paris 1995.
- Emmanuel Pernoud, *Louise Bourgeois Estampes*. Paris 1995.
- *Louise Bourgeois: The Locus of Memory, 1982–1993*, mit Texten von/with texts by Charlotta Kotik,
- Terrie Christian Leigh Sultan, Ausst.-Kat./Exh. cat., Brooklyn Museum, New York. New York 1994.
- Jan Hoet (Hg./ed.), *Documenta IX, vol. I, II*, Ausst.-Kat./Exh. cat., Stuttgart, New York 1992.


**Glenn Brown**

1966 geboren in Hexham, Northumberland, England, lebt und arbeitet in London
1984–1992 Studium an der Norwich School of Art in Norwich, am Bath College of Higher Education in Bath sowie am Goldsmiths College in London

1966 born in Hexham, Northumberland, England, lives and works in London
1984–1992 studies at Norwich School of Art, Norwich, at Bath College of Higher Education, Bath, and at Goldsmiths College, London

Einzelausstellungen/Solo Exhibitions (Auswahl/Selection)



2011 *Glenn Brown*, Galerie Max Hetzler, Berlin
*Etchings and Sculpture*, Gagosian Gallery, Genf/Geneva
2009 *Glenn Brown*, Gagosian Gallery, London
*Etchings (Portraits)*, Karsten Schubert Gallery, London
*Glenn Brown Retrospective*, Tate Liverpool, Liverpool; Fondazione Sandretto Re Rebaudengo, Turin; Ludwig Museum of Contemporary Art Budapest, Budapest
2008 *Editions and a Unique Sculpture*, Patrick Painter, Los Angeles
*Glenn Brown*, Kunsthistorisches Museum Wien, Wien/Vienna
2007 *Glenn Brown*, Gagosian Gallery, New York
2006 *Glenn Brown*, Galerie Max Hetzler, Berlin
2004 *Glenn Brown*, Serpentine Gallery, London
*Glenn Brown*, Gagosian Gallery, New York
2000 *Glenn Brown*, Domaine de Kerguéhennec, Centre d'Art Contemporain, Centre Culturel de Rencontre, Bignan
1999 *Glenn Brown*, Jerwood Gallery, London
1997 *Glenn Brown*, Galerie Ghislaine Hussenot, Paris
1996 *Glenn Brown*, Queen's Hall Arts Centre, Hexham
1995 *Glenn Brown*, Karsten Schubert Gallery, London

Bibliografie/Bibliography (Auswahl/Selection)


*Glenn Brown. Three Exhibitions*, mit Texten von/with texts by Michael Bracewell, David Freedberg und/and Rochelle Steiner. London 2010.

- Francesco Bonami, Christoph Grunenberg (Hg./ed.), *Glenn Brown*, Ausst.-Kat./Exh. cat., Tate Liverpool. London 2009.
- *Glenn Brown: Etchings (Portraits)* mit einem Text von/with a text by John-Paul Stonard, Ausst.-Kat./ Exh. cat., Karsten Schubert Galerie. London 2009.
- Wilfried Seipel (Hg./ed.), *Glenn Brown*, Ausst.-Kat./Exh. cat., Kunsthistorisches Museum Wien. Wien/Vienna 2008.
- *Glenn Brown*, mit einem Text von/with a text by Michael Bracewell, Ausst.-Kat./Exh. cat., Gagosian Gallery, New York. Ostfildern-Ruit 2007.
- Virginia Button, *The Turner Prize, Revised Edition*. London 2007.
- *Glenn Brown*, mit einem Text von/with a text by Tom Morton, Ausst.-Kat./Exh. cat., Galerie Max Hetzler. Berlin 2006.
- *Glenn Brown*, mit einem Text von/with a text by Alison Gingeras, Ausst.-Kat./Exh. cat., Serpentine Gallery. London 2004.
- *Glenn Brown*, mit einem Text von/with a text by David Freedberg. Ausst.-Kat./Exh. cat., Gagosian Gallery, New York. Toronto 2004.
- Sabine Folie, „Glenn Brown“, in: *Lieber Maler, male mir... Radikaler Realismus nach Picabia/ “Dear Painter, paint me ...” ... Painting the Figure since Late Picabia*, Ausst.-Kat./Exh. cat., Centre Georges
- Pompidou, Paris; Kunsthalle Wien, Wien/Vienna; Schirn Kunsthalle Frankfurt. Frankfurt a. M. 2002, S./pp. 86–95.
- Domaine de Kerguéhennec (Hg./ed.), *Glenn Brown*. Bignan 2000.



**Markus Schinwald**

1973 in Salzburg geboren, lebt und arbeitet in Wien
1993–1999 Studium an der Hochschule für künstlerische und industrielle Gestaltung in Linz und Kulturwissenschaften an der Humboldt Universität Berlin

1973 born in Salzburg, lives and works in Vienna
1993–1999 Studies at the Hochschule für künstlerische und industrielle Gestaltung, Linz, and Cultural Studies at the Humboldt Universität Berlin

Einzelausstellungen/Solo Exhibitions (Auswahl/Selection)

2011 *Markus Schinwald*, Kunstverein Hannover, Hannover; Lentos Kunstmuseum Linz, Linz
2010 *Markus Schinwald*, Yvon Lambert New York, New York
2009 *Markus Schinwald – Pocket History*, Mücsarnok Kunsthalle Budapest, Budapest
*Markus Schinwald*, Georg Kargl Fine Arts, Wien/Vienna
*Vanishing Lessons*, Kunsthaus Bregenz, Bregenz
2008 *Markus Schinwald*, migros museum für gegenwartskunst, Zürich/Zurich
*Markus Schinwald*, Galleria Giò Marconi, Mailand/Milan
2007 *Markus Schinwald*, Augarten Contemporary, Wien/Vienna
*Markus Schinwald*, CECCH – Centre d'édition contemporaine, Genf/Geneva
*Markus Schinwald*, Center for Contemporary Art, Thessaloniki

2006 *Markus Schinwald,* Aspen Art Museum, Aspen
*Markus Schinwald,* MAMbo – Museo d'Arte Moderna di Bologna, Bologna
*Markus Schinwald,* Argos – Center for Art & Media, Brüssel/Brussels
*Markus Schinwald,* CAC – Centre d'art contemporain de Brétigny, Brétigny sur Orge
2005 *Markus Schinwald – Korridor der Unsicherheiten,* Ausstellungshalle zeitgenössische Kunst, Münster
2004 *Tableau Twain,* Frankfurter Kunstverein, Frankfurt a. Main
*Dictio Pii,* Sprengel Museum, Hannover
2003 *Ceaseless blur,* TAV Gallery, Taipei
*Markus Schinwald,* Georg Kargl Fine Arts, Wien/Vienna
2000 *Oxygen, flipping through Kiesler,* MAK Center for Art and Architecture, Los Angeles

Bibliografie/Bibliography (Auswahl/Selection)


- Eva Schlegel (Hg./ed.), Markus Schinwald, mit Texten von/with texts by Philipp Kaiser, Thomas Macho, Mirjam Schaub. Nürnberg 2010.
- Brigitte Franzen, Susanne Neuburger (Hg./ed.), *Hyper Real. Die Passion des Realen in Malerei und Fotografie,* Ausst.-Kat./Exh. cat., MUMOK – Museum moderner Kunst Wien. Köln/Cologne 2010, S./pp. 296–297.
- Laura Hotman, Yilmaz Dziewior, Uta Grosenick (Hg./ed.), *The Art of Tomorrow.* Berlin 2010, S. /pp. 282–285.
- KÖR – Kunst im öffentlichen Raum Wien, Kunsthalle Wien (Hg./ed.), *Wem gehört die Stadt? Wien – Kunst im öffentlichen Raum seit 1968.* Nürnberg/Nuremberg 2009, S./pp. 78–79.
- *Subversive Spaces: Surrealism and Contemporary Art,* mit Texten von/with texts by Anna Dezeuze et al, Ausst.-Kat./Exh. cat., The Whitworth Art Gallery. Manchester 2009, S./pp. 38–39.
- *Markus Schinwald. Vanishing Lessons,* mit Texten von/with texts by Jörg Heiser et al, Ausst.-Kat./Exh.-cat., Kunsthaus Bregenz. Bregenz 2009.
- Gerald A. Matt (Hg./ed.), *Western Motel. Edward Hopper und die zeitgenössische Kunst,* Ausst.-Kat./Exh. cat., Kunsthalle Wien, Nürnberg/Nuremberg 2008, S./pp. 218–222.
- *DRESSing the MESSAGE. Transformationen von Kunst und Mode.* Ausst.-Kat./Exh. cat., Sprengel Museum Hannover. Hannover 2008, S./pp. 85–90.
- Belinda Grace Gardner, Gerald A. Matt (Hg./eds.), *True Romance. Allegorien der Liebe von der Renaissance bis heute,* Ausst.-Kat./Exh. cat., Kunsthalle Wien, Wien/Vienna; Villa Stuck, München/Munich; Kunsthalle zu Kiel, Kiel. Köln/Cologne 2007, S./p. 86.
- Agnes Husslein-Arco, Heike Munder, Thomas Trummer (Hg./ed.), *Markus Schinwald,* Ausst.-Kat./Exh. cat.,
- Belvedere Wien, Wien/Vienna; migros museum für gegenwartskunst, Zürich/Zurich. Zürich/Zurich 2007.
- Barbara J. Scheuermann (Hg./ed.), *Talking Pictures,* Ausst.-Kat./Exh. cat., Kunstsammlung Nordrhein-Westfallen. Düsseldorf 2007, S./pp. 67–77.
- Phillip Kaiser, Gabriel Schor (Hg./ed.), *Held Together with water. Art from the Sammlung Verbund.* Ausst.-Kat./Exh. cat., MAK – Österreichisches Museum für angewandte Kunst/Gegenwartskunst, Wien/Vienna. Osterfildern-Ruit 2007, S./p. 168–171.
- Gerald A. Matt (Hg./ed.), *Interviews.* Köln/Cologne 2007, S./pp. 300–307.

**Francesco Vezzoli**

1971 in Brescia, Italien, geboren, lebt und arbeitet in Mailand
1992–1995 BA, Fine Arts, Central Saint Martins College of Art and Design in London

1971 born in Brescia, Italy, lives and works in Milan
1992–1995 Studies at the Central St. Martin's School of Art in London

Einzelausstellungen/Solo Exhibitions (Auswahl/Selection)

2011 *Francesco Vezzoli – Sacrilegio*, Gagosian Gallery, New York
*Greed, A New Fragrance by Francesco Vezzoli*, La Conservera – Centro de Arte Contemporàneo, Ceutì (Murcia)
2010 *Francesco Vezzoli*, Garage Center for Contemporary Culture – GCCC, Moskau/Moscow
2009 *Francesco Vezzoli. Marlene Redux: A True Hollywood Story!*, Kunsthalle Wien, project space Karlsplatz, Wien/Vienna
*Dalí Dalí featuring Francesco Vezzoli*, Moderna Museet, Stockholm
*Francesco Vezzoli. À chacun sa vérité*, Jeu de Paume, Paris
*Greed: The New Fragrance by Francesco Vezzoli*, Gagosian Gallery, Rom/Rome
2007 *Francesco Vezzoli – Primadonnas*, Pinakothek der Moderne, München/Munich
*Francesco Vezzoli: A True Hollywood Story!*, The Power Plant, Toronto
2006 *Francesco Vezzoli*, Le Consortium, Dijon
*The Bruce Nauman Trilogy*, Galerie NEU, Berlin
*The Gore Vidal Trilogy*, Gagosian Gallery, Beverly Hills
2005 *Francesco Vezzoli. Trilogia della Morte (Trilogy of Death)*, Fondaziona Cini, Fondazione Prada, Madrid
*Francesco Vezzoli*, Museu Serralves Museu de Arte Contemporânea, Porto, Portugal
2004 *Francesco Vezzoli*, Fondazione Prada, Mailand/Milan
2002 *Die Handarbeiten von Francesco Vezzoli*, Galerie für Zeitgenössische Kunst, Leipzig
*The Films of Francesco Vezzoli*, New Museum, New York
*Francesco Vezzoli*, Castello di Rivoli Museo d'Arte Contemporanea, Turin
2000 *A Love Trilogy – Self-portrait with Marisa Berenson as Edith Piaf*, Galleria d'Arte Moderna di Bologna – GAM, Bologna

Bibliografie/Bibliography (Auswahl/Selection)


- Valentina Castellani (Hg./ed.), *Francesco Vezzoli: Ballets Russes Italian Style (The Shortes Musical You Will Never See Again)*, Ausst.-Kat./Exh. cat., The Museum of Contemporary Art, Los Angeles; Gagosian Gallery, New York. Minneapolis 2010.
- John Peter Nilsson, Matilda Olof-Ors (Hg./ed.), *Dalí Dalí featuring Francesco Vezzoli*, Ausst.-Kat./ Exh. cat., Moderna Museet, Stockholm. Göttingen 2009.
- Gerald A. Matt, Synne Genzmer (Hg./ed.), *Francesco Vezzoli: Marlene Redux*, Ausst.-Kat./Exh. cat., Kunsthalle Wien. Nürnberg/Nuremberg 2009.
- Alison McDonald (Hg./ed.), *Francesco Vezzoli: Right You Are (If You Think You Are)*. Mailand/Milan 2008.
- Gregory Burke (Hg./ed.), *Francesco Vezzoli: A True Hollywood Story!*, Ausst.-Kat./Exh. cat., The Power Plant. Toronto 2008.
- Ida Gianelli (Hg./ed.), *Francesco Vezzoli. Democrazy*, Ausst.-Kat./Exh. cat., MAXXI – Museo nazionale

- delle arti XXI secolo, Rom/Rome. Mailand/Milan 2007.
- Germano Celant (Hg.), *Francesco Vezzoli*, Ausst.-Kat./Exh. cat., Fondazione Prada. Mailand/Milan 2004.
- Jan Winkelmann (Hg./ed.), *The Needleworks of Francesco Vezzoli*, Ausst.-Kat./Exh. cat., Galerie für
- Zeitgenössische Kunst, Leipzig. Ostfildern-Ruit 2002.
- Marcella Beccaria (Hg./ed.), *Francesco Vezzoli*. Ausst.-Kat./Exh. cat., Castello di Rivoli Museo d'Arte Contemporanea, Rivoli. Turin 2002.


**Co-Stars**

**Philippe Halsman**
1906 geboren in Riga, Lettland. Gestorben 1979 in New York./Born 1906 in Riga, Latvia. Died 1979 in New York. Dalí lernte den berühmten Fotografen Halsman 1941 kennen. Bis zu Halsman's Tod 1979 arbeiteten sie immer wieder zusammen. 1954 veröffentlichten sie gemeinsam das Buch *Dalí's Mustache*./Dalí met Halsman, the famous photographer, in 1941. They worked together up to Halsman's death in 1979. In 1954, they published the book *Dalí's Mustache*.

**Jean-Michel Othoniel**
1964 geboren in Saint-Etienne, Frankreich. Lebt und arbeitet in Paris./Born 1964 in Saint-Etienne, France. Lives and works in Paris. Mit einer Reihe von Skulpturen aus Schwefel machte Jean-Michel Othoniel im Rahmen der documenta IX erstmals auf sich aufmerksam. Seit 1993 arbeitet der französische Bildhauer zunehmend mit Glas. Er gestaltete u. a. den Eingang zur U-Bahn-Station *Palais Royal – Musée du Louvre*./With a series of sculptures made from sulfur, the artist Jean-Michel Othoniel received international attention at documenta IX. Since 1993, the French sculptor has chosen to work increasingly with glass. He designed, inter alia, the entrance to the metro station *Palais Royal – Musée du Louvre*.



**Eric Schaal**
1905 geboren in München. Gestorben 1994 in Zürich./Born 1905 in Munich. Died 1994 in Zurich. Eric Schaals Fotografien von Dalí zählen neben denen Halsmans zu den bekanntesten. 1939 dokumentierte Schaal den *Dream of Venus*-Pavillon, den Dalí für die New Yorker Weltausstellung entwarf./Eric Schaal's photographs of Dalí and his work, alongside those of Halsman, count amongst the most well known. Schaal documented the *Dream of Venus* pavilion in 1939, which Dalí designed for the New York World Fair.

**Andy Warhol**
1928 geboren in Pittsburgh. Gestorben 1987 in New York./Born 1928 in Pittsburgh. Died 1987 in New York. 1965 besuchte Dalí Andy Warhols Factory. Dabei entstanden insgesamt zwei *Screentests* von Dalí./Dalí visited Andy Warhol's Factory in 1965, resulting in a total of two Screen Tests of Dalí by Warhol.

**Autoren/Authors**

Caroline Corbetta ist Kunstkritikerin und Kuratorin. Sie schreibt für *Vogue Italia, Domus, L'Uomo Vogue* und ist Mitherausgeberin des *Contemporary magazine*. Sie ist Dozentin an der Accademia Carrara in Bergamo und an der Accademia di Belle Arti di Brera in Mailand./Caroline Corbetta is an art critic and curator. She writes for *Vogue Italia, Domus, L'Uomo Vogue*, and is co-editor of *Contemporary magazine*. She is a lecturer at the Accademia Carrara in Bergamo and at the Accademia di Belle Arti di Brera in Milan.

Wolfgang Fetz ist künstlerischer Leiter des Magazin 4 – Kunstverein Bregenz und Leiter der Abteilung Kultur der Stadt Bregenz./Wolfgang Fetz is director of Magazin 4 – Kunstverein Bregenz. He serves as head of culture for the city of Bregenz, Austria.

Belinda Grace Gardner ist Journalistin, Kunstkritikerin und Kuratorin. Sie ist Lehrbeauftragte im Studienschwerpunkt Theorie und Geschichte an der HFBK Hamburg./Belinda Grace Gardner is a journalist, art critic and curator. She is a lecturer in gravity theory and history at the HFBK Hamburg.

Lucas Gehrmann ist Kunsthistoriker, freier Kurator und wissenschaftlicher Mitarbeiter der Kunsthalle Wien. Er ist Stellvertreter des künstlerischen Leiters der Kunstfabrik Wien./Lucas Gehrmann is an art historian, free curator and research associate at Kunsthalle Wien. He is deputy artistic director of the Art Factory in Vienna.

Synne Genzmer ist Kunsthistorikerin und Kuratorin der Kunsthalle Wien./Synne Genzmer is an art historian and curator at Kunsthalle Wien.

David Lomas ist Kunsthistoriker und Professor für Kunstgeschichte an der University of Manchester. Er ist Autor des Buches *The Haunted Self: Surrealism, Psychoanalysis, Subjectivity*. 2011 erscheint *Narcissus Reflected: The Narcissus Myth in Surrealist and Contemporary Art*./David Lomas is an art historian and professor of art history at the University of Manchester. He is the author of *The Haunted Self: Surrealism, Psychoanalysis, Subjectivity*, as well as *Narcissus Reflected: The Narcissus Myth in Surrealist and Contemporary Art*, coming out in 2011.

Gerald A. Matt ist Direktor und Kurator der Kunsthalle Wien. Er ist Gastprofessor an der Universität für angewandte Kunst in Wien und Dozent an der CIAM Hochschule in Köln./Gerald A. Matt is director and curator of Kunsthalle Wien. He is a visiting professor at the University of Applied Arts in Vienna and lecturer at the University of CIAM in Cologne.

Catherine Millet ist Autorin, Kunstkritikerin, Kuratorin und Chefredakteurin des französischen Kunstmagazins *Art Press*. Ihr 2001 veröffentlichtes Buch *Das sexuelle Leben der Catherine M.* machte international Furore. 2008 erschien *Eifersucht*./Catherine Millet is a writer, art critic, curator and editor-in-chief of the French art magazine *Art Press*. Its 2001 publication *The Sexual Life of Catherine M.* was an international sensation. *Jealousy: The other Life of Catherine M.* came out in 2008.

Katarzyna Uszynska ist Kunsthistorikerin, freie Kuratorin und Leiterin des Neuen Kunstvereins Wien./Katarzyna Uszynska is an art historian, free curator and director of Neuer Kunstverein Wien.

**Werk- und Abbildungsverzeichnis/**
**List of Works and Images**

**Louise Bourgeois**

Alle Werke und Worte von/all works and words of
Louise Bourgeois © Louise Bourgeois Trust

*Untitled*, 1943
Bleistift auf Papier/pencil on paper
12,7 × 15,2 cm
Courtesy Cheim & Read and Hauser & Wirth
Foto/photo: Christopher Burke
Abb. S./ill. p. 70

*Untitled (Clocks)*, 1944
Metall, Folienpapier auf Holz/metal, foil paper on wood
29,2 × 20,3 cm
Courtesy Cheim & Read and Hauser & Wirth
Foto/photo: Christopher Burke
Abb. S./ill. p. 74



*Untitled*, 1946
Tusche auf Papier/ink on paper
21,6 × 27,9 cm
Courtesy Cheim & Read and Hauser & Wirth
Foto/photo: Christopher Burke
Abb. S./ill. p. 72

*Untitled*, 1946
Tusche auf Papier/ink on paper
27,9 × 22,2 cm
Courtesy Cheim & Read and Hauser & Wirth
Foto/photo: Christopher Burke
Keine Abb./no ill.

*He Disappeared Into Complete Silence* (Plate 8), 1947
Gravüre auf Papier/engraving on paper
25,4 × 17,8 cm
Courtesy Cheim & Read and Hauser & Wirth
Foto/photo: Christopher Burke
Abb. S./ill. p. 69

*Untitled*, 1947
Bleistift auf Papier/pencil on paper
20,3 × 12,7 cm
Courtesy Cheim & Read and Hauser & Wirth
Foto/photo: Christopher Burke
Keine Abb./no ill.

*Untitled*, 1947
Tusche auf Illustrationskarton/ink on illustration board
24,8 × 35,6 cm
Courtesy Cheim & Read and Hauser & Wirth
Foto/photo: Christopher Burke
Abb. S./ill. p. 70

*Untitled*, 1947
Tusche auf Papier/ink on paper
21,6 × 8,9 cm
Courtesy Cheim & Read and Hauser & Wirth
Foto/photo: Christopher Burke
Keine Abb./no ill.

*Les Voleuse de Gratte Ciel*, 1949
Bleistift auf Papier/pencil on paper
20,3 × 12,7 cm
Courtesy Cheim & Read and Hauser & Wirth
Foto/photo: Christopher Burke
Keine Abb./no ill.

*Untitled*, c. 1960
Schwarzes Gummi, Nägel/black rubber, nails
8,3 × 7,9 × 4,4 cm
Privatsammlung/Private Collection, New York
Foto/photo: Christopher Burke
Abb. S./ill. p. 85

*Untitled*, 1964
Gips, bemalte Nägel/plaster, painted nails
12,7 × 13,3 × 11,4 cm
Privatsammlung/Private Collection, New York
Foto/photo: Christopher Burke
Abb. S./ill. p. 96

*Untitled*, 1965
Blei, zwei Teile/lead, two elements
10,8 × 17.1 × 2,5 cm
Courtesy Cheim & Read and Hauser & Wirth
Foto/photo: Christopher Burke
Abb. S./ill. p. 86

*Soft Landscape I*, 1967
Pigmentierter Harz/pigmented resin
10,2 × 30,5 × 27,9 cm
Courtesy Cheim & Read and Hauser & Wirth
Foto/photo: Christopher Burke
Abb. S./ill. p. 92

*Untitled (Germinal)*, 1967–1995
Bronze, Silbernitrat-Patina/bronze, silver nitrate patina
16,5 × 21,6 × 21,6 cm
Courtesy Cheim & Read and Hauser & Wirth
Foto/photo: Christopher Burke
Abb. S./ill. p. 90

*Hanging Janus*, 1968
Bronze, dunkel polierte Patina, hängend/bronze, dark and polished patina, hanging piece
17,5 × 27,9 × 15,9 cm
Courtesy Cheim & Read and Hauser & Wirth
Foto/photo: Christopher Burke
Abb. S./ill. p. 82

*Hanging Janus with Jacket*, 1968
Bronze, dunkel polierte Patina, hängend/bronze, dark and polished patina, hanging piece
27 × 52,4 × 16,2 cm
Courtesy Cheim & Read and Hauser & Wirth
Foto/photo: Christopher Burke
Abb. S./ill. p. 82

*Janus*, 1968
Bronze, dunkel polierte Patina, hängend/bronze, dark and polished patina, hanging piece
25,4 × 33 × 17,8 cm
Courtesy Cheim & Read and Hauser & Wirth
Foto/photo: Christopher Burke
Keine Abb./no ill.

*Untitled (Sleep II)*, 1968
Bronze, polierte Patina/bronze, polished patina
14 × 17,8 × 15,2 cm
Courtesy Cheim & Read and Hauser & Wirth
Foto/photo: Christopher Burke
Abb. S./ill. p. 94

*Femme Pieu*, c. 1970
Bemaltes Holz, Metallnägel/painted wood, metal pins
6,4 × 6,4 × 16,5 cm
Privatsammlung/Private Collection, New York
Foto/photo: Christopher Burke
Abb. S./ill. p. 88

*Fragile Goddess*, 1970
Bronze
26 × 14,3 × 13,7 cm
Courtesy Cheim & Read and Hauser & Wirth
Foto/photo: Christopher Burke
Abb. S./ill. p. 91

*Rabbit*, 1970
Bronze, Wandstück/bronze, wall piece
58,4 × 28,9 × 14,9 cm
Courtesy Cheim & Read and Hauser & Wirth
Foto/photo: Christopher Burke
Abb. S./ill. p. 81

*Untitled (Hand)*, 1970
Wachs, Textil/wax, cloth
4,4 × 19,1 × 12,7 cm
Courtesy Cheim & Read and Hauser & Wirth
Foto/photo: Christopher Burke
Abb. S./ill. p. 90

*Untitled*, 1970–1972
Bronze, fünf Teile/bronze, five elements
Je/each c. 15,9 × 5,7 × 8,9 cm
Courtesy Cheim & Read and Hauser & Wirth
Foto/photo: Christopher Burke
Abb. S./ill. p. 86

*Untitled*, 1973
Gummi/rubber
25,4 × 17,1 × 9,5 cm
Courtesy Cheim & Read and Hauser & Wirth
Foto/photo: Christopher Burke
Keine Abb./no ill.

*Fallen Woman*, 1981–1996
Weißer Marmor, Nylon, Garn/white marble, nylon, thread
8,3 × 12,7 × 8,3 cm
Privatsammlung/Private Collection, New York
Foto/photo: Christopher Burke
Abb. S./ill. p. 79

*Femme Couteau*, 1982
Schwarzer Marmor/black marble
14 × 77,5 × 20,3 cm
Privatsammlung/Private Collection, New York
Foto/photo: Christopher Burke
Keine Abb./no ill.

*Femme Maison*, 1982
Weißer Marmor/white marble
27,9 × 30,5 × 33 cm
Courtesy Cheim & Read and Hauser & Wirth
Foto/photo: Christopher Burke
Abb. S./ill. p. 83

*Femme Maison*, 1982
Plastikpuppe, Ton/plastic doll, clay
40,6 × 13,3 × 5,1 cm
Courtesy Cheim & Read and Hauser & Wirth
Foto/photo: Christopher Burke
Keine Abb./no ill.

*Nature Study*, 1986
Bronze, Silbernitrat-Patina/bronze, silver nitrate patina
15,2 × 25,4 × 17,8 cm
Courtesy Cheim & Read and Hauser & Wirth
Foto/photo: Christopher Burke
Abb. S./ill. p. 98

*The Worm*, 1989
Bronze, schwarz polierte Patina/bronze, black and polished patina
30,5 × 55,9 × 25,4 cm
Courtesy Cheim & Read and Hauser & Wirth
Foto/photo: Christopher Burke
Abb. S./ill. p. 94

*Untitled (No. 7)*, 1993
Bronze, Silbernitrat-Patina/bronze, silver nitrate patina
12,1 × 68,6 × 43,2 cm
Courtesy Cheim & Read and Hauser & Wirth
Foto/photo: Christopher Burke
Keine Abb./no ill.

*Femme Maison*, 1994
Weißer Marmor/white marble
11,4 × 31,1 × 6,7 cm
Courtesy Cheim & Read and Hauser & Wirth
Foto/photo: Christopher Burke
Abb. S./ill. p. 78

*Fallen Woman*, 1996
Porzelan, Blau und Gold/porcelain, blue and gold
8,3 × 30,5 × 7,6 cm
Courtesy Cheim & Read and Hauser & Wirth
Foto/photo: Christopher Burke
Abb. S./ill. p. 84

*In and Out*, 1997
Geschweißter Stahl, Blei/welded steel, lead
43,5 × 82,6 × 61,3 cm
Courtesy Cheim & Read and Hauser & Wirth
Foto/photo: Christopher Burke
Abb. S./ill. p. 88

*Untitled*, 1997
Stahl, Nylon, Garn, Gummi/steel, nylon, thread, rubber
16,5 × 10,2 × 25,4 cm
Privatsammlung/Private Collection, New York
Foto/photo: Christopher Burke
Abb. S./ill. p. 96

*Repairs in the Sky*, 1999
Wandrelief: Blei, Stahl, Textil, Garn/wall relief: lead, steel, fabric, thread
36,2 × 50,8 × 1,6 cm
Courtesy Cheim & Read and Hauser & Wirth
Foto/photo: Christopher Burke
Abb. S./ill. p. 92

*Hair*, 2000
Kaltnadel auf Papier/drypoint on paper
38,1 × 30,5 cm
Courtesy Harlan & Weaver, New York
Foto/photo: Christopher Burke
Abb. S./ill. p. 72

*Untitled*, 2001
Bronze mit Silbernitrat-Patina: drei Teile/bronze with silver nitrate patina: three parts
17,8 × 14,6 × 12,7 cm, 26,7 × 20,3 × 16,5 cm, 31,8 × 20,3 × 15,2 cm
Courtesy Cheim & Read and Hauser & Wirth
Foto/photo: Christopher Burke
Abb. S./ill. p. 84

*Ear*, 2002
Pinkfarbener Gummi/pink rubber
10,2 × 20,3 × 23,5 cm
Courtesy Cheim & Read and Hauser & Wirth
Foto/photo: Christopher Burke
Abb. S./ill. p. 98

*Femme Couteau*, 2002
Textil, Stahl/fabric, steel
35,6 × 68,6 × 17,8 cm
Courtesy Cheim & Read and Hauser & Wirth
Foto/photo: Christopher Burke
Abb. S./ill. p. 77

*Give or Take*, 2002
Bronze, Silbernitrat-Patina/bronze, silver nitrate patina
8,9 × 58,4 × 12,7 cm
Courtesy Cheim & Read and Hauser & Wirth
Foto/photo: Christopher Burke
Abb. S./ill. p. 80

*The Couple*, 2002
Glasperlen, Textil, Stahl/glass beads, fabric, steel
41,9 × 43,2 × 33,7 cm
Courtesy Cheim & Read and Hauser & Wirth
Foto/photo: Christopher Burke
Keine Abb./no ill.

*Untitled*, 2002
Textil, Stahl/fabric, steel
27,3 × 12,7 × 10,2 cm
Courtesy Cheim & Read and Hauser & Wirth
Foto/photo: Christopher Burke
Abb. S./ill. p. 99

*Lady in Waiting*, 2003
Wandteppich, Garn, Edelstahl, Stahl, Holz, Glas/tapestry, thread, stainless steel, steel, wood, glass
208,3 × 110,3 × 147,3 cm
Courtesy Cheim & Read and Hauser & Wirth
Foto/photo: Christopher Burke
Abb. S./ill. p. 76

*Arch of Hysteria*, 2004
Textil, hängend/fabric, hanging piece
21,6 × 53,3 × 12,1 cm
Courtesy Cheim & Read and Hauser & Wirth
Foto/photo: Christopher Burke
Abb. S./ill. p. 103

*Femme*, 2005
Wandteppich/tapestry
14 × 27,9 × 16,5 cm
Courtesy Cheim & Read and Hauser & Wirth
Foto/photo: Christopher Burke
Abb. S./ill. p. 77

*Femme*, 2005
Bronze, Silbernitrat-Patina/bronze, silver nitrate patina
14 × 22,9 × 15,2 cm
Courtesy Cheim & Read and Hauser & Wirth
Foto/photo: Christopher Burke
Abb. S./ill. p. 80

*Topiary*, 2005
Bronze, Silbernitrat-Patina/bronze, silver nitrate patina
17,1 × 28,6 × 26 cm
Courtesy Cheim & Read and Hauser & Wirth
Foto/photo: Christopher Burke
Abb. S./ill. p. 97

*Topiary*, 2005
Bronze, Silbernitrat-Patina/bronze, silver nitrate and polished patina
29,5 × 10,8 × 8,9 cm
Courtesy Cheim & Read and Hauser & Wirth
Foto/photo: Christopher Burke
Abb. S./ill. p. 95

*Femme*, 2006
Bronze, poliertes Silber, Nitrat-Patina/bronze, polished silver, nitrate patina
19,7 × 8,9 × 8,3 cm
Courtesy Cheim & Read and Hauser & Wirth
Foto/photo: Christopher Burke
Abb. S./ill. p. 97

nicht ausgestellt/not on display:

*Cell (Arch of Hysteria)*, 1992–1993
Stahl, Bronze, gegossenes Eisen, Textil/steel, bronze, cast iron, fabric
302,2 × 368,3 × 304,8 cm
Courtesy Collection Centro Andaluz de Arte Contemporaneo, Seville
Foto/photo: Armin Linke
Abb. S./ill. p. 102

**Glenn Brown**



Alle Werke von/all works by Glenn Brown


*Paranoïac-Critical Method*, 1998
Ilfochrome Classic Print
46,1 × 36 cm
Sammlung des Künstlers/Collection of the artist, London
Abb. S./ill. p. 142

*Oscillate Wildly (after "Autumn Cannibalism", 1936 by Salvador Dalí)*, 1999
Mit freundlicher Genehmigung der/with kind permission by the Gala-Salvador Dalí Foundation, Spanien/Spain
Öl auf Leinen/oil on linen
175,5 × 391,5 cm
Courtesy Thomas Dane
Abb. S./ill. p. 136–137

*International Velvet*, 2004
Öl auf Tafel/oil on panel
145,5 × 121,5 × cm
Sammlung des Künstlers/Collection of the artist, London
Abb. S./ill. p. 127

*Song to the Siren*, 2009
Öl auf geformter Tafel auf Stahlträger/oil on shaped panel on steel support
250 × 148 × 18 cm
Sammlung des Künstlers/Collection of the artist, London
Abb. S./ill. p. 131

*Come All Ye Rolling Minstrels*, 2009
Öl auf Tafel/oil on panel
140 × 109 cm
Privatsammlung/Private Collection
Abb. S./ill. p. 128

*Woman I*, 2011
Öl, Acryl auf Fiberglas, Stahl/oil, acrylic on fibreglass, steel
135 × 90 × 70 cm
Sammlung/Collection Douglas B. Andrews
Courtesy Galerie Max Hetzler, Berlin
Abb. S./ill. p. 130

*Two Personages in Love with a Woman (after "Autumnal Cannibalism", 1936 by Salvador Dalí, by kind permission of the Gala-Salvador Dalí Foundation) and (after "The Laughing Cavalier", 1624 by Frans Hals) for Phil King*, 2011
Giclee Print auf Hahnemühle Photo Rag Papier/Giclee print on Hahnemühle Photo Rag paper
54 × 120 cm
Sammlung des Künstlers/Collection of the artist, London
Abb. S./ill. p. 138–139

*If God Exists Then Everything Is His Will II*, 2011
Giclee Print auf Hahnemühle Photo Rag Papier/Giclee print on Hahnemühle Photo Rag paper
12 × 15 cm
Sammlung des Künstlers/Collection of the artist, London
Abb. S./ill. p. 140

*Love II*, 2011
Giclee Print auf Hahenmühle Photo Rag Papier/
Giclee Print on Hahnemuhle Photorag paper
15 × 12 cm
Sammlung des Künstlers/Collection the artist, London
Abb. S./ill. p. 141

*Nigger of the World*, 2011
Öl auf Tafel/oil on panel
172 × 138 cm
Privatsammlung/Private Collection
Abb. S./ill. p. 129

nicht ausgestellt/not on display:

*Dalí-Christ*, 1992
Öl auf Leinwand/oil on canvas
275 × 183 cm
Abb. S./ill. p. 158

*You Take My Place in this Showdown*, 1993
Öl auf Leinwand/oil on canvas
215 × 323 cm
Abb. S./ill. p. 158

*The Loves of Shepherd, after Tony Roberts*, 2000
Öl auf Leinwand/oil on canvas
219,5 × 336 cm
Abb. S./ill. p. 148

*Architecture and Morality*, 2004
Öl auf Tafel/oil on panel
140 × 98 cm
Abb. S./ill. p. 122

*Theatre*, 2006
Öl auf Holz/oil on wood
122 × 93 cm
Abb. S./ill. p. 126

*Natural Selection*, 2010
Öl auf Tafel/oil on panel
120 × 96 cm
Abb. S./ill. p. 123

**Salvador Dalí**

Alle Werke von Salvador Dalí/all works by Salvador Dalí


*Objet scatologique à fonctionnement symbolique (Scatological Object Functioning Symbolically)*,
Assemblage 1930 (Rekonstruktion/reconstruction 1973)
Damenschuh, Knetmasse, Milchglas, Bürste ohne Borsten, Zuckerwürfel, Löffel etc./women's shoe, modelling clay, milk glass, brush without bristles, sugar cubes, spoons, etc.
121,9 × 71,1 × 35,6 cm
Edition Clarac-Serou/Galerie du Dragon
Abb. S./ill. p. 87

44 Heliogravuren aus der Illustrationsfolge/
heliogravures from the illustration series to
*Les Chants de Maldoror*, 1933–1934
Heliogravur und Kaltnadel auf Büttenpapier mit Wasserzeichen „Arche"/heliogravur and dry-point on laid paper with watermark "Arche"
33,2 × 25,4 cm
Kunstmuseum Bern, Ankauf durch die Freunde des Kunstmuseums Bern über die/acquisition of the friends of Kunstmuseum Bern through Galerie Wolfgang Wittrock, Düsseldorf
Abb. S./ill. p. 58–68

*Moment of Transition*, 1934
Öl auf Leinwand/oil on canvas
54 × 64,5 cm
Sammlung Viktor und Marianne Langen/Collection Viktor and Marianne Langen
Abb. S./ill. p. 143

*La Tour*, 1936
Öl auf Leinwand/oil on canvas
65,5 × 54 cm
Kunsthaus Zürich, Schenkung aus der Sammlung Erna und Curt Burgauer/Endowment from the Erna and Curt Burgauer Collection
Abb. S./ill. p. 121

*Couple aux têtes pleines de nuages*, 1936
Öl auf Holztafel/oil on panel
2 Teile/parts
92,5 × 69,5 cm; 82,5 × 62,5 cm
MART – Museo di Arte Moderna e Contemporanea di Trento e Rovereto – Deposito Fondazione Isabella Scelsi, Rovereto
Abb. S./ill. p. 133

*Telephone-homard ou Telephone aphrodisiaque (Lobster telephone)*, 1936
Bemalte Bronze/painted bronze
C. 15 × 30 × 17 cm
Edition Clarac-Serou/Galerie du Dragon
Abb. S./ill. p. 9

*Flores surrealistas (Gala-Narciso)*, 1938
Pastell, Aquarellfarbe, Ölkreide auf Papier/pastel, water colour, oil pastels on paper
20,2 × 19 cm
Privatsammlung/Private Collection, Barcelona
Abb. S./ill. p. 125



*Estudio – Croquis para "Romeo y Julieta"*, 1942
Tusche und Feder auf Papier/india ink and pen on paper
15 × 20,7 cm
Privatsammlung/Private Collection, Courtesy Manuel Barbié, Barcelona
Abb. S./ill. p. 73

*Café de Chinitas*, 1943
Bleistift auf Papier/pencil on paper
57,2 × 78 cm
Courtesy Galería Manuel Barbié, Barcelona
Abb. S./ill. p. 71

*The Eye*, 1944
Öl auf Holztafel/oil on panel
60 × 85 cm
Privatsammlung/Private Collection, Courtesy Hauser & Wirth
Abb. S./ill. p. 135

*Homenaje a Lautréamont*, c. 1945
Tusche, Aquarell und Öl auf Karton/ink, water colour and oil on carton
16,5 × 18,2 cm
Privatsammlung/Private Collection
Courtesy Manuel Barbié, Barcelona
Abb. S./ill. p. 9

*Esfinge*, c. 1947
Bleistift auf Papier/pencil on paper
22,8 × 30 cm
Courtesy Galería Manuel Barbié, Barcelona
Abb. S./ill. p. 71

Entwurf für Umschlag-Rückseite des Ausstellungskatalogs Dalí Bignou Gallery, New York, 25. Nov. 1947 bis 3. Jan. 1948/sketch for the back cover of the Dalí exhibition catalogue, Bignou Gallery, New York, Nov. 25, 1947 through Jan. 3, 1948, 1947
Tusche auf Papier/ink on paper
24,5 × 15,6 cm
Kunstmuseum Bern, Legat Georges F. Keller 1981
Abb. S./ill. p. 2

Entwurf für Katalog-Titelseite der Dalí-Ausstellung in der Carstairs Gallery, New York, 25. Nov. 1947 bis 3. Jan. 1948/sketch for the cover of the Dalí exhibition catalogue, Carstairs Gallery, New York, Nov. 25, 1947 through Jan. 3, 1948, 1947
Tusche auf Papier/ink on paper
20,0 × 17,5 cm
Kunstmuseum Bern, Legat Georges F. Keller 1981
Abb. S./ill. p. 2

*Personaje surrealista/Boceto para la escenografía de "Don Juan Tenorio"*, 1950
Öl auf Karton/oil on carton
32 × 25 cm
Museo Nacional Centro de Arte Reina Sofía, Madrid
Archivo fotográfico Museo Nacional Centro de Arte Reina Sofía, Madrid
Abb. S./ill. p. 75

*Paisaje/Boceto para la escenografía de "Don Juan Tenorio"*, 1950
Gouache auf Karton/gouache on carton
38 × 52 cm
Museo Nacional Centro de Arte Reina Sofía, Madrid
Archivo fotográfico Museo Nacional Centro de Arte

Reina Sofía, Madrid
Abb. S./ill. p. 134

*Consola con florero de cisnes*, 1950
Öl auf Karton/oil on carton
33,5 × 24,5 cm
Museo Nacional Centro de Arte Reina Sofía, Madrid
Archivo fotográfico Museo Nacional Centro de Arte
Reina Sofía, Madrid
Abb. S./ill. p. 124

Entwurf für die Neueinrichtung des Schlafzimmers in Dalís Haus in Port Llegat/sketch for the re-accomodation of the bedroom in Dalí's house in Port Llegat, 1954
Gouache auf Karton/gouache on carton
13,7 × 19,0 cm
Kunstmuseum Bern
Abb. S./ill. p. 73

Entwurf für Katalog-Titelseite der Dalí-Ausstellung in der Carstairs Gallery, New York, Dez. 1954 bis Jan. 1955/sketch for cover of the Dalí exhibition catalogue, Carstairs Gallery, New York, Dec. 1954 through Jan. 1955, 1954
Tusche auf Papier/ink on paper
25,4 × 14,5 cm
Kunstmuseum Bern, Legat Georges F. Keller 1981
Abb. S./ill. p. 2

*Der Koloss von Rhodos*, 1954
Öl auf Leinwand/oil on canvas
68,8 × 39 cm
Kunstmuseum Bern, Legat Georges F. Keller 1981
Abb. S./ill. p. 120

Entwurf für Titel- und Rückseite des Katalogs der Dalí-Ausstellung in der Carstairs Gallery, New York, 4. Dez. 1956 bis 5. Jan. 1957/sketch for cover and back cover of the Dalí exhibition catalogue, Carstairs Gallery, New York, Dec. 4, 1956 through Jan. 5, 1957, 1956
Tusche auf unregelmässigem Papier auf Untergrund-Karton/ink on irregular paper on cardboard
c. 26,0 × 24,09 cm
Kunstmuseum Bern, Legat Georges F. Keller 1981
Abb. S./ill. p. 2

*Venus à la Giraffe*, 1973
Bemalte Bronze/painted bronze
57 × 27,5 × 9 cm
Privatsammlung, Wien/Private Collection, Vienna
Abb. S./ill. p. 89

*Paisaje con ciprés*, 1981
Öl auf Kupfer/oil on copper
37 × 53 cm
Museo Nacional Centro de Arte Reina Sofía, Madrid
Archivo fotográfico Museo Nacional Centro de Arte
Reina Sofía, Madrid
Abb. S./ill. p. 89

nicht ausgestellt/not on display:

*Das finstere Spiel/The lubrigous game*, 1929
Öl und Collage auf Karton/oil and collage on carton
44,4 × 30,3 cm
Abb. S./ill. p. 184

*Der große Masturbator/The Great Masturbator*, 1929
Öl auf Leinwand/oil on canvas
110 × 150 cm
Abb. S./ill. p. 184

*Teilhalluzination: Sechs Erscheinungen von Lenin/Partial Hallucination: Six Apparitions of Lenin on a Piano*, 1931
Öl auf Leinwand/oil on canvas
114 × 146 cm
Abb. S./ill. p. 158

*Das Greisenalter Wilhelm Tells/The Old Age of Wilhelm Tell*, 1931
Öl auf Leinwand/oil on canvas
98 × 140 cm
Abb. S./ill. p. 184

*Die Metamorphose des Narziss/Metamorphosis of Narcissus*, 1937
Öl auf Leinwand/oil on canvas
50,8 × 78,3 cm
Abb. S./ill. p. 184

*Das durchsichtige Scheinbild des falschen Bildes/ Transparent Simulacrum of a Feigned Illusion*, 1938
Öl auf Leinwand/oil on canvas
73,5 × 92 cm
Abb. S./ill. p. 155

*Bildnis meines toten Bruders/Portrait of My Dead Brother*, 1963
Öl auf Leinwand/oil on canvas
175 × 175 cm
Abb. S./ill. p. 155

**Salvador Dalí & Philippe Halsman**

Alle Werke von Philippe Halsman und Salvador Dalí/all works by Philippe Halsman and Salvador Dalí: Philippe Halsman © Phillipe Halsman/Magnum Photos; Salvador Dalí © Fundació Gala-Salvador Dalí, Figueres, 2011

*Dalí Atomicus, New York*, 1948
Silbergelatineprint/gelatin silver print
25,2 × 32,7 cm
Privatsammlung Wien/Private Collection, Vienna
Abb. S./ill. p. 207

*Dalí Skull, New York*, 1951
Silbergelatineprint/gelatin silver print
32,7 × 25,2 cm
Privatsammlung Wien/Private Collection, Vienna
Abb. S./ill. p. 206

*Dalí's Mustache, New York*, 1953
Silbergelatineprint/gelatin silver print
32,7 × 25,2 cm
Privatsammlung Wien/Private Collection, Vienna
Abb. S./ill. p. 209

*Dalí in Port Lligat*, 1964
Silbergelatineprint/gelatin silver print
32,7 × 25,2 cm
Privatsammlung Wien/Private Collection, Vienna
Abb. S./ill. p. 208



**Jean-Michel Othoniel**

*Es bello como el encuentro fortuito entre un paraguas y una máquina de coser*, 1993
16 mm-Video auf DVD, 5' 47" Min., s/w/16 mm on DVD Video, 5' 47" min., b/w
Courtesy Galeria Senda, Barcelona
© Jean-Michel Othoniel
Abb. S./ill. p. 287

**Eric Schaal**

Salvador Dalí, *Dream of Venus-Pavillon*, 1939
Pavillon, Weltausstellung, New York/pavilion, World Fair, New York
16 Fotografien/photographs
Fundació Gala-Salvador Dalí, Figueres
© Fundació Gala-Salvador Dalí, Figueres, 2011
Abb. S./ill. p. 24–36

**Markus Schinwald**

Alle Werke von/all works by Markus Schinwald
© Markus Schinwald

*Untitled (Aquarium#1)*, 2011
Glas, Epoxydharz, Holz/glas, epoxyd-resin, wood
140 × 70 × 70 cm
Courtesy der Künstler/the artist
Abb. S./ill. p. 43

nicht ausgestellt/not on display:

Installationsansichten/installation views
MAMbo – Museo Palazzo Poggi, Bologna, 2006
Abb. S./ill. pp. 38–41

*Curvings, Toes*, 2007
Mixed Media
Abb. S./ill. p. 42

**Francesco Vezzoli**

Alle Werke von/all works by Francesco Vezzoli


*Surrealiz (Who's afraid of Salvador Dalí?)*, 2008
Inkjetprint auf Leinwand, Metallstickerei, Papier/inkjet print on canvas, metallic embroidery, paper
113 × 173 × 8 cm
Privatsammlung/Private Collection
Courtesy Gagosian Gallery, Foto/photo: Robert McKeever
Abb. S./ill. p. 213

*Surrealiz (Le sommeil in Hollywood)*, 2008
Inkjetprint auf Leinwand, Metallstickerei, Papier/inkjet on canvas, metallic embroidery, paper
113 × 173 cm
Burger Collection
Courtesy Gagosian Gallery
Abb./ill. Installationsansicht/installation view: Francesco Vezzoli, *Dalí Dalí featuring Francesco Vezzoli*, Moderna Museet, Stockholm, 2009,
Abb. S./ill. pp. 214–215

*Surrealiz (Lucio Fontana as Marco Antonio)*, 2008
Inkjetprint auf Leinwand, Metallstickerei, Papier/inkjet print on canvas, metallic embroidery, paper
153 × 113 cm
Sammlung Maya und Fahed Hariri/Maya and Fahed Hariri Collection
Courtesy Gagosian Gallery, Foto/photo: Robert McKeever
Abb. S./ill. p. 212

*Le Surréalisme, c'est moi! (Portrait of Salvador Dalí with Jewels and Tears, After Horst)*, 2009
Inkjetprint auf Leinwand, Baumwoll- und Metallstickerei, Schmuck/inkjet on canvas, cotton and metallic embroidery, custom jewelry
106 × 77 × 4 cm
Sammlung/Collection Santiago Barberi Gonzalez, Kolumbien/Colombia
Courtesy Yvon Lambert, Foto/photo: Didier Barroso
Abb. S./ill. p. 210

*Greed*, 2009
Video, c. 1 min.
Regie/directed by Roman Polanski
Courtesy der Künstler/the artist
Abb. S./ill. pp. 216–219

Installationsansicht/installation view: Francesco Vezzoli, *Dalí Dalí featuring Francesco Vezzoli*, Moderna Museet, Stockholm, 2009
Courtesy Moderna Museet
Abb. S./ill. pp. 214–215

nicht ausgestellt/not on display:

*Gala as Sylvia in La Dolce Vita*, 2008
Inkjetprint auf Leinwand, Metallstickerei, Papier/inkjet on canvas, metallic embroidery, paper
120,6 × 96,5 cm
Abb. S./ill. p. 211

**Andy Warhol**

*Screen Tests: Salvador Dalí*, 1966
16 mm-Film, s/w, ohne Ton, 4 Min.
16 mm film, b/w, silent, 4 min.
The Andy Warhol Museum, Pittsburgh

Abb. S./ill. p. 205

**Ephemera**

Le Comte de Lautréamont
*Les Chants de Maldoror*, 1925
Französische Edition/French edition
Privatsammlung/Private Collection
Keine Abb. /no ill.

*Time*, 14/12/1936
Magazin/magazine
Privatsammlung/Private Collection
Abb. S./ill. p. 8

*Vogue*, 01/06/1939
Magazincover/magazine cover
Abb. S./ill. p. 237

Salvador Dalí
*The Secret Life of Salvador Dalí*, 1942
Erstausgabe/first edition
Privatsammlung/Private Collection
Keine Abb. /no ill.

*Chen Yu, Vogue*, 01/09/1945
Magazincover/magazine cover
Abb. S./ill. p. 237

*Vogue*, 01/04/1945
Magazincover/magazine cover
Abb. S./ill. p. 237

*Dalí News*, 1947
Zeitung/newspaper
Privatsammlung/Private Collection
Abb. S./ill. p. 4

*Correo de la radio*, 01/02/1953
Magazincover/magazine cover
Abb. S./ill. p. 238

*Photo Monde*, 02/1954
Magazincover/magazine cover
Abb. S./ill. p. 238

*Rock 'n' Roll, le parfum de chock!, United States Lines*, 1957
Werbeanzeige/advertisement
Abb. S./ill. p. 237

*Connaissance des Arts*, 02/1961
Magazin/magazine
Privatsammlung/Private Collection
Keine Abb./no ill.

*The Studio*, 09/1961
Magazincover/magazine cover
Abb. S./ill. p. 238

Salvador Dalí, *Le mythe tragique de l'Angelus de Millet: interpretation „paranoique-critique"*, 1963
Französische Ausgabe/French edition
Privatsammlung/Private Collection
Keine Abb./no ill.

*Gentlemen's Quaterly*, 10/1963
Magazincover/magazine cover
Abb. S./ill. p. 238

Salvador Dalí
*Journal d'un Genie*, 1964
Erstausgabe/first edition
Privatsammlung/Private Collection
Keine Abb./no ill.

*TV Guide*, 14/06/1968
Magazin/magazine
Privatsammlung/Private Collection
Keine Abb./no ill.

*Andy Warhol's Interview*, 05/1973
Magazin/magazine
Privatsammlung/Private Collection
Keine Abb./no ill.

*The Connoisseur, The Jewellery Issue*, November 1975
Magazin/magazine
Privatsammlung/Private Collection
Keine Abb./no ill.

nicht ausgestellt/not on display:

Still aus/still from
Alfred Hitchcock, *Spellbound*, 1945
Traumsequenz von/dream sequence by Salvador Dalí
© United Artists Inc.
Abb. S./ill. p. 225

Robert A. Heinlein, *Double Star*, 1974
Buchcover/book cover
Abb. S./ill. p. 148

Christopher Makos
*Dalí Kissing Andy*, 1979
s/w Fotografie/b/w photograph
© Christopher Makos
Abb. S./ill. p. 225

**Impressum/Colophon**

**Katalog/Catalogue**

Herausgeber/Editor:
Kunsthalle Wien, Gerald A. Matt

Redaktion/Editing:
Lucas Gehrmann, Synne Genzmer, Gerald A. Matt

Mitarbeit/Assistence:
Viola Wagner

Grafische Gestaltung/Graphic Design:
Funny Paper

Texte/Texts:
Wolfgang Fetz, Belinda Grace Gardner, Synne Genzmer, David Lomas, Gerald A. Matt, Catherine Millet (Wiederabdruck/Reprint), August Ruhs

Interviews:
Caroline Corbetta mit/with Francesco Vezzoli, Lucas Gehmann mit/with Markus Schinwald, Gerald A. Matt und/and Katarzyna Uszynka mit/with Glenn Brown

Übersetzungen/Translations:
Christian Breuer (I>D Interview Francesco Vezzoli), Jeremy Gaines (D>E August Ruhs, D>E Interview Markus Schinwald), Belinda Grace Gardner (D>E Belinda Grace Gardner), Chiara Redini (I>E Interview Francesco Vezzoli), James Rumball (D>E Gerald A. Matt), Natascha Unkart (E>D David Lomas), Nelson Wattie (D>E Wolfgang Fetz, D>E Synne Genzmer)

Bio- und Bibliografien/Bio- and Bibliographies:
Synne Genzmer, Viola Wagner

Lektorat/Proof-Reading:
Sandra Huber (Englisch/English), Eva Hubert und/and Silvia Jaklitsch (Deutsch/German)

Druck/Print:
Holzhausen Druck GmbH

Papier/Paper:
Arctic Volume white, 115 g

Schrift Umschlag/Font Cover:
Neutra Text TF

Schrift Fließtext/Font Continuous Text:
Lyon Text



Verlag für moderne Kunst Nürnberg GmbH
Luitpoldstraße 5, D-90402 Nürnberg
Tel.: +49 911 240 21 14
Fax: +49 911 240 21 19
www.vfmk.de



Printed in Austria
ISBN 978-3-86984-233-2

Bibliografische Information der Deutschen Nationalbibliothek/Die Deutsche Nationalbibliothek verzeichnet diese Publikation in der Deutschen Nationalbibliografie; detaillierte bibliografische Daten sind im Internet über http://dnb.d-nb.de abrufbar.

Bibliographic information published by Die Deutsche Bibliothek/Die Deutsche Bibliothek lists this publication in the Deutsche Nationalbibliografie; detailed bibliographic data is available in the internet at http://dnb.ddb.de

Vertrieb Großbritannien/Distribution in Great Britain
Cornerhouse Publications
70 Oxford Street, Manchester M1 5 NH, UK
Tel.: +44 161 200 15 03
Fax: +44 161 200 15 04

Vertrieb außerhalb Europas/Distribution outside Europe
D.A.P./Distributed Art Publishers, Inc., New York
155 Sixth Avenue, 2nd Floor, New York, NY 10013, USA
Tel.: +1 212 627 19 99, Fax: +1 212 627 94 84

**Ausstellung/Exhibition**

*Le Surréalisme, c'est moi! Hommage an Salvador Dalí.*
*Le Surréalisme, c'est moi! Homage to Salvador Dalí.*
*Louise Bourgeois, Glenn Brown, Markus Schinwald, Franceso Vezzoli*

22. Juni – 23. Oktober 2011/
June 22 – October 23, 2011

Kunsthalle Wien, halle 2
Museumsplatz 1
A – 1070 Wien/Vienna
www.kunsthallewien.at

Kurator/Curator:
Gerald A. Matt

Wissenschaftliche Mitarbeit/Research and Curatorial Consultant:
Lucas Gehrmann

Koordination/Coordination:
Synne Genzmer

Mitarbeit/Assistance:
Viola Wagner

Produktionsleitung/Production Manager:
Barbara Nowy

Presse, Marketing/Press, Marketing:
Claudia Bauer (Head), Katharina Murschetz (Press/Presse), Katharina Baumgartner (Marketing)
Kunstvermittlung/Educational Program:
Isabella Drozda, Michael Würges

Ausstellungsgrafik/Exhibition Design:
Karin Holzfeind

Technik/Technique:
Johannes Diboky

Installation Francesco Vezzoli:
Gioele Amaro

Restauratoren/Conservators:
Sascha Höchtl, Ursula Brandl-Pühringer

Die KUNSTHALLE wien ist die Institution der Stadt Wien für moderne und zeitgenössische Kunst und wird durch die Kulturabteilung MA7 unterstützt.

KUNSTHALLE wien is the institution of the City of Vienna devoted to modern and contemporary art and is supported by the Department of Cultural Affairs MA7.

WIEN KULTUR

Direktor/Director:
Gerald A. Matt

Geschäftsführerin/General Manager:
Bettina Leidl